Meet the *Southern Living* Foods Staff

On these pages we show the Foods Staff (left to right in each photograph) at work as they compile, test, taste, and photograph the recipes that appear each month in *Southern Living*.

Susan McIntosh, Assistant Foods Editor; and Susan Payne, Associate Foods Editor

Jean Wickstrom Liles, Foods Editor

Above: *Connie Shedd and Peggy Smith, Test Kitchens Staff*

Right: *Vivienne Johnson, Karren King, and Catherine Garrison, Editorial Assistants*

Carole King, Diane Hogan, and Carroll Sessions, Test Kitchens Staff

Deborah Lowery, Assistant Foods Editor; Margaret Chason, Associate Foods Editor; and Nola McKey, Assistant Foods Editor

Beverly Morrow, Photo Stylist; John O'Hagan, Photographer; Charles Walton, Senior Foods Photographer; and Jim Bathie, Photographer

Debby Maugans, Test Kitchens Staff; Nancy Nevins, Test Kitchens Director

Southern Living
1984 ANNUAL RECIPES

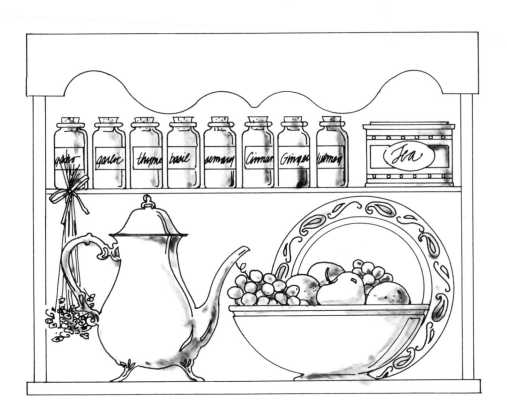

Oxmoor House, Inc., Birmingham

Copyright 1984 by Oxmoor House, Inc.
Book Division of Southern Progress Corporation
P.O. Box 2463, Birmingham, Alabama 35201

Southern Living® is a federally registered trademark of Southern Living, Inc. *Breakfasts & Brunches*™, *Summer Suppers*®, *Holiday Dinners*™, *Holiday Desserts*™, and *Cooking Light*™ are trademarks of Southern Living, Inc.

Library of Congress Catalog Number: 79-88364
ISBN: 0-8487-0638-2

Manufactured in the United States of America
First Printing 1984

Southern Living 1984 Annual Recipes

Southern Living®
    Foods Editor: Jean Wickstrom Liles
    Associate Foods Editors: Margaret Chason, Susan Payne
    Assistant Foods Editors: Deborah G. Lowery, Susan M. McIntosh, Nola McKey
    Test Kitchens Director: Nancy Nevins
    Test Kitchens Staff: Diane Hogan, Carole King, Debby Maugans, Carroll Sessions, Connie Shedd, Peggy Smith
    Photo Stylist: Beverly Morrow
    Editorial Assistants: Catherine Garrison, Vivienne Johnson, Karren King
    Production: Clay Nordan, Wanda Butler
    Photographers: Charles Walton: cover, ii, bottom right and left, iii top left and bottom right, 27, 28, 61, 62, 63, 64, 97, 98, 99 top, 100, 133, 134, 167, 168, 169, 170, 203, 204, 237, 238, 271, 272, 273, 274, 307, 308, 309, 310; John O'Hagan: i, ii top left, iii top right, iv, 99 bottom; Jim Bathie: ii top right; Courtland W. Richards: iii bottom left.

Oxmoor House, Inc.
    Executive Editor: Ann H. Harvey
    Editor: Annette Thompson
    Production: Jerry Higdon, Jim Thomas, Jane Bonds
    Copy Editor: Melinda E. West
    Editorial Assistants: Patty E. Howdon, Mary Ann Laurens, Karen P. Traccarella

    Designer: Carol Middleton
    Illustrator: Cindia Pickering

Cover: *A favorite of all Christmas sweets is candy—as fun to make as it is to eat. To satisfy your sweet cravings, we offer (clockwise from top): Peanut Brittle, Crystal Candy, Chocolate Velvets, Chocolate Bourbon Balls, Easy Holiday Mints, Chocolate-Covered Cherries, Holiday Mocha Fudge, and Spicy Praline Delights (recipes begin on page 298).*

Page i: *Topped with snowy white coconut, Coconut-Spice Cake (page 255) captures the rich flavor of the holiday season.*

Page iv: *Easy-to-eat finger food works best for open house treats. For your next party, try a spread of Chocolate-Tipped Butter Cookies (page 258), Chicken Salad Tarts (page 257), Fruitcake Fondue (page 258), and Spiced Nuts (page 257).*

Table of Contents

Chicken Salad with a Twist (page 221)

Stuffed Pork Chops (page 195)

Cream Cheese Tarts (page 74)

Our Year at Southern Living®

For eighteen years *Southern Living* has provided the South with delectable recipes and a rich source of entertaining ideas. Each year our foods staff test, taste, and publish hundreds of recipes that reflect the good food and the gracious lifestyle found in the South.

Now, for the sixth time, we offer a whole year of *Southern Living* recipes in a single volume. Overflowing with more than 1300 recipes, *1984 Annual Recipes* brings together all of the recipes published in *Southern Living* during 1984. This cookbook offers recipes for every occasion and for every type of cook.

Our food ideas come from the South's best cooks who submit thousands of their family's favorite recipes to *Southern Living* each month. Before we even receive these recipes, they have passed a taste test in homes throughout the South.

Once a food story idea originates and recipes are selected, these recipes are tested, tasted, and evaluated in our modern test kitchens by our staff of experienced home economists. Each recipe is examined in terms of taste, appearance, ease of preparation, and cost of ingredients. Only after this intensive testing process do the recipes appear in *Southern Living*. We select the "best of the best" for publication.

But before publication each recipe is edited in a clear and concise manner. In writing each recipe, the ingredients are listed in the order in which they are used in preparation and then an easy-to-follow

cooking procedure is given. Each recipe is checked several times for accuracy in measurements, bowl and pan sizes, oven time and temperature, and yield. We want nothing left uncertain when you get ready to prepare our recipe. At that point we're confident your finished dish will be as tasty and attractive as ours.

After the recipes for a story have been tested, our editors assist the photographers and photo stylist in preparing the setting and props for photography. Our food photographs serve as an invitation to the reader to enjoy our recipes and often suggest how to garnish and serve the dish. Whether the shot is taken in the studio or on location, the aim of each is to capture the actual appearance of the food so that you can duplicate it at home.

1984 Annual Recipes is organized into monthly chapters designed to spotlight seasonal foods and offer great entertaining ideas for each season. This winter you can take the chill away with one of our old-fashioned stews or add variety to your winter menus with meat pastries or whole grain breads. In March you'll get a headstart in the morning with *Breakfasts & Brunches*. You'll find delicious recipes for beignets, unusual omelets, and exotic coffees. Along with spring come some

luscious low-calorie desserts. And May promises new ideas for serving fresh vegetables. Put away the salt shaker and enjoy the season's bounty with low-sodium herbs.

Our July *Summer Suppers* offers sizzling suggestions for picnics and cookouts, but we also offer cooling off ideas with congealed salads, chilled desserts, and ice cream beverages. September

kicks off the football season and you can rally team spirit with our winning appetizers or a tailgate picnic. Usher in the holiday season in November with *Holiday Dinners* where you'll find fabulous entrées, spirited beverages, and more. To help you celebrate the merry holiday season, we've wrapped our traditional and favorite sweets into *Holiday Desserts*.

This year we gave special emphasis to piped meringues, shrimp curry, puff pastry, Christmas cookie cards, and other topics by including step-by-step instructions with photographs. Featured each

month are recipes for the microwave oven, low-calorie cooking, and recipes designed just for two.

As the foods staff put the finishing touches on the sixth edition of *Annual Recipes*, we salute *you,* our readers, for your generosity in sharing special recipes with us. From corresponding with you and from visiting in your homes or on the phone, we've learned what you cook and how you entertain. Most of you consider it an honor to have a recipe published in *Southern Living*. You've told us you've become an "instant celebrity" in your hometown and, as a result, are often invited for radio and newspaper interviews. One reader even wrote to say, "You have me flirting with fame."

Enjoy your *1984 Annual Recipes*. After a very busy and exciting year, our foods staff present to you the pick of the South's most treasured recipes.

Jean Wickstrom Liles

January

Reap The Bounty Of The Cabbage Patch

Cabbage is one group of fresh vegetables you can enjoy year-round. Its crisp, crunchy texture and varied shapes offer lots of versatility. You can toss it in a salad, stuff it with a ground beef filling, or stir-fry it in a wok—and that's just the beginning.

Bok choy, often called Chinese cabbage, has long, firm, tapering stalks resembling a cross between romaine lettuce and celery. From pale green to white, it has crisp, broad leaves and is good in cooked dishes as well as salads.

To keep the bright color of red cabbage, cook it with an acid, such as wine, apple juice, or vinegar. If it's cooked with baking soda or other alkaline ingredients, the cabbage will turn blue. Certain knives may also cause red cabbage to turn blue. That's why it's always a good idea to use a stainless steel knife.

SPICY CABBAGE ROLLS

1 large green cabbage
1 pound ground beef
3 tablespoons chopped onion
3 tablespoons chopped green pepper
3 tablespoons chopped celery
1 tablespoon Worcestershire sauce
¾ cup cooked rice
½ teaspoon salt
Dash of pepper
1 (6-ounce) can tomato paste
⅓ cup water
1 (10-ounce) can tomatoes with green chiles, undrained
¼ teaspoon salt
¼ teaspoon seasoned salt

Remove 10 large outer leaves of cabbage; reserve remaining cabbage for other uses. Cook leaves in boiling salted water 5 to 8 minutes or just until tender; drain and set aside.

Combine next 8 ingredients. Place equal portions of meat mixture in center of each cabbage leaf. Fold 2 opposite ends over and place rolls, seam side down, in a lightly greased 13- x 9- x 2-inch baking dish.

Combine remaining ingredients; pour over cabbage rolls. Cover and bake at 350° for 1 hour. Yield: 10 servings.

Susie Cole,
Lake Charles, Louisiana.

CHICKEN COLESLAW

2 cups shredded green cabbage
2 cups diced cooked chicken
1 cup unpeeled cubed red apple
1 cup seedless red grapes, halved
½ cup sliced celery
½ cup chopped walnuts
½ cup commercial sour cream
3 tablespoons mayonnaise
3 tablespoons honey
1 tablespoon lemon juice
⅛ teaspoon salt
Dash of pepper
Leaf lettuce (optional)

Combine first 6 ingredients in a large bowl; set aside.

Combine sour cream, mayonnaise, honey, lemon juice, salt, and pepper; stir until smooth. Pour over chicken mixture, and toss gently. Cover and chill 1 to 2 hours. To serve, spoon coleslaw into a lettuce-lined bowl, if desired. Yield: 6 servings.

Bobbie A. McGuire,
Norris, South Carolina.

GERMAN-STYLE RED CABBAGE

1 small red cabbage
1 small onion, chopped
2 tablespoons sugar
1 teaspoon salt
1 bay leaf
¼ cup water
2 tablespoons red wine vinegar
1 apple, peeled and chopped
3 slices bacon, cooked and crumbled

Cut cabbage into 6 wedges, removing core; place in a large saucepan. Add onion, sugar, salt, bay leaf, and water; bring to a boil. Cover, reduce heat, and simmer 20 minutes. Add vinegar and apple; cover and cook an additional 3 to 4 minutes or until apple is tender.

Remove cabbage to a serving platter with a slotted spoon. Strain pan liquid, reserving onion and apple; discard the bay leaf. Spoon onion and apple over cabbage; sprinkle with the crumbled bacon. Yield: about 6 servings.

Mary Jane Yost,
Huntsville, Alabama.

BUBBLING CABBAGE

1 medium savoy cabbage, coarsely chopped
1 cup lemon-lime carbonated beverage
5 anise seeds, crushed
⅛ teaspoon salt
⅛ teaspoon pepper
3 tablespoons butter or margarine

Combine first 5 ingredients in a large skillet; cover and cook over medium heat 8 to 10 minutes or until cabbage is tender. Add butter, and toss cabbage gently. Yield: 6 servings. *Katie Kent,*
Gladewater, Texas.

BOK CHOY-BROCCOLI STIR-FRY

2 tablespoons vegetable oil
1 medium onion, thinly sliced
½ to 1 tablespoon freshly grated gingerroot
2 cloves garlic, crushed
½ teaspoon salt
3 cups sliced fresh broccoli flowerets
1 to 1½ pounds bok choy, coarsely chopped
2 tablespoons lemon juice
1½ teaspoons sugar

Pour oil around top of a preheated wok, coating sides; heat at medium high (325°) for 2 minutes. Add onion, gingerroot, garlic, and salt; stir-fry 2 minutes.

Add broccoli and bok choy to wok; stir-fry 1 minute. Add lemon juice and sugar; stir-fry 3 minutes or until crisp-tender. Yield: 6 servings.

Joy M. Maurer,
Christmas, Florida.

Simmer A Pot Of Tempting Soup Or Stew

Nothing tastes better than a big bowl of homemade soup or stew on a blustery winter day. Simmered to perfection, these aromatic mixtures are robust and nutritious enough to serve as the mainstay of a meal.

Homemade soups and stews may be created from whatever ingredients you have on hand. The base for many soups is often a broth made by simmering the meaty bones from leftover roasted turkey, chicken, ham, or beef in water. When the broth has finished cooking, it should be strained. The tender meat clinging to the bones may be removed and added back to the broth along with a variety of vegetables.

What's the difference between a soup and a stew? Southern cooks maintain that stews are usually cooked in less liquid than a soup. Stews are often thickened with flour or dumplings. And, the meat and vegetables are usually cut into larger pieces.

When preparing soups and stews, the simmering step is the most critical. For example, a beef stew that has galloped along at a rolling boil for several hours will not taste or look as good as one that has been gently simmered with a slow, sporadic bubble or two breaking the surface. If roughly boiled, meat will toughen and become stringy and vegetables will break apart.

Most soups and stews can be made ahead and kept covered in the refrigerator for two or three days. Thick mixtures become even thicker upon standing, so you may have to dilute them with a little broth or water.

Remember that some ingredients, such as potatoes and dumplings, do not freeze well, so they should be cooked and added after thawing. Also, flour-thickened soups and stews may tend to separate if frozen a long time.

BEEF STEW WITH DUMPLINGS

¼ cup all-purpose flour
1½ teaspoons salt
¼ teaspoon pepper
2 pounds boneless beef chuck, cut into 1-inch cubes
3 tablespoons vegetable oil
1 medium onion, sliced
½ teaspoon sugar
½ teaspoon Worcestershire sauce
½ clove garlic, minced
1 small bay leaf
Pinch of ground allspice
5 cups water
3 large potatoes, quartered
4 large carrots, cut in half crosswise
6 small onions
3 stalks celery, cut into 1-inch pieces
3 tablespoons milk
1 egg
1 tablespoon chopped fresh parsley
1 cup biscuit mix

Combine first 3 ingredients; dredge meat in flour mixture, and brown in hot oil in a large Dutch oven. Stir in the next 7 ingredients; cover, reduce heat, and simmer 2 hours.

Add potatoes, carrots, onions, and celery; cover and cook over low heat 15 minutes.

Combine milk, egg, and parsley; stir well. Add milk mixture to biscuit mix, and stir just until all ingredients are moistened. Drop dough by tablespoonfuls on top of vegetables in stew. Cook, uncovered, over low heat 10 minutes; cover and cook an additional 10 minutes. Yield: 3 quarts. *Sandy French, Beaumont, Texas.*

Step 1—Dredge beef cubes in a mixture of flour, salt, and pepper. Brown meat on all sides in oil in a large Dutch oven, removing pieces as they brown.

Step 2—Return browned meat to Dutch oven; add sliced onion, seasonings, and 5 cups water. Cover, reduce heat, and simmer stew gently for 2 hours.

Step 3—Add potatoes, carrots, small onions, and celery; cover and cook over low heat 15 minutes.

Step 4—As vegetables cook, start dumplings by combining milk, egg, and parsley. Add to biscuit mix; stir until moistened.

Step 5—Drop batter by rounded tablespoonfuls onto gently simmering stew, placing on top of vegetables, not in liquid.

Step 6—Cook dumplings, uncovered, over low heat 10 minutes. Cover and cook 10 additional minutes.

HAMBURGER OVEN STEW

1½ pounds ground beef
1 medium onion, chopped
1 (16-ounce) can whole tomatoes, undrained
1 (16-ounce) can whole kernel corn, undrained
1 (16-ounce) can cut green beans, undrained
1 (10½-ounce) can beef broth, undiluted
1 cup water
6 medium potatoes, peeled and cubed
1 cup (4 ounces) shredded sharp Cheddar cheese
½ teaspoon celery seeds
½ teaspoon ground thyme
½ teaspoon chili powder
½ teaspoon salt
¼ teaspoon pepper
2 (11-ounce) cans refrigerator buttermilk biscuits

Combine ground beef and onion in a Dutch oven; cook over medium heat until meat is browned, stirring to crumble. Drain off drippings. Add next 6 ingredients; cook over medium heat 10 minutes, stirring occasionally.

Add cheese and seasonings; stir until cheese melts. Reduce heat and simmer, uncovered, for 1 hour and 20 to 30 minutes, stirring occasionally, or until liquid is almost gone.

Pour into a lightly greased 13- x 9- x 2-inch baking dish; arrange biscuits on top. Bake at 400° for 10 to 13 minutes. Yield: 10 servings. *Shirley Dunn, Allen, Oklahoma.*

HAM-AND-BEAN SOUP

1 pound dried Great Northern beans
6 cups water
1½ pounds cubed cooked ham
2 teaspoons salt
1 teaspoon dried whole thyme
½ teaspoon dried parsley flakes
4 peppercorns
3 cloves garlic, minced
1 bay leaf
2 cups water
4 medium potatoes, peeled and quartered
3 carrots, scraped and cut into ½-inch slices
1 medium onion, finely chopped

Sort and wash beans; place in a Dutch oven. Cover with water 2 inches above beans; let soak overnight. Drain. Combine beans, 6 cups water, and next 7 ingredients in a large Dutch oven; bring to a boil. Cover, reduce

heat, and simmer 1½ hours. Add 2 cups water and vegetables to soup. Cover and simmer about 30 minutes or until the vegetables are tender. Yield: about 1 gallon. *Gwen Tant, Senatobia, Mississippi.*

ITALIAN SAUSAGE-ZUCCHINI SOUP

1 pound Italian sausage
2 cups sliced celery
2 (28-ounce) cans tomatoes, undrained and coarsely chopped
1 cup chopped onion
1 teaspoon salt
1 teaspoon sugar
1 teaspoon dried whole oregano
1 teaspoon Italian seasoning
½ teaspoon dried whole basil
¼ teaspoon garlic powder
6 small zucchini, cut into ¼-inch slices
1 medium-size green pepper, chopped
1 cup water
1 cup red wine

Cook sausage in a Dutch oven until browned. Add celery and cook until tender; drain off drippings. Add next 8 ingredients. Cover, reduce heat, and simmer 20 minutes. Add remaining ingredients; cover and simmer 20 minutes or until vegetables are tender. Yield: 3 quarts. *Earlene Ramay, Englewood, Colorado.*

TURKEY-VEGETABLE SOUP

2 quarts turkey broth
2 cups chopped cooked turkey
1 (16-ounce) can whole tomatoes, undrained and coarsely chopped
1 (8¾-ounce) can whole kernel corn, drained
1 (8½-ounce) can English peas, drained
1 cup cooked navy beans
¼ cup chopped celery
2 tablespoons barley
1 tablespoon instant minced onion
1 tablespoon beef-flavored bouillon granules
1 tablespoon chicken-flavored bouillon granules
1 teaspoon hot sauce
Dash of garlic powder

Combine all ingredients in a large Dutch oven. Bring to a boil. Cover, reduce heat, and simmer 1 hour, stirring occasionally. Yield: 2½ quarts. *Mrs. Jack Hudgens, Sr., Welling, Oklahoma.*

CHICKEN STEW AND DUMPLINGS

1 (3-pound) broiler-fryer
5 cups water
2 tablespoons chopped fresh parsley
4 chicken-flavored bouillon cubes
3 cups water
1½ cups sliced carrots
½ cup barley
4 stalks celery, chopped
1 medium onion, chopped
1 teaspoon dried whole basil
1 clove garlic, minced
⅔ cup milk
2 tablespoons chopped fresh parsley
2 cups biscuit mix

Combine first 4 ingredients in a large Dutch oven; bring to a boil. Cover, reduce heat, and simmer 1 hour. Remove chicken; let cool. Bone chicken, and chop the meat. Return meat to broth. Add next 7 ingredients, and bring mixture to a boil. Cover, reduce heat, and simmer 25 minutes.

Combine milk and parsley; stir well. Add milk mixture to biscuit mix, and stir just until all ingredients are moistened. Drop dough by tablespoonfuls on top of vegetables and chicken in stew. Cook, uncovered, over low heat 10 minutes; cover and cook 10 minutes. Yield: 2 quarts. *Carol Poole, Winston-Salem, North Carolina.*

HEARTY CHEESE SOUP

½ cup finely diced onion
½ cup finely diced carrots
½ cup finely diced celery
¼ cup butter or margarine
¼ cup all-purpose flour
1 tablespoon cornstarch
4 cups milk
4 cups chicken broth
⅛ teaspoon baking soda
1 pound sharp process American cheese, cubed

Sauté onion, carrots, and celery in butter in a large Dutch oven 5 minutes or until tender. Add flour and cornstarch, stirring until smooth. Cook 1 minute, stirring constantly. Gradually add milk and chicken broth; cook over medium heat, stirring constantly, until thickened and bubbly.

Stir in soda and cheese. Reduce heat to low; cook, stirring constantly, just until cheese melts. Serve immediately. Yield: 2 quarts. *Kim Kelly, Austin, Texas.*

Tip: Rub hands with parsley to remove any odor.

CREAM OF MUSHROOM SOUP

1 pound fresh mushrooms, sliced
1 medium onion, finely chopped
¼ cup plus 2 tablespoons butter or
   margarine
¼ cup all-purpose flour
3 cups chicken broth
2 cups half-and-half
1 teaspoon salt
¼ teaspoon white pepper
½ cup dry sherry
¼ teaspoon Angostura bitters

Sauté mushrooms and onion in butter in a heavy saucepan over low heat for 10 minutes or until vegetables are tender. Add flour, stirring until smooth. Cook 1 minute, stirring constantly. Gradually add broth; cook over medium heat, stirring constantly, until thickened and bubbly.

Reduce heat to low; stir in remaining ingredients. Cook just until thoroughly heated, stirring frequently. Serve immediately. Yield: 1½ quarts.
Martha Heun,
Louisville, Kentucky.

Bake A Casserole Of Potatoes

Potatoes are great to serve in casseroles. Their mild flavor blends well with a wide range of foods and seasonings.

Select potatoes according to their use. General purpose or round red potatoes are best for boiling. Russet, Idaho, and other long, white potatoes are recommended for baking.

CHEESY POTATO-EGG CASSEROLE

6 large red potatoes (about 2½ pounds)
1 (10¾-ounce) can cream of chicken soup,
   undiluted
1 (8-ounce) carton commercial sour cream
¼ teaspoon curry powder
¼ teaspoon pepper
4 hard-cooked eggs, chopped
2 tablespoons fine, dry breadcrumbs
1 cup (4 ounces) shredded Cheddar cheese

Cook potatoes in boiling water 25 to 30 minutes or until tender; drain and cool to touch. Peel and cut into ¼-inch slices; set aside.

Combine soup, sour cream, curry powder, and pepper; mix well. Layer

half each of potato slices, eggs, and soup mixture in a greased 12- x 8- x 2-inch baking dish; repeat layers. Cover and bake at 350° for 30 minutes. Sprinkle with breadcrumbs and cheese; bake, uncovered, 5 minutes or until cheese melts. Yield: 8 servings.
Mrs. John W. Stevens,
Lexington, Kentucky.

POTATOES-AND-ZUCCHINI AU GRATIN

5 medium-size red potatoes (about 1¼
   pounds)
3 medium zucchini, cut into ¼-inch slices
3 tablespoons butter or margarine
3 tablespoons all-purpose flour
1 teaspoon chicken-flavored bouillon
   granules
1½ cups milk
1 cup (4 ounces) shredded Cheddar cheese
1 (2-ounce) jar diced pimiento, drained
½ teaspoon dried whole thyme
1 (2.8-ounce) can French-fried onion rings

Cook potatoes in boiling water 25 to 30 minutes or until tender; drain and cool to touch. Peel and cut into ¼-inch slices. Set aside.

Cook zucchini, covered, in a small amount of boiling water 5 minutes; drain well, and set aside.

Melt butter in a heavy saucepan over low heat; add flour and bouillon, stirring until smooth. Cook 1 minute, stirring constantly. Gradually add milk; cook over medium heat, stirring constantly, until thickened and bubbly. Remove from heat; add cheese, pimiento, and thyme, stirring until cheese melts.

Layer half each of potatoes, zucchini, and sauce mixture in a lightly greased 2-quart casserole; repeat layers. Cover and bake at 350° for 30 minutes. Sprinkle with fried onion rings; bake, uncovered, 5 minutes. Yield: 8 servings.
Georgia F. Chapman,
Bedford, Virginia.

MUSHROOM-POTATO CASSEROLE

6 medium-size red potatoes (about 1½
   pounds)
1 pound fresh mushrooms, sliced
3 tablespoons butter or margarine
1 (10¾-ounce) can cream of chicken soup,
   undiluted
¼ cup milk
¼ cup chopped onion
½ cup (2 ounces) shredded Cheddar
   cheese
¼ teaspoon paprika

Cook potatoes in boiling salted water 25 to 30 minutes or until tender. Drain and cool to touch. Peel and cut into ½-inch slices; set aside.

Sauté mushrooms in butter in a large skillet until tender; set aside.

Combine soup, milk, and onion in a small saucepan; cook over medium heat until mixture is thoroughly heated, stirring occasionally. Remove from heat; set aside.

Place potatoes in a lightly greased 1½-quart casserole; top with mushrooms, reserving ½ cup. Spoon soup mixture over mushrooms. Top with cheese and paprika. Bake at 350° for 15 minutes. Garnish with the reserved mushrooms. Yield: 6 servings.
Connie Millsap,
Birmingham, Alabama.

Enjoy Carrots Year-Round

One of the best things about carrots is that they're available throughout the year. What's more, carrots may be kept fresh in the refrigerator up to a month. So stock up on a supply of vitamin A-rich carrots to prepare as quick side dishes for your winter meals.

ZESTY CARROTS

7 medium carrots (about 1½ pounds),
   scraped
½ cup mayonnaise
2 tablespoons horseradish sauce
2 tablespoons grated onion
¼ teaspoon salt
¼ teaspoon pepper
¼ cup fine, dry breadcrumbs
1 tablespoon butter or margarine,
   melted
Paprika

Cut carrots into 2½- x ¼-inch strips. Cook carrots, covered, in a small amount of boiling water 5 minutes or until crisp-tender. Drain.

Arrange carrots in a shallow 1½-quart casserole. Combine next 5 ingredients, mixing well; spread evenly over carrots. Combine breadcrumbs and butter; sprinkle over mayonnaise mixture. Sprinkle with paprika. Bake at 375° for 15 minutes. Yield: 6 servings.
Betty Hornsby,
Columbia, South Carolina.

APRICOT CARROTS

2½ cups scraped, sliced carrots (about 1 pound)
¼ cup apricot preserves
1½ tablespoons butter or margarine
1 teaspoon lemon juice
¼ teaspoon grated orange rind
⅛ teaspoon ground nutmeg

Cook carrots, covered, in a medium saucepan in a small amount of boiling water 8 to 10 minutes or until crisp-tender; drain.

Combine remaining ingredients in a saucepan; cook over low heat, stirring constantly, until preserves melt. Stir in carrots; cook until thoroughly heated. Yield: 4 servings. *Mrs. John Andrew, Winston-Salem, North Carolina.*

SPECIAL CARROTS

1 pound carrots, scraped and diagonally sliced
½ cup chopped celery
¼ cup chopped onion
¼ cup Chablis or other dry white wine
2 tablespoons butter or margarine
2 tablespoons sugar
¼ teaspoon dried whole dillweed

Combine all ingredients in a medium saucepan. Bring to a boil; cover, reduce heat, and simmer 10 to 12 minutes or until vegetables are tender. Yield: about 6 servings. *Karen Beal, Key Largo, Florida.*

VEGETABLES WITH BUTTERMILK SAUCE

1 pound carrots, scraped and cut into ¼-inch slices
1 (16-ounce) package frozen English peas
1 cup water
½ teaspoon sugar
½ teaspoon salt
½ cup thinly sliced green onions with tops
Buttermilk Sauce

Combine first 5 ingredients in a large saucepan; bring to a boil. Cover, reduce heat, and simmer 10 minutes or until tender. Add onions; cook 1 minute. Drain vegetables; transfer to a serving dish. Serve with Buttermilk Sauce. Yield: 8 servings.

Buttermilk Sauce:

2 tablespoons butter or margarine
1 tablespoon all-purpose flour
¾ cup buttermilk
¼ cup mayonnaise
¼ teaspoon salt
Dash of pepper

Melt butter in a heavy saucepan over low heat; add flour, stirring until smooth. Cook 1 minute, stirring constantly. Gradually add buttermilk; cook over medium heat, stirring constantly, until thickened and bubbly. Stir in mayonnaise, salt, and pepper with a wire whisk until smooth and thoroughly heated. Yield: 1 cup. *Sarah Watson, Knoxville, Tennessee.*

CARROTS CAPRICE

1 pound carrots, scraped and cut into ¼-inch slices
½ cup water
¼ cup butter or margarine
2 teaspoons sugar
¼ teaspoon salt
¼ teaspoon ground nutmeg
2 tablespoons chopped fresh parsley
2 teaspoons lemon juice

Combine first 6 ingredients in a large saucepan. Bring to a boil; cover, reduce heat, and simmer 8 to 10 minutes or just until tender. Remove from heat; stir in parsley and lemon juice. Serve carrots with a slotted spoon. Yield: 4 servings. *Mrs. Robert M. Moyer, Fairfax, Virginia.*

Dried Fruit Brings The Taste Of Summer

Whether you dry your own or buy the commercially packaged kind, dried fruit is an excellent way to feast on summer flavors out of season. Dried plums and grapes (prunes and raisins) are the most popular dried fruit, but you'll find many delicious uses for dried pears, apricots, peaches, and apples as well. See page 146 for instructions on drying fruit.

You can eat dried fruit right from the package if you wish, but you may want to "plump" or rehydrate the fruit to make it softer and more chewable. Place the fruit in just enough boiling water to cover, and soak for 5 to 10 minutes. Or place the dried fruit in a vegetable steamer, and steam 3 to 5 minutes. Some types of fruit will take longer than others; just simmer or steam to desired softness.

If you plan to chop the fruit, it's easier to do it with kitchen shears or a knife before plumping. The fruit will still be somewhat sticky, so run the blades under hot water or brush them with vegetable oil occasionally during chopping. If you use a food processor or blender, it's best to freeze the fruit first. It will be less sticky and much easier to chop.

APRICOT-STUFFED CORNISH HENS

1½ cups chopped dried apricots
1½ cups boiling water
1 cup sliced fresh mushrooms
¾ cup chopped pecans
3 green onions, thinly sliced
3 tablespoons minced green pepper
¼ cup plus 2 tablespoons butter or margarine
3 cups cooked wild rice
1 tablespoon minced fresh parsley
½ teaspoon salt
¼ teaspoon pepper
⅛ teaspoon red pepper
2 pounds skinned and boned chicken breasts
4 (1- to 1½-pound) Cornish hens
Melted butter
½ cup apricot preserves
2 tablespoons Triple Sec or other orange-flavored liqueur
1 tablespoon vinegar

Soak apricots in boiling water for 20 minutes; drain well, and set aside.

Sauté mushrooms, pecans, onions, and green pepper in butter in a large skillet until vegetables are tender. Remove from heat; add apricots and next 5 ingredients. Set aside.

Cut chicken into uniform pieces. Position steel blade in food processor bowl; add chicken. Process about 1 minute, or until chicken is pureed. Remove chicken, and add to rice mixture, stirring well.

Remove giblets from hens; reserve for another use. Rinse hens with cold water, and pat dry. Stuff hens with rice mixture, and close cavities. Secure with wooden picks; truss. Place hens breast side up in a 13- x 9- x 2-inch baking pan. Spoon remaining stuffing around hens; brush hens with melted butter. Bake at 350° for 1 hour and 15 minutes, basting frequently with butter.

Combine preserves, Triple Sec, and vinegar in a small saucepan; cook over medium heat until thoroughly heated. Brush hens with the glaze, and bake an additional 15 minutes or until lightly browned. Arrange hens on platter, and spoon remaining glaze over each. Yield: 4 servings. *Joanne C. Champagne, Covington, Louisiana.*

PORK CHOPS STUFFED WITH PRUNES

8 pitted prunes
⅔ cup dry red wine
½ pound uncooked ground pork
½ cup minced onion
½ cup soft breadcrumbs
1 egg, slightly beaten
1 teaspoon minced fresh parsley
¼ teaspoon salt
⅛ teaspoon pepper
8 (1-inch-thick) pork chops
2 tablespoons vegetable oil
2 tablespoons butter or margarine
2 teaspoons dried whole rosemary, crushed
¾ cup dry white wine
1 cup orange juice
1 tablespoon cornstarch
1 teaspoon all-purpose flour
¼ cup water

Combine prunes and red wine in a small saucepan over low heat; simmer 5 to 8 minutes. Drain and set aside.

Combine the next 7 ingredients, and mix well; set aside.

Make pockets in pork chops, cutting from rib side to fat edge of each chop. (Do not cut through fat edge.) Stuff pockets of pork chops with the ground pork mixture. Press a prune into each pocket.

Heat oil and butter in a large skillet over medium heat. Brown pork chops on both sides. Transfer chops to a large baking dish; sprinkle with rosemary. Cover and bake at 350° for 1 hour.

Add white wine and orange juice to skillet drippings; bring to a boil, and cook 2 minutes. Combine cornstarch, flour, and water; stir into orange juice mixture. Cook, stirring constantly, until thickened. Serve sauce with pork chops. Yield: 8 servings. *Carrie Bartlett, Gallatin, Tennessee.*

PINEAPPLE-APRICOT BREAD

2½ cups all-purpose flour
1½ teaspoons baking powder
¼ teaspoon salt
¼ teaspoon baking soda
¾ cup sugar
⅓ cup butter or margarine, melted
1 egg
¼ cup milk
1 (8-ounce) can crushed pineapple, undrained
⅓ cup chopped dried apricots
¼ cup raisins
1 cup chopped pecans

Combine first 4 ingredients, and set mixture aside.

Combine sugar, butter, and egg; beat well. Add milk, pineapple, apricots, and raisins; beat well. Stir in flour mixture and pecans.

Pour mixture into a greased and floured 9- x 5- x 3-inch loafpan. Bake at 350° for 1 hour and 15 minutes or until a wooden pick inserted in center comes out clean. Cool 10 minutes in pan on a wire rack. Remove from pan. Yield: 1 loaf. *Brenda Heupel, Florence, Alabama.*

RUM-RAISIN SAUCE

¼ cup honey
3 tablespoons butter
1 cup golden raisins
Grated rind of 1 lemon
2 tablespoons lemon juice
1 cup water
½ cup sugar
1 tablespoon cornstarch
Dash of salt
2 tablespoons dark rum

Combine first 6 ingredients in a saucepan. Combine sugar, cornstarch, and salt; stir into honey mixture. Bring mixture to a boil, stirring constantly, and cook 5 minutes. Remove from heat, and stir in rum. Serve over ice cream. Yield: 2¼ cups. *Kathleen Stone, Houston, Texas.*

BAKED FRUIT PIES

2 cups or 1 (6-ounce) package dried mixed fruit
1 cup sugar
2 cups all-purpose flour
1 teaspoon salt
¾ cup shortening
4 to 5 tablespoons cold water
3 tablespoons butter or margarine, melted

Combine fruit and sugar in a medium saucepan; cover with water. Bring to a boil. Reduce heat and simmer, uncovered, about 1 hour or until fruit is tender. Cool. Mash slightly.

Combine flour and salt; cut in shortening until mixture resembles coarse meal. Sprinkle cold water, 1 tablespoon at a time, evenly over surface; stir with a fork until all dry ingredients are moistened. Shape into a ball.

Divide pastry in half; roll each portion to ⅛-inch thickness on a lightly floured surface. Cut into 5-inch circles.

Place about 2 tablespoons fruit mixture on half of each pastry circle. To seal pies, dip fingers in water, and moisten edges of circles; fold in half, making sure edges are even. Using a fork dipped in flour, press pastry edges firmly together.

Place pies on a baking sheet; brush with melted butter. Bake at 400° for 15 to 20 minutes or until golden brown. Yield: 1 dozen. *Susan A. Houston, Tucker, Georgia.*

BREAKFAST DATE SPREAD

1 (8-ounce) package cream cheese, softened
1 cup chopped walnuts
½ cup chopped dates
Honey (optional)

Beat cream cheese until smooth. Add walnuts and dates, mixing well. Spread mixture on toast; top each slice with honey, if desired. Yield: 2 cups. *Charles Walton, Birmingham, Alabama.*

DATE CUPCAKES

1 cup chopped dates
1 cup boiling water
2 tablespoons butter
1 cup sugar
1 egg
1¾ cups all-purpose flour
1 teaspoon baking soda
1 cup chopped pecans
1 teaspoon vanilla extract

Combine first 3 ingredients in mixing bowl; let cool. Stir in sugar and egg. Combine flour and baking soda; add to date mixture. Stir in chopped pecans and vanilla. Spoon batter into paper-lined muffin pans, filling two-thirds full. Bake at 375° for 25 minutes. Yield: about 1 dozen. *Paula Patterson, Houston, Texas.*

Tip: For ingredients listed in recipes: If the direction comes before the ingredient—for example, sifted flour—first sift the flour, then measure. If the direction comes after the ingredient—for example, pecans, chopped—first measure pecans, then chop.

Tender Ways With Round Steak

Since there is little fat or waste on round steak, you'll find it makes an economical beef entrée. It's less tender than popular steak cuts such as T-bone or sirloin, but cooking it with moist heat and spices makes it just as tasty.

The three cuts from a full round steak vary in price and tenderness, so it pays to be familiar with them all. Top round is the most tender; it's even tender enough to broil or pan fry.

The bottom round and the eye of the round are less tender cuts, so they should be cooked by moist heat. Simmer them in flavorful juices, wine, or broth. Cutting the steak in thin strips also increases tenderness.

STEAK-AND-VEGETABLE STIR-FRY

1 pound boneless round steak
¼ cup soy sauce
1 clove garlic, crushed
½ teaspoon ground ginger
¼ cup vegetable oil
1 cup thinly sliced green onions
½ cup green pepper, cut into 1-inch
    squares
½ cup sweet red pepper, cut into 1-inch
    squares
2 stalks celery, chopped
1 tablespoon cornstarch
1 cup water
2 medium tomatoes, cut into wedges
Hot cooked rice

Partially freeze steak; slice diagonally across the grain into 2- x ¼-inch strips. Combine next 3 ingredients in a shallow container, mixing well; add steak.

Heat oil in a large skillet. Add steak and soy sauce mixture to skillet; cook 2 to 3 minutes or until meat is browned. Stir in onions, pepper, and celery; cook 5 minutes, stirring constantly, until vegetables are crisp-tender. Remove meat and vegetables from skillet; set aside.

Combine cornstarch and water, stirring until cornstarch dissolves. Add cornstarch mixture to liquid in skillet; cook, stirring constantly, until smooth and thickened. Return meat, cooked vegetables, and tomato wedges to skillet; stir well to coat. Serve over rice. Yield: 4 servings. *Sue B. Freeman, Cadiz, Kentucky.*

COUNTRY-FRIED STEAK AND CREAM GRAVY

2 to 2½ pounds boneless round steak
1 teaspoon salt
½ teaspoon pepper
½ teaspoon garlic salt
½ cup all-purpose flour
½ cup milk
½ cup vegetable oil
¼ cup all-purpose flour
2 cups milk
½ teaspoon salt
¼ teaspoon pepper

Pound steak to ¼-inch thickness; cut into serving-size pieces.

Sprinkle steaks with 1 teaspoon salt, ½ teaspoon pepper, and garlic salt. Dredge steak in ½ cup flour, and dip in ½ cup milk. Return to flour, and dredge again. Brown steaks in hot oil in a large skillet. Remove from skillet, and drain on paper towels; set aside.

Pour off pan drippings, reserving 3 tablespoons. Add ¼ cup flour to drippings; cook over medium heat until bubbly, stirring constantly. Add 2 cups milk; cook until thickened, stirring constantly. Stir in ½ teaspoon salt and ¼ teaspoon pepper. Add steak to gravy; cover, reduce heat, and simmer 25 minutes. Remove cover, and cook an additional 5 minutes. Yield: 8 servings. *Mrs. Ross Sparkman, Jr., Moultrie, Georgia.*

GARLIC STEAK

2 pounds boneless round steak, about
    1 inch thick
½ cup all-purpose flour
¼ cup vegetable oil
2 medium onions, sliced
½ cup chopped fresh parsley
8 cloves garlic, crushed
2 (10¾-ounce) cans chicken broth,
    undiluted
1½ cups water
½ teaspoon salt
¼ teaspoon pepper
Hot cooked noodles

Dredge steak in flour; pound to ½-inch thickness. Cut steak into serving-size pieces. Brown steaks in hot oil in a Dutch oven. Remove from skillet, and set aside.

Add onions to pan drippings; sauté until tender. Return steak to Dutch oven; add remaining ingredients except noodles. Cover, reduce heat, and simmer 1½ to 2 hours or until steak is tender. Serve over noodles. Yield: 6 servings. *Richard Heyman, Sunnyvale, California.*

BEEF PARMIGIANA

3 tablespoons all-purpose flour
½ teaspoon salt
⅛ teaspoon pepper
1½ to 2 pounds boneless round
    steak
½ cup fine, dry breadcrumbs
¼ cup grated Parmesan cheese
½ teaspoon dried whole basil
1 egg, slightly beaten
1 tablespoon water
¼ cup vegetable oil
1 (15-ounce) can tomato sauce
1 clove garlic, crushed
1 tablespoon sugar
½ teaspoon dried whole oregano
3 (6- x 3-inch) slices mozzarella
    cheese, halved

Combine flour, salt, and pepper; mix well. Dredge steak in flour mixture; pound to ¼-inch thickness. Cut round steak into 6 pieces.

Combine breadcrumbs, Parmesan cheese, and basil; mix well. Combine egg and water; dip steak in egg mixture, and coat with crumb mixture.

Brown steak in hot oil in a large skillet. Remove from skillet, and drain on paper towels. Place in a lightly greased 13- x 9- x 2-inch baking dish. Combine tomato sauce, garlic, sugar, and oregano; pour over steak. Cover and bake at 350° for 1 hour. Remove from oven; uncover and place a cheese slice on each piece of steak. Return to oven; bake 5 minutes or until cheese melts. Yield: 6 servings. *Judy Mogridge, Augusta, Georgia.*

Pasta Dinners Are His Specialty

If he isn't busy hunting, scuba diving, or working with his Arabian horses, you'll probably find Harris Simpson of Atlanta in the kitchen. He may be cooking up a game dinner for some friends, mixing up his own tomato sauce, or hanging homemade pasta on the racks to dry.

Harris Simpson believes that the best meals come from your own kitchen. "The only sure way to get a good meal is to prepare it yourself," he says. Now he's even hooked on making all of his own pasta. "I made some out of curiosity, and it was so much better that I bought a pasta machine to start making my own."

Pasta dinners have become a favorite with Harris. He gets new ideas for sauces at restaurants, then comes home and tries to duplicate the ones he likes.

Whether you make your own pasta or not, you'll enjoy sampling some of these pasta toppers created by Harris. Following his recipes are some from other Southern men who like to be creative in the kitchen.

ITALIAN SAUSAGE AND PEPPERS

1 pound Italian sausage links, cut into
   1-inch pieces
4 medium-size green peppers, cut into
   2-inch pieces
1 large onion, cut into eighths
1 (32-ounce) jar meatless marinara sauce
Hot cooked whole wheat noodles
Grated Romano cheese
Chopped fresh parsley

Brown sausage in a Dutch oven over medium heat; remove and set aside. Reserve 3½ tablespoons drippings in Dutch oven, adding vegetable oil if necessary. Sauté green pepper and onion in reserved drippings until onion is tender. Add sausage and marinara sauce; reduce heat and simmer, uncovered, 10 minutes, stirring occasionally. Spoon sauce over whole wheat noodles; sprinkle each serving with Romano cheese and parsley. Yield: 8 servings.

CLAM SAUCE WITH LINGUINE

¼ cup finely chopped onion
6 cloves garlic, minced
½ cup olive oil
2 (6½-ounce) cans minced clams,
   undrained
½ cup Chablis or other dry white wine
1 teaspoon basil leaves, crushed
1 teaspoon dried whole thyme
¼ teaspoon salt
⅛ teaspoon coarsely ground pepper
1 (8-ounce) package linguine, cooked
½ cup chopped fresh parsley

Sauté onion and garlic in olive oil in a medium skillet.

Drain clams, reserving ½ cup juice. Add reserved clam juice and wine to skillet; bring to a boil. Cook over medium-high heat 10 minutes or until mixture is reduced by half. Stir in clams, basil, thyme, salt, and pepper; simmer an additional 5 minutes.

Pour sauce over linguine; toss well before serving. Sprinkle with parsley. Yield: 8 servings.

CHICKEN CACCIATORE

8 chicken breast halves, skinned and
   boned
Salt and pepper
All-purpose flour
⅓ cup olive oil
1 large onion, chopped
3 or 4 cloves garlic, minced
½ pound fresh mushrooms, sliced
2 (16-ounce) cans whole tomatoes,
   undrained and quartered
1 (4-ounce) jar whole pimientos,
   undrained and sliced
½ cup sweet vermouth
3 bay leaves
1 teaspoon dried whole thyme
1 teaspoon dried whole oregano
Salt to taste
¼ teaspoon freshly ground pepper
2 medium-size green peppers, cut into
   strips
Hot cooked spaghetti

Sprinkle chicken with salt and pepper; dredge in flour, shaking off excess. Heat oil in a Dutch oven over medium-high heat; add chicken, and sauté 4 to 5 minutes on each side or until golden brown. Remove chicken from Dutch oven; drain on paper towels.

Add onion and garlic to Dutch oven; sauté over medium heat 5 minutes. Stir in next 9 ingredients; add chicken, and bring to a boil. Reduce heat and simmer, uncovered, 30 minutes, stirring occasionally. Stir in green pepper; cook an additional 30 minutes, stirring occasionally. Remove bay leaves; serve over spaghetti. Yield: 8 servings.
Joe Maugans,
Birmingham, Alabama.

WEST TEXAS PIMIENTO CHEESE

4 cups (16 ounces) shredded Colby
   cheese
1 (4-ounce) jar diced pimiento,
   drained
1 cup mayonnaise
6 pimiento-stuffed olives, diced
¾ teaspoon lemon-pepper seasoning
½ teaspoon instant minced onion

Combine all ingredients; stir well. Cover and chill thoroughly. Yield: about 2½ cups.
Robert A. Hill,
Lubbock, Texas.

Tip: Organize your spice shelf and save much time by keeping the spices in alphabetical order. Store all spices in tightly covered containers to retain flavor and fragrance.

BROCCOLI-CHEESE CASSEROLE

2 (10-ounce) packages frozen chopped
   broccoli
1 (10¾-ounce) can cream of mushroom
   soup, undiluted
1 cup (4 ounces) shredded Cheddar
   cheese, divided
¼ cup milk
¼ cup mayonnaise
2 eggs, beaten
Dash of red pepper
Paprika

Cook broccoli according to package directions. Drain and spoon into a lightly greased 10- x 6- x 2-inch baking dish; set aside.

Combine soup, ½ cup cheese, milk, mayonnaise, eggs, and red pepper. Spoon soup mixture evenly over broccoli. Sprinkle with remaining ½ cup cheese and paprika. Bake at 350° for 45 minutes. Yield: 6 to 8 servings.
George Boyd,
Wilcoe, West Virginia.

Jazz Up Black-Eyed Peas

Southerners know they can bring good fortune to the new year by eating a generous helping of black-eyed peas on New Year's Day.

HOT-AND-SPICY BLACK-EYED PEAS

2 (16-ounce) cans black-eyed peas,
   undrained
½ (3½-ounce) package sliced pepperoni,
   diced
1 medium-size green pepper, diced
1 medium onion, diced
¼ teaspoon hot sauce
2 tablespoons hot taco sauce

Combine all ingredients in a Dutch oven over low heat, Cover and simmer for 1 hour, stirring occasionally. Yield: 8 servings.
Barbara H. Smith,
Centreville, Virginia.

Simply Delicious Pound Cakes

When we tested Yogurt Pound Cake in our kitchens, it was a hit. The cake came out of the pan beautifully, and when sliced, the texture was light and tender. Since the cake is so moist and delicious, we suggest simply dusting the top with powdered sugar. There's no need for frosting.

YOGURT POUND CAKE

1 cup butter or margarine, softened
1½ cups sugar
3 eggs
2¼ cups all-purpose flour
½ teaspoon baking soda
½ teaspoon salt
1 teaspoon grated lemon rind
1 teaspoon vanilla extract
1 (8-ounce) carton peach yogurt
Powdered sugar (optional)

Cream butter; gradually add sugar, beating until mixture is light and fluffy. Add eggs, one at a time, beating after each addition.

Combine flour, soda, and salt; add to creamed mixture, mixing just until blended. Add lemon rind, vanilla, and yogurt.

Pour batter into a greased and floured 10-inch Bundt pan. Bake at 350° for 1 hour or until a wooden pick inserted in center comes out clean. Cool in pan 15 minutes; remove from pan, and cool completely on a rack. Sprinkle cake with powdered sugar, if desired. Yield: one 10-inch cake. *Ethel Evans, St. Petersburg, Florida.*

CHOCOLATE POUND CAKE

1 cup shortening
2 cups sugar
4 eggs
3 cups all-purpose flour
½ teaspoon baking soda
½ teaspoon salt
1 cup buttermilk
1 (4-ounce) bar sweet baking chocolate, melted and cooled
2 teaspoons vanilla extract
1 teaspoon butter flavoring
Chocolate glaze (recipe follows)

Cream shortening; gradually add sugar, beating until mixture is light and fluffy. Add eggs, one at a time, beating after each addition.

Combine flour, soda, and salt; mix well. Add to creamed mixture alternately with buttermilk, beginning and ending with flour mixture. Mix just until blended after each addition. Stir in chocolate and flavorings, mixing just until blended.

Pour batter into a greased and floured 10-inch Bundt pan. Bake at 300° for 1½ hours. Cool in pan 10 to 15 minutes; invert onto a serving plate. Spoon chocolate glaze over top of warm cake. Cool before serving. Yield: one 10-inch cake.

Chocolate Glaze:

1 (4-ounce) bar sweet baking chocolate
1 tablespoon butter or margarine
1 cup sifted powdered sugar
3 tablespoons hot water

Melt chocolate and butter in top of a double boiler over boiling water. Add sugar and hot water, beating well. Yield: about 1 cup. *Mrs. L. L. Gray, Fort Worth, Texas.*

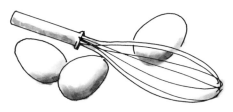

COCONUT CREAM POUND CAKE

1 cup butter or margarine, softened
½ cup shortening
2½ cups sugar
5 eggs
3 cups all-purpose flour
½ teaspoon baking powder
1 cup cream of coconut
1 teaspoon grated lemon rind
1 teaspoon vanilla extract

Cream butter and shortening; gradually add sugar, beating until light and fluffy. Add eggs, one at a time, beating after each addition.

Combine flour and baking powder; add to creamed mixture alternately with cream of coconut, beginning and ending with flour mixture. Mix just until blended after each addition. Stir in the lemon rind and vanilla.

Pour batter into a greased and floured 10-inch tube pan; bake at 350° for 1 hour and 15 minutes or until a wooden pick inserted in center comes out clean. Cool in pan 10 to 15 minutes; remove from pan, and cool completely on a rack. Yield: one 10-inch cake.

Agnes W. Ladd, Washington, D.C.

APPLE CIDER POUND CAKE

1 cup butter, softened
½ cup shortening
3 cups sugar
6 eggs
3 cups all-purpose flour
½ teaspoon baking powder
½ teaspoon salt
1½ teaspoons apple pie spice
1 cup apple cider
1 teaspoon vanilla extract

Cream butter and shortening; gradually add sugar, beating until light and fluffy. Add eggs, one at a time, beating after each addition.

Combine next 4 ingredients; add to creamed mixture alternately with apple cider, beginning and ending with dry ingredients. Mix just until blended after each addition. Stir in vanilla.

Pour batter into a greased and floured 10-inch tube pan. Bake at 325° for 1 hour and 20 minutes or until a wooden pick inserted in center comes out clean. Cool in pan 10 to 15 minutes; remove from pan, and cool completely on a rack. Yield: one 10-inch cake.

Mrs. Billie Taylor, Afton, Virginia.

From Our Kitchen To Yours

With deadlines constantly facing us, we're always trying to find a better way to organize our *Southern Living* test kitchens. Here are a variety of helpful tips on kitchen organization and grocery shopping.

Winter Clean-Up

With the Christmas rush behind, January is usually a relaxing month. Therefore, this is the best time of year for cleaning up, throwing out, and reorganizing. Check these suggestions:

—Clean out your pantry. Check all the canned items. Canned foods that are older than one year tend to lose their nutritional value and flavor.

—Organize your recipe files. Try those recipes you've been saving. Discard the ones you'll never make.

—Store utensils and small appliances near the spot in your kitchen where you'll be using them. For example, store your mixer, measuring spoons and cups, and mixing bowls near the area where you would mix a cake. Keep pot holders, cooking spoons, and pans near the range.

—Arrange wooden spoons and spatulas in a decorative container, and place near the range. You'll always have cooking spoons at your fingertips.

—Organize the utensil drawers. Invest in plastic drawer trays to store pancake or egg turners, wire whisks, specialty items such as a garlic press.

—Put those knives in a knife block. Storing knives in a drawer not only dulls the blades, it's dangerous.

—Clean out the freezer. Bring older items to the front and use them before recently purchased ones. Also, start labeling frozen foods with the date you bought them.

—Check your spices by smelling each one. If the aroma has faded, it's time to buy more. Storing spices and seasonings in the freezer keeps them fresh and away from the heat and humidity of the kitchen. The spices won't freeze solid.

—Vacuum the coils of your freezer and refrigerator. A build-up of dust can interfere with efficient cooling.

Shape-Up Grocery Shopping

You can save money on groceries and even reduce the number of trips to the store by trying these tips:

—Set a weekly grocery budget and stick to it.

—Plan weekly menus to fit your budget. Then make your grocery list from your meal plans. Never go shopping without a list; you'll end up spending too much.

—Plan on one major grocery trip a week. You may need to plan on a second trip later to pick up fresh vegetables, fruit, and milk. The more times you go to the store, the more you will spend.

—Look for advertised specials and coupons in your newspapers. Work them into your menus, if possible.

—When writing out your grocery list, try grouping the items under the following headings: Canned Vegetables and Soups, Canned Fruits, Cleaning Supplies, Baking Items, Imported or Specialty Items, Produce, Meats, Dairy Products, Frozen Foods, and Miscellaneous. We have found that these headings reduce the amount of time we spend in the grocery store.

—Organize your list so that it corresponds to the layout of the grocery store. For example, if the produce section is located at the front of the store, then start your list with produce.

—Don't go shopping when you're hungry. Everything looks good, and it's easy to go over your budget.

—Update your coupons. Many coupons expire at the end of the year. Make sure your coupons are organized according to product, so they'll be easy to locate when they're needed.

MICROWAVE COOKERY

Dress Up Franks In The Microwave

With a few extra ingredients and the help of your microwave oven, you can take plain frankfurters beyond the traditional hot dog. Rather than reserving franks as a convenient standby to be served only when you're in a pinch, turn them into these speedy appetizers, entrées, and side dishes.

When kids come in from play and want a hot snack or need to prepare their own dinner, let them make Frankfurter Sandwiches or Barbecued Frankfurters. The microwave oven gets the food hot, but the containers don't absorb as much heat as metal pans do. So with basic microwave instructions, children can safely prepare frankfurters in no time at all.

POLYNESIAN BEANS-AND-FRANKS

1 medium apple, peeled and chopped
¼ cup chopped onion
¼ cup chopped green pepper
1 tablespoon butter or margarine
2 (16-ounce) cans kidney beans, drained
1 (16-ounce) can baked beans, undrained
1 (8-ounce) can pineapple chunks, drained
½ pound frankfurters, cut into ½-inch slices
2 tablespoons vinegar
2 tablespoons corn syrup
½ teaspoon dry mustard
¼ teaspoon salt
⅛ teaspoon pepper

Combine apple, onion, green pepper, and butter in a 2½-quart casserole. Cover with heavy-duty plastic wrap, and microwave at HIGH for 2½ to 3 minutes. Stir in remaining ingredients, mixing well. Cover and microwave at HIGH for 8 to 10 minutes or until thoroughly heated, stirring after 4 minutes. Yield: 8 to 10 servings.

FRANK-FILLED POTATOES

6 medium-size baking potatoes
2 tablespoons butter or margarine
¼ cup chopped onion
¼ cup chopped green pepper
2 tablespoons all-purpose flour
1¾ cups milk
1 cup (4 ounces) shredded Cheddar cheese
2 tablespoons chopped pimiento
½ teaspoon salt
¼ teaspoon pepper
4 frankfurters, cut into ¼-inch slices
½ cup (2 ounces) shredded Cheddar cheese

Rinse potatoes, and pat dry; prick several times with a fork. Arrange potatoes in a circle on paper towels in microwave oven, leaving 1 inch between each potato. Microwave at HIGH for 16 to 18 minutes, turning and rearranging potatoes once. Let potatoes stand 5 minutes.

Place butter in a 4-cup glass measure; microwave at HIGH for 45 seconds or until butter melts. Add onion and green pepper, and cover with heavy-duty plastic wrap; microwave at HIGH for 2 minutes or until vegetables are crisp-tender. Add flour, stirring until smooth; gradually add milk, stirring well. Microwave at HIGH for 4 minutes or until thickened and bubbly; stir at 1-minute intervals. Stir in next 5 ingredients; stir until cheese melts.

Split tops of potatoes lengthwise, and fluff pulp with a fork. Spoon about ½ cup topping over each potato. Sprinkle potatoes with ½ cup Cheddar cheese. Yield: 6 servings.

FRANKFURTER SANDWICHES

1 tablespoon butter or margarine
½ cup chopped onion
1 (14-ounce) bottle extra-hot or regular catsup
2 tablespoons sweet pickle relish
1 tablespoon sugar
1 tablespoon vinegar
¼ teaspoon salt
¼ teaspoon pepper
1 pound frankfurters, cut into ½-inch slices
Hamburger buns

Place butter in a 1½-quart casserole. Microwave at HIGH for 35 seconds or until butter melts. Add onion, and cover with heavy-duty plastic wrap. Microwave at HIGH for 3 minutes or until crisp-tender. Stir in next 6 ingredients. Add frankfurters to sauce. Cover and microwave at HIGH for 3 to 4 minutes, stirring once. Serve in hamburger buns. Yield: 8 to 10 servings.

BARBECUED FRANKFURTERS

1 pound frankfurters
1 tablespoon all-purpose flour
2 tablespoons water
½ cup catsup
¼ cup finely chopped onion
1 tablespoon brown sugar
2 tablespoons vinegar
1 tablespoon plus 1 teaspoon
   Worcestershire sauce
1 teaspoon paprika
1 teaspoon chili powder
¼ teaspoon salt
½ teaspoon pepper
Hot dog buns

Pierce each frankfurter several times with a fork, and place in a 10- x 6- x 2-inch baking dish. Combine flour and water in a small bowl, stirring until smooth; stir in remaining ingredients except hot dog buns, mixing well. Pour mixture over frankfurters; cover with heavy-duty plastic wrap. Microwave at HIGH for 5 to 6 minutes, rearranging frankfurters and rotating the baking dish after 3 minutes.

To serve, place frankfurters in buns; top with sauce. Yield: 8 servings.

SAUCY APPETIZER FRANKS

1 (12-ounce) bottle chili sauce
3 tablespoons brown sugar
2 tablespoons minced onion
2 tablespoons bourbon
½ teaspoon ground ginger
⅛ teaspoon dry mustard
1 pound frankfurters, cut into ¾-inch
   slices

Combine first 6 ingredients in a 1½-quart casserole. Cover with heavy-duty plastic wrap, and microwave at HIGH for 1½ to 2½ minutes or until hot. Stir in frankfurters; cover and microwave at HIGH for 4 to 5 minutes, stirring once. Serve with wooden picks. Yield: 12 appetizer servings.

Make Salad-Fresh Dressings

If your taste for tossed salads is wilting, give these dressings a try. A tossed salad will be crispy and taste its best if you add the dressing at the last minute. Either toss it just before serving or serve the dressing at the table.

HOT BACON DRESSING

4 slices bacon
2 tablespoons cider vinegar
2 tablespoons water
1 tablespoon sugar
1 egg, beaten

Cook bacon in a large skillet until crisp; remove bacon, reserving drippings in skillet. Crumble bacon, and set aside. Add vinegar, water, and sugar to skillet; bring to a boil. Remove from heat. Gradually stir one-fourth of hot mixture into beaten egg; add egg mixture to skillet, stirring constantly, until blended. Cook over low heat, stirring constantly, until thickened. Stir in bacon. Serve dressing warm over salad greens. Yield: about ¾ cup. *Lynette Walther, East Palatka, Florida.*

TANGY FRENCH DRESSING

1 tablespoon instant minced onion
1 teaspoon salt
1 teaspoon celery seeds
1 teaspoon dry mustard
¼ cup sugar
¼ cup vinegar
¼ cup catsup
1 cup vegetable oil

Combine first 7 ingredients in a small mixing bowl; mix well. Gradually add oil in a slow, steady stream, beating constantly at high speed of an electric mixer until thickened. Cover and chill thoroughly. Serve over salad greens. Yield: 1½ cups. *Mrs. John Wyatt, Sr., Palmyra, Tennessee.*

GREEN PEPPER-ONION SALAD DRESSING

1 cup vegetable oil
1 cup vinegar
1 cup sugar
1 medium onion, cut into chunks
1 (2-ounce) jar diced pimiento, drained
1 small green pepper, cut into chunks
3 tablespoons prepared mustard
1 tablespoon Worcestershire sauce
2 teaspoons salt

Combine all ingredients in container of an electric blender; process until smooth. Place in an airtight container, and chill thoroughly. Serve over salad greens. Yield: 5 cups. *Clota Engleman, Spur, Texas.*

CREAMY ROQUEFORT DRESSING

1 (8-ounce) carton commercial sour
   cream
4 ounces Roquefort cheese, crumbled
2 teaspoons lemon juice
¼ teaspoon dry mustard
⅛ teaspoon pepper
4 drops of hot sauce

Combine all ingredients, stirring well. Cover and chill thoroughly. Serve over salad greens. Yield: 1½ cups.
Mrs. J. Edward Ebel, Louisville, Kentucky.

ITALIAN SALAD DRESSING

½ cup vegetable oil
2 tablespoons vinegar
2 tablespoons lemon juice
2 tablespoons water
1 teaspoon sugar
½ teaspoon dry mustard
½ teaspoon paprika
¼ teaspoon salt
¼ teaspoon seasoned salt
¼ teaspoon dried Italian seasoning
⅛ teaspoon red pepper

Combine all ingredients in a jar. Cover tightly, and shake jar vigorously. Chill thoroughly. Shake before serving. Serve over salad greens. Yield: 1 cup.
Ernestine Donaldson, De Funiak Springs, Florida.

EASY HOMEMADE MAYONNAISE

¼ cup sugar
2 teaspoons all-purpose flour
1 teaspoon dry mustard
½ teaspoon salt
¼ cup water
¼ cup vinegar
2 eggs, beaten
1 tablespoon butter or margarine

Combine first 4 ingredients in a saucepan; blend well. Gradually stir in water and vinegar. Add eggs, beating well with a wire whisk. Add butter. Cook over medium heat until mixture comes to a boil, beating constantly. Cover and chill. Yield: 1¼ cups.
Mrs. B. C. Forbes, Clover, South Carolina.

Tip: For salad success be sure lettuce is cold, crisp, and dry. Tear, don't cut, lettuce into bite-size pieces. Add the dressing just before serving.

COOKING LIGHT

These Recipes Are Light And Easy

If you are a dieter, don't be tempted by the increasing variety of convenience products designed to cut minutes away from busy schedules. Some of these processed foods should be avoided because they offer few nutrients other than fat, sugar, and sodium. But if you plan wisely, you can save time by using some convenience products and still keep calories under control.

You'll find several options when it comes to buying vegetables—fresh, canned, or frozen; with or without added salt; plain or in a butter or cream sauce. The best choice for maximum nutrients and fiber is to buy fresh vegetables. But in the dead of winter, a variety isn't always available. That's when frozen vegetables are helpful. What's more, frozen vegetables are a big time-saver.

Grocery shopping is less confusing when you take advantage of the nutrition labels on many processed and convenience items. By law, any product that makes a claim of being reduced in calories, fat, or salt, or fortified with any nutrient, must list certain information on the label, including calories per serving. In fact, many manufacturers voluntarily list nutrition information on their product's label.

If there is no nutrition label, you can still get an idea of the product's nutritive value by looking at the list of ingredients. They must be listed in order of quantity. For instance, a product that lists sugar as its first ingredient contains more sugar than any other ingredient and is probably high in calories.

HAMBURGER PIE

1 pound ground chuck
1 small onion, chopped
1 (4-ounce) can sliced mushrooms, drained
4 ounces Neufchâtel cheese, cubed
1 tablespoon all-purpose flour
½ teaspoon ground savory
½ teaspoon pepper
¼ teaspoon salt
1 (5.5-ounce) can refrigerated buttermilk biscuits
Vegetable cooking spray
1 cup low-fat cottage cheese
1 egg
Ground paprika

Combine ground chuck and onion in a large skillet; cook until meat is browned and onion is tender. Drain meat mixture in a colander, and pat dry with a paper towel; wipe pan drippings from skillet with a paper towel.

Return meat mixture to skillet; add mushrooms and Neufchâtel cheese. Cook over low heat, stirring constantly, until cheese melts. Stir in next 4 ingredients, blending well.

Split each biscuit in half; pat biscuit dough evenly into a 9-inch pieplate coated with cooking spray. Spoon meat mixture over dough. Combine cottage cheese and egg, mixing well; spread evenly over meat mixture. Sprinkle with paprika. Bake at 350° for 35 to 40 minutes. Yield: 8 servings (about 224 calories per serving).

MIXED VEGETABLE STEW

1½ pounds ground chuck
1 (16-ounce) package frozen mixed vegetables
1 (16-ounce) can whole tomatoes, undrained and cut into quarters
1 (4-ounce) can mushroom stems and pieces, undrained
2 cups tomato juice
2 tablespoons instant minced onion
1 teaspoon dried whole basil
½ teaspoon dried whole oregano
½ teaspoon pepper

Cook ground chuck in a Dutch oven until meat is browned, stirring to crumble; drain meat in a colander, and pat dry with a paper towel. Wipe pan drippings from Dutch oven with a paper towel.

Return meat to Dutch oven; stir in remaining ingredients. Bring to a boil; cover, reduce heat, and simmer 30 minutes. Yield: 8 cups (about 208 calories per 1-cup serving).

CHICKEN-VEGETABLE STIR-FRY

2 (10-ounce) packages frozen Chinese-style stir-fry vegetables
4 chicken breast halves, skinned and boned
Vegetable cooking spray
1 medium tomato, peeled and cut into thin wedges
2 cups hot cooked rice

Remove seasoning packets from frozen vegetables. Cut chicken breasts into 1-inch pieces; sprinkle 1 seasoning packet over chicken. Set aside.

Coat a wok with cooking spray. Cook vegetables in wok according to package directions, using remaining seasoning packet; set aside. Remove vegetables from wok, and set aside.

Coat wok with cooking spray; allow to heat at medium high (325°) for 2 minutes. Add chicken, and stir-fry 3 to 4 minutes. Return vegetables to wok; add tomato, and simmer 1 to 2 minutes or until thoroughly heated. Serve over rice. Yield: 4 servings (about 220 calories per serving plus 90 calories per ½ cup cooked rice).

OPEN-FACE SANDWICHES

1 tablespoon mustard with horseradish
2 tablespoons reduced-calorie mayonnaise
1 teaspoon sesame seeds
1 (10-ounce) package frozen broccoli spears
4 slices rye bread, toasted
4 (⁴/₅-ounce) slices lean cooked ham
4 (⅔-ounce) slices low-fat process American cheese

Combine first 3 ingredients, and set aside. Cook broccoli according to package directions, omitting salt; drain and set aside.

Spread mayonnaise mixture evenly over bread slices. Place 1 slice ham on each slice of bread. Arrange broccoli over ham; top with cheese slices. Broil until cheese melts. Yield: 4 servings (about 180 calories per serving).

MARINATED VEGETABLE SALAD

1 (1.3-ounce) package Italian reduced-calorie salad dressing mix
3 cups broccoli flowerets
2 cups cauliflower flowerets
2 small carrots, scraped and diagonally sliced
1 small cucumber, sliced
1 medium-size green pepper, thinly sliced

Prepare salad dressing according to package directions; set aside.

Combine remaining ingredients in a large, shallow container. Pour the salad dressing over vegetables; toss well. Cover and refrigerate overnight, tossing occasionally. Yield: 8 servings (about 47 calories per serving).

EASY TOMATO SOUP

Vegetable cooking spray
¼ cup chopped green pepper
2 tablespoons chopped onion
1 (10½-ounce) can low-sodium tomato
    soup with tomato pieces, undiluted
1¼ cups water
¼ teaspoon celery seeds
⅛ teaspoon freshly ground pepper
⅛ teaspoon dried whole basil
Commercial croutons (optional)

Coat a medium saucepan with cooking spray; place over medium-high heat until hot. Add green pepper and onion; sauté until tender. Stir in next 5 ingredients. Cover and cook over low heat about 5 minutes or until thoroughly heated. Garnish with croutons, if desired. Yield: 2⅓ cups (about 94 calories per 1-cup serving plus 6 calories per tablespoon croutons).

ANGEL CAKE WITH PINEAPPLE-ORANGE SAUCE

1 (14.5-ounce) package white angel food
    cake mix
½ teaspoon ground cardamom
¼ teaspoon ground nutmeg
Pineapple-Orange Sauce
Orange twists (optional)

Prepare cake mix according to package directions, adding cardamom and nutmeg to batter; bake according to package directions. Invert pan on funnel or bottle until cake is completely cooled (approximately 2 hours).

Loosen cake from sides of pan using a small metal spatula. Remove from pan. Serve with Pineapple-Orange Sauce; garnish with orange twists, if desired. Yield: 12 servings (about 131 calories per serving plus 40 calories per ¼-cup sauce).

Pineapple-Orange Sauce:

1 (15¼-ounce) can unsweetened pineapple
    chunks, undrained
1 teaspoon grated orange rind
¾ cup unsweetened orange juice
¼ cup Cointreau
1 tablespoon plus 1 teaspoon cornstarch
¼ teaspoon ground cardamom
1 (11-ounce) can mandarin oranges,
    drained

Drain pineapple, reserving juice. Combine pineapple juice and next 5 ingredients in a saucepan, mixing well; cook over medium heat, stirring constantly, until clear and thickened. Stir in pineapple chunks and mandarin oranges; cook until thoroughly heated. Yield: 3½ cups.

Serve Sandwiches For Two

Cooking for two is no problem with these quick sandwich ideas. You'll probably have most ingredients on hand.

CHEESY HAM-AND-TURKEY SPECIALS

4 thin slices cooked ham
4 thin slices cooked turkey
2 thick slices French bread
2 slices tomato
2 tablespoons crumbled blue cheese
2 (1-ounce) slices Swiss cheese

Place ham and turkey on top of each bread slice. Top with tomato slices, blue cheese, and Swiss cheese. Bake at 350° for 10 minutes or until cheese melts and sandwich is warm. Yield: 2 servings.

BACON, CHEESE, AND TOMATO SANDWICHES

1 medium tomato, peeled and chopped
4 slices bacon, cooked and crumbled
1 cup (4 ounces) shredded Cheddar
    cheese
2 tablespoons mayonnaise
2 hamburger buns, split

Combine first 4 ingredients; mix well. Spoon mixture onto each bun half; bake at 350°, uncovered, for 10 minutes or until cheese melts. Yield: 2 servings.
Mrs. Ron Kirkland,
Memphis, Tennessee.

VEGETABLE GARDEN HEROES

1 tablespoon butter or margarine,
    softened
Dash of garlic powder
2 French rolls, split lengthwise
¼ green pepper, sliced
1 small purple onion, thinly sliced and
    separated into rings
2 radishes, thinly sliced
½ cup sliced cauliflower flowerets
4 cherry tomatoes, halved
½ cup sliced broccoli flowerets
1 small carrot, grated
4 dill pickle slices
2 (1-ounce) slices Cheddar cheese
¼ cup commercial Thousand Island
    salad dressing

Combine butter and garlic powder, mixing well. Spread butter mixture on top half of each roll; set aside.

Scoop out centers from the bottom half of each roll, leaving a ½-inch shell. Layer next 9 ingredients (in order given) on rolls. Spoon 2 tablespoons dressing over each sandwich. Top with the remaining roll halves. Yield: 2 servings.
Cynthia Kannenberg,
Brown Deer, Wisconsin.

Bake Enchiladas With Spinach

This recipe for Spinach Enchiladas is one of the best Mexican dishes we've ever tasted. Fill tortillas with onion and Monterey Jack cheese, and spoon a spicy spinach sauce on top. A generous sprinkling of cheese, and the dish is ready for the oven.

SPINACH ENCHILADAS

1 (10-ounce) package frozen chopped
    spinach, thawed and pressed dry
1 (10¾-ounce) can cream of chicken soup,
    undiluted
1 (8-ounce) carton commercial sour cream
1 (4-ounce) can chopped green chiles,
    drained
2 tablespoons minced green onion
12 (4½-inch) corn tortillas
Vegetable oil
4 cups (16 ounces) shredded Monterey
    Jack cheese, divided
¾ cup minced onion

Combine first 5 ingredients in container of an electric blender or food processor, and process until smooth. Set mixture aside.

Fry tortillas, one at a time, in ¼ inch of hot oil about 5 seconds on each side or until softened. Drain tortillas well on paper towels.

Spoon 1 tablespoon each of cheese and onion on each tortilla; roll up and place in a lightly greased 12- x 8- x 2-inch baking dish. Spoon spinach mixture over tortillas. Sprinkle with remaining cheese. Bake, uncovered, at 325° for 30 minutes. Serve immediately. Yield: 6 servings.
Virginia Atkinson,
Omaha, Texas.

This Menu Is Easy On The Budget

If you're trying to feed your family economically, here's a menu that will help you whip up a fabulous meal and cut costs at the same time. The key is stretching expensive ingredients and using them where they'll have the most impact.

Pasta is an excellent meat-stretcher for our Chicken-Spaghetti Casserole. Save even more money by purchasing a whole chicken rather than one that's already cut up. You'll pay less per pound than if the butcher cuts it.

You can use your imagination with recipes and substitute less expensive ingredients if necessary. For example, substitute crunchy homemade croutons for 6 slices of bacon in our Fresh Spinach Salad.

Add the flavor of pecans to each serving of gingerbread for only pennies. When you use a sprinkling of pecans on top, it's much less expensive than stirring ½ cup of pecans into the cake.

Chicken-Spaghetti Casserole
Fresh Spinach Salad
Lemon-Glazed Carrots
Corn Muffins
Gingerbread Squares
Iced Tea

You'll save money with our menu of Chicken-Spaghetti Casserole, Fresh Spinach Salad, Lemon-Glazed Carrots, Corn Muffins, and Gingerbread Squares.

CHICKEN-SPAGHETTI CASSEROLE

1 (4-pound) broiler-fryer
1 bay leaf
8 ounces uncooked spaghetti
1 large onion, chopped
½ medium-size green pepper, coarsely chopped
2 stalks celery, chopped
2 cloves garlic, minced
3 tablespoons butter or margarine
1 (10¾-ounce) can cream of mushroom soup, undiluted
1 (28-ounce) can tomatoes, drained and chopped
1 teaspoon Worcestershire sauce
4 drops of hot sauce
⅛ teaspoon pepper
Salt to taste
1 cup (4 ounces) shredded medium Cheddar cheese

Place chicken and bay leaf in a large Dutch oven, and cover with salted water. Bring to a boil; cover, reduce heat, and simmer 1 hour or until tender. Remove chicken, and let cool. Discard bay leaf. Bone chicken, and cut meat into bite-size pieces; set aside.

Reserve ¼ cup chicken broth; set aside. Bring remaining broth to a boil. Break spaghetti into thirds, and cook in broth 12 to 15 minutes or until tender; drain well. Return spaghetti to Dutch oven; set aside.

Sauté onion, green pepper, celery, and garlic in butter until tender; add to spaghetti. Combine cream of mushroom soup and ¼ cup reserved broth; stir into spaghetti mixture. Add tomatoes and chicken; stir well. Add seasonings, mixing well.

Spoon the mixture into a lightly greased 13- x 9- x 2-inch baking dish. Top with cheese. Bake at 350° for 15 to 20 minutes or until cheese melts. Yield: 8 servings.
Mrs. Kris Ragan, Midlothian, Virginia.

FRESH SPINACH SALAD

½ cup vegetable oil
¼ cup red wine vinegar
1 teaspoon salt
⅛ teaspoon dried whole oregano
⅛ teaspoon freshly ground pepper
1 pound fresh spinach
6 slices bacon, cooked and crumbled
2 hard-cooked eggs, diced
1 small red onion, sliced and separated into rings

Combine first 5 ingredients in a jar. Cover tightly, and shake vigorously. Chill at least 30 minutes.

Remove stems from spinach; wash leaves thoroughly, and pat dry. Tear into bite-size pieces. Combine spinach, bacon, eggs, and onion in a large bowl.

Toss spinach mixture with chilled dressing until well coated. Yield: 8 servings.
Irene A. Murry, Herculaneum, Missouri.

LEMON-GLAZED CARROTS

2 pounds carrots, scraped and diagonally sliced
¼ cup butter or margarine
¼ cup firmly packed brown sugar
¼ cup lemon juice
½ teaspoon salt

Cook carrots in a small amount of boiling water 12 to 15 minutes or until crisp-tender; drain.

Melt butter in a small saucepan; add remaining ingredients. Bring mixture to a boil, stirring constantly; pour over carrots, and toss gently. Yield: 8 servings.
Stacey Wilson,
Reidsville, North Carolina.

CORN MUFFINS

1½ cups biscuit mix
½ cup cornmeal
2 tablespoons sugar
2 eggs
⅔ cup milk

Combine first 3 ingredients in a large bowl; make a well in center of mixture. Combine eggs and milk; add to dry ingredients, stirring just until moistened. Spoon into greased muffin pans. Bake at 400° for 20 to 23 minutes. Yield: about 1 dozen.
Lorraine Simpler,
Selbyville, Delaware.

GINGERBREAD SQUARES

½ cup shortening
½ cup sugar
1 egg, beaten
¾ cup molasses
2½ cups all-purpose flour
1½ teaspoons baking soda
½ teaspoon ground ginger
½ teaspoon ground cloves
½ teaspoon ground cinnamon
½ teaspoon salt
1 cup hot water
Whipped topping
1½ tablespoons finely chopped pecans

Cream shortening; gradually add sugar, beating until mixture is light and fluffy. Beat in egg and molasses.

Combine flour, soda, spices, and salt; add to creamed mixture alternately with hot water, beginning and ending with flour mixture; beat well.

Pour batter into a greased and floured 9-inch square pan. Bake at 350°

for 35 minutes or until a wooden pick inserted in center comes out clean.

Cut cake into squares; serve warm or at room temperature. Top each serving with a dollop of whipped topping; sprinkle with pecans. Yield: 9 servings.
Tulp Hoeksema,
Satellite Beach, Florida.

Hurry-Up Salad Ideas

Cut corners in the kitchen with Grapefruit-Avocado Salad. Make and chill the poppy seed dressing ahead of time; then just before dinner, arrange grapefruit sections and avocado slices on lettuce leaves and spoon the dressing on top.

GRAPEFRUIT-AVOCADO SALAD

3 grapefruit, peeled, seeded, and sectioned
2 avocados, peeled and sliced
Lettuce leaves
Poppy Seed Dressing

Arrange grapefruit sections and avocado slices on individual lettuce-lined plates. Serve with Poppy Seed Dressing. Yield: 6 servings.

Poppy Seed Dressing:

¾ cup sugar
⅓ cup cider vinegar
1 teaspoon salt
1 teaspoon dry mustard
1 teaspoon finely grated onion
1 cup vegetable oil
1 tablespoon poppy seeds

Combine first 5 ingredients in a small mixing bowl; beat with electric mixer until sugar dissolves. Continue to beat, slowly adding oil. Stir in poppy seeds. Cover and chill thoroughly; stir before serving. Yield: 1¾ cups. *Joan Sessoms,*
Hope Mills, North Carolina.

CARROT-TANGERINE SALAD

4 cups shredded carrots
2 tangerines, peeled and sectioned
½ cup raisins
1 teaspoon lemon juice
½ cup mayonnaise
Lettuce leaves

Combine first 4 ingredients; chill. Stir in mayonnaise before serving; serve on lettuce leaves. Yield: 8 servings.
Bettye Cortner,
Cerulean, Kentucky.

ORANGE-SPINACH SALAD

1 green apple, cored and cut into thin wedges
1 tablespoon lemon juice
1 pound fresh spinach, torn into bite-size pieces
½ pound fresh mushrooms, sliced
6 slices bacon, cooked and crumbled
1 (6-ounce) can frozen orange juice concentrate, thawed and undiluted
¾ cup mayonnaise

Toss apple wedges in lemon juice; drain. Combine apple wedges and next 3 ingredients in a large bowl; toss well.

Combine orange juice concentrate and mayonnaise; stir until smooth. Serve with salad. Yield: 8 servings.
Mrs. C. Shoemaker,
Boynton Beach, Florida.

EASY VEGETABLE SALAD

1 (1-pound) bunch broccoli
1 (16-ounce) can ripe olives, drained and sliced
1 (8-ounce) can sliced water chestnuts, drained
1 medium-size green pepper, cut into strips
1 medium onion, chopped
4 stalks celery, chopped
½ pound fresh mushrooms, sliced
1 pint cherry tomatoes, halved
1 (8-ounce) bottle commercial Italian salad dressing

Combine first 8 ingredients in a large bowl. Add dressing; toss gently. Chill 1 to 2 hours. Yield: 10 to 12 servings.
Mina De Kraker,
Holland, Michigan.

MIXED VEGETABLE SALAD

2 (10-ounce) packages frozen mixed vegetables
1 medium onion, chopped
3 stalks celery, chopped
⅓ cup mayonnaise
1 teaspoon dried whole dillweed
1 tablespoon plus 1 teaspoon lemon juice

Cook mixed vegetables according to package directions; drain and cool. Add onion and celery; set aside.

Combine remaining ingredients; stir until smooth. Pour over vegetables, and toss gently. Cover and chill 2 to 3 hours. Yield: 4 to 6 servings.

Marsha Webb,
Roswell, Georgia.

Southern Ways With Cornbread

Ask ten Southerners how to make cornbread, and you'll get ten different answers. The recipes here reflect the variety of this regional favorite: jalapeño cornbread, deep-fried hush puppies, and old-fashioned spoonbread.

HOT MEXICAN CORNBREAD

1½ cups yellow cornmeal
1 teaspoon salt
1 tablespoon baking powder
2 eggs, beaten
2 tablespoons chopped green pepper
1 (8-ounce) carton commercial sour cream
1 cup cream-style corn
¼ cup vegetable oil
1 to 2 jalapeño peppers, chopped
1 cup (4 ounces) shredded Cheddar
   cheese

Combine cornmeal, salt, and baking powder; mix well. Stir in remaining ingredients except cheese. Pour half the batter into a hot, greased 10½-inch cast-iron skillet; sprinkle evenly with half the cheese. Pour the remaining batter over cheese; top with remaining cheese. Bake at 350° for 35 to 40 minutes. Yield: 10 to 12 servings.

Mrs. Glenn Moore, Jr.,
Winchester, Tennessee.

HUSH PUPPIES WITH CORN

1 cup all-purpose flour
1 cup cornmeal
2 teaspoons baking powder
¾ teaspoon salt
¾ cup cream-style corn
½ cup chopped onion
1 egg, beaten
2 tablespoons vegetable oil
Vegetable oil

Combine first 4 ingredients in a large mixing bowl. Add corn, onion, egg, and 2 tablespoons oil; stir well.

Carefully drop batter by level tablespoonfuls into deep hot oil (370°); cook only a few at a time, turning once. Fry 3 to 5 minutes until hush puppies are golden brown. Drain well on paper towels. Yield: about 2½ dozen.

Debbie Baskin,
Shreveport, Louisiana.

CHEDDAR CORNBREAD

1 cup yellow cornmeal
1 cup all-purpose flour
2 tablespoons sugar
1 tablespoon baking powder
1 teaspoon salt
1 cup milk
2 eggs, beaten
2 cups (8 ounces) shredded Cheddar
   cheese

Combine first 5 ingredients in a large mixing bowl; set aside. Combine milk, eggs, and cheese; add to dry ingredients, mixing well. Pour batter into a hot, greased 10½-inch cast-iron skillet. Bake at 425° for 15 minutes or until cornbread is golden. Yield: 10 to 12 servings.

Mrs. T. L. Trimble,
Pensacola, Florida.

HONEY CORNBREAD

2½ cups yellow cornmeal
1 cup whole wheat flour
2½ teaspoons baking powder
1 teaspoon baking soda
1 teaspoon salt
2½ cups buttermilk
½ cup vegetable oil
2 eggs, beaten
2 tablespoons honey

Combine first 5 ingredients in a large mixing bowl; set aside. Combine buttermilk, oil, eggs, and honey; add to dry ingredients, mixing well. Pour batter into a greased 13- x 9- x 2-inch baking pan. Bake at 425° for 20 to 25 minutes or until golden brown. Cut into 2-inch squares to serve. Yield: about 2 dozen squares.

Nancy Chaney,
Tullahoma, Tennessee.

GOLDEN SPOONBREAD

2 cups water
1 cup yellow cornmeal
¼ cup shortening
2 tablespoons sugar
1 teaspoon salt
2 eggs, beaten
1 cup evaporated milk

Combine first 5 ingredients in a saucepan; cook over medium heat until mixture is thickened, stirring constantly. Remove from heat.

Combine eggs and milk; stir into cornmeal mixture. Pour into a lightly greased 1½-quart casserole.

Bake at 425° for 30 to 35 minutes or until a knife inserted in center comes out clean. Yield: 6 servings.

Kathleen Branson,
Thomasville, North Carolina.

Bake A Quick Coffee Cake

You'll find a delicate, sweet flavor in our Cardamom Coffee Cake. The cardamom laces the tender cake layer to make it irresistible.

CARDAMOM COFFEE CAKE

2 eggs, beaten
1⅓ cups milk
½ cup butter or margarine, melted
¼ teaspoon imitation butter flavoring
2 teaspoons vanilla extract
3 cups all-purpose flour
2 teaspoons baking powder
¾ teaspoon salt
1 cup sugar
1 teaspoon ground cardamom
½ cup sugar
½ cup firmly packed brown sugar
½ teaspoon ground cinnamon
Dash of ground nutmeg
2 tablespoons butter or margarine,
   softened

Combine first 5 ingredients; mix well. Combine flour, baking powder, salt, 1 cup sugar, and cardamom in a large bowl; gradually stir in milk mixture, mixing well. Pour into a greased and floured 13- x 9- x 2-inch baking pan.

Combine remaining ingredients, stirring with a fork until crumbly; sprinkle topping over batter. Bake at 375° for 30 minutes or until a wooden pick inserted in center comes out clean. Yield: 15 to 18 servings.

Mrs. W. C. McGee,
Raleigh, North Carolina.

Roll Out Some Elephant Ears

You don't have to be a professional baker to make these large, crisp Elephant Ears. These are delicious served as a snack or a sweet breakfast treat.

ELEPHANT EARS

1 package dry yeast
¼ cup warm water (105° to 115°)
2 cups all-purpose flour
1½ tablespoons sugar
½ teaspoon salt
1 cup butter or margarine
½ cup milk, scalded
1 egg yolk
2 tablespoons butter or margarine, melted
2 cups sugar
1 tablespoon plus ½ teaspoon ground cinnamon
¼ cup butter or margarine, melted
½ cup chopped pecans or walnuts

Dissolve yeast in ¼ cup warm water; let stand 5 minutes.

Combine flour, 1½ tablespoons sugar, and salt in a large mixing bowl. Cut 1 cup butter into flour mixture with a pastry blender until mixture resembles coarse meal. Combine milk, egg yolk, and yeast mixture; add to flour mixture, mixing well. Chill dough 2 hours.

Turn dough out onto a floured surface; knead 1 to 2 minutes. Cover and let rest 10 minutes.

Roll dough into an 18- x 10-inch rectangle on a lightly floured surface; brush with 2 tablespoons melted butter. Combine 2 cups sugar and cinnamon; sprinkle 1 cup of mixture over dough. Roll up jellyroll fashion, starting at long side; pinch long edge (do not seal ends). Place roll seam side down, and cut into eighteen 1-inch slices.

Sprinkle a portion of remaining cinnamon-sugar mixture lightly over waxed paper. Roll each slice out to ⅛-inch thickness, turning over once. Carefully transfer slices to an ungreased baking sheet. Spread each pastry with remaining melted butter; sprinkle with remaining cinnamon-sugar mixture and pecans. Bake at 400° for 10 minutes or until lightly browned. Cool on wire racks. Yield: 1½ dozen.
Mrs. J. Russell Buchanan,
Monroe, Louisiana.

Winter Salads With A New Twist

Tired of the same old salads? Liven up cabbage slaw with cheese, olives, and corn. Or for a change, serve a hot salad, such as marinated German Potato Salad. It's a sweet-and-sour variation of a basic winter favorite.

SAUCY BEAN SALAD

1 (10-ounce) package frozen green beans
1 (10-ounce) package frozen lima beans
1 (10-ounce) package frozen English peas
2 hard-cooked eggs, chopped
½ cup commercial sour cream
½ cup mayonnaise
¼ cup finely diced Cheddar cheese
¼ cup vegetable oil
1½ teaspoons grated onion
1 teaspoon prepared mustard
½ teaspoon Worcestershire sauce
⅛ teaspoon pepper
Dash of hot sauce
2 tablespoons sliced almonds, toasted

Cook green beans, lima beans, and English peas according to package directions; drain and cool.

Combine next 10 ingredients in a large bowl; stir well. Add vegetables to sauce, stirring well. Spoon salad into a serving bowl. Chill. Top with almonds before serving. Yield: 8 to 10 servings.
Mrs. Glen Miller,
Franklinton, Louisiana.

MEXICALI COLESLAW

4 cups shredded cabbage
1 (12-ounce) can golden whole kernel corn with sweet peppers, drained
½ cup finely chopped onion
½ cup cubed process American cheese
¼ cup sliced ripe olives
1 cup mayonnaise
2 tablespoons sugar
1 tablespoon plus 1 teaspoon prepared mustard
1 tablespoon salad vinegar
½ teaspoon celery seeds

Combine first 5 ingredients in a large mixing bowl. Combine remaining ingredients; mix well, and pour over cabbage mixture. Cover and chill 2 to 3 hours. Yield: 6 to 8 servings.
Mrs. R. V. Hargrove,
Oakdale, Louisiana.

GERMAN POTATO SALAD

10 medium potatoes, cooked, peeled, and sliced
4 hard-cooked eggs, chopped
4 stalks celery, chopped
2 small onions, chopped
Diced pimiento (optional)
4 slices bacon, diced
⅓ cup water
2 tablespoons cornstarch
½ to ¾ cup sugar
½ teaspoon salt
¼ teaspoon pepper
⅓ cup vinegar

Combine potatoes, eggs, celery, onion, and pimiento, if desired, in a large mixing bowl; mix gently.

Cook bacon in a skillet until crisp. Combine water and cornstarch, mixing well. Stir cornstarch mixture, sugar, salt, pepper, and vinegar into skillet. Cook over medium heat, stirring constantly, until thickened. Pour dressing over potato mixture; mix gently. Cover and chill overnight.

Spoon into a Dutch oven; cook over low heat until thoroughly heated. Serve immediately. Yield: 12 servings.
Mrs. Ben Harper,
Edmonton, Kentucky.

EGG-RICE SALAD

2 cups cooked rice
6 hard-cooked eggs, chopped
1 cup diced celery
¾ cup mayonnaise
¼ cup diced sweet pickle
¼ cup minced green onions
Lettuce leaves
Paprika (optional)

Combine first 6 ingredients, stirring well. Chill. Serve on lettuce leaves; sprinkle with paprika, if desired. Yield: 6 servings.
Mrs. Kenneth Tubbs,
Oak Grove, Louisiana.

Tip: The reason some hard-cooked eggs have discolored yolks is that the eggs have been cooked at too high a temperature, or they have not been cooled rapidly following cooking. The greenish color comes from sulfur and iron compounds in the eggs. These form at the surface of the yolks when they have been overcooked. This, however, does not interfere with the taste or nutritional value of the eggs.

Whole Grain Breads—You Know They're Good

When it comes to cornmeal, you don't have to describe the taste to a Southerner. This gritty flour bakes into corn sticks, muffins, and loaves, all labeled as the South's favorite bread. Stone-ground cornmeal includes the germ of the kernel, unlike most commercially ground meal, and produces a coarser bread. Since the germ is perishable, store meal in the refrigerator to keep it fresh.

Whole wheat and rye flours also are ground with the germ, so it's best to refrigerate them. If you don't plan to use the flour often, package it in an airtight container and store it in the freezer.

When baking with whole grain flour, you'll find that breads are coarser, more compact, and will take longer to rise. This is because whole grains have low gluten-forming ability; gluten is a protein substance that gives bread dough elasticity and structure. Combining whole grain flour with all-purpose or high-protein bread flour will yield higher-rising breads.

Before measuring whole grain flour, be certain to stir it gently to evenly distribute any bran that may have settled to the bottom. Sifting isn't necessary. Just spoon the flour into a measuring cup, and level with a knife.

WHOLE WHEAT BAGELS

2 packages dry yeast
2 cups warm water (105° to 115°)
2 tablespoons honey
2 cups whole wheat flour
2 teaspoons salt
3 to 3½ cups all-purpose flour
3½ quarts water
1 teaspoon salt
Sesame seeds

Dissolve yeast in 2 cups warm water in a large bowl; add honey, stirring well. Stir in whole wheat flour and salt; mix well. Gradually stir in enough all-purpose flour to form a soft dough.

Turn dough out onto a heavily floured surface (dough will be sticky), and knead 8 to 10 minutes until smooth and elastic. Place dough in a greased bowl, turning to grease top. Cover and let rise in a warm place (85°), free from drafts, 1½ hours or until dough is doubled in bulk.

Punch dough down. Divide dough into 12 equal pieces. Roll each into a smooth ball. Punch a hole in the center of each ball with a floured finger. Gently pull dough away from center to make a 1½- to 2-inch hole. Place shaped bagels on lightly greased baking sheets. Cover and let rise 15 minutes. Broil bagels 5 inches from heat for 2 minutes on each side.

Bring 3½ quarts water and salt to a boil in a large Dutch oven; reduce heat and drop bagels, one at a time, into water. Simmer 3 minutes on each side.

Place bagels on lightly greased baking sheets. Sprinkle with sesame seeds; lightly press seeds into bagels. Bake at 425° for 20 to 25 minutes or until golden brown. Yield: about 1 dozen.
Nell Hamm,
Louisville, Mississippi.

ANGEL CORN STICKS

1½ cups cornmeal
1 cup all-purpose flour
1 package dry yeast
1 tablespoon sugar
1 teaspoon salt
1½ teaspoons baking powder
½ teaspoon baking soda
2 eggs, beaten
2 cups buttermilk
½ cup vegetable oil

Combine first 7 ingredients in a large bowl. Combine eggs, buttermilk, and oil; add to dry ingredients, stirring until batter is smooth.

Spoon the batter into well-greased cast-iron corn-stick pans, filling half full. Bake at 450° for 12 to 15 minutes. Yield: 3 dozen.
Cora Cahee,
Clarksville, Tennessee.

ROUND OATMEAL BREAD

1¼ cups quick-cooking oats, uncooked
½ cup molasses
¼ cup shortening
1½ teaspoons salt
1⅔ cups boiling water
2 packages dry yeast
½ cup warm water (105° to 115°)
2 eggs, beaten
About 5 cups all-purpose flour
2 tablespoons butter or margarine, melted
1 tablespoon quick-cooking oats, uncooked

Combine first 5 ingredients, mixing well; cool to lukewarm (105° to 115°). Dissolve yeast in warm water in a large bowl; let stand 5 minutes. Add oats mixture, eggs, and 3 cups flour; mix well. Stir in enough of the remaining flour to form a soft dough.

Turn dough out onto a floured surface, and knead about 5 minutes until smooth and elastic. Divide dough in half; shape each into a round loaf. Place loaves in two well-greased 10-inch pieplates. Cover and let rise in a warm place (85°), free from drafts, about 1 hour or until doubled in bulk.

Gently brush each loaf with 1 tablespoon melted butter, and sprinkle with 1½ teaspoons uncooked oats. Bake at 350° for 45 minutes or until loaves sound hollow when tapped. Remove loaves from pieplates, and cool completely on wire racks. Yield: 2 loaves.
Ruth Chellis,
Easley, South Carolina.

BANANA-OATMEAL MUFFINS

1½ cups whole wheat flour
1½ cups quick-cooking oats, uncooked
1 cup all-purpose flour
1 cup sugar
⅓ cup wheat germ
2 teaspoons baking soda
1 teaspoon salt
2 teaspoons ground cinnamon
3 eggs, slightly beaten
1 (8-ounce) can crushed pineapple, undrained
2 cups mashed banana
½ cup vegetable oil

Combine first 8 ingredients in a large bowl; make a well in center of mixture. Add eggs, pineapple, banana, and oil, stirring just until moistened. Spoon into greased muffin pans, filling two-thirds full. Bake at 350° for 20 to 22 minutes or until done. Yield: about 2½ dozen.
Bunny Stevenson,
San Marcos, Texas.

Tip: Read labels to learn the weight, quality, and size of food products. Don't be afraid to experiment with new brands. Store brands can be equally good in quality and nutritional value, yet lower in price. Lower grades of canned fruit and vegetables are as nutritious as higher grades. Whenever possible, buy most foods by weight or cost per serving rather than by volume or package size.

RYE BREAD

5 cups bread flour
4 cups medium rye flour
1 tablespoon sifted cocoa
2 cups milk, scalded
1 tablespoon salt
⅓ cup molasses
¼ cup butter or margarine
2 packages dry yeast
1 (12-ounce) can beer (at room
temperature)
½ teaspoon fennel seeds

Combine flour and cocoa in a large bowl; set aside.

Combine milk, salt, molasses, and butter; stir until butter melts. Cool to lukewarm (105° to 115°).

Dissolve yeast in beer in a large bowl; stir well. Add milk mixture, fennel seeds, and 4 cups of flour mixture; beat well. (Mixture will be thin.) Cover and let rise in a warm place (85°), free from drafts, about 30 minutes.

Stir in enough remaining flour to form a stiff dough. Turn dough out onto a lightly floured surface; knead about 5 minutes until smooth and elastic. Place dough in a greased bowl, turning to grease top. Cover and let rise in a warm place (85°), free from drafts, 30 minutes or until doubled in bulk.

Punch dough down, and turn out onto a lightly floured surface. Let dough rest 10 minutes.

Divide dough in half, and shape each into a loaf. Place loaves in two 9- x 5- x 3-inch loafpans. Cover and let rise in a warm place (85°), free from drafts, 15 to 20 minutes or until the dough is doubled in bulk.

Bake at 400° for 45 to 50 minutes or until bread sounds hollow when tapped. Remove loaves from pans, and cool on wire racks. Yield: 2 loaves.
Mae Harkey,
Mount Pleasant, North Carolina.

Serve The Meat In A Crust

Dress meats in a flaky brown crust to warm up your winter meals. Meat pastries like our Chicken Breasts Wellington provide a spectacular entrée, while offerings such as Chicken Pot Pie serve the whole meal in a crust. Whether the crust is on the bottom, top, or all around the filling, you'll enjoy the added taste and texture of the crust.

The shiny, glazed surface on meat pies is no accident. Many recipes call for a beaten egg, sometimes mixed with water, to be brushed over the pastry before baking. Brush it on gently so you don't mar the smooth surface. The egg also contributes to the crust's rich golden color, so be sure to watch the pastry carefully as it bakes; cover it with aluminum foil if the crust begins browning too quickly.

Make your meat pies extra special by adding a little decoration (see page 22). Flute pastry edges like a piecrust, or press the edges with the tines of a fork. Weaving the top crust into a lattice or attaching pastry cutouts are two other ways to add interest. When joining two pieces of dough, dampen the pieces with water or beaten egg to help them stick together better.

CHICKEN POT PIE

¼ cup butter or margarine
⅓ cup all-purpose flour
2¾ cups chicken broth
½ teaspoon salt
½ teaspoon pepper
3½ cups chopped cooked chicken
1 (10-ounce) package frozen mixed
vegetables, thawed
½ cup chopped celery
3 hard-cooked eggs, chopped
Pastry (recipe follows)
1 egg, beaten
1 teaspoon water

Melt butter in a heavy saucepan over low heat; add flour, stirring until smooth. Cook 1 minute, stirring constantly. Gradually add chicken broth; cook over medium heat, stirring constantly, until mixture is thickened and bubbly. Stir in salt and pepper. Stir in chicken, vegetables, and eggs. Spoon chicken mixture into a lightly greased 12- x 8- x 2-inch baking dish.

Roll out pastry on a lightly floured surface to ⅛-inch thickness. Cut pastry into ¾-inch-wide strips using a fluted pastry wheel. Arrange the strips lattice-fashion across top of casserole. Combine egg and water; lightly brush pastry with egg mixture. Bake pie at 400° for 35 to 40 minutes or until golden. Yield: 6 to 8 servings.

Pastry:

1½ cups all-purpose flour
¾ teaspoon salt
½ cup plus 1½ tablespoons
shortening
4 to 5 tablespoons cold water

Combine flour and salt; cut in shortening with pastry blender until mixture resembles coarse meal. Sprinkle cold water, 1 tablespoon at a time, evenly over surface; stir with a fork until all ingredients are moistened. Shape into a ball. Yield: enough pastry for one 12- x 8-inch lattice crust.   *Lorene Carlisle,*
Columbus, Georgia.

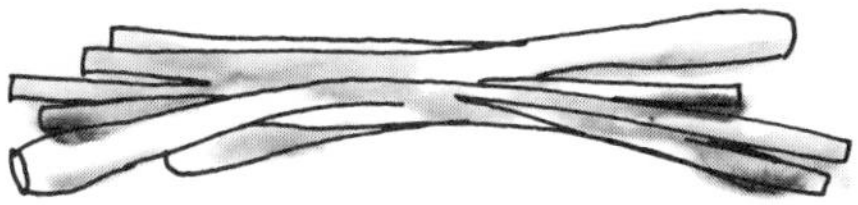

NATCHITOCHES MEAT PIES

2 teaspoons shortening
2 teaspoons all-purpose flour
1½ pounds ground pork
½ pound ground beef
2 large onions, finely chopped
6 green onions, chopped
1 tablespoon chopped fresh parsley
1 teaspoon salt
¼ teaspoon rubbed sage
⅛ teaspoon garlic salt
⅛ teaspoon pepper
Dash of red pepper
Pastry (recipe follows)
Vegetable oil

Combine shortening and flour in a large Dutch oven; cook over medium heat, stirring constantly, until roux is the color of a copper penny. Add pork, beef, onions, parsley, and seasonings. Cook over medium heat until meat is browned and onions are tender, stirring occasionally. Drain well and cool.

Divide pastry into 22 equal portions. Roll out each portion into a 5-inch circle. Place about 2 tablespoons meat mixture in center of each circle, and fold pastry in half. Moisten edges with water, and press with a fork to seal.

Heat 1 inch of oil to 375°. Fry pies in hot oil until golden, turning once. Drain on paper towels. Yield: 22 pies.

Pastry:

4 cups all-purpose flour
2 teaspoons baking powder
1 teaspoon salt
½ cup shortening, melted
½ cup plus 2 tablespoons milk
2 eggs, slightly beaten

Combine flour, baking powder, and salt. Add melted shortening, stirring until blended. Combine milk and eggs, stirring well. Pour milk mixture into flour mixture; stir just until blended, adding more milk if necessary. Yield: enough pastry for 22 pies.
Col. Bob F. Wilson,
Shreveport, Louisiana.

Each Chicken Breast Wellington hides carrots, mushrooms, and chicken beneath the crust. Fold pastry over filling, and attach decorative strips.

Cut pastry scraps into decorations for the top crust of Supreme Ham Tart. Moisten the back of the cutouts; then gently press them onto crust.

Give Cornish Meat Pies a new shape: Center the filling on dough circles; then join sides on top. Seal and flute edges.

CHICKEN BREASTS WELLINGTON

½ cup butter or margarine, softened
½ (8-ounce) package cream cheese, softened
1 cup all-purpose flour
4 chicken breast halves, skinned and boned
2 tablespoons butter or margarine
Salt and pepper
¼ cup canned chicken broth
¼ cup water
1 large carrot, scraped and cut into ¼-inch slices
¾ cup sliced fresh mushrooms
1 tablespoon butter or margarine
1 egg
1 teaspoon water
Velouté Sauce

Combine ½ cup butter and cream cheese; mix well. Add flour; stir with a fork until all dry ingredients are moistened. Remove a 1-inch ball of dough; divide remaining dough into 4 portions. Chill 1 hour.

Sauté chicken in 2 tablespoons butter for 2 minutes on each side; remove from pan. Sprinkle lightly with salt and pepper; set aside.

Combine chicken broth, water, and carrot in a small saucepan; bring to a boil. Cover, reduce heat, and simmer 8 to 10 minutes or until crisp-tender. Drain and set aside.

Sauté mushrooms in 1 tablespoon butter; drain and set aside.

Roll out the 4 large portions of pastry on a lightly floured surface into ⅛-inch-thick circles. On each, arrange one-fourth of the carrot slices, one-fourth of the mushrooms, and 1 chicken piece. Fold 2 opposite edges over filling; then fold over 2 remaining opposite edges. Invert and transfer to an ungreased baking sheet. Roll out 1-inch ball of pastry to ⅛-inch thickness; cut into 8 thin strips. Place 2 strips on top of each Wellington forming a letter X. Beat together egg and water. Brush tops with egg mixture; prick several times with a fork. Bake at 425° for 15 to 18 minutes or until golden. Serve with Velouté Sauce. Yield: 4 servings.

Velouté Sauce:

¾ cup canned chicken broth
¾ cup water
3 tablespoons butter or margarine
3 tablespoons all-purpose flour
¼ teaspoon salt
⅛ teaspoon pepper

Combine chicken broth and water, and set aside.

Melt butter in a heavy saucepan over low heat; add flour, stirring until smooth. Cook, stirring constantly, until lightly browned. Gradually add broth; cook over medium heat, stirring constantly, until thickened. Stir in salt and pepper, and cook, stirring constantly, over medium heat until mixture is reduced to 1¼ cups. Yield: 1¼ cups.

Karen Dodson,
Lake Park, Georgia.

SUPREME HAM TART

½ pound ground cooked ham
½ pound ground fresh pork
½ cup cracker crumbs
1 egg, slightly beaten
¼ teaspoon onion powder
⅛ teaspoon salt
⅛ teaspoon seasoned pepper
Golden Butter Pastry
2½ tablespoons brown sugar
½ teaspoon dry mustard
1 tablespoon vinegar
1 egg, beaten
1 (8-ounce) can whole berry cranberry sauce

Combine first 7 ingredients; mix well, and set aside.

Roll out half of pastry to fit a 9-inch round tart pan. Fit pastry into pan, letting excess pastry overlap sides of pan. Spread ham filling evenly over pastry. Combine sugar, mustard, and vinegar; spread over filling. Roll out remaining pastry to fit over top of pan; place over filling. Roll over top of pan with a rolling pin to trim excess pastry from the edges.

Cut decorative flowers and leaves from pastry scraps. Moisten bottom of cutouts, and arrange on pastry. Prick pastry with a wooden pick several times around edges of flowers and leaves for steam to escape. Brush top crust with beaten egg.

Set pan in a larger pan (in case there are any drippings). Bake at 425° for 1 hour. Cover with foil halfway during baking, if necessary, to prevent excess browning. Remove from oven, and let stand 10 minutes. Remove sides of tart pan. Serve with cranberry sauce. Yield: one 9-inch tart.

Golden Butter Pastry:

3 cups all-purpose flour
¾ teaspoon salt
½ cup plus 2 tablespoons butter or margarine
½ cup warm water
1 egg yolk

Combine flour and salt in a bowl; cut in butter with a pastry blender until mixture resembles coarse meal.

Combine water and egg yolk, mixing well. Sprinkle mixture, 1 tablespoon at a time, evenly over surface; stir with a fork until all dry ingredients are moistened. Shape into a ball; chill. Yield: enough pastry for one double-crust 9-inch tart.

CORNISH MEAT PIES

1 pound boneless sirloin steak, cut into ½-inch cubes
3 medium potatoes, chopped
1 medium onion, chopped
2 medium carrots, chopped
¼ cup water
¾ teaspoon salt
¼ teaspoon pepper
Pastry (recipe follows)
1 egg, beaten
1 teaspoon water

Combine first 7 ingredients. Divide pastry into 8 equal portions; roll out each portion into a 6½-inch circle. Spoon ½ cup meat mixture on center of each circle. Beat together egg and water; brush edges of circles with beaten egg, making a ¾-inch border. Gently lift sides of circle to meet at the top. Firmly press edges together; flute.

Place pies on ungreased baking sheets; bake at 350° for 1 hour or until lightly browned. Yield: 8 servings.

Pastry:

3 cups all-purpose flour
1½ teaspoons salt
1 cup shortening
½ cup plus 2 tablespoons cold water

Combine flour and salt in a bowl; cut in shortening with pastry blender until mixture resembles coarse meal. Sprinkle cold water, 1 tablespoon at a time, evenly over surface; stir with a fork until all dry ingredients are moistened. Yield: enough pastry for 8 meat pies.
Ethel Evans,
St. Petersburg, Florida.

MEAT-AND-POTATO PIE

Pastry for 8-inch double-crust pie
1 pound ground beef
1 medium onion, chopped
2 cups coarsely grated potato
1½ cups beef broth
¼ teaspoon salt
¼ teaspoon pepper
3 tablespoons cornstarch
¼ cup water

Roll half of pastry to ⅛-inch thickness on a lightly floured surface; fit into an 8-inch pieplate. Set aside.

Combine ground beef and onion in a large skillet; cook until ground beef is browned. Drain off pan drippings. Add potato, broth, salt, and pepper; cover and simmer 15 minutes or until potato is tender. Dissolve cornstarch in water; stir into meat mixture. Bring mixture to a boil; cook 1 minute. Spoon mixture into pastry shell.

Roll out remaining pastry to ⅛-inch thickness; carefully place over pie, leaving a 1-inch overhang at edge of dish. Seal and flute edges; cut slits in top for steam to escape. Bake at 425° for 30 to 35 minutes or until golden brown. Yield: one 8-inch pie. *Susan Simonson, Greenville, South Carolina.*

Enjoy The Zest Of Citrus

A juicy orange is good by itself, but that's only one way you can enjoy citrus. When oranges and grapefruit as well as lemons and limes are plentiful, try one of these tasty ideas.

With citrus, the word zest has double meaning. In addition to flavor, zest also refers to the colored part of the peel, which contains aromatic oils. The white part of the peel beneath it has a bitter taste. When a recipe calls for grated citrus rind, use the fine grids on your grater or a hand-held citrus peeler to remove the zest in tiny, colorful shreds.

An easy way to section citrus is to peel the fruit with a knife, cutting deep enough to remove all of the bitter white rind; then cut along either side of each section, between the pulp and membrane, to the center of the fruit. Remove each section, leaving the membrane attached to the core.

LEMON MERINGUE CREAM CUPS

2 egg whites
Pinch of salt
1 teaspoon lemon juice
½ cup sugar
Lemon Cream Filling
Whipped cream (optional)
Grated lemon rind (optional)

Beat egg whites (at room temperature), salt, and lemon juice until foamy. Gradually add sugar, 1 tablespoon at a time, beating until stiff peaks form. (Do not underbeat.)

Place a sheet of unglazed brown paper on a cookie sheet. (Do not use recycled paper.) Spoon meringue into 6 equal portions on paper. Using back of spoon, shape meringue into circles about 3 inches in diameter; shape each circle into a shell with sides about 1 to 1½ inches high.

Bake at 275° for 1 hour. Turn off oven; let stand in oven several hours or until meringues are cool.

Carefully peel off paper. Spoon Lemon Cream Filling into shells. Garnish with whipped cream and lemon rind, if desired. Yield: 6 servings.

Lemon Cream Filling:

3 eggs
½ cup sugar
3 tablespoons lemon juice
1½ teaspoons grated lemon rind
½ cup whipping cream, whipped

Beat eggs until thick and lemon colored. Add sugar and lemon juice; beat well. Stir in lemon rind. Cook over low heat, stirring constantly, until thickened; cool thoroughly. Fold in whipped cream. Yield: about 1½ cups.
Mrs. Henry DeBlieux, Sr.,
Natchitoches, Louisiana.

SLICE OF LEMON PIE

Pastry for 9-inch double-crust pie
1¼ cups sugar
2 tablespoons all-purpose flour
⅛ teaspoon salt
¼ cup butter or margarine, softened
3 eggs
½ cup water
1 teaspoon grated lemon rind
1 medium lemon, peeled and thinly sliced
1 egg white
1 tablespoon sugar
¼ teaspoon ground cinnamon

Roll half of pastry to ⅛-inch thickness on a lightly floured surface; fit into a 9-inch pieplate. Set aside.

Combine 1¼ cups sugar, flour, and salt, stirring well. Cream butter; gradually add sugar mixture, beating well.

Add eggs, one at a time, and water, beating until smooth. Stir in lemon rind and lemon slices; spoon into prepared pastry shell.

Roll out remaining pastry to ⅛-inch thickness, and place over filling. Trim edges; seal and flute. Cut slits to allow steam to escape; brush with egg white. Combine 1 tablespoon sugar and cinnamon, and sprinkle over pastry. Bake at 400° for 30 to 35 minutes. Yield: one 9-inch pie. *Mrs. Roger Williams, Arden, North Carolina.*

ORANGE-COCONUT CREAM

1 (3-ounce) package orange-flavored
  gelatin
1 cup boiling water
Grated rind of 1 orange
1 cup orange juice
2 teaspoons lemon juice
1 cup whipping cream
⅓ cup sugar
½ cup flaked coconut
Additional whipped cream (optional)
Orange slices (optional)

Dissolve gelatin in boiling water. Stir in orange rind, orange juice, and lemon juice. Chill until consistency of unbeaten egg white.

Beat 1 cup whipping cream until foamy; gradually add sugar, beating until stiff. Fold sweetened whipped cream and coconut into gelatin mixture. Spoon into stemmed glasses, and chill until firm. Garnish with additional whipped cream and orange slices, if desired. Yield: 6 to 8 servings.

Pat Boschen,
Ashland, Virginia.

COLD LEMON-LIME SOUFFLE

4 eggs
3 egg yolks
¾ cup sugar
2 envelopes unflavored gelatin
½ cup lemon juice
¼ cup lime juice
1 cup whipping cream, whipped
Grated rind of 1 lemon
Grated rind of 1 lime

Beat eggs and yolks 10 minutes at medium speed of an electric mixer; gradually add sugar, beating 10 additional minutes.

Combine gelatin, lemon juice, and lime juice in top of a double boiler; bring water to a boil. Reduce heat to low; cook until mixture thickens, stirring constantly. Cool slightly. Gradually stir about one-fourth of juice mixture into egg mixture; add to remaining juice mixture, mixing well. Fold in whipped cream and lemon and lime rind.

Spoon mixture into a 1-quart soufflé dish, and chill until firm. Yield: about 6 servings. *Mrs. Karl Koenig,*
Dallas, Texas.

LEMONADE FRUIT SALAD

4 oranges, peeled, seeded, and sectioned
2 apples, peeled and cut into chunks
1 cup sliced celery
1 (15¼-ounce) can pineapple chunks,
  drained
1 (6-ounce) can frozen lemonade
  concentrate, thawed and undiluted

Combine all ingredients; toss well. Chill salad before serving. Yield: 6 to 8 servings. *Carolyn Grover,*
Anderson, South Carolina.

CHUNKY FRUIT-AND-COCONUT
SALAD

4 medium-size oranges, peeled, seeded,
  and sectioned
2 medium apples, unpeeled and chopped
2 medium bananas, sliced
1 cup seedless green grapes, halved
1 cup flaked coconut
1 (8-ounce) can pineapple chunks, drained
½ cup chopped pecans
½ cup whipping cream
1½ tablespoons sugar
⅛ teaspoon almond extract

Combine first 7 ingredients in a large bowl; toss gently.

Beat whipping cream until foamy; gradually add sugar, beating until soft peaks form. Stir in almond extract.

Fold whipped cream mixture into fruit; chill salad before serving. Yield: 8 to 10 servings. *Mrs. Harry Zimmer,*
El Paso, Texas.

GRAPEFRUIT WINTER SALAD

1 ripe avocado, peeled and cubed
2 bananas, sliced
Lemon juice
1 cup finely shredded green cabbage
1 cup finely shredded red cabbage
2 pink grapefruit, peeled and sectioned
Commercial blue cheese salad dressing

Sprinkle avocado and bananas with lemon juice; set aside.

Combine the cabbage, tossing well. Mound cabbage in center of a serving platter. Arrange avocado, bananas, and grapefruit around cabbage. Serve with blue cheese dressing. Yield: 4 servings.
Mrs. James E. Shearer,
El Paso, Texas.

Tip: Chill gelatin mixtures quickly for aspics or molds by pouring in metal pans and placing in freezer about 15 minutes.

Sweeten It With Molasses

Years ago, molasses was the staple sweetening ingredient in most kitchens. Today, many people still enjoy it to add old-fashioned flavor to breads, cakes, beans, and ham.

Capture the flavor of this dark syrup in Molasses-Nut Bread. We recommend serving this bread with butter or cream cheese for a delicious morning snack.

MOLASSES-NUT BREAD

1 egg
½ cup molasses
⅓ cup sugar
3 tablespoons butter or margarine,
  melted
1½ teaspoons grated lemon rind
1 tablespoon lemon juice
2 cups all-purpose flour
¾ teaspoon baking powder
½ teaspoon baking soda
½ teaspoon salt
⅔ cup buttermilk
½ cup chopped pecans

Combine first 6 ingredients in a large mixing bowl, beating well.

Combine flour, baking powder, soda, and salt; add to egg mixture alternately with buttermilk, beginning and ending with flour mixture. Mix well after each addition. Stir in pecans.

Spoon batter in a greased and floured 8½- x 4½- x 3-inch loafpan. Bake at 350° for 50 to 55 minutes or until a wooden pick inserted in center comes out clean. Cool in pan 10 minutes; remove loaf from pan, and let cool completely. Yield: 1 loaf. *Sarah Watson,*
Knoxville, Tennessee.

MOLASSES-GLAZED HAM

1 (6- to 8-pound) fully cooked ham
About 20 whole cloves
¼ cup molasses
¼ cup prepared mustard
¼ teaspoon ground cinnamon
¼ teaspoon ground nutmeg

Remove skin from ham; place ham, fat side up, on a baking rack. Score fat in a diamond design, and stud with cloves. Insert meat thermometer, making sure it does not touch fat or bone. Bake ham at 325° for 1 hour and 15 minutes. Remove ham from oven.

Combine remaining ingredients; baste ham with molasses mixture. Return ham to oven, and bake an additional 30 to 40 minutes or until meat thermometer registers 140°, basting frequently with glaze. Yield: 12 to 15 servings.

Thelma Robinson,
Birmingham, Alabama.

OLD-FASHIONED BAKED BEANS

1 pound dried navy beans
2 quarts water
1 teaspoon salt
⅓ cup firmly packed brown sugar
¼ cup molasses
1 teaspoon celery salt
1 teaspoon dry mustard
½ teaspoon freshly ground pepper
2 large onions, thinly sliced
4 slices bacon, cut into 1-inch pieces

Sort and wash beans; place in a large Dutch oven. Cover with 2 quarts water. Bring to a boil; cover, reduce heat, and simmer 2 minutes. Remove from heat, and let stand 1 hour. Add salt to beans. Bring to a boil; cover, reduce heat, and simmer 1 hour. Drain, reserving 1½ cups liquid; set beans aside.

Combine reserved bean liquid, brown sugar, molasses, celery salt, dry mustard, and pepper; stir well. Set aside.

Layer half of beans, onion, bacon, and molasses mixture in a 3-quart casserole; repeat layers. Cover and bake at 300° for 3 to 3½ hours. Yield: 10 servings.

Ann M. Klein,
Savannah, Georgia.

BOURBON-PECAN CAKE

6 cups chopped pecans
1 (9-ounce) box raisins
4 cups all-purpose flour, divided
1 teaspoon ground nutmeg
1 teaspoon ground cinnamon
1 teaspoon ground cloves
1½ cups butter or margarine,
   softened
2 cups sugar
6 eggs
½ cup molasses
1 teaspoon baking soda
1 cup bourbon, divided

Combine pecans and raisins. Dredge with ½ cup flour; stir well. Set aside.

Combine remaining 3½ cups flour and spices; set aside.

Cream butter in a large mixing bowl; gradually add sugar, beating until light and fluffy. Add eggs, one at a time, beating well after each addition.

Combine molasses and soda; add to creamed mixture. Add flour mixture to creamed mixture alternately with ½ cup bourbon, beginning and ending with flour mixture. Mix well after each addition. Stir in pecan mixture.

Spoon batter into a waxed paper-lined and greased 10-inch tube pan. Bake at 325° for 2 hours to 2 hours and 15 minutes or until a wooden pick inserted in center comes out clean. Cool completely in pan. Remove from pan.

Moisten several layers of cheesecloth with remaining ½ cup bourbon; cover cake completely with cheesecloth. Wrap with foil; store in cool place at least one week, remoistening cheesecloth as needed. Yield: one 10-inch cake.

Bobbie Collins,
Shelbyville, Tennessee.

Be Creative With Canned Pineapple

Pineapple has always been popular in the South. Try one of these recipes for upside-down cake, bacon-wrapped pineapple, and a pineapple-and-cream cheese ball to add the tangy-sweet flavor to your desserts and appetizers.

BACON-WRAPPED PINEAPPLE CHUNKS

1 cup catsup
¼ cup dark corn syrup
1 tablespoon Worcestershire sauce
1 tablespoon prepared horseradish
⅛ teaspoon hot sauce
1 (15¼-ounce) can pineapple chunks,
   drained
About 1 pound bacon, cut in half
   crosswise
1 (11-ounce) can mandarin oranges,
   drained (optional)

Combine first 5 ingredients in a saucepan, stirring well. Bring to a boil; reduce heat and simmer, uncovered, 10 minutes, stirring frequently. Remove from heat; set sauce aside.

Wrap each pineapple chunk with a piece of bacon, securing with a wooden pick. Place on a rack in a shallow roasting pan; bake at 400° for 15 minutes. Baste with sauce; return to oven, and bake an additional 15 to 20 minutes, or until bacon is cooked. Before serving, secure a mandarin orange slice to bottom of each pineapple chunk, if desired. Serve with remaining sauce. Yield: 35 to 40 appetizer servings. *Jamie Pinion, Moulton, Alabama.*

FRUITED CHICKEN SALAD

3 cups chopped cooked chicken
1 cup diced celery
1 cup orange sections
1 (8-ounce) can pineapple tidbits, drained
½ cup slivered almonds, toasted
2 tablespoons vegetable oil
2 tablespoons orange juice
2 tablespoons vinegar
½ teaspoon salt
Dash of ground marjoram
¾ to 1 cup mayonnaise

Combine first 5 ingredients, and toss gently. Combine oil, orange juice, vinegar, and seasonings; pour over chicken mixture, and toss gently. Chill 1 hour.

Drain off liquids; stir mayonnaise into salad. Yield: 6 servings.

Cyndi Copenhaver,
Virginia Beach, Virginia.

PINEAPPLE-PECAN UPSIDE-DOWN CAKE

½ cup butter or margarine
1 cup firmly packed brown sugar
1 (15½-ounce) can pineapple slices,
   undrained
About ¼ cup pecan halves
3 eggs, separated
1 cup sugar
1 cup sifted cake flour
1 teaspoon baking powder
⅛ teaspoon salt

Melt butter in a 10-inch cast-iron skillet. Sprinkle evenly with brown sugar. Drain pineapple, reserving ⅓ cup pineapple juice; set juice aside. Arrange pineapple slices in a single layer over brown sugar. Place a pecan half in the center of each pineapple slice; set aside.

Beat egg yolks until thick and lemon colored; gradually add sugar, beating well. Combine flour, baking powder, and salt; add to egg mixture. Stir in reserved pineapple juice.

Beat egg whites (at room temperature) until stiff peaks form; fold into flour mixture. Spoon batter evenly over pineapple slices. Bake at 375° for 30 minutes or until cake tests done. Cool for 5 minutes; invert cake onto a plate. Yield: one 10-inch cake.

Linda H. Sutton,
Winston-Salem, North Carolina.

PINEAPPLE-CHEESE BALL

2 (8-ounce) packages cream cheese, softened
1 (8-ounce) can crushed pineapple, drained
¼ cup finely chopped green pepper
2 tablespoons finely chopped onion
1 teaspoon seasoned salt
¾ cup chopped pecans

Combine first 5 ingredients, mixing well. Shape mixture into a ball. Refrigerate several hours or overnight. Roll in chopped pecans. Serve with crackers. Yield: 1 cheese ball.

Mrs. John Andrew,
Winston-Salem, North Carolina.

PINEAPPLE GLAZE

2 tablespoons brown sugar
1 tablespoon cornstarch
1 (15¼-ounce) can crushed pineapple, undrained
¼ cup soy sauce
¼ teaspoon garlic salt
¼ teaspoon ground ginger

Combine brown sugar and cornstarch in a small saucepan. Stir in pineapple, soy sauce, garlic salt, and ginger; cook mixture over low heat, stirring constantly, until thickened. Serve over ham or chicken. Yield: about 1⅔ cups.

Mary J. Ealey,
Smithfield, Virginia.

Stir-Fry Enough For Two

Stir-frying makes cooking for two easier than ever before. In just a few minutes you can prepare an exciting main or side dish.

The wok is the traditional cooking utensil for stir-frying, but a large skillet may be substituted. With this rapid cooking process, meats brown but stay juicy, and vegetables keep their bright color and fresh flavor.

Ingredients for stir-frying can be chopped, measured, and assembled ahead of time, then refrigerated until they are used. Meats should be cut into small pieces or thin strips. Thick, fibrous vegetables like carrots or celery will cook more evenly if sliced diagonally. It is best to add the more delicate vegetables last to prevent overcooking.

STIR-FRIED BEEF

6 ounces boneless round steak
2 teaspoons vegetable oil
1¼ cups cauliflower flowerets
½ green pepper, cut into ¾-inch pieces
1 tablespoon soy sauce
½ small clove garlic, minced
2 teaspoons cornstarch
½ cup beef broth
⅓ cup chopped green onions with tops
1 cup hot cooked rice

Partially freeze steak; slice diagonally across the grain into 2- x ¼-inch strips.

Pour oil into a preheated wok or skillet; allow to heat at medium high (325°) for 2 minutes. Add beef, and stir-fry until browned. Add cauliflower, green pepper, soy sauce, and garlic. Cover, reduce heat, and simmer 10 minutes or until vegetables are crisp-tender.

Combine cornstarch and broth, stirring well; add to meat mixture. Stir in onions; cook, stirring constantly, until thickened; serve over rice. Yield: 2 servings. *Mrs. Glenn A. Davenport,*
Paducah, Kentucky.

CHICKEN IN SOY AND WINE

4 small boneless chicken breast halves, skinned and cut into 1-inch pieces
1 egg white
1 tablespoon cornstarch
⅛ teaspoon grated fresh gingerroot
2 tablespoons vegetable oil
½ cup chopped walnuts
2 tablespoons soy sauce
1 tablespoon dry white wine
1 teaspoon cornstarch
1 tablespoon water
1 cup hot cooked rice

Combine first 4 ingredients in a small mixing bowl; mix well, and set aside.

Pour oil into a preheated wok or large skillet; allow to heat at medium high (325°) for 1 minute. Add walnuts; stir-fry 1 minute or until lightly browned. Remove walnuts from skillet, and set aside. Add chicken mixture to skillet; stir-fry 2 to 3 minutes or until lightly browned. Add soy sauce and wine; cook an additional minute.

Combine cornstarch and water; stir well. Add cornstarch mixture and walnuts to chicken; reduce heat and simmer, stirring constantly, until thickened. Serve over rice. Yield: 2 servings.

Mrs. Robert McDowell,
Winchester, Virginia.

CHINESE-STYLE DINNER

1 tablespoon vegetable oil
1 stalk celery, sliced diagonally into 1-inch pieces
1 small onion, thinly sliced and separated into rings
¼ small head cabbage, coarsely shredded
¾ cup chicken broth
2 tablespoons soy sauce
1 tablespoon cornstarch
2 large boneless chicken breast halves, skinned and cut into 1-inch pieces
1 cup hot cooked rice

Pour oil into a preheated wok or large skillet; heat at medium high (325°) for 2 minutes. Add vegetables; stir-fry 2 minutes. Remove vegetables from skillet. Combine chicken broth, soy sauce, and cornstarch; stir well. Add chicken to skillet, and stir-fry 3 minutes or until lightly browned; add vegetables and chicken broth mixture. Cover, reduce heat, and simmer 3 minutes or until thickened. Serve over rice. Yield: 2 servings.

Jandra Smithen,
Tulsa, Oklahoma.

ORIENTAL VEGETABLES

⅓ cup olive or vegetable oil
½ pound fresh mushrooms, thinly sliced
1 small onion, thinly sliced
1 medium zucchini, cut into 3-inch strips
½ teaspoon sugar
½ teaspoon coarsely ground black pepper
2 tablespoons soy sauce
1 cup hot cooked rice

Pour oil into a preheated wok or large skillet; allow to heat at medium high (325°) for 2 minutes. Add vegetables, sugar, and pepper; stir-fry 4 to 5 minutes. Add soy sauce; reduce heat and simmer an additional 1 to 2 minutes or until vegetables are crisp-tender. Serve over rice. Yield: 2 servings.

Mrs. H. Maxcy Smith,
St. Petersburg, Florida.

Right: *Enjoy the variety of winter cabbage in Chicken Coleslaw and Bok Choy-Broccoli Stir-Fry (recipes on page 2).*

Page 28: *Try these meat pies to satisfy hearty appetites. Front to back: Chicken Breasts Wellington (page 22), Natchitoches Meat Pies (page 21), Supreme Ham Tart (page 22), and Chicken Pot Pie (page 21).*

Freshen Menus With Spinach

These spinach dishes will help perk up your winter meals. Each begins with tender, freshly washed spinach that's steamed in the water that clings to the leaves. This way, less riboflavin and vitamin C are lost.

SPINACH TIMBALES

2 pounds fresh spinach
2 eggs, beaten
1 cup milk
¼ cup butter or margarine, melted
1 tablespoon prepared horseradish
¼ to ½ teaspoon salt
Dash of pepper
Dash of ground nutmeg

Remove stems from spinach; wash leaves thoroughly in lukewarm water. Drain and place in Dutch oven (do not add water); cover and cook over high heat 3 to 5 minutes. Drain well, and chop. Combine 2½ cups chopped spinach (reserve remaining spinach for other uses) and remaining ingredients, and stir well.

Spoon mixture into 6 greased ½-cup baking molds or custard cups. Place molds in a 13- x 9- x 2-inch baking pan; pour hot water into pan to a depth of 1 inch. Bake, uncovered, at 350° for 45 minutes or until set. Unmold on a serving platter. Yield: 6 servings.

Daisy Cotton,
Edcouch, Texas.

CREAMED SPINACH WITH NOODLES

1 pound fresh spinach
3 slices bacon
3 tablespoons all-purpose flour
1½ cups milk
1 tablespoon finely chopped onion
¾ teaspoon salt
Dash of pepper
2 cups medium egg noodles, cooked and drained
1 cup (4 ounces) shredded Cheddar cheese

Remove stems from spinach; wash leaves thoroughly in lukewarm water. Drain and place in Dutch oven (do not add water); cover and cook over high heat 3 to 5 minutes. Drain spinach well; chop and set aside.

Cook bacon in a large skillet until crisp; remove bacon, reserving drippings in skillet. Crumble bacon, and set aside.

Add flour to pan drippings, stirring until smooth. Cook over medium heat 1 minute, stirring constantly. Gradually add milk; cook, stirring constantly, until thickened and bubbly. Stir in the chopped spinach, onion, salt, and pepper; set aside.

Arrange noodles on a serving platter; top with spinach mixture. Sprinkle with cheese and crumbled bacon; serve immediately. Yield: 6 servings.

Sarah Watson,
Knoxville, Tennessee.

HOT CREAM OF SPINACH SOUP

¾ pound fresh spinach
4 scallions or green onions, thinly sliced
1 tablespoon butter or margarine
1 quart chicken broth, divided
3 tablespoons butter or margarine
3 tablespoons all-purpose flour
¼ teaspoon pepper
Pinch of ground nutmeg
Pinch of dried whole basil
1 cup half-and-half
Croutons (optional)

Remove stems from spinach; wash leaves thoroughly in lukewarm water. Drain and set aside.

Sauté scallions in 1 tablespoon butter in a Dutch oven for 1 minute. Add spinach (do not add water); cover and cook over high heat 3 to 5 minutes. Spoon spinach mixture into container of electric blender; add 1 cup broth. Process until smooth; set aside.

Melt 3 tablespoons butter in a Dutch oven over low heat; add flour, stirring until smooth. Cook 1 minute, stirring constantly. Gradually add remaining 3 cups broth; cook over medium heat, stirring constantly, until thickened and bubbly. Add spinach mixture, pepper, nutmeg, and basil; bring to a boil. Cover, reduce heat, and simmer 5 minutes. Stir in half-and-half; cook, stirring constantly, until thoroughly heated. Ladle into bowls; top with croutons, if desired. Yield: about 6 cups.

Debbie Dockery,
Brevard, North Carolina.

Get The Most From Peanut Butter

Peanut butter makes a great sandwich, but why stop there? The appealing aroma, creamy texture, and rich flavor of this Southern spread makes it ideal for baking into cookies and pie or stirring into soup.

CREAM OF PEANUT BUTTER SOUP

1 cup chopped celery
½ medium onion, chopped
2 tablespoons butter or margarine
2 tablespoons all-purpose flour
7 cups chicken broth
1 cup creamy peanut butter
1 cup milk or half-and-half
Chopped chives (optional)

Sauté celery and onion in butter in a large Dutch oven until tender; add flour, stirring until smooth. Cook 1 minute, stirring constantly. Gradually add chicken broth; bring mixture to a boil. Add peanut butter and milk; reduce heat and simmer 10 minutes, stirring constantly (do not boil). Garnish soup with chives, if desired. Serve hot. Yield: about 7½ cups. *Mrs. T. J. Compton,*
Lampasas, Texas.

PEANUT BUTTER TEMPTATIONS

½ cup butter or margarine, softened
½ cup creamy peanut butter
½ cup sugar
½ cup firmly packed brown sugar
1 egg
½ teaspoon vanilla extract
1¼ cups all-purpose flour
¾ teaspoon baking soda
½ teaspoon salt
48 miniature peanut butter cup candies

Cream butter and peanut butter; gradually add sugar, beating until light and fluffy. Add egg and vanilla, beating well. Combine flour, soda, and salt; add to creamed mixture, mixing well. Chill dough 1 hour.

Shape dough into forty-eight 1-inch balls; place in lightly greased 1¾-inch muffin pans, shaping each into a shell. Bake at 350° for 12 minutes (dough will rise during baking). Remove from oven, and immediately press a miniature peanut butter cup evenly into each hot crust. Cool before removing from pan. Yield: 4 dozen. *Marilyne Hubert,*
Tifton, Georgia.

PEANUT BUTTER MERINGUE PIE

¾ cup creamy peanut butter
¾ cup sifted powdered sugar
1 baked 9-inch pastry shell
½ cup sugar
⅓ cup all-purpose flour
½ teaspoon salt
2 cups milk
3 eggs, separated
1 tablespoon butter or margarine
½ teaspoon vanilla extract
¼ teaspoon cream of tartar
¼ cup plus 2 tablespoons sugar

Combine peanut butter and powdered sugar. Stir with a fork until mixture resembles coarse meal. Spread mixture in cooled pastry shell; set aside.

Combine ½ cup sugar, flour, and salt in a heavy saucepan; gradually add milk, stirring until well blended. Cook over medium heat, stirring constantly, until mixture is thickened and bubbly. Remove pan from heat.

Beat egg yolks until thick and lemon colored. Gradually stir about one-fourth of hot milk mixture into yolks; add to remaining hot mixture, stirring constantly. Cook over medium heat, stirring constantly, about 4 minutes until thickened. Remove from heat; stir in butter and vanilla. Pour over peanut butter mixture in pastry shell.

Combine egg whites (at room temperature) and cream of tartar; beat until foamy. Gradually add remaining sugar, 1 tablespoon at a time, beating until stiff peaks form. Spread meringue over hot filling, sealing to edge of pastry. Bake at 350° for 12 to 15 minutes or until golden brown. Cool to room temperature. Yield: one 9-inch pie.
Mrs. B. F. Turner,
West Palm Beach, Florida.

PEANUT BUTTER-CINNAMON COOKIES

½ cup butter or margarine, softened
½ cup creamy peanut butter
½ cup sugar
½ cup firmly packed brown sugar
1 egg
1 teaspoon vanilla extract
1¼ cups all-purpose flour
½ teaspoon baking soda
½ teaspoon salt
1 teaspoon ground cinnamon

Cream butter and peanut butter; gradually add sugar, beating until light and fluffy. Add egg and vanilla, and beat well.

Combine flour, soda, salt, and cinnamon; add to creamed mixture, mixing well. Shape dough into thirty-six 1-inch balls; place 2 inches apart on lightly greased cookie sheets. Dip a fork in water, and flatten cookies to ¼-inch thickness. Bake at 350° for 12 to 14 minutes. Let cool 2 minutes on cookie sheets. Remove to wire racks, and let cool completely. Yield: 3 dozen.
Brenda Nelson,
Sandersville, Georgia.

PEANUT BUTTER ICE CREAM SAUCE

1 cup firmly packed brown sugar
⅓ cup milk
¼ cup light corn syrup
1 tablespoon butter, softened
¼ cup creamy peanut butter

Combine first 4 ingredients in a medium saucepan. Cook over medium heat, stirring until sugar dissolves. Remove from heat; add peanut butter, beating until smooth. Serve warm over ice cream. Yield: about 1¼ cups.
Mrs. J. David Stearns,
Mobile, Alabama.

Snacks From Your Pantry

When the craving for a snack hits, you want something you can fix in a hurry. All of these recipes can be prepared in 5 to 20 minutes, and you probably have all the ingredients on hand in your kitchen.

EASY NACHOS

1 (12-ounce) package tortilla chips
1 (16-ounce) can refried beans
½ cup chopped green onions
1 cup (4 ounces) shredded Cheddar cheese
1 (11.5-ounce) jar pickled hot jalapeño pepper slices

Place about 3 dozen tortilla chips on ungreased baking sheets. Spread 2 teaspoons refried beans on each chip; sprinkle with green onions and cheese. Top each with a slice of jalapeño pepper. (Reserve remaining tortilla chips and jalapeño slices for other uses.) Bake at 350° for 5 minutes. Yield: about 3 dozen.
Karen Dorsett,
Austin, Texas.

PIZZA-BURGER SNACKS

1 medium onion, chopped
1 clove garlic, minced
1 teaspoon olive or vegetable oil
¾ pound ground beef
½ teaspoon salt
¼ teaspoon pepper
1 (8-ounce) can tomato sauce
6 English muffins, split and toasted
1 teaspoon dried whole oregano
1½ cups (6 ounces) shredded Monterey Jack cheese

Sauté onion and garlic in oil in a skillet; add beef, salt, and pepper, and cook until beef is browned, stirring to crumble. Drain off drippings. Add tomato sauce; cook until thoroughly heated. Spoon meat mixture over muffins. Sprinkle with oregano and cheese. Bake at 375° until cheese melts. Cut into quarters. Yield: 12 servings.
Janet McIntire,
Marietta, Georgia.

TASTY GRILLED SANDWICHES

4 slices bread, toasted
8 slices process American cheese
4 slices tomato
4 slices onion
2 slices bacon, halved
Mayonnaise (optional)

Arrange toast on a baking sheet; place 2 slices cheese on each slice of toast. Top each sandwich with a tomato slice, an onion slice, and bacon. Bake at 425° for 12 to 15 minutes or until bacon is cooked. Top with mayonnaise, if desired. Yield: 4 servings.
Dona G. Mandeville,
San Antonio, Texas.

PRETZEL POPCORN

2 quarts freshly popped popcorn, unsalted
1 cup broken pretzel sticks
1 cup dry roasted salted peanuts
⅓ cup butter or margarine, melted
½ teaspoon soy sauce
½ (.56-ounce) package imitation bacon-onion dip mix

Combine popcorn, pretzels, and peanuts in a large bowl; set aside.

Combine butter and soy sauce; pour over popcorn mixture, stirring until evenly coated. Sprinkle with dip mix, tossing gently. Spread mixture in a 15- x 10- x 1-inch jellyroll pan. Bake at 350° for 8 to 10 minutes. Yield: about 10 cups.
Mrs. O. V. Elkins,
Chattanooga, Tennessee.

TUNA-CURRY DIP

1 (8-ounce) carton commercial sour cream
1 (6½-ounce) can tuna, drained and
  flaked
¼ teaspoon curry powder
¼ teaspoon pepper
Hot sauce

Combine first 4 ingredients, mixing well. Stir in hot sauce to taste. Serve immediately or chill, if desired. Serve dip with assorted raw vegetables. Yield: 1½ cups.   *Annette Crane,*
Dallas, Texas.

Tex-Mex Means Good And Spicy

If there are any authorities on Tex-Mex foods, it's those who live in the Southwest. They've adopted tortillas, chiles, spicy-hot sauces, and other Mexican foods and come up with a cooking style that has become popular throughout the South.

CHILE RELLENOS CASSEROLE

1 pound ground beef
½ cup chopped onion
½ teaspoon salt
¼ teaspoon pepper
2 (4-ounce) cans whole green chiles,
  drained and cut in half
1½ cups (6 ounces) shredded sharp
  Cheddar cheese
4 eggs, beaten
1½ cups milk
¼ cup all-purpose flour
¼ teaspoon salt
Dash of pepper
⅛ teaspoon hot sauce

Combine the first 4 ingredients in a medium skillet; cook until meat is browned, stirring to crumble. Drain off pan drippings.

Layer half each of green chiles and cheese in a lightly greased 10- x 6- x 2-inch baking dish; top with meat mixture. Sprinkle with the remaining cheese and chiles.

Combine remaining ingredients, stirring well. Pour over casserole. Bake, uncovered, at 350° for 45 to 50 minutes or until set. Let stand 5 minutes before serving. Yield: 6 servings.
Mrs. W. Fred Norman,
Houston, Texas.

SOUTH-OF-THE-BORDER LASAGNA

1 pound ground beef
4 (7-inch) flour tortillas
Vegetable oil
1 (15-ounce) can tomato sauce
1 (1¼-ounce) package taco seasoning mix
1 (4-ounce) can chopped green chiles,
  drained and divided
1 (6-ounce) can frozen avocado dip,
  thawed
1 cup (4 ounces) shredded Monterey Jack
  cheese, divided
1 jalapeño pepper, sliced and seeded
  (optional)
1 hot red pepper, sliced and seeded
  (optional)
Fresh parsley sprigs (optional)

Cook ground beef in a skillet until browned, stirring to crumble; drain well, and set aside.

Fry tortillas, one at a time, in ¼ inch hot oil (375°) about 5 seconds on each side or just until softened. Drain well on paper towels; set aside.

Combine tomato sauce and taco seasoning mix in a medium saucepan; bring to a boil. Reduce heat and simmer, uncovered, 10 minutes. Remove from heat; reserve ¼ cup sauce mixture. Add beef and half of green chiles to remaining sauce mixture.

Place a tortilla and half of meat mixture in a greased 8- or 9-inch cakepan. Layer with a tortilla, avocado dip, ½ cup cheese, and remaining green chiles. Top with a tortilla, remaining meat sauce, remaining tortilla, and ¼ cup reserved sauce. Bake, uncovered, at 350° for 40 minutes. Sprinkle with remaining ½ cup cheese, and bake 5 minutes or until cheese melts. Garnish top with pepper slices and parsley, if desired. Yield: 4 servings.   *Dottie Placke,*
Katy, Texas.

BEEF-AND-GARBANZO DINNER

½ pound ground beef
¼ cup chopped onion
¼ cup chopped green pepper
1 (15-ounce) can garbanzo beans,
  drained
1 (14½-ounce) can stewed tomatoes,
  drained
1 teaspoon cumin powder
1 teaspoon chili powder
¼ teaspoon salt
⅛ teaspoon pepper
2 tablespoons all-purpose flour
3 tablespoons water
¼ cup (1 ounce) shredded Cheddar cheese
Crushed tortilla chips

Combine ground beef, onion, and green pepper in a large skillet; cook until meat is browned, stirring to crumble. Drain off pan drippings. Stir in next 6 ingredients; bring to a boil. Reduce heat and simmer 15 minutes.

Combine flour and water, stirring until smooth. Add to meat mixture; cook, stirring constantly, until thickened. Sprinkle with cheese; cook just until cheese melts. Serve over tortilla chips. Yield: 4 servings.
Joyce Holeman,
Austin, Texas.

CHEESY JALAPENO QUICHE

½ pound cooked ham, chopped
4 slices bacon, cooked and crumbled
1 cup (4 ounces) shredded Swiss cheese
1 cup (4 ounces) shredded Cheddar cheese
¼ cup chopped onion
1 medium tomato, peeled and chopped
1 to 2 canned jalapeño peppers, seeded
  and chopped
2 tablespoons chopped fresh mushrooms
1 tablespoon dried parsley flakes
Pastry shell (recipe follows)
4 eggs, beaten
1 teaspoon dry mustard
½ cup commercial sour cream

Layer first 9 ingredients in prepared pastry shell. Combine eggs, mustard, and sour cream, mixing well. Pour into pastry shell. Bake at 450° for 30 to 35 minutes or until filling is set. Cover edge of pastry with aluminum foil, if necessary, to prevent excessive browning. Yield: one 10-inch quiche.

Pastry Shell:

1½ cups all-purpose flour
½ teaspoon salt
¼ cup plus 2 tablespoons butter or
  margarine, softened
2½ tablespoons shortening
4 to 5 tablespoons cold water

Combine flour and salt; cut in butter and shortening with a pastry blender until mixture resembles coarse meal. Sprinkle cold water, 1 tablespoon at a time, evenly over surface; stir with a fork until all the dry ingredients are moistened. Shape into a ball.

Roll dough to ⅛-inch thickness on a lightly floured surface. Line a 10-inch quiche dish with pastry; trim excess pastry around edges. Prick bottom and sides of pastry with a fork. Bake at 400° for 3 minutes; remove from oven, and gently prick with a fork. Bake 5 more minutes. Yield: one 10-inch shell.
Mrs. Lexie Freeman,
Fort Worth, Texas.

ENCHILADAS TERRIFICAS

1 (2½- to 3-pound) broiler-fryer
1 stalk celery, chopped
1 medium onion, chopped
1 tablespoon vegetable oil
1 (10-ounce) package frozen chopped
    broccoli
1 (8-ounce) carton commercial sour
    cream
1 (10¾-ounce) can cream of chicken
    soup, undiluted
Salt and pepper to taste
1 dozen corn tortillas
Vegetable oil
1 teaspoon paprika
1 cup (4 ounces) shredded Cheddar cheese
Additional commercial sour cream
    (optional)
Sliced ripe olives (optional)

Place chicken and celery in a Dutch oven; cover with water, and bring to a boil. Cover, reduce heat, and simmer 1 hour or until chicken is tender. Remove chicken from broth, reserving ¼ cup broth. (Reserve remaining broth for other uses.) Remove chicken from bone, and shred with a fork; set aside.

Sauté onion in 1 tablespoon hot oil until tender; set aside. Cook broccoli according to package directions. Drain well, and set aside.

Combine chicken, onion, broccoli, 1 carton sour cream, soup, and 2 tablespoons chicken broth in a large saucepan, mixing well; bring to a boil. Reduce heat and simmer 5 minutes, stirring frequently. Stir in salt and pepper. Remove from heat, and set aside.

Fry tortillas, one at a time, in ¼ inch hot oil (375°) about 5 seconds on each side or just until softened. Drain well on paper towels; set aside.

Place remaining 2 tablespoons chicken broth in a lightly greased 13- x 9- x 2-inch baking dish. Rotate dish to coat with broth. Place about ¼ cup chicken mixture on each tortilla; roll up tightly, and place, seam side down, in prepared dish. Spoon remaining chicken mixture evenly over top. Sprinkle with paprika.

Bake, uncovered, at 350° for 15 minutes. Sprinkle with cheese. Serve with additional sour cream and olives, if desired. Yield: 6 servings.
Marylou Coffin,
Albuquerque, New Mexico.

Tip: Use a timer when cooking. Set the timer so it will ring at various intervals, and check the progress of the dish. However, try to avoid opening the oven door unless necessary.

CHICKEN ACAPULCO

1 medium onion, chopped
1 tablespoon butter or margarine
3 cups chopped cooked chicken
1 (10¾-ounce) can cream of chicken soup,
    undiluted
1 (8-ounce) carton commercial sour cream
1 (4.5-ounce) jar sliced mushrooms,
    drained
1 (4-ounce) can chopped green chiles,
    drained
½ cup sliced almonds, toasted
½ teaspoon dried whole oregano
¼ teaspoon salt
⅛ teaspoon pepper
10 (7-inch) flour tortillas
1 (10¾-ounce) can cream of chicken soup,
    undiluted
1 cup (4 ounces) shredded sharp Cheddar
    cheese
⅓ cup milk

Sauté onion in butter in a large saucepan until tender. Stir in the next 9 ingredients, mixing well. Spoon about ½ cup chicken mixture in center of each tortilla; roll up and place, seam side down, in a lightly greased 13- x 9- x 2-inch baking dish.

Combine remaining ingredients; spoon over tortillas. Bake, uncovered, at 350° for 35 minutes. Yield: 5 servings.
Kay Hall,
Richardson, Texas.

GREEN CHILE-AND-FISH CASSEROLE

1½ pounds flounder fillets
Salt
Pepper
Paprika
Red pepper
3 tablespoons butter or margarine
1 teaspoon lemon juice
2 (4-ounce) cans chopped green chiles,
    drained
1 cup (4 ounces) shredded Monterey Jack
    cheese
1 cup (4 ounces) shredded sharp Cheddar
    cheese

Sprinkle fillets lightly with salt, pepper, paprika, and red pepper.

Place butter in electric skillet; heat at medium high (350°) until butter melts. Stir in lemon juice. Add fillets; cook 3 to 4 minutes, turning once, or until fish flakes easily when tested with a fork.

Place fillets in a lightly greased 13- x 9- x 2-inch baking dish. Sprinkle green chiles evenly over fillets; top with cheese. Bake, uncovered, at 350° for 5 to 7 minutes or until cheese melts. Yield: 6 servings. *Mrs. Harry Zimmer,*
El Paso, Texas.

Let's Cook The Light Way

Who would think a dieter could indulge in pasta, pizza, or dessert and enjoy it with a clear conscience? If you're interested in losing weight but want something more exciting than a green salad and tuna, *Southern Living's Cooking Light Cookbook* may be what you're looking for.

Here's a sampling of one of the menus followed by several of the recipes you'll find in the cookbook.

Marinated Beef Kabobs With Rice
Broccoli With Horseradish Sauce
Cheesy Italian Salad
Glazed Strawberry Dessert

MARINATED BEEF KABOBS WITH RICE

1½ pounds lean boneless sirloin
    steak
1 large purple onion, cut into
    1-inch cubes
2 medium-size green peppers, cut
    into 1-inch squares
1 pound small yellow squash, cut
    into 1-inch-thick slices
1 (8-ounce) bottle Italian reduced-calorie
    salad dressing
¼ cup Burgundy or other dry
    red wine
Vegetable cooking spray
3 cups hot cooked rice

Trim all visible fat from meat; cut meat into 1½-inch cubes. Place meat and vegetables in a shallow container; set aside.

Combine salad dressing and wine; pour over meat and vegetables. Cover and marinate in the refrigerator overnight, stirring occasionally. Drain, reserving the marinade.

Alternate meat and vegetables on six 12-inch skewers. Coat grill with cooking spray. Grill kabobs over medium-hot coals for 15 minutes or until desired degree of doneness, turning and basting frequently with marinade. Serve over rice. Yield: 6 servings (about 206 calories per serving plus 90 calories per ½ cup cooked rice).

BROCCOLI WITH HORSERADISH SAUCE

1 (1½-pound) bunch fresh broccoli
¼ cup plus 2 tablespoons plain low-fat yogurt
¼ cup plus 2 tablespoons reduced-calorie mayonnaise
1½ teaspoons prepared mustard
½ teaspoon prepared horseradish
Paprika (optional)

Trim off large leaves of broccoli; remove tough ends of lower stalks. Wash the broccoli thoroughly, and separate it into spears.

Arrange broccoli in steaming rack with stalks to center of rack. Place over boiling water; cover and steam 10 to 15 minutes or to desired degree of doneness. Arrange broccoli spears in serving dish; keep warm.

Combine next 4 ingredients in a small saucepan; cook until thoroughly heated, stirring constantly (do not boil). Spoon sauce over broccoli; sprinkle with paprika, if desired. Yield: 6 servings (about 73 calories per serving).

CHEESY ITALIAN SALAD

3 small zucchini, finely chopped
4 green onions, thinly sliced
6 large fresh mushrooms, finely chopped
1 hard-cooked egg, finely chopped
1 clove garlic, crushed
1 (2-ounce) package blue cheese, crumbled
½ cup Italian reduced-calorie salad dressing
1 small head lettuce

Combine all ingredients except lettuce in a medium bowl. Cover and refrigerate for 2 hours, stirring occasionally.

Cut lettuce into 6 wedges; place on serving plates. Divide vegetable mixture on top of lettuce. Yield: 6 servings (about 96 calories per serving).

GLAZED STRAWBERRY DESSERT

7 cups fresh strawberries, divided
1 cup water
½ cup sugar
2 tablespoons cornstarch
⅛ teaspoon ground cinnamon
Fresh mint (optional)

Place 1 cup strawberries and water in container of electric blender; process until pureed. Transfer to a small saucepan, and bring to a boil; cover, reduce heat, and simmer 5 minutes. Strain, reserving liquid; discard pulp. Return liquid to saucepan.

Combine sugar, cornstarch, and cinnamon in a small bowl; add to strawberry liquid, and stir until smooth. Bring to a boil, and cook until mixture thickens, stirring constantly.

Place 1 cup strawberries in each dessert dish; spoon sauce over top and chill. Garnish with mint, if desired. Yield: 6 servings (about 133 calories per serving).

WHOLE WHEAT PIZZA

½ cup warm water (105° to 115°)
1 tablespoon vegetable oil
1 teaspoon sugar
½ teaspoon salt
½ package (about 1 teaspoon) dry yeast
¾ cup all-purpose flour
¾ cup whole wheat flour
Vegetable cooking spray
½ pound ground chuck
½ teaspoon salt
1 cup pizza sauce (recipe follows)
1 cup (4 ounces) shredded mozzarella cheese, divided
¾ cup sliced fresh mushrooms
¼ cup sliced green onions
1 green pepper, sliced into thin rings (optional)
2 tablespoons grated Parmesan cheese
Crushed red pepper (optional)

Combine water, oil, sugar, and ½ teaspoon salt in a medium mixing bowl. Sprinkle yeast over mixture, stirring until dissolved. Gradually add flour, mixing well after each addition.

Turn dough out onto a lightly floured surface, and knead about 4 minutes or until smooth and elastic. Shape into a ball, and place in a bowl coated with cooking spray, turning to grease top. Cover and let rise in a warm place (85°), free from drafts, 1 hour or until doubled in bulk.

Coat a 12-inch pizza pan with cooking spray; set aside. Punch dough down. Lightly coat hands with cooking spray, and pat dough evenly into pizza pan. Bake at 425° for 5 minutes.

Combine ground chuck and ½ teaspoon salt in a skillet; cook over medium heat until meat is browned, stirring to crumble. Drain beef well on paper towels.

Spread 1 cup pizza sauce evenly over pizza crust, leaving a ½-inch border around edges. Sprinkle ¾ cup mozzarella cheese over top.

Sprinkle meat over cheese on pizza crust; top with mushrooms, green onions, and green pepper, if desired. Bake at 425° for 15 minutes.

Sprinkle with remaining ¼ cup mozzarella cheese and Parmesan cheese; bake 5 minutes. Sprinkle with crushed red pepper, if desired. Yield: 10 slices (about 171 calories per slice).

Pizza Sauce:

1 (28-ounce) can whole tomatoes, undrained
1 (6-ounce) can tomato paste
1 large onion, chopped
3 tablespoons chopped fresh parsley
2 cloves garlic, minced
1 small green pepper, chopped
1½ teaspoons dried whole oregano
¼ teaspoon pepper

Place tomatoes in container of an electric blender; process until smooth. Pour into a small Dutch oven. Stir in remaining ingredients; bring to a boil. Reduce heat and simmer, uncovered, 1 hour or until sauce is reduced to about 3 cups. Divide into 1-cup portions; freeze 2 portions for later use. Yield: 3 cups or enough for three 12-inch pizzas.

CHINESE VEGETABLE MEDLEY

Vegetable cooking spray
1 teaspoon vegetable oil
1 (6-ounce) package frozen Chinese pea pods, thawed and drained
6 water chestnuts, sliced
½ cup diagonally sliced carrots
¼ cup sliced bamboo shoots
1 teaspoon sugar
1 teaspoon soy sauce
½ teaspoon cornstarch
¼ cup chicken broth

Coat a nonstick wok or skillet with cooking spray; add oil, and heat at medium high (325°) until hot. Add vegetables, and stir-fry 2 to 3 minutes or until vegetables are crisp-tender.

Combine sugar, soy sauce, cornstarch, and chicken broth; add to vegetables. Cook, stirring constantly, until thickened. Yield: 4 servings (about 60 calories per serving).

Tip: Clean, dry coffee cans make ideal baking containers for gift breads.

TROPICAL CARROTS

4 medium carrots, cut into 3- x ¼-inch strips (about 2 cups)
½ cup water
¾ cup unsweetened pineapple tidbits, undrained
2 teaspoons cornstarch
¼ teaspoon ground ginger

Combine carrots and water in a small saucepan; cover and cook until carrots are crisp-tender.

Combine pineapple, cornstarch, and ginger in a small bowl; mix well. Add pineapple mixture to carrots; cook over low heat, stirring constantly, until thickened. Serve immediately. Yield: 4 servings (about 59 calories per serving).

CELERY-PARMESAN TOSS

3 cups diagonally sliced celery
1 tablespoon reduced-calorie margarine
⅓ cup minced fresh parsley
¼ cup grated Parmesan cheese
Chopped pimiento (optional)

Cook celery in a small amount of boiling water 8 minutes or until crisp-tender; drain. Return to saucepan, and stir in margarine; cover and cook over low heat 2 minutes.

Remove from heat, and toss with parsley and cheese. Sprinkle mixture with chopped pimiento, if desired. Serve immediately. Yield: 6 servings (about 40 calories per serving).

BEAN-STUFFED TOMATOES

2 (9-ounce) packages frozen French-style green beans
1 (4-ounce) can sliced mushrooms, drained
⅓ cup Italian reduced-calorie salad dressing
¼ cup sliced green onions
⅛ teaspoon dried whole basil
⅛ teaspoon pepper
6 medium tomatoes

Cook green beans according to package directions, omitting salt; drain well. Combine beans and next 5 ingredients in a medium bowl. Cover and chill for 3 to 4 hours.

Cut off top of each tomato; scoop out pulp, leaving shells intact (reserve pulp for other uses). Invert tomato shells on paper towels to drain.

To serve, fill tomato shells with bean mixture. Yield: 6 servings (about 74 calories per serving).

Combine fresh brussels sprouts with orange wedges and savory seasonings for a quick and colorful dish appropriately called Orange Brussels Sprouts.

Fix Fresh Vegetables In A Hurry

Ever wonder what side dishes to cook when you're in a hurry for supper? We suggest Orange Brussels Sprouts for a delicious and colorful side dish.

Festive Cauliflower is another quick vegetable that takes only a few ingredients and a minimum amount of time. Keep the cauliflower whole to make the dish especially attractive.

ORANGE BRUSSELS SPROUTS

1 pound fresh brussels sprouts
1 small orange, unpeeled and cut into wedges
⅓ cup fresh orange juice
1 tablespoon white wine vinegar
1 tablespoon butter or margarine
1 teaspoon sugar
½ teaspoon salt
½ teaspoon dried whole dillweed

Wash brussels sprouts thoroughly; drain. Combine brussels sprouts and remaining ingredients in a saucepan; bring to a boil. Cover, reduce heat, and simmer 8 to 10 minutes or until tender. Yield: 4 servings. *Rebecca Shay, Murrells Inlet, South Carolina.*

FESTIVE CAULIFLOWER

1 medium head cauliflower
½ teaspoon salt
¼ cup mayonnaise
1 tablespoon chopped pimiento
1 tablespoon chopped green pepper
3 slices bacon, cooked and crumbled

Remove outer leaves and stalk of cauliflower; wash thoroughly. Leave cauliflower whole.

Bring 1 inch of water and salt to a boil in a large saucepan; add cauliflower. Cover and cook 10 to 12 minutes. Drain cauliflower, and place in a serving dish; keep warm.

Combine mayonnaise, pimiento, and green pepper; spread over hot cauliflower. Sprinkle with bacon. Yield: 4 to 6 servings.
Ann Thomas,
Huntsville, Alabama.

SAUCY BROCCOLI SPEARS

1 (1¼-pound) bunch fresh broccoli
2 tablespoons butter or margarine,
  melted
2 tablespoons lemon juice
¼ to ½ teaspoon salt
½ teaspoon paprika
1½ teaspoons prepared horseradish

Trim off large leaves of broccoli. Remove tough ends of stalks, and wash broccoli thoroughly. Cook broccoli, covered, in a small amount of boiling water for 10 to 12 minutes or until tender; drain and place in a serving dish. Combine the remaining ingredients, and spoon over broccoli. Serve immediately. Yield: 4 servings.
Mrs. John R. Armstrong,
Farwell, Texas.

SAUTEED MUSHROOMS

⅓ cup butter or margarine
1 teaspoon lemon juice
½ teaspoon vinegar
¼ teaspoon salt
⅛ teaspoon pepper
1 pound fresh mushrooms, sliced

Combine first 5 ingredients in a large skillet. Add mushrooms; sauté 5 minutes, stirring occasionally. Yield: 4 servings.
Pat Boschen,
Ashland, Virginia.

ZUCCHINI SAUTE

3 medium zucchini, cut into 2-inch
  strips
1 small onion, finely chopped
3 tablespoons butter or margarine
1 tablespoon soy sauce
¼ cup slivered almonds, toasted
2 tablespoons chopped fresh parsley

Sauté zucchini and onion in butter in a large skillet until crisp-tender. Spoon vegetables into a serving dish; sprinkle with soy sauce, and toss. Top with slivered almonds and parsley. Yield: 4 to 6 servings.
Sophie Baugher,
Shrewsbury, Pennsylvania.

Pork Roast With A New Look

The reputation of pork has changed over the past few years—it's much leaner and lower in calories than before. What's more, pork combines well with a variety of seasonings and is suited for the family supper or a special company dinner.

It's important to cook pork thoroughly, but not until it's overdone. The surest method is to insert a meat thermometer into the thickest part of the meat, making sure thermometer does not touch fat, and cook the roast until the thermometer registers 170°.

ROAST PORK TENDERLOIN

1 teaspoon dried whole rosemary,
  crushed
1 teaspoon dried whole thyme
1 large clove garlic, minced
2 (1½- to 2-pound) pork tenderloins
¼ cup butter or margarine, melted

Combine herbs and garlic; set aside. Brush tenderloins with butter, and roll in herb mixture, coating evenly. Place tenderloins, fat side up, on a rack in a shallow roasting pan. Insert meat thermometer into thickest part of tenderloin, making sure thermometer does not touch fat. Drizzle any remaining butter over meat.

Bake roast at 375° for 1 hour to 1 hour and 15 minutes or until meat thermometer registers 170°. Yield: 10 to 12 servings.
Lucille James,
New Orleans, Louisiana.

RIO GRANDE PORK ROAST

1 (4- to 5-pound) boneless pork loin
  roast, rolled and tied
½ teaspoon salt
½ teaspoon garlic salt
½ teaspoon chili powder
1 cup apple jelly
1 cup catsup
2 tablespoons vinegar
1 teaspoon chili powder
½ cup crushed corn chips

Rub roast on all sides with salt, garlic salt, and ½ teaspoon chili powder. Place roast, fat side up, on a rack in a shallow roasting pan. Insert meat thermometer into thickest part of roast, making sure thermometer does not touch fat. Bake at 325° for 2 hours or until thermometer registers 165°.

Combine jelly, catsup, vinegar, and 1 teaspoon chili powder in a small saucepan. Bring to a boil; reduce heat and simmer, uncovered, 2 minutes.

Brush roast with jelly mixture. Sprinkle with corn chips. Return to oven; bake at 325° for 10 to 15 minutes or until thermometer registers 170°. Serve with sauce. Yield: 12 to 15 servings.
Betty Rabe,
Plano, Texas.

PORK LOIN STUFFED WITH WILD RICE

⅓ cup uncooked wild rice
1⅓ cups water
⅔ cup grated carrots
½ cup golden raisins
½ cup chopped dry roasted pistachio nuts
6 scallions or green onions with tops,
  sliced
1 apple, peeled, cored, and finely chopped
¼ cup butter or margarine
2 tablespoons lime juice
½ teaspoon salt
¼ teaspoon white pepper
¼ teaspoon ground cardamom
1 (2½- to 3-pound) boneless pork loin
  roast, rolled and tied
½ cup Sauterne or other dry white wine
2 tablespoons blueberry preserves
Pinch of dried whole thyme

Combine rice and water in a heavy saucepan; bring to a boil. Cover, reduce heat, and simmer 12 minutes. Drain and set aside.

Sauté next 5 ingredients in butter and lime juice about 3 minutes or until carrots are tender. Remove from heat; stir in rice, salt, pepper, and cardamom, mixing gently. Set aside.

Untie roast, and spoon half of rice mixture lengthwise between loins. Retie roast securely with string at 2- to 3-inch intervals; place, fat side down, on rack in a shallow roasting pan. Spoon remaining stuffing into a greased shallow 1-quart casserole. Set aside.

Combine Sauterne, preserves, and thyme; pour over roast. Insert meat thermometer into thickest part of roast, making sure thermometer does not touch stuffing or fat. Bake at 325° for 1 hour and 45 minutes or until thermometer registers 170°. Cover and bake reserved stuffing at 325° for 25 to 30 minutes. Remove string, and slice roast to serve. Yield: 6 to 8 servings.
Mrs. Clifford Graham,
Fayette, Alabama.

BROWN SUGAR BRAISED PORK

1 (4- to 5-pound) Boston butt pork roast
⅓ cup Dijon mustard
½ cup firmly packed brown sugar
2 tablespoons vegetable oil
2 medium onions, thinly sliced
1 (10½-ounce) can beef broth, undiluted
¼ teaspoon pepper
2 teaspoons cornstarch
1 tablespoon cold water

Brush pork with mustard; coat with brown sugar. Brown pork on all sides in hot oil in a Dutch oven. Transfer roast to a platter.

Add onion to Dutch oven; cover and cook 5 minutes, stirring occasionally.

Return meat to Dutch oven; add broth and pepper. Cover and bring to a boil; remove from heat. Bake at 325° for 1 hour. Turn roast over; insert meat thermometer into roast, making sure thermometer does not touch bone or fat. Cover and bake an additional 1½ hours or until thermometer registers 170°. Remove pork to a serving platter.

Combine cornstarch and water, stirring until smooth; set aside. Bring pan drippings in Dutch oven to a boil; stir in cornstarch mixture. Return to a boil, and cook 1 minute or until thickened, stirring constantly. Serve sauce over pork roast. Yield: 8 servings.
Evelyn E. Walden,
Memphis, Tennessee.

Bake A Batch Of Drop Cookies

The next time you're longing for a cookie, try a batch of drop cookies. Our readers like them chunky with candy, spread with frostings, or paired together like a sandwich.

BUTTERSCOTCH-PECAN COOKIES

½ cup butter or margarine, softened
1 cup sugar
1 egg
½ teaspoon vanilla extract
1½ cups all-purpose flour
½ teaspoon baking powder
½ teaspoon baking soda
¼ teaspoon salt
1¼ cups chopped pecans
1 (6-ounce) package butterscotch morsels, finely chopped

Cream butter; gradually add sugar, beating until light and fluffy. Add egg and vanilla; beat well. Combine flour, baking powder, soda, and salt; add to creamed mixture, mixing well (batter will be stiff). Stir in pecans and chopped butterscotch morsels.

Drop dough by rounded teaspoonfuls, 2 inches apart, onto ungreased cookie sheets. Bake at 350° for 15 to 18 minutes. Remove from cookie sheets; cool completely on wire racks. Yield: 6 dozen.
Patrick J. Scussel,
Marietta, Georgia.

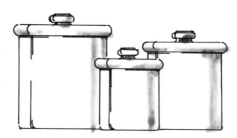

CHOCOLATE DROP COOKIES

½ cup shortening
1 cup firmly packed brown sugar
1 egg, beaten
2 (1-ounce) squares semisweet chocolate, melted
1 teaspoon vanilla extract
1⅔ cups sifted cake flour
½ teaspoon baking soda
½ teaspoon salt
½ cup milk
½ cup chopped pecans or walnuts
Chocolate-Coffee Frosting

Cream shortening and sugar until light and fluffy. Add egg, chocolate, and vanilla; mix well.

Combine flour, soda, and salt; add to creamed mixture alternately with milk, mixing well. Stir in pecans.

Drop dough by teaspoonfuls, about 1½ inches apart, onto greased cookie sheets. Bake at 350° for 10 to 12 minutes or until done. Cool partially on wire racks. Frost with Chocolate-Coffee Frosting while cookies are still warm. Yield: about 4 dozen.

Chocolate-Coffee Frosting:

¼ cup plus 2 tablespoons cocoa
¼ cup plus 2 tablespoons hot coffee
¼ cup plus 2 tablespoons butter or margarine, melted
1 teaspoon vanilla extract
3 cups sifted powdered sugar

Combine first 4 ingredients; blend until smooth. Gradually add powdered sugar, mixing well. Yield: enough for about 4 dozen cookies.
Patty Fitts,
Birmingham, Alabama.

FRESH APPLE COOKIES

½ cup shortening
1⅓ cups firmly packed brown sugar
1 egg
¼ cup milk
2 cups all-purpose flour
1 teaspoon baking soda
½ teaspoon salt
1 teaspoon ground cinnamon
½ teaspoon ground nutmeg
½ teaspoon ground cardamom
1 cup raisins
1 cup chopped pecans
1 cup finely chopped unpeeled apple
Vanilla frosting (recipe follows)

Cream shortening; gradually add sugar, beating well. Add egg and milk; beat well. Combine flour, soda, salt, and spices; add to creamed mixture, mixing well. Stir in the raisins, pecans, and apple.

Drop dough by rounded teaspoonfuls, 1½ inches apart, onto greased cookie sheets. Bake at 400° for 12 to 15 minutes. Cool on wire racks. Frost with vanilla frosting. Yield: 4½ dozen.

Vanilla Frosting:

1½ cups sifted powdered sugar
⅛ teaspoon salt
2½ tablespoons milk
1 tablespoon butter or margarine, melted
½ teaspoon vanilla extract

Combine all ingredients in a small mixing bowl; beat until smooth. Yield: enough for 4½ dozen cookies.
Cynthia Shipley,
Dallas, Texas.

MONSTER COOKIES

½ cup butter or margarine, softened
1 cup sugar
1 cup plus 2 tablespoons firmly packed brown sugar
3 eggs
2 cups peanut butter
¼ teaspoon vanilla extract
¾ teaspoon light corn syrup
4½ cups regular oats, uncooked
2 teaspoons baking soda
¼ teaspoon salt
1 cup candy-coated milk chocolate pieces
1 (6-ounce) package semisweet chocolate morsels

Cream butter; gradually add sugar, beating well. Add eggs, peanut butter, vanilla, and corn syrup, beating well. Add oats, soda, and salt, stirring well. Stir in the remaining ingredients. (Dough will be stiff.)

Pack dough into a ¼-cup measure. Drop dough, 4 inches apart, onto lightly greased cookie sheets. Lightly press each cookie into a 3½-inch circle with fingertips. Bake at 350° for 12 to 15 minutes (centers of cookies will be slightly soft). Cool slightly on cookie sheets; remove to wire racks, and cool completely. Yield: 2½ dozen.

Barbara Vandergriff,
Birmingham, Alabama.

DEVIL DOGGIES

¼ cup plus 2 tablespoons butter or
    margarine, softened
1 cup sugar
1 egg
1 cup milk
2 cups all-purpose flour
¼ cup plus 2 tablespoons cocoa
1¼ teaspoons baking soda
¼ teaspoon salt
1 teaspoon vanilla extract
Cream filling (recipe follows)

Cream butter and gradually add sugar, beating well. Add egg and milk; beat well. Combine flour, cocoa, soda, and salt; gradually add to creamed mixture, mixing well. Stir in vanilla.

Drop dough by heaping teaspoonfuls, 2 inches apart, onto ungreased cookie sheets. Bake at 400° for 8 minutes or until done. Cool cookies completely on wire racks.

Spread bottom side of half of cookies with cream filling; place on top of the remaining cookies. Yield: about 3½ dozen.

Cream Filling:

¾ cup butter or margarine, softened
¾ cup sifted powdered sugar
½ cup marshmallow creme
1 teaspoon vanilla extract

Cream butter and powdered sugar in a small mixing bowl until light and fluffy. Add marshmallow creme and vanilla; mix well. Yield: about 1½ cups.

Ann Devendra,
Bellaire, Ohio.

Tip: Have your oven thermostat professionally checked at least once a year. Another way to occasionally check oven temperature is to prepare a cake mix according to package directions; the cake should cook the entire recommended time and test done (a wooden pick inserted in the center should come out clean).

From Our Kitchen To Yours

A fire in the kitchen is too often a reality. Here are some safety tips to help prevent fires in your kitchen:

Safety in the Kitchen

—What should you do if grease catches fire? If the fire is contained in the cooking utensil, first turn the heat off and then put the lid over the pan. If a lid is unavailable, throw some baking soda on the fire. But never use water. Water will splatter the grease and spread the flames. And, don't attempt to move the skillet to the sink or outdoors, as the movement will add air to fire, causing it to ignite.

In our kitchens, we always use deep fat frying thermometers to keep the oil at the proper temperature.

—Don't wear long, flowing sleeves or blouses with bows or scarves when cooking. These clothing items can touch a burner and quickly ignite.

—Never use a dish towel to handle a hot utensil. The loose ends of the towel may catch on fire. Also, don't use a wet pot holder—it may cause a steam burn.

—Don't store frequently used items over the stove. It's too easy to catch your clothes on fire or get burned when you reach over a hot burner to get something.

—Don't overload the electrical outlets. The heat may cause a fire in the wiring.

—Keep a fire extinguisher in your kitchen. Look for an extinguisher labeled ABC that is equipped to handle all kinds of home fires.

—Before frying chicken or fish, carefully pat dry each piece with paper towels. Remember that water may cause the oil to splatter and burn skin.

—Use kitchen tongs to turn food that is frying. Food can slip off a fork and splatter the grease.

—When removing the cover from a pan, lift the lid from the back first. This lets the steam escape away from you.

—Keep handles of pots and pans turned inward towards the back of the stove. This puts the handles out of the reach of children and keeps you from bumping them and causing spills.

—If you do burn yourself and the area is red but with no blisters, run cold water over the burn or put ice on it. Applying butter or margarine is not recommended. If the pain persists, apply sunburn lotion or spray. For additional treatment, apply an antiseptic ointment.

A Final Safety Note

Keep a list of the following phone numbers by each telephone in your home: fire department, police department, doctor's office, poison control center, hospital emergency room, ambulance service, and a family member or close friend who could be notified in case of emergency.

Enjoy A Cajun Favorite

While growing up in Baton Rouge, Wes Bowman of Birmingham always enjoyed his mother's Red Beans and Rice. Wes adds garlic salt, a pinch of cinnamon, and extra Worcestershire sauce to the Cajun specialty. Then he thickens it by mashing most of the beans against the side of the pot—the recipe's secret, he says.

RED BEANS AND RICE

1 pound dried red beans
3 quarts water
1 pound diced cooked ham
1 large onion, chopped
½ cup Worcestershire sauce
1 teaspoon garlic salt
½ teaspoon pepper
⅛ teaspoon red pepper
⅛ teaspoon ground cinnamon
3 bay leaves
Hot cooked rice

Sort and wash beans. Combine beans and water in a large Dutch oven; bring to a boil. Cover, reduce heat to medium, and cook 40 minutes.

Add next 8 ingredients; cover, reduce heat, and simmer 2 hours, stirring occasionally. Mash most of beans against side of Dutch oven with back of a spoon; stir well. Cover and bring to a boil; reduce heat to medium high and cook, uncovered, 1 hour or until desired degree of doneness, stirring occasionally. Discard bay leaves. Serve over rice. Yield: 6 servings. *Wes Bowman, Birmingham, Alabama.*

Microwave A Soup In Minutes

With the help of the microwave oven, you can serve steaming bowls of nourishing homemade soup in no time at all. In fact, all of these soups can be microwaved in about 25 minutes or less.

Speed isn't the only reason for preparing soups in the microwave oven. Vegetables in microwaved soups have a fresher taste and texture than those that simmer on top of the range for hours, losing flavor and vitamins.

If your family is always on the go, you may want to prepare a large amount of soup and store it in the refrigerator. Individual mugs or bowls of the refrigerated soup can be quickly reheated in the microwave. Stir the soup before tasting to make sure the heat is evenly distributed.

Several of the soups included here are prepared in extra-large casseroles—especially those with a lot of liquid. This allows plenty of room for boiling and stirring of the soups.

BEEFY VEGETABLE SOUP

1 pound ground beef
⅔ cup chopped celery
⅔ cup chopped onion
1 (16-ounce) can cut green beans, drained
1 (16-ounce) can cut wax beans, drained
1 (16-ounce) can whole tomatoes, drained and chopped
2 cups tomato juice
2 cups water
2 teaspoons beef-flavored bouillon granules
1 teaspoon salt
1 teaspoon dried parsley flakes
¼ teaspoon dried whole oregano
¼ teaspoon dried whole thyme
¼ teaspoon pepper
⅛ teaspoon garlic powder
1½ teaspoons Worcestershire sauce

Combine beef, celery, and onion in a 4½-quart casserole. Cover and microwave at HIGH for 6 to 7 minutes or until beef is browned, stirring once. Drain off pan drippings, reserving 3 tablespoons in dish. Add remaining ingredients. Cover and microwave at HIGH for 15 minutes or until flavors are blended, stir at 5-minute intervals. Yield: about 2½ quarts.

POTATO-BACON SOUP

4 slices bacon, chopped
3 medium potatoes, peeled and cut into ½-inch cubes
2 stalks celery, chopped
4 green onions, chopped
¼ cup water
¼ teaspoon pepper
2½ cups milk, divided
¼ cup all-purpose flour
1 teaspoon onion salt

Place bacon in a 2-quart casserole. Cover and microwave at HIGH for 4½ to 5½ minutes, or until browned; drain.

Add potatoes, celery, onions, water, and pepper. Cover and microwave at HIGH for 10 to 12 minutes or until vegetables are tender, stirring mixture after 5 minutes.

Combine ½ cup milk and flour, stirring well; stir into potato mixture. Add remaining 2 cups milk and onion salt to potatoes. Microwave, uncovered, at HIGH for 7 to 10 minutes, or just until thickened, stirring twice. Yield: about 2 quarts.

CORN CHOWDER

¼ pound bulk pork sausage
½ cup chopped onion
½ cup chopped green pepper
4 cups milk, divided
¼ cup all-purpose flour
1 tablespoon chopped fresh parsley
1 teaspoon onion salt
⅛ teaspoon pepper
1 egg, slightly beaten
1 (17-ounce) can cream-style corn
1 (17-ounce) can whole kernel corn, drained
¼ cup diced pimiento, drained

Combine sausage, onion, and green pepper in a 3-quart casserole. Microwave at HIGH for 2½ to 3 minutes or until sausage is browned, stirring once.

Combine 1 cup milk and flour, stirring well; stir into sausage mixture. Add parsley, onion salt, and pepper; microwave at HIGH for 2 to 3 minutes or until thick and bubbly, stirring once. Stir in remaining 3 cups milk.

Gradually add a small amount of milk mixture to egg; add to remaining milk mixture, stirring well. Stir in remaining ingredients. Microwave at HIGH for 7 to 9 minutes or just until slightly thickened, stirring after 4 minutes. Yield: about 2 quarts.

FISH CHOWDER

1½ cups coarsely shredded cabbage
1 (8-ounce) can tomato sauce
1 cup hot water
1 cup thinly sliced carrots
4 green onions, chopped
1½ teaspoons onion salt
¼ teaspoon red pepper
1 pound frozen fish fillets, thawed and cut into 1-inch pieces
1 (16-ounce) package frozen cut okra
1 cup hot water
¾ cup uncooked instant rice

Combine first 7 ingredients in a 3-quart casserole. Cover and microwave at HIGH for 8 minutes, stirring mixture after 4 minutes.

Add remaining ingredients. Cover and microwave at HIGH for 11 to 13 minutes, stirring after 6 minutes. Yield: about 6½ cups.

Dress Up The Simple Potato

Next time you crave a hot baked potato, try one stuffed with sour cream and onion for a change. Bake them as usual—then scoop out the pulp and mix in the onion and sour cream. After spooning the mixture into its original shells, garnish Baked Stuffed Potatoes with paprika and strips of cheese.

BAKED STUFFED POTATOES

3 large baking potatoes
Vegetable oil
¼ cup butter or margarine, melted
¼ cup milk
3 tablespoons commercial sour cream
2 tablespoons chopped onion
1½ teaspoons parsley flakes
¼ teaspoon dry mustard
⅛ teaspoon salt
⅛ teaspoon pepper
2 slices process American cheese, cut into thin strips
Paprika

Scrub potatoes thoroughly, and rub skins with oil; bake at 400° for 1 hour or until done.

Allow potatoes to cool to touch. Cut potatoes in half lengthwise; carefully scoop out pulp, leaving shells intact. Spoon pulp into a mixing bowl. Add remaining ingredients except cheese and paprika; beat with an electric mixer until fluffy. Stuff shells with potato mixture; garnish with cheese strips, and sprinkle with paprika. Bake at 400° for 15 minutes. Yield: 6 servings.

Mrs. John C. Williams,
Hurtsboro, Alabama.

JALAPENO POTATOES

4 medium-size red potatoes
¼ cup butter or margarine
1 tablespoon all-purpose flour
1 cup milk
1 (6-ounce) roll jalapeño cheese
½ cup chopped green pepper
1 (2-ounce) jar diced pimiento, drained

Scrub potatoes; cook in boiling water about 30 minutes or until tender. Drain and cool slightly; peel and cut into ¼-inch slices.

Melt butter in a heavy saucepan over low heat; add flour, stirring until smooth. Cook 1 minute, stirring constantly. Gradually add milk; cook over medium heat, stirring constantly, until thickened and bubbly. Add cheese, stirring until cheese melts and sauce is smooth.

Layer half of potatoes, green pepper, and pimiento in a lightly greased 1½-quart casserole. Repeat with remaining ingredients. Pour cheese sauce over potatoes. Bake, uncovered, at 350° for 40 to 45 minutes. Yield: 4 to 6 servings.

Geraldine Graves,
Marion, Louisiana.

SOUR CREAM POTATOES

8 medium-size red potatoes
⅓ cup chopped onion
⅓ cup butter or margarine
1 cup (4 ounces) shredded Cheddar cheese
1 (16-ounce) carton commercial sour cream
1 teaspoon salt
½ teaspoon pepper

Scrub potatoes; cook in boiling water about 30 minutes or until tender. Drain and cool slightly. Peel and cut potatoes into ½-inch cubes.

Sauté onion in butter in a small skillet until tender. Combine potatoes, sautéed onion, and remaining ingredients in a large bowl; mix gently.

Spoon potato mixture into a lightly greased 12- x 8- x 2-inch baking dish. Bake at 350° for 30 minutes or until bubbly. Yield: 10 servings.

Barbara D. Walker,
Rocky Mount, North Carolina.

There's Chocolate And Caramel In The Cake

Brown Mountain Cake is a delicious blend of chocolate and rich caramel. If you are looking for a scrumptious cake for a special occasion, this cake will bring in showers of compliments. But be prepared to share the recipe.

BROWN MOUNTAIN CAKE

1 cup butter or margarine, softened
2 cups sugar
3 eggs
3 cups all-purpose flour
1 cup buttermilk
½ cup warm water
3 tablespoons cocoa
1 teaspoon baking soda
1 teaspoon vanilla extract
Caramel frosting (recipe follows)
Grated chocolate (optional)
Pecan halves (optional)

Cream butter; gradually add sugar, beating until light and fluffy. Add eggs, one at a time, beating well after each addition. Add flour alternately with buttermilk, beginning and ending with flour. Combine water, cocoa, and soda, stirring well; add to flour mixture, beating well. Stir in vanilla.

Pour batter into 2 greased and floured 9-inch round cakepans. Bake at 350° for 35 to 40 minutes or until a wooden pick inserted in center comes out clean. Cool in pans 10 minutes; remove from pans, and cool completely on wire racks.

Spread caramel frosting between layers and on top and sides of cake. Sprinkle with grated chocolate, and garnish with pecan halves, if desired. Yield: one 2-layer cake.

Caramel Frosting:

1 cup butter
2 cups sugar
1 cup evaporated milk
1 teaspoon vanilla extract

Melt butter in a heavy saucepan over medium heat; add sugar and milk. Cook mixture over medium heat, stirring constantly, until candy thermometer registers 234° (soft ball stage). Remove from heat, and add vanilla (do not stir); cool 10 minutes.

Beat on medium speed of electric mixer about 10 minutes until thick enough to spread. Spread immediately on cooled cake. Yield: enough for one 2-layer cake.

Gail Sewell,
Kingsport, Tennessee.

Beef Up A Dish

Meatballs and burgers are two of the oldest uses for ground beef. The recipes here offer tasty variations on these favorite standbys.

PARTY BURGERS

2 pounds ground beef
1 cup soft breadcrumbs
¾ cup Burgundy
1 (4-ounce) can mushroom stems and pieces, drained
2 teaspoons onion salt
1 teaspoon dry mustard
1 teaspoon Worcestershire sauce
¼ teaspoon garlic powder
¼ teaspoon pepper
8 hamburger buns (optional)

Combine first 9 ingredients, mixing well. Shape into 8 patties. Broil or grill 4 to 5 inches from heat 5 minutes on each side or until desired degree of doneness. Serve in hamburger buns, if desired. Yield: 8 servings.

Mrs. R. P. Vinroot,
Matthews, North Carolina.

BEEF BALLS HEIDELBERG

1½ pounds ground beef
1½ teaspoons caraway seeds
1 tablespoon vinegar
1½ cups soft rye breadcrumbs
¼ cup chopped onion
⅓ cup milk
1 egg, beaten
1 teaspoon salt
1 tablespoon vegetable oil
1 (16-ounce) can whole potatoes, drained and cut into ¼-inch slices
1 (16-ounce) can sauerkraut, undrained

Combine first 8 ingredients, mixing well. Shape mixture into 1½-inch balls; brown in oil over medium heat in a large skillet. Add potatoes and sauerkraut; cover, reduce heat, and simmer 10 minutes. Yield: 6 servings.

Norma Cowden,
Shawnee, Oklahoma.

Mold Candies For Your Valentine

Making fancy candies is easy and fun, and you get to eat the end product—or wrap it up as a gift to give on Valentine Day or for other special occasions.

Molding candy is a kitchen craft that is sweeping the South. You'll find the colored candies and specialty molds in kitchen shops, department stores, or in catalogs from large cake-decorating companies.

Choosing the Candy

The candies most often used in molding are chocolate-flavored compounds intended especially for making candy at home. These compounds, often called "summer coatings," were developed with qualities that make candymaking simple, even for the novice. They melt easily, harden quickly after molding, and are not as adversely affected by high temperatures and humidity as most other candies.

Summer coatings are available in a rainbow of colors in either chunk or wafer form. The advantage to the wafer form is that it does not have to be chopped before melting.

For the taste of real chocolate, you can also mold candy with either semi-sweet or milk chocolate in the chunk, block, or chip forms. Candies molded with real chocolate will melt more easily than those made of summer coatings, so store in a cool, dry place. If they become too soft at room temperature, refrigerate until ready to serve. Candy made with real chocolate can develop "bloom" if exposed to extremes in temperature. Bloom is a gray discoloration on the surface of the chocolate; but it only affects the appearance of the chocolate, not the flavor or quality.

When using real chocolate, you obviously won't have the various colors of summer coating. To add color, we suggest painting detail on the mold with summer coating and filling the remainder of the mold with the chocolate.

You can also melt and color white chocolate found in many large department stores, but it's more expensive and time-consuming than purchasing the summer coating. White chocolate is not real chocolate either, but a substance similar in makeup to summer coating. To color white chocolate, melt it like real chocolate and stir in paste food coloring to achieve desired color. (Liquid coloring will cause the chocolate to thicken and lump.)

Surprise friends with a gift of candy you've made yourself. For a festive look, nestle candies into tiny paper cups, and arrange them in a basket or gift box.

About Candy Molds

The molds for this type of candymaking come in a variety of shapes and sizes. The best are made of transparent plastic, which allows you to see underneath and check for air bubbles or a poor paint job on multicolored candies.

If you use a mold several times in one day, it needn't be cleaned between uses because candy will come out cleanly and leave the mold ready for another filling. When finished with the mold, wash in warm water, dry, and store it flat. Detergents and hot water will dry out the mold and can crack it.

Melting the Candy

Chop or grate any large chunks of candy or chocolate before melting. Because it can scorch easily, always heat it in a double boiler over hot, not boiling, water until almost melted. Then remove the top of the double boiler from water, and stir until melted. When you're melting small amounts of many different colors, use small jars (one for each color of candy) set in an electric skillet filled with water to simulate a double boiler. Let the jars stand in warm water while you paint designs. If candy hardens too much, reheat slowly just until melted.

Be careful not to let any steam or water droplets get into the candy or chocolate, or it will thicken and be hard to work with. All cooking utensils should be absolutely dry.

If you wish to add flavoring to the candy, do so as you melt it. Use only oil-base flavorings; water-base flavorings, such as regular peppermint extract found in grocery stores, will cause the mixture to harden and lump.

Filling the Molds

If you're only using one color of candy per mold, simply spoon in the melted candy. Greasing molds is not necessary and would harm the finished appearance of the candy. Underfill rather than overfill molds so that the finished candy won't have a base larger than the design. Tap molds on a table to level them and to bring any bubbles to the surface. Let candy harden (refrigeration or freezing will hasten the process); then invert the mold, and tap it

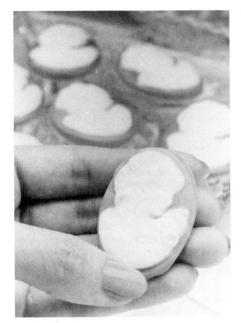

It doesn't take special skill to achieve magnificent detail as in these cameo candies.

For Valentine Day, you'll enjoy special card molds and three-dimensional hearts.

To make molded candies, melt the desired colors of candy in separate jars set in a skillet of hot water to simulate a double boiler; don't boil the water.

Paint melted candy onto mold; freeze the mold until candy hardens between each change of color. Freeze finished candies until firm; then invert mold to release them.

gently for the candy to fall out. Store molded candy in a cool, dry place.

For multicolored candy, use a small paintbrush to paint details directly onto the mold. Freeze mold a few minutes after painting each color to harden candy so that the first color won't run when you paint the next. Use good quality brushes that won't lose their bristles as you paint, and use a separate brush for each color of candy. If there are a lot of narrow lines in the design, you'll find that piping melted candy from a decorating bag does a quicker and neater job than painting; just use any metal decorating tip with a small round hole. Once detail is painted, fill remainder of the mold with chocolate or summer coating, and freeze until firm; then unmold. Store in a cool, dry place.

Serve A Hot Fireside Drink

Chilly evenings call for a cozy fire, good friends, and a toasty beverage. On those occasions, serve mugs of Hot Cranberry Punch or Hot Spiced Wine.

HOT CRANBERRY PUNCH

1 quart cranberry juice cocktail
1 (12-ounce) can frozen lemonade
  concentrate, undiluted
2 cups water
¼ cup sugar
½ teaspoon ground allspice
¼ teaspoon salt
¼ teaspoon ground cinnamon
½ cup brandy

Combine first 7 ingredients in a Dutch oven, mixing well. Place over medium heat, stirring until sugar dissolves. Stir in brandy; reduce heat and simmer until mixture is thoroughly heated. Serve hot. Yield: 2 quarts.

Mrs. E. L. Warstler,
Kill Devil Hills, North Carolina.

HOT SPICED WINE

1 cup water
½ cup sugar
1 lemon, sliced
1 orange, sliced
12 whole allspice
12 whole cloves
1 (3-inch) stick cinnamon
1 (25.4-ounce) bottle Burgundy or other
  dry red wine

Combine water, sugar, lemon slices, and orange slices in a Dutch oven. Tie spices in a cheesecloth bag; add to sugar mixture, and bring to a boil. Reduce heat and simmer 5 minutes. Add wine; return to a boil. Reduce heat and simmer 10 minutes. Discard spice bag. Serve hot. Yield: 4½ cups.

Cyndi Turner,
Humboldt, Tennessee.

Tip: Wine should be stored at an even temperature of 50° to 60°. It is important that bottles of corked table wines be kept on their sides so that the corks are kept moist and airtight. Bottles with screw caps may remain upright.

HOT APPLE CIDER NOG

2 eggs, beaten
½ cup sugar
1 cup apple cider or apple juice
¼ teaspoon salt
¼ teaspoon ground cinnamon
⅛ teaspoon ground nutmeg
3 cups milk, scalded
½ cup whipping cream, whipped
Ground nutmeg

Combine first 6 ingredients in a medium saucepan, mixing well. Gradually add scalded milk, stirring constantly with a wire whisk. Cook over low heat, stirring constantly, until thoroughly heated (do not boil). Ladle into mugs. Top each serving with a dollop of whipped cream; sprinkle with nutmeg. Serve hot. Yield: about 4½ cups.

Gail Weeks,
Moultrie, Georgia.

HOT SPICED CIDER MIX

1 cup orange-flavored drink mix
1 cup sugar-sweetened apple-flavored drink mix
1 cup sugar
½ cup instant tea mix
1 (6-ounce) package sugar-sweetened lemonade-flavored mix
½ teaspoon ground cinnamon
¼ teaspoon ground cloves
¼ teaspoon ground allspice

Combine all ingredients in a large bowl, and mix well. Store in an airtight container until ready to use.

For each serving, place 1 tablespoon plus 1 teaspoon mix in a cup. Add 1 cup boiling water, and stir well. Serve hot. Yield: 42 servings.

Eleanor Rowland,
Newport News, Virginia.

Green Onions Fill This Quiche

When you want a simple, hot dish for lunch or supper, serve slices of Cheesy Green Onion Quiche. The filling of cheese, bacon, eggs, and sour cream is similar to that of a traditional Quiche Lorraine. But the addition of mild-flavored green onions and two types of cheese—Swiss and Cheddar—makes it deliciously different.

CHEESY GREEN ONION QUICHE

Pastry for 9-inch quiche dish or pieplate
8 slices bacon, cooked and crumbled
¾ cup (3 ounces) shredded Cheddar cheese
¾ cup (3 ounces) shredded Swiss cheese
4 eggs, beaten
1 (8-ounce) carton commercial sour cream
½ cup half-and-half
¼ cup sliced green onions
1 tablespoon all-purpose flour
¾ teaspoon salt
⅛ teaspoon pepper
Dash of red pepper

Line a 9-inch quiche dish or pieplate with pastry; trim excess pastry around edges. Prick bottom and sides of pastry with a fork. Bake at 400° for 3 minutes; remove from oven, and gently prick with a fork. Bake 5 minutes longer.

Sprinkle bacon and cheese into pastry shell. Combine remaining ingredients, and mix well. Pour into pastry shell. Bake at 375° for 40 to 45 minutes or until set. Yield: one 9-inch quiche.

Grace Bravos,
Timonium, Maryland.

Sausage Makes These Dishes

Beckon your family to a meal with the tantalizing aroma of sizzling sausage. And with these recipes, you can serve sausage at any time of the day.

Most of the recipes here call for mild-flavored sausage. But you can always substitute a hot and spicy version.

PANCAKE-SAUSAGE ROLLUPS

1 (12-ounce) package blueberry pancake mix (canned blueberries included)
1¾ cups milk
¼ cup vegetable oil
1 egg
Vegetable oil
1 pound mild bulk pork sausage
1 (8-ounce) carton commercial sour cream
Blueberry syrup

Combine dry ingredients of pancake mix, milk, ¼ cup oil, and egg in a large bowl; stir with a wire whisk until smooth. Rinse blueberries packaged with pancake mix, and drain well. Fold blueberries into batter.

Brush the bottom of a 10-inch crêpe pan or heavy skillet with vegetable oil; place over medium heat until just hot, not smoking.

Pour ¼ cup batter into pan; quickly tilt pan in all directions so that batter covers pan, making a 7-inch pancake. Turn pancakes when tops are covered with bubbles and edges are slightly dry. Set pancakes aside, and keep warm.

Cook sausage in a skillet until browned, stirring to crumble meat; drain well.

Spoon 2 tablespoons sausage and 1 tablespoon sour cream into center of each pancake; roll up and place, seam side down, in a 13- x 9- x 2-inch baking dish. Bake at 400° for 10 minutes. Serve hot with blueberry syrup. Yield: 6 servings.

Mary Belle Purvis,
Greeneville, Tennessee.

SAUSAGE SURPRISE

2 pounds smoked sausage, cut into ¾-inch slices
1 large onion, cut into eighths
1 medium cabbage, cut into small chunks
½ cup water
1 pound carrots, cut into ½-inch slices
5 medium potatoes, peeled and cut into ¾-inch cubes

Brown sausage in a Dutch oven; remove and drain on paper towels. Drain off drippings, reserving 1 tablespoon in Dutch oven.

Sauté onion in reserved drippings 3 to 5 minutes; add sausage, cabbage, and water. Cover and cook over low heat 10 minutes. Stir in carrots and potatoes; cover and cook an additional 20 minutes or until the vegetables are tender. Yield: 8 servings.

Sharyl Langley,
Sulphur, Louisiana.

EGG-AND-SAUSAGE TORTILLAS

8 flour tortillas
½ pound mild bulk pork sausage
½ cup chopped green onions
4 eggs
2 tablespoons whipping cream
½ teaspoon salt
¼ teaspoon pepper
2 tablespoons butter or margarine
½ cup (2 ounces) shredded sharp Cheddar cheese
Commercial picante sauce

Wrap tortillas tightly in foil; bake at 350° for 15 minutes.

Combine sausage and green onions in a large skillet; cook until sausage is browned and onion is tender, stirring to crumble meat. Drain well; set aside.

Combine eggs, whipping cream, salt, and pepper, beating well. Melt 2 tablespoons butter in a heavy skillet over medium heat; add egg mixture and cook, stirring often, until eggs are firm but still moist. Add sausage mixture and cheese, stirring well.

Spoon an equal amount of sausage-egg mixture into center of each warm tortilla. Roll up tortillas; serve immediately with picante sauce. Yield: 8 servings.
Kathleen Stone,
Houston, Texas.

Remember Teacakes?

When these Old-Fashioned Teacakes were prepared in our test kitchens, many of us were reminded of childhood days. We think you and the children in your home will enjoy this teacake recipe. Cut the dough into large rounds with a large biscuit cutter, or use shaped cookie cutters to make a special treat for your children.

OLD-FASHIONED TEACAKES

1 cup butter or margarine, softened
2 cups sugar
3 eggs
2 tablespoons buttermilk
5 cups all-purpose flour
1 teaspoon baking soda
1 teaspoon vanilla extract
Additional sugar

Cream butter; gradually add 2 cups sugar, beating well. Add eggs, one at a time, beating well after each addition. Add buttermilk, and beat well. Combine flour and soda; gradually stir into creamed mixture. Stir in vanilla. Chill dough several hours or overnight.

Roll dough to ¼-inch thickness on a lightly floured surface; cut into rounds with a large biscuit cutter or a 3½-inch cookie cutter. Place rounds 1 inch apart on lightly greased cookie sheets; sprinkle with additional sugar. Bake at 400° for 7 to 8 minutes or until edges are lightly browned. Remove cookies to wire racks, and let cool completely. Yield: about 4 dozen.
Willie Mae Alexander,
Antioch, Tennessee.

Sweet Endings Make The Meal

Favorite desserts add a special touch on holidays, birthdays, and other celebrations, but they can also make the most ordinary meals seem special. These desserts will help end any occasion on a sweet note.

LIME FLUFF PIE

1 (3-ounce) package lime-flavored gelatin
1 cup boiling water
¼ cup sugar
¼ cup frozen limeade concentrate, thawed and undiluted
⅓ cup cold water
1 (8-ounce) package cream cheese, softened
1 (1.5-ounce) envelope whipped topping mix
Crispy Rice Crust

Combine gelatin, boiling water, and sugar; stir until dissolved. Stir in limeade concentrate and cold water; set mixture aside.

Beat cream cheese until smooth in a large mixing bowl. Add ¼ cup gelatin mixture, one tablespoon at a time, beating after each addition. Gradually add remaining gelatin mixture, beating until smooth. Chill 1 hour and 15 minutes or until thickened, stirring occasionally.

Prepare whipped topping mix according to package directions, omitting vanilla; fold into gelatin mixture. Chill 45 minutes or until the mixture mounds. Pour filling into Crispy Rice Crust. Refrigerate pie at least 3 hours. Yield: one 9-inch pie.

Crispy Rice Crust:

4 cups bite-size crispy rice squares cereal, crushed
¼ cup firmly packed brown sugar
¼ cup plus 2 tablespoons butter or margarine, melted

Combine cereal crumbs and sugar in a small mixing bowl; stir in butter. Press mixture evenly into a 9-inch pieplate. Bake at 300° for 10 minutes; cool. Yield: one 9-inch pie crust.
Varniece R. Warren,
Hermitage, Arkansas.

CREAMY COCONUT CAKE

½ cup shortening
½ cup butter or margarine, softened
2 cups sugar
5 eggs, separated
2 cups all-purpose flour
1 teaspoon baking soda
¼ teaspoon salt
1 cup buttermilk
1 teaspoon vanilla extract
⅔ cup flaked coconut
Pinch of cream of tartar
Coconut-Pecan Frosting

Cream shortening, butter, and sugar until light and fluffy. Add egg yolks, one at a time, beating well after each addition. Combine flour, soda, and salt. Add to creamed mixture alternately with buttermilk, beginning and ending with flour mixture; beat well after each addition. Stir in vanilla and coconut.

Beat egg whites (at room temperature) until frothy; add cream of tartar, and continue beating until egg whites are stiff but not dry. Fold egg whites into batter.

Spoon batter into 3 greased and floured 9-inch cakepans. Bake at 350° for 25 to 30 minutes or until a wooden pick inserted in center comes out clean. Cool in pans 10 minutes; remove layers from pans, and let cool completely.

Spread Coconut-Pecan Frosting between layers and on top and sides of cake. Store in refrigerator. Yield: one 3-layer cake.

Coconut-Pecan Frosting:

1 (8-ounce) package cream cheese, softened
½ cup butter or margarine, softened
1 (16-ounce) package powdered sugar, sifted
1 teaspoon vanilla extract
Dash of salt
½ cup flaked coconut
½ cup chopped pecans

Beat cream cheese and butter until light and fluffy. Gradually add sugar, beating until smooth. Add vanilla and salt; beat until thoroughly blended. Stir in coconut and pecans. Yield: enough for one 3-layer cake.
Mrs. Leonard G. Voegeli,
Amber, Oklahoma.

Tip: Tinted coconut makes a child's cake more festive. Fill a pint jar one-third to one-half full of coconut. Add a few drops of liquid food coloring to 1 to 2 tablespoons of water, and add to coconut; cover jar, and shake well to distribute color evenly.

Bake Oysters In A Casserole

Many oyster fans like to eat this delicately flavored shellfish raw—right out of the rough, oblong shell. But if you prefer your oysters cooked, try combining them with spinach, corn, or wild rice for a flavorful side-dish casserole.

OYSTER-AND-WILD RICE CASSEROLE

1 (6-ounce) package long grain and
  wild rice
½ cup cream of chicken soup, undiluted
½ cup half-and-half
1 tablespoon finely chopped onion
1 teaspoon curry powder
½ teaspoon dried whole thyme
Dash of Worcestershire sauce
¼ cup dry sherry
1 pint oysters, drained
8 mushroom caps
1 tablespoon lemon juice
Fresh parsley sprigs (optional)

Prepare rice according to package directions; set aside.

Combine next 6 ingredients in a small bowl; mix well.

Pour sherry in a lightly greased 10- x 6- x 2-inch baking dish; top with half of rice. Pour one-third soup mixture over rice. Arrange oysters and mushroom caps over soup mixture. Sprinkle with lemon juice. Top with remaining rice and soup mixture. Bake at 350° for 45 minutes. Garnish with parsley sprigs, if desired. Yield: 6 to 8 servings.
Fred T. Marshall,
Hollywood, Maryland.

OYSTER-AND-CORN BAKE

¼ cup butter or margarine, melted
1½ cups fine cracker crumbs
2 tablespoons chopped fresh parsley
⅓ cup chopped onion
⅓ cup chopped celery
2 tablespoons butter or margarine
1 pint oysters
1 (8¾-ounce) can whole kernel corn,
  drained
1 (2-ounce) jar diced pimiento, drained
1 teaspoon Worcestershire sauce
½ teaspoon salt
Pinch of pepper

Combine ¼ cup butter, crumbs, and parsley; mix well. Set aside.

Sauté onion and celery in 2 tablespoons butter in a skillet until tender. Drain oysters, reserving ¼ cup liquid. Stir in the reserved oyster liquid, corn, pimiento, Worcestershire sauce, salt, and pepper into sautéed vegetables.

Place 1 cup crumb mixture in a lightly greased 10- x 6- x 2-inch baking dish. Arrange oysters over crumbs; spoon vegetable mixture on top. Cover with remaining crumb mixture; bake at 375° for 30 minutes or until golden brown. Yield: 6 servings. *Kathryn Bibelhauser, Louisville, Kentucky.*

OYSTER-AND-SPINACH CASSEROLE

1 (10-ounce) package frozen chopped
  spinach
½ pint oysters, drained
¼ cup grated Parmesan cheese
⅛ teaspoon garlic powder
⅛ teaspoon pepper
3 slices bacon, cooked and crumbled
2 tablespoons butter or margarine, melted
1 tablespoon lemon juice

Cook spinach according to package directions, omitting salt; drain well.

Place spinach in a lightly greased 1-quart casserole; arrange oysters over spinach. Sprinkle with cheese, garlic powder, and pepper; top with bacon. Combine butter and lemon juice; pour over oyster mixture. Bake at 450° for 5 to 7 minutes. Yield: 4 servings.
David L. Nickel,
Irvington, Virginia.

Easy Jambalaya From The Oven

If you are looking for an easy version of jambalaya, try this combination using canned celery and onion soups, canned tomatoes and green chiles, smoked sausage, and shrimp. This recipe may become one of your favorites because the simple ingredients can be quickly assembled, mixed, and baked in one dish.

OVEN JAMBALAYA

2¼ cups water
1½ cups uncooked regular rice
1 (10¾-ounce) can cream of celery soup,
  undiluted
1 (10¾-ounce) can cream of onion soup,
  undiluted
1 (10-ounce) can tomatoes and green
  chiles, undrained and chopped
1 pound smoked sausage, cut into ½-inch
  slices
1 pound fresh shrimp, peeled and
  deveined

Combine first 5 ingredients in a lightly greased shallow 3-quart baking dish; cover and bake at 350° for 40 minutes. Stir in sausage and shrimp. Cover and bake an additional 20 minutes or until rice is done. Yield: 8 servings.
Susie Baldone,
Houma, Louisiana.

Freeze A Banana Pop

The next time your family wants something sweet, offer fruit treats that are good for them—frozen Banana Pops. They're quick to make and convenient to keep on hand.

BANANA POPS

3 bananas
2 tablespoons orange juice
1 (6-ounce) package semisweet chocolate
  morsels
1 tablespoon shortening
¾ cup finely chopped pecans or flaked
  coconut

Peel bananas, and slice in half crosswise; brush bananas with orange juice. Insert wooden skewers in cut end of bananas, and place on a waxed paper-lined cookie sheet. Freeze until firm.

Combine chocolate and shortening in top of double boiler; bring water to a boil. Reduce heat to low; cook until chocolate melts. Cool slightly. Spoon chocolate evenly over frozen bananas; immediately roll coated bananas in pecans. Serve at once, or wrap in plastic and freeze. Yield: 6 servings.

Tip: Ripe bananas can be refrigerated to keep them an additional 3 to 5 days. Or peel, mash, and freeze in airtight containers for use in baking.

March

Catch The Rich Flavor Of Smoked Fish

The pungent aroma of hickory scents the air. Whet your appetite with the anticipation of smoked fish—salmon, mackerel, mullet, or fresh trout. Come along with us and see which version of smoking suits you. For information on charcoal-grilling fish, see "From Our Kitchen to Yours" on page 48.

The Quick Way to Smoke Fish

Phil Youngberg of Atlanta says the all-day process of smoking fish isn't for him, so he uses a regular hooded charcoal grill to turn salmon and mackerel into tasty smoked treats in less than an hour. He points out that using a hooded grill instead of a smoker allows the fish to cook faster since it doesn't take as long to heat up the grill.

The whole concept of smoking fish, according to Phil, is to cook the fish at as low a temperature as possible. "Let the coals burn down until they're white. Put the fish as far away from the heat source as possible. Then cover the food and restrict the air that gets in. This will bring the temperature of the coals down," he explains. "The fish is done when it reaches an internal temperature of 170°F to 180°F."

Several steps make Phil's smoking process different from that of ordinary grilling. First of all, he uses only a large handful of charcoal briquets and piles them high in one corner of the grill. When the coals burn down and are completely white, he covers them with a handful of soaked wood chips.

He prepares the fish by brushing with oil and salting liberally. The salt prevents dehydration, and oil holds in and replaces lost moisture.

To use the grill for smoking, Phil carefully places the fish on the grill in the opposite corner from the coals. Thicker pieces of fish should be placed closest to the coals, but never directly over them. Then close the top and side vents to about ¼ to ⅛ inch to trap smoke and lower the temperature inside the grill.

Since fish cooks so quickly in the grill, there is plenty of smoke left to prepare additional fish. "You can usually smoke two or three batches with the same wood chips," says Phil. "Then freeze what you don't need immediately." Fish freezes well after smoking

and will keep up to three months, he says. Be sure to wrap the fish well in moisture-vapor proof wrapping paper before placing it in the freezer. To re-heat, remove the freezer paper, wrap the fish in foil, and heat at 300° for 20 to 30 minutes.

Smoking fish is simply for flavor and not a method of preservation. Smoked fish should be kept refrigerated, but no longer than three days.

SMOKED SALMON OR MACKEREL

4 salmon steaks or fillets, about 1 inch thick or 2½ pounds pan-dressed mackerel
Vegetable oil
Salt

Soak oak or hickory chips in water 1 to 24 hours.

Brush fish liberally with vegetable oil on both sides; sprinkle with salt. Refrigerate fish while preparing grill.

Prepare charcoal fire by piling charcoal in one corner of grill; let burn 15 to 20 minutes or until flames disappear and coals are white. Add 6 to 8 pieces of soaked hickory to coals.

Arrange fish away from coals on opposite side of grill; cover with grill hood. Open air vents halfway.

Cook 35 to 45 minutes or until fish flakes easily with a fork. (The salmon steaks and fillets will cook quicker than the pan-dressed mackerel.) Place additional wood chips on coals, if necessary. Yield: 4 servings.

SMOKED FISH DIP

½ pound Smoked Mackerel
1 (8-ounce) carton commercial sour cream
2 tablespoons lemon juice
2 teaspoons chopped chives
1 teaspoon instant minced onion
½ teaspoon salt
¼ teaspoon dried whole rosemary, crushed
⅛ teaspoon freshly ground black pepper
Dash of ground cloves
Chopped fresh parsley

Remove skin and bones from the mackerel; flake fish with a fork. Combine fish and next 8 ingredients. Refrigerate for at least 1 hour. Sprinkle with parsley; serve with assorted crackers. Yield: about 2 cups.

SMOKY SEAFOOD SALAD

1½ pounds Smoked Mackerel
1 (10-ounce) package frozen English peas, thawed
4 ounces Swiss cheese, cut into julienne strips
1 cup chopped red onion
⅓ cup mayonnaise
¾ teaspoon salt
¼ teaspoon pepper
Lettuce leaves
4 slices bacon, cooked and crumbled
Cherry tomatoes
Green pepper rings

Remove skin and bones from fish; flake fish with a fork. Combine fish, peas, cheese, and onion; toss well. Combine mayonnaise, salt, and pepper; add to fish mixture, and mix well. Chill 1 hour. Spoon fish mixture into lettuce-lined bowl. Sprinkle with bacon; garnish with cherry tomatoes and green pepper rings. Yield: 4 to 6 servings.

Smoke Mullet the Old-Fashioned Way

"A lot of people turn up their noses at mullet. But smoking it, I think, is one of the best things you can do with it." That's the opinion of Wesley Nall of Auburndale, Florida. He, like many other cooks, has been smoking mullet for years.

Because mullet has dark meat and is a little oilier than most fish, it doesn't dry out as quickly when it's smoked. Wesley usually buys the mullet at the local fish market, where it's one of the most inexpensive fish available.

When he's away from home, Wesley smokes mullet in a dome-topped water smoker. But he prefers to use the old-fashioned smoker in his backyard. The 55-gallon barrel is cradled in a heavy iron frame. One-third of the barrel is sectioned off for the fire. Wesley first builds the fire with charcoal, which he says helps maintain a constant temperature. When the coals turn white, he adds hardwood to provide the smoke. He recommends soaking the wood only if it's aged; if it's green, he uses it dry. He places a water pan on the grill, directly above the coals, to add moisture to the fish.

Long before he begins the fire, Wesley butterflies the mullet. "I like this method of dressing because it exposes more of the meat and allows the smoke to permeate the fish." He says that leaving the scales on the fish helps hold the meat together and retains the juices that would otherwise drip out.

When it's time to smoke the fish, Wesley places them on the smoker, scale side down. As they smoke, he rearranges them on the grill, but doesn't turn them over. "Don't open the smoker more than once or twice if the temperature is right," he warns.

SMOKED MULLET

8 whole mullet (1 pound each)
1 gallon water
1½ cups noniodized salt
1 cup firmly packed dark brown sugar
1 tablespoon onion powder
5 bay leaves, crushed
Pepper

Remove head of each fish by cutting under dorsal fin to center, just behind the head. Repeat procedure on other side. Remove head and internal organs.

Cut along bottom of fish, from head to tail. Push thumb under membrane and ribs, moving from back of fish toward head. Spread 2 halves of fish apart. Remove loose ribs (backbone stays in fish). Scrape along backbone with a knife, removing debris. Rinse.

Combine next 5 ingredients, stirring well. Pour into two 13- x 9- x 2-inch dishes. Place 4 mullet in each dish. Cover and refrigerate 45 minutes to 2 hours, depending on degree of saltiness desired (do not reduce amount of salt); rotate fish, and stir mixture once. Rinse fish well; pat dry with paper towels. Place cooling racks on baking sheets; arrange fish on racks. Refrigerate for 2 to 3 hours to dry. Rub pepper on both sides of each fish.

Prepare charcoal fire in smoker, and let burn 10 to 15 minutes. Cover coals with large pieces of green hickory. Place water pan in the smoker, and fill with water. Arrange the fish on rack, scale side down. Cover and cook 3 to 4 hours, rotating fish occasionally (do not turn). Add hot water to water pan, if necessary. Yield: 8 servings.

On the River in Arkansas

A light morning mist slowly lifts off the Little Red River near Heber Springs, Arkansas, one of the best trout streams in the South; John Linn, part owner and manager of the Red River Trout Dock, is already at his smoker. John leaves the smoker, along with all the utensils and ingredients, on the trout dock all the time. "Once the weather starts to warm up, I just keep the smoker going. To me, it's the best way to fix trout, better than frying or broiling," says John.

Knowing what kind of fish are best for smoking is important. "I use trout the most because that's what's caught here, but it's a lean fish, so it's got to be marinated and basted as it cooks." John often smokes farm-raised catfish, also lean, along with the trout.

John prefers to use a dome-topped water smoker. He fills the pan in the bottom of the smoker with about five pounds of charcoal. The charcoal is topped with a layer of fresh, green hickory that he cuts himself. "You don't have to soak green hickory, but if you use the dry chips, they need to soak for a couple of hours."

Next, the water pan over the charcoal and hickory is filled and the grill racks are lightly oiled to keep the fish from sticking. John places the catfish steaks on the lower rack and arranges trout steaks on the top rack.

"One good thing about smoking fish this way, I can put them on over low coals, and then forget it while we fish. You may have to add more hickory, but you don't have to watch it too carefully." In domed smokers, the grill racks are farther from the fire, so it takes longer for the fish to cook.

SMOKED CATFISH

7 pounds catfish, cut into 1½-inch-thick steaks (with skin on)
2 cups water
½ cup firmly packed brown sugar
¼ cup salt
2 tablespoons concentrated liquid crab and shrimp boil
¼ teaspoon dried whole dillweed

Place fish in a large shallow dish. Combine remaining ingredients; pour over fish. Cover; marinate at least 8 hours or overnight in refrigerator, turning occasionally.

Prepare charcoal fire in smoker, and let burn 10 to 15 minutes. Cover coals

with large pieces of green hickory. Place water pan in smoker. Add hot water to fill pan.

Place lower food rack on appropriate shelf in smoker. Arrange fish on food rack. Cover with smoker lid, and cook 3 to 4 hours or until desired degree of doneness. Yield: 10 to 12 servings.

Note: Smoked Catfish and Smoked Trout may be cooked simultaneously on different racks.

SMOKED TROUT

7 pounds trout, cut into 1½-inch-thick steaks (with skin on)
2 cups water
½ cup firmly packed brown sugar
¼ cup salt
¼ teaspoon red pepper

Place fish in a large shallow dish. Combine remaining ingredients; pour over fish. Cover; marinate at least 8 hours or overnight in refrigerator, turning occasionally.

Prepare charcoal fire in smoker, and let burn 10 to 15 minutes. Cover coals with large pieces of green hickory. Place water pan in smoker. Add hot water to fill pan.

Place upper food rack on appropriate shelf in smoker. Arrange trout steaks on food rack. Cover with smoker lid, and cook 3 to 4 hours or until desired degree of doneness. Yield: 10 to 12 servings.

SMOKED TROUT SPREAD

2 cups Smoked Trout, boned and flaked
4 hard-cooked eggs, finely chopped
½ cup chopped sweet pickles
½ cup finely chopped onion
½ cup chopped celery
½ cup mayonnaise
½ cup prepared mustard

Combine first 5 ingredients; mix well. Combine mayonnaise and mustard; fold into fish mixture. Chill. Serve on crackers or bread. Yield: 3½ cups.

Tip: Disposable pans for heating vegetables, breads, or other foods on the grill are easily made from heavy-duty aluminum foil: Tear off a length of foil and turn up edges to make 1½- to 2-inch sides; pinch corners to prevent leaking.

From Our Kitchen To Yours

While testing recipes for the story "Catch the Rich Flavor of Smoked Fish" on page 46, our test kitchens home economists thought we'd offer some tips on charcoal-grilling fish. If you have a big catch, you'll probably want to cook the fish more than one way. Grilling is an excellent alternative. And if your catch is from the local grocery store or fish market, we included some tips on buying fresh fish.

Charcoal-Grilling Fish

Starting the fire—To grill fish, prepare your charcoal grill basically as you would for any other barbecue. Start the fire in advance so the coals will be hot by the time you're ready to cook. One method to use when lighting the fire is to mound the briquets into a cone shape. Lightly spray the briquets with a commercial lighter fluid. Let the fluid soak in about a minute before lighting. Never use gasoline.

The coals are ready for cooking when they're covered with a gray ash. Spread the coals evenly into an area slightly larger than the area the fish will cover.

Greasing the grill—Before you put the fish on to cook, thoroughly grease the metal cooking grid. Fish is so lean and fragile that it will stick to an ungreased grid during cooking. In the test kitchens, we've found spraying the grid with vegetable cooking spray to be easy and quick. If you prefer, you could grease with shortening or vegetable oil.

A fish basket also comes in handy for grilling fish. The basket holds the fish and keeps it from sticking to the grill. Grease the part of the basket where fish will lie. Arrange the fish in the basket, and fasten shut. Place the basket flat on the grill. When the fish needs to be turned, simply flip the basket.

Grilling the fish—Baste the fish often with melted butter or a basting sauce during cooking to keep it moist.

Don't overcook the fish. The fish is ready when it flakes easily with a fork.

The Right Fish for Charcoal-Grilling

Almost any type of fish is suitable for the grill. "Lean" fish, such as scamp, snapper, flounder, and grouper, need more basting during cooking to keep them moist and flavorful. You may want to baste "fat" fish, such as mackerel, croaker, and amberjack, for extra flavor, but it's not essential.

Also, choose fish—steaks, pan-dressed fish, or fillets—about 1 inch thick for grilling. Thinner pieces tend to dry out.

Make Sure the Fish You Buy Is Fresh

When buying fish, whether whole fish (as it comes from the water) or drawn fish (entrails only removed), the fish should show certain signs of freshness. The eyes should be very clear and bright with no signs of redness. The gills, however, should be bright red. The flesh needs to be firm and pliable with no signs of drying out. The skin should have no faded markings. Probably the best sign of freshness is the odor. The odor should always be mild with no offensive smell. For fillets or steaks, check the flesh, skin, and odor.

Dessert Is Easy With Cream Pies

Cream pies don't call for a lot of fancy ingredients—basically just milk, eggs, sugar, and cornstarch.

The secret of a perfect consistency lies in having just the right amount of thickeners in the filling—cornstarch and egg yolks. There are a few pointers to keep in mind, however, to be sure fillings turn out smooth and creamy.

Never add cornstarch directly to a hot mixture, because the cornstarch will lump. In these recipes, the cornstarch is blended with cold liquid ingredients before the cooking process is begun. Cook the filling until it comes to a full boil; then boil and stir it for 1 minute. (Overcooking can make the mixture thin and runny.) Remember that the filling may look too thin while it's cooking, but it will thicken as it cools.

BASIC PASTRY

1½ cups all-purpose flour
½ teaspoon salt
½ cup shortening
3 to 4 tablespoons cold water

Combine flour and salt; cut in shortening with pastry blender until mixture resembles coarse meal. With a fork, stir in enough cold water, 1 tablespoonful at a time, to moisten dry ingredients. Shape dough into a ball.

Roll out dough to ⅛-inch thickness on a lightly floured surface. Place in a 9-inch pieplate; trim off excess pastry around edges. Fold edges under and flute. Prick bottom and sides of shell with a fork. Bake at 425° for 12 to 15 minutes or until golden brown. Yield: one 9-inch shell.

BANANA CREAM PIE

¾ cup sugar
¼ cup cornstarch
⅛ teaspoon salt
3 cups milk
3 egg yolks, beaten
1½ tablespoons butter or margarine
1 teaspoon vanilla extract
2 small bananas
1 Basic Pastry shell
3 egg whites
¼ teaspoon plus ⅛ teaspoon cream of tartar
¼ cup plus 2 tablespoons sugar

Combine first 3 ingredients in a heavy saucepan. Combine milk and egg yolks; gradually stir into sugar mixture. Cook over medium heat, stirring constantly, until mixture thickens and boils. Cook 1 minute, stirring constantly. Remove from heat; stir in butter and vanilla. Slice bananas into baked pastry shell. Pour filling over bananas. Cover the filling with waxed paper.

Beat egg whites (at room temperature) and cream of tartar at high speed of an electric mixer for 1 minute. Gradually add remaining sugar, 1 tablespoon at a time, beating 2 to 4 minutes until stiff peaks form and sugar dissolves. Remove waxed paper; spread meringue over hot filling, sealing to edge of pastry. Bake at 350° for 12 to 15 minutes or until golden brown. Cool. Yield: one 9-inch pie.

BUTTERSCOTCH CREAM PIE

¾ cup firmly packed dark brown sugar
¼ cup cornstarch
⅛ teaspoon salt
3 cups milk
3 egg yolks
1½ tablespoons butter or margarine
1 teaspoon vanilla extract
1 Basic Pastry shell
3 egg whites
¼ teaspoon plus ⅛ teaspoon cream of tartar
¼ cup plus 2 tablespoons sugar

Combine brown sugar, cornstarch, and salt in a heavy saucepan. Combine milk and egg yolks; gradually stir into sugar mixture. Cook over medium heat, stirring constantly, until mixture thickens and boils. Cook 1 minute, stirring constantly. Remove from heat; stir in butter and vanilla. Immediately pour into baked shell. Cover filling with waxed paper.

Beat egg whites (at room temperature) and cream of tartar at high speed of an electric mixer for 1 minute. Gradually add remaining sugar, 1 tablespoon at a time, beating until stiff peaks form and sugar dissolves. Remove waxed paper; spread meringue over hot filling, sealing to edge of pastry. Bake at 350° for 12 to 15 minutes or until golden. Cool. Yield: one 9-inch pie.

COCONUT CREAM PIE

¾ cup sugar
¼ cup cornstarch
⅛ teaspoon salt
3 cups milk
3 egg yolks, beaten
¾ cup flaked coconut, divided
1½ tablespoons butter or margarine
1 teaspoon vanilla extract
1 Basic Pastry shell
3 egg whites
¼ teaspoon plus ⅛ teaspoon cream of tartar
¼ cup plus 2 tablespoons sugar

Combine first 3 ingredients in a heavy saucepan. Combine milk and egg yolks; gradually stir into sugar mixture. Cook over medium heat, stirring constantly, until mixture thickens and boils. Cook 1 minute, stirring constantly. Remove from heat; stir in ½ cup coconut, butter, and vanilla. Immediately pour filling into baked pastry shell. Cover the filling with waxed paper.

Beat egg whites (at room temperature) and cream of tartar at high speed of an electric mixer for 1 minute. Gradually add remaining sugar, 1 tablespoon at a time, beating 2 to 4 minutes until stiff peaks form and sugar dissolves. Remove waxed paper from filling; spread meringue over hot filling, sealing to edge of pastry. Sprinkle meringue with ¼ cup coconut. Bake at 350° for 12 to 15 minutes or until golden brown. Cool. Yield: one 9-inch pie.

Tip: Pans used for pastry never need greasing. The pastry shell or crumb crust will not stick to the sides.

CHOCOLATE CREAM PIE

1 cup sugar
¼ cup cocoa
¼ cup cornstarch
Pinch of salt
3 cups milk
3 egg yolks
1¼ teaspoons vanilla extract
1 Basic Pastry shell
½ cup whipping cream
3 tablespoons powdered sugar
¼ cup chopped almonds, toasted

Combine first 4 ingredients in a heavy saucepan. Combine milk and egg yolks; gradually stir into sugar mixture. Cook over medium heat, stirring constantly, until mixture thickens and boils. Cook 1 minute, stirring constantly. Remove from heat; stir in vanilla. Immediately pour into baked pastry shell. Cover filling with waxed paper. Let cool 30 minutes; chill until firm.

Beat whipping cream until foamy; gradually add powdered sugar, beating until soft peaks form. Spoon whipped cream around edge of pie; sprinkle with almonds. Yield: one 9-inch pie.

FRUIT-TOPPED VANILLA CREAM PIE

1 cup sugar
⅓ cup cornstarch
¼ teaspoon salt
1 quart milk
4 egg yolks, beaten
2 tablespoons butter or margarine
1½ teaspoons vanilla extract
1 Basic Pastry shell
2 to 3 kiwi, peeled and sliced
1 cup sliced fresh strawberries
1 whole strawberry
½ cup strawberry jelly

Combine sugar, cornstarch, and salt in a heavy saucepan. Combine milk and egg yolks; gradually stir into sugar mixture. Cook over medium heat, stirring constantly, until mixture thickens and boils. Cook 1 minute, stirring constantly. Remove from heat; stir in butter and vanilla. Immediately pour into baked pastry shell. Cover filling with waxed paper. Let pie cool 30 minutes; chill until firm.

Arrange fruit attractively on pie. Cook jelly over low heat until jelly melts, stirring constantly. Spoon jelly evenly over fruit. Refrigerate 1 hour before serving. Yield: one 9-inch pie.

Breads Filled With Fruit And Nuts

Fruit-and-nut breads are favorites with many cooks. You can usually stir up the batter quickly, and the finished loaves are great for breakfast, snacks, or a simple dessert.

STRAWBERRY BREAD

3 cups all-purpose flour
1 tablespoon ground cinnamon
1 teaspoon baking soda
1 teaspoon salt
1¼ cups vegetable oil
3 eggs
2 cups sugar
2 (10-ounce) packages frozen strawberries, thawed and drained
1 cup chopped pecans

Combine first 4 ingredients; set aside. Combine oil, eggs, and sugar in a large bowl of electric mixer; mix well. Gradually add dry ingredients to creamed mixture, stirring just until all ingredients are moistened. Stir in strawberries and chopped pecans.

Spoon mixture into 2 greased and floured 8½- x 4½- x 3-inch loafpans. Bake at 350° for 1 hour or until a wooden pick inserted in center comes out clean. Cool in pans 10 minutes; remove to wire rack, and cool completely. Yield: 2 loaves. *Marcia Strickland, Hinsdale, Illinois.*

APPLE BUTTER BREAD

2 cups self-rising flour
1 cup sugar
1½ teaspoons ground cinnamon
2 eggs
1 cup butter or margarine, melted
¾ cup apple butter
2 tablespoons milk
½ cup chopped pecans
½ cup golden raisins

Combine flour, sugar, and cinnamon; set aside.

Combine eggs, butter, apple butter, and milk; beat well. Stir in pecans and raisins. Add flour mixture, stirring just until dry ingredients are moistened.

Spoon batter into a greased and floured 9- x 5- x 3-inch loafpan. Bake at 350° for 1 hour and 5 minutes or until a wooden pick inserted in center comes out clean. Cool in pan 10 minutes; remove to wire rack, and cool completely. Yield: 1 loaf. *Charlene Keebler, Savannah, Georgia.*

LEMON-CREAM TEA LOAF

1 (8-ounce) package cream cheese, softened
½ cup butter or margarine, softened
1¼ cups sugar
2 eggs
2¼ cups all-purpose flour
1 tablespoon baking powder
½ teaspoon salt
¾ cup milk
⅔ cup chopped pecans
1 teaspoon grated lemon rind
2 to 3 tablespoons lemon juice
⅓ cup sifted powdered sugar

Combine cream cheese and butter, creaming well. Gradually add sugar, beating until light and fluffy. Add eggs, one at a time, beating mixture well after each addition.

Combine flour, baking powder, and salt; add to creamed mixture alternately with milk, beginning and ending with flour mixture. Mix well after each addition. Stir in pecans.

Pour batter into 2 greased and floured 8½- x 4½- x 3-inch loafpans. Bake at 350° for 45 minutes or until a wooden pick inserted in center comes out clean. Combine lemon rind, lemon juice, and powdered sugar, mixing until smooth; pour over hot loaves. Cool in pans 10 minutes; remove to wire rack, and cool completely. Yield: 2 loaves.
Mabel Hoffman,
Eden, New York.

WHOLE WHEAT-BANANA NUT BREAD

¼ cup plus 2 tablespoons butter or margarine, softened
¾ cup firmly packed dark brown sugar
2 eggs
1½ cups whole wheat flour
¾ cup all-purpose flour
2 teaspoons baking powder
1 teaspoon baking soda
1 teaspoon salt
3 tablespoons buttermilk
2 cups mashed ripe banana
1 cup chopped pecans

Cream butter; gradually add sugar, beating well. Add eggs, one at a time, beating well after each addition.

Combine flour, baking powder, soda, and salt; add to creamed mixture alternately with buttermilk, beginning and ending with flour mixture. Stir in banana and pecans.

Spoon batter into a greased and floured 9- x 5- x 3-inch loafpan. Bake at 350° for 1 hour and 10 minutes or until

a wooden pick inserted in center comes out clean. Cool in pan 5 minutes; remove to wire rack, and cool completely. Yield: 1 loaf.
Marguerite Harlow,
Aberdeen, Mississippi.

These Entrées Serve Two

With ground beef, steak, chicken breasts, and pork chops, you can prepare delicious entrées planned just right to serve two.

MARINATED STEAK TERIYAKI

¼ cup vegetable oil
2 tablespoons soy sauce
1 tablespoon cider vinegar
1 tablespoon honey
1 tablespoon finely chopped green onions
1 teaspoon ground ginger
1 small clove garlic, minced
¾ pound sirloin steak

Combine first 7 ingredients; pour into a shallow dish. Add meat, turning to coat. Cover and marinate in refrigerator 24 hours, turning occasionally.

Remove meat from marinade. Broil 6 inches from heat 5 to 7 minutes on each side or until desired degree of doneness. Yield: 2 servings.
Mary V. Kramer,
Nashua, New Hampshire.

BARBECUED MEAT LOAF

¼ cup chopped onion
1 tablespoon butter or margarine
¾ pound ground beef
½ cup soft breadcrumbs
1 egg, beaten
2 tablespoons milk
½ teaspoon salt
¼ teaspoon rubbed sage
Dash of pepper
1 tablespoon commercial barbecue sauce

Sauté onion in butter in a small skillet until tender. Combine next 7 ingredients in a bowl; add onion, and mix lightly. Place mixture in a lightly greased 10- x 6- x 2-inch baking dish, and shape into a loaf. Bake at 350° for 30 minutes; brush loaf with barbecue sauce. Bake an additional 15 minutes or until done. Yield: 2 servings.
Elizabeth M. Verbeck,
St. Petersburg, Florida.

CHICKEN-ZUCCHINI STIR-FRY

2 teaspoons cornstarch
2 tablespoons water
2 chicken breast halves, skinned and boned
2 tablespoons vegetable oil
1 tablespoon dry sherry
½ teaspoon salt
2 tablespoons vegetable oil
1 carrot, scraped and cut into thin strips
1 medium onion, cut into thin strips
1 medium zucchini, cut into thin strips
½ pound fresh mushrooms, sliced
1 tablespoon cornstarch
1 tablespoon dry sherry
½ cup water
½ teaspoon salt
Hot cooked rice

Dissolve 2 teaspoons cornstarch in 2 tablespoons water. Cut chicken into thin strips; dredge in cornstarch mixture.

Pour 2 tablespoons oil around top of preheated wok, coating sides; allow to heat at medium high (325°) for 2 minutes. Add chicken; stir-fry 2 minutes or until lightly browned. Add 1 tablespoon sherry and ½ teaspoon salt; stir well. Remove chicken from wok; set aside.

Heat 2 tablespoons oil in wok. Add carrot and onion; stir-fry 1 to 2 minutes. Add zucchini and mushrooms; stir-fry until vegetables are crisp-tender. Return chicken to wok. Combine next 4 ingredients; pour over chicken mixture, and toss gently. Reduce heat to low (225°); simmer 3 minutes or until thickened, stirring often. Serve over rice. Yield: 2 servings.
Caroline P. Hembel,
Saluda, South Carolina.

APPLE-KRAUT PORK CHOPS

1 tablespoon vegetable oil
2 (½-inch-thick) pork chops
1 cup drained sauerkraut
¼ cup water
½ teaspoon caraway seeds
½ cup applesauce
2 tablespoons chopped onion
1 tablespoon brown sugar
⅛ teaspoon pepper

Heat oil in a heavy skillet; brown pork chops on both sides. Remove pork chops from skillet, and set aside. Drain off the pan drippings.

Add sauerkraut, water, and caraway seeds to skillet, stirring well; place pork chops on top. Combine remaining ingredients, and spoon over pork chops. Cover, reduce heat, and simmer 35 to 40 minutes. Yield: 2 servings.
Mae McClaugherty,
Marble Falls, Texas.

BREAKFASTS&BRUNCHES™

Rise And Shine With A Southern Morning Meal

All over the South, folks begin the morning in a different ways—with coffee and a doughnut, around the family table, breakfast on the run, or at a buffet brunch spread. No matter what your life-style, you'll find just the right recipes for you in this edition of our *Breakfasts & Brunches* special section.

Regardless of how rushed Southerners are during the week, the weekends bring relaxed mornings and time to savor the company of good friends over a fabulous brunch. We found such a party in Irmo, South Carolina, so please join us as we share these recipes and entertaining secrets.

Come On Over for Brunch

According to Roland and Molly Hughes, it's their business to entertain. Whether guests are neighbors or from as far away as Hong Kong, the family's business headquartered at their home brings a varied group of visitors.

Molly says that when she and Roland host a party, her goal is to have as much done in advance as possible. They also find that casual entertaining, such as brunches, covered dish suppers, and dessert parties, is what they enjoy most.

The Hughes begin brunch with appetizers in a cozy shaded area in front of the house. Guests whet their appetites with strawberries and dip, fresh vegetables and cheese appetizer, and a refreshing sip of Strawberry Cooler.

Brunch is served buffet-style on the patio. A spread of blue cheese quiche, phyllo pastry treats filled with spinach and cheese, a showy layered vegetable torte, frozen tomato salad, and bran muffins offers a delicious variety. For dessert there is spectacular Royal Mocha Freeze.

Strawberry Cooler
Cheesy Sour Cream Appetizer
Fresh Vegetables
Creamy Fruit Dip
Fresh Strawberries
Spinach-Filled Phyllo Triangles
Blue Cheese Quiche
Frozen Tomato Salad
Layered Vegetable Torte
Bran Muffins   Preserves
Royal Mocha Freeze
Ice Water

STRAWBERRY COOLER

3¾ cups fresh strawberries
¾ cup sugar
4½ cups orange juice
1½ cups ginger ale
4½ cups ice cubes

Combine strawberries, sugar, and 1 cup orange juice in container of an electric blender; process until smooth.

Combine strawberry mixture, remaining orange juice, and ginger ale. Pour one-fourth of mixture in container of electric blender, and add one-fourth of ice; process until mixture is slushy. Repeat procedure until all ingredients are used. Yield: about 4 quarts.

CHEESY SOUR CREAM APPETIZER

1⅔ cups Cheddar cheese cracker crumbs
3 tablespoons butter or margarine, melted
3 hard-cooked eggs, grated
3 cloves garlic, crushed
1 (16-ounce) carton commercial sour cream
¼ cup finely chopped green pepper
3 tablespoons lemon juice
1 teaspoon Worcestershire sauce
½ teaspoon Beau Monde seasoning
½ teaspoon paprika
¼ teaspoon salt
Dash of hot sauce
Fresh parsley sprigs
Tomato rose

Combine Cheddar cheese cracker crumbs and butter, mixing well. Firmly press one-third of crumbs into the bottom of a buttered 8-inch springform pan, reserving the remaining crumbs.

Combine next 10 ingredients, mixing well. Spread half of sour cream mixture in springform pan; sprinkle with one-third of crumb mixture. Repeat layers with remaining ingredients. Chill thoroughly. Remove sides of springform pan. Garnish with fresh parsley and a tomato rose. Serve with assorted vegetables. Yield: 12 servings.

CREAMY FRUIT DIP

1 (8-ounce) carton commercial sour cream
1 to 2 tablespoons sweetened strawberry-flavored drink mix
Fresh strawberries

Combine sour cream and drink mix, mixing well. Chill. Serve with strawberries or other fresh fruit. Yield: 1 cup.

Tip: Hull strawberries after washing so that they won't absorb too much water and become mushy.

SPINACH-FILLED PHYLLO TRIANGLES

2 (10-ounce) packages chopped frozen spinach
¾ cup minced onion
½ cup butter or margarine
½ pound fresh Parmesan cheese, grated
3 eggs, beaten
½ cup (2 ounces) shredded mozzarella cheese
½ cup (2 ounces) shredded Monterey Jack cheese
¼ cup crumbled blue cheese
¼ cup soft breadcrumbs
½ teaspoon salt
½ teaspoon ground nutmeg
¼ teaspoon pepper
1 (16-ounce) package frozen phyllo pastry, thawed
Melted butter
Fresh spinach leaves

Thaw spinach; place on paper towels, and squeeze until barely moist.

Sauté onion in ½ cup butter in a large skillet; add spinach, and cook 5 minutes. Remove vegetables from skillet; cool. Add next 9 ingredients to spinach mixture; stir well.

Cut sheets of phyllo lengthwise into 3½-inch strips. Working with one at a time, brush each phyllo strip with melted butter. Keep remaining strips covered, according to package directions. Place 2 teaspoons spinach mixture at base of phyllo strip, folding the right bottom corner over it into a triangle. Continue folding back and forth into a triangle to end of strip. Repeat process with the remaining phyllo.

Place triangles, seam side down, on baking sheets. Brush tops with melted butter, and bake at 450° for 10 to 15 minutes. Drain well on paper towels. Serve on spinach leaves. Yield: 8 dozen.

Tip: Onions offer outstanding nutritive value. They are a good source of calcium and vitamins A and C. They contain iron, riboflavin, thiamine, and niacin, have a high percentage of water, and supply essential bulk. They are low in calories and have only a trace of fat.

BLUE CHEESE QUICHE

⅓ cup fine, dry breadcrumbs
½ cup chopped leeks
1 tablespoon butter or margarine
2 (8-ounce) packages cream cheese, cut into 1-inch cubes
½ cup crumbled blue cheese
⅓ cup commercial sour cream
2 tablespoons chopped fresh parsley
4 eggs
⅛ teaspoon salt
⅛ teaspoon white pepper
Fresh parsley sprigs
Pimiento strips
Lettuce leaves
Cherry tomatoes

Line bottom and sides of a greased 10-inch quiche dish with breadcrumbs. Place in freezer until ready to fill.

Sauté leeks in butter until tender.

Position knife blade in food processor bowl; add leeks, cream cheese, blue cheese, sour cream, and parsley. Top with cover and process 4 to 6 seconds. Stop processor, remove cover, and scrape sides of bowl with a rubber spatula. Replace cover and process an additional 4 to 5 seconds or until smooth. Add eggs and seasonings; process 20 to 25 seconds or until well combined.

Pour filling into prepared quiche dish, and bake at 350° for 25 to 30 minutes or until set. Garnish with parsley, pimiento, lettuce leaves, and cherry tomatoes. Yield: one 10-inch quiche.

FROZEN TOMATO SALAD

1 envelope unflavored gelatin
⅓ cup cold water
2 (16-ounce) cans stewed tomatoes, drained
1⅓ cups commercial sour cream
1 tablespoon finely chopped green onions
Juice of 1 lemon
1 teaspoon Worcestershire sauce
2 drops of hot sauce
¼ teaspoon salt
Dash of cracked black pepper
Lettuce leaves

Soften gelatin in ⅓ cup water.

Combine gelatin mixture and next 8 ingredients in container of an electric blender; process until smooth. Pour into oiled muffin tins; freeze. Let stand 5 to 10 minutes before serving. Serve on lettuce leaves. Yield: 16 to 18 servings.

LAYERED VEGETABLE TORTE

1 (13¾-ounce) package hot roll mix
2 (10-ounce) packages frozen chopped broccoli
2 eggs, beaten
½ teaspoon salt
⅛ teaspoon pepper
¾ teaspoon lemon juice
¼ teaspoon ground nutmeg
¼ teaspoon dried whole oregano
3 cups cauliflower flowerets (about ¾ pound)
1 medium onion, chopped
1 tablespoon butter or margarine
½ cup whipping cream
2 eggs, beaten
½ teaspoon garlic salt
½ teaspoon dried whole dillweed
2½ pounds carrots, diagonally sliced
2 eggs, beaten
¼ cup mayonnaise
2 teaspoons Worcestershire sauce
½ teaspoon dried whole thyme
½ teaspoon salt
1 teaspoon vinegar
⅛ teaspoon hot sauce
2 tablespoons butter, melted
Fresh parsley sprigs

Prepare hot roll mix according to package directions up to the first rising.

Cook broccoli in lightly salted water for 5 minutes. Drain well; pat dry with a paper towel. Combine broccoli and 2 eggs, mixing well. Add next 5 ingredients, stirring well; set aside.

Cook cauliflower in lightly salted water for 5 minutes; drain well. Position knife blade in processor bowl, and top with cover; puree cauliflower. Set aside. Sauté onion in butter until tender; stir in cream. Bring to a boil, and continue to cook over high heat until mixture is slightly thickened, stirring constantly; set aside. Combine cauliflower and 2 eggs, mixing well. Add onion mixture, garlic salt, and dillweed, stirring well. Set aside.

Cook carrots in lightly salted water for 10 minutes; drain well. Position knife blade in processor bowl, and top with cover; puree carrots. Combine carrots and 2 eggs, mixing well. Add next 6 ingredients, mixing well. Set aside.

Punch dough down; turn out onto a lightly floured surface, and knead 2 minutes. Divide dough in half, and cover one portion. Roll out remaining half into an 8-inch circle on a lightly floured surface. Cut a hole in center of circle with a 2-inch biscuit cutter. Carefully fit circle into the bottom of a greased and floured 10-inch tube pan with removable bottom. Spread broccoli mixture evenly over dough. Layer cauliflower evenly over broccoli. Spread carrot mixture evenly over cauliflower. Roll out remaining half of dough into a 10-inch circle. Cut a hole in the center of the circle with a 2-inch biscuit cutter. Carefully fit circle over carrot mixture, sealing edges. Indent top of dough with knife so that top is divided into 12 wedges. (Do not cut through dough.) Brush with melted butter. Let rise in a warm place (85°), free from drafts, 40 minutes or until top is doubled in bulk.

Wrap bottom of pan with foil. Bake at 350° for 1 hour. Cover top with foil to prevent overbrowning, if necessary. Cool in pan 5 minutes. Loosen torte from sides of pan with a knife. Grasp center tube of pan, lift, and remove torte from pan. Cool an additional 15 minutes. Invert torte onto a plate; then invert again onto platter. Garnish with parsley. Yield: 12 servings.

BRAN MUFFINS

4 cups wheat bran flakes cereal with
  raisins
2½ cups all-purpose flour
1½ cups sugar
2½ teaspoons baking soda
1 teaspoon salt
2 eggs, beaten
2 cups buttermilk
½ cup vegetable oil

Combine first 5 ingredients in a large bowl; make a well in center of mixture. Add eggs, buttermilk, and oil; stir just until moistened. Spoon the batter into greased miniature muffin pans, filling two-thirds full. Bake at 400° for 12 minutes. Yield: about 6½ dozen.

ROYAL MOCHA FREEZE

1 pint whipping cream
1 (5.5-ounce) can chocolate syrup
⅓ cup brandy
1 quart coffee ice cream, softened
1 (6-ounce) package semisweet chocolate
  morsels
¾ cup chopped almonds, toasted
Whipped cream
Chocolate leaves
Maraschino cherries

Combine whipping cream, chocolate syrup, and brandy; beat until thickened. Place ice cream in a large plastic or metal freezer container; fold chocolate mixture into ice cream. Stir in chocolate morsels and almonds. Freeze, uncovered, about 3 hours. Remove from freezer, and stir well. Cover and freeze.

Spoon into parfait glasses and garnish with whipped cream, chocolate leaves, and maraschino cherries. Yield: about 12 servings.

Brew The Best Coffee

You can wake up to more flavorful coffee. And if you don't believe it, just check the number of coffee specialty shops around, the variety of coffee blends available, and the latest grinders and brewers designed for the coffee gourmet.

The key to the best tasting coffee is buying fresh coffee beans and grinding them just before brewing. Hand grinders were once the only choice for home-ground coffee, but electric grinders now offer a quick and efficient way to grind the beans. They come with a variety of options and with the capacity to grind large or small amounts.

Hand grinders still come in novelty shapes and sizes. You can select the grind by adjusting a small screw. The heavier models with grinding wheels on the side work best.

Espresso coffee has become one of the most recent fascinations for gourmet coffee enthusiasts. The rich, thick coffee is made with dark roasted beans in special espresso makers, one cup at a time. It's a strong coffee made by steam forced through the ground coffee to get a concentrate.

Cappuccino is a mixture of one-third espresso and two-thirds hot, foamy cream. Espresso-cappuccino makers are specially designed with a steam nozzle to warm and foam the milk or cream for topping the espresso.

CHOCOLATE CASTLE CAPPUCCINO

3 cups cold water
¼ cup finely ground French roast coffee
About ½ cup chocolate syrup
1 cup whipping cream
Grated chocolate
5 (4-inch) sticks cinnamon

Pour water in reservoir of espresso-cappuccino maker; add coffee to filter. Brew espresso according to manufacturer's instructions, and fill coffee cups one-third full. Add 1 tablespoon plus 1 teaspoon chocolate syrup to each cup of espresso, stirring well.

Pour whipping cream in a small, deep, chilled metal or ceramic pitcher. Place steam nozzle of cappuccino maker in the bottom of the pitcher. Slowly release steam completely. Lower pitcher until end of nozzle is just below surface of cream. Continue to steam until whipping cream foams and doubles in volume. Pour foamed whipping cream over brewed espresso, filling cups full. Sprinkle each serving with grated chocolate. Place a cinnamon stick in each cup. Serve immediately. Yield: 5 servings.

Note: If the steamed cream does not become frothy and double in volume, pour over espresso and stir to mix before serving.
Phillip Waldon,
Carbon Hill, Alabama.

Use cinnamon and orange rind to spice up coffee for Viennese Orange Coffee. Or try a cool, refreshing glass of Kona Luscious—a mixture of cold Kona coffee, pineapple juice, and ice cream. For the best flavor, grind the coffee beans with an electric or hand grinder just before brewing. Hand grinders with grinding wheels on the side work best.

CAFE MOCHA CREAM

½ cup medium to coarsely ground
  Colombian coffee
4½ cups cold water
About 3 tablespoons chocolate syrup
About ½ cup crème de cacao
Sweetened whipped cream
Grated chocolate

Brew coffee and water in a drip coffee maker or percolator. (Use medium grind for drip coffee maker, coarse grind for percolator.)

Pour brewed coffee into 6-ounce coffee cups. Add 1 teaspoon chocolate syrup and 1 tablespoon crème de cacao to each serving, stirring to mix. Top each serving with whipped cream, and sprinkle with grated chocolate. Serve immediately. Yield: 4½ cups.

CHOCOLATE-ALMOND COFFEE

½ cup whole Colombian coffee beans
1 tablespoon cocoa
¼ teaspoon ground nutmeg
¼ cup coarsely chopped almonds, toasted
¼ teaspoon almond extract
4½ cups cold water

Combine coffee beans, cocoa, and nutmeg; toss well. Place mixture in container of a coffee grinder; process to a medium grind.

Assemble drip coffee maker according to manufacturer's instructions. Layer almonds in paper filter or filter basket; top with ground coffee mixture. Pour almond extract over coffee mixture. Add water to coffee maker and brew. Serve immediately with cream and sugar to taste. Yield: 4½ cups.

KONA LUSCIOUS

⅔ cup medium or coarsely ground Kona
  coffee
4½ cups cold water
2 cups pineapple juice, chilled
1 quart vanilla ice cream, softened

Brew the coffee and water in a drip coffee maker or percolator. (Use medium grind for a drip coffee maker, coarse grind for a percolator.) Chill 4 cups of brewed coffee.

Combine chilled coffee, pineapple juice, and ice cream; beat at low speed of electric mixer until smooth and frothy. Serve immediately. Yield: 9 cups.
     Bobbie Chandler,
Birmingham, Alabama.

VIENNESE ORANGE COFFEE

½ cup whole Colombian coffee beans
2 teaspoons grated orange rind
¼ teaspoon ground cinnamon
½ teaspoon brandy extract
4½ cups cold water

Place coffee beans in container of a coffee grinder; process to medium grind. Assemble drip coffee maker according to manufacturer's instructions. Place orange rind in paper filter or filter basket; top with ground coffee beans. Sprinkle with cinnamon; pour brandy extract over coffee mixture.

Add water to coffee maker, and brew. Serve immediately with cream and sugar to taste. Yield: 4½ cups.

Fresh Ideas For Tabletops

Want to give morning tables more sparkle and shine? Then turn to your china cabinet and linen closet. Grandmother's crystal and your wedding china can be teamed with a few everyday pieces to create an entirely new look.

Perhaps you have some beautiful fine china that has always been set aside for formal occasions. You may be surprised to see how well it blends when layered with contrasting oven-to-table ware. Try combining solid patterns with florals or pastels with darker colors. And don't hesitate to experiment with a pattern-on-pattern effect. You'll find that the possibilities are limitless.

Bring out that potpourri of salt and pepper shakers you may have collected. Using a different set of shakers by each place setting would be helpful and also look unique.

Those crystal wine goblets and decanter that are impressively arranged on the dining room sideboard will look even better on your breakfast table. Fill the decanter with orange juice and pour your morning beverage in style.

Place the decanter on top of your prized silver trivet. Laying a simple rose or spring flower by its side will make it pretty enough for a centerpiece. The trivet will also protect your table from water marks.

Other silver pieces will add to the sparkle, so go ahead and use your sterling flatware, napkin rings, and trays.

Your favorite piece of lace or linen tied around an ordinary glass dish can instantly transform it into a truly elegant accent piece for the table. Start by wrapping a big bowl of fresh fruit; the result will be lovely.

Doughnuts And Beignets Fresh From Your Kitchen

The best doughnuts don't have to come from the local bakery. With our recipes, you can make them fresh and delicious right in your own kitchen.

You can make jelly doughnuts with an assortment of your favorite jams, jellies, and preserves. For each one, just pinch together two thin rounds of dough with the jelly filling in between. After they're fried, drain the doughnuts well on paper towels and sprinkle with powdered sugar.

CHOCOLATE-COVERED DOUGHNUTS

1 package dry yeast
2 tablespoons warm water (105° to 115°)
¾ cup warm milk (105° to 115°)
¼ cup sugar
1 egg
3 tablespoons shortening
½ teaspoon salt
2½ cups bread flour, divided
Vegetable oil
Chocolate glaze (recipe follows)

Dissolve yeast in warm water in a large mixing bowl. Add next 5 ingredients and 1 cup flour; beat at medium speed of an electric mixer 2 minutes or until blended. Stir in remaining flour.

Cover and let rise in a warm place (85°), free from drafts, 1 hour or until doubled in bulk. Punch dough down; turn dough out onto a well-floured surface, and knead several times or until smooth and elastic. Roll dough out to ½-inch thickness, and cut with a floured 2½-inch doughnut cutter. Place doughnuts on a lightly floured surface. Cover and let rise in a warm place, free from drafts, 30 minutes or until doughnuts are doubled in bulk.

Heat 2 to 3 inches of oil to 375°; drop in 4 or 5 doughnuts at a time. Cook 1 minute on each side or until golden. Drain on paper towels. Dip warm doughnuts in chocolate glaze; cool. Yield: 1½ dozen.

Chocolate Glaze:

2 tablespoons butter or margarine
1 (1-ounce) square unsweetened chocolate
1 cup sifted powdered sugar
2 to 3 tablespoons hot water
¼ teaspoon vanilla extract

Melt butter and chocolate in a saucepan; remove from heat. Add remaining ingredients, and beat well. Keep warm, stirring occasionally. Yield: ½ cup.

JELLY-FILLED DOUGHNUTS

½ cup milk
¼ cup sugar
1 teaspoon salt
¼ cup plus 2 tablespoons butter or margarine
2 packages dry yeast
½ cup warm water (105° to 115°)
4 egg yolks
4 cups all-purpose flour, divided
Jelly, jam, or preserves
2 egg whites
Vegetable oil
Sifted powdered sugar

Combine milk, sugar, salt, and butter in a small saucepan; cook over low heat until butter melts. Cool to lukewarm (105° to 115°).

Dissolve yeast in warm water in a large mixing bowl. Add egg yolks, 2 cups flour, and milk mixture; beat at medium speed of an electric mixer about 2 minutes until smooth. Stir in remaining flour. (Dough will be sticky.)

Cover and let rise in a warm place (85°), free from drafts, 1 hour or until doubled in bulk. Punch dough down; turn dough out onto a lightly floured surface, and knead several times or until smooth and elastic.

Divide dough in half; keep one portion covered. Roll other portion to ¼-inch thickness, and cut into twelve 3-inch rounds; place on a lightly floured baking sheet. Place ½ teaspoon jelly in center of each round. Roll out remaining dough to ¼-inch thickness, and cut into twelve 3-inch rounds. (These will be tops of jelly-filled rounds.) Brush edges of each jelly-filled round with egg white. Place tops over jelly-filled rounds; pinch edges to seal. Cover and let rise in a warm place, free from drafts, 45 minutes or until doubled.

Heat 2 to 3 inches of oil to 375°; carefully drop in 2 to 3 doughnuts at a time. Cook about 1 minute on each side or until golden brown. Drain well on paper towels. Sprinkle with powdered sugar. Yield: 2 dozen.

Tip: Small amounts of jelly left in jars may be combined, melted, and used to glaze a ham.

BEIGNETS

1 package dry yeast
3 tablespoons warm water (105° to 115°)
¾ cup milk
¼ cup sugar
¼ cup shortening
1 teaspoon salt
1 egg, beaten
About 3 cups all-purpose flour
Vegetable oil
Sifted powdered sugar

Dissolve yeast in warm water in a large mixing bowl, stirring well; let stand 5 minutes. Scald milk; stir in sugar, shortening, and salt. Cool mixture to lukewarm (105° to 115°). Add milk mixture, egg, and 2 cups flour to yeast mixture; mix well. Stir in enough remaining flour to make a soft dough.

Turn dough out onto a floured surface, and knead about 8 to 10 minutes until smooth and elastic. Place in a well-greased bowl, turning to grease top. Cover and let rise in a warm place (85°), free from drafts, about 1 hour or until doubled in bulk.

Punch dough down; turn out onto a lightly floured surface. Roll dough into a 12- x 10-inch rectangle; cut into 2-inch squares. Place on a floured surface; cover and let rise in a warm place, 30 minutes or until doubled in bulk.

Heat 3 to 4 inches of oil to 375°; drop in 3 to 4 beignets at a time. Cook 1 minute on each side or until golden. Drain on paper towels; sprinkle with powdered sugar. Yield: 2½ dozen.

WHOLE WHEAT DOUGHNUTS

1 cup buttermilk
¼ cup butter or margarine, melted
2 eggs
1 teaspoon vanilla extract
2¼ cups all-purpose flour
2 cups whole wheat flour
1 cup sugar
2 teaspoons baking powder
½ teaspoon baking soda
½ teaspoon ground nutmeg
¼ teaspoon salt
Vegetable oil
2 cups sifted powdered sugar
3 tablespoons water
½ teaspoon vanilla extract

Combine buttermilk, butter, eggs, and 1 teaspoon vanilla in a large bowl, beating well.

Combine next 7 ingredients; gradually add to buttermilk mixture, mixing well.

Place dough on a heavily floured surface; roll out to ½-inch thickness. Cut with a floured 2½-inch doughnut cutter.

Heat 3 to 4 inches of oil to 375°; drop in 3 or 4 doughnuts at a time. Cook 3 to 4 minutes on each side or until golden brown. Drain on paper towels.

Combine powdered sugar, water, and ½ teaspoon vanilla, beating until smooth. Dip warm doughnuts in the glaze; cool. Yield: about 2 dozen.
*Marlene F. Cline,
Harrisonburg, Virginia.*

SPICE DOUGHNUTS

2 tablespoons shortening
¾ cup sugar
2 eggs
3½ cups all-purpose flour
1 tablespoon plus 2 teaspoons baking powder
1 teaspoon salt
1 teaspoon ground cinnamon
½ teaspoon ground nutmeg
¾ cup milk
Vegetable oil
2 cups sifted powdered sugar
3 tablespoons water
½ teaspoon vanilla extract

Cream shortening; gradually add ¾ cup sugar, beating well. Add eggs, beating well. Combine flour, baking powder, salt, and spices; add to creamed mixture alternately with milk, beginning and ending with flour mixture.

Place dough on a lightly floured surface; roll out to ½-inch thickness. Cut with a floured 2½-inch doughnut cutter. Place doughnuts on a lightly floured surface; cover and let rest 15 minutes.

Heat 3 to 4 inches of oil to 375°; drop in 3 to 4 doughnuts at a time. Cook about 1 minute on each side or until golden brown. Drain on paper towels.

Combine powdered sugar, water, and vanilla; beat until smooth. Dip warm doughnuts in glaze; cool. Yield: about 1½ dozen. *Flora Bowie,
Splendora, Texas.*

OLD-FASHIONED POTATO DOUGHNUTS

3 tablespoons shortening
1 cup sugar
1 egg
¼ cup milk
1 cup cooked, mashed potatoes
3 cups all-purpose flour
1½ tablespoons baking powder
½ teaspoon salt
1 teaspoon ground nutmeg
¼ teaspoon ground cinnamon
Vegetable oil
1 cup sugar
1½ teaspoons ground cinnamon

Cream shortening and 1 cup sugar; add egg and beat well. Stir in milk and potatoes. Combine next 5 ingredients; add to potato mixture, stirring well.

Place dough on a lightly floured surface; knead lightly. Roll out to ½-inch thickness. Cut with a floured 2½-inch doughnut cutter.

Heat 3 to 4 inches of oil to 375°; drop in 3 to 4 doughnuts at a time. Cook about 1 minute on each side or until golden brown. Drain on paper towels.

Combine 1 cup sugar and 1½ teaspoons cinnamon; sprinkle over doughnuts. Yield: about 2 dozen.
*Mrs. Charles H. Gleason,
Marrero, Louisiana.*

Whip Up A Quick Breakfast

When your morning schedule is hectic, you can still whip up a special breakfast for your family or guests. Try an omelet, and you'll have a delightful meal in a matter of minutes.

FLUFFY OMELET

4 eggs, separated
2 tablespoons water
¼ teaspoon salt
1 tablespoon butter or margarine
Cheese sauce (recipe follows)

Beat egg whites (at room temperature) until foamy; add water and salt. Beat until stiff peaks form. Beat egg yolks in a medium bowl until thick and lemon colored. Fold whites into yolks.

Heat a heavy skillet over medium heat until hot enough to sizzle a drop of water. Add butter, and rotate skillet to coat bottom.

Spread egg mixture in skillet, leaving sides slightly high. Cover, reduce heat, and cook 8 to 10 minutes or until puffed and set. Bake at 325° for 10 minutes or until a knife inserted in center comes out clean. Loosen omelet with a spatula; fold omelet in half. Gently slide omelet onto a plate; spoon cheese sauce over top. Yield: 2 servings.

Cheese Sauce:

1 tablespoon butter or margarine
1 tablespoon all-purpose flour
½ cup milk
⅛ teaspoon salt
½ cup (2 ounces) shredded sharp Cheddar cheese

Melt butter in a heavy saucepan over low heat; add flour and cook 1 minute, stirring constantly. Gradually add milk; cook over medium heat, stirring constantly, until thickened and bubbly. Add salt and cheese; stir until cheese melts. Yield: ¾ cup.

Kathy Y. Edlefson,
Houma, Louisiana.

SHRIMP-AND-CHEDDAR OMELET

¼ pound unpeeled small fresh shrimp
2 scallions or green onions, finely chopped
1 tablespoon butter or margarine
6 eggs
2 tablespoons milk
½ teaspoon salt
⅛ teaspoon pepper
1 tablespoon butter or margarine
½ cup (2 ounces) shredded Cheddar cheese
Green onion fans (optional)

Peel and devein shrimp. Sauté shrimp and scallions in 1 tablespoon butter in a heavy skillet until the shrimp turn pink; set aside, reserving 2 shrimp for garnish, if desired.

Combine eggs, milk, salt, and pepper; beat well. Heat a 10-inch omelet pan or heavy skillet until it is hot enough to sizzle a drop of water. Add 1 tablespoon butter; rotate pan to coat bottom. Pour egg mixture into pan. As mixture starts to cook, gently lift edges of omelet with a spatula and tilt pan so uncooked portion flows underneath.

Spoon shrimp mixture and cheese over half of omelet when eggs are set and top is still moist and creamy.

Loosen omelet with a spatula, and fold unfilled side over filling; remove from heat. Cover and let stand 1 to 2 minutes or until cheese melts. Gently slide omelet onto a serving plate; garnish with green onion fans and reserved shrimp, if desired. Serve immediately. Yield: 3 servings.

Sandy Buckley,
Ormond Beach, Florida.

BREAKFAST BURRITOS

½ pound bulk pork sausage
2 large potatoes, peeled and grated
1 medium-size green pepper, chopped
½ cup chopped onion
8 eggs, beaten
8 (8-inch) flour tortillas
¼ cup butter or margarine, melted
2½ cups (10 ounces) shredded Cheddar cheese
Taco sauce

Cook sausage until browned; drain, reserving drippings in skillet. Set sausage aside. Add vegetables to skillet, and cook until potatoes are browned. Add eggs; cook, stirring occasionally, until eggs are firm but still moist. Stir in the sausage.

Wrap tortillas tightly in foil; bake at 350° for 15 minutes. Spoon an equal amount of egg mixture in center of each tortilla; roll up.

Place filled tortillas in a lightly greased 13- x 9- x 2-inch baking dish; brush with butter, and cover with foil. Bake at 375° for 10 minutes; sprinkle burritos with cheese. Cover and bake 5 minutes or until cheese melts. Serve with taco sauce. Yield: 4 servings.

Stephen H. Badgett,
Memphis, Tennessee.

Linger Over A Cool Drink

One sure way to get your day off to a good start is to sip away the morning blahs with a refreshing beverage. Cold and full of flavor, you'll find these thirst quenchers are a great way to wake up.

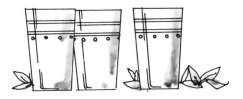

RASPBERRY SPARKLE PUNCH

1 (10-ounce) package frozen raspberries, thawed
1 (6-ounce) can frozen lemonade concentrate, thawed and undiluted
2 cups water
1 (32-ounce) bottle lemon-lime carbonated beverage, chilled
Fresh mint sprigs (optional)

Process raspberries in food mill or container of electric blender; strain, discarding seeds.

Combine raspberry pulp, lemonade concentrate, and water; chill.

To serve, combine raspberry mixture and lemon-lime beverage; stir well. Serve over ice. Garnish with mint sprigs, if desired. Yield: 7 cups.

Mrs. Rudolph Watts,
Glasgow, Kentucky.

STRAWBERRY-MINT COOLER

4 cups tonic water, divided
1 cup strawberry or raspberry jam
1 cup chopped fresh mint
½ cup lemon juice

Combine 2 cups tonic water, jam, and mint in a saucepan; bring to a boil. Boil 3 minutes. Let stand 1 hour; strain.

Combine remaining 2 cups tonic water, strained jam mixture, and lemon juice. Serve over shaved ice. Yield: 5 cups.

Ruth Tulp Hoeksema,
Satellite Beach, Florida.

PONCHE DE PINA

1 cup sugar
1½ cups water
4 (3-inch) sticks cinnamon
12 whole cloves
1 (46-ounce) can pineapple juice, chilled
1½ cups orange juice, chilled
½ cup lemon juice, chilled

Combine first 4 ingredients in a saucepan; bring to a boil. Reduce heat; simmer 30 minutes. Cool; discard cinnamon and cloves. Combine sugar syrup and fruit juice; stir well. Serve over ice. Yield: 2 quarts.   *Marie Weeks,*
Gilmer, Texas.

VEGETABLE JUICE DELIGHT

1 (46-ounce) can cocktail vegetable juice
1 (10½-ounce) can beef broth, undiluted
¼ to ½ teaspoon pepper
2 tablespoons lemon juice
2 teaspoons Worcestershire sauce
¼ teaspoon hot sauce
Celery stalks (optional)

Combine first 6 ingredients; chill thoroughly. Garnish each serving with a celery stalk, if desired. Yield: 7 cups.
Ferrilyn Welsh,
Warner Robins, Georgia.

MOCHA PUNCH

4 cups hot coffee
½ cup sugar
¼ teaspoon almond extract
1 quart chocolate ice cream
1 quart vanilla ice cream
1 cup whipping cream, whipped
Ground nutmeg

Combine coffee and sugar; stir until sugar dissolves. Chill. Add almond extract; stir well. Scoop ice cream into coffee mixture; stir well. Fold in whipped cream. Pour into serving glasses; sprinkle with nutmeg. Yield: 3 quarts.   *Sandra Souther,*
Gainesville, Georgia.

SPARKLING CHAMPAGNE PUNCH

4 (6-ounce) cans frozen lemonade concentrate, thawed and undiluted
4 (6-ounce) cans frozen pineapple juice concentrate, thawed and undiluted
6 cups water
Ice cubes or ice ring
2 (33.8-ounce) bottles ginger ale
1 (28-ounce) bottle tonic water
1 (25.4-ounce) bottle champagne

Combine first 3 ingredients; chill well. To serve, pour the juice mixture over ice in a large punch bowl. Gently stir in ginger ale, tonic water, and champagne. Yield: 1½ gallons. *Mrs. R. D. Hicks,*
Ozark, Alabama.

BOURBON SLUSH

9 cups water
2 to 3 cups bourbon
1 (12-ounce) can frozen orange juice concentrate, thawed and undiluted
1 (12-ounce) can frozen lemonade concentrate, thawed and undiluted
1¾ cups sugar
1 tablespoon instant tea
3 (16-ounce) bottles lemon-lime carbonated beverage

Combine first 6 ingredients; stir well. Freeze overnight or until firm. Remove from freezer 30 minutes before serving (mixture should be slushy); combine with lemon-lime beverage, stirring well. Yield: 1½ gallons. *Edna W. Douglas,*
Roodhouse, Illinois.

LIME PUNCH

1 (3-ounce) package lime-flavored gelatin
2 cups boiling water
½ cup lime juice
2 (12-ounce) cans frozen limeade concentrate, thawed and undiluted
1 teaspoon almond extract
3 (32-ounce) bottles lemon-lime carbonated beverage
3 to 4 cups vodka

Dissolve gelatin in boiling water. Stir in remaining ingredients. Serve over ice. Yield: about 1 gallon. *Carolyn Look,*
El Paso, Texas.

For Breakfast On The Run

If breakfast for your family means grabbing a bite on the run or even packing and eating it on the way to work or school, you'll enjoy these new quick-breakfast ideas.

WAKE-UP SANDWICHES

½ cup whipped cream cheese
2 tablespoons milk
1 (3-ounce) package thinly sliced corned beef, chopped
½ cup (2 ounces) shredded Swiss cheese
2 hard-cooked eggs, chopped
3 English muffins, split and toasted
1 hard-cooked egg, sliced
Chopped fresh parsley

Combine cream cheese and milk, stirring until smooth. Stir in corned beef, Swiss cheese, and chopped eggs. Spread corned beef mixture on English muffin halves. Serve cold or broil 2 to 3 minutes or until thoroughly heated. Garnish each half with an egg slice and parsley. Yield: 6 servings.   *Dorothy L. Bedell,*
Fort Myers, Florida.

HOMEMADE GRANOLA

4 cups regular oats, uncooked
½ cup wheat germ
½ cup flaked coconut
½ cup sesame seeds
½ cup sunflower kernels
½ cup honey
⅓ cup vegetable oil
1 teaspoon ground cinnamon
1 teaspoon vanilla extract
1 cup chopped pecans
1 cup chopped dates

Combine first 9 ingredients in a large bowl; mix well. Spread mixture on a lightly greased 15- x 10- x 1-inch jellyroll pan. Bake at 350° for 25 to 30 minutes, stirring every 10 minutes. Stir in pecans and dates. Cool; store in an airtight container in refrigerator. Yield: 9 cups.   *Ranaé Phelps,*
Balch Springs, Texas.

BREAKFAST RAISIN MUFFINS

1½ cups water
1 cup golden raisins
1 teaspoon baking soda
1½ cups all-purpose flour
¾ cup sugar
1 teaspoon ground nutmeg
1 teaspoon ground cinnamon
¼ cup vegetable oil
1 egg, beaten

Bring water to a boil; add raisins, and return to a boil. Cover, reduce heat, and simmer 20 minutes, stirring occasionally. Drain, reserving liquid; add water to measure ½ cup, if necessary. Dissolve soda in liquid.

Combine next 4 ingredients; stir in raisins, and make a well in center of mixture. Combine oil, egg, and soda mixture; add to dry ingredients, stirring just until moistened.

Spoon batter into greased muffin pans, filling two-thirds full. Bake at 350° for 20 to 25 minutes. Yield: about 1 dozen.   *Carole Steindoeff,*
Spring, Texas.

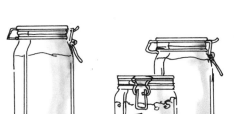

TAKE-ALONG
BREAKFAST COOKIES

¾ cup all-purpose flour
½ teaspoon baking soda
½ teaspoon salt
⅔ cup butter or margarine, softened
⅔ cup sugar
1 egg, slightly beaten
1 teaspoon vanilla extract
1½ cups regular oats, uncooked
1 cup (4 ounces) shredded Cheddar cheese
½ cup wheat germ
6 slices bacon, cooked and crumbled

Combine flour, soda, and salt; mix well, and set aside.

Cream butter and sugar; beat in egg and vanilla. Add flour mixture, mixing

well. Stir in oats, cheese, wheat germ, and bacon.

Drop dough by rounded tablespoonfuls onto ungreased cookie sheets. Bake at 350° for 16 minutes. Cool 1 minute on cookie sheets. Yield: 2 dozen.
Mrs. Lundy W. Lovelace,
Chattanooga, Tennessee.

BANANA-PINEAPPLE
MILK SHAKE

2 ripe bananas, cut into chunks
2 cups milk
⅓ cup drained crushed pineapple
¼ cup instant nonfat dry milk
    powder
½ teaspoon vanilla extract
Dash of ground nutmeg
4 ice cubes

Combine all ingredients in container of electric blender; process until frothy. Serve shake immediately. Yield: about 4½ cups.   *Marian Cox,*
Deming, New Mexico.

COOKING LIGHT

Don't Skip Breakfast—Make It Light

Many dieters skip breakfast to avoid extra calories. But if you don't eat breakfast, you may be so hungry by lunchtime that you'll forget your good intentions and overeat.

On days when you don't have time to cook, stop for a few minutes to have a bowl of whole grain cereal (no added sugar) with fruit and skim milk. Or top a slice of whole wheat bread with low-fat cheese. Put the bread under the broiler to melt the cheese, and you'll have a quick breakfast to take with you.

Don't have the misconception that a vitamin pill can replace breakfast. A vitamin supplement simply does not provide all that the body needs, such as fiber and many trace vitamins and minerals present in food.

High doses of some vitamins can be dangerous. The fat-soluble vitamins (vitamins A, D, E, and K) are stored within the body and cannot be excreted. As these vitamins build up in the body, serious health problems can result.

When a person takes supplements of the water-soluble vitamins (vitamin C and the B vitamins), any amount not needed by the body is usually excreted. But over long periods of time, high doses of some water-soluble vitamins (including vitamin C) may be harmful.

The best advice is to eat a variety of nutritious foods each day, with a total calorie intake of at least 1200 calories for women and at least 1600 calories for men. Unless your doctor or dietician recommends otherwise, you may not need vitamin or mineral supplements.

Shredded Wheat Pancakes
Mandarin Sauce
Hot Mocha

SHREDDED WHEAT PANCAKES

¾ cup all-purpose flour
½ cup crushed shredded whole wheat
    cereal biscuits
1 tablespoon baking powder
2 teaspoons sugar
¼ teaspoon salt
1 egg, beaten
1 cup skim milk
1 tablespoon vegetable oil
Vegetable cooking spray

Combine first 5 ingredients, and set aside. Combine egg, milk, and oil; stir well. Add to dry ingredients, stirring just until moistened.

For each pancake, pour ¼ cup batter onto a hot griddle coated with cooking spray. Turn pancakes when the tops are covered with bubbles and the edges are browned. Yield: 9 pancakes (about 79 calories each).

BREAKFASTS & BRUNCHES

MANDARIN SAUCE

¾ cup plus 2 tablespoons unsweetened white grape juice
2 teaspoons cornstarch
1 (11-ounce) can mandarin oranges, drained
½ teaspoon grated lemon rind
⅛ teaspoon ground cinnamon

Combine grape juice and cornstarch in a small saucepan, stirring until cornstarch dissolves. Cook over medium heat, stirring constantly, until smooth and thickened. Stir in oranges, lemon rind, and cinnamon; cook until thoroughly heated. Serve sauce warm over pancakes. Yield: about 1⅓ cups (about 14 calories per tablespoon).

HOT MOCHA

1¾ cups strong hot coffee
¼ teaspoon ground cinnamon
⅛ teaspoon ground nutmeg
2 tablespoons sugar
3 tablespoons cocoa
¼ cup water
2 cups skim milk
½ teaspoon vanilla extract

Combine coffee, cinnamon, and nutmeg; stir well. Set aside. Combine sugar and cocoa in a saucepan; add water, stirring well. Bring mixture to a boil. Cook 3 minutes, stirring constantly. Stir in milk; heat to boiling point (212°). Remove saucepan from heat, and stir in vanilla and coffee mixture. Serve immediately. Yield: 4 cups (about 75 calories per 1-cup serving).

**Spanish Scrambled Eggs
Chilled Fruit Medley
Whole Wheat Biscuits
Sugarless Fruit Spread**

SPANISH SCRAMBLED EGGS

Vegetable cooking spray
¼ cup chopped green pepper
¼ cup finely chopped green onions with tops
6 eggs
¼ cup skim milk
⅛ teaspoon pepper
⅛ teaspoon hot sauce
½ cup chopped tomato
¼ cup (1 ounce) extra-sharp Cheddar cheese
Pimiento strips
Fresh parsley sprigs

Coat a large skillet with cooking spray; place over medium-low heat until hot. Add green pepper and onions; cook until vegetables are tender, stirring occasionally. Drain and set aside.
Combine eggs, milk, pepper, and hot sauce; beat well, and pour into skillet. Cook over low heat, stirring gently to allow uncooked portions to flow underneath. Cook until eggs are set but still moist. Stir in vegetables and tomato; cook until thoroughly heated. Sprinkle with cheese. Garnish with pimiento strips and parsley. Yield: 6 servings (about 109 calories per serving).

CHILLED FRUIT MEDLEY

1 small banana, peeled and sliced
1 medium apple, unpeeled and sliced
¼ cup unsweetened orange juice
6 fresh strawberries, quartered
2 medium oranges, peeled, seeded, and sectioned
1 grapefruit, peeled, seeded, and sectioned

Combine first 3 ingredients in a medium bowl; toss gently. Add strawberries, oranges, and grapefruit; cover and chill. To serve, arrange fruit on individual plates. Yield: 6 servings (about 68 calories per serving). *Frances Bowles, Mableton, Georgia.*

WHOLE WHEAT BISCUITS

1¼ cups all-purpose flour
¾ cup whole wheat flour
1 tablespoon sugar
1 teaspoon baking powder
½ teaspoon baking soda
¼ teaspoon salt
3 tablespoons reduced-calorie margarine
1 package dry yeast
¼ cup warm water (105° to 115°)
⅔ cup buttermilk
Vegetable cooking spray

Combine first 6 ingredients in a medium bowl; cut in margarine using a pastry blender until mixture resembles coarse meal. Dissolve yeast in warm water. Combine yeast mixture and buttermilk; add to flour mixture, stirring until moistened. Cover and refrigerate overnight.
Turn dough out onto a lightly floured surface, and knead 1 minute. Roll dough to ½-inch thickness; cut with a 2-inch biscuit cutter. Place biscuits on a baking sheet coated with cooking spray. Bake at 425° for 12 minutes or until golden brown. Yield: 1½ dozen (about 68 calories each).

SUGARLESS FRUIT SPREAD

1 cup drained unsweetened crushed pineapple
1 cup pitted whole dates
¼ cup dried apricot halves
2 to 3 tablespoons lemon juice

Combine all ingredients in container of an electric blender; process until smooth. Store in refrigerator. Yield: about 1¼ cups (about 36 calories per tablespoon). *Lorraine Evans, Alexandria, Virginia.*

Right: *Enjoy these cream pie flavors. Front to back: Fruit-Topped Vanilla Cream Pie, Chocolate Cream Pie, and Coconut Cream Pie (recipes on page 49).*

Page 64: *Here are four ways to highlight the spicy flavor of onions: Vidalia-Tomato Salad (page 65), Tarragon Leeks (page 66), Green Onion Relish (page 65), and Crisp Fried Onion Rings (page 65).*

Right: *Sip away the morning blahs with Lime-Punch (page 58), an eye-opening beverage with the addition of vodka.*

Below: *For an attractive and scrumptious breakfast, garnish Shrimp-and-Cheddar Omelet (page 57) with green onion fans and sautéed shrimp.*

Far right: *Take your time at breakfast and enjoy a tall glass of Raspberry Sparkle Punch (page 57). It tastes as refreshing as it looks.*

Your Pick Of Fresh Onions!

We rarely think about singling out onions for praise; yet we would have a hard time cooking without them. The fact is, onions are virtually indispensable in the kitchen and are used more in soups, salads, and main courses than any other vegetable.

Being able to identify the types of onions can save time and money at the market. Basically, there are two main categories—green and dried. Green onions, such as scallions, are harvested while their tops are tender and before the underground bulbs have fully developed. Dry onions have crisp outer skin, are juicy on the inside, and are more fully developed than green onions.

There are many different types of dry onions. Spanish onions are giant size and round. They usually have yellow skins and taste mild and slightly sweet. Granex onions, often referred to in stores as Bermuda onions, are medium to large in size, round or semiflat, with either white or yellow skins. The mild flavor of both the Spanish and Granex onions makes them ideal for either eating raw or frying into onion rings.

A Grano onion is a long, slim, yellow onion that is shaped like a top. Small white onions, still another type, are not as sweet as the Granex or Spanish onion; they are best used in pickles, stews, or baked in a sauce. Red-purple onions add robust taste to salads and are delicious marinated.

Perhaps the most famous Southern onion is the Vidalia. It's mild, sweet, and simply delicious either cooked or raw. What a Vidalia really is even causes debate among the experts. Technically, it's a Texas Granex, but Georgians claim that when it's planted in the soil around the town of Vidalia, it takes on special qualities.

Shallots, garlic, chives, and leeks are also members of the onion group. A shallot is a small, brown-skinned clustered bulb that tastes like a cross between a garlic and an onion. A head of garlic, the most pungent member of the onion group, is made up of small cloves. Chives look like tiny green onions with pencil-thin green tops that are snipped and used as an herb. Leeks have straight, thick stems and leaves and roots that are ropelike. Leeks are somewhat milder and sweeter than most types of onions.

Ever wonder how to chop, mince, or slice onions without crying? We have found that placing the onion under cold running water, cutting off the top first, and then peeling down the skin will help. Refrigerating onions for several hours before cutting is also helpful. A food processor will make the task a lot easier but will probably not solve the weeping problem completely.

Store green onions in the refrigerator, being sure to keep them dry. Moisture can cause the leaves to turn yellow and become slimy. Use them within three to five days.

Dry onions are stored best in a cool, ventilated, dry place. Although fresh onions are available all year long, they can be sliced or chopped and frozen for convenient use.

SPICY BAKED ONIONS

2 dozen small white boiling onions
⅓ cup butter or margarine, melted
1 tablespoon brown sugar
½ teaspoon salt
¼ teaspoon ground nutmeg
⅛ teaspoon red pepper
Dash of white pepper
¼ cup chopped almonds, toasted

Cook onions in boiling water 5 minutes. Drain; place onions in a lightly greased shallow 2-quart baking dish.

Combine next 6 ingredients; drizzle over onions, and stir gently. Cover and bake at 375° for 45 minutes, stirring at 15-minute intervals. Sprinkle onions with almonds. Yield: 6 servings.
Claire Wash,
Greenwood, South Carolina.

CRISP FRIED ONION RINGS

2 large Spanish onions
1 cup all-purpose flour
1 teaspoon sugar
½ teaspoon baking soda
½ teaspoon salt
¼ teaspoon ground nutmeg
¼ teaspoon pepper
1 cup buttermilk
1 egg
Vegetable oil

Peel onions; cut into ½-inch slices, and separate into rings. Place rings in a bowl, and cover with water; refrigerate 1 hour. Drain; dry with paper towels.

Combine dry ingredients; add buttermilk and egg, beating until smooth.

Dip rings into batter; fry in deep hot oil (375°) 2 to 3 minutes until golden brown on both sides. Drain well on paper towels. Yield: 4 to 6 servings.

CLASSIC ONION SOUP

6 medium-size yellow onions, thinly sliced
¼ cup butter or margarine
2 tablespoons vegetable oil
6 cups beef broth
1 teaspoon sugar
Dash of ground nutmeg
¼ cup dry sherry
6 slices French bread, toasted
About ¾ cup (3 ounces) shredded mozzarella cheese

Sauté onion in butter and oil in a Dutch oven over medium heat until tender, stirring frequently. Add broth, sugar, and nutmeg; bring to a boil. Cover, reduce heat, and simmer 10 minutes. Add sherry, stirring well.

Ladle soup into individual baking dishes; top each with a slice of toasted bread and about 2 tablespoons cheese. Bake at 300° for 10 minutes or until cheese melts. Serve immediately. Yield: about 9 cups.
Nancy Everett,
Cleveland, Tennessee.

GREEN ONION RELISH

1 (16-ounce) can stewed tomatoes, drained and mashed
1 cup chopped celery
1 cup sliced green onions with tops
½ cup finely chopped green pepper
½ cup coarsely chopped pickled hot pepper rings
¼ teaspoon ground cumin

Combine all ingredients; mix well. Cover and refrigerate. Drain before serving. Serve with corn chips. Yield: 2¼ cups.
Mrs. Gary Witschy,
Marietta, Georgia.

VIDALIA-TOMATO SALAD

3 medium tomatoes, thinly sliced
3 medium Vidalia onions, thinly sliced
1 teaspoon salt
1 teaspoon dried whole basil
1 teaspoon freshly ground pepper
¼ cup plus 2 tablespoons olive oil
2 tablespoons cognac
2 tablespoons chopped fresh parsley

Arrange tomato and onion slices on serving platter, overlapping edges.

Combine next 5 ingredients; stir well. Spoon over tomatoes and onions; sprinkle with parsley. Chill 1 to 2 hours. Yield: 6 to 8 servings. *Pam McIntyre,*
Vidalia, Georgia.

TARRAGON LEEKS

6 medium leeks
4 cups water
2 tablespoons butter or margarine
¼ cup grated Parmesan cheese
1 tablespoon chopped fresh parsley
½ teaspoon dried whole tarragon leaves
¼ teaspoon seasoned salt

Remove roots, tough outer leaves, and tops from leeks, leaving 1½ to 2 inches of dark leaves. Split leeks in half lengthwise to within 1 inch of bulb end. Bring water to a boil in a large heavy skillet; add leeks. Cover, reduce heat, and simmer 10 to 15 minutes or until tender; drain. Arrange leeks on a serving platter.

Melt butter in a small saucepan; add remaining ingredients, stirring well. Spoon over leeks. Yield: 6 servings.

HOME-STYLE SCRAMBLED EGGS

1 cup chopped tomatoes
1 cup diced cooked potatoes
1 cup chopped zucchini
2 tablespoons butter or margarine
6 eggs, beaten
¼ cup minced fresh chives
3 tablespoons water
½ teaspoon salt
2 tablespoons butter or margarine

Sauté tomatoes, potatoes, and zucchini in 2 tablespoons butter in a large skillet. Remove vegetables; keep warm.

Combine eggs, chives, water, and salt; melt remaining 2 tablespoons butter in skillet. Add egg mixture; cook over medium heat until partially set, lifting edges with a spatula to allow uncooked portion to flow underneath. Add vegetables; cook until eggs are set but still moist. Yield: 4 to 6 servings.
Carolyn Collins,
Winston-Salem, North Carolina.

Put A Little Meat In Your Salad

When you're not in the mood for a big meal, main-dish salads can be a cool, crisp change. Vegetables or pasta combined with tuna, chicken, or even salami make a light yet filling entrée.

TANGY SHRIMP-RICE SALAD

4½ cups water
1½ pounds unpeeled small shrimp, uncooked
1½ cups cooked regular rice
1 (16-ounce) can cut green beans, drained
½ cup pitted ripe olives, sliced
¼ cup sliced water chestnuts
⅓ cup chopped green onions
½ cup commercial Italian salad dressing
3 tablespoons chili sauce
½ teaspoon dried whole basil
¼ teaspoon pepper
⅛ teaspoon garlic powder
Salad greens

Bring water to a boil; add shrimp, and return to a boil. Reduce heat and simmer 3 to 5 minutes. Drain well; rinse with cold water. Cool shrimp; peel and devein. Combine shrimp and next 5 ingredients; toss well.

Combine next 5 ingredients; mix well. Pour over rice mixture; chill. Serve over salad greens. Yield: 4 servings.
Karen C. Stratton,
Little Rock, Arkansas.

TUNA-MACARONI SALAD

2 cups cooked elbow or shell macaroni
1 (7-ounce) can tuna, drained and flaked
1 hard-cooked egg, chopped
½ cup (2 ounces) cubed Cheddar cheese
½ cup frozen English peas, thawed
½ cup mayonnaise
2 to 3 tablespoons chopped dill pickle
2 tablespoons minced onion
Lettuce leaves

Combine first 8 ingredients; mix well. Chill well. Serve on lettuce leaves. Yield: 4 to 6 servings.
Mrs. Loyd E. Weddle,
Hopkinsville, Kentucky.

CURRIED CHICKEN SALAD

3 cups chopped cooked chicken
1 (11-ounce) can mandarin oranges, drained
1 (8-ounce) can sliced water chestnuts, drained
1 cup chopped celery
½ cup mayonnaise
2 teaspoons lemon juice
2 teaspoons soy sauce
1 teaspoon curry powder
Salt to taste
Lettuce leaves

Combine first 9 ingredients; mix well. Chill 2 hours. Serve on lettuce leaves. Yield: 4 to 6 servings.
Elyce Waddington,
Crystal River, Florida.

CHEF'S SALAD BOWL

1 medium head iceberg lettuce, torn
1 tomato, chopped
1 green pepper, diced
2 cups chopped cooked chicken
1 cup (4 ounces) cubed Cheddar cheese
2 hard-cooked eggs, sliced
⅓ cup sliced scallions or green onions
¼ cup sunflower kernels, toasted
Creamy Garlic-Herb Salad Dressing

Combine first 8 ingredients in a large salad bowl; toss lightly. Serve with Creamy Garlic-Herb Salad Dressing. Yield: 6 servings.

Creamy Garlic-Herb Salad Dressing:
¾ cup commercial sour cream
¾ cup mayonnaise
1 tablespoon commercial steak sauce
1 tablespoon barbecue sauce
1 tablespoon plus 1½ teaspoons soy sauce
1 large clove garlic, crushed
1½ teaspoons dried whole thyme
1½ teaspoons pepper

Combine all ingredients; mix well. Chill. Yield: about 1¾ cups.
Mrs. Derrick A. Luttrell,
Jackson, Mississippi.

ANTIPASTO SALAD

1 medium zucchini, thinly sliced
1 cup cauliflower flowerets
1 green onion, sliced
¾ cup commercial Italian salad dressing
6 slices salami, cut into thin strips (about 6 ounces)
1 cup (4 ounces) cubed Provolone cheese
2 medium tomatoes, cut into wedges
1 ripe avocado, peeled and sliced
1 small head leaf lettuce, torn
1 tablespoon grated Parmesan cheese

Combine zucchini, cauliflower, and green onion in a shallow container. Pour Italian salad dressing over vegetables, and toss lightly. Cover and chill at least 4 hours.

Combine marinated vegetables and next 5 ingredients in a large bowl; toss gently. Sprinkle with Parmesan cheese. Yield: 6 servings. *Louise Walker,*
Lexington, Tennessee.

Tip: Leftover vegetables go nicely in a salad. Or make a chef's salad with leftover meats, cheese, and cold cuts cut in strips and tossed with leftover vegetables, greens, and salad dressing.

COOKING LIGHT

Take Advantage Of Spring Vegetables

A smart dieter knows the advantage of eating fresh vegetables often. They provide important vitamins (including A, C, and the B vitamins) and minerals. Fiber-rich vegetables also help control appetites since they are filling, but low in calories.

If you appreciate fresh vegetables, you're in for a special treat when spring arrives. There is usually an abundant supply of fresh asparagus, artichokes, and English peas.

In most parts of the country, fresh asparagus is only available from late February through June, although you may be lucky enough to find a few stalks during the fall months. Artichokes and English peas may be available year-round but are at their peak during the spring.

Our recipes for artichokes call for cooking the vegetable in boiling water. However, artichokes can be steamed by placing them upside down on a steaming rack and cooking for 30 to 40 minutes. Before cooking them, be sure to follow the directions for trimming the leaves and removing the fuzzy center (the choke).

To eat an artichoke, pull off the leaves, one at a time, and pull the fleshy end of each leaf through your front teeth, scraping off the edible part of the leaf. (Discard the remaining fibrous part of the leaf.) After eating each of the artichoke's leaves, you'll reach the bottom or "heart" of the artichoke, which is considered by many to be the very best part of this vegetable.

MARINATED ASPARAGUS

2 pounds fresh asparagus
1 medium-size green pepper,
  coarsely chopped
5 green onions with tops,
  chopped
1 stalk celery, finely chopped
¾ cup unsweetened apple cider
½ cup red wine vinegar
½ clove garlic, minced
¼ teaspoon paprika
Leaf lettuce
Pimiento strips (optional)

Snap off tough ends of asparagus. Remove scales with a knife or vegetable peeler, if desired. Cook asparagus, covered, in boiling water 6 to 8 minutes or until crisp-tender; drain. Place asparagus in a 13- x 9- x 2-inch baking dish.

Combine next 7 ingredients; pour over asparagus. Chill asparagus 4 hours or overnight. Drain marinade before serving. Serve on leaf lettuce; garnish with pimiento, if desired. Yield: 8 servings (about 35 calories per serving).

ASPARAGUS SOUP

2 pounds fresh asparagus
Vegetable cooking spray
1 tablespoon reduced-calorie margarine
¼ cup minced onion
¼ cup chopped fresh parsley
1 teaspoon ground coriander
1 tablespoon all-purpose flour
2½ cups chicken broth
½ cup skim milk
2 to 3 teaspoons lemon juice
White pepper to taste
Lemon slices (optional)

Snap off tough ends of asparagus. Remove scales from stalks with a knife or vegetable peeler, if desired. Cook asparagus, covered, in boiling water 10 minutes or until tender. Cut about 2 inches from tops of asparagus and reserve; set the stalks aside.

Coat a large saucepan with cooking spray; add margarine, and place over medium heat until melted. Add onion, parsley, and coriander to saucepan, and sauté until onion is tender. Reduce heat to low, and add flour; cook 1 minute, stirring constantly. Gradually add chicken broth; cook over medium heat 5 minutes, stirring constantly. Remove from heat, and add the reserved asparagus stalks.

Pour broth mixture into container of electric blender; process until smooth. Pour mixture into a heavy saucepan; stir in skim milk and reserved asparagus tips. Add lemon juice and pepper; cook until thoroughly heated. Garnish with lemon slices, if desired. Yield: 4 cups (about 92 calories per 1-cup serving).

ARTICHOKES WITH HERB-MAYONNAISE DIP

½ cup reduced-calorie mayonnaise
¼ cup chopped fresh parsley
3 tablespoons water
1 tablespoon lemon juice
1 teaspoon minced shallot
½ teaspoon dried whole basil
½ teaspoon Dijon mustard
4 whole artichokes
Lemon wedge

Combine first 7 ingredients, stirring gently; chill.

Wash artichokes by plunging up and down in cold water. Cut off the stem end, and trim about ½ inch from top of each artichoke. Remove any loose bottom leaves. With scissors, trim away about a fourth of each outer leaf. Rub top and edges of leaves with a lemon wedge to prevent discoloration.

Place artichokes in a large Dutch oven with about 1 inch of water. Cover and bring to a boil; reduce heat and simmer 30 minutes or until leaves pull out easily. Spread leaves apart; scrape out the fuzzy thistle center (choke) with a spoon.

Arrange artichokes on serving plates, and serve with dip. Yield: 4 servings (about 42 calories per artichoke plus 22 calories per tablespoon dip).

SHRIMP-STUFFED ARTICHOKES

5 cups water
1½ pounds unpeeled medium-size fresh
  shrimp
1 (8-ounce) bottle Italian reduced-calorie
  salad dressing
½ cup chopped celery
½ cup chopped green pepper
2 tablespoons minced fresh parsley
2 tablespoons minced green onions
2 tablespoons minced sweet pickle
2 teaspoons capers
6 medium artichokes
Lemon wedge

Bring water to a boil; add shrimp, and return to a boil. Reduce heat and simmer 3 to 5 minutes. Drain and rinse with cold water. Peel and devein shrimp.

Combine shrimp and next 7 ingredients in an airtight container; cover and refrigerate overnight.

Wash artichokes by plunging up and down in cold water. Cut off the stem end, and trim about ½ inch from top of each artichoke. Remove any loose bottom leaves. With scissors, trim away about a fourth of each outer leaf. Rub top and edges of leaves with a lemon wedge to prevent discoloration.

Place artichokes in a large Dutch oven with about 1 inch of water. Cover and bring to a boil; reduce heat and simmer 35 to 45 minutes or until leaves pull out easily. Spread leaves apart; scrape out the fuzzy thistle center (choke) with a spoon. Chill artichokes.

Arrange artichokes on serving plates; spread leaves apart, and stuff shrimp mixture into center. Yield: 6 servings (about 138 calories per serving).

March 67

ONIONS STUFFED WITH PEAS

6 medium onions
1¼ cups fresh English peas
⅓ cup chicken broth
¼ teaspoon pepper
½ cup chicken broth
2 tablespoons Chablis or other dry
    white wine
⅔ cup reduced-calorie mayonnaise
2 teaspoons lemon juice
¼ teaspoon dried whole tarragon
⅛ teaspoon white pepper

Peel onions, and cut a slice from top of each. Remove center of onions, leaving ¼-inch-thick shells. Chop onion centers, reserving ½ cup. Cook onion shells, covered, in boiling water 5 minutes; remove onion shells, and drain upside down on a wire rack.

Combine chopped onion, peas, ⅓ cup chicken broth, and pepper in a saucepan; cover and cook 15 to 20 minutes or until tender. Fill onion shells with pea mixture; place in a shallow baking dish. Combine ½ cup chicken broth and wine; pour around onions.

Combine remaining ingredients; stir with a wire whisk until smooth. Spoon over pea mixture in each onion. Broil onions 3 inches from heat 3 minutes or until lightly browned. Yield: 6 servings (about 125 calories per serving).

DELUXE ENGLISH PEAS

2 pounds fresh English peas
Vegetable cooking spray
1 tablespoon reduced-calorie margarine
1 cup sliced celery
2 tablespoons finely chopped onion
4 ounces fresh mushrooms, sliced
1 (2-ounce) jar diced pimiento, drained
¼ teaspoon salt
¼ teaspoon ground savory
Freshly ground pepper

Shell and wash peas; add water to cover. Bring peas to a boil; cover, reduce heat, and simmer 8 to 12 minutes or until tender. Drain and set aside.

Coat a medium skillet with cooking spray; add margarine. Place skillet over medium heat until margarine melts. Add celery and onion; sauté 3 minutes. Add next 5 ingredients, and cook until celery is crisp-tender. Add peas; cook until thoroughly heated, stirring occasionally. Yield: 4 servings (about 104 calories per serving).

Chicken Gets A Squeeze Of Citrus

Whether chicken is stir-fried, baked, or braised, it always gets along splendidly with the tart taste of citrus. A slice of lemon, a sprinkling of lime juice, or a handful of orange sections makes the difference between plain chicken and some of the tastiest dishes you've ever tried.

A squeeze of fresh lime turned chicken into a big winner: Chicken With Lime Butter won first place in the 1983 National Chicken Cooking Contest.

CHICKEN WITH LIME BUTTER

6 chicken breast halves, boned and
    skinned
½ teaspoon salt
½ teaspoon pepper
⅓ cup vegetable oil
Juice of 1 lime
½ cup butter or margarine
½ teaspoon minced fresh or freeze-dried
    chives
½ teaspoon dried whole dillweed

Sprinkle chicken with salt and pepper; sauté in hot oil about 4 minutes or until lightly browned. Turn chicken, cover, and reduce heat to low; cook 10 minutes or until chicken is tender. Remove chicken from skillet, and set aside; drain pan drippings from skillet.

Pour lime juice into skillet, and cook over low heat until bubbly. Add butter; stir until butter becomes opaque and mixture slightly thickens. Stir in chives and dillweed. Spoon sauce over chicken. Yield: 6 servings.

Karen Johnson,
Wichita, Kansas.

ORANGE-CHICKEN STIR-FRY

3 tablespoons vegetable oil
3 pounds boneless chicken breasts,
    skinned and cut into 1-inch pieces
2 tablespoons grated orange rind
1 teaspoon freshly grated gingerroot
¼ teaspoon hot sauce
4 green onions, cut into ¼-inch slices
1 cup orange juice
⅓ cup soy sauce
¼ cup sugar
1½ tablespoons cornstarch
2 oranges peeled, seeded, and sectioned
Hot cooked rice

Pour oil around top of preheated wok, coating sides; heat at medium high

(325°) for 2 minutes. Add chicken and stir-fry 2 minutes or until lightly browned. Remove from wok, and drain well on paper towels. Add orange rind, gingerroot, and hot sauce; stir-fry 1½ minutes.

Return chicken to skillet; stir-fry 3 minutes. Combine onions, orange juice, soy sauce, sugar, and cornstarch; mix well. Add orange juice mixture and orange sections to chicken; stir-fry 3 minutes or until thickened. Serve over rice. Yield: 6 to 8 servings.

DeLea Lanadier,
Montgomery, Louisiana.

ISLAND CHICKEN BREASTS

¼ cup honey
¼ cup orange marmalade
½ teaspoon ground ginger
4 chicken breast halves, skinned
1 (8-ounce) can pineapple chunks, drained
1 orange, peeled and sectioned

Combine first 3 ingredients; stir well. Place chicken in a lightly greased 13- x 9- x 2-inch baking dish; brush with half of marmalade mixture. Bake, uncovered, at 350° for 50 minutes, basting occasionally with the remaining marmalade mixture. Spoon pineapple chunks and orange sections over chicken; bake an additional 10 minutes. Yield: 4 servings.   *Thelma Olson,*
Lexington, Oklahoma.

TAHITIAN CHICKEN

Vegetable cooking spray
¼ cup butter or margarine, melted
¼ cup all-purpose flour
¼ teaspoon salt
1 (2½- to 3-pound) broiler-fryer, cut up
    and skinned
1 (6-ounce) can frozen orange juice
    concentrate, thawed and undiluted
¼ cup soy sauce
2 tablespoons butter or margarine
½ teaspoon ground ginger

Coat a 13- x 9- x 2-inch baking dish with cooking spray. Pour melted butter into dish, spreading evenly.

Combine flour and salt; dredge chicken in flour mixture, and place in baking dish. Cover and bake at 350° for 30 minutes.

Combine remaining ingredients in a saucepan; cook over medium heat, stirring constantly, until butter melts and mixture is blended. Spoon glaze over chicken. Bake, uncovered, an additional 30 minutes, basting occasionally. Yield: 4 servings.   *Mildred Sheppard,*
Crawfordville, Florida.

SWEET LEMON-CHICKEN

3 tablespoons all-purpose flour
1 teaspoon salt
1 (3-pound) broiler-fryer, cut up
  and skinned
2 tablespoons vegetable oil
1 (12-ounce) can frozen lemonade
  concentrate, thawed and undiluted
½ cup water
¼ cup firmly packed brown sugar
3 tablespoons catsup
2 teaspoons vinegar
2 tablespoons cornstarch
2 tablespoons water

Combine flour and salt; dredge chicken in flour mixture.

Heat oil in a large skillet; add chicken and cook over medium heat until lightly browned, turning once.

Combine thawed lemonade, ½ cup water, brown sugar, catsup, and vinegar; pour mixture over chicken in skillet. Cover and cook over low heat 30 minutes or until chicken is tender. Remove chicken to a serving platter; cover and keep warm.

Combine cornstarch and water, stirring well; gradually add to lemonade mixture in skillet, stirring until smooth. Cook over low heat until thickened and bubbly. Spoon the mixture over chicken. Yield: about 6 servings.
Sandra Smith,
Winston-Salem, North Carolina.

Make Dinner In A Jiffy

These menus are great for days when you don't have much time to prepare dinner. Each dish requires only a few simple steps, and the entire meal is ready before you know it.

The secret to preparing dinner quickly is to organize your time. Start with the dish that takes the longest to make, and determine when it will be ready to serve. Then plan when you'll prepare the other dishes so everything will be ready at the same time.

Cheesy Broiled Flounder
Sesame Broccoli
Quick Yeast Muffins
Ice Cream With
Easy Hot Fudge Sauce
Iced Tea

CHEESY BROILED FLOUNDER

2 pounds flounder fillets
2 tablespoons lemon juice
½ cup grated Parmesan cheese
¼ cup butter or margarine, softened
3 tablespoons mayonnaise
3 green onions, chopped
¼ teaspoon salt
Dash of hot sauce
Lemon twists (optional)
Fresh parsley sprigs (optional)

Place fillets in a single layer on rack of a greased broiler pan; brush with lemon juice. Combine next 6 ingredients in a small bowl; set aside.

Broil fillets 4 to 6 minutes or until fish flakes easily when tested with a fork. Remove from oven; spread with cheese mixture. Broil an additional 30 seconds or until cheese is lightly browned and bubbly. Garnish with lemon twists and parsley, if desired. Yield: 6 servings. *Debbie R. Brown,*
Austin, Texas.

SESAME BROCCOLI

1 (1½-pound) bunch fresh broccoli
2 tablespoons vegetable oil
2 tablespoons vinegar
2 tablespoons soy sauce
2 tablespoons sesame seeds, toasted
1 tablespoon sugar

Trim off large leaves of broccoli. Remove tough ends of lower stalks, and wash broccoli thoroughly. Remove flowerets from stems; slice stems thinly. Cook, covered, in a small amount of boiling water 10 minutes or until crisp-tender; drain. Arrange broccoli in a serving dish.

Combine remaining ingredients in a small saucepan; bring to a boil. Pour over broccoli. Yield: 6 servings.
Anna Gerich,
Clearwater, Florida.

QUICK YEAST MUFFINS

1 package dry yeast
2 cups lukewarm water (105° to 115°)
¾ cup butter or margarine, melted
¼ cup sugar
1 egg
4 cups self-rising flour

Dissolve yeast in warm water, and set mixture aside.

Combine butter, sugar, and egg in a large bowl; beat well. Stir in yeast mixture. Gradually add flour, stirring well. Cover and store in refrigerator until ready to bake. (Mixture may be stored in the refrigerator for two days in an airtight container.)

To bake, spoon batter into greased muffin pans, filling two-thirds full. Bake at 350° for 30 minutes. Yield: 2 dozen.

Note: In this recipe, the yeast does not require time to rise.
Mrs. P. D. Spradlin,
Russellville, Arkansas.

EASY HOT FUDGE SAUCE

3 tablespoons cocoa
1 cup sugar
1 (5.33-ounce) can evaporated milk
1 tablespoon butter or margarine
1 teaspoon vanilla extract

Combine cocoa and sugar in a small saucepan; stir in milk. Bring to a boil, stirring constantly. Remove from heat; add butter and vanilla, stirring until butter melts. Serve warm over ice cream. Yield: 1⅓ cups. *Beckie Webster,*
Roanoke, Virginia.

Quick Skillet Supper
Tossed Salad With
Sweet-and-Sour Dressing
Commercial Rolls
Scalloped Apples
Iced Tea

QUICK SKILLET SUPPER

1 pound ground beef
1 teaspoon dried whole dillweed
½ teaspoon salt
¼ teaspoon pepper
2 (16-ounce) cans mixed vegetables,
  drained
1 (10½-ounce) can beef broth, undiluted
1 cup uncooked elbow macaroni
1 (8-ounce) carton commercial sour
  cream
1 (3-ounce) can French fried onion
  rings, divided

Cook ground beef in a large skillet until browned, stirring to crumble; drain off pan drippings. Stir in next 6 ingredients; bring to a boil. Cover, reduce heat, and simmer 15 minutes or until macaroni is tender.

Stir in sour cream and ½ can onion rings. Cook until mixture is thoroughly heated. Sprinkle with remaining onion rings. Yield: about 6 servings.
Peggy H. Amos,
Martinsville, Virginia.

SWEET-AND-SOUR DRESSING

1½ cups vegetable oil
⅓ cup catsup
¾ cup firmly packed brown sugar
½ cup red wine vinegar
1 small onion, chopped
1 teaspoon commercial steak sauce

Combine all ingredients; beat well with a wire whisk. Serve over salad greens. Store in refrigerator. Yield: 3⅔ cups.
Mrs. E. W. Hanley,
Palm Harbor, Florida.

SCALLOPED APPLES

2 (20-ounce) cans apple slices, drained
1 tablespoon lemon juice
¼ cup plus 2 tablespoons firmly packed brown sugar
2 tablespoons all-purpose flour
¼ teaspoon salt
¼ teaspoon ground cinnamon
¼ teaspoon ground cloves
2½ tablespoons butter or margarine, softened
Whipped cream (optional)

Spoon apples into a lightly greased 12- x 8- x 2-inch baking dish; sprinkle with lemon juice.
Combine next 6 ingredients; stir until well blended. Sprinkle mixture over apples. Bake at 400° for 30 minutes. Serve with a dollop of whipped cream, if desired. Yield: 6 to 8 servings.
Rebecca M. Burnett,
Jeffersontown, Kentucky.

MICROWAVE COOKERY

Microwave A Savory Sauce

Making a sauce can be a slow, tedious process—but not with a microwave oven. Besides being quick and easy to prepare, microwaved sauces won't scorch and rarely lump.

A glass measure or casserole dish is perfect for making sauces in the microwave. Just be sure the utensil is large enough to prevent the sauce from boiling over. A 4-cup glass measure or a 1-quart casserole is usually large enough. Large glass measuring cups are handy because you can measure, mix, microwave, and pour the sauce using the same container.

While microwaved sauces do not require constant attention, they will need to be stirred occasionally to mix the cooked portion near the outside of the dish with the uncooked portion in the center. Stirring with a wire whisk at 1-minute intervals is sufficient.

Don't worry about your sauce scorching, curdling, or sticking to the dish in the microwave. Just be sure to stir when indicated and add hot mixtures to yolk-thickened sauces slowly and carefully.

GARLIC-CHEESE SAUCE

1 tablespoon butter or margarine
1 tablespoon all-purpose flour
½ cup milk
¼ teaspoon garlic powder
Dash of pepper
¼ cup (1 ounce) shredded Cheddar cheese

Place butter in a 2-cup glass measure. Microwave at HIGH for 35 seconds or until melted. Add flour, stirring until smooth. Gradually add milk, stirring well. Microwave at HIGH for 1½ to 2 minutes or until thickened and bubbly. Stir in remaining ingredients. Microwave at HIGH for 30 to 35 seconds or until cheese melts. Stir well. Serve over beef, vegetables, or eggs. Yield: ¾ cup.

MUSTARD SAUCE

½ cup sugar
2 tablespoons dry mustard
1 teaspoon salt
2 egg yolks, beaten
2 (5.33-ounce) cans evaporated milk, divided
⅓ cup vinegar

Combine sugar, dry mustard, and salt; stir into egg yolks. Add ¼ cup evaporated milk; stir mixture with a wire whisk until smooth.
Microwave remaining milk at HIGH in a 4-cup glass measure 1½ minutes or until hot (do not boil). Add a small amount of hot milk to yolk mixture, stirring constantly. Add yolk mixture to remaining hot milk, stirring constantly; microwave at HIGH for 1½ to 2 minutes, stirring every 30 seconds until smooth and slightly thickened.
Stir in vinegar; microwave at HIGH for 1½ minutes or until creamy and thickened, stirring after 1 minute. Let stand 4 to 5 minutes before serving. Serve over pork. Yield: 2 cups.

PARSLEY-GARLIC SAUCE

½ cup butter or margarine
2 egg yolks
2 cloves garlic, crushed
1½ tablespoons lemon juice
1 tablespoon minced fresh parsley
1 tablespoon chopped chives
¼ teaspoon dry mustard
⅛ teaspoon red pepper
Dash of salt

Place butter in a 1-cup glass measure; microwave at HIGH for 1 minute or until melted. (Do not allow the butter to boil.) Set aside.
Combine remaining ingredients in container of electric blender; blend until thick and lemon colored. Turn blender to low speed; add butter to yolk mixture in a slow, steady stream. Turn blender to high speed and blend until sauce is smooth and thickened. Serve over seafood, beef, or vegetables. Yield: ¾ cup.

DILL SAUCE

2 tablespoons butter or margarine
2 tablespoons all-purpose flour
1 cup chicken broth
¼ cup commercial sour cream
2 teaspoons dried whole dillweed

Place butter in a 4-cup glass measure. Microwave at HIGH for 45 seconds or until melted. Add flour, stirring until smooth. Gradually add broth, stirring well. Microwave at HIGH for 2 minutes; stir well. Microwave at HIGH for 2 minutes, stirring at 1-minute intervals until thickened and bubbly. Add sour cream and dillweed, stirring until smooth. Serve over vegetables. Yield: 1½ cups.

MUSHROOM SAUCE

2 cups sliced fresh mushrooms
2 tablespoons butter or margarine
¼ cup water
¼ cup dry sherry
1½ teaspoons cornstarch
⅛ teaspoon lemon-pepper seasoning

Place mushrooms and butter in a 1-quart casserole. Cover casserole, and microwave at MEDIUM HIGH (70% power) for 3 minutes.
Combine water, sherry, cornstarch, and seasoning. Gradually add to mushrooms, stirring constantly. Cover and microwave at MEDIUM HIGH for 3 to 4 minutes or until thickened, stirring after 2 minutes. Serve over beef or poultry. Yield: 2 cups.

CURRY SAUCE

2 tablespoons butter or margarine
3 tablespoons minced green onions
1¼ teaspoons curry powder
½ teaspoon sugar
⅛ teaspoon ground ginger
2 tablespoons all-purpose flour
1 cup milk
1 teaspoon lemon juice
⅛ teaspoon salt
Dash of white pepper

Place butter in a 4-cup glass measure. Microwave at HIGH for 45 seconds or until melted. Stir in next 4 ingredients, and microwave at HIGH for 1½ minutes or until onion is tender. Add flour, stirring until smooth. Gradually add milk, stirring well. Microwave at HIGH for 2 minutes; stir well. Microwave at HIGH for 2 minutes, stirring at 1-minute intervals until thickened and bubbly. Stir in lemon juice, salt, and pepper. Serve over poached eggs, poultry, or vegetables. Yield: 1¼ cups.

The Main Dish Is A Casserole

Main dish casseroles offer a number of advantages for economical cooks. They help to stretch expensive or leftover meat and are usually simple and can be put together quickly.

CHICKEN-ASPARAGUS CASSEROLE

2 (15-ounce) cans asparagus, drained
1 (8-ounce) can sliced water chestnuts, drained
¾ cup sliced almonds, toasted
3½ cups diced, cooked chicken
1 (10¾-ounce) can cream of celery soup, undiluted
¾ cup mayonnaise
½ cup Chablis or other dry white wine
1 (5.33-ounce) can evaporated milk
¼ cup grated Parmesan cheese

Layer asparagus, water chestnuts, almonds, and chicken in a lightly greased 12- x 8- x 2-inch baking dish. Combine next 4 ingredients, mixing well. Spoon mixture over chicken, and sprinkle with cheese. Bake at 350° for 20 minutes. Yield: 6 servings. *Nancy M. Duncan, Roanoke, Virginia.*

TURKEY-SPINACH CASSEROLE

6 slices bacon
½ cup chopped onion
1½ cups cooked regular rice
1 (10-ounce) package frozen chopped spinach, cooked and well drained
1 (2-ounce) jar diced pimiento, drained
¼ cup sliced water chestnuts
¼ teaspoon salt
1 (10¾-ounce) can cream of mushroom soup, undiluted
½ cup commercial sour cream
1 pound sliced cooked turkey
¾ cup soft breadcrumbs
1 tablespoon butter or margarine, melted

Cook bacon in a large skillet until crisp; remove bacon, reserving 2 tablespoons drippings in skillet. Crumble bacon, and set aside.

Sauté onion in bacon drippings until tender; remove from heat. Add rice, spinach, pimiento, water chestnuts, half of bacon, and salt; stir well. Combine soup and sour cream; stir half of soup mixture into spinach mixture. Spoon spinach mixture into a lightly greased 12- x 7- x 2-inch baking dish; arrange turkey slices on top. Spoon remaining soup mixture over turkey. Combine breadcrumbs and butter; mix well, and sprinkle around edges of casserole. Sprinkle remaining bacon over center of casserole. Bake, uncovered, at 350° for 30 minutes. Yield: 6 servings.
Carolyn Look,
El Paso, Texas.

CRAB-AND-SHRIMP CASSEROLE

1 (6-ounce) package long grain and wild rice
3 tablespoons grated onion
½ cup chopped green pepper
½ cup chopped celery
2 tablespoons butter or margarine
1 (6-ounce) can crabmeat, drained and flaked
2 (4½-ounce) cans shrimp, drained
1 (10¾-ounce) can cream of mushroom soup, undiluted
1 (2-ounce) jar diced pimiento, drained
1 tablespoon lemon juice

Prepare rice according to directions on the package.

Sauté onion, pepper, and celery in butter 4 to 5 minutes or until crisp-tender. Combine rice, sautéed vegetables, and remaining ingredients; mix well. Spoon mixture into a greased 2-quart baking dish. Bake at 325° for 30 minutes. Yield: 6 servings.
Charlene Keebler,
Savannah, Georgia.

Mixes To Make Now And Enjoy Later

Mixes offer the convenience of making tasty foods in a minimum amount of time. And when you make your own mixes you also save money.

GROUND BEEF MIX

4 medium onions, chopped
3 cloves garlic, minced
2 cups chopped celery
1 large green pepper, chopped
¼ cup vegetable oil
4 pounds ground beef
2 (14-ounce) bottles catsup
1 (15-ounce) can tomato sauce
¼ cup Worcestershire sauce
1 tablespoon salt
1 teaspoon pepper

Sauté first 4 ingredients in hot oil in a Dutch oven until tender. Add ground beef; cook until browned, stirring to crumble meat. Drain off pan drippings. Stir in remaining ingredients; simmer, uncovered, 20 minutes. Cool. Spoon mixture into 2- or 3-cup freezer containers. Label and freeze. Mix can be stored up to 3 months. Yield: 14 cups.
Note: Additional recipes using Ground Beef Mix are on page 72.

GROUND BEEF STROGANOFF

3 cups Ground Beef Mix (above), thawed
1 (10¾-ounce) can cream of mushroom soup, undiluted
2 (4-ounce) cans sliced mushrooms, undrained
½ cup commercial sour cream
Hot cooked noodles
Chopped fresh parsley

Combine first 3 ingredients in a large skillet; bring to a boil. Reduce heat and simmer 5 minutes. Stir in sour cream; cook just until thoroughly heated. Serve over hot cooked noodles. Sprinkle with parsley. Yield: 4 servings.

BEEFBURGER ON BUNS

2 cups Ground Beef Mix (above), thawed
4 hamburger buns, toasted

Heat Ground Beef Mix in a saucepan. Spoon mixture onto bottom half of each bun; cover with top of each bun. Yield: 4 servings.

CHILI CON CARNE

2 cups Ground Beef Mix (page 71), thawed
1 (16-ounce) can kidney beans, undrained
1 tablespoon chili powder
Dash of hot sauce
Dash of red pepper

Combine all ingredients in a saucepan; bring to a boil. Reduce heat and simmer 5 minutes. Yield: 4 servings.

EASY SPAGHETTI

3 cups Ground Beef Mix (page 71), thawed
⅛ teaspoon dried whole oregano
⅛ teaspoon dried whole basil
Dash of garlic salt
Hot cooked spaghetti
Grated Parmesan cheese

Combine first 4 ingredients in a saucepan; bring to a boil. Reduce heat and simmer 5 minutes. Serve sauce over hot cooked spaghetti; sprinkle with Parmesan cheese. Yield: 3 to 4 servings.

BEEF-AND-NOODLES CASSEROLE

2 cups Ground Beef Mix (page 71), thawed
2 cups cooked narrow egg noodles
1 (8½-ounce) can mixed vegetables, drained
½ cup (2 ounces) shredded Cheddar cheese
½ teaspoon dried parsley flakes

Combine first 3 ingredients; spoon into a lightly greased 1-quart casserole. Sprinkle with cheese and parsley. Bake casserole, uncovered, at 350° for 15 minutes. Yield: 4 servings.

PEPPERS STUFFED WITH BEEF

4 medium-size green peppers
2 cups Ground Beef Mix (page 71), thawed
2 cups cooked regular rice
½ cup (2 ounces) shredded Cheddar cheese

Cut off tops of green peppers; remove seeds. Cook peppers 4 minutes in boiling water to cover; drain.
Combine beef mix and rice. Fill peppers with beef mixture, and place in a shallow baking dish. Cover and bake at 375° for 25 minutes; sprinkle with cheese. Bake, uncovered, an additional 5 minutes. Yield: 4 servings.

ROLLED OATS MIX

4 cups regular oats, uncooked
4 cups all-purpose flour
1½ cups instant nonfat dry milk powder
3 tablespoons baking powder
1½ teaspoons salt
1½ cups shortening

Combine first 5 ingredients in a large bowl; cut in shortening with pastry blender until mixture resembles coarse meal. Store in a tightly covered container. Yield: about 10 cups.

CINNAMON OATMEAL COOKIES

2¾ cups Rolled Oats Mix (above)
¾ cup sugar
1 teaspoon ground cinnamon
1 egg, beaten
¼ cup water
1 teaspoon vanilla extract
⅓ cup raisins

Combine first 3 ingredients, stirring well. Add egg and water, stirring just until moistened (dough will be stiff). Stir in vanilla and raisins. Drop the dough by rounded teaspoonfuls onto lightly greased cookie sheets. Bake at 350° for 12 to 15 minutes. Cool on wire racks. Yield: about 3 dozen.

OATMEAL MUFFINS

2¼ cups Rolled Oats Mix (above)
½ cup firmly packed brown sugar
⅔ cup water
1 egg, beaten
¼ cup raisins

Combine all ingredients, stirring just until moistened. Spoon into greased muffin pans, filling two-thirds full. Bake at 425° for 15 minutes or until a wooden pick inserted in the center comes out clean. Yield: 1 dozen.

Tip: Use the water-displacement method for measuring shortening if the water that clings to the shortening will not affect the product. Do not use this method for measuring shortening for frying. To measure ¼ cup shortening using this method, put ¾ cup water in a measuring cup; add shortening until the water reaches the 1-cup level. Be sure that the shortening is completely covered with water. Drain off the water before using the shortening.

PEANUT BUTTER-OATMEAL COOKIES

1 cup peanut butter
¾ cup sugar
1 egg, beaten
¼ cup water
1 teaspoon ground cinnamon
1 teaspoon vanilla extract
1 cup Rolled Oats Mix (page 72)

Combine first 6 ingredients; stir until smooth. Add Rolled Oats Mix, blending well (dough will be stiff). Cover and chill 1 hour. Shape into 1-inch balls; place 3 inches apart on greased cookie sheets. Dip a fork in flour; flatten cookies to ¼-inch thickness. Bake at 350° for 12 to 15 minutes. Cool on wire racks. Yield: 4 dozen.

Food Fit For A Bake Sale

Bake sales offer an excellent way for groups and clubs to earn money and have fun too. With planning and some extra effort, your next one can be the most successful sale yet.

Pound cake is particularly handy for bake sales; since they aren't glazed or frosted, they won't be sticky to handle when a customer is ready to take them home. If whole cakes aren't selling, you can slice pound cake during the last hour of the sale. Have a clean knife, plastic bags, and plenty of napkins on hand just in case.

Cookies and brownies are always popular items. Tie two or three in a package with colorful curly ribbon and see how quickly they sell. Select those cookies that won't crumble or break easily during handling.

An eye-catching food display will draw more customers. Use a clean, pretty table covering, set a plant or flowers on the table, and package each food item attractively. For bread loaves, it's simple to line a cardboard box with pretty tissue paper; then the box serves as a container as well.

Cover cardboard rounds with foil or wrapping paper for cakes. Keep each item for sale well covered, and protect the food from excessive handling.

BANANA-JAM BREAD

½ cup shortening
1 cup sugar
2 eggs
1 cup mashed ripe banana
1 teaspoon lemon juice
2 cups all-purpose flour
1 tablespoon baking powder
½ teaspoon salt
½ cup strawberry jam
1 cup chopped pecans

Cream the shortening; gradually add sugar, beating until light and fluffy. Add eggs, one at a time, beating well after each addition.

Combine banana and lemon juice; stir into creamed mixture.

Combine flour, baking powder, and salt; add to creamed mixture, stirring just until moist. Stir in jam and pecans.

Spoon batter into 2 greased and floured 8½- x 4½- x 3-inch loafpans. Bake at 350° for 50 minutes or until wooden pick inserted in center comes out clean. Cool in pans 10 minutes; remove from pans, and cool completely on wire racks. Yield: 2 loaves.

Faye Parker,
Laurens, South Carolina.

CINNAMON SUGAR COOKIES

½ cup butter or margarine, softened
1 cup sugar
2 eggs
1 teaspoon grated lemon rind
2 cups all-purpose flour
1 teaspoon baking powder
½ teaspoon baking soda
½ teaspoon salt
¼ cup sugar
½ teaspoon ground cinnamon

Cream butter; gradually add 1 cup sugar, beating well. Add eggs and lemon rind, beating well. Combine flour, baking powder, soda, and salt; stir into creamed mixture. Chill 2 hours.

Combine ¼ cup sugar and cinnamon, mixing well. Roll dough into 1-inch balls; roll in cinnamon-sugar mixture. Place about 2 inches apart on lightly greased cookie sheets. Bake at 375° for 8 to 10 minutes or until lightly browned. Cool on wire racks. Yield: about 3 dozen. *Harriet O. St. Amant, Fayetteville, North Carolina.*

SPICED BUTTERMILK POUND CAKE

1 cup butter, softened
2 cups sugar
4 eggs
3 cups all-purpose flour
½ teaspoon baking powder
½ teaspoon baking soda
¼ teaspoon salt
2 teaspoons ground cinnamon
1 teaspoon ground cloves
½ teaspoon ground nutmeg
1 cup buttermilk
1 cup chopped walnuts
1 teaspoon vanilla extract

Cream butter; gradually add sugar, beating until mixture is light and fluffy. Add eggs, one at a time, beating well after each addition.

Combine flour, baking powder, soda, salt, and spices. Add buttermilk to creamed mixture alternately with flour mixture, beginning and ending with the flour mixture. Stir in the chopped walnuts and vanilla.

Pour batter into a greased and floured 10-inch tube pan. Bake at 350° for 1 hour and 15 minutes or until cake tests done. Cool in pan 10 to 15 minutes; remove from pan, and cool completely. Yield: one 10-inch cake.

Charlene Keebler,
Savannah, Georgia.

CHOCOLATE CHIP-PEANUT BUTTER BROWNIES

⅓ cup butter or margarine, softened
½ cup peanut butter
½ cup sugar
½ cup firmly packed brown sugar
2 eggs
1 cup all-purpose flour
1 teaspoon baking powder
¼ teaspoon salt
1 teaspoon vanilla extract
1 (6-ounce) package chocolate morsels

Cream butter and peanut butter. Gradually add sugar, beating well. Add the eggs, one at a time, beating well after each addition.

Combine flour, baking powder, and salt; add to the creamed mixture, stirring well. Stir in vanilla and the chocolate morsels.

Pour batter into a greased 8-inch square baking pan. Bake at 350° for 30 to 35 minutes. Cool and cut into squares. Yield: 1½ dozen.

Mary B. Quesenberry,
Dugspur, Virginia.

Serve A Slice Of Cheesecake

Rich and creamy cheesecake is always a favorite dessert. And mixed with flavors like raspberry, chocolate, or blueberry, who could refuse a bite?

FROZEN CHEESECAKE WITH RASPBERRY SAUCE

1¼ cups graham cracker crumbs
3 tablespoons sugar
⅓ cup butter or margarine, melted
3 (3-ounce) packages cream cheese, softened
1 cup sugar
3 eggs, separated
1 teaspoon vanilla extract
1 cup whipping cream, whipped
Raspberry Sauce

Combine graham cracker crumbs, 3 tablespoons sugar, and butter; mix well. Firmly press mixture into a buttered 9-inch pieplate; chill.

Beat cream cheese in a large mixing bowl until light and fluffy; gradually add 1 cup sugar, beating well.

Beat egg yolks until thick and lemon colored; stir in vanilla. Add to cream cheese mixture, beating well.

Beat the egg whites (at room temperature) until stiff peaks form; fold into cream cheese mixture. Fold in the whipped cream. Pour filling into graham cracker crust; cover cake, and freeze until firm.

Remove cheesecake from freezer 10 minutes before serving. Spoon Raspberry Sauce over each serving. Yield: one 9-inch cheesecake.

Raspberry Sauce:

1 (10-ounce) package frozen raspberries, thawed and undrained
1½ teaspoons cornstarch
1 teaspoon sugar

Combine raspberries, cornstarch, and sugar in a saucepan; cook over low heat, stirring constantly, until smooth and thickened. Put mixture through a food mill. Cool. Yield: about ⅔ cup.

Carol Anne Bartek,
Austin, Texas.

Tip: Before starting a recipe, make sure you have the equipment needed to prepare it. Be sure to use the correct pan size, especially when preparing cakes, pies, or breads.

RICH CHOCOLATE CHEESECAKE

3 cups graham cracker crumbs
1 cup butter, melted
1 (12-ounce) package semisweet chocolate morsels
4 (8-ounce) packages cream cheese, softened
2 cups sugar
4 eggs
1 tablespoon cocoa
2 teaspoons vanilla extract
1 (16-ounce) carton commercial sour cream
Whipped cream

Combine graham cracker crumbs and melted butter, mixing well; firmly press on bottom and sides of a 10-inch springform pan.

Place chocolate morsels in top of double boiler; bring water to a boil. Reduce heat to low; cook until chocolate melts.

Beat cream cheese with an electric mixer until light and fluffy; gradually add sugar, mixing well. Add eggs, one at a time, beating well after each addition. Stir in melted chocolate, cocoa, and vanilla; beat until blended. Stir in sour cream, blending well. Pour into prepared pan. Bake at 300° for 1 hour and 40 minutes (center may be soft but will firm when chilled). Let cool to room temperature on a wire rack; chill at least 5 hours. Garnish each serving with whipped cream. Yield: one 10-inch cheesecake.   *Vivian Padgett,*
St. Simons Island, Georgia.

BLACK FOREST CHEESECAKE

1½ cups chocolate wafer crumbs
¼ cup butter or margarine, melted
3 (8-ounce) packages cream cheese, softened
1½ cups sugar
4 eggs
⅓ cup kirsch or other cherry-flavored liqueur
4 (1-ounce) squares semisweet chocolate
½ cup commercial sour cream
Whipped cream
Maraschino cherries with stems

Combine chocolate wafer crumbs and butter, mixing well; firmly press into bottom and 1 inch up sides of a 9-inch springform pan.

Beat cream cheese with electric mixer until light and fluffy; gradually add sugar, mixing well. Add eggs, one at a time, beating well after each addition. Stir in kirsch, and mix until blended. Pour into prepared pan. Bake at 350° for 1 hour. Let cake cool to room temperature on a wire rack.

Place chocolate in top of a double boiler; bring water to a boil. Reduce heat to low; cook until chocolate melts. Cool slightly. Stir in sour cream. Spread chocolate mixture evenly over top. Chill thoroughly. Garnish with whipped cream and cherries. Yield: one 9-inch cheesecake.   *Louise E. Ellis,*
Talbott, Tennessee.

CREAM CHEESE TARTS

2 (8-ounce) packages cream cheese, softened
1 cup sugar
2 eggs
1 teaspoon vanilla extract
12 vanilla wafers
Blueberry pie filling or whipped cream

Beat cream cheese in a medium mixing bowl until soft and creamy. Gradually add sugar, beating until light and fluffy. Add eggs, one at a time, beating well after each addition. Stir in vanilla. Place a vanilla wafer in each paper-lined muffin cup; spoon cream cheese mixture over wafer, filling cups full. Bake at 350° for 20 minutes. Leave in muffin pans, and refrigerate overnight.

To serve, remove paper liners, if desired, and top with a small amount of blueberry pie filling or whipped cream. (Reserve leftover pie filling for other uses.) Yield: 12 servings.
Rebecca T. Wine,
Florence, Alabama.

Wake Up To Muffins

Special Peach Muffins were some of the best muffins we've tried. The fruit flavor comes from dried peaches and peach yogurt. A pecan topping makes these muffins even more appealing.

SPECIAL PEACH MUFFINS

2 cups all-purpose flour
½ cup sugar
2 teaspoons baking powder
½ teaspoon baking soda
½ teaspoon salt
½ teaspoon ground cinnamon
½ teaspoon ground nutmeg
Dash of ground mace
1 egg, beaten
⅓ cup vegetable oil
⅓ cup milk
1 (8-ounce) carton peach yogurt
½ cup finely chopped dried peaches
2 tablespoons all-purpose flour
2 tablespoons brown sugar
2 tablespoons chopped pecans
½ teaspoon ground cinnamon
2 tablespoons butter or margarine, softened

Combine first 8 ingredients in a large bowl; make a well in center of mixture. Combine egg, oil, milk, yogurt, and dried peaches; add to dry ingredients, stirring just until moistened. Spoon batter into greased muffin pans, filling two-thirds full.

Combine 2 tablespoons flour, brown sugar, pecans, and ½ teaspoon cinnamon in a small mixing bowl. Cut butter into flour mixture with a pastry blender until mixture resembles coarse meal; sprinkle 1 heaping teaspoon over each muffin. Bake at 400° for 20 minutes or until golden. Serve warm or at room temperature. Yield: 1½ dozen.
Grace Bravos,
Timonium, Maryland.

STREUSEL-TOPPED ORANGE MUFFINS

2 cups biscuit mix
¼ cup sugar
1 egg, beaten
½ cup orange juice
2 tablespoons vegetable oil
½ cup orange marmalade
½ cup chopped pecans
3 tablespoons sugar
1 tablespoon all-purpose flour
½ teaspoon ground cinnamon
¼ teaspoon ground nutmeg
Orange-Pecan Butter

Combine biscuit mix and ¼ cup sugar; make a well in center of mixture. Combine egg, orange juice, and oil; add to dry ingredients, stirring just until moistened. Gently stir in marmalade and pecans.

Spoon into paper-lined muffin pans, filling two-thirds full. Combine 3 tablespoons sugar, flour, and spices; sprinkle

1 teaspoon over each muffin. Bake at 400° for 18 to 20 minutes. Serve with Orange-Pecan Butter. Yield: 1 dozen.

Orange-Pecan Butter:
½ cup butter or margarine, softened
1 tablespoon sifted powdered sugar
1 tablespoon orange juice
3 tablespoons finely chopped pecans, toasted

Cream butter until light and fluffy; blend in sugar and orange juice. Stir in pecans. Cover and store in refrigerator. Yield: ½ cup. *Peggy Cranford, Winston-Salem, North Carolina.*

DATE-NUT MUFFINS

1½ cups all-purpose flour
½ cup sugar
2 teaspoons baking powder
½ teaspoon salt
½ cup chopped dates
½ cup chopped pecans
1 egg, beaten
½ cup milk
¼ cup butter or margarine, melted

Combine first 4 ingredients in a bowl; stir in dates and pecans. Make a well in center of mixture. Combine egg, milk, and butter. Add to dry ingredients; stir just until moistened. Spoon into greased muffin pans, filling three-fourths full. Bake at 400° for 18 to 20 minutes. Yield: 10 muffins. *Jean Sessions, Enterprise, Alabama.*

BANANA MUFFINS

1¾ cups all-purpose flour
¾ cup sugar
1¼ teaspoons cream of tartar
¾ teaspoon baking soda
½ teaspoon salt
2 ripe bananas, mashed
2 eggs, beaten
½ cup vegetable oil
¾ cup chopped pecans

Combine first 5 ingredients in a large bowl; make a well in center of mixture. Combine remaining ingredients; add to dry ingredients; stir just until moistened. Spoon batter into greased muffin pans, filling three-fourths full. Bake at 400° for 18 minutes or until golden brown. Yield: 1½ dozen.
Lorene Carlisle, Columbus, Georgia.

Pasta, Rice, And Grits: Basic But Good

Don't forget those standard kitchen staples of pasta, rice, and grits. They can serve as the key ingredients for an economical main or side dish, so be sure to keep a variety on hand.

Whenever you cook pasta, keep these tips in mind: Gradually add the uncooked pasta to a large quantity of boiling water. Then cook the pasta just until it no longer tastes raw. It should be tender but firm.

SPAGHETTI-AND-HERB MEATBALLS

2 (6-ounce) cans tomato paste
2 (8-ounce) cans tomato sauce
1 quart water
1 clove garlic, minced
1 small onion, minced
¼ teaspoon dried whole oregano
¼ teaspoon dried whole basil
¼ teaspoon anise seeds
1 bay leaf
1½ pounds ground beef
½ pound bulk pork sausage
½ cup cracker crumbs
1 tablespoon shredded Cheddar cheese (optional)
¼ teaspoon dried whole oregano
¼ teaspoon dried whole basil
¼ teaspoon anise seeds
Hot cooked spaghetti

Combine the first 9 ingredients in a large Dutch oven; bring to a boil over medium heat. Reduce heat and simmer, uncovered, for 45 minutes, stirring the sauce occasionally.

Combine next 7 ingredients; mix well. Shape into 1-inch meatballs. Cook over medium heat until browned; drain.

Add meatballs to sauce, and simmer 20 minutes. Remove the bay leaf. Serve sauce over spaghetti. Yield: 8 servings.
Coleen Lester, Welch, Oklahoma.

GRITS-SAUSAGE CASSEROLE

1 cup quick-cooking grits
1 pound bulk pork sausage
1 small onion, chopped
⅓ cup chopped green pepper
1½ cups (6 ounces) shredded sharp Cheddar cheese, divided

Cook grits according to package directions; set aside.

Crumble sausage in a large skillet; add onion and green pepper. Cook over medium heat until meat is browned and vegetables are tender, stirring occasionally. Drain well.

Combine grits, meat mixture, and 1 cup cheese. Spoon into lightly greased 10- x 6- x 2-inch baking dish. Bake at 350° for 15 minutes. Sprinkle with remaining ½ cup cheese; bake an additional 5 minutes or until cheese melts. Yield: 8 servings. *Mrs. Kirby Smith, Clio, Alabama.*

SLICED CHEESE GRITS

1 cup quick-cooking grits
1 quart milk
¼ cup butter or margarine
½ teaspoon salt
3 tablespoons butter or margarine, melted
1 cup (4 ounces) shredded Swiss cheese
⅓ cup grated Parmesan cheese

Combine first 4 ingredients in top of double boiler; bring water to a boil. Cook over boiling water 20 to 30 minutes, stirring occasionally, until grits are thick. Add additional water to the double boiler, if necessary.

Spread grits mixture evenly in a lightly greased 13- x 9- x 2-inch baking pan. Let stand at room temperature until grits are firm. Cut grits into 12 rectangular slices. Arrange slices, long sides slightly overlapping, in a lightly greased 9-inch square baking dish. Drizzle melted butter over grits; sprinkle with cheese. Bake at 400° for 25 minutes. Serve grits hot. Yield: 8 servings.
Evelyn D. Thompson, Fayetteville, Ohio.

HAM-AND-RICE CASSEROLE

4 cups chopped, peeled tomatoes
3 cups chopped cooked ham
½ cup water
2 medium-size green peppers, chopped
2 small onions, chopped
1 small clove garlic, minced
¾ cup uncooked regular rice
2 tablespoons butter or margarine, melted
2 tablespoons catsup
1 teaspoon salt
¼ teaspoon pepper

Combine all ingredients, and stir well. Spoon into a lightly greased 3-quart casserole. Cover and bake at 350° for 1 hour. Yield: 6 to 8 servings.
Mrs. Dan Scott, Pleasant Hill, Missouri.

FIESTA RICE

1 small bunch green onions, chopped
½ cup chopped celery
½ cup chopped green pepper
¼ cup butter or margarine
1½ cups uncooked regular rice
1 (10¾-ounce) can cream of chicken soup,
  undiluted
1 (10¾-ounce) can cream of celery soup,
  undiluted
1 cup water
1 (8-ounce) can sliced water chestnuts,
  drained
1 (2-ounce) jar diced pimiento, drained
1 (3-ounce) can sliced mushrooms, drained
Additional pimiento (optional)
Green onion fan (optional)

Sauté onions, celery, and green pepper in butter until tender. Stir in next 7 ingredients. Spoon mixture into a lightly greased 2-quart casserole. Cover and bake at 350° for 1 hour or until rice is done. Garnish with pimiento and a green onion fan, if desired. Yield: 8 servings. *Mrs. Richard Herrington, Hermitage, Tennessee.*

EASY FRIED RICE

1 tablespoon vegetable oil
1 (4½-ounce) can shrimp, drained and
  rinsed
1 egg, beaten
½ cup diced cooked ham
4 green onions, sliced
3 cups cooked regular or wild rice
1 to 2 tablespoons soy sauce

Heat oil to 350° in wok or electric skillet. Add shrimp, and stir-fry 1 minute; set aside. Add egg and stir-fry until firm but still moist; set aside.
Add ham and onions; stir-fry 1 minute. Stir in rice, soy sauce, and shrimp; cook, stirring constantly, 1 additional minute. Stir in egg; serve immediately. Yield: 6 servings. *Mrs. Steve Toney, Helena, Arkansas.*

GLORIOUS MACARONI

1 (8-ounce) package seashell macaroni
¼ cup chopped onion
1 (2-ounce) jar diced pimiento, drained
1 tablespoon butter or margarine
2 cups (8 ounces) shredded Cheddar
  cheese
1 (10¾-ounce) can cream of mushroom
  soup, undiluted
½ cup mayonnaise
1 (2½-ounce) jar sliced mushrooms,
  drained

Cook macaroni according to package directions; drain.
Sauté onion and pimiento in butter until onion is crisp-tender.
Combine macaroni, onion mixture, and remaining ingredients; mix well. Spoon into a lightly greased 2-quart shallow casserole. Bake at 350° for 30 minutes. Yield: 6 servings.
Mrs. Paul H. Farmer, Swainsboro, Georgia.

Peppers Make It Hot

Add a touch of Mexico to breads, vegetables, and main dishes with hot peppers. Peppers come in a number of varieties with a range of hotness and versatility.
You should be very careful in handling hot peppers since they can burn your eyes and skin. Be sure to wash your hands well after you've finished. When handling fresh jalapeño peppers, you may even want to wear some rubber gloves.

MEXICAN STEAK

1¼ pounds boneless round steak
2 tablespoons butter or margarine
1 (4-ounce) can chopped green chiles,
  drained
1 (8-ounce) jar taco sauce
½ cup (2 ounces) shredded Monterey Jack
  cheese

Trim excess fat from steak. Cut steak into 4 pieces, and pound to ¼-inch thickness. Brown steak in butter, and place in a lightly greased shallow 2-quart casserole. Top with chiles and taco sauce. Cover and bake at 350° for 40 minutes. Sprinkle steak with cheese, and bake, uncovered, an additional 5 minutes. Yield: 4 servings. *Kay Hall, Richardson, Texas.*

JALAPENO-CHEESE LOAF

1 package dry yeast
1 cup warm water (105° to 115°)
1 egg, beaten
2 tablespoons butter or margarine,
  softened
4 to 4½ cups all-purpose flour, divided
1 tablespoon sugar
¾ teaspoon salt
¼ teaspoon garlic salt
3 small canned or fresh jalapeño peppers,
  seeded and chopped
1 cup (4 ounces) shredded sharp Cheddar
  cheese
1 (4-ounce) jar diced pimiento, drained
¼ cup minced onion

Dissolve yeast in warm water in a large bowl; let stand for 5 minutes. Combine yeast, egg, and butter; mix until butter melts.
Combine 3 cups flour, sugar, salt, and garlic salt. Gradually add flour mixture to yeast mixture, beating at medium speed of electric mixer until smooth. Beat in peppers, cheese, pimiento, onion, and enough of the remaining flour to form a soft dough.
Turn dough out onto a well-floured surface, and knead 5 to 10 minutes or until smooth and elastic. Place dough in a greased bowl, turning to grease top. Cover and let rise in a warm place (85°), free from drafts, 1 hour or until doubled in bulk. Punch dough down.
Turn dough out onto a well-floured surface, and knead 1 minute. Shape dough into a loaf; place in a greased 9- x 5- x 3-inch loafpan. Cover and let rise in a warm place (85°), free from drafts, 30 minutes or until doubled in bulk. Bake at 400° for 40 to 45 minutes or until loaves sound hollow when tapped. Remove from pans; let cool on wire racks. Yield: 1 loaf. *Doris Curls, Anniston, Alabama.*

CHICKEN ENCHILADAS WITH SPICY SAUCE

¼ cup butter or margarine
¼ cup all-purpose flour
2 cups chicken broth
1 (8-ounce) carton commercial sour cream
2 canned jalapeño peppers, seeded and
  chopped
12 corn tortillas
Vegetable oil
1 whole chicken breast, cooked and
  chopped
2 cups (8 ounces) shredded Monterey Jack
  cheese, divided
¾ cup chopped onion
Chopped fresh parsley
Spicy Sauce

Melt butter in a heavy saucepan over low heat; add flour, stirring until smooth. Cook 1 minute, stirring constantly. Gradually add chicken broth; cook over medium heat, stirring constantly, until mixture is thickened and bubbly. Stir in the sour cream and chopped peppers. Pour half of sour cream sauce into a lightly greased 12- x 8- x 2-inch baking dish; set aside dish and remaining sour cream sauce.

Fry tortillas, one at a time, in 2 tablespoons oil in a medium skillet 5 seconds on each side or just until tortillas are softened; add additional oil, if necessary. Drain on paper towels.

Place about 1 tablespoon each of chicken, cheese, and onion on each tortilla; roll up each tortilla, and place seam side down in reserved baking dish. Pour remaining sour cream sauce over top. Bake at 425° for 20 minutes. Sprinkle remaining cheese on top; bake an additional 5 minutes or until cheese melts. Garnish with parsley, and serve with Spicy Sauce. Yield: 6 servings.

Spicy Sauce:

1 large tomato, finely chopped
½ cup finely chopped onion
2 canned jalapeño peppers, seeded
  and chopped
¼ cup tomato juice
½ teaspoon salt

Combine all ingredients; stir well. Chill until serving time. Yield: 1 cup.
Anita Cox,
Fort Worth, Texas.

HOT CHEESE HOMINY

¼ cup chopped onion
2 tablespoons butter or margarine
2 (15½-ounce) cans hominy, drained
2 (4-ounce) cans chopped green chiles,
  drained
1 (8-ounce) carton commercial sour
  cream
1 teaspoon chili powder
¼ teaspoon salt
⅛ teaspoon pepper
1½ cups (6 ounces) shredded Cheddar
  cheese, divided

Sauté onion in butter in a large skillet 5 minutes. Add next 6 ingredients and ½ cup cheese; mix well.

Pour mixture into a lightly greased 10- x 6- x 2-inch baking dish; bake at 400° for 20 minutes. Sprinkle remaining 1 cup cheese over top, and bake an additional 5 minutes or until cheese melts. Yield: 8 servings.
Carol Barclay,
Portland, Texas.

CHILE SQUASH

1 medium onion, chopped
2 tablespoons butter or margarine
1 zucchini, cut into ¼-inch slices
1 yellow squash, cut into ¼-inch slices
1 (4-ounce) can chopped green chiles,
  drained
1 medium tomato, peeled and chopped
½ teaspoon salt
⅛ teaspoon pepper

Sauté onion in butter in a large skillet 2 minutes. Add remaining ingredients; stir gently. Cover and cook 5 minutes or until crisp-tender, stirring occasionally. Yield: 6 servings.
Darlene Landry Burke,
Albuquerque, New Mexico.

Handle Spinach With Care

Fresh spinach is delicate, so treat it gently to retain its flavor and texture. First, remember that spinach wilts easily and shouldn't be washed until just before it's used. The easiest way to prepare the leaves is to dunk them in lukewarm water; then blot with paper towels. Never let leaves stay long in water because they will become limp and flavorless.

COTTAGE CHEESE-AND-SPINACH CASSEROLE

1 pound fresh spinach
2 eggs, beaten
1 (8-ounce) carton cottage cheese
½ teaspoon seasoned salt
¼ teaspoon pepper
¼ cup (1 ounce) shredded Cheddar
  cheese
1 teaspoon sesame seeds, toasted

Remove stems from spinach; wash leaves in lukewarm water. Place spinach in Dutch oven (do not add water); cover and cook over high heat 3 to 5 minutes. Drain spinach well; chop and set aside.

Combine next 4 ingredients; mix well. Stir in spinach. Spoon mixture into a lightly greased 1-quart casserole. Bake, uncovered, at 350° for 20 minutes. Sprinkle with cheese and sesame seeds; bake an additional 5 minutes. Yield: about 4 servings. *Mrs. J. S. Grant,*
Sanford, North Carolina.

SPINACH SUPREME

1½ pounds fresh spinach
½ cup chopped onion
½ cup chopped celery
2 tablespoons chopped green pepper
¼ cup butter or margarine
1 (10¾-ounce) can cream of mushroom
  soup, undiluted
6 ounces process American cheese, diced
Pinch of garlic powder
1 cup soft breadcrumbs, divided

Remove stems from spinach; wash leaves in lukewarm water. Place spinach in Dutch oven (do not add water); cover and cook over high heat 3 to 5 minutes. Drain spinach well; chop coarsely, and set aside.

Sauté onion, celery, and green pepper in butter until tender. Stir in soup; cook over medium heat, stirring constantly, until thoroughly heated. Add cheese and garlic powder; stir until cheese melts. Stir in spinach and ¾ cup breadcrumbs; pour mixture into a lightly greased 10- x 6- x 2-inch baking dish. Sprinkle remaining ¼ cup breadcrumbs over top; bake at 350° for 15 to 20 minutes. Yield: 6 servings.
Pauline Withem,
Shreveport, Louisiana.

FRESH SPINACH SALAD

1 pound fresh spinach
1 small red onion, sliced
3 hard-cooked eggs, finely chopped
6 slices bacon, cooked and crumbled
Dressing (recipe follows)

Remove stems from spinach; wash leaves in lukewarm water, and pat dry. Tear into bite-size pieces. Combine spinach, onion, eggs, and bacon in a large bowl. Serve with dressing. Yield: 6 to 8 servings.

Dressing:

1 small onion, chopped
1 cup vegetable oil
⅓ cup vinegar
⅓ cup sugar
1 tablespoon prepared mustard
1 teaspoon celery seeds
½ teaspoon salt
½ teaspoon pepper

Combine all ingredients in container of electric blender, and process well. Chill thoroughly. Stir before serving. Yield: 2 cups. *Marie W. Harris,*
Sevierville, Tennessee.

SPINACH SOUFFLE

1½ pounds fresh spinach
2 tablespoons butter or margarine
2 tablespoons all-purpose flour
¾ cup milk
1 teaspoon chopped onion
1½ cups (6 ounces) shredded Cheddar
  cheese
3 eggs, separated

Remove stems from spinach; wash leaves in lukewarm water. Place spinach in Dutch oven (do not add water); cover and cook over high heat 3 to 5 minutes. Drain spinach well; coarsely chop, and set aside.

Melt butter in a heavy saucepan over low heat; add flour, stirring until smooth. Cook 1 minute, stirring constantly. Gradually stir in milk; cook over medium heat, stirring constantly, until thickened and bubbly. Add onion and cheese, stirring until cheese melts. Beat egg yolks, and stir about one-fourth of hot mixture into yolks, mixing well. Add yolk mixture and spinach to sauce mixture, stirring constantly.

Beat egg whites (at room temperature) until stiff but not dry; fold into sauce mixture. Pour into a greased 1½-quart casserole; place casserole in a shallow baking pan. Fill pan 1 inch deep with water; bake at 350° for 45 to 50 minutes or until a knife inserted in center comes out clean. Yield: 8 servings.
Mrs. John A. Wyatt,
Palmyra, Tennessee.

Sunny Ideas For Breakfast

For most folks, a good breakfast is the start of a good day. If your family likes to take time to savor a traditional morning meal, get out your apron and try one of these appealing ideas.

ORANGE FRENCH TOAST

2 eggs
⅔ cup orange juice
3 tablespoons powdered sugar
1 teaspoon ground cinnamon
8 slices white bread
2 tablespoons butter or margarine, divided

Combine eggs, orange juice, powdered sugar, and cinnamon in container of electric blender; blend well. Pour egg mixture into a shallow container. Dip each slice of bread in the mixture, coating well on each side.

Melt 1 tablespoon butter in a large skillet; fry 4 bread slices until golden brown on each side. Repeat procedure with remaining butter and bread. Yield: 4 servings.
Audrey Hasenbein,
Gardendale, Alabama.

FRIED GRITS

4 cups water
½ teaspoon salt
1 cup uncooked quick-cooking grits
2 tablespoons cooked, crumbled bacon
¼ cup plus 1 tablespoon butter or
  margarine, divided

Bring water and salt to a boil; stir in grits. Cook grits until done, following package directions. Remove from heat. Add bacon and 1 tablespoon butter; stir until butter melts.

Pour grits into a greased 8½- x 4½- x 3-inch loafpan. Cool; cover and refrigerate overnight.

Remove grits by inverting pan; cut loaf into ½-inch slices. Melt remaining ¼ cup butter in a large skillet; fry slices over medium heat 5 to 7 minutes or until lightly browned, turning once. Yield: about 8 servings.

Dorothy McGinley,
Wilmington, Delaware.

BAKED CHEESE-AND-GARLIC GRITS

4 cups water
½ teaspoon salt
1 cup uncooked quick-cooking grits
1½ cups (6 ounces) shredded sharp
  Cheddar cheese
½ cup butter or margarine
½ cup milk
1 clove garlic, minced
2 eggs, beaten

Bring water and salt to a boil; stir in grits. Cook grits until done, following package directions. Remove from heat, and add next 4 ingredients; stir until butter and cheese melt.

Add a small amount of hot grits to eggs, stirring well; stir egg mixture into remaining grits. Pour grits into a lightly greased 2-quart baking dish. Bake at 325° for 1 hour. Yield: 8 servings.
Marian Cox,
Deming, New Mexico.

OPEN-FACE EGG SANDWICHES

1½ tablespoons butter or margarine
1½ tablespoons all-purpose flour
¾ cup milk
¾ cup (3 ounces) shredded Cheddar
  cheese
Salt and pepper
4 eggs
2 tablespoons water
2 tablespoons butter or margarine, divided
4 tomato slices, cut ¼ inch thick
4 slices buttered toast
Chopped fresh parsley (optional)

Melt 1½ tablespoons butter in a heavy saucepan over low heat; add flour, stirring until smooth. Cook 1 minute, stirring constantly. Gradually add milk; cook over medium heat, stirring constantly, until thickened and bubbly. Add cheese, ⅛ teaspoon salt, and dash of pepper, stirring until smooth. Set sauce aside.

Combine eggs, water, ¼ teaspoon salt, and dash of pepper; beat well with a fork. Melt 1 tablespoon butter in a 10-inch skillet. Add egg mixture, and cook over low heat until eggs are partially set; stir occasionally until the eggs are firm but still moist.

Fry tomato slices in remaining 1 tablespoon butter, 1 minute on each side. Place a tomato slice on each piece of toast. Spoon eggs over tomato, and top with cheese sauce. Garnish with parsley, if desired. Yield: 4 servings.
G. C. MacDonald,
Shalimar, Florida.

Tip: It's a good idea to learn as much as you can about the metric system of measuring since these measurements are now appearing on some foods. To give you an idea of some new measurements: 1 cup flour equals 140 grams; 1 cup butter equals 200 grams; and 1 cup sugar equals 190 grams.

Welcome Guests With Vegetable Appetizers

Get out the silver and light the candles—it's time to have a party. And if you're tired of serving the same old appetizers when you entertain, serve some of our refreshing new-style vegetable appetizers.

Several of these appetizers call for piping filling from a decorating bag. Of course, you can spread the mixtures with a knife or the back of a spoon, but piping makes the filling look pretty, and it's also the quickest, easiest, and neatest way to complete the task. If you've never used a decorating bag before, we hope you'll try one with these recipes.

DILLED BABY CARROTS

¾ cup white wine vinegar
¼ cup water
¼ cup honey
½ teaspoon dried whole dillweed
½ teaspoon mixed pickling spices
Dash of salt
½ pound baby carrots, scraped
Sprigs of fresh dill (optional)

Combine first 6 ingredients in a large saucepan; bring to a boil. Add carrots; cover, reduce heat, and simmer 10 to 12 minutes or until crisp-tender. Remove from heat, and pour mixture into a plastic container; set container in a bowl of ice water to cool quickly. Chill. Serve with a slotted spoon. Garnish with sprigs of dill, if desired. Yield: 12 to 15 appetizer servings.

CHEESY CUCUMBER SLICES

1½ cups (6 ounces) shredded farmer's cheese
2½ tablespoons commercial sour cream
3 tablespoons minced onion
½ teaspoon dried herb seasoning
3 small cucumbers
Paprika
Sprigs of fresh thyme (optional)

Combine first 4 ingredients in container of electric blender; process until smooth. Chill.

Score cucumbers lengthwise down the skin using a lemon zester. Slice crosswise into ⅛-inch slices; arrange on a serving platter. Spoon cheese mixture into decorating bag fitted with tip number 4B; pipe mixture on each cucumber slice. Sprinkle with paprika and top with sprig of thyme, if desired. Yield: about 4½ dozen.

ENDIVE BOATS

2 small heads Belgian endive
½ cup whipped cream cheese, softened
1 (2-ounce) package blue cheese, crumbled
½ teaspoon dried whole dillweed
Few drops of milk
Pimiento strips

Peel leaves from core of endive. Wash leaves, and pat dry with paper towels. Place in plastic food storage bag, and refrigerate.

Combine cream cheese, blue cheese, and dillweed; stir with a fork until blended. Stir a few drops of milk into cheese mixture, if necessary, to make cheese a piping consistency. Spoon cheese mixture into decorating bag fitted with tip number 18. Pipe about 1 teaspoon cheese mixture down inside spine of each endive leaf. Top with a pimiento strip. Refrigerate until ready to serve. Yield: about 1½ dozen.

STUFFED SNOW PEAS

2 dozen fresh or frozen snow peas
¾ cup whipped cream cheese, softened
2 tablespoons orange juice
1½ teaspoons prepared horseradish
⅛ teaspoon freshly ground pepper
Grated orange rind

Thaw snow peas, if frozen. Trim ends from snow peas. Place snow peas in a steaming basket. Plunge basket into boiling water, and remove immediately. Place snow peas in a bowl of ice water to cool quickly. Remove from water and refrigerate.

Combine cream cheese, orange juice, horseradish, and pepper; stir until smooth. Chill at least 1 hour.

Using a sharp knife, carefully slit one side of each pea pod. Spoon cream cheese mixture into decorating bag fitted with tip number 18. Pipe about 1½ teaspoons cream cheese mixture into each snow pea. Sprinkle with grated orange rind. Refrigerate until ready to serve. Yield: 2 dozen.

CAVIAR POTATOES

7 small new potatoes
1 (8-ounce) carton commercial sour cream
About 1½ tablespoons black caviar
About 1½ tablespoons gold caviar

Cook potatoes in boiling water to cover 15 minutes or just until tender. Remove from water; chill potatoes. Slice potatoes crosswise into ¼-inch slices. Place potato slices on serving platter. Top each slice with 1 teaspoon sour cream and ¼ teaspoon caviar. Yield: about 3 dozen.

TOMATO BITES

1 pint cherry tomatoes
Few drops of milk
4 ounces goat cheese, softened
Fresh basil or oregano leaves

Wash tomatoes; set tomatoes on cutting board, stem end down. Slice off top third of tomatoes.

Stir a few drops of milk into cheese, if necessary, to make cheese a piping consistency. Spoon cheese into decorating bag fitted with tip number 18. Pipe about ½ teaspoon cheese on bottom portion of each tomato. Insert basil or oregano leaf into cheese so that it stands upright. Top with tomato caps, placing caps slightly off center of bottom portions to make leaves show. Refrigerate until ready to serve. Yield: about 2 dozen.

Note: Dried whole basil or oregano leaves may be sprinkled over cheese instead of using fresh herbs, if desired.

Pass The Pork Chops!

If you're looking for new ideas for pork chops, you'll love trying these delicious variations.

As with any stuffed pork chop recipe, you'll find it best to cut the pocket from the rib or bone side to the fat edge, being careful not to cut through the fat edge. This way the stuffing is sealed inside the chop, and the need for skewering the edges closed is eliminated. Be certain to cook the meat until it is well done and all pink is gone. A meat thermometer should register at least 170°F.

When selecting pork chops, look for meat that is pink to delicate rose with a moderate amount of marbling (fat streaks distributed throughout the meat). If you don't plan to use them within the next two days, package and freeze the chops.

CHEESE-STUFFED PORK CHOPS

1 (4-ounce) can mushroom stems and pieces, chopped and undrained
1 cup (4 ounces) shredded Swiss cheese
¼ cup chopped fresh parsley
½ teaspoon salt
4 (1-inch-thick) pork chops
½ cup fine, dry breadcrumbs
¼ teaspoon salt
Dash of pepper
1 egg, beaten
3 tablespoons vegetable oil

Drain mushrooms, reserving the liquid; set liquid aside. Combine mushrooms, cheese, parsley, and ½ teaspoon salt; mix well, and set aside.

Make pockets in pork chops, cutting from rib side just to beginning of fat edge of each chop. Stuff pockets of pork chops with cheese mixture.

Combine breadcrumbs, ¼ teaspoon salt, and pepper, stirring well. Dip pork chops in the beaten egg, and dredge in breadcrumb mixture.

Heat oil in a skillet over medium heat; brown pork chops on both sides. Add water to reserved mushroom liquid to equal 1 cup. Pour over pork chops. Cover, reduce heat, and simmer 1 hour or until pork chops are tender. Yield: 4 servings.
Jayne Perala,
Salem, Virginia.

LEMON-HERB PORK CHOPS

¼ cup lemon juice
2 tablespoons vegetable oil
3 to 4 cloves garlic, minced
1 teaspoon salt
¼ teaspoon ground thyme
¼ teaspoon dried whole oregano
¼ teaspoon pepper
6 (1-inch-thick) pork chops

Combine first 7 ingredients in a shallow dish; stir well. Add pork chops. Cover and marinate 12 hours in refrigerator, turning meat occasionally.

Remove pork chops from marinade, reserving marinade. Grill over hot coals 30 minutes on each side or until well done, basting chops with marinade. Yield: 6 servings.
Connie Burgess,
Knoxville, Tennessee.

ORIENTAL PORK CHOPS

1 (8-ounce) jar commercial sweet-and-sour sauce, divided
4 (½-inch-thick) pork chops
1 (11-ounce) can mandarin oranges, drained
1 large green pepper, cut into strips
Hot cooked rice

Heat ¼ cup sweet-and-sour sauce in a skillet over medium heat; brown pork chops in sauce on both sides. Transfer pork chops to a lightly greased 9-inch square baking dish; top with oranges and green pepper. Pour remaining sweet-and-sour sauce over pork chops. Bake, uncovered, at 350° for 45 minutes or until done. Serve chops over hot cooked rice. Yield: 4 servings.
Kathryn Knight,
Sarasota, Florida.

PORK CHOPS WITH DILL-CREAM GRAVY

½ cup thinly sliced green onions
½ cup sliced fresh mushrooms
3 tablespoons butter or margarine
6 (¾-inch-thick) pork chops
1 teaspoon salt
¼ teaspoon pepper
½ cup Chablis or other dry white wine
1 teaspoon Worcestershire sauce
1 teaspoon dried whole dillweed
⅓ cup water
2 tablespoons all-purpose flour
1 (8-ounce) carton commercial sour cream
Hot cooked rice

Sauté onions and mushrooms in butter in a large skillet until tender. Remove from skillet; set aside.

Sprinkle pork chops with salt and pepper; place in large skillet, and brown on both sides. Combine sautéed vegetables, wine, Worcestershire sauce, and dillweed; pour over chops. Cover, reduce heat, and simmer 40 minutes or until pork chops are tender. Remove chops from skillet, and set aside.

Combine water and flour, stirring until smooth; add to pan drippings in skillet. Cook over low heat, stirring constantly, until thickened and bubbly. Stir in sour cream, and cook until thoroughly heated.

Serve pork chops over hot cooked rice; spoon gravy over the chops, as desired. Yield: 6 servings.
Mrs. Lloyd E. Reynolds,
York, Pennsylvania.

ORANGE PORK CHOPS

4 (1-inch-thick) pork chops
Salt and pepper
Paprika
2 tablespoons vegetable oil
⅓ cup water
½ cup sugar
½ teaspoon cornstarch
½ teaspoon ground cinnamon
1 tablespoon plus 1 teaspoon grated orange rind
1 cup orange juice
1 teaspoon whole cloves
Hot cooked rice

Sprinkle pork chops with salt, pepper, and paprika.

Heat oil in a skillet over medium heat; brown pork chops on both sides. Add water to skillet. Cover, reduce heat, and simmer 40 to 45 minutes or until chops are tender, turning once.

Combine sugar, cornstarch, and cinnamon in a medium saucepan; stir in orange rind, orange juice, and cloves. Cook over medium heat, stirring constantly, until thickened and bubbly. Serve pork chops and sauce over rice. Yield: 4 servings.
Mrs. Joseph T. Mollick,
Longwood, Florida.

Stir Up A Cool, Crisp Salad

Need some new ideas for a refreshing salad? With these recipes, you can put together a salad from canned ingredients, fresh fruit, or vegetables.

SWISS-APPLE SALAD

3 large red apples, unpeeled and diced
2 tablespoons lemon juice
1 cup seedless green grapes, halved
¾ cup diced Swiss cheese
½ cup sliced celery
½ cup coarsely chopped pecans
⅓ cup mayonnaise
Lettuce leaves

Sprinkle apples with lemon juice, and toss lightly. Add the next 5 ingredients, and mix well. Serve on lettuce leaves. Yield: 6 servings.
Violet Moore,
Montezuma, Georgia.

CHEDDAR-PEA SALAD

1 (16-ounce) can small English peas,
    drained
1 cup cubed Cheddar cheese
½ cup chopped celery
¼ to ½ cup sliced pimiento-stuffed olives
1 hard-cooked egg, chopped
1 tablespoon grated onion
¼ cup mayonnaise

Combine all ingredients; mix well.
Cover salad, and chill at least 1 hour.
Yield: 4 servings.   *Edna Mae Gibson,*
Marietta, Georgia.

GARDEN PATCH POTATO SALAD

8 cups cubed cooked potatoes
2 cups chopped zucchini
1 cup sliced celery
¾ cup shredded carrot
3 tablespoons minced onion
1 (16-ounce) carton commercial sour
    cream
2 tablespoons vinegar
1 tablespoon sugar
1 teaspoon salt
¼ to ½ teaspoon dillweed
¼ teaspoon celery seeds
⅛ teaspoon pepper

Combine first 5 ingredients in a large
bowl; toss lightly, and set aside. Combine remaining ingredients; stir until
blended. Add sour cream mixture to
vegetables, stirring well. Chill thoroughly. Yield: 8 to 10 servings.
Irene Murry,
Herculaneum, Missouri.

FOUR-BEAN SALAD

1 (16-ounce) can golden wax beans,
    drained
1 (16-ounce) can green beans, drained
1 (15-ounce) can lima beans, drained
1 (15-ounce) can red kidney beans,
    drained
1 large green pepper, cut into 1-inch
    strips
1 medium onion, thinly sliced and
    separated into rings
1 pint cherry tomatoes, halved
1 medium cucumber, thinly sliced
½ cup red wine vinegar
½ cup vegetable oil
½ cup sugar
2 tablespoons chopped fresh tarragon or
    ½ teaspoon dried whole tarragon
2 tablespoons chopped fresh basil or ½
    teaspoon dried whole basil
2 tablespoons chopped fresh parsley
½ teaspoon salt
½ teaspoon dry mustard
Lettuce leaves (optional)

Combine first 8 ingredients in a large
bowl; toss gently.
Combine next 8 ingredients in a jar.
Cover tightly, and shake vigorously;
pour marinade over vegetables, tossing
gently. Cover vegetables, and chill at
least 4 hours or overnight. Serve in a
lettuce-lined bowl, if desired. Yield: 12
to 15 servings.   *Wanda Juraschek,*
Vienna, Virginia.

COOKING LIGHT

Have Fun Dieting With Desserts

If you're interested in losing weight,
dessert is probably the first thing you'll
try to give up. One piece of pecan pie
can exceed 400 calories; a slice of
cheesecake is about 500 calories. To
help you diet without feeling deprived,
we've collected a variety of luscious
spring desserts that each serving is
under 200 calories.

Fruit is one of the best dessert
choices for dieters. It's generally high in
vitamins, minerals, and fiber and rela-
tively low in calories. Our Fresh Fruit
Compote calls for papaya, a refreshing
tropical fruit high in vitamins A and C.
If you're unable to find papaya, you can
substitute two additional oranges or
apples and maintain about the same calorie count.

Remember that you cannot lose
weight and keep eating rich pecan pie
and creamy chocolate cheesecake. The
truth of the matter is the only way to
lose weight is to take in fewer calories
than your body burns up. That means
giving up those rich desserts that are
high in calories but low in vitamins,
minerals, and protein. A good diet plan
should provide fewer calories than you
normally eat and should include a variety of foods: fruit and vegetables;
breads and cereals; milk and cheese;
and meat, fish, poultry, and dried
beans. By including each of these
groups daily, you'll be more likely to
get the necessary vitamins and minerals.

In "Cooking Light," we recommend
foods you will enjoy eating for a lifetime—not just for a week or two in
order to quickly lose a few pounds. For
most people, weight control must be a
lifetime effort. A successful dieter will

learn to adjust his habits by eating food
more slowly, eating fewer snacks, and
avoiding situations where he knows he'll
eat too much of the wrong food.

Don't overlook the value of exercise
in your weight control program. Exercise helps improve self-esteem and body
tone. By burning up extra calories, exercise aids in weight loss. Once you've
reached your desired body weight, regular strenuous exercise helps keep un-
wanted pounds from creeping back.

FRESH FRUIT COMPOTE

1 large seedless orange, peeled and
    sectioned
1 ripe papaya, peeled and cut into ¾-inch
    cubes
2 cups cubed fresh pineapple
1 medium apple, unpeeled and cut into
    ¾-inch cubes
1 small banana, sliced
¼ cup Grand Marnier or other
    orange-flavored liqueur
¼ cup unsweetened orange juice

Combine fruit in a large bowl, tossing
lightly. Combine liqueur and orange
juice; pour over fruit, mixing well.
Cover and chill at least 1 hour. Yield: 8
servings (about 94 calories per serving).

STRAWBERRIES JULIET

4 cups whole fresh strawberries, divided
⅓ cup frozen whipped topping, thawed
⅓ cup plain low-fat yogurt
1 tablespoon sugar

Slice enough strawberries to measure
¼ cup; crush with a fork. Add whipped
topping, yogurt, and sugar; mix well.

Spoon remaining strawberries evenly
into dessert dishes. Top each serving
with strawberry-yogurt mixture. Chill 1
hour. Yield: 4 servings (about 104 calories per serving).   *Lockie Burge,*
Sulphur Rock, Arkansas.

FANCY FRUIT MEDLEY

2 (8-ounce) cans unsweetened pineapple
    chunks, undrained
1 tablespoon cornstarch
2 teaspoons sugar
½ teaspoon vanilla extract
⅓ cup plain low-fat yogurt
1 cup seedless green grapes, halved
1 cup halved fresh strawberries

Drain pineapple, reserving juice. Set
pineapple aside.

Combine pineapple juice, cornstarch, and sugar in a saucepan; cook over medium heat, stirring constantly, until mixture comes to a boil. Cook 1 minute, stirring constantly. Stir in vanilla; cool 10 minutes. Stir in yogurt; fold in fruit. Chill several hours. Yield: 6 servings (about 94 calories per serving).

Frankie Frost,
Lancaster, Texas.

PEACH-YOGURT ICE

2 (16-ounce) cans unsweetened sliced
   peaches, undrained
2 envelopes unflavored gelatin
2 (8-ounce) cartons vanilla low-fat yogurt
2 tablespoons dark rum
Kiwi slices (optional)

Drain peaches, reserving liquid; set aside. Soften gelatin in ⅓ cup reserved peach liquid; set aside. Place remaining peach liquid in a small saucepan; bring to a boil. Add gelatin mixture to boiling liquid; remove from heat, and stir until completely dissolved. Set aside to cool.

Place peaches in container of electric blender, and process until smooth. Add yogurt and rum; process until thoroughly blended. Combine gelatin mixture and yogurt mixture; stir well. Pour into a 9-inch square pan; freeze until firm, stirring several times during freezing process. Let stand at room temperature 10 minutes before serving. Garnish with kiwi, if desired. Yield: 5 cups (about 176 calories per 1-cup serving).

PINEAPPLE SHERBET

2 cups buttermilk
⅓ cup sugar
1 (8-ounce) can unsweetened crushed
   pineapple, undrained
2 teaspoons vanilla extract
½ teaspoon lemon juice
2 egg whites

Combine first 5 ingredients in a medium mixing bowl; mix well. Pour into a 9-inch square pan, and place in freezer about 30 minutes or until slushy.

Beat egg whites (at room temperature) in a medium mixing bowl until soft peaks form; fold pineapple mixture into egg whites. Pour into pan; freeze 25 minutes or until just firm but not frozen. Spoon into mixing bowl; beat with electric mixer until fluffy. Pour back into pan; freeze until firm. Yield: 3 cups (about 104 calories per ½-cup serving).

Doris Clark,
Hurst, Texas.

PINEAPPLE PARFAIT

1 (8-ounce) can unsweetened crushed
   pineapple, undrained
1 envelope unflavored gelatin
¼ cup sugar
1 tablespoon all-purpose flour
3 eggs, separated
1 cup skim milk
1 teaspoon grated orange rind

Drain pineapple, reserving ½ cup juice; set aside. Soften gelatin in reserved pineapple juice; set aside.

Combine sugar and flour in a medium saucepan, mixing well. Beat egg yolks and milk; stir into sugar mixture. Cook over low heat, stirring constantly, 6 to 8 minutes or until mixture coats a spoon. Remove from heat; stir in gelatin mixture, pineapple, and orange rind until well blended.

Beat egg whites (at room temperature) until stiff peaks form. Fold into pineapple mixture. Spoon into parfait glasses; chill until firm. Yield: 6 servings (about 117 calories per serving).

STIRRED CUSTARD OVER FRUIT

2 eggs, slightly beaten
2½ tablespoons sugar
1⅓ cups skim milk
¼ teaspoon almond extract
¼ teaspoon vanilla extract
2 cups fresh strawberries, halved
2 kiwi, peeled and sliced
1 (11-ounce) can mandarin oranges,
   drained

Combine eggs, sugar, and milk in top of a double boiler, mixing well. Bring water to boil in bottom of double boiler. Reduce heat to low; cook custard over hot water, stirring occasionally, until custard thickens and coats a metal spoon. Remove from heat; stir in flavorings. Place pan in a bowl of ice water; cover with waxed paper, and chill thoroughly.

Combine fruit; chill. Divide fruit among 6 individual serving dishes; spoon custard over fruit. Yield: 6 servings (about 128 calories per serving).

Crêpes Are Simply Elegant

Crêpes begin with the simplest of ingredients and evolve into the most elegant creations. The thin, delicate pancakes invite only the best fillings and sauces. And you can fold them a number of ways to create impressive desserts, appetizers, and entrées.

It's not necessary to use a special crêpe pan for making crêpes. A 6- or 8-inch skillet with low, sloping sides works nicely. Brush the pan with oil periodically to prevent crêpes from sticking. Skillets with nonstick surfaces usually don't need to be greased.

When you're making crêpes, it's a good idea to do plenty, since they keep well. After the crêpes cool, stack them between waxed paper and sandwich the stack between two paper plates. Wrap the entire package—plates and all—in aluminum foil, or slip it into a freezer bag. In the refrigerator, crêpes can be stored for two to three days. They'll keep up to four months in the freezer.

BASIC CREPES

1½ cups all-purpose flour
¼ teaspoon salt
2 cups milk
3 eggs
2 tablespoons butter or margarine, melted
Vegetable oil

Combine flour, salt, and milk; mix well. Add the eggs and butter; beat until smooth. Refrigerate batter at least 2 hours. (This allows flour particles to swell and soften so the crêpes will be light in texture.)

Brush bottom of a 6- or 8-inch crêpe pan or heavy skillet with oil; place the pan over medium heat until just hot, not smoking.

Pour 2 to 3 tablespoons batter into pan; quickly tilt pan in all directions so batter covers pan in a thin film. Cook about 1 minute or until lightly browned.

Lift edge of crêpe to test for doneness. Crêpe is ready for flipping when it can be shaken loose from pan. Flip crêpe, and cook about 30 seconds on other side. (This side is rarely more than spotty brown and is the side on which the filling is placed.)

Place crêpes on a towel to cool. Stack between layers of waxed paper to prevent sticking. Repeat until all batter is used. Yield: 2 dozen 6-inch crêpes or 1½ dozen 8-inch crêpes.

SAUTEED CRAB CREPES

1 pound fresh crabmeat, drained and
　flaked
¼ cup chopped green pepper
¼ cup chopped green onions
2 tablespoons minced celery
1 clove garlic, minced
¼ cup butter or margarine
1 (2-ounce) jar chopped pimiento, drained
1 to 2 tablespoons dry white wine
1 tablespoon minced fresh parsley
1 teaspoon seafood seasoning
¼ teaspoon salt
¼ teaspoon dry mustard
Dash of hot sauce
1 egg, beaten
3 tablespoons mayonnaise
8 (8-inch) Basic Crêpes (page 83)
Mushroom-Wine Sauce
Chopped fresh parsley (optional)

Sauté first 5 ingredients in butter in a
large skillet until vegetables are tender.
Remove from heat. Stir in the next 7
ingredients.

Combine egg and mayonnaise in a
bowl; stir in crabmeat mixture. Fill each
crêpe with a heaping one-fourth cup
crabmeat mixture. Roll up, and place
seam side down in a lightly greased 13-
x 9- x 2-inch baking dish; spoon Mushroom-Wine Sauce over crêpes. Cover
and bake at 350° for 15 to 20 minutes.
Garnish with chopped fresh parsley, if
desired. Yield: 4 servings.

Mushroom-Wine Sauce:

½ pound fresh mushrooms, sliced
2 tablespoons finely chopped green onions
¼ cup plus 1 tablespoon butter or
　margarine, divided
3 tablespoons all-purpose flour
1½ cups milk
¼ cup dry white wine
1 tablespoon minced fresh parsley
½ teaspoon salt
Pinch of dried whole tarragon
¼ teaspoon white pepper

Sauté mushrooms and onions in 2 tablespoons butter in a heavy skillet until
tender. Remove from skillet; set aside.
Melt 3 tablespoons butter in a heavy
saucepan over low heat. Add flour, stirring until smooth. Cook 1 minute, stirring constantly. Gradually add milk and
white wine; cook over medium heat,
stirring constantly, until thickened and
bubbly. Stir in sautéed vegetables and
remaining ingredients. Yield: 2 cups.

*Tip: To retain white color of fresh
mushrooms, slice just before using or
dip in lemon juice.*

CHEESY PARTY WEDGES

1 cup (4 ounces) shredded Cheddar cheese
1 (3-ounce) package cream cheese,
　softened
3 tablespoons mayonnaise
¼ teaspoon Worcestershire sauce
Dash of garlic powder
2 tablespoons chopped pimiento-stuffed
　olives
1 tablespoon minced onion
8 (6-inch) Basic Crêpes (page 83)
Sliced pimiento-stuffed olives

Combine first 7 ingredients, mixing
well. Spread 2 tablespoons cheese mixture over each crêpe. Stack crêpes on a
serving plate; garnish with olive slices.
Chill at least 1 hour. Cut into wedges.
Yield: 12 to 16 appetizer servings.

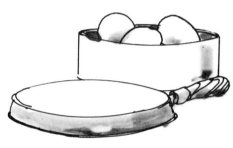

DESSERT CREPES

1½ cups all-purpose flour
1 tablespoon sugar
¼ teaspoon salt
2 cups milk
1 teaspoon vanilla extract
3 eggs
2 tablespoons butter or margarine, melted
Vegetable oil

Combine first 5 ingredients, beating
until smooth. Add eggs, and beat well;
stir in butter. Refrigerate 2 hours. (This
allows flour particles to swell and soften
so crêpes are light in texture.)
Brush bottom of a 6-inch crêpe pan
or heavy skillet with oil; place over medium heat until just hot, not smoking.
Pour 2 tablespoons batter into pan;
quickly tilt pan in all directions so batter covers pan in a thin film. Cook 1
minute or until lightly browned.
Lift edge of crêpe to test for doneness. Crêpe is ready for flipping when it
can be shaken loose from pan. Flip
crêpe, and cook about 30 seconds on
other side. (This side is rarely more
than spotty brown and is the side on
which the filling is placed.)
Place crêpes on a towel to cool. Stack
between layers of waxed paper to prevent sticking. Repeat until all batter is
used. Yield: 2 dozen 6-inch crêpes.

RASPBERRY CREPES SUZETTE

¼ cup unsalted butter, softened
2 tablespoons sugar
1½ tablespoons Grand Marnier or other
　orange-flavored liqueur
1 tablespoon grated orange rind
1 (10-ounce) package frozen raspberries,
　thawed
2 teaspoons cornstarch
⅓ cup red currant jelly
3 tablespoons unsalted butter
¼ teaspoon ground cardamom
8 Dessert Crêpes (page 84)
3 to 4 tablespoons rum

Cream ¼ cup butter; gradually add
sugar, beating until light and fluffy. Stir
in Grand Marnier and orange rind, and
set aside.
Drain raspberries, reserving juice.
Process raspberries in a food mill; discard seeds. Set berry pulp aside.
Combine berry juice and cornstarch
in a saucepan; mix well. Add berry
pulp, jelly, 3 tablespoons butter, and
cardamom; cook over low heat, stirring
constantly, until sauce is smooth and
slightly thickened. Set aside.
Spoon about 1½ teaspoons orange
butter on each crêpe, spreading evenly
to outer edges. Fold crêpes in half, and
then into quarters.
Spoon half of raspberry sauce into
chafing dish; arrange crêpes in sauce.
Spoon remaining sauce over crêpes;
place over low heat until heated.
Heat rum in a small saucepan; remove from heat. Ignite rum with a long
match, and pour over crêpes. Spoon
sauce over crêpes until flames die. Serve
immediately. Yield: 4 servings.

CHOCOLATE DESSERT CREPES

½ cup all-purpose flour
1 tablespoon cocoa
1 tablespoon sugar
Dash of salt
¾ cup milk
½ teaspoon vanilla extract
1 egg
2 teaspoons butter or margarine, melted
Vegetable oil

Combine first 4 ingredients. Add milk
and vanilla; beat until smooth. Add
egg, and beat well; stir in butter. Refrigerate 2 hours. (This allows flour particles to swell and soften so crêpes are
light in texture.)
Brush bottom of a 6-inch crêpe pan
or heavy skillet with oil; place over medium heat until just hot, not smoking.

Pour 2 tablespoons batter into pan; quickly tilt pan in all directions so batter covers pan in a thin film. Cook crêpe about 1 minute.

Lift edge of crêpe to test for doneness. Crêpe is ready for flipping when it can be shaken loose from pan. Flip crêpe, and cook about 30 seconds on other side. (This side is rarely more than spotty brown and is the side on which the filling is placed.)

Place crêpes on a towel to cool. Stack between layers of waxed paper to prevent sticking. Repeat until all batter is used. Yield: 1 dozen 6-inch crêpes.

COFFEE ICE CREAM CREPES

½ cup whipping cream
1 tablespoon Kahlúa or other
  coffee-flavored liqueur
1 quart coffee-flavored ice cream
1 dozen Chocolate Dessert Crêpes
  (page 84)
Sliced almonds, toasted

Beat whipping cream until foamy; add Kahlúa, beating until stiff peaks form. Set aside.

Spoon about ⅓ cup ice cream down center of each crêpe; fold right and left sides over, and place seam side up on a serving plate. Top each crêpe with a dollop of the whipped cream; sprinkle with almonds. Yield: 6 servings.

Fresh Ideas For Spring Greens

Delicate lettuce, frilly escarole, and tender spinach—three good ways to add green color and fresh flavor to spring menus. Here are some of our readers' suggestions for tossing them into salads or gently cooking for simple side dishes.

Remember that salad greens should never be cut with a knife because it may discolor and bruise the leaves. Gently tearing the greens is better and makes a prettier salad.

Escarole and spinach are ideal for cooking. But don't get carried away and cook them in too much water. The water that clings to their leaves after they are washed is enough. No additional water is needed. Also, their cooking time is very brief—just a matter of a few minutes. Overcooking will drain the leaves of color and cause them to become too limp.

ESCAROLE-AND-BACON SALAD

2 large heads escarole, washed and
  torn
5 green onions, thinly sliced
8 slices bacon
⅓ cup cider vinegar
½ teaspoon salt
⅛ teaspoon coarsely ground black pepper
1½ tablespoons honey

Place escarole and onions in a large salad bowl; set aside.

Cook bacon in a large skillet until crisp; remove bacon, reserving drippings in skillet. Crumble bacon, and sprinkle over escarole. Add remaining ingredients to hot drippings; stir well. Quickly pour over escarole; toss gently. Serve immediately. Yield: 8 servings.
Anita McLemore,
Knoxville, Tennessee.

EASY COOKED ESCAROLE

1 large head escarole
1 tablespoon olive oil
1 clove garlic, minced
Salt and pepper to taste

Remove and discard stems from escarole; wash leaves thoroughly, and tear into large pieces. Place escarole leaves in a large saucepan (do not add water); cover and cook over medium heat 5 minutes or until wilted. Drain well.

Heat oil in a medium skillet; add garlic, and sauté 2 to 3 minutes. Add drained escarole, salt, and pepper. Cook, stirring constantly, until escarole is well heated. Yield: 4 servings.
Vivian Riegelman,
Charlotte, North Carolina.

BOSTON TOSSED SALAD

½ cup olive oil
¼ cup corn oil
¼ cup wine vinegar
½ teaspoon lemon-pepper seasoning
¼ teaspoon chopped fresh parsley
1 head Boston lettuce, washed and
  torn
1 (11-ounce) can mandarin oranges,
  drained
½ red onion, thinly sliced and separated
  into rings
12 large fresh mushrooms, sliced

Combine first 5 ingredients in a jar. Cover tightly, and shake vigorously.

Combine remaining ingredients; toss gently. Serve with salad dressing. Yield: 6 servings.
Evelyn Hamblen,
New Orleans, Louisiana.

CHEESY TOPPED SPINACH

2 pounds fresh spinach
1 tablespoon half-and-half
Dash of salt
Dash of pepper
2 small onions, chopped
2 tablespoons butter or margarine
1 cup (4 ounces) shredded Swiss
  cheese
3 large tomatoes, peeled and chopped

Remove stems from spinach. Wash leaves thoroughly; tear into bite-size pieces. Place spinach in a large saucepan (do not add water); cover and cook over high heat 3 minutes. Drain well. Return spinach to pan; add half-and-half, salt, and pepper. Cook over low heat until thoroughly heated, stirring occasionally.

Sauté onion in butter in a medium skillet 5 minutes or until tender. Remove from heat, and stir in cheese and tomatoes. Place spinach in a lightly greased 2-quart casserole; top with cheese mixture. Broil 6 inches from heat for 3 to 5 minutes or until lightly browned. Yield: 6 servings.
Cecilia Breithaupt,
Boerne, Texas.

Asparagus Signals Spring

One of the most welcome signs of spring is fresh asparagus in supermarkets. These crisp, slender stalks stimulate a number of tasty serving ideas.

ASPARAGUS WITH ALMOND BUTTER

1 pound fresh asparagus spears
½ cup sliced almonds
¼ cup butter or margarine
2 tablespoons peeled, grated cucumber
1 teaspoon lemon juice

Snap off tough ends of asparagus. Remove scales with a knife or vegetable peeler, if desired. Cook asparagus, covered, in a small amount of boiling water 6 to 8 minutes or until crisp-tender; drain. Arrange in a serving dish.

Sauté almonds in butter over low heat until golden brown. Stir in cucumber and lemon juice. Pour over asparagus. Yield: 4 servings.
Audrey Bledsoe,
Smyrna, Georgia.

ASPARAGUS-PIMIENTO LOAF

1 pound fresh asparagus spears
1 whole pimiento, cut into strips
¼ cup butter or margarine
⅓ cup all-purpose flour
1½ cups milk
1 tablespoon prepared mustard
½ teaspoon salt
½ teaspoon dried whole thyme
5 eggs, separated
3 slices bacon, cooked and crumbled
Commercial sour cream

Snap off tough ends of asparagus. Remove scales from stalks with a knife or vegetable peeler, if desired. Cook asparagus, covered, in a small amount of boiling water about 3 minutes; drain.

Arrange pimiento strips in a decorative design in a lightly greased 12- x 8- x 2-inch baking dish. Arrange asparagus in dish.

Melt butter in a heavy saucepan over low heat; add flour and cook 1 minute, stirring constantly. Gradually add milk; cook over medium heat, stirring constantly, until thickened and bubbly. Stir in mustard, salt, and thyme.

Beat egg yolks until thick and lemon colored. Gradually stir about one-fourth of hot mixture into yolks; add to remaining hot mixture, stirring constantly.

Beat egg whites (at room temperature) until stiff peaks form; fold into cooked mixture. Pour over asparagus.

Place baking dish in a shallow baking pan; pour hot water into pan to a depth of 1 inch. Bake, uncovered, at 350° for 35 to 40 minutes or until a knife inserted halfway between center and edge of dish comes out clean. Remove dish from water. Loosen edges of loaf with a knife; invert onto a serving platter. Sprinkle with bacon. Serve immediately with warm sour cream. Yield: 6 servings.
Edna Earle Moore,
Hueytown, Alabama.

TANGY ASPARAGUS

1½ pounds fresh asparagus spears
2 tablespoons butter or margarine
½ cup soft breadcrumbs
⅛ teaspoon garlic salt
⅛ teaspoon pepper
1 (8-ounce) carton commercial sour cream
2 tablespoons prepared horseradish

Snap off tough ends of asparagus. Remove scales from stalks with a knife or vegetable peeler, if desired. Cook asparagus, covered, in a small amount of boiling water 6 to 8 minutes or until crisp-tender; drain. Arrange asparagus in a lightly greased 12- x 8- x 2-inch baking dish.

Melt butter in a small skillet; add breadcrumbs, garlic salt, and pepper. Cook, stirring frequently, until breadcrumbs are lightly browned. Combine sour cream and horseradish; pour over asparagus. Top with breadcrumbs. Bake, uncovered, at 350° for 10 minutes. Yield: 6 servings. *Pat Sanders,*
Austin, Texas.

MARINATED ASPARAGUS

1 pound fresh asparagus spears
1 cup Italian salad dressing
½ cup Chablis or other dry white wine
1 tablespoon tarragon vinegar
¼ teaspoon dried whole basil
⅛ teaspoon dried whole oregano
⅛ teaspoon pepper
1 clove garlic, crushed
Romaine lettuce leaves

Snap off tough ends of asparagus. Remove scales with a knife or a vegetable peeler. Cook asparagus, covered, in a small amount of boiling water 6 to 8 minutes or until crisp-tender; drain.

Combine next 7 ingredients in a jar; cover tightly, and shake vigorously.

Place asparagus in a shallow dish; pour dressing over asparagus. Cover and chill overnight. Drain well. Arrange spears on lettuce. Yield: 4 servings.
Katie Kent,
Gladewater, Texas.

Gulf Coast Specialties To Try At Home

Even if you don't make it to the Gulf Coast this summer, you can still enjoy some of the outstanding dishes from the area. We ate our way from Lil' Ray's in Waveland, Mississippi, to Roussos restaurant in Mobile, Alabama, and here are some of the recipes we found.

■ You'll get a sampling of real, old-fashioned Southern hospitality when you visit Laurie's Southern Tearoom in Gulfport. Cheerful hostesses greet you with a smile, serve refreshing entrées such as Congealed Salad With Crabmeat-and-Asparagus, and serve tea after lunch from a silver tea service.

CONGEALED SALAD WITH CRABMEAT-AND-ASPARAGUS

1 envelope unflavored gelatin
2 tablespoons water
3 (3-ounce) packages lime-flavored gelatin
1 teaspoon salt
3 cups water
2 (15-ounce) cans cut asparagus, undrained
2 cups mayonnaise
¼ cup vinegar
2 cups (8 ounces) shredded Cheddar cheese
4 to 5 drops of hot sauce
1 pound fresh crabmeat, drained and flaked
Lettuce leaves

Combine unflavored gelatin and 2 tablespoons water; let stand 5 minutes.

Combine unflavored and flavored gelatin, salt, and 3 cups water in a saucepan; bring to a boil, stirring constantly. Remove from heat; chill until consistency of unbeaten egg white.

Drain asparagus, reserving juice from 1 can. Combine the reserved juice, mayonnaise, vinegar, cheese, hot sauce, and crabmeat. Fold into the chilled gelatin mixture.

Pour half of gelatin mixture into a 13- x 9- x 2-inch dish. Top with drained asparagus and remaining gelatin mixture. Chill until firm. Cut into squares, and serve on a bed of lettuce leaves. Yield: 12 servings.

■ Shrimp Melba and Seafood Gumbo are just two of the delicious specialties at Mary Mahoney's Old French House Restaurant in Biloxi.

SHRIMP MELBA

¼ cup plus 2 tablespoons water
¼ cup butter, melted
2 teaspoons chopped fresh parsley
1 teaspoon paprika
32 large fresh shrimp, peeled and deveined
1 cup frozen English peas, thawed
1 cup sliced almonds
½ cup sliced green onions with tops
½ cup sliced fresh mushrooms
3 tablespoons butter
2 cups cooked saffron rice
Salt to taste
Fresh mushrooms (optional)
Cherry tomatoes (optional)
Watercress (optional)
Lemon wedges (optional)

Combine water, ¼ cup butter, parsley, and paprika in a broiling pan; add shrimp, tossing well to coat. Broil shrimp 4 inches from heat 3 to 4 minutes; turn and broil an additional 3 to 4 minutes or until done.

Sauté peas, almonds, onions, and mushrooms in 3 tablespoons butter in a large skillet 5 minutes or until almonds are toasted. Add rice and salt; cook until thoroughly heated.

To serve, spoon shrimp over rice mixture. Garnish with mushrooms, cherry tomatoes, watercress, and lemon wedges, if desired. Yield: 4 servings.

SEAFOOD GUMBO

¼ cup plus 1 tablespoon bacon drippings
¼ cup plus 2 tablespoons all-purpose flour
2 medium onions, finely chopped
1½ cups finely chopped celery
1 clove garlic, minced
1 (28-ounce) can whole tomatoes, undrained
1 (16-ounce) can tomato sauce
5 to 6 cups water
1 tablespoon salt
1 teaspoon pepper
2 pounds fresh shrimp, peeled and deveined
1½ pounds fresh crabmeat, drained
1 (16-ounce) package frozen cut okra
1 pint oysters, undrained (optional)
3 tablespoons Worcestershire sauce
Hot cooked rice

Combine bacon drippings and flour in a large Dutch oven; cook over medium heat, stirring constantly, 10 to 15 minutes or until roux is the color of a copper penny. Stir in onion, celery, and garlic; cook 5 minutes, uncovered, stirring occasionally. Add tomatoes, tomato sauce, water, salt, and pepper; simmer over medium heat 1 hour, stirring occasionally. Add shrimp, crabmeat, and okra; simmer 20 minutes. Add oysters, if desired, and Worcestershire sauce; simmer 10 minutes. Serve over hot cooked rice. Yield: 4½ quarts.

■ When Ray Kidd boils shrimp at Lil' Ray's in Waveland, he always follows a secret technique taught to him by his father. "Most people overcook shrimp," explains Ray. "I throw the shrimp into boiling water. Then when the water comes back to a boil, I throw in ice to stop the cookin'. That's the only way to get really good boiled shrimp."

RAY KIDD'S BOILED SHRIMP

5 quarts water
5 pounds medium unpeeled fresh shrimp
⅓ cup ground red pepper
⅓ cup powdered seafood boil
3 tablespoons creole seasoning
2 teaspoons garlic powder
1 lemon, halved
1 stalk celery, cut into 3-inch pieces
½ cup salt
Ice cubes

Bring water to a boil in a large Dutch oven; add next 7 ingredients. Return to a boil; remove from heat, and stir in salt. Add enough ice cubes to stop cooking process; let stand 3 minutes, stirring frequently. Drain; serve immediately. Yield: 10 to 12 servings.

■ The White Pillars Restaurant in Biloxi, built around 1900, was styled after the Gunston Hall in Virginia to recapture the spirit of the antebellum South. Plan to spend a leisurely evening at the White Pillars where the expert staff will treat you to such elegant dishes as Carpetbagger Steak, Roast Long Island Duckling, and Kentucky Bourbon Pie.

ROAST LONG ISLAND DUCKLING

2 (4- to 4½-pound) dressed ducklings
1 teaspoon salt
¼ teaspoon pepper
1 teaspoon dried whole tarragon
2 stalks celery, cut into 2-inch pieces
2 carrots, scraped and cut into 2-inch pieces
2 apples, cored and coarsely chopped
¼ cup chopped green onions
1 orange, seeded and coarsely ground
2 tablespoons butter
1 cup orange marmalade
½ cup firmly packed brown sugar
¼ cup rum

Remove giblets and neck from ducklings; reserve for other use, if desired. Rub cavities of each duckling with ½ teaspoon salt, ⅛ teaspoon pepper, and 1½ teaspoons tarragon; stuff each with half the celery, carrots, and apples. Close cavities of ducklings with skewers. Place ducklings, breast side up, on rack in a shallow roasting pan. Bake, covered, at 375° for 1 hour. Cover ducklings loosely with aluminum foil; bake an additional 1 to 1½ hours or until drumsticks and thighs move easily. Let cool to touch.

Strain drippings, reserving ½ cup stock, and set aside.

Remove and discard stuffing; halve ducklings by cutting down both sides of backbones as close as possible to bone. Then, cut ducklings in half down breast sides, removing breast bones. Place duckling halves in a large baking dish; set aside, and keep warm.

Sauté onions and orange in butter until tender; stir in reserved stock, marmalade, and brown sugar. Bring to a boil and cook 5 minutes, or until thickened, stirring constantly. Stir in rum.

Reheat ducklings if necessary; top with sauce. Yield: 4 servings.

KENTUCKY BOURBON PIE

2 eggs, slightly beaten
1 cup sugar
½ cup all-purpose flour
½ cup butter, melted and cooled
1 cup chopped pecans
1 (6-ounce) package semisweet chocolate morsels
1 teaspoon vanilla extract
1 unbaked 9-inch pastry shell
1 cup whipping cream
1 tablespoon bourbon
¼ cup sifted powdered sugar

Combine first 4 ingredients in a medium mixing bowl; beat with an electric mixer just until blended. Stir in pecans, chocolate morsels, and vanilla. Pour filling into pastry shell, and bake at 350° for 45 to 50 minutes.

Beat whipping cream and bourbon until foamy; gradually add powdered sugar, beating until soft peaks form. Serve pie warm with whipped cream. Yield: one 9-inch pie.

CARPETBAGGER STEAK

½ cup fresh oysters, drained and chopped
¼ cup chopped fresh mushrooms
2 teaspoons chopped fresh parsley
1 tablespoon butter
2 slices bacon, cooked and crumbled
¼ cup crumbled blue cheese
2 tablespoons Sauterne or other dry white wine
1 (¾-pound) boneless sirloin strip steak

Sauté oysters, mushrooms, and parsley in butter until mushrooms are tender; drain. Stir in bacon, cheese, and Sauterne; set aside.

Make pocket in side of steak. Stuff pocket with oyster mixture; secure with wooden picks.

Broil steaks about 6 inches from heat 8 to 10 minutes on each side or until desired degree of doneness. Yield: 1 to 2 servings.

■ People who eat at Aunt Jenny's Catfish Restaurant in Ocean Springs will not go away hungry. The specialty is catfish, fried up with a nice, light batter, and served with spicy hush puppies.

AUNT JENNY'S HUSH PUPPIES

1¾ cups self-rising white cornmeal
1½ cups self-rising flour
1½ cups yellow cornmeal
2 teaspoons baking powder
½ teaspoon salt
½ teaspoon garlic powder
¾ teaspoon red pepper
1½ cups milk
¾ cup buttermilk
1 egg, beaten
½ cup minced onion
¼ cup diced canned jalapeño
   peppers
Vegetable oil

Combine first 7 ingredients in a large mixing bowl. Add milk, buttermilk, and egg; mix until blended. Stir in the onion and peppers.

Carefully drop batter by level tablespoonfuls into deep hot oil (370°). Fry 3 to 5 minutes, turning once, until hush puppies are golden brown. Drain on paper towels. Yield: about 4½ dozen.

■ Jocelyn's is a quaint restaurant just off U.S. 90 in Ocean Springs. Many of the locals visit Jocelyn's as often as they can for the homey atmosphere and the delicious food. Shrimp-and-Corn Soup is an outstanding appetizer frequently offered as a daily special.

SHRIMP-AND-CORN SOUP

¼ cup bacon drippings
2 tablespoons all-purpose flour
1 cup chopped celery
1 cup chopped green pepper
1 cup chopped onion
1 tablespoon minced garlic
2 teaspoons salt
½ teaspoon pepper
1 teaspoon dried whole thyme
1 (16-ounce) can whole tomatoes,
   undrained and chopped
1 (6-ounce) can tomato paste
6 cups water
2 (10-ounce) packages frozen whole
   kernel corn
2 pounds fresh medium shrimp, peeled,
   deveined, and cut in half

Combine bacon drippings and flour in a large Dutch oven; cook over medium heat, stirring constantly, 10 to 15 minutes or until roux is the color of a copper penny. Add next 7 ingredients, and cook, uncovered, 15 minutes, stirring occasionally. Add tomatoes, tomato paste, water, and corn. Bring to a boil; reduce heat and simmer, uncovered, 45 minutes. Stir in shrimp; simmer, uncovered, 10 minutes. Yield: 3½ quarts.

■ At The Landmark Townsquare in Bay St. Louis, you can enjoy the house specialty of Oyster Landmark in a charming restored home.

OYSTER LANDMARK

2 to 3 large cloves garlic, minced
2 tablespoons chopped green onions
¼ cup butter
½ teaspoon salt
¼ teaspoon pepper
16 fresh Select oysters, drained
2 cups sliced fresh mushrooms
Hot cooked noodles
Grated Parmesan cheese
Diced pimiento

Sauté garlic and green onions in butter in a heavy skillet 4 to 5 minutes or until tender. Stir in salt and pepper. Add the oysters and mushrooms, and cook over medium heat 5 to 8 minutes or until edges of oysters begin to curl. To serve, spoon over noodles, and sprinkle with Parmesan cheese and pimiento. Yield: 2 servings.

■ The Roussos take a lot of pride in the dishes they serve at their restaurant in Mobile. The specialty is seafood, including Roussos Sautéed Crabmeat.

ROUSSOS SAUTEED CRABMEAT

¾ cup chopped green onions with tops
½ pound fresh mushrooms, sliced
¼ cup butter
1 pound fresh lump crabmeat, drained
   and flaked
¼ to ⅓ cup cream sherry
Fresh parsley sprigs
Lemon wedges

Sauté onions and mushrooms in butter until tender. Add crabmeat and sherry; cook until thoroughly heated. Garnish with parsley and lemon wedges. Yield: 2 to 4 servings.

■ Eva and Binh Ly give meticulous attention to the dishes served at The Blue Rose in Pass Christian. Chicken Hawaiian is an especially popular luncheon dish and is always served on a bed of fresh lettuce with a variety of colorful vegetable garnishes surrounding it.

CHICKEN HAWAIIAN

1 large fresh pineapple
1½ cups chopped, cooked chicken
1 cup chopped celery
1 cup halved green grapes
½ cup coarsely chopped pecans, toasted
¼ cup mayonnaise
⅛ teaspoon salt
⅛ teaspoon pepper

Cut pineapple lengthwise into quarters. Scoop out pulp, leaving shells ¼ to ½ inch thick; set aside.

Cut enough pineapple pulp into bite-size pieces to measure 1 cup, discarding cores; reserve remaining pineapple for other uses. Combine 1 cup pineapple and remaining ingredients; toss gently. Spoon mixture into the pineapple shells. Yield: 4 servings.

MICROWAVE COOKERY

Dinner For Two In A Hurry

Wine and candlelight are all that's needed to complete this microwave menu for two. And when you're finished, there won't be a messy roasting pan or range top to clean.

To streamline the process, prepare the dessert a day ahead and place it in the refrigerator. With that out of the way, we suggest cooking the hens first. While they are microwaving and then standing the required six minutes, you can prepare the ingredients for the remaining recipes and begin cooking the fresh broccoli.

Prepare the soup last. Since it's thickened with flour and an egg yolk, it might become lumpy if allowed to sit very long. For best results, serve it immediately as an appetizer, straight from the microwave oven.

You might notice when preparing the hens that we refer to the use of a microwave rack and a microwave meat thermometer. Both should be readily available in kitchen shops or microwave specialty stores. The rack is placed inside a glass baking dish; it lifts the hens to allow the juices to drain.

Since the hens do not turn as brown as those that are conventionally cooked, it can be difficult to tell when they're done. Insert the microwave meat thermometer between the leg and thigh of the hen. It should register 185° when the hens are fully cooked. When placed in the center of the stuffing, the thermometer should register 165°.

If you prefer not to use the thermometer, carefully determine the doneness by looking for juices that run clear when the meat between the thigh and leg is pierced with a fork.

Curried Mushroom Soup
Orange-Glazed Stuffed
Cornish Hens
Lemon-Broccoli Goldenrod
Make-Ahead Kahlúa Delight

CURRIED
MUSHROOM SOUP

2 tablespoons butter or margarine
4 green onions with tops, chopped
¼ teaspoon curry powder
1 tablespoon all-purpose flour
1 cup chicken broth
1 cup milk
⅓ pound fresh mushrooms, chopped
¼ teaspoon salt
¼ teaspoon white pepper
¼ cup half-and-half
1 egg yolk

Place butter in a deep 1½-quart casserole. Microwave at HIGH for 45 seconds or until butter melts. Stir in onions and curry powder; microwave at HIGH for 1 minute or until onion is tender. Add flour, stirring until smooth. Gradually add broth and milk, stirring well. Microwave at HIGH for 4 minutes; stir well with a wire whisk. Add mushrooms, salt, and pepper. Microwave at HIGH for 2 to 3 minutes or until slightly thickened.

Combine half-and-half and egg yolk, stirring well. Gradually add about one-fourth of hot mixture to yolk mixture, stirring constantly; add to remaining hot mixture. Microwave at HIGH for 1½ minutes, stirring every 30 seconds until smooth and slightly thickened. Serve immediately. Yield: about 2⅔ cups.

ORANGE-GLAZED STUFFED
CORNISH HENS

¼ cup butter or margarine
⅓ cup orange marmalade
1 tablespoon orange juice
¼ teaspoon browning and seasoning sauce
3 tablespoons butter or margarine
2 tablespoons chopped onion
2 tablespoons diced celery
¼ cup chicken broth
1 cup herb-seasoned stuffing mix
2 (1¼-pound) Cornish hens, completely thawed

Place ¼ cup butter in a 2-cup glass measure; microwave at HIGH for 55 seconds or until melted. Stir in the orange marmalade, juice, and browning sauce. Microwave at HIGH for 45 seconds or until mixture is thoroughly heated. Set aside.

Combine 3 tablespoons butter, onion, and celery in a deep 1-quart casserole. Cover with heavy-duty plastic wrap, and microwave at HIGH for 2 minutes or until onion is tender. Stir in broth; microwave at HIGH for 40 seconds. Add stuffing mix, tossing gently until moistened. Set aside.

Remove giblets from hens, and reserve for use in another recipe. Rinse hens with cold water, and pat dry. Stuff hens lightly with stuffing mixture. Close cavities, and secure with wooden picks; truss. Twist the wing tips behind back. Make a small slit in back skin on each hen for release of steam.

Place hens, breast side down, on a microwave rack placed inside a 12- x 8- x 2-inch baking dish. Brush hens with marmalade mixture. Cover hens with a tent of waxed paper. Microwave at HIGH for 10 minutes.

Turn hens breast side up, and give each a half turn on rack. Brush hens with glaze, and cover with waxed paper tent. Microwave at HIGH for 3 minutes. Brush with glaze. Cover with tent, and microwave at HIGH an additional 4 to 7 minutes or until juices run clear when pierced with a fork between leg and thigh. Microwave meat thermometer should register 185° when inserted in center between leg and thigh and 165°

when inserted in center of stuffing. Brush hens with remaining glaze. Cover hens with foil, and let stand 4 to 6 minutes before serving. Yield: 2 servings.

LEMON-BROCCOLI GOLDENROD

¾ pound fresh broccoli
¼ cup water
⅓ cup mayonnaise
1 tablespoon lemon juice
½ teaspoon grated onion
⅛ teaspoon dried whole thyme
1 teaspoon grated lemon rind

Trim off large leaves of broccoli, and remove tough ends of lower stalks. Wash broccoli, and slice into separate spears. Arrange broccoli spears in a circle in a glass pieplate, placing stem ends toward the outside. Add water. Cover with heavy-duty plastic wrap, and microwave at HIGH for 4 to 6 minutes or until spears are tender. Drain well, and arrange on serving platter.

Combine mayonnaise, lemon juice, onion, and thyme in a 1-cup glass measure. Microwave at HIGH for 30 to 40 seconds or until thoroughly heated. Pour over broccoli. Sprinkle with lemon rind. Yield: 2 servings.

MAKE-AHEAD
KAHLUA DELIGHT

½ cup semisweet chocolate morsels
¼ cup sugar
2 tablespoons water
1 egg
2 tablespoons Kahlúa or other coffee-flavored liqueur
¼ teaspoon instant coffee granules
½ cup whipping cream, whipped
Additional whipped cream

Place chocolate morsels in a small glass bowl. Microwave at HIGH for 1½ minutes or until melted, stirring once. Set chocolate aside.

Combine sugar and water in a 1-cup glass measure. Microwave at HIGH for 1 minute or until boiling. Stir well until sugar dissolves.

Beat egg on medium speed of electric mixer. Gradually stir melted chocolate into egg; stir in Kahlúa and coffee granules. While beating at medium speed of electric mixer, slowly pour hot sugar syrup in a slow stream over egg mixture. Continue beating until blended. Fold in whipped cream.

Spoon into 2 cordial cups or stemmed glasses. Refrigerate at least 2 hours. Garnish with additional whipped cream before serving. Yield: 2 servings.

Plan For Leftover Ham

Leftover ham can do a lot more than fill the space between two slices of bread. Our readers mix it with vegetables and canned soup for a casserole and toss it with macaroni for a refreshing main-dish salad.

A cooked cured ham will keep in the refrigerator up to five days. Freezing is generally not recommended because of flavor and texture changes. But if the ham is frozen for no more than two months in an airtight container, these changes may not be a problem, especially if you combine the ham with other ingredients in a cooked dish.

Strips of ham are tossed with Cheddar cheese and cooked macaroni for Hearty Macaroni Salad, a perfect entrée for springtime luncheons.

HEARTY MACARONI SALAD

1 cup uncooked elbow macaroni
¾ pound cooked ham, cut into 1-inch strips
1½ cups diced sharp Cheddar cheese
1 cup chopped celery
½ cup chopped onion
½ cup chopped sweet pickle
½ cup commercial sour cream
2 tablespoons prepared mustard
Celery leaves (optional)

Cook macaroni according to package directions; drain. Rinse with cold water; drain well.

Combine macaroni and next 7 ingredients; toss gently. Cover and chill. Garnish with celery leaves, if desired. Yield: 6 servings. *Shirley Hodge, Delray Beach, Florida.*

CHEESY HAM DINNER

2 tablespoons chopped onion
2 tablespoons butter or margarine
3 tablespoons all-purpose flour
1½ cups milk
1 cup (4 ounces) shredded Cheddar cheese
1 (8½-ounce) can English peas, drained
¾ pound cubed cooked ham
1 (4-ounce) can mushroom stems and pieces, drained
2 tablespoons chopped ripe olives
Dash of chili powder
Dash of red pepper
Dash of black pepper
Hot cooked rice

Sauté onion in butter in a Dutch oven until tender. Reduce heat to low; add flour, and cook 1 minute, stirring constantly. Gradually add milk; cook over medium heat, stirring constantly, until mixture is thickened and bubbly. Add next 8 ingredients; cook over low heat 5 minutes, stirring often. Serve over hot cooked rice. Yield: 6 to 8 servings. *Craig R. McNees, Sarasota, Florida.*

CREAMY HAM MEDLEY

½ cup chopped onion
¼ cup thinly sliced celery
¼ cup chopped green pepper
2 tablespoons butter or margarine
2 tablespoons all-purpose flour
1 cup milk
1 cup cream-style cottage cheese
1 cup cubed cooked ham
2 cups cooked narrow egg noodles
½ teaspoon salt
⅛ teaspoon pepper
Paprika

Sauté vegetables in butter in a heavy saucepan until tender. Reduce heat to low; add flour, and cook 1 minute, stirring constantly. Gradually add milk and cottage cheese; cook over medium heat, stirring constantly, until mixture is thickened and bubbly. Stir in ham, noodles, salt, and pepper.

Spoon mixture into a greased 1-quart casserole; sprinkle with paprika. Bake at 350° for 25 minutes or until bubbly. Yield: 4 servings. *Jennie Kinnard, Mabank, Texas.*

SKILLET HAM-AND-VEGETABLES

½ pound cooked ham, cut into ½-inch strips
½ pound fresh mushrooms, sliced
4 small green onions, chopped
2 medium carrots, scraped and thinly sliced
2 medium tomatoes, peeled and chopped
2 medium potatoes, peeled and chopped
2 stalks celery, chopped
1 medium-size green pepper, cut into strips
1 (8-ounce) can tomato sauce
¼ cup commercial Italian salad dressing
1 tablespoon lemon juice
Dash of salt
Dash of pepper
Hot cooked rice

Combine all ingredients except rice in an electric skillet. Cover and cook at 350° for 15 to 20 minutes or until vegetables are tender, stirring occasionally. Serve over rice. Yield: 4 to 6 servings.

Gary Smith,
Jekyll Island, Georgia.

HAM RING

1 pound ground cooked ham
½ pound ground pork
1 cup soft breadcrumbs
¾ cup milk
1 egg, beaten
1 tablespoon prepared mustard
¼ cup firmly packed brown sugar
1 teaspoon prepared mustard
Cherry Sauce

Combine first 6 ingredients; press into a lightly greased 4-cup ring mold. Combine brown sugar and 1 teaspoon mustard; crumble over ham ring. Bake at 325° for 1 hour. Invert onto platter; serve hot with Cherry Sauce. Yield: 8 servings.

Cherry Sauce:

¼ cup sugar
2 tablespoons cornstarch
1 (16-ounce) can pitted dark sweet cherries, undrained
¼ cup Burgundy or other dry red wine

Combine sugar and cornstarch in a small saucepan. Drain cherries, and gradually add juice to sugar mixture. Cook over medium heat, stirring constantly, until thickened. Stir in cherries and Burgundy, and cook until heated. Yield: about 2¼ cups.

Evelyn Weisman,
Kingsville, Texas.

HAM BALLS

1½ pounds ground pork
1 pound ground cooked ham
2 cups cracker crumbs
2 eggs, beaten
½ cup milk
½ teaspoon salt
Raisin Sauce

Combine first 6 ingredients; chill. Shape into ten 2½-inch balls; place in a greased 13- x 9- x 2-inch baking dish. Bake at 350° for 15 minutes. Pour Raisin Sauce over ham balls; cover and bake 30 minutes. Uncover and bake 30 minutes, basting occasionally with pan drippings. Yield: 5 servings.

Raisin Sauce:

1 cup firmly packed brown sugar
½ cup vinegar
½ cup water
¼ cup raisins
1 teaspoon dry mustard

Combine all ingredients in a small saucepan. Cook mixture over medium heat until the sugar dissolves, stirring constantly. Yield: about 1¼ cups.

Sara Sellers,
New Providence, New Jersey.

VEGETABLE-AND-HAM CASSEROLE

2 large potatoes, peeled and thinly sliced
1 medium onion, thinly sliced
3 carrots, scraped and sliced
2 cups chopped cooked ham
1 (10¾-ounce) can cream of celery soup, undiluted
½ cup milk
Dash of freshly ground pepper
⅓ cup grated Parmesan cheese

Layer half each of potatoes, onion, carrots, and ham in a greased 2-quart baking dish.
Combine soup, milk, and pepper. Pour half of sauce over vegetable mixture in dish. Layer remaining vegetables and ham over sauce; top with remaining sauce. Cover and bake at 375° for 1 hour. Remove cover, and sprinkle with Parmesan cheese; bake an additional 10 minutes. Yield: 6 servings.

Carol Bowen,
Tifton, Georgia.

Make Frozen Fish The Entrée

Whether you live close to the water or inland, you can enjoy delicious fresh-tasting fish any time of the year with frozen fish fillets.

Unless you plan to cook frozen fish within a day or two after purchase, it should be placed in the freezer immediately. Thaw frozen fish in the refrigerator overnight or under cold running water. Never thaw fish at room temperature or in warm water. The thinner edges thaw faster than the thick pieces and may spoil before the entire piece of fish is defrosted.

BAKED FILLETS IN LEMON-CELERY SAUCE

2 (1-pound) packages frozen perch or flounder fillets, thawed
1 (10¾-ounce) can cream of celery soup, undiluted
¼ cup butter or margarine, melted
3 tablespoons finely chopped green pepper
2 tablespoons lemon juice
Paprika

Arrange fillets in a lightly greased 12- x 8- x 2-inch baking dish. Combine soup, butter, green pepper, and lemon juice; pour over fish. Sprinkle with paprika. Bake, uncovered, at 350° about 20 minutes or until fish flakes easily with a fork. Place fish under broiler 2 to 3 minutes or until lightly browned. Yield: 6 to 8 servings. *Sallie Speights, Lafayette, Louisiana.*

BROILED FISH FILLETS PIQUANTE

2 tablespoons butter or margarine, melted
1 tablespoon lemon juice
1 teaspoon minced onion
½ teaspoon salt
¼ teaspoon white pepper
¼ teaspoon dried whole marjoram
¼ teaspoon ground savory
1 (1-pound) package frozen perch fillets, thawed
1 tablespoon minced fresh parsley

Combine first 7 ingredients; stir well. Place fish in a lightly greased 11- x 7- x 2-inch shallow baking pan. Spoon half of butter mixture over fish. Broil 5 to 6 inches from heat 5 minutes or until fish flakes easily with a fork; transfer to a serving platter. Pour remaining butter mixture over fish; sprinkle with parsley. Yield: 4 servings. *Betty Wilkinson, Dothan, Alabama.*

CREAMY BAKED FILLETS

1 (1-pound) package frozen perch or halibut fillets, thawed
Freshly ground pepper
1½ tablespoons butter or margarine
1 (10¾-ounce) can cream of shrimp soup, undiluted
¼ cup grated Parmesan cheese
Paprika

Place fillets in a lightly greased 9-inch baking dish. Sprinkle with pepper; dot with butter. Spoon soup over fillets; sprinkle with cheese and paprika. Bake, uncovered, at 350° about 20 minutes or until fish flakes easily with a fork. Yield: 4 servings. *Kenneth Lawrence, Nashville, Tennessee.*

CRISPY FRIED FISH

⅓ cup cornmeal
½ teaspoon salt
⅛ teaspoon pepper
1 (1-pound) package frozen perch or
   flounder fillets, thawed
Vegetable oil

Combine cornmeal, salt, and pepper. Dredge fillets in cornmeal mixture. (Do not pat fish dry before dredging.)

Fry fillets in deep hot oil (375°) for 4 to 5 minutes or until golden brown; drain the fillets well on paper towels. Yield: about 4 servings.

Elizabeth Grimes,
Fremont, North Carolina.

BAKED FISH WITH BARBECUE SAUCE

3 tablespoons chopped onion
3 tablespoons chopped green pepper
1 tablespoon vegetable oil
1 (8-ounce) can tomato sauce
2 tablespoons brown sugar
2 tablespoons lemon juice
¼ teaspoon Worcestershire sauce
1 (1-pound) package frozen perch fillets,
   thawed
½ teaspoon salt
¼ teaspoon pepper

Sauté onion and green pepper in oil in a heavy saucepan until tender. Stir in next 4 ingredients. Bring to a boil; cover, reduce heat, and simmer 15 minutes, stirring occasionally.

Place fish fillets in a greased 12- x 8- x 2-inch baking dish; sprinkle with salt and pepper. Spoon sauce on top. Bake, uncovered, at 350° for 10 to 15 minutes or until fish flakes easily with a fork. Yield: about 4 servings.

Mrs. R. E. Bunker,
Bartlett, Texas.

From Our Kitchen To Yours

Learning how to achieve perfect results in baking takes some know-how. We put special emphasis on standardizing our mixing methods, baking times, and tests for doneness so you can end up with the same product. Tests for doneness can be vague at times, so we have some tips to reduce your guesswork when baking.

Tests for Doneness

Yeast Breads—Most yeast breads are baked at temperatures between 350°F and 425°F. For bread to be done on the inside when it reaches a golden brown color, oven temperature should not be higher than 450°F.

To be sure the bread is evenly baked, place the pan in the center of the oven. If more than one pan is to be baked in the same oven, leave space around each pan so heat can circulate freely.

The outward appearance is not always an accurate indication of doneness. Tap the crust lightly with your knuckles and listen for a hollow sound.

Cakes and Quick Breads—Many of our recipes for cakes and quick breads contain the words "when a wooden pick inserted in center comes out clean." Insert the pick in the thickest part of the cake or bread, for this is the last part to bake. The pick should come out clean, dry, and free of crumbs.

Quick breads often have a crack down the center of the loaf. Try to avoid this crack when testing for doneness because there's often some wetness near the crack, which might give a false reading.

Another sign to watch for when testing for doneness: Cakes and quick breads will pull away from sides of the pan when they are ready.

When testing cakes or quick breads, be careful to close the oven door as soon as possible after testing to prevent losing oven heat. Remember that unnecessary jarring can cause a cake to fall if it's not done.

Soufflés and Custards—Soufflés are very delicate and need to be tested carefully. Try to prevent any moving of the dish or sudden drafts of cold air. A soufflé will be done "when a knife inserted halfway between the center and the edge comes out clean." If a soufflé is removed from the oven too early, it will collapse.

A custard is done when "set." Use the same knife test for a custard that is used for a soufflé. When the custard is set, it does not jiggle or appear to be soupy when gently shaken.

Cookies—Cookies are often the most difficult to test for doneness. Since personal preference varies as to soft or crisp cookies, recipes give a range in baking time. Often the phrase "until lightly browned" is used to indicate doneness, too.

Let cookies cool completely before storing. To keep cookies fresh, store soft and chewy ones in an airtight container. Store crisp cookies in a jar with a loose-fitting lid.

He's A Connoisseur Of Cajun Cooking

Unlike many men who sit down with the newspaper after a busy day at work, Dr. Herbert Plauché of Baton Rouge heads for the kitchen. "My way to relax is to stir up something good," he says. He dons an apron and lets his imagination go to work, using whatever ingredients he can find.

Seafood Gumbo and Redfish Court Bouillon are two of his Cajun specialties. Each begins with a roux, which, he says, is the basis of almost any Cajun recipe. "It gives the dish character," he explains.

Herbert's recipes are followed by favorite recipes from other men who also like to cook.

SEAFOOD GUMBO

¾ cup vegetable oil
1 cup all-purpose flour
2 large onions, chopped
4 stalks celery, chopped
1 (16-ounce) can whole tomatoes,
   undrained and chopped
4 cloves garlic, minced
½ cup chopped fresh parsley
1 teaspoon dried whole thyme
1 teaspoon red pepper
1 bay leaf
4 (14½-ounce) cans chicken broth,
   undiluted
2 pounds medium shrimp, peeled and
   deveined
1 pound fresh crabmeat
2 to 3 dozen fresh oysters, shucked
1 pound fresh crab claws (optional)
1½ teaspoons salt
½ teaspoon pepper
Hot cooked rice
Chopped fresh parsley
Chopped green onions
Gumbo filé

Heat oil in a large Dutch oven. Add flour, and cook over medium heat 10 to 15 minutes, stirring constantly, until roux is the color of a copper penny. Stir in onions and celery; cook 10 minutes, stirring occasionally. Add next 6 ingredients and cook 10 minutes, stirring occasionally. Stir in chicken broth; bring to a boil. Cover, reduce heat, and simmer 30 minutes, stirring occasionally.

Add shrimp and 1 pound crabmeat; cover and simmer 15 minutes. Add oysters and crab claws, if desired; cover and simmer 15 minutes. Stir in salt and pepper. Remove bay leaf. Serve gumbo over hot cooked rice. Garnish each serving with chopped parsley, green onions, and ¼ teaspoon gumbo filé. Yield: about 5 quarts.

REDFISH COURT BOUILLON

1 (4-pound) redfish
2 quarts water
¾ cup vegetable oil
1 cup all-purpose flour
2 medium onions, chopped
4 stalks celery, chopped
½ cup chopped green pepper
2 (16-ounce) cans tomatoes, undrained and chopped
½ cup chopped fresh parsley
½ cup chopped green onions
3 tablespoons grated lemon rind
2 bay leaves
1 teaspoon dried whole thyme
1 to 1½ teaspoons salt
½ teaspoon ground allspice
½ teaspoon pepper
½ teaspoon red pepper
4 whole cloves
Hot cooked rice
Chopped fresh parsley (optional)
Chopped green onions (optional)

Fillet fish, reserving head and bones. Cut fillets into 3- x 2-inch pieces, and set aside in refrigerator. Combine head, bones, and 2 quarts water in a large Dutch oven; bring to a boil. Cover, reduce heat, and simmer 1 hour. Strain stock through layers of cheesecloth; repeat procedure, if necessary. Set aside 1 quart stock; discard head and bones.

Heat oil in a large Dutch oven; add flour, and cook over medium heat 10 minutes, stirring constantly, until roux is the color of light peanut butter. Add onion, celery, and green pepper; cook 15 minutes, stirring occasionally. Add reserved fish stock and next 11 ingredients; bring to a boil. Cover, reduce heat, and simmer 1 hour, stirring occasionally. Add fish; cover and simmer an additional 30 minutes, stirring occasionally. Serve mixture over hot cooked rice. Sprinkle each serving with parsley and green onions, if desired. Yield: about 3 quarts.

Tip: Cooked rice freezes well. It can be stored in the refrigerator up to one week, or in the freezer as long as three months.

SPICY BARBECUED SPARERIBS

5 pounds spareribs
1 cup firmly packed brown sugar
½ cup catsup
⅓ cup soy sauce
¼ cup Worcestershire sauce
¼ cup chili sauce
2 cloves garlic, crushed
2 teaspoons prepared mustard
⅛ teaspoon pepper

Cut ribs into serving-size pieces. Combine remaining ingredients, mixing well; pour into a large shallow dish. Add ribs; cover and refrigerate at least 2 hours, turning ribs occasionally.

Drain ribs, reserving marinade. Place ribs, bone side down, on grill over slow coals. Grill 30 minutes, turning ribs frequently. Brush ribs with sauce; cook an additional 30 minutes, basting and turning frequently. Yield: 4 to 6 servings.
Patrick Christman,
Panama City, Florida.

SWEET-AND-SOUR LEMON CHICKEN

8 chicken breast halves, skinned and boned
¼ cup vegetable oil
2 tablespoons soy sauce
1 tablespoon gin or vodka
3 egg whites
1 cup all-purpose flour
Peanut oil
1 cup chicken broth
½ cup vinegar
¾ cup sugar
2 tablespoons cornstarch
1 tablespoon water
Grated rind and juice of 1 lemon
3 small carrots, cut into julienne strips
3 green onions, cut into strips
½ large green pepper, cut into strips
1 (8-ounce) can crushed pineapple, drained
1 teaspoon lemon extract (optional)
¼ head of lettuce, shredded

Place chicken in a shallow container. Combine next 3 ingredients; pour over chicken, turning to coat. Cover and refrigerate 30 minutes.

Drain chicken, and discard marinade. Beat egg whites (at room temperature) until foamy. Add chicken to egg whites, and toss to coat; dredge in flour.

Heat ½ inch peanut oil in a large skillet to 350°; add chicken and fry 20 to 25 minutes, turning once. Drain chicken well on paper towels.

Combine next 6 ingredients in a medium saucepan; cook over low heat, stirring constantly, until thickened and

bubbly. Add carrots, green onions, green pepper, and pineapple; stir well. Remove from heat, and stir in lemon extract, if desired. Set aside.

Cut chicken crosswise into 1-inch slices. Arrange on shredded lettuce on a platter. Pour sauce over chicken. Serve immediately. Yield: 4 servings.
Trey Obenshain,
Augusta, Georgia.

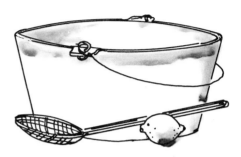

CRISPY FRIED FLOUNDER

2 eggs, beaten
¾ cup plus 2 tablespoons milk
1½ cups cornmeal
¾ teaspoon salt
¼ teaspoon garlic powder
½ teaspoon pepper
¼ teaspoon red pepper
3 pounds flounder fillets, cut into serving-size portions
All-purpose flour
Vegetable oil
Fresh parsley sprigs (optional)
Fluted lemon halves (optional)

Combine first 7 ingredients in a large bowl; mix well. Dredge fish in flour, coating both sides lightly. Dip fish into batter. Fry in deep hot oil (330°) until fillets float to the top and are golden brown; drain well. Serve hot. Garnish with parsley and lemon, if desired. Yield: 6 servings.
Jeff Leonard,
Manassas, Virginia.

BARBECUED SHRIMP

2 pounds unpeeled jumbo shrimp
¾ cup butter or margarine
¼ cup fresh lime juice

Peel and devein shrimp. Melt butter; stir in lime juice. Dip shrimp in butter mixture. Thread tail and neck of each shrimp on skewers so shrimp will lie flat. Grill over medium-hot coals 3 to 4 minutes on each side. Serve butter mixture with shrimp. Yield: 6 servings.
Bruce A. Gearhart,
Indian Harbour Beach, Florida.

Nestle Eggs Into A Bread Ring

In many countries, festive breads are a part of the Easter celebration. Many Greeks prepare egg-filled loaves like this one.

EASTER EGG BREAD

1 package dry yeast
½ cup warm water (105° to 115°)
½ cup boiling water
1 teaspoon ground cinnamon
3 eggs
¾ cup sugar
¼ cup butter or margarine, melted
½ cup warm milk (105° to 115°)
About 6 cups all-purpose flour
1 teaspoon baking powder
½ teaspoon salt
1 egg yolk, beaten
10 hard-cooked eggs, unshelled and dyed
1½ cups sifted powdered sugar
2 to 3 tablespoons milk
Decorator candies

Dissolve yeast in warm water; let stand 5 minutes.

Combine boiling water and cinnamon, stirring well; set aside.

Combine 3 eggs and ¾ cup sugar in a large mixing bowl; beat well. Add butter, and beat until blended. Skim off ¼ cup clear cinnamon water, and add to egg mixture. Discard remaining cinnamon water. Stir in yeast mixture and ½ cup warm milk, blending well.

Combine flour, baking powder, and salt; mix well. Gradually stir dry ingredients into batter to make a soft dough.

Turn dough out onto a lightly floured surface, and knead 8 to 10 minutes or until smooth and elastic.

Divide dough into quarters. Roll each quarter into a 22-inch rope. Pinch 2 ropes together at one end to seal. Twist ropes together. Shape twist into a ring, and pinch ends together to seal. Place on a greased baking sheet. Repeat with remaining 2 ropes.

Cover and let rise in a warm place (85°), free from drafts, 1½ hours or until doubled in bulk. Brush rings with beaten egg yolk. Bake at 350° for 25 minutes or until golden brown. Gently push 5 dyed eggs into each loaf immediately when loaves are removed from oven. Combine powdered sugar and 2 to 3 tablespoons milk, stirring well. Drizzle over bread while warm; sprinkle with decorator candies. Yield: 2 loaves.
Tina Jebeles,
Birmingham, Alabama.

Delightful Desserts To Make Ahead

If you're a chocolate fan, here's a dessert you'll love: Chocolate Supreme is rich with sweet baking chocolate. Like our other chilled desserts, Chocolate Supreme should be made ahead of time, making last-minute meal preparation easier.

CHOCOLATE SUPREME

1 (4-ounce) bar sweet baking chocolate
3 tablespoons water
1 teaspoon vanilla extract
1 (4-ounce) container frozen whipped
  topping, thawed
½ cup chopped almonds, toasted
Additional frozen whipped topping,
  thawed (optional)
Sliced almonds, toasted (optional)

Combine chocolate and water in a small heavy saucepan; cook over low heat, stirring constantly, until chocolate melts. Cool; stir in vanilla. Fold in next 2 ingredients; spoon into individual serving dishes. Chill 1 to 2 hours; garnish with additional whipped topping and sliced almonds, if desired. Yield: 4 to 6 servings.
Lisa Cobb,
Rusk, Texas.

LAYERED ICE CREAM DESSERT

4 (1-ounce) squares sweet baking chocolate
½ cup butter or margarine
⅔ cup sugar
1 (5.33-ounce) can evaporated milk
⅛ teaspoon salt
2 teaspoons vanilla extract
24 chocolate wafers, crushed
¼ cup butter or margarine, melted
½ gallon vanilla ice cream, softened
1 cup whipping cream, whipped
¼ cup chopped pecans

Melt chocolate and ½ cup butter in top of a double boiler; stir in sugar, evaporated milk, and salt. Bring mixture to a boil; reduce heat and cook 4 minutes, stirring constantly. Remove from heat; stir in vanilla. Let cool.

Combine chocolate wafer crumbs and melted butter; press firmly into a 13- x 9- x 2-inch pan. Cool. Spread ice cream evenly over crumb mixture; top with chocolate sauce. Spread with whipped cream; sprinkle with pecans. Cover and freeze until firm. Let stand at room temperature 5 minutes before slicing. Yield: 15 servings.
Robert L. Ralston,
Parkersburg, West Virginia.

BANANA PUDDING

1 cup sugar
¼ cup cornstarch
¼ teaspoon salt
2 cups milk
3 eggs, separated
2 tablespoons butter or margarine
1 teaspoon vanilla extract
24 vanilla wafers
3 large ripe bananas, sliced
¼ teaspoon cream of tartar
¼ cup plus 2 tablespoons sugar
½ teaspoon vanilla extract

Combine sugar, cornstarch, and salt in top of a double boiler; stir in milk, and bring water to a boil. Reduce heat to low; cook, stirring constantly, 10 to 12 minutes or until slightly thickened.

Beat egg yolks until thick and lemon colored. Gradually stir about one-fourth of hot mixture into yolks; add to remaining hot mixture, stirring constantly. Cook, stirring constantly, until mixture thickens. Remove from heat, and gently stir in butter and 1 teaspoon vanilla.

Layer half of vanilla wafers in a 2½-quart baking dish; top with half of bananas. Pour half of filling over bananas. Repeat layers.

Combine egg whites (at room temperature) and cream of tartar; beat until foamy. Gradually add ¼ cup plus 2 tablespoons sugar, 1 tablespoon at a time, beating until stiff peaks form.

Beat in remaining ½ teaspoon vanilla. Spread meringue over filling, sealing to edge of dish. Bake at 350° for 10 to 12 minutes or until golden brown. Let cool to room temperature; chill. Yield: 6 servings.
Peggy McEwen,
Columbiana, Alabama.

LEMON TWIRL PIE

1 tablespoon grated lemon rind
¾ cup lemon juice
½ cup butter or margarine
½ cup sugar
¼ teaspoon salt
5 eggs
½ gallon vanilla ice cream, softened
2 (9-inch) graham cracker crusts
¼ cup chopped almonds, toasted

Combine first 5 ingredients in a small saucepan; cook over low heat, stirring constantly, until thoroughly heated.

Beat eggs until thick and lemon colored. Gradually stir about one-fourth of hot mixture into eggs; add to remaining hot mixture, stirring constantly. Cook over medium heat, stirring constantly, until mixture boils. Remove from heat, and let cool.

Spread one-fourth of ice cream in each pie crust; pour half of lemon mixture over each, spreading evenly. Top each with one-fourth of ice cream; sprinkle each with half of almonds. Freeze. Yield: two 9-inch pies.

Patsy Murphy,
Miami, Florida.

LEMON-CREAM CHEESE DESSERT

3 cups round toasted oat cereal, finely crushed
⅓ cup butter or margarine, melted
1 tablespoon sugar
1 teaspoon ground cinnamon
1 (8-ounce) package cream cheese, softened
1 (14-ounce) can sweetened condensed milk
¼ cup lemon juice
1 teaspoon vanilla extract

Combine crumbs, butter, sugar, and cinnamon; mix well. Reserve 2 tablespoons mixture; press remaining crumb mixture into an 8-inch square baking pan. Bake at 375° for 9 minutes.

Beat cream cheese in a mixing bowl until light and fluffy. Gradually add sweetened condensed milk, beating until smooth. Stir in lemon juice and vanilla, mixing until well blended.

Spoon filling into prepared crust. Sprinkle the reserved crumb mixture over filling. Chill at least 4 hours. Yield: 9 servings.

Delaine Haraway,
Killen, Alabama.

ORANGE FLAN

¾ cup sugar
½ cup sugar
2 eggs, slightly beaten
2 tablespoons Grand Marnier or other orange-flavored liqueur
½ teaspoon vanilla extract
¼ teaspoon ground nutmeg
¼ teaspoon ground cinnamon
¼ teaspoon ground allspice
Dash of salt
2 cups milk, scalded and cooled

Sprinkle ¾ cup sugar evenly in a heavy skillet; place over low heat. Caramelize sugar by stirring often until sugar melts and is a light golden brown. Divide syrup evenly among six 6-ounce custard cups, tipping each cup quickly to evenly coat the bottom. Allow syrup to harden in cups about 10 minutes.

Combine next 8 ingredients in a mixing bowl, blending well. Gradually add scalded milk, stirring constantly.

Pour over caramelized sugar in custard cups. Place cups in a 13- x 9- x 2-inch baking pan; pour about 1 inch of hot water into baking pan.

Bake at 350° for 45 to 50 minutes or until knife inserted in center comes out clean. Remove custard cups from water; cool. Chill thoroughly. Unmold flans onto individual dessert plates to serve. Yield: 6 servings.

Sheree Garvin,
Wilkesboro, North Carolina.

Spice Up The Biscuits

Biscuits are a Southern specialty and with the recipes here, you can bring some unique flavor to the table. Our readers used their creativity by stirring sausage, pepperoni, Roquefort cheese, herbs, and other ingredients into basic biscuit dough.

PEPPERONI BISCUITS

2 cups biscuit mix
¾ cup shredded pepperoni
⅔ cup milk

Combine all ingredients; stir with a fork just until the dry ingredients are moistened.

Turn dough out onto a lightly floured surface; knead 5 times. Roll dough to ½-inch thickness; cut with a 2½-inch biscuit cutter. Place biscuits on a lightly greased baking sheet. Bake at 450° for 8 to 10 minutes or until golden brown. Yield: 10 biscuits.

Mrs. Harlan J. Stone,
Ocala, Florida.

SAUSAGE BISCUIT BITES

¾ pound hot bulk pork sausage
2⅔ cups all-purpose flour
2 tablespoons sugar
1 teaspoon baking powder
½ teaspoon baking soda
½ teaspoon salt
½ cup shortening
1 package dry yeast
¼ cup warm water (105° to 115°)
1 cup buttermilk
Melted butter or margarine

Cook sausage in a skillet until browned, stirring to crumble; drain well, and set aside.

Combine next 5 ingredients, mixing well; cut in shortening with a pastry blender until mixture resembles coarse meal. Dissolve yeast in warm water; let stand 5 minutes. Add yeast mixture to buttermilk, stirring well. Add buttermilk mixture to dry ingredients, stirring just until the dry ingredients are moistened. Knead in sausage. Turn dough out onto a lightly floured surface; knead lightly 3 to 4 times.

Roll dough to ½-inch thickness; cut with a 1¾-inch round cutter. Place biscuits on an ungreased baking sheet. Brush tops with melted butter. Bake at 425° for 10 minutes or until golden brown. Yield: 3 dozen biscuits.

Note: To freeze, place uncooked biscuits on an ungreased baking sheet; cover and freeze until firm. Transfer frozen biscuits to plastic bags. To bake, place frozen biscuits on an ungreased baking sheet; bake at 425° for 10 minutes.

Martha Martin,
Vardaman, Mississippi.

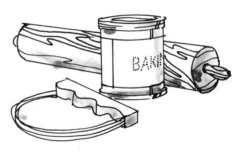

HERBED ROQUEFORT BISCUITS

1 (3-ounce) package Roquefort cheese, crumbled
2 tablespoons minced green onion tops
1 teaspoon dried whole basil
½ teaspoon dried whole thyme
2 cups all-purpose flour
1 tablespoon baking powder
½ teaspoon salt
¼ teaspoon baking soda
¼ cup plus 2 tablespoons cold, unsalted butter, cut into pieces
¾ cup buttermilk

Combine first 4 ingredients in a small bowl; set aside.

Combine flour, baking powder, salt, and soda in a medium bowl. Cut in cheese mixture and butter with a pastry blender until mixture resembles coarse meal; stir in buttermilk. Turn dough out onto a floured surface, and knead lightly 7 to 8 times.

Roll dough to ½-inch thickness; cut with a 2½-inch biscuit cutter. Place biscuits on a lightly greased baking sheet. Bake at 450° for 13 to 15 minutes. Yield: 14 biscuits.

Alma Stanton,
Richmond, Virginia.

RYE BISCUITS

1½ cups all-purpose flour
1½ cups rye flour
2 tablespoons baking powder
½ teaspoon salt
1 teaspoon caraway seeds
¾ cup shortening
1 cup plus 2 tablespoons milk

Combine the first 5 ingredients, and mix well; cut in shortening with a pastry blender until mixture resembles coarse meal. Add milk, stirring until dry ingredients are moistened. Turn dough out onto a lightly floured surface; knead lightly 8 to 10 times.

Roll dough to ½-inch thickness; cut with a 2-inch biscuit cutter. Place biscuits on an ungreased baking sheet. Bake at 450° for 10 to 12 minutes. Yield: about 15 biscuits.

Note: To freeze, place uncooked biscuits on an ungreased baking sheet; cover and freeze until firm. Transfer frozen biscuits to plastic bags. To bake, place frozen biscuits on an ungreased baking sheet; bake at 400° for 20 to 23 minutes.

Patricia Boschen,
Ashland, Virginia.

Count On Eggs For Brunch

Whether you want a quick entrée or one to make ahead, eggs are the answer for a delicious brunch main dish. Whip up an omelet, a casserole, or a cheesy seafood quiche with our recipes.

SMOKED OYSTER OMELETS

½ cup chopped fresh mushrooms
¼ cup chopped shallots
1 tablespoon butter or margarine
¼ cup dry white wine or vermouth
1 (3.66-ounce) can smoked oysters, drained and chopped
¼ cup peeled chopped tomato
2 tablespoons chopped fresh parsley
½ teaspoon lemon juice
Salt and pepper to taste
8 eggs
¼ cup water
2 tablespoons butter or margarine

Sauté mushrooms and shallots in 1 tablespoon butter in a skillet until tender. Add wine; cook over medium heat until liquid is absorbed. Stir in next 5 ingredients; cook until heated.

Combine eggs and ¼ cup water; mix just until blended.

Heat a 10-inch omelet pan or heavy skillet over medium heat until hot enough to sizzle a drop of water. Add 1 tablespoon butter; rotate pan to coat bottom. Pour in half of egg mixture. As mixture starts to cook, gently lift edges of omelet with a spatula, and tilt pan so uncooked portion flows underneath.

When egg mixture is set, spoon half of oyster mixture over half of omelet. Loosen omelet with a spatula; fold in half, and slide onto a serving plate. Repeat with remaining ingredients. Yield: 4 servings. *Cynthia Stewart Neely,*
Charlotte, North Carolina.

QUICK CRAB QUICHE

Pastry for 9-inch deep-dish pie
3 eggs, beaten
1 (6-ounce) can crabmeat, drained and flaked
1 (2.8-ounce) can fried onion rings, crushed
1 (8-ounce) carton commercial sour cream
1 cup (4 ounces) shredded Cheddar cheese

Line a 9-inch deep-dish pieplate with pastry. Trim excess pastry around edges; fold edges under, and flute. Prick bottom and sides of pastry with a fork. Bake at 400° for 3 minutes; remove from oven, and gently prick with a fork. Bake 5 minutes longer. Cool.

Combine remaining ingredients, mixing well. Spoon into pastry shell; bake at 350° for 35 minutes or until set. Let stand 10 minutes before serving. Yield: one 9-inch quiche. *Peggy C. Brown,*
Winston-Salem, North Carolina.

SPINACH-CHEESE PUFF

12 slices day-old bread
2 cups (8 ounces) shredded Cheddar cheese
1 (10-ounce) package frozen chopped spinach, thawed
1 (4½-ounce) jar sliced mushrooms, drained
4 eggs
2½ cups milk
1 tablespoon grated onion
½ teaspoon prepared mustard
¼ teaspoon salt
1 teaspoon seasoned salt
Dash of red pepper
Dash of pepper

Trim crusts from bread. Arrange 6 bread slices in a greased 13- x 9- x 2-inch baking dish; sprinkle cheese over bread. Drain spinach, and squeeze to remove excess liquid. Arrange spinach and mushrooms over cheese; place 6 remaining bread slices on top.

Combine remaining ingredients; beat well, and pour over casserole. Cover; chill several hours or overnight.

Uncover and bake at 325° for 1 hour. Serve immediately. Yield: 6 servings.
Mrs. John L. Paul,
Columbia, South Carolina.

Bake A Batch Of Chocolate Snaps

A handful of crisp chocolate cookies with a glass of cold milk makes a great afternoon snack.

CHOCOLATE-MINT SNAPS

4 (1-ounce) squares unsweetened chocolate
1¼ cups shortening
2 cups sugar
2 eggs
⅓ cup corn syrup
2½ tablespoons water
2 teaspoons peppermint extract
1 teaspoon vanilla extract
4 cups all-purpose flour
2 teaspoons baking soda
½ teaspoon salt
¼ cup plus 2 tablespoons sugar

Melt chocolate over hot water in top of double boiler. Remove from heat.

Cream shortening; gradually add 2 cups sugar, beating until light and fluffy. Add melted chocolate, eggs, corn syrup, water, and flavorings; mix well. Combine flour, soda, and salt; add to creamed mixture, beating until blended.

Shape dough into 1-inch balls, and roll in remaining sugar. Place on ungreased cookie sheets; bake at 350° for 10 minutes. Cool 5 minutes; remove to wire racks, and cool completely. Yield: 10½ dozen. *Lawrence L. Clapp,*
Contonment, Florida.

Right: Make use of the South's plentiful produce with party appetizers. From front to back: Endive Boats, Caviar Potatoes, Tomato Bites, Dilled Baby Carrots, Stuffed Snow Peas, and Cheesy Cucumber Slices (recipes on page 80).

Page 100: *It's easy to enjoy desserts while dieting with Peach-Yogurt Ice (page 83) or Strawberries Juliet (page 82).*

Far left: *Serve Orange Pork Chops (page 81) on a bed of rice to capture more of the clove- and cinnamon-flavored orange sauce.*

Above: *Sautéed Crab Crêpes (page 84) are filled with crabmeat and baked with a topping of Mushroom-Wine Sauce.*

Right: *The Gulf Coast offers an abundance of fish and shellfish. Sautéed Crabmeat (page 88) is a house specialty at a local restaurant in Mobile, Alabama.*

Sunday Night Favorites

When you've cooked a large meal for Sunday lunch, it's hard to get excited about cooking supper. So give yourself a break and put together one of these simple main dishes. They'll turn Sunday supper into a relaxing occasion you'll look forward to.

SAUSAGE STRATA

6 slices white bread, crusts removed
1 pound bulk pork sausage
1 teaspoon prepared mustard
¾ cup (3 ounces) shredded Swiss cheese
3 eggs, slightly beaten
1¼ cups milk
⅔ cup half-and-half
¼ teaspoon salt
Dash of pepper
1 teaspoon Worcestershire sauce

Line a buttered 13- x 9- x 2-inch baking dish with bread.

Crumble sausage in a medium skillet; cook over medium heat until browned, stirring occasionally. Drain well. Add mustard, stirring well. Spread sausage over bread; sprinkle with cheese.

Combine remaining ingredients; beat well, and pour over sausage and cheese. Bake at 350° for 25 minutes or until set. Cut into squares, and serve immediately. Yield: 6 to 8 servings.

Joy M. Hall,
Lucedale, Mississippi.

SPANISH OMELET

8 eggs
½ cup water
¼ teaspoon salt
1 (4-ounce) can chopped green chiles, drained
¼ cup finely chopped onion
¼ cup butter or margarine, divided
1 cup (4 ounces) shredded Monterey Jack or Cheddar cheese
1 (8-ounce) jar taco or picante sauce

Combine eggs, water, and salt; beat well. Stir in chiles and onion.

For each omelet, melt 1 tablespoon butter in an 8-inch omelet pan or heavy skillet until just hot enough to sizzle a drop of water; pour in one-fourth of egg mixture. As mixture starts to cook, gently lift edges of omelet and tilt pan to allow uncooked portion to flow underneath. When egg mixture is set and no longer flows freely, sprinkle ¼ cup cheese over half of omelet. Fold omelet in half, and place on a warm platter. Repeat procedure with remaining ingredients. Serve with taco sauce. Yield: 4 servings.

Mrs. Gary Ferguson,
Corsicana, Texas.

CORNBREAD SKILLET CASSEROLE

2 eggs, slightly beaten
1 cup yellow cornmeal
2 teaspoons baking soda
1 teaspoon salt
1 (17-ounce) can cream-style corn
1 cup milk
¼ cup vegetable oil
1 pound ground beef
2 cups (8 ounces) shredded Cheddar cheese
1 large onion, chopped
2 to 4 jalapeño peppers, finely chopped

Combine first 7 ingredients in a bowl, and set aside. Cook ground beef until browned; drain well, and set aside.

Pour half of cornmeal mixture into a greased 10½-inch cast-iron skillet. Sprinkle evenly with beef; top with cheese, onion, and peppers. Pour remaining batter over top. Bake at 350° for 45 to 50 minutes. Let stand 5 minutes before serving. Yield: 6 to 8 servings.

Stephen H. Badgett,
Memphis, Tennessee.

BUTTERMILK PANCAKES

1 cup all-purpose flour
1 teaspoon baking soda
1 tablespoon sugar
½ teaspoon salt
1 egg
1 cup plus 2 tablespoons buttermilk
1 tablespoon vegetable oil

Combine first 4 ingredients. Combine egg, buttermilk, and oil; slowly stir into dry ingredients.

For each pancake, pour about ¼ cup batter onto a hot, lightly greased griddle. Turn pancakes when tops are covered with bubbles and edges are brown. Serve with syrup. Yield: eight 4-inch pancakes.

Mrs. Theron L. Trimble,
Pensacola, Florida.

Tip: To determine the size or capacity of a utensil, fill a liquid measure with water, and pour into utensil. Repeat until utensil is full, noting amount of water used. To determine the dimensions, measure from the inside edges.

Stuff Chicken With Crab

Next time you have company for dinner, serve Crab-Stuffed Chicken. It's not only delicious, but elegant.

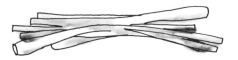

CRAB-STUFFED CHICKEN

2 tablespoons butter or margarine
¼ cup all-purpose flour
¾ cup milk
¾ cup chicken broth
⅓ cup Chablis or other dry white wine
⅓ cup chopped green onions
1 tablespoon butter or margarine
1 (6-ounce) package frozen crabmeat, thawed and drained
1 (4-ounce) can mushroom stems and pieces, drained and chopped
½ cup cracker crumbs
1 tablespoon chopped fresh parsley
½ teaspoon salt
¼ teaspoon pepper
8 chicken breast halves, boned and skinned
1 cup (4 ounces) shredded Swiss cheese
1 teaspoon paprika
Hot cooked rice

Melt 2 tablespoons butter in a heavy saucepan over low heat; add flour, stirring until smooth. Cook 1 minute, stirring constantly. Combine milk, broth, and wine; gradually add to flour mixture. Cook over medium heat, stirring constantly, until thickened and bubbly. Set sauce aside.

Sauté green onions in 1 tablespoon butter until tender. Stir in crabmeat, mushrooms, cracker crumbs, parsley, salt, and pepper. Stir in 2 tablespoons sauce.

Place each chicken breast half on a sheet of waxed paper. Flatten chicken to ¼-inch thickness, using a meat mallet or rolling pin.

Spoon ¼ cup crabmeat mixture in center of each chicken breast half. Fold opposite ends over and place, seam side down, in a greased 13- x 9- x 2-inch baking dish. Pour remaining sauce over the chicken.

Cover dish, and bake at 350° for 1 hour. Sprinkle with cheese and paprika; bake an additional minute or until cheese melts. Serve over hot cooked rice. Yield: 8 servings.

Maxine C. Moses,
Birmingham, Alabama.

Southern Breads With A Tradition

If you're a true Southerner, you're already well acquainted with buttermilk biscuits, golden corn sticks, and spoonbread. But if you can't find a recipe that compares to one your grandmother made, try one of the following.

FLUFFY BUTTERMILK BISCUITS

2 cups self-rising flour
1½ teaspoons baking powder
1½ teaspoons sugar
⅓ cup shortening
1 cup buttermilk
Melted butter or margarine

Combine flour, baking powder, and sugar; mix well. Cut in shortening with a pastry blender until mixture resembles coarse meal.

Add buttermilk, stirring until dry ingredients are moistened. Turn dough out onto a floured surface; knead lightly 3 or 4 times. Dough will be soft.

Roll dough to ½-inch thickness; cut with a 2½-inch biscuit cutter. Place biscuits on a greased baking sheet. Brush tops of biscuits with melted butter, and bake at 375° for 18 to 20 minutes or until lightly browned. Brush with melted butter. Yield: 9 biscuits.
Mildred Bickley,
Bristol, Virginia.

HUSH PUPPIES

1 cup cornmeal
½ cup all-purpose flour
2 teaspoons baking powder
1 teaspoon garlic salt
½ teaspoon salt
½ cup minced onion
1 green onion with top, chopped
1 egg, beaten
1 cup milk
Vegetable oil

Combine first 5 ingredients in a mixing bowl. Add remaining ingredients; stir well. Let batter stand 5 minutes.

Carefully drop batter by level tablespoonfuls into deep hot oil (370°); cook only a few at a time, turning once. Fry 3 to 5 minutes or until hush puppies are golden brown. Drain well on paper towels. Yield: about 2 dozen.
Mrs. John Woods,
Memphis, Tennessee.

SKILLET CORNBREAD

1½ cups yellow cornmeal
2 tablespoons sugar
1 teaspoon salt
½ teaspoon baking soda
1 egg, beaten
1½ cups buttermilk
2 to 3 tablespoons bacon drippings

Combine dry ingredients; add egg and buttermilk, mixing well.

Grease a 9-inch cast-iron skillet with bacon drippings; heat in a 400° oven for 3 minutes or until very hot.

Pour batter into hot skillet, and bake at 400° for 20 to 25 minutes or until golden brown. Yield: 8 to 10 servings.
Mrs. Joe V. Pool,
Ennis, Texas.

BLUE RIBBON CORN STICKS

½ cup all-purpose flour
½ cup yellow cornmeal
1 to 2 tablespoons sugar
2 teaspoons baking powder
¼ teaspoon salt
1 egg, beaten
½ cup milk
2 tablespoons vegetable oil

Combine dry ingredients; mix well. Add egg, milk, and oil; stir until batter is smooth.

Place a well-greased cast-iron corn stick pan in a 425° oven for 3 minutes or until very hot. Remove pan from oven; spoon batter into pan, filling two-thirds full. Bake at 425° for 10 to 12 minutes or until lightly browned. Yield: 12 corn sticks.
Jane Hancock,
Madison, Alabama.

OLD VIRGINIA SPOONBREAD

3 cups milk, divided
¾ cup cornmeal
2 eggs, separated
2 tablespoons butter or margarine
1 teaspoon baking powder
1 teaspoon salt

Scald 2 cups milk in top of double boiler. Combine remaining 1 cup milk and cornmeal; mix well. Add cornmeal mixture to scalded milk; cook over low heat 30 minutes, stirring frequently. Remove from heat.

Beat egg yolks until thick and lemon colored. Gradually stir about one-fourth of the hot mixture into yolks. Add egg yolk mixture, butter, baking powder, and salt to the remaining hot mixture, stirring constantly.

Beat egg whites (at room temperature) until stiff but not dry. Gently fold into cornmeal mixture. Pour into a lightly greased 2-quart baking dish. Bake at 375° for 25 to 30 minutes. Yield: 6 servings.
Mrs. C. Robert Bauer,
Charlottesville, Virginia.

A Unique Vegetable Soup

One look at this recipe and you'll know that it isn't an ordinary vegetable soup. Just simmer a rich spiced broth from beef ribs, strain the stock, and stir in the rib meat, barley, tomatoes, carrots, peas, leeks, and cabbage. Curry powder and tarragon add to the unique flavor. Serve the soup hot with crusty bread and a refreshing fruit salad.

HEARTY VEGETABLE-BEEF SOUP

3 pounds beef short ribs
1½ quarts water
2 stalks celery with leaves, thinly sliced
1 medium onion, quartered
3 sprigs fresh parsley
2 teaspoons salt
10 whole black peppercorns
1 bay leaf
1 (28-ounce) can whole tomatoes, undrained
¾ cup thinly sliced carrots
½ cup fine barley
1 teaspoon salt
¼ teaspoon curry powder
¾ teaspoon minced fresh tarragon or ¼ teaspoon dried whole tarragon
1 (10-ounce) package frozen English peas, thawed
1 cup thinly sliced leeks
1 cup shredded cabbage

Combine first 8 ingredients in a large Dutch oven; bring to a boil. Cover, reduce heat, and simmer 2 hours. Remove short ribs, and cool. Remove fat and bones from meat. Cut meat into ½-inch pieces; set aside.

Strain soup stock; skim off fat. Return stock to Dutch oven; add meat and next 5 ingredients. Bring to a boil. Cover, reduce heat, and simmer 20 minutes. Add remaining ingredients; cover and simmer soup 10 minutes. Yield: about 13 cups.
Ella Brown,
Proctor, Arkansas.

May

Put Your Saltshaker Back On The Shelf

Nutritionists tell us that too much salt in our diets is a major cause of hypertension (high blood pressure). However, salt is the major source of sodium, and sodium is necessary for maintaining fluid balance within the cells. The average American consumes far more salt (and sodium) than needed, and in some people, the extra sodium may cause high blood pressure. Since sodium is present naturally in many foods, most people can get all the sodium their bodies need without additional salt.

Try substituting herbs and spices for the regular salt-laden foods such as bouillon cubes and granules, garlic salt, bacon drippings, soy sauce, and regular butter or margarine. Our Minted Green Beans is an example of cooking without such ingredients. Fresh green beans are glazed with cider vinegar, mint jelly, unsalted margarine, and rosemary.

A combination of several fresh herbs is used for Herbed Zucchini. If fresh herbs aren't available, use one-third to one-fourth as much dried herbs.

VEGETABLE STIR-FRY

1½ teaspoons cornstarch
1½ teaspoons sugar
½ teaspoon ground ginger
⅛ teaspoon pepper
½ cup water
1 tablespoon lemon juice
2 tablespoons instant minced onion
½ teaspoon instant minced garlic
2 tablespoons water
1 (1-pound) bunch broccoli
2 tablespoons vegetable oil
1 cup diagonally sliced carrots
2 cups coarsely shredded cabbage

Combine cornstarch, sugar, ginger, and pepper; stir in ½ cup water and lemon juice, mixing well. Set aside.

Combine onion, garlic, and 2 tablespoons water in a small bowl; let stand at least 10 minutes.

Trim off large leaves of broccoli. Remove tough ends of lower stalks, and wash the broccoli thoroughly. Remove flowerets from stems, and set aside. Slice stems thinly, and set aside.

Pour oil around top of preheated wok; allow to heat at medium high (325°) for 2 minutes. Drain onion and garlic; add to wok, and stir-fry 2 minutes. Add broccoli and carrots; stir-fry 4 to 5 minutes or until crisp-tender. Add cabbage; stir-fry 2 minutes. Stir cornstarch mixture into wok; cook, stirring constantly, until thickened. Yield: 6 servings (about 26 milligrams sodium per serving).
Beverly George, Metairie, Louisiana.

MINTED GREEN BEANS

1 pound fresh green beans
3 tablespoons cider vinegar
1 tablespoon plus 1 teaspoon unsalted margarine
1 tablespoon mint jelly
¾ teaspoon minced fresh rosemary
Lemon twist (optional)
Additional fresh rosemary (optional)

Remove strings from beans; wash thoroughly. Cook beans, covered, in a small amount of boiling water 12 to 15 minutes or just until tender; drain.

Add next 4 ingredients to beans; cook until thoroughly heated, stirring gently to coat beans. Garnish with lemon twist and fresh rosemary, if desired. Yield: 4 servings (about 8 milligrams sodium per serving).
Mary M. Kruse, Mesa, Arizona.

GLAZED ONIONS

1¼ pounds small white onions, peeled
⅓ cup unsalted margarine
2 tablespoons sugar

Cook onions in boiling water to cover 10 to 15 minutes or just until tender; drain thoroughly.

Melt margarine in a large skillet over medium-low heat. Add sugar and onions, stirring to coat; cook 15 minutes or until onions are golden brown, stirring occasionally. Yield: 4 servings (about 14 milligrams sodium per serving).
Susan Bradberry, Texarkana, Arkansas.

CORN-STUFFED PEPPERS

6 small green peppers
2 cups fresh cut corn (about 4 ears)
¼ cup water
3 green onions with tops, chopped
1 medium tomato, peeled, seeded, and diced
2 teaspoons minced fresh basil
¼ teaspoon freshly ground pepper

Cut off tops of green peppers; remove seeds and membrane. Cook peppers, covered, in boiling water 5 minutes; drain and set aside.

Combine corn and ¼ cup water in a medium saucepan. Bring to a boil; cover, reduce heat, and simmer 7 to 8 minutes or just until corn is tender. Drain; add green onions, tomato, basil, and pepper, tossing lightly. Spoon corn mixture into peppers; arrange in a 12- x 8- x 2-inch baking dish. Cover and bake at 350° for 10 minutes or until thoroughly heated. Yield: 6 servings (about 8 milligrams sodium per serving).

VEGETABLE-STUFFED SQUASH

4 small (about ½ pound) yellow squash
2 bay leaves
½ cup finely chopped tomato
2 tablespoons finely chopped green onions
⅛ teaspoon celery seeds
⅛ teaspoon freshly ground pepper

Wash squash thoroughly, and place in a large saucepan with bay leaves. Cover with water, and bring to a boil. Cover, reduce heat, and simmer 5 minutes or until tender but still firm. Drain in a colander, and let cool to touch. Discard bay leaves.

Cut squash in half lengthwise; gently scoop out pulp, leaving firm shells. Drain and chop squash pulp; combine pulp and remaining ingredients. Place squash shells in a 10- x 6- x 2-inch baking dish; spoon vegetable mixture into shells. Cover and bake at 350° for 15 to 20 minutes or until thoroughly heated. Yield: 4 servings (about 2 milligrams sodium per serving).

HERBED ZUCCHINI

3 medium zucchini
½ cup water
1 teaspoon minced fresh parsley
1 teaspoon minced fresh chives
1 teaspoon minced fresh basil
1 teaspoon minced fresh rosemary
1 teaspoon minced fresh dillweed
Freshly ground pepper to taste

Cut zucchini in half lengthwise. Place water in a large skillet; arrange zucchini in skillet, cut sides up. Combine herbs and pepper; sprinkle over zucchini.

Bring water to a boil; cover, reduce heat, and simmer 4 to 6 minutes or until zucchini is crisp-tender. Carefully transfer to a serving platter. Yield: 6 servings (about 1 milligram sodium per serving).
Linda Jones, Stafford, Texas.

RATATOUILLE

4 cloves garlic, minced
1 tablespoon vegetable oil
6 small zucchini, thinly sliced
3 medium tomatoes, peeled and chopped
1 medium eggplant (about 1¼ pounds), peeled and chopped
1 medium-size green pepper, chopped
2 tablespoons minced fresh basil
1 tablespoon minced fresh oregano
Freshly ground pepper to taste
6 green onions with tops, chopped
2 tablespoons minced fresh parsley

Sauté garlic in oil in a Dutch oven 1 minute. Add next 7 ingredients; cover and cook over medium heat 10 minutes, stirring occasionally. Stir in green onions; cook, uncovered, 2 minutes. Transfer to a serving dish; sprinkle with parsley. Yield: 8 servings (about 6 milligrams sodium per serving).

Frankie Frost,
Lancaster, Texas.

Scoop Up A Rainbow Of Desserts

It's hard to beat that quick way to satisfy an ice cream craving—eating it right out of the carton! But this array of ice cream desserts may start some new cravings on their own.

Keep in mind that no matter what flavor of ice cream these recipes specify, you can substitute your own favorites.

When making layered or rolled ice cream desserts, be sure to let the ice cream soften slightly before spreading. Then freeze each new layer before adding another, so layers will not run together. Return the completed dish to the freezer to firm up completely. For individual balls, it's usually easiest to scoop them with ice cream firm from the freezer.

BAKED ALASKA

1 (10-inch) commercial angel food cake
1 pint strawberry ice cream, softened
1 pint pistachio ice cream, softened
6 egg whites
¼ teaspoon cream of tartar
½ cup sugar

Slice cake horizontally into 3 layers. Place one layer on freezer-to-oven serving plate. Spread strawberry ice cream over first layer. Top with second cake layer; spread pistachio ice cream over cake. Top with third cake layer; freeze until firm.

Beat egg whites (at room temperature) and cream of tartar until foamy. Gradually add sugar, 1 tablespoon at a time, beating until stiff peaks form. Remove cake from freezer; quickly spread meringue over entire surface, making sure edges are sealed to plate.

Bake at 500° for 2 to 3 minutes or until meringue peaks are browned. Slice dessert, and serve immediately. Yield: 12 to 15 servings.

STRAWBERRY ICE CREAM ROLL

4 eggs, separated
¾ cup sugar, divided
½ teaspoon lemon extract
¾ cup all-purpose flour
¾ teaspoon baking powder
¼ teaspoon salt
2 to 3 tablespoons powdered sugar
2 pints strawberry ice cream, softened
Sifted powdered sugar
Whipped cream (optional)
Fresh strawberries (optional)

Grease a 15- x 10- x 1-inch jellyroll pan, and line with waxed paper; grease and flour waxed paper. Set aside.

Beat egg yolks until thick and lemon colored. Gradually add ¼ cup sugar, beating constantly. Beat in extract.

Beat egg whites (at room temperature) until foamy. Gradually add remaining ½ cup sugar, 1 tablespoon at a time, beating until stiff peaks form. Fold egg yolk mixture into egg whites. Combine flour, baking powder, and salt; gently fold flour mixture, one-third at a time, into egg mixture. Pour batter into prepared pan; bake at 400° for 12 to 13 minutes.

Sift 2 to 3 tablespoons powdered sugar in a 15- x 10- x 1-inch rectangle on a linen towel. When cake is done, immediately loosen from sides of pan and turn out on sugar. Peel off waxed paper. Starting at long end, roll up cake and towel together; cool on a wire rack, seam side down.

Unroll cake and remove towel; spread with ice cream, and reroll. Wrap in plastic wrap, and freeze 4 hours or until firm. Sprinkle cake with powdered sugar, and garnish with whipped cream and strawberries, if desired. Yield: 12 to 15 servings.

Beverly Brannon,
Vidor, Texas.

LAYERED ICE CREAM DESSERT

2 cups gingersnap crumbs
⅓ cup butter or margarine, melted
1½ pints chocolate fudge ice cream, slightly softened
1½ pints mint-chocolate chip ice cream, slightly softened
1½ pints strawberry ice cream, slightly softened
2 (16½-ounce) cans dark sweet pitted cherries, undrained
1½ pints French vanilla ice cream, slightly softened
¾ cup coarsely chopped pecans

Combine gingersnap crumbs and butter. Press mixture firmly into a 9-inch springform pan. Freeze until firm.

Spread chocolate fudge ice cream over crumb crust; freeze until firm. Spread mint-chocolate chip ice cream over frozen ice cream; freeze until firm. Spread strawberry ice cream over frozen ice cream; freeze until firm. Drain cherries and pat dry; arrange cherries over strawberry ice cream; freeze until firm. Spread French vanilla ice cream over frozen cherries. Sprinkle chopped pecans on top; freeze until firm. Cover tightly, and freeze overnight. Remove from freezer 10 minutes before serving; remove sides of springform pan, and slice into wedges. Yield: 10 to 12 servings.

Candy Carrigan,
Birmingham, Alabama.

FROZEN RAINBOW DELIGHT

2 cups whipping cream
3 tablespoons powdered sugar
18 soft macaroon cookies, crumbled
1 cup chopped pecans
1 teaspoon vanilla extract
1 quart raspberry sherbet
1 quart lime sherbet
1 quart orange sherbet

Beat whipping cream until foamy; gradually add sugar, beating until soft peaks form. Fold in macaroon crumbs, pecans, and vanilla.

Spread half of macaroon mixture in bottom of a two-piece 10-inch tube pan. Spread raspberry sherbet evenly over macaroon mixture; freeze 30 minutes. Repeat with other sherbets, freezing 30 minutes between layers. Top with remaining macaroon mixture, and freeze until firm.

Let frozen dessert stand at room temperature 10 minutes before serving. Remove side piece of tube pan; slice. Yield: 16 servings.

Mrs. Bert E. Uebele, Jr.,
Boca Raton, Florida.

EASY ICE CREAM BALLS

½ gallon peppermint or vanilla
  ice cream
14 chocolate cream-filled sandwich
  cookies, crushed
2 (1-inch) squares semisweet chocolate
½ cup butter or margarine
1 (5.33-ounce) can evaporated milk
2 cups sifted powdered sugar
Whipped cream (optional)
Maraschino cherries (optional)

Scoop ice cream into 2½-inch balls. Lightly roll in cookie crumbs. Cover and freeze until firm.

Combine chocolate and butter in top of a double boiler; bring water to a boil. Reduce heat to low; cook until chocolate melts. Stir in milk and sugar. Cook, stirring constantly, until sauce is thickened and smooth.

Arrange ice cream balls in individual serving dishes. Garnish with whipped cream and cherries, if desired. Spoon warm sauce over ice cream balls just before serving. Yield: 18 ice cream balls. *Cyndi Turner,*
Humboldt, Tennessee.

NUTMEG-ALMOND FLOAT

1 quart cold milk
⅓ cup sugar
¼ teaspoon ground nutmeg
Dash of salt
1 teaspoon almond extract
½ teaspoon vanilla extract
2 pints vanilla ice cream
Whipped cream
Maraschino cherries

Combine first 6 ingredients; stir until sugar dissolves. Spoon ice cream evenly into 6 chilled glasses. Pour milk mixture over ice cream. Top each with whipped cream and a cherry. Yield: 6 servings.
Linda H. Sutton,
Winston-Salem, North Carolina.

Recipes For The Harvest

Gardening and cooking naturally go together—for what could be better than a recipe featuring the flavor of carefully tended tomatoes, crisp snap beans, or juicy sweet corn. And your garden might include more than vegetables; a section can be set aside for growing basil, dill, and tarragon. Fresh herbs enhance the natural flavor of foods.

Whether you are a gourmet cook, on a low-sodium diet, or simply an avid gardener, you will discover that fresh herbs add interest to recipes as well as to your garden. Start experimenting with a few familiar herbs such as parsley or mint. Soon you will be adding fresh burnet to soup and dillweed to sauces. And don't forget that you can capture the flavor of fresh herbs for later use by drying or freezing them. You can also make homemade vinegars with them.

TOMATOES VINAIGRETTE

4 large tomatoes
¼ cup plus 2 tablespoons chopped fresh
  parsley or 2 tablespoons dried parsley
  flakes
1 clove garlic, crushed
¼ cup plus 2 tablespoons olive oil
2 tablespoons vinegar
1½ teaspoons minced fresh basil or ½
  teaspoon dried whole basil
1 teaspoon salt
⅛ teaspoon pepper
Additional chopped fresh parsley
  (optional)

Slice tomatoes; place in a serving bowl. Sprinkle with ¼ cup plus 2 tablespoons parsley. Combine next 6 ingredients in a jar; cover tightly, and shake vigorously. Pour over tomatoes. Chill 3 hours. Sprinkle with additional parsley, if desired. Yield: 8 servings.

GARDEN-STUFFED YELLOW SQUASH

6 medium-size yellow squash
1 cup chopped onion
1 cup chopped tomato
½ cup chopped green pepper
½ cup (2 ounces) shredded Cheddar
  cheese
2 slices bacon, cooked and crumbled
½ teaspoon salt
Dash of pepper
Butter or margarine

Wash squash thoroughly; cover with water and bring to a boil. Cover, reduce heat, and simmer 8 to 10 minutes or until tender but still firm. Drain and cool slightly. Trim off stems. Cut squash in half lengthwise; remove and reserve pulp, leaving a firm shell.

Chop pulp; combine pulp and remaining ingredients except butter. Place squash shells in a 13- x 9- x 2-inch baking dish. Spoon vegetable mixture into shells; dot with butter. Bake at 400° for 20 minutes. Yield: 6 servings.

COLD GREEN BEAN SALAD

½ pound new potatoes, peeled and cubed
1 pound fresh green beans
3 tablespoons olive oil
1 tablespoon white wine vinegar
1 tablespoon lemon juice
1 tablespoon fresh basil or 1 teaspoon
  dried whole basil
½ teaspoon salt
⅛ teaspoon garlic powder
⅛ teaspoon coarsely ground black pepper

Cook potatoes in boiling water to cover 15 to 20 minutes; drain well.

Remove strings from beans; cut beans into 1½-inch pieces. Wash thoroughly. Cover beans with water, and bring to a boil. Reduce heat, cover, and simmer 10 minutes or until crisp-tender. Drain.

Combine potatoes and beans, tossing gently. Combine remaining ingredients, stirring well; pour over vegetables, tossing gently to coat. Cover and chill at least 4 hours. Yield: 4 to 6 servings.

WATERMELON RIND PICKLES

1 large watermelon, quartered
Pickling salt
2 tablespoons plus 2 teaspoons whole
  cloves
16 (1½-inch) sticks cinnamon
½ teaspoon mustard seeds
8 cups sugar
1 quart vinegar (5% acidity)

Remove flesh from melon (reserve for other use); peel watermelon. Cut rind into 1-inch cubes.

Place rind in a large crock or plastic container. Add water by the quart until it covers the rind; add ¼ cup pickling salt for each quart water, stirring until salt dissolves. Cover and let stand in a cool place overnight. Drain well.

Place rind in a 10-quart Dutch oven; cover with cold water. Bring to a boil, and cook until rind is almost tender. Drain and set aside.

Tie cloves, cinnamon, and mustard seeds in a cheesecloth bag. Combine spice bag, sugar, and vinegar in a Dutch oven. Bring to a boil; remove from heat and let stand 15 minutes. Add rind to syrup. Bring to a boil; reduce heat to low and cook until rind is transparent. Remove spice bag.

Pack rind into hot sterilized jars, leaving ½-inch headspace. Cover at once with metal lids, and screw bands tight. Process in boiling-water bath 5 minutes. Yield: about 6 pints.

CORN RELISH

About 18 ears fresh corn
7 quarts water
1 small head cabbage, chopped
1 cup chopped onion
1 cup chopped green pepper
1 cup chopped sweet red pepper
1 to 2 cups sugar
2 tablespoons dry mustard
1 tablespoon celery seeds
1 tablespoon mustard seeds
1 tablespoon salt
1 tablespoon ground turmeric
1 quart vinegar (5% acidity)
1 cup water

Remove husks and silks from corn. Bring 7 quarts water to a boil; add corn. Bring water to a second boil; cook 5 minutes. Cool. Cut corn from cob, measuring about 2 quarts of kernels.

Combine corn kernels and remaining ingredients in a large saucepan; simmer over low heat 20 minutes. Bring mixture to a boil. Pack into hot sterilized jars, leaving ¼-inch headspace.

Cover at once with metal lids, and screw bands tight. Process in boiling-water bath 15 minutes. Yield: 6 pints.

COLD DILL SOUP

1 pint half-and-half
2 (8-ounce) cartons plain yogurt
2 cucumbers, peeled, seeded, and diced
3 tablespoons minced fresh dillweed or 1 tablespoon dried whole dillweed
2 tablespoons lemon juice
1 tablespoon chopped green onions
½ teaspoon salt
⅛ to ¼ teaspoon white pepper
Sliced cucumber (optional)
Sprigs of fresh dillweed (optional)

Combine first 8 ingredients, stirring well; chill thoroughly. Stir well; garnish with sliced cucumber and dill sprigs, if desired. Yield: 4 cups.

SAVORY CARROT SOUP

1 medium onion, chopped
2 tablespoons butter or margarine
4 carrots, scraped and coarsely chopped
4 cups chicken broth
1 (2- x 1-inch) strip lemon rind
1 tablespoon minced fresh savory or 1 teaspoon dried whole savory
2 teaspoons sugar
½ to 1 teaspoon curry powder
¼ teaspoon salt
¼ teaspoon pepper
3 tablespoons dry sherry
Thinly sliced carrot strips (optional)

Sauté onion in butter in a large skillet until tender. Add next 8 ingredients. Cover, reduce heat, and simmer 20 minutes or until carrots are tender.

Pour half of mixture into container of electric blender; process until smooth. Pour into a bowl or pitcher; repeat with remaining mixture. Stir in sherry. Cover and chill.

Garnish soup with carrot strips, if desired. Yield: about 5 cups.

BURNET-CELERY SOUP

6 stalks celery, finely chopped
6 green onions, finely chopped
3 medium potatoes, peeled and cubed
1 quart milk
2 tablespoons chopped fresh burnet or 2 teaspoons dried whole burnet
½ teaspoon salt
⅛ teaspoon pepper
3 tablespoons whipping cream
1 tablespoon butter or margarine
Sliced celery (optional)
Fresh burnet leaves (optional)

Combine first 5 ingredients in a large saucepan; simmer 30 minutes (do not boil). Pour half of mixture into blender and process 30 seconds; strain through a sieve. Repeat with remaining mixture. Return to saucepan. Stir in salt, pepper, whipping cream, and butter. Heat thoroughly (do not boil), stirring occasionally. Chill before serving. Garnish with sliced celery and burnet leaves, if desired. Yield: 5 cups.

MIXED HERB VINEGAR

½ cup chopped fresh rosemary
½ cup chopped fresh thyme
4 shallots, thinly sliced
1 sprig fresh parsley, chopped
12 peppercorns
3¾ cups white vinegar (5% acidity)
Sprigs of fresh rosemary and thyme (optional)

Place first 5 ingredients in a wide-mouth glass jar. Place vinegar in medium saucepan; bring to a boil. Pour vinegar over herbs; cover with a metal lid and screw band tight. Let stand at room temperature for 2 weeks.

Strain vinegar into decorative jars, discarding herb residue; add additional sprigs of fresh rosemary and thyme, if desired. Seal jars with a cork or other airtight lid. Yield: 4 cups.

TARRAGON VINEGAR

1 cup chopped fresh tarragon
3¾ cups white vinegar (5% acidity)
Fresh tarragon sprigs (optional)

Place chopped tarragon in a wide-mouth glass jar. Place vinegar in a medium saucepan; bring to a boil. Pour vinegar over chopped tarragon; cover with a metal lid and screw band tight. Let mixture stand at room temperature for 2 weeks.

Strain vinegar into decorative jars, discarding herb residue; add additional sprigs of fresh tarragon, if desired. Seal jars with a cork or other airtight lid. Yield: 4 cups.

MINT SAUCE

½ cup vinegar
1 cup water
½ cup chopped fresh mint leaves, divided
½ cup water
¼ cup lemon juice
2½ tablespoons sugar
Dash of salt

Combine vinegar, 1 cup water, and ¼ cup mint in a small saucepan; bring to a boil. Reduce heat and simmer until liquid is reduced by half; strain. Add ½ cup water, lemon juice, sugar, and salt (sauce will be thin). Chill. To serve, stir in remaining ¼ cup mint and serve over fish or lamb. Yield: about 1½ cups.

DILL SAUCE

2 tablespoons butter or margarine
2 tablespoons all-purpose flour
1 cup fish broth or chicken broth
1 egg yolk, beaten
¼ cup commercial sour cream
2 tablespoons minced fresh dillweed or 2 teaspoons dried whole dillweed
Sprigs of fresh dillweed (optional)

Melt butter in a heavy saucepan over low heat; add flour, stirring until smooth. Cook 1 minute, stirring constantly. Gradually add fish stock; cook over medium heat, stirring constantly, until thickened and bubbly. Gradually stir about one-fourth of hot mixture into egg yolk; add to remaining hot mixture, stirring constantly. Cook 5 minutes, stirring constantly. Remove from heat; stir in sour cream and 2 tablespoons dillweed. Cook over low heat just until heated (do not boil). Garnish with sprigs of fresh dillweed, if desired. Serve sauce over fish or seafood. Yield: about 1¼ cups.

GARLIC PESTO

5 ounces fresh spinach
6 cloves garlic, crushed
1 cup fresh parsley sprigs
⅔ cup grated Parmesan cheese
½ cup finely chopped walnuts
4 anchovy fillets
3 tablespoons minced fresh tarragon
    or 1 tablespoon dried whole
    tarragon
1 tablespoon minced fresh basil or
    1 teaspoon dried whole basil
½ teaspoon salt
½ teaspoon pepper
¾ cup olive oil
1 (16-ounce) package thin spaghetti
Pimiento strips (optional)
Fresh basil leaves (optional)

Remove stems from spinach. Wash leaves thoroughly in lukewarm water; tear into bite-size pieces.

Position knife blade in food processor bowl; add spinach and next 9 ingredients, and top with cover; process until smooth. With processor running, pour oil through food chute in a slow, steady stream until combined.

Prepare spaghetti according to package directions; drain well. Toss spaghetti with garlic mixture. Garnish with pimiento and basil leaves, if desired. Yield: 8 to 10 servings.

SALSA PICANTE

2 fresh jalapeño peppers
12 sprigs fresh coriander, chopped or 1
    tablespoon plus 1 teaspoon dried whole
    cilantro
3 medium tomatoes, cored and cut into
    eighths
1 bunch green onions, cut into 1-inch
    pieces
1 small green tomato, cored and cut into
    eighths
1 medium avocado, peeled and cut into
    chunks
¼ cup olive oil
2 to 3 tablespoons lime juice
1 teaspoon garlic powder
1 teaspoon ground cumin
1 teaspoon salt
¼ teaspoon sugar

Place peppers on a baking sheet; broil 3 to 4 inches from heat, turning often with tongs, until peppers are blistered on all sides. Immediately place peppers in a plastic bag; fasten securely, and let steam 10 to 15 minutes. Remove peel of each pepper. Cut a small slit in side of each pepper, and rinse under cold water to remove seeds. (Wear rubber plastic gloves when rinsing and cutting peppers if you have sensitive skin.) Remove stems from peppers; quarter each pepper, and set aside.

Combine peppers and remaining ingredients in container of electric blender or food processor. Process 10 to 15 seconds or until chopped to desired texture. Chill before serving. Serve as a dip or with salad or black beans. Yield: about 3 cups.

GARLIC BUTTER

½ cup butter or margarine, softened
2 tablespoons chopped fresh chives
2 or 3 cloves garlic, minced
Dash of salt

Cream butter until light and fluffy; blend in remaining ingredients. Chill before serving. Yield: ½ cup.

Strawberries—Sweet And Juicy

When you pop a fresh, juicy strawberry in your mouth, it seems to burst with sweet flavor. Eating strawberries whole or sliced is the simplest way to enjoy them, but here are new ideas for some irresistible spring desserts.

STRAWBERRIES WITH STRAWBERRY CREAM

4 cups strawberries, hulled
¼ cup plus 2 tablespoons sugar
⅓ cup Cointreau or other orange-flavored
    liqueur
½ cup whipping cream
3 tablespoons sugar
3 strawberries, halved (optional)

Combine first 3 ingredients; mix gently. Cover and chill 2 hours. Drain.

Process enough strawberries in blender to make ½ cup puree; set aside. Beat whipping cream until foamy; gradually add 3 tablespoons sugar, beating until stiff peaks form. Gently fold in strawberry puree.

Spoon strawberries into 6 individual serving containers. Top each serving with a dollop of the whipped cream mixture and a strawberry half, if desired. Yield: 6 servings.

Audrey Bledsoe,
Smyrna, Georgia.

STRAWBERRIES ROMANOFF

4 cups strawberries, hulled
¼ cup plus 2 tablespoons sifted powdered
    sugar, divided
2 tablespoons rum
2 tablespoons Cointreau or other
    orange-flavored liqueur
1 cup whipping cream
2 tablespoons kirsch or other
    cherry-flavored liqueur

Combine strawberries, ¼ cup powdered sugar, rum, and Cointreau; mix gently. Cover and chill 2 hours.

Beat whipping cream until foamy; gradually add remaining 2 tablespoons sugar and kirsch. Spoon strawberries into individual serving dishes. Top each with a dollop of cream mixture. Yield: 6 servings.

Susan Kamer-Shinaberry,
Charleston, West Virginia.

STRAWBERRY SWIRL

1 cup graham cracker crumbs
1 tablespoon sugar
¼ cup butter or margarine, melted
2 cups sliced strawberries
2 tablespoons sugar
4½ cups miniature marshmallows
½ cup milk
1 cup whipping cream
1 (3-ounce) package strawberry-flavored
    gelatin
1 cup boiling water

Combine cracker crumbs, 1 tablespoon sugar, and butter; mix well. Press mixture into a 9-inch square baking pan; chill at least 1 hour.

Combine strawberries and 2 tablespoons sugar; stir gently. Let stand 30 minutes; drain, reserving juice. Set strawberries aside. Add enough water to juice to make 1 cup; set aside.

Combine marshmallows and milk in a small saucepan; cook over medium heat, stirring constantly, until marshmallows melt. Cool completely. Beat whipping cream until stiff peaks form; gently fold into marshmallow mixture.

Dissolve gelatin in boiling water; stir in reserved strawberry juice mixture. Chill until the consistency of unbeaten egg white; stir in strawberries.

Pour marshmallow mixture into gelatin; fold in slightly, leaving a swirled effect. Pour into prepared crust; chill until set. Yield: 9 servings.

Carrie J. Regan,
Fort Walton Beach, Florida.

DEEP-FRIED STRAWBERRIES

1 cup pancake mix
½ cup plus 2 tablespoons milk
24 large strawberries
Vegetable oil
Sherry Sauce

Combine pancake mix and milk, stirring well. Dip strawberries in batter, and deep fry in hot oil (375°) until golden brown. Drain on paper towels. Serve strawberries immediately with Sherry Sauce. Yield: 2 dozen.

Sherry Sauce:

1 cup sifted powdered sugar
⅓ cup water
1 tablespoon plus ¾ teaspoon cornstarch
¼ cup sherry

Combine sugar and water in a small saucepan; bring to a boil. Combine cornstarch and sherry, stirring until cornstarch dissolves. Gradually stir cornstarch mixture into hot mixture; cook over medium heat, stirring constantly, until sauce is smooth and thickened. Yield: about ¾ cup.

Adeline Larrieu,
Homosassa Springs, Florida.

Entertain With A Spicy Curry

Coriander, turmeric, cumin, fenugreek, red pepper, black pepper, white pepper, caraway seeds, allspice, cinnamon, cloves, ginger, mace, mustard, fennel . . . some or all of these spices are combined for the distinctive flavor of curry. But the beauty of curry is that the spice mixture varies.

In India and Far Eastern countries, fresh spices used for curry are ground daily and vary according to preferred seasonings and degree of hotness desired. Even commercial brands of curry powder offer different blends of spices.

Curry dishes involve more than sprinkling curry powder over food or stirring it into a sauce. Traditionally, curry is a creamy sauce with chunks of seafood, poultry, meat, or vegetables simmered until thick. It's usually served over rice to capture all of the flavorful sauce and then topped with any of a number of chopped vegetables, nuts, and fruit.

Curry is fun to serve at a guest participation party. Invite your guests to help chop ingredients for the condiments while you prepare the curry sauce.

Step 1—Sauté celery, apple, and onion in butter for the chunky base to Charleston-Style Shrimp Curry.

Step 2—Traditionalists prefer mixing their own spices, but you can substitute commercial curry powder.

Step 3—Cream is the liquid stirred into most curries, though some use broth or water. After adding cream, simmer 10 minutes.

Step 4—Stir in cooked shrimp when the sauce is ready, and continue cooking just until thoroughly heated.

CHARLESTON-STYLE SHRIMP CURRY

9 cups water
3 pounds large fresh shrimp
1 large onion, finely chopped
½ cup finely chopped apple
½ cup finely chopped celery
¼ cup butter or margarine
1 cup water
2 cups whipping cream
2 tablespoons curry powder
½ teaspoon salt
⅛ teaspoon pepper
Hot cooked rice

Bring 9 cups water to a boil; add shrimp, and return to a boil. Reduce heat and simmer 3 to 5 minutes. Drain well; rinse with cold water. Chill. Peel and devein shrimp; set aside.

Sauté onion, apple, and celery in butter for 5 minutes; add 1 cup water.

Cook, uncovered, over low heat for 25 minutes or until most of the liquid is absorbed. Stir in whipping cream, curry powder, salt, and pepper; simmer, uncovered, 10 minutes. Add shrimp, and simmer until thoroughly heated. Serve over rice.

Serve curry with several of the following condiments: flaked coconut, toasted almonds, peanuts, raisins, fig preserves, chutney, pickle relish, crumbled bacon, bananas, chopped hard-cooked egg, chopped green pepper, and chopped onion. Yield: 8 to 10 servings.

Mrs. Richard Atwell,
Thomasville, Georgia.

Tip: When browning food in a skillet, dry the food first on paper towels.

SHRIMP MALAI CURRY

½ cup frozen grated coconut, thawed
1 cup water
1 medium onion, chopped
1 green chile pepper, finely chopped
2 tablespoons vegetable oil
1 teaspoon ground coriander
1 teaspoon garlic powder
1 teaspoon ground cumin
½ teaspoon salt
½ teaspoon ground turmeric
½ teaspoon paprika
¼ teaspoon ground cloves
¼ teaspoon chili powder
¼ teaspoon ground cinnamon
1 pound large shrimp, peeled and
    deveined
Hot cooked rice

Combine coconut and water; set aside. Sauté onion and chile pepper in oil in a large skillet until tender. Combine next 9 ingredients and add to skillet, blending well. Stir in coconut and water; cook over low heat 2 minutes. Add the shrimp and cook over low heat 15 minutes, stirring occasionally. Serve over rice. Yield: 4 servings.
Sambhu N. Banik,
Bethesda, Maryland.

CURRIED SHRIMP

9 cups water
3 pounds medium-size fresh shrimp
¼ cup butter or margarine
1½ to 2 teaspoons curry powder
½ cup diced celery
½ cup chopped green pepper
¼ cup chopped fresh parsley
¼ cup plus 1 tablespoon all-purpose
    flour
¾ teaspoon salt
½ teaspoon garlic salt
3 cups milk
1½ cups (6 ounces) shredded Cheddar
    cheese
¼ cup chopped pimiento
Hot cooked rice

Bring water to a boil; add shrimp, and return to a boil. Reduce heat and simmer 3 to 5 minutes. Drain well; rinse with cold water. Chill. Peel and devein shrimp; set aside.

Melt butter in a heavy saucepan over low heat; stir in curry powder. Add celery, green pepper, and parsley; cook 2 minutes over medium-high heat, stirring occasionally. Add flour, salt, and garlic salt; stir until smooth. Cook 1 minute, stirring constantly. Reduce heat to medium; gradually add milk. Cook, stirring constantly, until thickened and bubbly. Add cheese, and stir until cheese melts.

Reduce heat to low; add shrimp and pimiento. Cook, stirring constantly, just until thoroughly heated. Serve over rice. Yield: 10 servings. *Julia Garmon,*
Alexandria, Virginia.

CHICKEN CURRY

1 (2½-pound) broiler-fryer
2 small onions, chopped
3 tablespoons vegetable oil
½ teaspoon ground allspice
½ teaspoon garlic powder
¼ teaspoon ground cardamom
¼ teaspoon ground cloves
¼ teaspoon black pepper
¼ teaspoon red pepper
1 teaspoon salt
¼ teaspoon ground turmeric
Juice of 1 lime
Hot cooked rice

Place chicken in a Dutch oven, and cover with water. Bring to a boil; cover, reduce heat, and simmer 1 hour or until tender. Remove chicken and let cool, reserving 1 cup broth. Bone chicken and chop meat; set aside.

Sauté onion in oil in a medium skillet for 1 minute. Combine next 8 ingredients; add to skillet, and sauté an additional 2 minutes. Stir in 1 cup of reserved broth and lime juice; remove from heat.

Place chicken in a lightly greased 12- x 8- x 2-inch baking dish; pour onion mixture over chicken. Cover and refrigerate several hours or overnight.

Bake at 350° for 15 to 20 minutes or until thoroughly heated. Serve over hot cooked rice. Yield: 6 servings.
Peter Phillips,
Amston, Connecticut.

REGAL CURRIED CHICKEN

7 chicken breast halves, skinned, boned,
    and cut into bite-size pieces
¼ cup all-purpose flour
¼ cup plus 2 tablespoons butter or
    margarine
1 cup finely chopped onion
1 small clove garlic, crushed
1 tablespoon plus 1½ teaspoons
    curry powder
½ teaspoon ground ginger
½ teaspoon salt
1½ cups chicken broth
1 medium cucumber, peeled and
    diced
¼ cup raisins
2 tablespoons chopped chutney
Hot cooked rice

Dredge chicken in flour; brown in butter in a large skillet. Remove chicken to a 2-quart casserole, reserving pan drippings in skillet.

Sauté onion and garlic in pan drippings until onion is tender. Stir in curry powder, ginger, and salt, blending well. Add next 4 ingredients, and stir well. Pour over chicken in casserole. Cover and bake at 350° for 1 hour. Serve over hot cooked rice.

Serve curry with several of the following condiments: flaked coconut, toasted almonds, chopped peanuts, pineapple chunks, chutney, diced tomato, chopped banana, and chopped hard-cooked egg. Yield: 6 to 8 servings.
Mrs. Delbert R. Snyder,
Williamsburg, Virginia.

Treat Yourself To Homemade Goodies

Why not fill your cookie jars and candy dishes with an assortment of sweet treats? Our recipes will not only satisfy the craving you have for homemade goodies, but they are also quick and easy to make.

CINNAMON CHEWS

⅓ cup shortening
½ cup sugar
1 egg, separated
2 tablespoons milk
1 cup all-purpose flour
¼ teaspoon salt
¼ teaspoon ground cinnamon
¼ teaspoon vanilla extract
¼ cup chopped pecans or walnuts
3 tablespoons sugar
¼ teaspoon ground cinnamon

Cream shortening; gradually add ½ cup sugar, beating until light and fluffy. Add egg yolk and milk; beat well.

Combine flour, salt, and ¼ teaspoon cinnamon; gradually add to creamed mixture. Stir in vanilla. Spread in an ungreased 11- x 7- x 1½-inch baking pan. Beat egg white slightly; brush over dough. Combine chopped pecans, 3 tablespoons sugar, and ¼ teaspoon cinnamon; sprinkle over dough. Bake at 350° for 18 to 20 minutes; cut into squares. Cool in pan. Yield: 2 dozen.
Louise Holmes,
Winchester, Tennessee.

HAZELNUT COOKIES

1 cup butter or margarine, softened
½ cup sifted powdered sugar
2 cups all-purpose flour
1 cup finely chopped hazelnuts, toasted
Sifted powdered sugar

Cream butter; add ½ cup powdered sugar, beating until light and fluffy. Gradually add flour; beat well. Stir in hazelnuts. Chill 30 minutes.

Shape dough into 1-inch balls; place on ungreased cookie sheets. Bake at 400° for 12 to 14 minutes. Remove immediately from sheets and roll in powdered sugar. Yield: 3½ dozen.

Betty R. Butts,
Kensington, Maryland.

MIXED RAISIN CANDY

4 cups sugar
2 cups whipping cream
2 tablespoons light corn syrup
1 (9-ounce) package raisins
2 cups chopped pecans or walnuts
1 cup flaked coconut
2½ cups semisweet chocolate morsels
¼ cup plus ½ tablespoon shortening

Combine first 3 ingredients in a heavy saucepan; stir well. Bring to a boil, stirring often; cook to soft ball stage (234°). Remove from heat; cover and chill 1 to 2 hours. Stir in raisins, pecans, and coconut; shape into 1-inch balls.

Combine chocolate and shortening in top of a double boiler; bring water to a boil. Reduce heat to low; cook until chocolate melts. Place several candy balls in chocolate mixture; roll with spoon to coat evenly. Remove with a wooden pick or spoon, allowing excess chocolate to cool. Continue process until all candy balls are coated. Cover and store in refrigerator. Yield: 8 dozen.

Rhonda Acton,
Crab Orchard, Kentucky.

CREAM CHEESE FUDGE

4 (1-ounce) squares unsweetened chocolate
2 (3-ounce) packages cream cheese, softened
4 cups sifted powdered sugar
½ teaspoon vanilla extract
1 cup chopped pecans or walnuts
16 pecan halves

Place chocolate in top of double boiler; bring water to a boil. Reduce heat to low; cook until chocolate melts.

Combine cream cheese and sugar; beat until smooth. Add chocolate and vanilla, beating well. Stir in chopped pecans. Press mixture into a lightly greased 8-inch square pan. Chill until firm, and cut into squares. Top each square with a pecan half. Store in refrigerator. Yield: 16 squares.

Susan Fondren,
Germantown, Tennessee.

CHOCOLATE DROPS

2 (16-ounce) packages powdered sugar, sifted
1½ cups sweetened condensed milk
½ cup butter or margarine, melted
1 teaspoon vanilla extract
2 cups chopped pecans
1 cup flaked coconut
1 (12-ounce) package semisweet chocolate morsels
3 tablespoons shortening

Combine sugar, sweetened condensed milk, butter, and vanilla; mix until smooth. Stir in pecans and coconut. Roll mixture into 1-inch balls, and chill at least 1 hour.

Combine chocolate and shortening in top of a double boiler; bring water to a boil. Reduce heat to low; cook until chocolate melts. Place several candy balls in chocolate mixture; roll with spoon to coat evenly. Remove from mixture with a wooden pick or spoon, allowing excess chocolate to drain off. Place on waxed paper to cool. Continue process until all candy balls are coated. Cover and store in refrigerator. Yield: 9 dozen.

Evelyn Roberts,
Columbus, Georgia.

Offer A Refreshing Spring Soup

A bowl of chilled Gazpacho or Green Onion Soup is a welcome addition to springtime meals. Offer either one as an appetizer for dinner, or alongside a salad or sandwich for lunch.

Whenever you have soup, top it with a simple garnish. You may use an ingredient that's called for in the recipe, such as green onion strips on the Green Onion Soup. Other good ideas are celery leaves, carrot curls, croutons, or a dollop of sour cream.

CREAM OF ASPARAGUS SOUP

2 (10-ounce) packages frozen asparagus spears
1 cup water
¼ cup chopped onion
2 tablespoons butter or margarine
2 tablespoons all-purpose flour
1 cup milk
1 cup half-and-half
½ teaspoon salt
⅛ teaspoon white pepper
Croutons (optional)

Combine first 3 ingredients in a saucepan; bring to a boil. Separate asparagus with a fork; cover, reduce heat, and simmer 5 minutes or until tender. Drain. Place asparagus in container of electric blender; process until smooth.

Melt butter in a heavy saucepan over low heat; add flour, stirring until smooth. Cook 1 minute, stirring constantly. Gradually add milk and half-and-half; cook over medium heat, stirring constantly, until mixture is thickened and bubbly. Stir in asparagus puree, salt, and pepper; cook until thoroughly heated. Garnish with croutons, if desired. Yield: 4½ cups.

Note: Soup may be served cold. Add additional milk for a thinner soup.

Mrs. Ed Stetz, Jr.,
Johnstown, Pennsylvania.

CREAM OF GREEN BEAN SOUP

½ pound fresh green beans
3 cups chicken broth
2 small potatoes, peeled and quartered
½ cup chopped fresh chives
¼ cup butter or margarine
2 small cloves garlic, crushed
½ teaspoon salt
⅛ teaspoon pepper
¼ cup commercial sour cream
1 tablespoon lemon juice

Wash beans; trim ends, and remove strings, if necessary. Cut beans into 2-inch lengths.

Combine the beans and next 5 ingredients in a large saucepan; bring to a boil. Cover, reduce heat, and simmer 20 to 25 minutes or until vegetables are tender. Stir in salt and pepper.

Place about one-third of bean mixture in container of an electric blender; process until smooth. Repeat procedure with remaining mixture. Return to saucepan; stir in the sour cream and lemon juice. Cook until soup is thoroughly heated, stirring constantly (do not boil). Yield: about 8 cups.

Thomas Farmer,
Richmond, Virginia.

GAZPACHO

3 cups peeled, seeded, and finely chopped
  tomato
2 cups tomato juice, chilled
1 cup seeded, finely chopped cucumber
1 cup finely chopped green pepper
½ cup finely chopped onion
2 tablespoons minced fresh green chiles
2 tablespoons olive oil
1 teaspoon garlic salt
1 teaspoon dried whole cilantro or parsley
  flakes
2 teaspoons lemon juice
¼ to ½ teaspoon salt
¼ teaspoon white pepper
¼ cup minced fresh parsley (optional)

Combine first 12 ingredients; cover
and chill 8 hours or overnight. Stir
gently before serving; sprinkle with
fresh parsley, if desired. Yield: 6 cups.
*Cathy Hardy,
Tustin, California.*

GREEN ONION SOUP

12 green onions with tops, thinly sliced
3 medium potatoes, peeled and thinly
  sliced
4 cups chicken broth
1 (10¾-ounce) can cream of celery soup,
  undiluted
¾ cup evaporated milk
1 tablespoon butter or margarine
½ teaspoon salt
¼ teaspoon white pepper
Green onion strips (optional)

Combine first 3 ingredients in a large
saucepan; cover and cook 10 minutes or
until vegetables are tender. Strain well,
reserving liquid in saucepan.

Combine vegetables, cream of celery
soup, and evaporated milk in container
of electric blender; process until
smooth. Add to reserved liquid. Stir in
butter, salt, and pepper; cook over low
heat, stirring often, until thoroughly
heated. Serve hot or cold. Garnish with
green onion strips, if desired. Yield: 7½
cups.
*Violet Moore,
Montezuma, Georgia.*

CREAMY POTATO SOUP

3 small potatoes, peeled and diced
1 medium onion, chopped
2 tablespoons butter or margarine
6 cups milk
1½ teaspoons salt
¼ teaspoon pepper
1 teaspoon chicken-flavored bouillon
  granules
1 to 1½ teaspoons dried whole oregano
1½ cups instant mashed potato flakes

Cook potatoes in boiling water to
cover 15 minutes or until tender; drain.
Sauté onion in butter in a Dutch oven
until tender. Stir in next 5 ingredients;
cook over low heat, stirring constantly,
until hot. Remove from heat. Stir in
potato flakes and potatoes, and serve.
Yield: 9 cups.
*Polly Hughes,
Tarpon Springs, Florida.*

LEEK-AND-POTATO SOUP

4 slices bacon, coarsely chopped
6 leeks, thinly sliced
¼ cup chopped onion
2 tablespoons all-purpose flour
4 cups chicken broth
3 large potatoes, peeled and thinly sliced
2 tablespoons chopped fresh chervil or 2
  teaspoons dried whole chervil
1 tablespoon chopped fresh parsley
2 egg yolks, beaten
1 (8-ounce) carton commercial sour cream

Cook bacon in a Dutch oven over
medium heat 5 minutes. Add leeks and
onion; sauté 5 minutes. Reduce heat to
low; add flour, stirring until smooth.
Cook 1 minute, stirring constantly.
Gradually add broth; cook over medium
heat, stirring constantly, until thickened. Add potatoes, chervil, and parsley; cover and simmer 45 minutes.

Combine egg yolks and sour cream,
stirring well; gradually add to soup.
Simmer, stirring constantly, 10 minutes.
Yield: 9 cups.
*Peggy Collins,
San Antonio, Texas.*

MICROWAVE COOKERY

Assemble A Vegetable Casserole

Microwave cooking offers convenience when it comes to vegetable casseroles. You can prepare the entire dish
in less than 30 minutes and retain valu-
able nutrients in the vegetables as well.

It's best to precook the raw vegetables before assembling the casserole so
that the vegetables will be evenly done.
Simply place the prepared vegetables in
a bowl with a small amount of water;
cover and microwave the designated
length of time. Stirring occasionally also
helps promote even cooking.

This quick-cooking method preserves
vitamins and minerals lost when vegetables are cooked in more water for a
longer period of time. To microwave
vegetables, only a small amount of
water is needed since moisture from the
produce helps to cook them, too.

When assembling casseroles, be certain to use the correct size container.
Cooking time differs according to the
depth and size of the dish, so it's best to
use the size container specified.

To ensure that microwaves penetrate
evenly, rotate the dish as it cooks. Just
give the casserole half- or quarter-turns
at intervals during microwaving.

With some experimenting, you can
convert your conventional vegetable
casserole recipes to microwave recipes.
Less liquid evaporates during microwave cooking, so reduce the liquid in
the original recipe by about half. If the
casserole contains cheese or sour cream,
cook at MEDIUM HIGH (70% power)
or lower to prevent curdling.

Also, casseroles will not brown in the
microwave. If the conventional recipe
calls for buttered, soft breadcrumbs, use
fine, dry breadcrumbs instead.

SCALLOPED CARROTS-AND-CELERY

¼ cup water
¼ teaspoon salt
1½ pounds carrots, scraped and
  diagonally sliced
3 tablespoons butter or margarine
½ cup diagonally sliced celery
3 tablespoons minced onion
3 tablespoons all-purpose flour
¼ teaspoon salt
¼ teaspoon dry mustard
1¼ cups milk
¾ cup (3 ounces) shredded Cheddar
  cheese
2 tablespoons butter or margarine
⅓ cup fine, dry breadcrumbs

Place water and salt in a 2-quart casserole. Add carrots, and cover with
heavy-duty plastic wrap. Microwave at
HIGH for 9 to 10 minutes, stirring after
5 minutes. Drain carrots, and set aside.

Place 3 tablespoons butter in a 1½-
quart casserole. Microwave at HIGH
for 50 seconds or until melted. Add celery and onion; cover and microwave at
HIGH for 3 minutes or until tender.

Add flour, salt, and dry mustard to
sautéed vegetables; blend until smooth.
Gradually stir in milk. Microwave at
HIGH for 1½ minutes; stir well. Microwave at HIGH for 2 to 3 minutes, stirring at 1-minute intervals until

thickened and bubbly. Add the cheese, stirring until melted. Stir in carrots.

Place 2 tablespoons butter in a 1-cup glass measure. Microwave at HIGH for 45 seconds or until melted. Combine butter and breadcrumbs; sprinkle over casserole. Microwave at MEDIUM (50% power) 2 to 4 minutes. Yield: 6 servings.

CREAMY POTATO CASSEROLE

8 medium potatoes, peeled and cut into 1-inch cubes
⅓ cup water
2 (3-ounce) packages cream cheese, softened
1 (8-ounce) carton commercial sour cream
¼ cup chopped chives
½ teaspoon salt
¼ teaspoon garlic salt
½ cup butter or margarine
Paprika
Fresh parsley sprigs

Place potatoes in a 2-quart glass bowl. Add water, and cover with heavy-duty plastic wrap. Microwave at HIGH for 12 to 14 minutes or until potatoes are tender, stirring after 6 minutes. Drain potatoes, and mash.

Beat cream cheese with an electric mixer until smooth. Add potatoes and the next 4 ingredients; beat just until combined.

Place butter in a shallow 1¾-quart casserole. Microwave at HIGH for 1 minute or until melted. Add potato mixture, stirring until well combined. Sprinkle with paprika. Cover casserole with heavy-duty plastic wrap, and microwave at HIGH for 3 to 4 minutes, giving dish a half-turn after 1½ minutes. Reduce heat to MEDIUM (50% power), and microwave for 8 to 10 minutes or until thoroughly heated, giving dish a half-turn after 4 minutes. Let stand 3 to 5 minutes. Garnish with parsley. Yield: 6 to 8 servings.

ZUCCHINI-EGG CASSEROLE

¼ cup water
¼ teaspoon salt
1 pound zucchini, coarsely chopped
2 tablespoons butter or margarine
1 cup sliced fresh mushrooms
⅓ cup chopped onion
4 eggs, beaten
1½ cups (6 ounces) shredded Cheddar cheese
1 (2-ounce) jar diced pimiento, drained
¼ teaspoon garlic salt
⅛ teaspoon pepper

Combine first 3 ingredients in a 2-quart bowl. Cover with heavy-duty plastic wrap. Microwave at HIGH for 8 to 10 minutes, stirring after 5 minutes. Drain well, and set zucchini aside.

Add butter to bowl. Microwave at HIGH for 45 seconds or until melted. Add mushrooms and onion; cover and microwave at HIGH for 1½ to 2 minutes, stirring after 30 seconds. Add zucchini to sautéed vegetables.

Combine remaining ingredients; stir into vegetables. Pour into a greased 10- x 6- x 2-inch baking dish. Cover with waxed paper, and microwave at MEDIUM HIGH (70% power) for 4 minutes. Remove waxed paper and stir; microwave at MEDIUM HIGH an additional 4 to 6 minutes or until center is set. Let stand for 2 minutes; serve immediately. Yield: 4 to 6 servings.

CHEDDAR-SQUASH BAKE

4 slices bacon
4 cups thinly sliced yellow squash
⅔ cup chopped onion
¼ cup water
2 eggs, separated
½ cup commercial sour cream
2 tablespoons all-purpose flour
¼ teaspoon salt
¼ teaspoon pepper
¼ teaspoon onion powder
1½ cups (6 ounces) shredded Cheddar cheese
1 tablespoon butter or margarine
¼ cup fine, dry breadcrumbs

Place bacon on a bacon rack in a 12- x 8- x 2-inch baking dish; cover with paper towels. Microwave at HIGH for 3½ to 4½ minutes or until bacon is crisp. Drain, crumble, and set aside.

Place squash and onion in a 2-quart casserole; add water. Cover with heavy-duty plastic wrap; microwave at HIGH for 7 to 9 minutes, stirring after 4 minutes. Drain and cool slightly.

Beat egg yolks until thick and lemon-colored; stir in next 5 ingredients. Beat egg whites (at room temperature) until stiff peaks form; fold into yolk mixture.

Layer half each of squash, egg mixture, and cheese in a lightly greased deep 1½-quart casserole. Sprinkle bacon on top. Layer remaining squash, egg mixture, and cheese. Microwave at MEDIUM HIGH (70% power) for 6 minutes, stirring after 3 minutes.

Place butter in a 1-cup glass measure. Microwave at HIGH for 35 seconds or until melted. Combine butter and breadcrumbs; sprinkle over casserole. Microwave at MEDIUM HIGH (70% power) for 2 to 3 minutes. Let stand 5 minutes. Yield: 6 to 8 servings.

Say Cheese For Flavor

Whether it's creamy Monterey Jack, sharp Cheddar, or nutty-tasting Swiss, cheese adds zest to party foods, protein to meatless main dishes, and a tasty topping or filling to casseroles. In the following recipes, some of our readers share their ideas for using cheese to make food more interesting.

A little Parmesan cheese and softened butter offer a quick and easy way to add an elegant touch to your next dinner party. Just mix the cheese and butter with seasonings, spoon into pretty butter molds, and chill. If you don't have molds to use, shape the mixture into a cylinder, and cut into slices after chilling. If you wish, you can cut the slices with canapé cutters.

BAKED LENTILS WITH CHEESE

1½ cups dried lentils, washed and sorted
2 (8-ounce) cans tomato sauce
2 cups water
1 medium onion, chopped
2 cloves garlic, crushed
1½ teaspoons salt
2 bay leaves
¼ teaspoon pepper
¼ teaspoon ground sage
¼ teaspoon dried whole thyme
¼ teaspoon dried whole marjoram
2 carrots, thinly sliced
1 cup thinly sliced celery
1 medium-size green pepper, chopped
2 tablespoons chopped fresh parsley
1½ cups (6 ounces) shredded Cheddar cheese

Combine first 11 ingredients in a lightly greased 2½-quart casserole; cover and bake at 375° for 30 minutes.

Add vegetables to casserole; cover and bake 30 minutes or until vegetables are tender. Stir in parsley; sprinkle cheese on top. Bake, uncovered, 5 minutes. Yield: 6 servings. *Barbie Hatfield, Mena, Arkansas.*

SPICY MEXICAN BEAN CASSEROLE

1 (8-ounce) carton commercial sour cream
1 cup cream-style cottage cheese
2 cups (8 ounces) shredded Monterey Jack cheese
¼ cup chopped green onions
2 tablespoons chopped green chiles
¼ teaspoon salt
¼ cup chopped onion
2 tablespoons chopped green pepper
1 clove garlic, minced
1 tablespoon vegetable oil
1 (16-ounce) can whole tomatoes, undrained and coarsely chopped
2 (16-ounce) cans red kidney beans, drained
1 (8-ounce) can tomato sauce
1½ teaspoons chili powder
1 (2¼-ounce) can sliced ripe olives, drained
2 cups crushed corn chips, divided
1 cup (4 ounces) shredded sharp Cheddar cheese

Combine first 6 ingredients, mixing well; set aside.

Sauté ¼ cup chopped onion, green pepper, and garlic in hot oil in a large saucepan until tender. Stir in tomatoes, beans, tomato sauce, and chili powder; bring to a boil. Reduce heat and simmer 5 minutes; stir in olives.

Sprinkle ½ cup corn chips in a lightly greased 2½-quart casserole. Layer with half each of sour cream mixture and bean mixture. Sprinkle with ¾ cup corn chips; layer with remaining sour cream mixture and bean mixture. Bake, uncovered, at 350° for 30 minutes. Sprinkle with remaining ¾ cup corn chips and Cheddar cheese; bake an additional 5 minutes. Yield: 6 to 8 servings.

CHILI-CHEESE ROLL

1 (16-ounce) package process cheese, softened
2 (3-ounce) packages cream cheese, softened
3 cloves garlic, crushed
1 cup finely chopped pecans
Chili powder

Combine process cheese and cream cheese in a large bowl; beat on medium speed of an electric mixer until smooth. Add garlic and pecans; mix well.

Divide mixture into 2 equal portions. Shape each into an 8-inch log, and roll in chili powder. Cover and chill several hours or overnight. Serve with crackers. Yield: 2 cheese logs.

Mrs. C. H. Althage,
San Antonio, Texas.

CHEESE-EGG-ZUCCHINI CASSEROLE

2 medium zucchini, cut into ¼-inch slices
1 small onion, thinly sliced
1 tablespoon vegetable oil
3 tomatoes, peeled and chopped
1 (4-ounce) can chopped green chiles, drained
⅛ teaspoon salt
3 eggs, beaten
1 cup (4 ounces) shredded Monterey Jack cheese

Cook zucchini in a small amount of water in a saucepan 5 minutes. Drain and set aside.

Sauté onion in vegetable oil in a skillet until tender; stir in tomatoes, green chiles, and salt.

Layer half each of zucchini, tomato mixture, eggs, and cheese in a 2-quart casserole. Repeat layers. Bake at 350° for 25 minutes. Yield: 6 servings.

Pamela Deutsch,
Dallas, Texas.

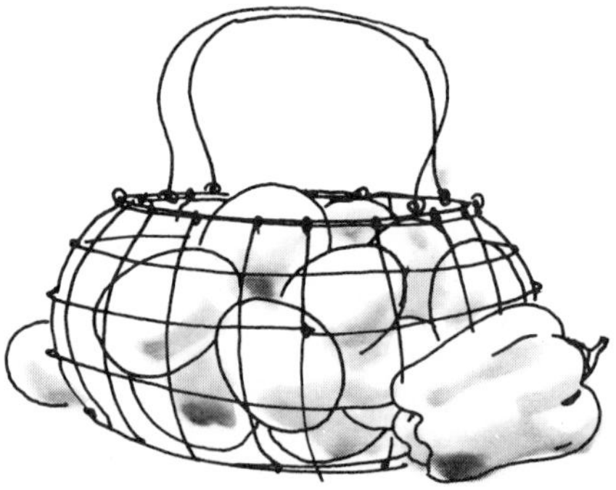

VEGETARIAN OMELET

¼ cup commercial Italian salad dressing
½ cup shredded carrots
¼ cup chopped green onions
¼ cup chopped green pepper
½ cup chopped, peeled cucumber
1 medium tomato, coarsely chopped
8 eggs
¼ cup milk
½ to ¾ teaspoon salt
¼ teaspoon coarsely ground black pepper
2 tablespoons butter or margarine, divided
1 cup (4 ounces) shredded Swiss cheese, divided
1 cup alfalfa sprouts, divided
Plain yogurt (optional)
Snipped chives (optional)

Heat salad dressing in a small saucepan. Add carrots, green onions, and green pepper; cook just until tender, stirring occasionally. Remove from heat; stir in cucumber and tomato.

Combine eggs, milk, salt, and pepper in a medium bowl; mix just until blended.

Heat an 8-inch omelet pan or heavy skillet over medium heat until hot enough to sizzle a drop of water. Add ½ tablespoon butter; rotate pan to coat bottom. Pour one-fourth of egg mixture into skillet. As mixture begins to cook, lift edges with a spatula, and tilt pan so uncooked portion flows underneath.

When egg mixture is set, spoon one-fourth of vegetable mixture over half of omelet; top with ¼ cup cheese and ¼ cup sprouts. Loosen omelet with spatula, and fold in half. Slide omelet onto a warm serving plate. Garnish with a dollop of yogurt, and sprinkle with chives, if desired.

Repeat with remaining ingredients, making 4 omelets. Serve immediately. Yield: 4 servings.

CHEESE BUTTER

¼ cup butter or margarine, softened
¼ cup grated Parmesan cheese
⅛ teaspoon salt
⅛ teaspoon white pepper

Combine all ingredients, mixing well. Spoon into small butter molds, or shape butter into a cylinder. Chill until firm. Serve with rolls or use on vegetables. Yield: about ¼ cup.

Ruth E. Cunliffe,
Lake Placid, Florida.

Dressing Up The Salad

It's so easy to mix up your own salad dressing using fresh ingredients you have on hand. Use our recipes to crown your salads with a spicy dressing. They're thick with mayonnaise, sour cream, catsup, and buttermilk.

DOWN-HOME BUTTERMILK DRESSING

2 cups mayonnaise
2 cups buttermilk
2 tablespoons minced onion
2 tablespoons minced parsley
½ teaspoon garlic powder

Combine all ingredients, mixing well. Chill several hours or overnight. Serve over salad greens. Yield: 3¾ cups.

Gwen Granderson,
Kingsland, Arkansas.

TANGY SALAD DRESSING

1 (8-ounce) carton commercial sour
  cream
2 tablespoons chopped pimiento
1 tablespoon minced green onion
1 teaspoon Dijon mustard
½ teaspoon sugar
½ teaspoon salt
¼ teaspoon celery seeds
⅛ teaspoon garlic powder

Combine all ingredients, mixing well. Cover and chill. Serve over salad greens. Yield: about 1¼ cups.

Joy Hall,
Lucedale, Mississippi.

CURRIED DRESSING

1 cup mayonnaise
½ cup commercial sour cream
¼ cup chopped fresh parsley
1 tablespoon grated onion
1½ teaspoons lemon juice
½ teaspoon Worcestershire
  sauce
¼ teaspoon curry powder
¼ teaspoon paprika
¼ teaspoon salt

Combine all ingredients, mixing well. Cover and chill. Serve over salad greens or with raw vegetables. Yield: about 1½ cups.

Judy Mogridge,
Augusta, Georgia.

TOSSED SALAD DRESSING

2 cups catsup
½ cup mayonnaise
2 tablespoons cider vinegar
1 small onion, finely chopped
¼ cup finely chopped celery
1 teaspoon prepared mustard
5 drops hot sauce
2 hard-cooked eggs, finely
  chopped
¼ cup sweet pickle relish
1 small clove garlic, crushed

Combine all ingredients, mixing well. Cover and chill. Serve over salad greens. Yield: 3 cups.

Pauline Sumners,
Huntsville, Alabama.

Some Thirst Quenchers For Two

Whether it's a hot afternoon in the sun or a cozy evening indoors, when the beverage craving hits, give in to it. With only a quick stir of a spoon or pulse of the blender, you can sip on these tasty thirst quenchers. How about an old-fashioned Strawberry Soda or an Apricot Shake that's high in nutrients and low in sugar? And don't worry—you won't have leftovers. All recipes are sized just for the two of you.

ALMOND-COFFEE DELIGHT

¼ cup amaretto
¼ cup Kahlúa or other coffee-flavored
  liqueur
1½ cups vanilla ice cream
5 to 7 ice cubes

Combine all ingredients in container of an electric blender; process until frothy. Serve immediately. Yield: about 2¼ cups.

Patricia Boschen,
Ashland, Virginia.

FROSTED MARGARITAS

Lime wedge
Salt
¼ cup plus 2 tablespoons tequila
¼ cup fresh lime juice
2 tablespoons Triple Sec
¼ cup sifted powdered sugar
1½ cups coarsely cracked ice

Rub rim of 2 cocktail glasses with wedge of lime. Place salt in saucer; spin rim of each glass in salt.

Combine remaining ingredients in container of an electric blender; process until mixture reaches desired consistency. Pour into the prepared glasses. Yield: 2 servings.

Mrs. Charles P. McGinty,
Cape Girardeau, Missouri.

EASY BLOODY MARY

¼ cup plus 2 tablespoons vodka
½ teaspoon Worcestershire sauce
⅛ teaspoon hot sauce
Dash of pepper
¼ teaspoon lime juice
1⅔ cups cocktail vegetable juice

Combine all ingredients; stir well. Chill. Yield: 2 cups.

Lois Schlatter,
Rochester, Michigan.

STRAWBERRY SODA

1 cup milk
½ cup fresh or frozen whole strawberries
½ cup vanilla ice cream, softened
2 tablespoons sugar
1 cup ginger ale, chilled

Combine first 4 ingredients in container of an electric blender, and process until smooth. Pour mixture into 2 glasses; add ginger ale. Serve immediately. Yield: 3 cups.

Mrs. Harlan J. Stone,
Ocala, Florida.

PEANUT BUTTER COOLER

3 cups milk
¼ cup honey
¼ cup creamy peanut butter
½ teaspoon vanilla extract
Whole strawberries (optional)

Combine first 4 ingredients in container of an electric blender; process until smooth. Serve immediately. Garnish with whole strawberries skewered on party picks, if desired. Yield: about 3¼ cups.

Harriett A. Chilton,
Falls Church, Virginia.

APRICOT SHAKE

2¾ cups milk
½ cup dried apricots
2 tablespoons plus 1½ teaspoons sugar
1 teaspoon vanilla extract
Apricot flowers (optional)

Combine the first 4 ingredients in container of an electric blender; process until smooth.

Garnish beverage with an apricot flower threaded on a straw, if desired. To make apricot flower, place 1 whole dried apricot, moist side down, on an absorbent paper towel. Roll apricot with a rolling pin to slightly flatten it. (Paper towel will absorb excess moisture from apricot.) Cut slits all around apricot using kitchen shears, cutting to but not through center. Hold apricot, drier side down, and pinch center of apricot to make top of apricot bunch into petals. Thread center of flower onto straw, pinching flower so it adheres to straw. Serve drink immediately. Yield: about 3 cups.

Bettina H. Hambrick,
Muskogee, Oklahoma.

Dainty Food For Teas And Showers

Spring is the time for fresh flowers and lots of parties. If you plan on hosting a tea, bridal shower, or reception, then turn to these recipes. They offer some attractive suggestions that will make food the center of attention.

SHRIMP CANAPES

20 slices white bread
2 tablespoons butter or margarine, melted
½ teaspoon dried whole thyme
¼ pound frozen, cooked shrimp, thawed and minced
½ cup (2 ounces) shredded Swiss cheese
⅓ cup mayonnaise
¼ teaspoon salt
Radish slices
Small sprigs of fresh dillweed (optional)

Cut each slice of bread into 2 decorative shapes using 2-inch cutters. Make breadcrumbs from leftover bread pieces; set aside ½ cup. Reserve any remaining breadcrumbs for use in other recipes.

Combine butter and thyme; brush over bread cutouts. Place cutouts on cookie sheets; broil 6 inches away from heat for 1 minute or until lightly browned. Cool.

Combine the ½ cup reserved breadcrumbs, shrimp, cheese, mayonnaise, and salt; mix well and spread on bread cutouts. Bake at 425° for 7 minutes or until bubbly; garnish each canapé with a radish slice and a sprig of dillweed, if desired. Yield: about 3½ dozen.

Carolyn Look,
El Paso, Texas.

Serve guests these pretty party foods: (front) Gingered Tea Sandwiches and Cucumber Delights, (back, left) Ham-Filled Party Puffs, and (back, right) Currant Scones.

HAM-FILLED PARTY PUFFS

1 cup water
½ cup butter
1 cup all-purpose flour
4 eggs
1 (3-ounce) package cream cheese, softened
⅓ cup commercial sour cream
2 (4½-ounce) cans deviled ham
3 tablespoons prepared horseradish
¾ teaspoon white pepper
¾ teaspoon onion powder

Combine water and butter in a medium saucepan; bring mixture to a boil. Reduce heat to low and add flour, stirring vigorously until mixture leaves sides of pan and forms a smooth ball. Remove saucepan from heat, and allow mixture to cool slightly.

Add eggs, one at a time, beating after each addition with a wooden spoon until dough is smooth.

Drop dough by rounded teaspoonfuls 2 inches apart on ungreased baking sheets. Bake at 400° for 25 minutes or until golden brown and puffed. Cool away from drafts.

Beat cream cheese with an electric mixer until smooth. Add remaining ingredients, and beat well; cover mixture, and chill 1 hour.

Cut off top of each pastry puff; pull out and discard the soft dough inside. Fill each pastry bottom with about 1 tablespoon ham mixture; then cover with pastry tops. Yield: 4½ dozen.

GINGERED TEA SANDWICHES

1 (3-ounce) package cream cheese, softened
1 tablespoon milk
1 tablespoon minced crystallized ginger
1 (8-ounce) can date-nut bread
Additional cream cheese, softened (optional)

Combine cream cheese and milk; beat until smooth. Stir in ginger.

Cut bread into fourteen ¼-inch slices. Spread cream cheese mixture on half the bread slices; top with remaining bread. Chill well. Cut each sandwich into quarters. Use additional cream cheese to make rosette garnishes, if desired. Yield: 14 appetizer servings.

Claire Bastable,
Chevy Chase, Maryland.

CURRANT SCONES

3 cups all-purpose flour
1 tablespoon baking powder
2 tablespoons sugar
2 tablespoons butter
½ cup currants
1 egg
¾ cup milk
Additional milk

Combine first 3 ingredients, mixing well. Cut in butter with a pastry blender until mixture resembles coarse meal. Stir in currants.

Combine egg and ¾ cup milk, beating well. Add to flour mixture, stirring until dry ingredients are moistened. Turn dough out onto a lightly floured surface; knead lightly 8 to 10 times.

Roll dough to ½-inch thickness; cut with a 2-inch biscuit cutter. Place scones on an ungreased baking sheet. Brush tops lightly with additional milk. Bake at 450° for 10 minutes or until scones are golden brown. Serve with butter and jam. Yield: 1 dozen.

Vivienne Johnson,
Birmingham, Alabama.

CREAMY ORANGE DIP

1 (8-ounce) package cream cheese,
  softened
1 (7-ounce) jar marshmallow creme
2 tablespoons grated orange rind
¼ cup orange juice
¼ teaspoon ground ginger

Combine all ingredients; beat mixture until smooth. Serve with strawberries and angel food cake cubes. Yield: about 1½ cups.

Brenda Heupel,
Florence, Alabama.

LEMON-PEPPER CHEESE PATTY

2 (8-ounce) packages cream cheese,
  softened
2 cloves garlic, crushed
2 teaspoons caraway seeds
2 teaspoons dried whole basil
2 teaspoons dried whole dillweed
2 teaspoons chopped chives
2 to 3 tablespoons lemon-pepper
  marinade

Combine first 6 ingredients; mix well. Shape into a 5- x 1-inch round patty; coat top and sides with lemon-pepper marinade. Cover and chill 10 to 12 hours; serve cheese patty with assorted crackers. Yield: one 5-inch round.

Mrs. C. E. McWilliams,
Montgomery, Alabama.

QUICK PATE SPREAD

1 (8-ounce) package cream cheese,
  softened
1 (8-ounce) package liverwurst
2 tablespoons finely chopped onion
1 teaspoon chicken-flavored bouillon
  granules

Beat cream cheese until light and fluffy. Add remaining ingredients, mixing well. Chill. Serve spread with crackers. Yield: 2 cups.   *Cathy Darling,*
Grafton, West Virginia.

CUCUMBER DELIGHTS

1 (5-ounce) can chunk white chicken,
  drained and flaked
1 hard-cooked egg, finely chopped
½ cup mayonnaise
¼ cup finely chopped onion
¼ cup finely chopped green pepper
2 tablespoons finely chopped pecans,
  toasted
Dash of salt
Dash of white pepper
5 dozen cucumber slices
5 dozen pecan halves, toasted

Combine first 8 ingredients; cover and refrigerate at least 2 hours.

Spread 1 teaspoon chicken mixture on each cucumber slice; top each with a toasted pecan half. Yield: 5 dozen.

Pam Brown,
Euless, Texas.

HAZELNUT-LEMON LOGS

1 cup butter or margarine, softened
¾ cup firmly packed light brown
  sugar
1 teaspoon grated lemon rind
1 tablespoon lemon juice
2½ cups all-purpose flour
¼ teaspoon salt
½ cup finely chopped hazelnuts

Cream butter; gradually add sugar, beating until light and fluffy. Stir in lemon rind and juice. Combine flour and salt. Add to creamed mixture; beat well. Cover and chill at least 1 hour.

Shape dough into 2½-inch-long cookies, using a heaping teaspoonful of dough for each cookie. Lightly roll each cookie in nuts; place about 2 inches apart on ungreased cookie sheets. Bake at 400° for 8 to 10 minutes or until cookies are lightly browned. Cool on wire racks. Yield: about 4 dozen.

Mrs. Earl L. Faulkenberry,
Lancaster, South Carolina.

PARTY CITRUS PUNCH

¼ cup citric acid
½ cup boiling water
6 cups sugar
5 quarts cold water
1 (46-ounce) can pineapple juice, chilled
1 (6-ounce) can frozen orange juice
  concentrate, thawed and undiluted
1 quart ginger ale, chilled

Combine citric acid and ½ cup boiling water, stirring until the powder dissolves.

Combine sugar and cold water, stirring until sugar dissolves. Stir in the citric acid mixture, pineapple juice, and orange juice concentrate.

Add ginger ale just before serving. Serve over ice. Yield: about 2 gallons.

Betty Baird,
Utica, Kentucky.

Try These Entrées For Supper

Do you find yourself short on entrée ideas for supper? If you're cooking for two, we suggest Steak de Burgo. But if you're expecting a larger crowd, we suggest Picadillo, a Mexican-style dish of spicy beef wrapped in flour tortillas.

STEAK DE BURGO

1 clove garlic, minced
½ teaspoon dried whole basil
2 large fresh mushrooms, fluted
2 tablespoons butter or margarine
2 (1¼- to 1½-inch-thick) tenderloin steaks
Salt
Freshly ground pepper
2 thick slices French bread, toasted

Sauté garlic, basil, and mushrooms in butter in a large skillet until garlic is browned and mushrooms are tender; remove mushrooms, and set aside. Sprinkle both sides of steaks with salt and pepper. Add steak to skillet; cook over medium-high heat 4 minutes on each side or until desired degree of doneness. To serve, place steak on bread; top each serving with a mushroom. Spoon pan drippings over steaks, and serve immediately. Yield: 2 servings.

Cheryl Keener,
Lenoir, North Carolina.

THICK SPAGHETTI SAUCE

2 pounds ground beef
1 cup minced onion
2 cloves garlic, minced
2 (16-ounce) cans tomatoes, undrained and chopped
1 (6-ounce) can tomato paste
¼ cup chopped fresh parsley or 2 tablespoons dried parsley flakes
2 or 3 bay leaves
1 teaspoon salt
1½ teaspoons ground oregano
1 teaspoon brown sugar
¼ teaspoon ground thyme
1 cup water
Hot cooked spaghetti
Grated Parmesan cheese

Cook ground beef, onion, and garlic in a heavy Dutch oven over medium heat until meat is browned; drain off drippings. Stir in next 9 ingredients. Simmer, uncovered, 3 hours or until sauce is thickened, stirring occasionally. Remove bay leaves.

Serve sauce over spaghetti; sprinkle with cheese. Yield: 6 to 8 servings.

Margaret Myers,
Amherst, Virginia.

PICADILLO

2 tablespoons olive oil
1 medium onion, finely chopped
4 small cloves garlic, crushed
1½ pounds lean ground beef
3 large tomatoes, peeled and chopped
1 medium-size green pepper, chopped
¾ cup raisins
½ cup sliced pimiento-stuffed olives
1 teaspoon salt
2 teaspoons vinegar
¼ teaspoon ground cloves
About 20 (6-inch) flour tortillas
Vegetable oil
Commercial taco sauce

Heat olive oil in a large skillet; add onion and garlic, and sauté until tender. Add ground beef; cook over medium heat until browned, stirring to crumble. Drain off pan drippings.

Add next 7 ingredients; stir well. Simmer, uncovered, 20 to 25 minutes, stirring occasionally, until most of the liquid is gone.

Fry tortillas, one at a time, in ¼ inch hot oil (375°) for 5 seconds on each side or just until softened. Drain tortillas on paper towels.

Spoon 2 to 3 tablespoons beef mixture on each tortilla; roll up tightly. Place on serving dish. Serve with taco sauce. Yield: 10 servings.

Elizabeth J. Cooper,
Houston, Texas.

OVEN-FRIED CHICKEN

1½ cups pancake mix
1 teaspoon salt
2 teaspoons paprika
½ teaspoon onion salt
½ teaspoon garlic powder
¼ teaspoon pepper
½ cup milk
2 eggs, beaten
1 (2½- to 3-pound) broiler-fryer, cut up and skinned
⅓ cup butter or margarine, melted

Combine first 6 ingredients; set aside ½ cup. Store remaining mix in an airtight container for later use.

Combine milk and eggs. Dip chicken in egg mixture; then dredge in ½ cup pancake mixture. Place chicken on a rack in a shallow baking pan; drizzle with melted butter. Bake, uncovered, at 350° for 1 hour or until done. Yield: 4 servings.

Gloria McCluskey,
Pensacola, Florida.

Try These Chocolate Chip Favorites

Chocolate chip cookies and a glass of cold milk—what could be better for an after-school or bedtime snack? Giant Chocolate Chip Cookies are oversized versions of the basic cookie, while Chocolate Chip Melt-a-Ways and Chocolate Chip-Oatmeal Cookies are two other variations.

CHOCOLATE CHIP MELT-AWAYS

1 cup butter or margarine, softened
1 cup vegetable oil
1 cup sugar
1 cup sifted powdered sugar
2 eggs
4 cups all-purpose flour
1 teaspoon baking soda
1 teaspoon cream of tartar
1 teaspoon salt
1 teaspoon vanilla extract
1 (12-ounce) package semisweet chocolate morsels
Additional sugar

Combine first 5 ingredients in a large mixing bowl; beat until smooth. Combine flour, soda, cream of tartar, and salt; add to butter mixture. Beat until

smooth; stir in vanilla and chocolate morsels. Shape mixture into 1-inch balls; roll in sugar. Place 2 inches apart on ungreased cookie sheets; bake at 375° for 10 to 12 minutes or until lightly browned. Cool cookies on wire racks. Yield: about 8½ dozen.

Carol S. Noble,
Burgaw, North Carolina.

CHOCOLATE CHIP-PEANUT BUTTER SQUARES

⅓ cup butter or margarine, melted
½ cup sugar
½ cup firmly packed brown sugar
½ cup chunky peanut butter
½ teaspoon vanilla extract
1 egg, beaten
¼ cup milk
1½ cups all-purpose flour
½ teaspoon baking soda
½ teaspoon salt
1 (6-ounce) package semisweet chocolate morsels

Combine first 7 ingredients; mix well.

Combine flour, soda, and salt; add dry ingredients and chocolate morsels to peanut butter mixture, stirring well. Pour batter into a greased 9-inch square pan. Bake at 375° for 25 minutes. Cool completely; cut into squares. Yield: 3 dozen.

Lynette L. Walther,
East Palatka, Florida.

MERINGUE-CHOCOLATE CHIP BARS

1½ cups all-purpose flour
½ cup firmly packed brown sugar
½ cup butter or margarine, melted
1 (6-ounce) package semisweet chocolate morsels
1½ cups chopped pecans
3 egg whites
1 cup firmly packed brown sugar

Combine flour and ½ cup brown sugar in a small bowl. Stir in butter, blending well. Press mixture evenly into an ungreased 13- x 9- x 2-inch baking pan. Sprinkle with the chocolate chips and pecans.

Beat egg whites (at room temperature) until foamy. Gradually add 1 cup brown sugar, beating until stiff peaks form. Carefully spread meringue over chocolate chips and pecans. Bake at 375° for 18 to 20 minutes. Cool, and cut into squares. Yield: 4 dozen.

Debbie Kremers,
Virginia Beach, Virginia.

CHOCOLATE CHIP-OATMEAL COOKIES

1 cup butter or margarine, softened
¾ cup sugar
¾ cup firmly packed brown sugar
2 eggs
1 teaspoon vanilla extract
1½ cups all-purpose flour
1 teaspoon baking soda
½ teaspoon baking powder
½ teaspoon salt
2 cups quick-cooking oats, uncooked
1 (12-ounce) package semisweet chocolate morsels
1 cup chopped pecans

Cream butter; gradually add sugar, beating until light and fluffy. Add eggs and vanilla, beating well. Combine flour, soda, baking powder, and salt; add to creamed mixture, beating well. Stir in remaining ingredients.

Drop dough by heaping teaspoonfuls onto ungreased cookie sheets; bake at 375° for 8 to 10 minutes. Cool slightly on cookie sheets; remove to wire racks. Yield: about 7½ dozen. *Billie Taylor, Afton, Virginia.*

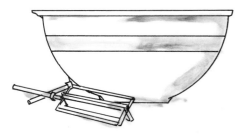

GIANT CHOCOLATE CHIP COOKIES

1 cup butter or margarine, softened
1 cup firmly packed brown sugar
½ cup sugar
2 eggs
2¼ cups all-purpose flour
1 teaspoon baking soda
½ teaspoon salt
1 teaspoon vanilla extract
1½ cups semisweet chocolate morsels
¾ cup chopped pecans

Cream butter; gradually add sugar, beating until light and fluffy. Add eggs, and beat until blended.

Combine flour, soda, and salt. Add to creamed mixture, mixing well. Stir in vanilla, chocolate morsels, and pecans.

Divide mixture into thirds. Spoon each third onto an ungreased cookie sheet, spreading into an 8½-inch circle. Bake at 375° for 12 to 14 minutes or until lightly browned. Gently remove from cookie sheets, and let cool on wire racks. Yield: three 10-inch cookies.

Serve The Entrée In A Shell

Sleek green zucchini and fat red tomatoes make delicious side dishes, but when sliced and stuffed with a filling, they make attractive entrées.

BAKED AVOCADO-AND-CRABMEAT

4 avocados
Lemon juice
8 small cloves garlic
2 tablespoons butter
2 tablespoons all-purpose flour
1 cup half-and-half
1 pound fresh crabmeat, drained and flaked
½ cup chopped fresh mushrooms
2 tablespoons dry sherry
½ teaspoon salt
¼ teaspoon white pepper
Pinch of sugar
½ cup (2 ounces) shredded sharp Cheddar cheese

Cut avocados in half lengthwise; remove seed, and peel. Brush with lemon juice. Place a garlic clove and 1 tablespoon lemon juice in each avocado half; set aside.

Melt butter in a heavy saucepan over low heat; add flour, stirring until smooth. Cook 1 minute, stirring constantly. Gradually add the half-and-half; cook over medium heat, stirring constantly, until sauce is thickened and bubbly. Stir in next 6 ingredients.

Remove garlic and lemon juice from avocado halves and discard; fill each avocado half with crabmeat mixture. Place avocados in a 13- x 9- x 2-inch baking pan. Bake at 350° for 10 minutes. Sprinkle with cheese; bake an additional 5 minutes. Yield: 8 servings.
Hazel Sellers, Albany, Georgia.

TURKEY-TOMATO CUPS

1 small avocado, peeled and chopped
2 tablespoons lemon juice
3 cups chopped, cooked turkey
¼ cup thinly sliced celery
¼ cup chopped pimiento-stuffed olives
½ cup commercial Italian salad dressing
2 tablespoons chopped pimiento
½ teaspoon curry powder
6 medium tomatoes

Toss the avocado in lemon juice. Add the next 6 ingredients, and mix well.

With stem end up, cut each tomato into 4 wedges, cutting to, but not through, base of tomato. Spread wedges slightly apart. Spoon turkey filling into shells. Yield: 6 servings. *Dixie Barger, Enid, Oklahoma.*

TACO-BAKED POTATOES

4 medium baking potatoes
Vegetable oil
1 pound ground beef
½ cup chopped onion
1 (1¼-ounce) package taco seasoning mix
1 cup water
¼ cup commercial sour cream

Wash potatoes, and rub with oil. Bake at 400° for 1 hour or until soft when pierced with a fork.

Cook ground beef and onion in a large skillet until beef is browned, stirring to crumble. Drain well. Add seasoning mix and water; reduce heat and simmer 15 to 20 minutes, stirring occasionally. Split tops of potatoes lengthwise, and fluff pulp with a fork. Spoon topping over potatoes. Top each potato with 1 tablespoon sour cream. Yield: 4 servings. *Paula Rawlins, Charlotte, North Carolina.*

ITALIAN STUFFED ZUCCHINI

6 medium zucchini
½ pound lean ground beef
½ cup chopped onion
½ cup minced green pepper
2 tablespoons minced fresh oregano or 2 teaspoons dried whole oregano
1 clove garlic, minced
1 tablespoon vegetable oil
1 (10¾-ounce) can tomato soup, undiluted and divided
1 cup grated Parmesan cheese, divided

Wash zucchini; cut in half lengthwise. Scoop out pulp, leaving a ¼-inch shell. Chop pulp, and set aside.

Sauté next 5 ingredients in oil until meat is browned and vegetables are tender. Stir in zucchini pulp, ¼ cup tomato soup, and ½ cup cheese.

Place zucchini shells in two 13- x 9- x 2-inch baking dishes. Spoon meat mixture into shells; pour remaining soup over zucchini. Sprinkle with remaining ½ cup cheese. Cover and bake at 375° for 30 minutes or until zucchini is tender. Uncover and bake an additional 5 minutes. Yield: 6 servings.
Mrs. Hugh F. Mosher, Huntsville, Alabama.

How About A Picnic?

Spring is a great time to pack your basket, head to a favorite spot, and enjoy a delicious picnic. We selected a menu featuring three cold salads: chicken, potato, and marinated vegetable. You'll probably want to carry them in an ice chest. Be sure to include some extra ice to serve with the beverage, Tropical Cooler.

TAHITIAN CHICKEN SALAD

3 cups chopped, cooked chicken
1 (15¼-ounce) can pineapple chunks, drained
1 cup sliced celery
⅓ cup dry roasted peanuts
¼ to ⅓ cup mayonnaise
1 tablespoon sweet pickle relish
½ teaspoon curry powder
Lettuce leaves
Seedless green grape clusters (optional)

Combine first 4 ingredients; set aside. Combine mayonnaise, relish, and curry powder; add to chicken mixture, and toss gently. Serve on lettuce leaves, and garnish with grape clusters, if desired. Yield: 6 servings.   *Frances Bowles, Mableton, Georgia.*

NEW POTATO SALAD

2 pounds new potatoes
½ cup sliced celery
3 hard-cooked eggs, sliced
1 (8-ounce) carton commercial sour cream
1 tablespoon chopped fresh dillweed or 1 teaspoon dried whole dillweed
2 tablespoons vinegar
1 teaspoon sugar
2 teaspoons prepared horseradish
½ teaspoon salt
½ teaspoon dry mustard
⅛ teaspoon freshly ground pepper

Cook potatoes in boiling water to cover 20 minutes or until tender. Drain well, and let cool. Peel potatoes, and slice into ½-inch slices.

Combine potatoes, celery, and eggs in a large bowl; toss gently.

Combine remaining ingredients in a small bowl. Pour over potato mixture; stir gently to coat. Chill thoroughly. Yield: 6 to 8 servings. *Jan Thompson, Highland, Maryland.*

REFRIGERATED VEGETABLE SALAD

1 (16-ounce) can French-style green beans, drained
1 (16-ounce) can chow mein vegetables, drained
1 (8-ounce) can sliced water chestnuts, drained
1 cup chopped celery
1 cup chopped onion
¾ cup sugar
¾ cup vinegar
½ cup vegetable oil

Combine first 5 ingredients in a large bowl; set aside.

Combine remaining ingredients; pour over vegetables, tossing gently. Cover and chill 8 hours or overnight. Yield: 6 to 8 servings.   *Carolyn Look, El Paso, Texas.*

CHOCOLATE CHIP COOKIES

½ cup butter or margarine, softened
½ cup sugar
¼ cup firmly packed dark brown sugar
1 egg
1 teaspoon vanilla extract
1½ cups all-purpose flour
½ teaspoon baking soda
¼ teaspoon salt
1 (6-ounce) package semisweet chocolate morsels
½ cup chopped pecans

Cream butter; gradually add sugar, beating until light and fluffy. Add egg and vanilla, beating well. Combine flour, soda, and salt; add to creamed mixture, beating well. Stir in chocolate morsels and pecans.

Drop dough by heaping teaspoonfuls onto ungreased cookie sheets. Bake at 350° for 10 to 12 minutes. Cool slightly on cookie sheets; remove to wire racks to cool completely. Yield: 4 dozen.

Ann McEwen, Birmingham, Alabama.

TROPICAL COOLER

3 tablespoons sugar
1 tablespoon instant tea
1¾ cups water
1 (12-ounce) can apricot nectar, chilled
1 (6-ounce) can frozen lemonade concentrate, thawed
2 (12-ounce) cans lemon-lime carbonated beverage, chilled

Combine first 3 ingredients; stir until sugar dissolves. Add remaining ingredients; mix well. Serve over ice. Yield: 1½ quarts.   *Azine G. Rush, Monroe, Louisiana.*

Slice At The Touch Of A Button

A food processor will help to save time when slicing vegetables and fruit. The key to pretty, uniform slices is placing the cut or whole produce in the food chute carefully.

For recipes like Relish Salad, which calls for slices of whole tomatoes and onion, look for small produce that will fit in the food chute. If it won't squeeze through the top of the opening, remove the lid and try to position the produce from the bottom, since that opening on some models is slightly larger than the top. Some processors offer the option of a larger feed tube to permit slicing of larger produce. If the food is still too large, cut it in half to slice.

We also suggest slicing the carrots and celery at the same time. Carrots and celery require the same amount of pressure applied during slicing, so the cut pieces should be similar in thickness. You can cut different textured foods at the same time, such as green onions and celery, as well. Just be sure to wedge the onions securely in between the celery stalks.

Most of the food slices from the processor will be thinner than if the food was sliced by hand. Since processor slicing blades offer only one thickness, variations are created by the amount of pressure applied during cutting. You'll get thicker slices by pressing firmly on the food pusher as the blade cuts, and thinner slices by using light pressure.

Our staff enjoyed the paper-thin sliced apples in our recipe for Apple Crisp. The apples are simply peeled, cored, quartered, and placed in the food chute with the cut side against the slicing blade. Alternate the thick and thin sides of the apple pieces when stacking them in the processor.

You can prepare special kinds of cuts in the processor, such as julienne or matchstick strips and French-cut green beans. See the step-by-step photographs for the technique of preparing julienne-cut carrots with a regular slicing blade. Use the same procedure with potatoes for French fries or with cucumbers for tasty salads.

For French-cut beans, string the beans and trim the ends, leaving 2- to 2½-inch pieces. Pack firmly in the food chute, layering the beans horizontally, and slice.

When slicing any food in the processor, don't be concerned if pieces become caught between the processor lid and the blade. This is normal, and most of the trapped food will end up in the work bowl as you continue to slice. Remove any pieces that are left, and cut by hand.

For processor models with several slicing blades, check the manufacturer's instructions for the best blade to use with different produce.

RELISH SALAD

3 small firm tomatoes
1 small cucumber
1 small onion
2 medium carrots, scraped and cut into
  4-inch pieces
3 stalks celery, cut into 4-inch pieces
½ cup tarragon vinegar
⅓ cup water
¼ cup sugar
1 teaspoon paprika
1 teaspoon dried whole basil, crushed
½ teaspoon salt
¼ teaspoon pepper

Select vegetables that are small enough to fit food chute. Remove stem end of tomatoes.

Position slicing blade in processor bowl. Halve larger tomatoes before slicing, if necessary. Place tomato in food chute. Slice, applying medium pressure with food pusher. Drain well.

Position slicing blade in bowl. Slice ends from cucumber. Place cucumber upright in food chute; slice, applying firm pressure with food pusher.

Insert onion through bottom of food chute. Slice, applying firm pressure with food pusher.

Place carrot pieces and celery pieces upright in food chute. Slice, applying firm pressure with food pusher.

Combine remaining ingredients in a jar. Cover tightly, and shake vigorously. Pour over vegetables; cover, and chill at least 4 hours or overnight. Yield: 6 to 8 servings.   *Maybelle Ferrell,*
Dunnellon, Florida.

HONEY-GLAZED CARROTS

12 medium (about 1½ pounds) carrots,
  scraped and cut into 2- to 2½-inch
  pieces
3 tablespoons butter or margarine
¼ cup honey
1 teaspoon grated orange rind
3 tablespoons orange juice
1½ teaspoons salt
¼ teaspoon ground ginger

Position slicing blade in processor bowl. Arrange carrots horizontally in the food chute; slice, applying firm

Save time cutting carrots julienne style for Honey-Glazed Carrots by using the food processor. Garnish with orange wedges and green carrot tops, if desired.

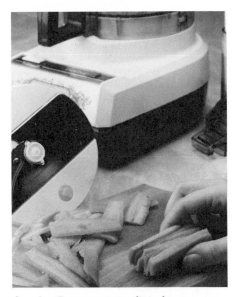

Step 2 —Remove carrot slices from processor bowl and stack, placing cut sides together and keeping ends even.

pressure with food pusher. Stack carrot slices, keeping ends even. Position slicing blade in processor; place slices in bottom of the food chute with cut sides parallel to chute sides. Reattach processor lid, and slice again.

Sauté carrots in butter in a medium saucepan about 5 minutes. Combine remaining ingredients. Pour over carrots, and cook over medium-high heat 15 minutes or until the liquid evaporates. Yield: about 6 servings.
Kate Schoenfelder,
Maryland Heights, Missouri.

Step 1 —To prepare julienne-style carrots, start with large carrots scraped and cut into 2-inch pieces. Layer carrots horizontally in the processor food chute, and slice.

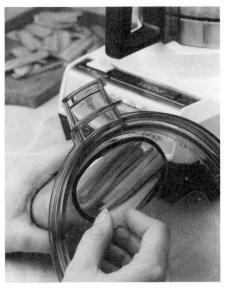

Step 3—Place stacks of slices in the bottom of the food chute, holding food pusher in place. Process using slicing blade.

APPLE CRISP

6 large cooking apples, peeled, cored, and quartered
½ cup sugar
¼ teaspoon ground nutmeg
¼ teaspoon ground cinnamon
1 cup all-purpose flour
1 cup firmly packed brown sugar
½ cup butter or margarine, softened

Position slicing blade in food processor bowl, and top with cover. Arrange apple quarters in food chute with cut side against the blade; slice, applying firm pressure with food pusher. Place sliced apples in a lightly greased 13- x 9- x 2-inch baking dish. Combine ½ cup sugar, nutmeg, and cinnamon. Sprinkle over the sliced apples.

Position plastic mixing blade in food processor bowl; place flour, brown sugar, and butter in bowl. Top with cover, and process until mixture resembles coarse meal. Sprinkle mixture over apples. Bake, uncovered, at 300° for 1 hour. Serve warm with ice cream, if desired. Yield: 8 servings.

Patricia Burch,
Wichita Falls, Texas.

These Vegetables Are Glazed

An easy, delicious way to prepare both carrots and beets is to cook them in a glaze. The clear honey glaze enhances the bright orange color in Honey-Kissed Carrots, while a strawberry jam glaze makes Ivy League Beets even redder.

HONEY-KISSED CARROTS

1 pound carrots, scraped and cut into ½-inch slices
1¼ cups water
⅓ cup golden raisins
⅓ cup honey
2 tablespoons butter

Combine carrots and water in a medium saucepan; cover and simmer 15 minutes or until tender. Add remaining ingredients; cook, uncovered, over medium heat an additional 10 minutes or until carrots are glazed, stirring occasionally. Yield: 4 servings.

Barbara Carson,
Hollywood, Florida.

IVY LEAGUE BEETS

1 pound fresh beets
1 tablespoon cornstarch
⅓ cup water
¼ cup strawberry jam
2 tablespoons lemon juice
¼ teaspoon salt
¼ teaspoon pumpkin pie spice
2 tablespoons butter or margarine

Leave root and 1 inch of stem on beets; scrub with a vegetable brush. Place beets in a saucepan; cover with water, and bring to a boil. Cover, reduce heat, and simmer 35 to 40 minutes or until tender. Drain; rinse beets with cold water, and drain again. Trim off beet roots and stems, and rub off skins; cut beets into ¼-inch slices.

Combine next 6 ingredients in a medium saucepan; cook, stirring constantly, until thickened and bubbly. Stir in beets and butter; cook until beets are glazed and thoroughly heated. Yield: about 4 servings.

Mrs. B. J. Davis,
Lilburn, Georgia.

From Our Kitchen To Yours

Entertaining at home can be fun and easy. Whether you're having a luncheon, a casual get-together, or a formal dinner, planning is the key to success. We'd like to share some tips on selecting a menu and getting organized for the occasion.

Selecting Foods To Fit the Occasion

When we're planning a party menu, we look for foods that vary in color, shape, flavor, and texture. We try to imagine how the plates are going to look when filled with the actual food. Stay away from serving all white foods or lightly browned baked goods. Your selections should come in different colors, shapes, and sizes. In addition, be careful not to include foods that have conflicting flavors.

Your guests will find it easier to serve themselves from a buffet if most of the food is precut. However, eye appeal can be added by leaving at least one item such as a torte or prime rib roast to be sliced as the guests go through the line.

Select a menu that will hold up throughout the party. One trick for keeping sandwiches fresh is to cover them with a damp paper towel until serving time. Avoid crumbly, soft, or sticky items. This is important if guests will be standing up and you don't plan to offer forks.

We find many hostesses prefer to serve "fork food" when possible; it's easier to manage, and guests can relax more. And remember, forks can be arranged attractively on the buffet. Try wrapping each fork with a napkin tied with a piece of ribbon or yarn. Arrange bundles of napkins in a lacy wicker basket or on a silver tray.

Throwing a party is easier when some of the food can be prepared ahead, perhaps as much as a week. You may even want to consider selecting recipes that use convenience foods for speed.

Getting Organized

More and more hosts and hostesses like to entertain as a group. Team effort can be a big help, allowing the main hostess to assign last-minute foods to others. This will free her to work with the table arrangement and other preparations. But if you're the only hostess, then start with a list of what you need to buy.

Purchase foods like canned goods, frozen products, and supplies early. Begin with the items on your menu that have lasting power or that freeze well. Many drop cookies and bar cookies can be frozen if they're stored in airtight containers. Get a head start on sandwiches by preparing the filling early, or begin chopping ingredients for a dip. Melon balls for a fruit salad can be scooped out a day ahead; just remember to keep them tightly sealed and drained so they won't get mushy.

Presenting Your Food

You may have noticed at well-planned parties that the food is the center of attention. To achieve this effect, position food tables where they can easily be reached. If a crowd is expected at your party, putting round skirted tables throughout the house can scatter guests as well as tie color schemes or themes together. Remember if you run out of space, you can always arrange trays on a desk, side table, or étagère.

Flowers or a centerpiece always add color. Many hostesses prefer to use an edible centerpiece of fresh fruit or vegetables. You might want to try your hand at making a shrimp tree or fresh vegetable wreath to wow your guests.

Traffic Flow

To keep the crowd moving and to avoid congestion, never invite more people than your house can comfortably hold. If your guest list keeps growing, you may want to stagger the times on your invitations, or simply move the party outdoors. You could even plan a brunch on the deck or around the pool or tennis court.

But always remember the most important rule for entertaining—just jump right in and enjoy the occasion. The more you entertain, the better hostess you'll become.

Peas Fresh From The Pod

May is the time to put aside canned or frozen English peas and enjoy this vegetable fresh from the pod. Fresh peas offer more flavor and better texture than the packaged form.

Snow peas are a somewhat less common variety of peas. Like English peas, fresh snow peas are most plentiful between May and September. Since the pea itself is extremely small and the pod is tender, the entire snow pea may be eaten raw or used in cooking.

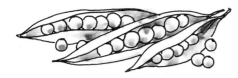

QUICK CREOLE PEAS

2 pounds fresh English peas
¼ cup chopped onion
¼ cup chopped green pepper
2 tablespoons butter or margarine
1 cup peeled, chopped tomato
¼ teaspoon salt
Dash of pepper

Shell and wash peas; cover with water, and bring to a boil. Cover, reduce heat, and simmer 8 to 12 minutes; drain, reserving 2 tablespoons liquid.

Sauté onion and green pepper in butter in a medium skillet until tender. Stir in peas, tomato, salt, pepper, and reserved pea liquid; cook, stirring constantly, until thoroughly heated. Yield: 4 servings.

Note: Two cups frozen peas may be substituted for fresh peas.

Leoda M. Baker,
McEwen, Tennessee.

SKILLET SNOW PEAS WITH CELERY

1 tablespoon cornstarch
1 teaspoon sugar
½ teaspoon salt
1 tablespoon soy sauce
½ cup water
1 pound fresh snow peas
½ cup chopped green onions with tops
¾ cup diagonally sliced celery
2 tablespoons vegetable oil

Combine first 5 ingredients, stirring well; set aside.

Wash pea pods; trim ends, and remove any tough strings. Sauté peas, green onions, and celery in oil in a large skillet 2 minutes. Stir in cornstarch mixture; cook, stirring constantly, 2 minutes or until thickened. Yield: 4 to 6 servings.

Kay Castleman Cooper,
Burke, Virginia.

Canned Seafood Makes It Quick

Cans of salmon, tuna, clams, or crabmeat can be a lifesaver when you need a main dish in a hurry. Since the seafood is precooked, just stir it in with the other ingredients, heat, and your entrée is ready.

TUNA LASAGNA

½ cup chopped onion
1 clove garlic, minced
1 tablespoon vegetable oil
2 (7-ounce) cans tuna, drained and flaked
1 (10¾-ounce) can cream of celery soup, undiluted
½ cup milk
½ teaspoon dried whole oregano
¼ teaspoon pepper
9 uncooked lasagna noodles
1 (6-ounce) package mozzarella cheese slices
1 (8-ounce) package process cheese, thinly sliced
⅓ cup grated Parmesan cheese

Sauté onion and garlic in oil in a medium skillet until tender. Stir in next 5 ingredients; simmer, uncovered, 5 minutes, stirring occasionally.

Cook lasagna noodles according to package directions; drain.

Place 3 noodles in a lightly greased 12- x 8- x 2-inch baking dish, slightly overlapping lengthwise edges. Spoon half of tuna mixture over noodles. Cut mozzarella cheese slices into eighths. Layer half of mozzarella and half of process cheese slices over tuna mixture. Repeat layers with 3 noodles, remaining tuna mixture, and cheese slices. Arrange remaining 3 noodles on top. Cover and bake at 350° for 20 minutes. Sprinkle with Parmesan cheese; bake, uncovered, 5 minutes. Yield: about 6 servings.

Mrs. Robert H. Kirk,
Winchester, Virginia.

TUNA-RICE PIE

1 cup uncooked rice
1 (10-ounce) package frozen chopped broccoli
1 egg, beaten
1 (11-ounce) can Cheddar cheese soup, undiluted
2 teaspoons Worcestershire sauce
1 (2½-ounce) jar sliced mushrooms, drained
1 (6½-ounce) can tuna, drained and flaked
Black olive slices
Fresh parsley sprigs

Cook rice according to package directions, omitting salt; set aside.

Cook broccoli according to package directions; drain well and set aside.

Combine rice and egg; mix well. Press firmly on bottom and sides of a buttered 10- x 6- x 2-inch baking dish; set aside. Combine soup and Worcestershire sauce in a large saucepan; bring to a boil, stirring constantly. Remove from heat; stir in broccoli, mushrooms, and tuna. Pour into rice shell; cover and bake at 375° for 20 to 25 minutes. Garnish with olive slices and parsley. Yield: 6 servings.

Adrian Palmer,
Chattanooga, Tennessee.

CRABMEAT SOUP

1 (10¾-ounce) can cream of mushroom soup, undiluted
1 (10¾-ounce) can cream of asparagus soup, undiluted
1 cup water
1 cup milk
½ cup whipping cream
1 (6-ounce) can crabmeat, drained and flaked

Combine first 4 ingredients in a small Dutch oven; cook over medium heat until thoroughly heated. Stir in whipping cream and crabmeat; heat thoroughly. Yield: 5½ cups.

Jacquelyn Christopher,
Asheville, North Carolina.

LINGUINE WITH CLAM SAUCE

8 ounces uncooked linguine
2 (6½-ounce) cans minced clams, undrained
½ medium onion, chopped
¼ cup olive oil
1 tablespoon chopped fresh parsley
½ teaspoon garlic powder

Cook linguine in a Dutch oven according to package directions. Drain and return to Dutch oven. Set aside. Drain clams, reserving liquid; set aside.

Sauté onion in olive oil in a medium saucepan until tender. Add clam liquid, and simmer 15 minutes. Stir in clams, parsley, and garlic powder. Heat thoroughly. Add clam mixture to linguine, tossing well. Continue to cook until mixture is thoroughly heated. Yield: 4 servings.
Betsy Rose,
Greensboro, North Carolina.

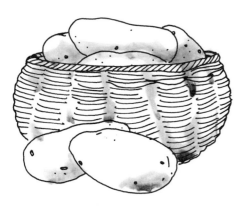

SALMON-TOPPED POTATOES

4 large baking potatoes
Vegetable oil
2 tablespoons butter or margarine
2 tablespoons all-purpose flour
1 cup milk
1 (7¾-ounce) can salmon, drained and flaked
¾ cup (3 ounces) shredded Cheddar cheese
¼ cup chopped green onions
1 hard-cooked egg, chopped
½ teaspoon salt
¼ teaspoon dry mustard

Wash potatoes, and rub with oil. Bake at 400° for 1 hour or until done.

Melt butter in a large skillet over low heat; add flour, stirring until smooth. Cook 1 minute, stirring constantly. Gradually add milk. Cook over medium heat, stirring constantly, until thickened and bubbly.

Stir in next 6 ingredients; cook, stirring constantly, until cheese melts.

Split tops of potatoes lengthwise, and fluff pulp with a fork. Spoon topping over potatoes. Yield: 4 servings.

Unmold A Shapely Salad

Delicate, pretty, and delicious is the way to describe these congealed salads. Molded into elaborate shapes or cut into squares, they are best when assembled a day ahead.

An easy way to get a congealed salad to unmold perfectly every time is to invert the mold on your serving dish; then wrap it with a hot towel. In a matter of seconds, the salad will slip out of the container.

SUNSHINE-PIMIENTO SALAD

1 (6-ounce) package lemon-flavored gelatin
2 cups boiling water
1 (5-ounce) jar process pimiento cheese spread
1⅓ cups mayonnaise
1 (15¼-ounce) can crushed pineapple, undrained
1 cup chopped celery
½ cup shredded carrot

Dissolve gelatin in boiling water. Add pimiento cheese spread, beating with a wire whisk until smooth. Let cool.

Add mayonnaise, beating with a wire whisk until smooth. Stir in pineapple, celery, and carrot; mix well. Pour into a lightly oiled 8-cup mold; chill until firm. Yield: 12 servings.
Violet King,
Pomona, Kansas.

CUCUMBER-PINEAPPLE SALAD

1 (6-ounce) package lemon-flavored gelatin
1½ cups boiling water
1 (8-ounce) package cream cheese, softened
1 (8-ounce) carton commercial sour cream
½ cup mayonnaise
1 teaspoon lemon juice
1 teaspoon Worcestershire sauce
1 (15½-ounce) can crushed pineapple, drained
1 cup grated, seeded cucumber
¾ cup chopped celery
1 (4-ounce) jar diced pimiento, drained
1 tablespoon prepared horseradish
1 tablespoon grated onion
Cucumber slices (optional)

Dissolve gelatin in boiling water; cool slightly. Beat cream cheese until smooth. Gradually add gelatin mixture; beat well. Add sour cream, mayonnaise, lemon juice, and Worcestershire sauce.

Chill until consistency of unbeaten egg white. Stir in next 6 ingredients. Pour into a lightly oiled 7-cup mold. Chill until firm. Unmold on a bed of cucumber slices, if desired. Yield: about 12 servings.
Cheryl Richardson,
Fairfax Station, Virginia.

CREAMY ORANGE SALAD

1 (3-ounce) package orange-flavored gelatin
1 cup boiling water
2 tablespoons grated orange rind
1 cup orange juice
½ cup whipping cream, whipped

Dissolve gelatin in boiling water; add orange rind and juice, stirring well. Chill until consistency of unbeaten egg white. Fold in whipped cream.

Spoon into a lightly oiled 4-cup mold; chill until firm. Yield: 6 to 8 servings.
Marion Gilmore,
Lake Placid, Florida.

CONGEALED BROCCOLI SALAD

2 (10-ounce) packages frozen chopped broccoli
2 envelopes unflavored gelatin
⅔ cup cold water
2 cups chicken broth
2 cups mayonnaise
3 to 4 tablespoons lemon juice
1 teaspoon Worcestershire sauce
Dash of garlic powder
4 hard-cooked eggs, grated
Paprika
Lettuce leaves

Cook broccoli according to package directions; drain well, and set aside.

Soften gelatin in water; set aside. Bring broth to a boil in a medium saucepan; remove from heat. Stir in gelatin mixture and next 4 ingredients.

Place drained broccoli and grated eggs in a lightly oiled 13- x 9- x 2-inch baking dish. Top with gelatin mixture; sprinkle with paprika. Chill until firm. Cut into squares, and serve on lettuce leaves. Yield: 15 servings.
Mrs. Bob Nester,
Charleston, West Virginia.

Tip: For perfect hard-cooked eggs, place eggs in a saucepan and cover with water; bring to a boil, lower heat to simmer, and cook 14 minutes. Pour off hot water and add cold water; shells will come off easily.

You Can't Beat A Burger

What could be better for a casual supper at home than juicy burgers? For a change of pace, try one of our burgers made with added sauce or seasonings.

BURGERS DELUXE

2 (8-ounce) cans tomato sauce with mushrooms
1¼ teaspoons sugar
½ teaspoon dried whole oregano
1½ pounds ground beef
½ teaspoon salt
¼ teaspoon pepper
6 hamburger buns, split and toasted
6 slices process American cheese
6 slices onion
6 slices dill pickle

Combine tomato sauce, sugar, and oregano in a small saucepan. Reserve ⅓ cup of mixture; set aside. Cook remaining mixture over low heat, stirring occasionally, until thoroughly heated. Remove from heat, and keep warm.

Combine beef, ⅓ cup reserved sauce, salt, and pepper; mix well. Shape into 6 patties about ¾ inch thick. Place burgers on the rack of a broiler pan. Broil 5 inches from heat for 5 minutes on each side or until burgers reach desired degree of doneness.

Place patties on bottom half of buns; top each with a slice of cheese, onion, and pickle. Broil until cheese melts. Spoon sauce over patties, and cover with top half of buns. Yield: 6 servings. *Mabel Baldwin Couch, Chelsea, Oklahoma.*

BEEF-AND-VEGETABLE BURGERS

1½ cups finely chopped fresh mushrooms
¾ cup finely chopped green pepper
¾ cup minced onion
¼ cup finely chopped carrot
1½ pounds ground beef
2½ teaspoons soy sauce
6 hamburger buns, split

Combine first 6 ingredients; mix well. Shape mixture into 6 patties about ¾ inch thick. Place patties in a skillet over medium heat; cook about 15 minutes or until desired degree of doneness, turning once. Serve in hamburger buns. Yield: 6 servings. *Marcia Kight, Paducah, Kentucky.*

HEARTY SAUCED PORK BURGERS

2 pounds ground pork
¼ cup fine, dry breadcrumbs
1 egg, beaten
2 tablespoons water
2 tablespoons catsup
½ teaspoon salt
¼ teaspoon onion powder
¼ teaspoon dried whole oregano
8 hamburger buns, split and toasted (optional)
Pepper-Onion Sauce

Combine first 8 ingredients; mix well. Shape mixture into 8 patties about ¾ inch thick.

Broil or grill 4 to 5 inches from heat 5 minutes on each side or until desired degree of doneness. Serve in hamburger buns, if desired. Serve with Pepper-Onion Sauce. Yield: 8 servings.

Pepper-Onion Sauce:

⅓ cup finely chopped onion
⅓ cup finely chopped green pepper
3 tablespoons butter or margarine
¾ cup catsup
2 tablespoons brown sugar
1 teaspoon horseradish
½ teaspoon salt

Sauté onion and green pepper in butter until tender. Stir in remaining ingredients; cook until thoroughly heated. Yield: 1¼ cups. *Sharon M. Crider, Evansville, Wisconsin.*

Fresh And Fruity Salads

Warm weather is the time to enjoy these fresh fruit salads. Bright in color, they enhance meals with luscious flavors and are good sources of vitamin C.

SWEET-AND-SOUR FRUIT SALAD

1 fresh pineapple
4 bananas, sliced
3 large red apples, unpeeled and coarsely chopped
3 oranges, peeled, seeded, and sectioned
2 cups seedless green grapes
Sweet-and-Sour Fruit Dressing

Cut pineapple lengthwise into quarters; cut pulp away from skin. Cut pulp into bite-size chunks, discarding core. Combine fruit in a large bowl; add Sweet-and-Sour Fruit Dressing, and toss gently. Cover and chill. Yield: 12 to 15 servings.

Sweet-and-Sour Fruit Dressing:

4 egg yolks
1½ cups sugar
½ cup milk
1 teaspoon dry mustard
½ cup vinegar

Combine first 4 ingredients in a medium saucepan; cook over low heat, stirring constantly, until smooth and thickened. Stir in vinegar. Cool. Yield: about 1½ cups. *Barbara Bracey, Franklin, Tennessee.*

CONGEALED MELON BALL SALAD

Melon Ball Layer:

1 envelope plus 1 teaspoon unflavored gelatin
¼ cup cold water
¾ cup hot water
3 tablespoons sugar
½ cup orange juice
1 tablespoon grated lemon rind
¼ cup lemon juice
1 cup watermelon balls
1 cup cantaloupe balls or honeydew balls
½ cup seedless green grapes
3 peaches, peeled and sliced

Soften gelatin in cold water; let stand 5 minutes. Add hot water and sugar; stir until gelatin dissolves. Add next 3 ingredients; mix well. Chill mixture until consistency of unbeaten egg white. Fold in fruit; pour into a lightly oiled 8-cup mold. Chill until set.

Cottage Cheese Layer:

1 envelope unflavored gelatin
¼ cup cold water
¾ cup hot water
⅓ cup lemon juice
¼ cup plus 1 tablespoon sugar
2 cups cream-style cottage cheese
Lettuce leaves

Soften gelatin in cold water; let stand 5 minutes. Add hot water, lemon juice, and sugar; mix well. Place cottage cheese in container of electric blender; process until smooth. Gradually stir cottage cheese into lemon juice mixture; pour over melon ball layer. Chill until firm. Unmold salad on lettuce leaves. Yield: 8 to 10 servings. *Martha Gentry, Bardstown, Kentucky.*

FRESH MANGO SALAD

3 mangoes, peeled, seeded, and coarsely chopped
2 bananas, sliced
2 oranges, peeled, sectioned, and seeded
¼ cup vegetable oil
2 tablespoons honey
Juice of 1 lime
Lettuce leaves

Combine first 3 ingredients in a large bowl, tossing gently. Combine oil, honey, and lime juice; pour over fruit, and toss gently. Cover and chill. To serve, remove fruit with a slotted spoon; arrange on lettuce leaves. Yield: 6 to 8 servings.   *T. O. Davis, Waynesboro, Mississippi.*

TROPICAL FRUIT SALAD WITH FRESH MINT DRESSING

1 medium pineapple
1 kiwi, peeled and thinly sliced
1 large banana, peeled and cut into ½-inch chunks
2 medium peaches, peeled and sliced
1 cup whole strawberries, halved
3 tablespoons slivered almonds, toasted
Fresh Mint Dressing

Cut pineapple in half lengthwise. Scoop out pulp, leaving shells ¼ to ½ inch thick; set aside.
Cut pineapple into bite-size pieces, discarding core. Combine pineapple chunks, kiwi, banana, peaches, and strawberries; toss gently, and spoon into pineapple shells. Sprinkle with toasted almonds. Serve with Fresh Mint Dressing. Yield: 4 to 6 servings.

Fresh Mint Dressing:

1 cup sugar
⅓ cup water
½ cup loosely packed fresh mint leaves

Combine sugar and water in a small saucepan; bring to a boil, stirring occasionally. Remove from heat.
Combine sugar mixture and mint leaves in container of electric blender; process until leaves are finely chopped. Chill 2 to 3 hours. Yield: ⅔ cup.

Try This Cook's Salad And Fixings

Your family will rave over these toppings and salad. Combine endive and iceberg lettuce with fresh vegetables for a salad, then serve it with croutons and Artichoke Dressing.

TOSSED MIXED GREEN SALAD

2 cups torn endive lettuce
½ head iceberg lettuce, torn
½ pound fresh mushrooms, sliced
4 cups torn leaf lettuce
¾ cup thinly sliced radishes
Crispy Italian Croutons
Artichoke Dressing

Layer first 5 ingredients in a large bowl. Cover and chill; toss before serving. Top with Crispy Italian Croutons; serve with Artichoke Dressing. Yield: 8 to 10 servings.

Crispy Italian Croutons:

5 slices pumpernickel bread
¼ cup butter or margarine
½ teaspoon garlic salt
1 tablespoon dried Italian seasoning

Cut bread into ¾-inch squares. Melt butter in a large skillet; stir in garlic salt and Italian seasoning. Add bread, tossing to coat well. Spread evenly on an ungreased baking sheet. Bake at 300° for 30 minutes or until very crisp. Yield: about 3 cups.

Artichoke Dressing:

1 (4½-ounce) jar marinated artichoke hearts, undrained and sliced
1 (2-ounce) can anchovies, undrained and chopped
¼ cup red wine vinegar
¼ cup sliced ripe olives
¼ cup sliced pimiento-stuffed olives
2 tablespoons capers
Freshly ground pepper

Combine all ingredients, stirring mixture. Yield: about 1⅔ cups.
Susan Houston, Tucker, Georgia.

Tip: For an interesting change, use fresh pineapple, cantaloupe, or other shells as containers for dips and spreads. Pineapple halves scooped out are beautiful for serving cheese dips or salads. Other fruit like melon shells are nice for salads or appetizers.

These Mousses Are Smooth And Creamy

An airy, light mousse is an intriguing way to begin or end a meal. Busy hostesses claim them as favorite appetizers and desserts since they can be made ahead and refrigerated.

COFFEE MOUSSE

1 envelope unflavored gelatin
¼ cup sugar
2 tablespoons instant coffee granules
⅛ teaspoon salt
2 eggs, separated
1¼ cups milk
½ teaspoon vanilla extract
¼ cup sugar
1 cup whipping cream, whipped
¼ cup finely chopped walnuts
Additional whipped cream (optional)

Combine first 4 ingredients in a medium saucepan. Combine egg yolks and milk, blending well. Stir into gelatin mixture, and let stand 1 minute. Cook over low heat, stirring constantly, until smooth and thickened. Remove from heat, and stir in vanilla. Chill until consistency of unbeaten egg white.
Beat egg whites (at room temperature) until foamy; gradually add ¼ cup sugar, 1 tablespoon at a time, beating until stiff peaks form. Gently fold whites into the coffee mixture.
Gently fold whipped cream and walnuts into egg white mixture. Spoon into individual serving dishes; chill until set. Top with additional whipped cream, if desired. Yield: 4 servings.
Mrs. Marshall M. DeBerry, Franklin, Virginia.

HORSERADISH MOUSSE

1 (3-ounce) package lemon-flavored gelatin
½ cup boiling water
1 tablespoon vinegar
¼ teaspoon salt
¾ cup prepared horseradish
⅛ teaspoon hot sauce
1 cup whipping cream, whipped

Dissolve gelatin in boiling water; stir in vinegar and salt. Chill until consistency of unbeaten egg white. Stir in horseradish and hot sauce.
Gently fold whipped cream into horseradish mixture. Spoon into a lightly oiled 3-cup mold, and chill until set. Serve with roast beef. Yield: 12 appetizer servings.   *Connie Weathers, Dalton, Georgia.*

MUSTARD MOUSSE

1 envelope unflavored gelatin
1 cup water
¾ cup sugar
1½ tablespoons dry mustard
¼ teaspoon salt
4 eggs, beaten
½ cup cider vinegar
1 cup whipping cream, whipped

Sprinkle gelatin over water in top of a double boiler; bring water to a boil. Combine sugar, mustard, and salt; add to gelatin mixture. Stir in eggs and vinegar. Reduce heat to low; cook, stirring constantly, until thickened. Let mixture cool to room temperature.

Gently fold whipped cream into mustard mixture; pour into a lightly oiled 6-cup ring mold. Chill until set. Unmold on a serving platter. Serve with cubed ham and pineapple chunks. Yield: 24 appetizer servings.

Mrs. Harry H. Lay, Jr.,
Fairmount, Georgia.

Snack On Tiny Quiches

These quiches may be small, but each one is packed with flavor. The classic quiche filling of cheese, cream, and eggs is nestled inside delicate pastry shells made crisp with sesame seeds.

TARRAGON COCKTAIL QUICHES

1 cup (4 ounces) shredded Cheddar
   cheese
2 tablespoons chopped fresh
   chives
2 tablespoons chopped fresh
   tarragon or 2 teaspoons
   dried whole tarragon
Pastry shells (recipe follows)
2 eggs, beaten
½ cup half-and-half
¼ teaspoon salt
¼ teaspoon pepper
⅛ teaspoon ground nutmeg
Dash of hot sauce

Combine cheese, chives, and tarragon; spoon evenly into pastry shells.

Combine remaining ingredients; stir well. Pour into pastry shells, filling three-fourths full. Bake at 350° for 30 to 35 minutes or until set. Yield: 3 dozen appetizer servings.

Pastry Shells:

½ cup butter, softened
½ (8-ounce) package cream cheese,
   softened
1 cup plus 2 tablespoons all-purpose flour
1½ tablespoons sesame seeds
¼ teaspoon salt

Combine butter and cream cheese, mixing well. Stir in flour, sesame seeds, and salt; shape mixture into thirty-six 1-inch balls. Place in a lightly greased 1¾-inch muffin pan, shaping each into a shell. Yield: 3 dozen.

Martha Schofield,
Chapel Hill, North Carolina.

Curious About Spaghetti Squash?

The first thing you notice about spaghetti squash is that it doesn't look like other squash.

When cooked, the flesh of the spaghetti squash can be fluffed up into strands and removed with a fork. You'll find the squash strands have a very delicate, almost bland flavor, similar to spaghetti or lasagna noodles.

Spaghetti squash can be cooked several different ways. Instructions are provided in the following recipes for baking the squash in the oven or steaming on top of the range. But you can also steam squash halves in the oven. Just place the halves, cut side down, in a shallow pan filled with an inch or two of water; bake at 375° for 30 minutes.

To microwave a spaghetti squash, cut it in half lengthwise and remove the seeds. Place the halves, cut side down, in a large baking dish filled with ¼ cup of water. Cover the squash with plastic wrap, and microwave at HIGH for 8 to 10 minutes or until the strands can be removed with a fork.

PEPPERONI-SQUASH TOSS

1 large spaghetti squash
2 cloves garlic, minced
1 medium onion, sliced and separated into
   rings
1 large green pepper, sliced into strips
2 tablespoons vegetable oil
1 (3½-ounce) package sliced pepperoni
1 (15-ounce) can tomato sauce
1 teaspoon dried whole oregano
1 teaspoon dried whole basil

Wash squash; cut in half lengthwise, and discard seeds. Place squash, cut side down, in a Dutch oven; add 2 inches water. Bring water to a boil; cover and cook for 20 to 25 minutes or until tender.

Drain squash, and cool. Using a fork, remove spaghetti-like strands; measure 5 cups of strands, and set aside.

Sauté garlic, onion, and green pepper in oil in a large skillet just until onion is tender; add pepperoni and cook 2 minutes. Stir in tomato sauce, oregano, and basil; cook 5 additional minutes or until thoroughly heated. Toss with squash strands. Yield: 8 servings.

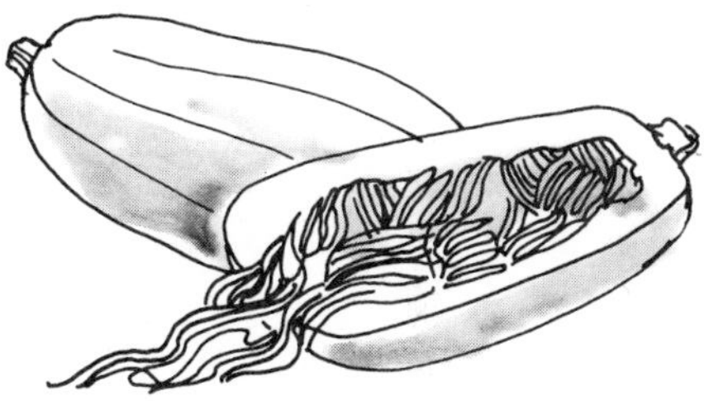

SPAGHETTI SQUASH LASAGNA

1 large spaghetti squash
½ pound ground beef
½ teaspoon dried whole basil
⅛ teaspoon garlic powder
1 (8-ounce) can tomatoes, undrained
1 (6-ounce) can tomato paste
1 (12-ounce) carton cream-style cottage
   cheese
1 egg, beaten
¼ teaspoon salt
¼ teaspoon pepper
¼ cup grated Parmesan cheese
½ pound sliced mozzarella cheese

Wash squash; pierce squash several times with a large fork. Place squash on a jellyroll pan or cookie sheet. Bake at 350° for 1 hour or until tender.

Allow squash to cool; cut squash in half, and remove seeds. Using a fork, remove spaghetti-like strands; measure 4 cups of strands, and set aside.

Cook ground beef in a large skillet until browned, stirring to crumble; drain off pan drippings. Add basil, garlic powder, tomatoes, and tomato paste; simmer, uncovered, 30 minutes or until thickened, stirring occasionally.

Combine cottage cheese, egg, salt, pepper, and Parmesan cheese; mix well.

Layer half each of the squash strands, cottage cheese mixture, mozzarella cheese, and meat sauce in a lightly greased 12- x 8- x 2-inch baking dish. Repeat layers. Bake at 375° for 30 minutes; let stand 10 minutes before serving. Yield: 6 to 8 servings.

SAUTEED VEGETABLES WITH SPAGHETTI SQUASH

1 medium spaghetti squash
1 small onion, chopped
2 tablespoons butter or margarine
2 medium zucchini, sliced
½ cup grated carrot
½ cup chopped green pepper
2 medium tomatoes, coarsely chopped
3 tablespoons chopped fresh parsley
¼ teaspoon salt
⅛ teaspoon pepper
Grated Parmesan cheese

Wash squash; cut in half lengthwise, and discard seeds. Place squash, cut side down, in a Dutch oven; add 2 inches water. Bring to a boil; cover and cook 20 to 25 minutes until tender.

Drain squash and cool. Using a fork, remove spaghetti-like strands; measure about 3 cups of strands, and set aside.

Sauté onion in butter in a large skillet for 2 minutes. Add zucchini, carrot, and green pepper; sauté 5 minutes. Stir in tomatoes, parsley, salt, and pepper; reduce heat to low, and cook 5 minutes.

Combine vegetables and squash strands, tossing gently. Sprinkle with cheese before serving. Yield: 6 servings.

Fresh Vegetables From The Garden

Summer is the time to enjoy garden-fresh vegetables. Squash, green peppers, green beans, and tomatoes can brighten your warm-weather meals.

GREEN BEANS WITH ZUCCHINI

1 pound fresh green beans
½ cup minced onion
¼ cup butter or margarine
2 medium zucchini, cut into ¼-inch slices
4 slices bacon, cooked and crumbled
¾ teaspoon salt
Dash of pepper

Wash beans; trim ends, and remove strings. Cut beans into 1½-inch pieces. Cook beans in boiling water 15 to 20 minutes or until crisp-tender. Drain.

Sauté onion in butter in a large skillet 3 minutes. Add zucchini and cook over medium-high heat 3 to 4 minutes, stirring constantly. Stir in green beans, bacon, salt, and pepper; cook for 1 minute. Yield: 6 servings. *Dorothy Youk, Durham, Kansas.*

SPANISH-STYLE GREEN BEANS

1 pound fresh green beans
½ cup chopped green pepper
¼ cup chopped onion
1 tablespoon vegetable oil or olive oil
2 medium tomatoes, peeled and chopped
¼ to ½ teaspoon dried whole basil
¼ teaspoon dried whole rosemary
½ to 1 teaspoon salt
¼ teaspoon pepper

Wash beans; trim ends, and remove strings. Cut beans into 1½-inch pieces. Cook beans in boiling water 15 to 20 minutes or until crisp-tender. Drain.

Sauté green pepper and onion in hot oil until tender. Add tomatoes, basil, rosemary, salt, pepper, and beans; mix well. Heat thoroughly. Yield: 6 to 8 servings. *Treva Musick, Tolar, Texas.*

SQUASH MEDLEY

2 tablespoons butter or margarine
1 medium onion, thinly sliced
1 large zucchini, thinly sliced
4 medium-size yellow squash, thinly sliced
1 medium-size green pepper, cut into thin strips
3 medium tomatoes, peeled and quartered
1 teaspoon salt
Dash of pepper
1 cup grated Parmesan cheese

Melt butter in preheated wok or large skillet, coating sides and bottom; allow to heat at medium high (325°) for 2 minutes. Add onion; stir-fry briefly. Stir in zucchini, yellow squash, and green pepper; cook 2 to 3 minutes or until crisp-tender. Add tomatoes, salt, and pepper; stir well. Sprinkle cheese over vegetables, and toss gently until the cheese melts. Yield: 6 servings. *Mrs. Melvin J. Cheatham, Gladys, Virginia.*

CHEDDAR-SQUASH BAKE

2 pounds yellow squash
¼ teaspoon salt
2 eggs, separated
1 (8-ounce) carton commercial sour cream
2 tablespoons all-purpose flour
1½ cups (6 ounces) shredded Cheddar cheese
4 slices bacon, cooked and crumbled
⅓ cup fine, dry breadcrumbs
1 tablespoon butter or margarine, melted

Wash squash thoroughly; trim off ends. Place in boiling water to cover. Cook 15 minutes or until crisp-tender. Drain and cool slightly. Thinly slice squash; sprinkle with salt.

Beat egg yolks until thick and lemon colored; stir in sour cream and flour. Beat egg whites until stiff peaks form; fold into yolk mixture.

Layer half of the squash, egg mixture, and cheese in a 12- x 8- x 2-inch lightly greased baking dish. Sprinkle with bacon. Layer remaining squash, egg mixture, and cheese. Combine breadcrumbs and butter; sprinkle over top. Bake at 350° for 20 minutes. Yield: 8 to 10 servings. *Carol T. Keith, Fincastle, Virginia.*

Stuff A Turkey Breast For Dinner

If you enjoy roast turkey but find that a whole turkey leaves you with too many leftovers, try our Stuffed Turkey Breast With Seasoned Dressing.

STUFFED TURKEY BREAST WITH SEASONED DRESSING

1 medium onion, finely chopped
½ cup butter or margarine
1 cup water
2 chicken-flavored bouillon cubes
2 teaspoons green pepper flakes
2 teaspoons dried parsley flakes
1 teaspoon dried celery flakes
1 teaspoon poultry seasoning
8 slices day-old bread, cut into ½-inch cubes
1 (6-pound) whole turkey breast
¼ teaspoon salt
¼ teaspoon pepper
¼ cup butter or margarine, melted

Sauté onion in ½ cup butter in a large skillet. Add next 6 ingredients; simmer 5 minutes, stirring to dissolve bouillon cubes. Add bread, and stir until mixture is moistened.

Bone turkey breast, leaving skin intact. Cut a pocket two-thirds through each side toward the center; sprinkle each pocket with salt and pepper. Stuff pockets with bread mixture, and secure with wooden picks. Place turkey, skin side up, in a shallow baking pan. Insert meat thermometer, making sure it rests in meaty part of turkey. Bake at 325° for 1 hour and 15 minutes or until thermometer registers 185°. Baste turkey with remaining ¼ cup butter. Yield: 10 to 12 servings. *Mrs. E. T. Williams, Baton Rouge, Louisiana.*

Terrines, Pretty Inside And Out

Puree the meat and layer the vegetables for the fanciest meat loaf you'll ever serve. With chicken, pork, or fish as the base, terrines offer eye-opening chilled dinner appetizers or entrées that can be made ahead.

A food processor is a great time-saver when it comes to preparing terrines.

You can puree the meat base, add the seasonings, and stir in the eggs and cream (which bind the mixture together) all in the same processor bowl.

Terrines are named for the earthenware container in which they were traditionally prepared and baked, but today, you'll find a wide assortment of special terrine dishes and pans on the market. For the following recipes we found that an ordinary loafpan or a metal ring mold works just as well.

Some terrine pans work much like a springform pan; the sides snap loose so the chilled terrine can be unmolded onto the serving platter without inverting. We found the terrine loaves to be sturdy enough to be inverted without cracking or breaking. For Jeweled Pork Terrine, it works best to invert and remove the mold before chilling, since the fat particles that collect on the romaine leaves are more easily blotted off at room temperature.

Step 1—To assemble Jeweled Pork Terrine, line the loafpan with romaine leaves simmered just until pliable. Layer the bottom first; then drape the leaves lengthwise over sides of the pan.

Step 2—Spread one-fourth of pork puree in the prepared pan; then alternate layers of vegetables and pork puree.

Step 3—Layer vegetable strips lengthwise, alternating colors. Top the last layer of vegetables with remaining pork mixture; then fold the romaine leaves over the top.

Step 4—To cook the terrine in a water bath, fill a baking pan with enough hot water to cover half of the terrine. Place the terrine in the pan of water, cover with foil, and bake.

Step 5—After baking, allow the terrine to cool; then pour off excess liquid. Invert onto a platter and pat dry. Cover and refrigerate overnight.

Step 6—Place a simple garnish of steamed green onion stems and tomato roses on top of the terrine. Slice with an electric knife to serve.

Before serving a terrine, set it out at room temperature for at least 30 minutes so that the flavors will be more pronounced. An electric knife will help make pretty, neat slices and keep the vegetables intact. If the terrine is to be served with a sauce, place the slices on top of the sauce to show the inside.

JEWELED PORK TERRINE

1 bunch romaine lettuce
About 5 small carrots
2½ cups broccoli flowerets
1 large green pepper, cut into ½-inch
    strips
2 medium-size red peppers, cut into
    ½-inch strips
1½ pounds boneless uncooked pork, cut
    into 1-inch cubes
2 tablespoons Dijon mustard
1 tablespoon dry mustard
2 teaspoons salt
2 teaspoons white pepper
1 teaspoon ground thyme
1 clove garlic, crushed
3 cups whipping cream
3 eggs
Green onion stems, steamed
Tomato roses

Trim stems and tough stalks from romaine leaves; cook leaves in boiling water 1½ to 2 minutes or until pliable. Remove romaine with a slotted spoon. Spread on paper towels, and gently pat dry; set aside.

Scrape carrots; use a knife to make several lengthwise notches on carrots. Place in boiling water to cover; reduce heat, and cook 15 minutes or until tender. Drain on paper towels, and pat dry; set aside.

Steam broccoli 8 minutes or until crisp-tender. Drain well on paper towels, and set aside.

Steam green and red pepper strips 5 to 10 minutes or until tender. Drain on paper towels, and set aside.

Position knife blade in processor bowl. Add half of pork and half of seasonings; top with cover. Process 1 to 1½ minutes or until smooth. Remove food pusher. Slowly pour 1½ cups whipping cream and 1 egg through food chute with processor running, blending just until mixture is smooth. Spoon pork mixture into a large bowl. Repeat procedure with the remaining pork, seasonings, whipping cream, and eggs. Stir pork mixtures together; cover bowl and set aside in refrigerator.

Line the bottom and sides of a buttered 9- x 5- x 3-inch loafpan with romaine, dull side up. Allow leaves to hang over sides of pan. Spread one-fourth of the pork mixture in loafpan. Arrange one-third of vegetables over pork mixture to create desired pattern when sliced. Repeat layers with remaining pork mixture and vegetables, ending with pork mixture. Fold overhanging romaine leaves over last pork layer. Cover pan tightly with foil; punch a hole in foil to allow steam to escape.

Place loafpan in a 13- x 9- x 2-inch baking pan. Fill baking pan with enough hot water to reach halfway up sides of loafpan. Bake at 350° for 1 hour and 5 minutes or until firm and springy to touch. Remove foil from loafpan, and allow terrine to cool. When warm to the touch, pour off excess liquid. Cool completely; invert onto a platter, and pat dry. Cover and refrigerate overnight.

Let terrine stand at room temperature 30 minutes. Garnish terrine with green onion stems and tomato roses. Slice with an electric knife. Yield: 15 to 18 servings.

CHICKEN-VEGETABLE TERRINE

3 medium carrots
2½ cups broccoli flowerets
¼ pound fresh green beans
2 medium-size red peppers, cut
    into half-inch strips
½ pound fresh mushrooms,
    halved
2 tablespoons butter or
    margarine
1¼ pounds boneless chicken
    breasts (about 4 boneless
    breast halves), skinned and
    cut into 1-inch pieces
1¼ teaspoons salt
⅛ teaspoon white pepper
¼ teaspoon onion powder
¾ teaspoon ground turmeric
1 teaspoon hot sauce
1½ cups whipping cream
⅓ cup dry white wine
2 egg whites
1 (7-ounce) jar pimiento-stuffed
    olives, drained
Tarragon-Tomato Sauce

Scrape carrots; cut in half, and quarter lengthwise. Steam 12 minutes or until crisp-tender. Drain on paper towels, and pat dry; set aside.

Steam broccoli 8 minutes or until crisp-tender. Drain on paper towels, and pat dry; set aside.

Wash beans; trim ends and remove strings. Cook in a small amount of boiling water 10 minutes or until crisp-tender. Drain beans on paper towels, and pat dry; set aside.

Steam pepper strips 5 minutes or until crisp-tender. Drain on paper towels, and pat dry; set aside.

Sauté mushrooms in butter in a heavy skillet 3 minutes or until just tender. Drain on paper towels; set aside.

Position knife blade in processor bowl; add half of chicken and all of seasonings. Top with cover; process 1½ minutes or until smooth. Remove food pusher. Slowly pour ¾ cup whipping cream, 3 tablespoons wine, and 1 egg white through food chute with processor running, blending just until mixture is smooth. Spoon chicken mixture into a large bowl. Repeat procedure with remaining chicken, whipping cream, wine, and egg white. Stir chicken mixtures together in bowl.

Place ¾ cup chicken mixture in a well-oiled 9- x 5- x 3-inch loafpan. Arrange 1 layer of vegetables over chicken mixture, creating desired pattern when sliced. Repeat alternating layers of remaining chicken mixture and vegetables, ending with chicken mixture. Arrange vegetables to create desired layers when sliced. (Alternate vegetable colors and shapes for interest.) Cover pan tightly with foil; punch a hole in the foil to allow steam to escape.

Place loafpan in a 13- x 9- x 2-inch baking pan. Fill baking pan with enough hot water to reach halfway up sides of loafpan. Bake at 350° for 1 hour and 15 minutes or until firm and springy to touch. Remove foil from loafpan, and allow terrine to cool. When warm to the touch, pour off excess liquid. Cool completely; cover and refrigerate overnight.

Invert terrine onto a platter; let stand at room temperature 30 minutes. Slice with an electric knife. To serve, spoon a small amount of Tarragon-Tomato Sauce on each serving plate; place terrine slices over sauce. Yield: 15 to 18 servings.

Tarragon-Tomato Sauce:

1 clove garlic, minced
1 tablespoon olive oil
¾ teaspoon dried whole tarragon,
    crushed
⅛ teaspoon pepper
2 (8-ounce) cans tomato
    sauce

Sauté garlic in oil in a heavy skillet for 2 minutes. Reduce heat to medium; stir in remaining ingredients. Cook, stirring constantly, until sauce is thoroughly heated. Yield: 1½ cups.

CHICKEN TERRINE RING

1 large red pepper, coarsely chopped
¾ cup chopped green onions with tops
Carrot flowers
Green onion stems
Pimiento strips
1¾ pounds boneless chicken breasts (about 5 boneless breast halves), skinned and cut into cubes
2 teaspoons salt
1 teaspoon hot sauce
1 teaspoon ground ginger
1 teaspoon ground nutmeg
2½ cups whipping cream
2 egg whites
White Wine Sauce

Steam pepper and chopped green onions 5 minutes. Remove vegetables from steamer, and place between paper towels. Gently pat dry, and set aside.

Steam carrot flowers and green onion stems 2 minutes; place between paper towels, and gently pat dry. Arrange carrot flowers, onion stems, and pimiento in desired design in the bottom of a well-oiled 4½-cup ring mold; set aside.

Position knife blade in processor bowl; add half of chicken and half of seasonings, and top with cover. Process 1½ minutes or until smooth. Remove food pusher. Slowly pour 1¼ cups whipping cream and 1 egg white through food chute with processor running, blending just until mixture is smooth. Spoon chicken mixture into a large bowl.

Repeat procedure with the remaining chicken, whipping cream, egg white, and seasonings. Stir both chicken mixtures together.

Carefully spread half of chicken mixture smoothly in bottom and on sides of mold with a spoon. Stir red pepper and chopped onion into half of the remaining chicken mixture; spoon evenly into mold. Spread remaining chicken mixture evenly over mold.

Cover mold tightly with foil; punch a hole in foil to allow steam to escape. Place mold in a 13- x 9- x 2-inch baking pan. Fill pan with enough hot water to reach two-thirds of the way up sides of mold. Bake at 350° for 1 hour or until firm and springy to touch.

Remove foil from mold, and allow the terrine to cool. When warm to the touch, pour off excess liquid. Cool terrine completely; then cover and refrigerate overnight.

Invert terrine onto a platter; let stand at room temperature 30 minutes. Slice with an electric knife. To serve, spoon a small amount of White Wine Sauce on each serving plate; place terrine slices over sauce. Yield: 8 to 10 servings.

White Wine Sauce:

3 tablespoons butter or margarine
3 tablespoons all-purpose flour
2 cups milk
¼ cup white wine
¼ teaspoon onion salt
2 tablespoons minced fresh parsley

Melt butter in a heavy saucepan over low heat; add flour, stirring until smooth. Cook 1 minute, stirring constantly. Gradually add milk; cook over medium heat, stirring constantly, until mixture is thickened and bubbly. Stir in remaining ingredients. Yield: 1⅔ cups.

LAYERED SALMON-AND-SPINACH TERRINE

1 pound fresh spinach
6 green onions with tops, finely chopped
3 tablespoons butter
½ pound lightly smoked salmon (pink salmon preferred)
1½ pounds sole fillets or any other mild-flavored lean white fish
1 teaspoon salt
¼ teaspoon ground nutmeg
¼ teaspoon white pepper
2 cups finely crumbled, lightly packed French bread
2 cups whipping cream
2 eggs
¼ cup lemon juice
Sour Cream Sauce
Fresh parsley sprigs (optional)

Remove stems from spinach; wash leaves thoroughly, and pat dry. Finely chop leaves. Sauté spinach and onions in butter 1 to 2 minutes or until vegetables are limp. Set aside.

Carefully remove bones from salmon; set salmon aside.

Cut sole into 2-inch pieces. Position knife blade in processor bowl; add half of sole, and top with cover. Process 45 seconds or until smooth. Add half of next 7 ingredients to processor bowl; replace cover, and process 30 seconds or until mixture is smooth. (Mixture should hold shape softly.) Spoon fish mixture into a large bowl. Repeat with the remaining sole, seasonings, breadcrumbs, cream, egg, and lemon juice. Stir the fish mixtures together.

Spread 1 cup of pureed sole mixture in a buttered 9- x 5- x 3-inch loafpan. Smooth layer with the back of a spoon.

Place salmon and 1 cup sole mixture in bowl of a food processor; process 30 seconds or just until mixture is smooth. Carefully spread salmon mixture over first layer; smooth with a spoon. Spread 1 cup sole mixture over second layer. Combine spinach mixture with 2 cups pureed sole mixture; spread spinach mixture over third layer. Smooth with the back of a spoon. Spread remaining sole mixture over spinach layer; smooth top with back of a spoon.

Cover top of terrine with buttered waxed paper cut just larger than the top of pan. Fit foil over waxed paper and top of pan and crimp tightly to top of pan. (Do not cover sides of dish with foil.) Carefully prick holes through foil and waxed paper in several places to allow steam to escape.

Place loafpan in a 13- x 9- x 2-inch baking pan. Fill baking pan with hot water to reach halfway up sides of loafpan. Bake at 350° for 1 hour and 15 minutes to 1 hour and 25 minutes or until terrine starts to rise above the rim of the loafpan and top is firm and springy to the touch.

Remove waxed paper and foil; allow terrine to cool. When warm to the touch, pour off excess liquid. Cool completely; cover and refrigerate overnight.

Invert terrine onto a platter; let stand at room temperature 30 minutes. Slice with an electric knife. To serve, spoon a small amount of Sour Cream Sauce on each serving plate; place terrine slices over sauce, and garnish with parsley, if desired. Yield: 15 to 18 servings.

Sour Cream Sauce:

1 (8-ounce) carton commercial sour cream
2 teaspoons Dijon mustard
1 teaspoon lemon juice
½ teaspoon salt
Dash of white pepper

Combine all ingredients, stirring well. Yield: 1 cup.

Page 134: *Pipe and bake meringue into these showy desserts. From front to back: Spanish Wind Cakes (page 157) with Meringue Flowers (page 156) for garnish, Chocolate-Almond Meringue Fingers (page 158), and Summer Berry Basket (page 158).*

Above: *Layers of seasoned pork puree and colorful vegetables make attractive slices of romaine-wrapped Jeweled Pork Terrine (page 130). Place servings of Chicken Terrine Ring (page 132) atop the sauce to show off the speckles of red pepper and green onion inside.*

Left: *Serve creamy Charleston-Style Shrimp Curry (page 109) over rice, and top it with condiments like chopped green pepper, raisins, peanuts, pickle relish, chopped banana, and fresh coconut.*

Puff Pastry Rises To Any Occasion

Although puff pastries may seem difficult to make, they're not. The repetition of a simple rolling, folding, and chilling process alternates layers of dough with layers of butter and gives the dough its characteristic lightness.

Puff pastry is time-consuming. Two hours of refrigeration are essential between each rolling and folding stage—chilling keeps the butter firm and helps the layers rise evenly. Flour used in pastry recipes should be chilled also.

As you roll and fold the dough, sprinkle it lightly with flour to keep it from sticking, but add as little extra flour as possible. Excess flour can toughen the pastry. After the rolling, folding, and chilling processes are completed, the dough may be refrigerated for a couple of days before shaping it. If longer storage is needed, wrap it in plastic, and freeze it in an airtight container for up to two months. Thaw the dough overnight in the refrigerator before using it.

Keep the dough smooth and level when rolling it out for final shaping. If some parts of the dough are thicker than others when it's rolled out, those areas may be greatly peaked after the dough bakes and rises.

Baking sheets for puff pastry are usually not greased. When baking larger items, sprinkle the baking sheet with water to keep the dough from retracting. Just before baking, brush the pastry with an egg yolk glaze to give it a pretty shine; then freeze the pastry, uncovered, for 10 minutes to firm up the butter in the dough. Bake it immediately after removal from the freezer.

If any scraps of dough remain, lay them out on the counter, piecing them into a solid sheet of dough, edges just touching or barely overlapping. Roll the scraps with a rolling pin to make pieces stick together, then fold in half, and roll again. If the sheet of dough scraps is not large enough for a recipe, just cut it into squares or diamonds, freeze 10 minutes; then bake at 425° until puffed and golden brown.

To make puff pastry, roll the dough into a 15-inch circle, and place prepared square of butter in center. Fold sides of dough over butter, making a thick square.

Roll dough into a 20- x 8-inch rectangle, then fold dough into thirds; roll and fold dough again, then chill 2 hours. Repeat entire rolling, folding, and chilling process 2 additional times.

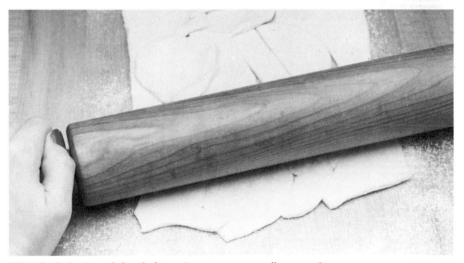

After final shaping of dough for recipes, you can reroll scraps. Lay scraps on counter, piecing them into a solid sheet of dough. Roll scraps with a rolling pin to make pieces stick together, then fold in half and roll again. Cut and bake as desired.

BASIC PUFF PASTRY

¼ cup butter
1¾ cups all-purpose flour, chilled
½ cup cold water
¾ cup butter, softened
¼ cup all-purpose flour, chilled

Cut ¼ cup butter into 1¾ cups flour with pastry blender until mixture resembles coarse meal. Sprinkle ½ cup cold water evenly over surface; stir with a fork until dry ingredients are moistened. Shape into a ball, and wrap in waxed paper. Chill 15 minutes.

Combine ¾ cup butter and remaining ¼ cup flour; stir with a wooden spoon until smooth. Shape butter mixture into a 6-inch square on waxed paper. Chill 5 minutes.

Roll dough into a 15-inch circle on a lightly floured surface or pastry cloth; place butter mixture in center of dough. Fold left side of dough over butter; fold right side of dough over left. Fold upper and lower edges of dough over butter, making a thick square.

Working quickly, place dough, folded side down, on a lightly floured surface or pastry cloth; roll dough into a 20- x 8-inch rectangle. Fold rectangle into thirds to resemble a folded letter, beginning with short side. Roll dough into another 20- x 8-inch rectangle; again fold rectangle into thirds. Wrap dough in waxed paper, and chill about 2 hours.

Repeat rolling, folding, and chilling process 2 additional times. Chill for 2 hours or overnight. Yield: one recipe Basic Puff Pastry.

Although puff pastry seems difficult to make, it's not. Bake puff pastry into these dessert delights: (clockwise from front) Strawberry Tart, Almond Combs, Cream Horns, more Almond Combs, and Lemon in Pastry Shell.

APPLE FOLDOVERS

1 recipe Basic Puff Pastry (page 135)
1 egg yolk
1 teaspoon water
6 cups sliced apples
¾ cup firmly packed brown sugar
¾ cup chopped pecans
3 tablespoons butter or margarine, melted
1½ tablespoons lemon juice
2 teaspoons cornstarch
Sifted powdered sugar

Roll pastry into a 17- x 13-inch rectangle. Cut pastry into 4-inch squares; place squares on ungreased baking sheets. Combine egg yolk and water; brush edges of pastry with yolk mixture. Fold each square of pastry into a triangle; press edges together with a fork. Bake at 425° for 13 to 15 minutes or until puffed and golden brown. Let foldovers cool on a wire rack.

Combine apples, brown sugar, pecans, butter, lemon juice, and cornstarch in a medium saucepan, stirring until cornstarch dissolves; bring to a boil. Reduce heat to low; cook, uncovered, about 10 minutes or until apples are tender.

Slice foldovers in half horizontally, not cutting completely through long side of pastry. Spoon hot filling into foldovers; sprinkle tops with powdered sugar. Yield: 1 dozen.

Tip: Evaporated milk and sweetened condensed milk are two of the forms in which milk is sold. They are different and cannot be interchanged within a recipe. Using evaporated milk in a recipe calling for sweetened condensed milk will result in disaster. Evaporated milk is unsweetened milk thickened by removing some of its water content. Sweetened condensed milk is sweetened with sugar and thickened by evaporation of some of its water content.

ALMOND COMBS

½ recipe Basic Puff Pastry (page 135)
½ cup ground almonds
1 egg, beaten
2 tablespoons sugar
1 egg yolk
1 teaspoon water
¾ cup sifted powdered sugar
1 to 2 teaspoons milk

Roll pastry into a 12-inch square. Cut pastry into 4-inch squares.

Combine almonds, 1 egg, and 2 tablespoons sugar. Spoon about 1 tablespoon almond mixture in a strip down center of each square. Combine egg yolk and water; brush one side of each square with yolk mixture. Fold over opposite side, and press gently to seal. Make even 1-inch cuts along sealed edge, about ¼ inch apart; spread to form a comb. Place pastries on an ungreased baking sheet. Brush remaining yolk mixture over pastries. Freeze 10 minutes. Bake at 425° for 15 minutes or until puffed and golden brown. Transfer to a wire rack.

Combine powdered sugar and milk; drizzle mixture over hot pastries. Yield: 9 servings.

CREAM HORNS

½ recipe Basic Puff Pastry (page 135)
1 egg yolk
1 teaspoon water
1 cup whipping cream
3 tablespoons powdered sugar
1 tablespoon grated semisweet chocolate

Roll pastry into a 15- x 9-inch rectangle. Cut into nine 15- x 1-inch strips. Starting at tip of mold, wrap one strip around an ungreased 4-inch metal cream horn mold, winding strip spiral-fashion and overlapping edges about ¼ inch. Place on lightly greased baking sheet, end of strip down. Repeat with remaining strips. Combine egg yolk and water; brush over entire pastry. Freeze 10 minutes.

Bake at 425° for 12 minutes or until puffed and golden brown. Remove from oven, and gently slide molds from pastry. Turn oven off. Return pastry to oven for 10 minutes. Remove from oven; cool completely on a wire rack.

Combine whipping cream and powdered sugar; beat at high speed of an electric mixer until stiff peaks form. Spoon whipped cream into a decorating bag fitted with metal tip No. 4B. Pipe whipped cream into pastry horns. Sprinkle grated chocolate over tops of cream horns. Chill until ready to serve. Yield: 9 servings.

LEMON IN PASTRY SHELL

1 recipe Basic Puff Pastry (page 135)
2 egg yolks
2 teaspoons water
Lemon filling (recipe follows)
Lemon slices
Mint leaves

Line a 4-cup mixing bowl with a 24- x 14-inch piece of foil, letting excess foil extend out of bowl. Fill bowl with crumpled paper towels, lightly packed. Fold excess foil over paper towels; secure with freezer tape. Remove foil mold from bowl, and set aside.

Roll half of pastry to ⅛-inch thickness; store remaining pastry, covered, in refrigerator. Cut out a circle from pastry about 10 inches in diameter. Sprinkle a baking sheet with water, and shake off excess water. Place pastry circle on baking sheet. Place flat side of foil mold in center of pastry. Cover pastry scraps, and refrigerate.

Roll remaining pastry to ⅛-inch thickness, and cut out a circle about 13 inches in diameter. Combine egg yolks and water; brush over edges of both pastry rounds. Carefully place large pastry round over foil mold; seal and crimp edges. (If an air pocket forms, gently separate pastry rounds, and push air out of opening.) Gently brush yolk mixture over pastry mold.

Roll pastry scraps, and cut out a 4-inch circle. Brush circle with yolk mixture, and place coated side on top of pastry mold. Carefully cut a perforated seam around outside edge of top pastry round. Cut decorative shapes from remaining pastry; brush with yolk mixture, and arrange on pastry mold. Brush

with remaining yolk mixture. Freeze 10 minutes. Bake at 400° for 15 to 17 minutes or until puffed and firm.

Remove from oven. Carefully cut away top circle of pastry, using perforated edge as a guide; place top on baking sheet. Cut a hole in top of foil, and gently pull paper towels from foil mold. Crumple foil, and carefully remove from pastry. Return pastry to oven, and bake an additional 10 minutes or until golden brown. Carefully remove pastry from baking sheet, and cool completely on wire rack.

Transfer pastry to serving platter, and spoon lemon filling into cavity of pastry. Cover and chill several hours or until firm. Garnish with lemon slices and mint; top with pastry cap, slightly off center. Yield: 8 to 10 servings.

Lemon Filling:

3 eggs, separated
1 envelope unflavored gelatin
1 cup water
½ cup sugar
1 tablespoon lemon rind
2 tablespoons lemon juice
¼ teaspoon salt
⅓ cup sugar
1 cup whipping cream, whipped

Beat egg yolks; combine yolks and next 6 ingredients in a saucepan, stirring well. Cook over medium heat, stirring constantly, until mixture begins to bubble. Remove from heat; cool.

Beat egg whites (at room temperature) until foamy; gradually add ⅓ cup sugar, beating until stiff peaks form. Fold egg whites and whipped cream into yolk mixture. Yield: about 3½ cups.

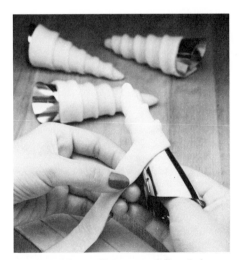

To shape Cream Horns, carefully wind strips of pastry around metal cream horn molds, overlapping edges about ¼ inch. Bake and fill as recipe directs.

For Lemon in Pastry Shell, the pastry is shaped around a prepared dome of foil filled with lightly packed, crumpled paper towels. After baking, slice away the center decorative lid using the perforated edge as a guide, and punch a hole in the foil. Carefully pull paper towels out, then crumple foil and remove it, too.

NAPOLEONS

1 recipe Basic Puff Pastry (page 135)
Napoleon Cream
1 cup sifted powdered sugar
1 teaspoon vanilla extract
1 to 2 tablespoons hot water
½ cup semisweet chocolate morsels
1 teaspoon shortening

Divide puff pastry in half lengthwise. Roll each half into a 15- x 6-inch rectangle. Sprinkle two baking sheets with water; shake off excess water. Carefully transfer pastry to baking sheets.

Prick pastry well with a fork. Trim sides with a sharp knife, if necessary, to make edges even. Freeze 10 minutes. Bake at 425° for 15 minutes or until pastry is puffed and golden brown. Gently remove pastries from baking sheets with spatulas, and cool on wire racks. Trim sides of pastry again, if necessary, to make edges even. Split each layer in half horizontally, using a long serrated knife. Set aside the prettiest bottom layer for top of Napoleon.

Place one pastry strip on serving platter, browned side down; spread evenly with one-third of Napoleon Cream. Repeat layering twice. Top with reserved bottom layer, browned side up.

Combine powdered sugar, vanilla, and enough hot water to make glaze of a smooth spreading consistency. Spoon glaze over top pastry layer, spreading evenly.

Combine chocolate and shortening in top of a double boiler; bring water to a boil. Reduce heat to low; cook until chocolate melts. Let cool slightly, then spoon into a decorating bag fitted with metal tip No. 2. Pipe five lengthwise strips of chocolate evenly across top of glaze. Pull a wooden pick crosswise through chocolate at 1-inch intervals, reversing the pulling direction each time. Refrigerate 30 minutes before serving. To serve, cut into 1½-inch crosswise slices, using a serrated knife. Yield: 10 servings.

Napoleon Cream:

¾ cup sugar
¼ cup cornstarch
⅛ teaspoon salt
1½ cups milk
4 egg yolks
1½ teaspoons vanilla extract
½ cup whipping cream, whipped

Combine first 3 ingredients in a heavy saucepan, stirring until cornstarch is evenly blended. Stir in milk. Cook over low heat, stirring constantly, until mixture is thickened.

Beat egg yolks until thick and lemon-colored. Gradually stir about one-fourth of hot mixture into yolks; add to remaining hot mixture, stirring constantly. Cook, stirring constantly, until mixture thickens. Remove from heat, and stir in vanilla. Cover filling with a sheet of waxed paper, and chill thoroughly. Gently fold whipped cream into chilled filling. Yield: 2⅔ cups.

STRAWBERRY TART

½ recipe Basic Puff Pastry (page 135)
1 egg yolk
1 teaspoon water
¾ cup sugar
3 tablespoons cornstarch
¾ cup lemon-lime carbonated beverage
Red food coloring
1 pint whole strawberries
Additional strawberries (optional)
Fresh mint sprigs (optional)

Roll dough into a 14½- x 7½-inch rectangle. Sprinkle a baking sheet with water, and shake off excess water. Place dough on baking sheet.

Working quickly, cut a ¾-inch-wide strip from each long side of pastry. Brush strips with water, and lay them, moist side down, on top of each long side of pastry rectangle, edges flush together. To complete pastry border, repeat procedure on short sides of rectangle, trimming away excess pastry at corners. Prick pastry generously with a fork, excluding the border.

Combine egg yolk and 1 teaspoon water; brush border of pastry with egg mixture. Freeze 10 minutes. Bake at 425° for 15 minutes or until puffed and golden brown. Gently remove pastry from baking sheet with spatulas, and let cool on a wire rack. Transfer prepared pastry to serving platter.

Combine sugar and cornstarch in a medium saucepan. Gradually stir in carbonated beverage. Cook over low heat, stirring constantly, until smooth and thickened. Stir in a few drops of red food coloring.

Wash 1 pint strawberries, and remove stems. Arrange strawberries in pastry shell, stem end down. Spoon glaze over berries. Chill. To serve, garnish platter with additional strawberries and mint sprigs, if desired. Yield: 8 servings.

Pack A Light Picnic

When warm weather arrives, it's time to call up some friends for a picnic. Here are two delicious calorie-trimmed menus perfect for a dieter's picnic.

While enjoying the outdoors, take advantage of the opportunity to get in some exercise. The best type of exercise for cardiovascular conditioning is classified as aerobic; such exercises require a constant supply of energy throughout the activity. Brisk walking is one of the best aerobic exercises, since it requires no special skills, training, or equipment other than a good pair of walking shoes.

The other type of exercise, anaerobic, requires only short bursts of energy and does not increase cardiovascular endurance as does aerobic exercise. Some anaerobic activities are calisthenics, tennis, weight training, and bowling.

Check with your doctor before you start a strenuous exercise program. And it is best to exercise regularly, three to five times a week for 15 to 60 minutes a day, instead of just exercising once every week or so.

Chilled Gazpacho
Pita Sandwiches
New Potato Salad
Melon Mélange

CHILLED GAZPACHO

1 (12-ounce) can tomato juice
3 medium tomatoes, peeled, seeded, and chopped
2 tablespoons lemon juice
½ teaspoon garlic salt
¼ teaspoon freshly ground pepper
Hot sauce to taste
1 medium cucumber, peeled and finely chopped
1 medium-size green pepper, finely chopped
½ cup finely chopped celery
⅓ cup minced green onions
Cucumber slices

Combine first 6 ingredients in container of electric blender; process until smooth. Combine tomato mixture, chopped cucumber, green pepper, celery, and green onions; chill thoroughly.

To serve, ladle soup into bowls; garnish with cucumber slices. Yield: 6 servings (about 43 calories per serving).

PITA SANDWICHES

1 medium cucumber
1 medium-size yellow squash
1 medium carrot, scraped and grated
2 cups alfalfa sprouts
⅓ cup crumbled feta cheese
¼ cup Thousand Island reduced-calorie
    salad dressing
¼ cup low-fat cottage cheese
1 tablespoon minced fresh oregano
¼ teaspoon freshly ground pepper
Leaf lettuce
3 (6-inch) whole wheat pita bread rounds,
    cut in half

Cut cucumber and squash in half lengthwise; slice thinly. Combine cucumber, squash, and next 7 ingredients; toss. Place leaf lettuce in each bread half, and fill with sandwich mixture. Yield: 6 servings (about 115 calories per serving).

NEW POTATO SALAD

1½ pounds small new potatoes
1 (1.3-ounce) package Italian
    reduced-calorie salad dressing mix
½ cup thinly sliced celery
3 tablespoons minced green onions
3 tablespoons minced fresh parsley
1 tablespoon chopped pimiento
Leaf lettuce

Cook potatoes in boiling water 10 to 15 minutes or until tender; drain and cool. Cut potatoes into ¼-inch slices; layer in a shallow serving dish.

Prepare salad dressing mix according to package directions; combine salad dressing and next 4 ingredients. Pour evenly over potatoes; cover and chill the salad thoroughly. Serve on lettuce leaves. Yield: 6 servings (about 95 calories per serving).

MELON MELANGE

1 medium honeydew
2 cups watermelon balls
1 cup cantaloupe balls
1 cup fresh blueberries
2 tablespoons lime juice
Mint leaves (optional)

Cut a thin slice from side of honeydew; place honeydew, cut side down,

on platter. Cut off top third of honeydew; scoop out seeds. Using a melon ball cutter, scoop out honeydew into balls, leaving a ½-inch-thick shell. Set aside 2 cups honeydew balls, reserving remaining balls for other uses.

Combine honeydew and next 4 ingredients. Spoon into honeydew shell; garnish with mint leaves, if desired. Yield: 6 servings (about 121 calories per serving). *Mrs. Robert M. Neumann, Bartlesville, Oklahoma.*

**Crudité Platter With Dip
Pasta Salad
Commercial Breadsticks
Plum Slush**

CRUDITE PLATTER WITH DIP

1 (12-ounce) carton low-fat cottage cheese
⅓ cup packed fresh parsley sprigs
2 tablespoons chopped green onions
1 clove garlic, minced
1 tablespoon anchovy paste
1 teaspoon Worcestershire sauce
½ teaspoon dry mustard
Hot sauce to taste
Fresh parsley sprigs (optional)
3 medium-size yellow squash, diagonally
    sliced
6 ounces fresh snow peas, trimmed

Combine first 8 ingredients in container of electric blender; process until smooth. Chill thoroughly. Garnish dip with parsley, if desired; serve with squash and snow peas. Yield: 6 servings (about 29 calories per serving plus 11 calories per tablespoon dip).

PASTA SALAD

4 ounces uncooked linguine
2 medium carrots, scraped and cut into
    2- x ¼-inch strips
1 medium zucchini, cut into 2- x ¼-inch
    strips
1 stalk celery, diagonally sliced
1 cup cherry tomatoes, halved
1 cup sliced fresh mushrooms
1 (15-ounce) can chick-peas, drained
½ cup Italian reduced-calorie salad
    dressing
¼ teaspoon fresh ground pepper

Cook linguine according to package directions, omitting salt. Drain in a colander; rinse with cold water, and drain. Let cool to room temperature.

Combine linguine and remaining ingredients in a large bowl; toss. Cover and chill thoroughly. Yield: 6 servings (about 166 calories per 1-cup serving).

PLUM SLUSH

1¼ cups light rosé
1¼ cups unsweetened white grape
    juice
3 cups peeled, sliced fresh plums
1 (3-inch) stick cinnamon
½ teaspoon vanilla extract

Combine first 4 ingredients in a medium saucepan. Bring to a boil; cover, reduce heat, and simmer 15 minutes. Remove from heat; discard cinnamon. Stir in vanilla. Process mixture in container of electric blender until smooth; pour into a plastic container. Cover and freeze until firm.

Remove container from freezer at least 1 hour before serving; spoon slushy mixture into glasses. Yield: 6 servings (about 82 calories per ¾-cup serving).

Add Variety To The Bread Basket

If you're longing for the special flavor of homemade bread, this varied assortment of quick-to-prepare recipes is sure to please you. Baking powder, baking soda, or eggs, rather than yeast, are used as leavening agents so the dough can be mixed up in no time.

CHEESE-AND-PEPPER MUFFINS

3 tablespoons finely chopped green pepper
¼ cup finely chopped onion
1 (2-ounce) jar diced pimiento, drained
¾ cup (3 ounces) shredded sharp Cheddar
    cheese
2½ cups all-purpose flour
¼ cup yellow cornmeal
2 tablespoons baking powder
1 teaspoon salt
¼ teaspoon red pepper
¼ cup sugar
2 eggs, beaten
1½ cups milk
¼ cup shortening, melted

Combine first 10 ingredients in a medium mixing bowl; make a well in center of mixture. Combine eggs, milk, and shortening; add to dry ingredients, stirring just until moistened. Spoon into greased muffin pans, filling two-thirds full. Bake at 400° for 20 to 25 minutes. Yield: 1½ dozen. *Jeannine Allen, McAllen, Texas.*

OATMEAL MUFFINS

1 cup regular oats, uncooked
1 cup buttermilk
½ cup firmly packed brown sugar
½ cup vegetable oil
1 egg, beaten
1 cup all-purpose flour
1 teaspoon baking powder
½ teaspoon baking soda
½ teaspoon salt

Combine oats and buttermilk; let stand 1 hour. Add sugar, oil, and egg to oat mixture; mix well. Combine flour, baking powder, soda, and salt in a large bowl; make a well in center of mixture. Add oat mixture to dry ingredients, stirring just until moistened.

Spoon into greased muffin pans, filling two-thirds full. Bake at 400° for 20 to 25 minutes. Yield: 1 dozen.
Mrs. Richard Herrington,
Hermitage, Tennessee.

MEXICAN CORNBREAD

1½ cups cornmeal
1 cup canned cream-style corn
1 cup buttermilk
½ cup vegetable oil
2 eggs, beaten
1 tablespoon baking powder
1 teaspoon salt
1 teaspoon sugar
2 jalapeño peppers, seeded and minced
¼ cup finely chopped onion
2 tablespoons minced green pepper
1 cup (4 ounces) shredded sharp Cheddar cheese

Combine all ingredients except cheese in a large bowl; stir well. Pour half of mixture into a greased 10-inch iron skillet; top with cheese. Add remaining cornmeal mixture. Bake cornbread at 450° for 30 minutes or until done. Yield: 10 to 12 servings.
Marie Johnson,
Hamburg, Arkansas.

SWEET POTATO BISCUITS

1 cup all-purpose flour
2 tablespoons baking powder
½ teaspoon salt
2 tablespoons sugar
⅓ cup shortening
1 cup cooked, mashed sweet potatoes
2 tablespoons milk

Combine first 4 ingredients; cut in shortening until mixture resembles coarse meal. Add sweet potatoes, and stir until evenly distributed. Sprinkle milk over flour mixture; stir until dry ingredients are moistened.

Turn dough out onto a heavily floured surface; pat to ½-inch thickness. Cut dough with a 2-inch biscuit cutter. Place biscuits on a lightly greased baking sheet. Bake at 450° for 10 minutes or until lightly browned. Yield: 1 dozen.
Mrs. E. R. Hendrix,
Augusta, Georgia.

FRY BREAD

2 eggs, beaten
1 cup milk
4 cups all-purpose flour
2 teaspoons baking powder
¾ teaspoon salt
Vegetable oil or shortening

Combine eggs and milk in a medium bowl. Stir in flour, baking powder, and salt; mix well. Turn dough out onto a floured surface. Roll dough to ¼-inch thickness; cut into 3-inch squares. Gently place dough squares, a few at a time, in deep hot oil (375°); fry until golden brown, turning once. Drain on paper towels. Serve warm with butter and honey. Yield: about 2 to 2½ dozen.
Frieda Ralstin,
Wellston, Oklahoma.

YELLOW SQUASH BREAD

1½ cups all-purpose flour
1 teaspoon baking powder
½ teaspoon baking soda
¼ teaspoon salt
2 teaspoons ground cinnamon
2 eggs
¾ cup sugar
½ cup vegetable oil
2 teaspoons vanilla extract
1⅓ cups shredded yellow squash

Combine the first 5 ingredients; set aside. Combine eggs, sugar, oil, and vanilla in a large bowl; beat well. Stir in the shredded squash. Add dry ingredients, stirring just until moistened.

Pour batter into a greased and floured 9- x 5- x 3-inch loafpan. Bake at 350° for 50 minutes or until a wooden pick inserted in center comes out clean. Cool in pan 10 minutes; remove to wire rack, and cool. Yield: 1 loaf.
Marie Davis,
Morganton, North Carolina.

Stir-Fry The Entrée

Nothing beats a stir-fry recipe for a quick and satisfying entrée. Bite-size morsels of meat and vegetables are cooked in a matter of minutes in the wok then served over hot, fluffy rice for a complete meal.

BEEF WITH ORIENTAL VEGETABLES

1 pound boneless sirloin steak
2 tablespoons soy sauce
2 tablespoons sugar
¼ teaspoon pepper
¼ teaspoon dried onion flakes
2 tablespoons vegetable oil
½ teaspoon salt
1 tablespoon soy sauce
1 tablespoon sugar
1 carrot, thinly sliced
1 medium onion, chopped
1 stalk celery, sliced
½ cup shredded cabbage
1 (14-ounce) can Chinese vegetables, drained
2 to 3 large fresh mushrooms, sliced
1 (6-ounce) package frozen Chinese pea pods, thawed and drained
½ cup water
1 teaspoon cornstarch
Hot cooked rice

Partially freeze steak; slice diagonally across grain into 3- x ¼-inch strips, and set aside. Combine next 4 ingredients; add steak, stirring until coated.

Pour oil around top of preheated wok, coating sides; allow to heat at medium high (325°) for 1 minute. Add steak; stir-fry 2 to 3 minutes or until browned. Remove steak from wok.

Combine salt, 1 tablespoon soy sauce, and 1 tablespoon sugar; mix well. Add carrot, onion, celery, and soy sauce mixture to wok; stir-fry 2 minutes or until vegetables are crisp-tender. Add steak, cabbage, Chinese vegetables, and mushrooms; stir-fry 1 to 2 minutes. Add pea pods; stir-fry 1 minute. Combine water and cornstarch; mix well. Add to wok, and cook 1 minute, stirring constantly, until thickened. Serve over rice. Yield: 4 servings.
Bill Clark,
Georgetown, Tennessee.

Tip: Experiment with new cooking methods. Oriental stir-fry cooking is not only intriguing as a change-of-pace menu idea, it's more energy efficient and nutritious than boiling or steaming. Cut foods into small pieces so that they can cook quickly.

STIR-FRY
BEEF-AND-VEGETABLES

¼ cup soy sauce
2 tablespoons cider vinegar
2½ teaspoons cornstarch
1 teaspoon sugar
2 beef-flavored bouillon cubes
⅓ cup boiling water
1 (1-pound) flank steak
¼ cup vegetable oil, divided
2 cloves garlic, halved
2 cups sliced fresh mushrooms
2 medium-size green peppers, cut into
    strips
1 large onion, sliced and separated into
    rings
1 (8-ounce) can water chestnuts, drained
    and sliced
Hot cooked rice

Combine soy sauce, vinegar, cornstarch, and sugar; stir until cornstarch dissolves. Dissolve bouillon cubes in boiling water, and add to cornstarch mixture. Set aside.

Partially freeze steak; slice diagonally across grain into 3- x ¼-inch strips, and set aside.

Pour 2 tablespoons oil around top of preheated wok, coating sides; allow to heat at medium high (325°) for 1 minute. Add garlic; stir-fry 1 minute. Discard garlic. Add steak to wok; stir-fry 2 minutes or just until browned. Remove steak from wok, and set aside.

Pour remaining 2 tablespoons oil around top of wok, coating sides; allow to heat at medium high 1 minute. Add mushrooms, green pepper, onion, and water chestnuts; stir-fry 2 minutes.

Pour cornstarch mixture over vegetables. Cook, stirring constantly, until slightly thickened. Return steak to wok; stir well. Serve over rice. Yield: 4 to 6 servings.   *Ann Sparks,*
Lexington, Kentucky.

CHICKEN-VEGETABLE STIR-FRY

½ cup soy sauce
¼ cup vegetable oil or sesame seed oil
2 teaspoons sesame seeds
6 chicken breast halves, skinned and
    boned
2 cups fresh broccoli flowerets
1 onion, thinly sliced and separated into
    rings
½ pound fresh snow peas
½ cup thinly sliced celery
½ cup sliced fresh mushrooms
1 tablespoon cornstarch
½ cup water
Hot cooked brown rice

Combine first 3 ingredients, stirring well; set aside. Cut chicken breasts into 2-inch strips, and add to marinade, mixing well. Cover and refrigerate for at least 30 minutes.

Preheat wok to medium high (325°). Add chicken mixture, and stir-fry 2 to 3 minutes. Remove chicken from wok, and set aside. Add broccoli and onion; stir-fry 2 minutes. Add snow peas, celery, and mushrooms; stir-fry 2 minutes or until vegetables are crisp-tender. Add chicken to wok. Combine cornstarch and water; add to wok. Cook, stirring constantly, until thickened. Serve over brown rice. Yield: 6 servings.   *Cynthia Newberry,*
Gainesville, Florida.

STIR-FRIED PORK IN
GARLIC SAUCE

1 pound lean boneless pork
2 teaspoons cornstarch
1 teaspoon salt
1 tablespoon plus 1 teaspoon soy
    sauce
2 teaspoons sesame oil
2 tablespoons vegetable oil
4 large fresh mushrooms, sliced
4 green onions, sliced
¼ cup sliced water chestnuts
2 teaspoons minced garlic
2 teaspoons minced fresh ginger
2 to 3 teaspoons crushed red
    pepper
2 tablespoons water
2 teaspoons cornstarch
2 tablespoons soy sauce
1 tablespoon plus 1 teaspoon sherry
2 teaspoons sugar
½ teaspoon salt
1 teaspoon commercial hoisin sauce
Hot cooked rice

Partially freeze pork; slice diagonally across grain into 2- x ¼-inch strips, and set aside.

Combine next 3 ingredients; add pork, stirring until meat is coated. Let stand 15 minutes.

Pour sesame and vegetable oil around top of preheated wok, coating sides; allow to heat at medium high (325°) for 1 minute. Add pork; stir-fry 3 to 4 minutes or until browned. Remove pork; add mushrooms, onions, water chestnuts, garlic, ginger, and red pepper; stir-fry 1 minute. Add pork, and stir-fry an additional 2 minutes.

Combine water and 2 teaspoons cornstarch; mix well. Add cornstarch mixture and remaining ingredients except rice to wok; cook 1 minute, stirring constantly, until thickened. Serve over rice. Yield: 4 servings.   *Fred Ralls,*
Dallas, Texas.

Berries! Berries! Berries!

When you get your hands on some fresh raspberries, blueberries, or blackberries, you'll want to eat them plain. But try to save some for our featured berry recipes. We think you'll love the results.

BLACKBERRY PIE

¾ cup sugar
2½ tablespoons cornstarch
1 cup water
3½ tablespoons blackberry-flavored gelatin
4 cups fresh blackberries
1 baked 9-inch pastry shell
Frozen whipped topping, thawed

Combine sugar, cornstarch, and water in a heavy saucepan; cook over medium heat, stirring constantly, until thickened. Remove from heat. Add gelatin, stirring until dissolved. Gently stir in blackberries. Pour into pastry shell; chill until firm. Garnish each slice with dollop of whipped topping. Yield: one 9-inch pie.   *Reba Lawing,*
Marion, North Carolina.

BLUEBERRY-ORANGE
NUT BREAD

3 eggs
1 tablespoon grated orange rind
⅔ cup orange juice
½ cup milk
½ cup butter or margarine, melted
3 cups all-purpose flour
¾ cup sugar
1 tablespoon baking powder
¼ teaspoon baking soda
½ teaspoon salt
1 cup fresh blueberries
½ cup chopped walnuts

Combine first 5 ingredients; beat at medium speed of electric mixer 30 seconds. Combine flour, sugar, baking powder, soda, and salt in a large bowl; make a well in center of mixture. Add egg mixture, stirring just until moistened. Fold in blueberries and walnuts.

Pour batter into a greased and floured 9- x 5- x 3-inch loafpan; bake at 350° for 1 hour or until a wooden pick inserted in center comes out clean. Cool in pan 10 minutes; remove from pan, and cool completely. Yield: 1 loaf.
Susan Key,
Houston, Texas.

BLUEBERRY CREAM PIE

¾ cup sugar
¼ cup cornstarch
½ teaspoon salt
2½ cups milk
3 egg yolks
1 tablespoon butter or margarine
1 teaspoon vanilla extract
2 cups fresh blueberries
1 baked 9-inch pastry shell
1 cup whipping cream
¼ cup sifted powdered sugar

Combine sugar, cornstarch, and salt in a heavy saucepan; stir well to remove lumps. Gradually add milk, stirring until blended. Cook over medium heat, stirring constantly, until mixture thickens and comes to a boil; cook 1 minute, stirring constantly. Remove mixture from heat.

Beat egg yolks until thick and lemon colored. Gradually stir about one-fourth of hot mixture into yolks; add to remaining hot mixture, stirring constantly. Cook over medium heat 2 minutes, stirring constantly. Remove from heat; add butter and vanilla; stir until butter melts. Gently stir in blueberries. Cool and pour into pastry shell.

Beat whipping cream until foamy; gradually add powdered sugar, beating until soft peaks form. Spread over pie. Chill. Yield: one 9-inch pie.

Mrs. M. Lyle Cashion,
Deer Creek, Illinois.

RASPBERRY SAUCE FLAMBE

2 cups fresh raspberries
¼ cup sugar
1 tablespoon cornstarch
¼ cup water
1½ teaspoons lemon juice
2 tablespoons amaretto
2 tablespoons brandy
Vanilla ice cream

Combine raspberries and sugar; stir gently. Let stand 1 hour. Drain raspberries, reserving juice. Press raspberries through a sieve or food mill, discarding seeds; set raspberry pulp aside.

Combine raspberry juice and cornstarch in a heavy saucepan; stir until smooth. Add raspberry pulp, water, and lemon juice; cook over low heat, stirring constantly, until mixture is smooth and thickened.

Combine amaretto and brandy in a small, long-handled pan; heat just until warm. Ignite with a long match, and pour over raspberry mixture. Stir gently until flames die down. Serve immediately over ice cream. Yield: 6 servings.

Celebrate Tomato Time

This is the season for juicy, red, vine-ripened tomatoes. They're great simply sliced and sprinkled with herbs. But you can also serve them sautéed with onions and green peppers, covered with marinated cucumbers, or cooked Creole-style with fresh corn.

When selecting tomatoes, look for fairly firm ones that are free of blemishes. Vine-ripened tomatoes have the best flavor, but if picked while still pink, you can ripen them indoors. Just place the tomatoes in a window or on the kitchen counter where they receive indirect sunlight. Once tomatoes have ripened, they may be kept in the refrigerator for several days.

SCALLOPED TOMATOES

1 cup diced celery
½ cup chopped onion
1 tablespoon butter or margarine
2 tablespoons all-purpose flour
3½ cups peeled, chopped tomatoes, drained
1 tablespoon sugar
1 teaspoon salt
2 teaspoons prepared mustard
Dash of pepper
3 slices white bread, toasted and cut into cubes

Sauté celery and onion in butter 5 minutes or until onion is tender. Blend in flour, stirring until smooth. Add next 5 ingredients and half of toast cubes. Spoon mixture into a lightly greased 1½-quart casserole. Bake at 350° for 30 minutes. Sprinkle with remaining toast cubes; bake an additional 15 to 20 minutes. Yield: 6 servings. *Carol T. Keith,*
Roanoke, Virginia.

SESAME TOMATOES

3 large tomatoes
½ cup (2 ounces) shredded Cheddar cheese
½ cup soft breadcrumbs
1½ tablespoons sesame seeds

Cut tomatoes in half crosswise. Broil 6 inches from heat about 5 minutes.

Combine remaining ingredients; lightly press mixture over cut surface of tomato halves. Broil 6 inches from heat an additional 2 minutes or just until topping is lightly browned. Yield: 6 servings. *Mrs. William R. Wager,*
Southport, North Carolina.

TOMATO-PEPPER SAUTE

6 large green peppers, cut into ¼-inch strips
2 medium onions, chopped
¼ cup vegetable oil
4 large tomatoes, peeled and cut into wedges
1 teaspoon salt
1¼ teaspoons dried whole basil

Sauté green pepper and onion in oil over medium heat for 10 minutes. Add remaining ingredients, stirring well. Cover, reduce heat, and simmer 15 minutes. Yield: 10 to 12 servings.

Grace Owens,
Pride, Louisiana.

CREOLE-STYLE TOMATOES-AND-CORN

2 slices bacon, chopped
1 large onion, chopped
1 medium-size green pepper, chopped
2½ cups peeled, chopped tomatoes
½ bay leaf
2 cups fresh corn cut from cob
¼ teaspoon salt
⅛ teaspoon pepper

Cook bacon in a large skillet until crisp; remove bacon, reserving drippings in skillet. Crumble bacon, and set aside.

Sauté onion and green pepper in drippings until tender. Add tomatoes and bay leaf; bring to a boil. Reduce heat and simmer 5 minutes, stirring occasionally. Stir in corn; return to a boil. Reduce heat and simmer an additional 5 minutes, stirring occasionally. Stir in salt and pepper. Remove bay leaf, and sprinkle vegetables with bacon before serving. Yield: 6 servings.

Ruby Bonelli,
Bastrop, Texas.

DILLED CUCUMBER ON TOMATOES

1 large cucumber, peeled and thinly sliced
⅓ cup vegetable oil
3 tablespoons vinegar
1½ teaspoons minced fresh dillweed or ½ teaspoon dried whole dillweed
½ teaspoon salt
¼ teaspoon sugar
⅛ teaspoon pepper
Bibb lettuce leaves
3 medium tomatoes, sliced

Place cucumber in a shallow bowl, and set aside.

Combine next 6 ingredients, and mix well with a wire whisk; pour over cucumbers, tossing gently. Cover and chill at least 6 hours.

Arrange lettuce on a serving platter; top with tomato slices. Spoon cucumber mixture over tomatoes. Yield: 6 servings. *Susan McLemore, Knoxville, Tennessee.*

Stuff Eggs With Devilish Fillings

Stuffed eggs are so popular at picnics, buffets, and family reunions that the name "deviled" seems undeserved. But spicy fillings such as the ones found here helped stuffed eggs earn this name.

Hard-cook your eggs just right by placing them in a saucepan and covering with water at least 1 inch above the eggs. Bring the water to a boil, then cover the pan with a lid. Turn off the heat and remove pan from the burner, if necessary, to prevent further boiling. The eggs should stand in hot water for at least 15 minutes. Drain and cool eggs in cold water before shelling.

SAUCY SHRIMP-CURRIED EGGS

8 hard-cooked eggs
⅓ cup mayonnaise
¼ teaspoon salt
½ teaspoon paprika
¼ teaspoon curry powder
¼ teaspoon dry mustard
1½ cups water
½ pound unpeeled medium shrimp
2 tablespoons butter or margarine
2 tablespoons all-purpose flour
1 (10½-ounce) can cream of celery soup, undiluted
¾ cup milk
½ cup (2 ounces) shredded sharp Cheddar cheese
¼ teaspoon curry powder
1 cup soft breadcrumbs
1 tablespoon butter or margarine, melted

Slice eggs in half lengthwise, and carefully remove yolks. Mash yolks, and stir in next 5 ingredients. Stuff egg whites with yolk mixture; arrange in a lightly greased 10- x 6- x 2-inch baking dish. Set eggs aside.

Bring 1½ cups water to a boil; add shrimp, and return to a boil. Reduce heat and simmer 1 minute. Drain well, and rinse with cold water. Peel, devein, and chop shrimp; set aside.

Melt 2 tablespoons butter in a large saucepan; add flour, stirring until smooth. Cook 1 minute, stirring constantly. Gradually stir in soup and milk; cook over medium heat, stirring constantly, until mixture is bubbly. Add cheese and ¼ teaspoon curry powder; stir until cheese melts. Stir in chopped shrimp; pour over stuffed eggs. Combine breadcrumbs and 1 tablespoon melted butter; mix well. Sprinkle over shrimp mixture; bake at 350° for 15 to 20 minutes. Yield: 8 servings. *Mrs. M. J. Alleman, Prairieville, Louisiana.*

PIMIENTO-DEVILED EGGS

8 hard-cooked eggs
1 (5-ounce) jar sharp process cheese spread with pimientos
1 tablespoon milk
1 tablespoon chopped chives
Dash of salt
Dash of pepper
Parsley or chives

Slice eggs in half lengthwise, and carefully remove yolks. Mash yolks, and stir in next 5 ingredients. Stuff egg whites with the yolk mixture. Garnish eggs with parsley or with additional chives. Yield: 8 servings. *Sandy Hayes, Morristown, Tennessee.*

SPICY MUSTARD EGGS

6 hard-cooked eggs
2 tablespoons butter or margarine, softened
2 tablespoons mayonnaise
1 teaspoon Dijon mustard
½ teaspoon white pepper
¼ teaspoon curry powder
Chopped chives
Paprika

Slice eggs in half lengthwise, and carefully remove yolks. Mash yolks, and stir in butter and mayonnaise. Add mustard, pepper, and curry powder; stir well. Stuff egg whites with the yolk mixture; garnish with chives and paprika. Yield: 6 servings. *Tony Jones, Atlanta, Georgia.*

CREAMY STUFFED EGGS

12 hard-cooked eggs
1 (3-ounce) package cream cheese, softened
¼ cup plus 1 tablespoon mayonnaise
½ teaspoon chicken-flavored bouillon granules
½ teaspoon prepared horseradish
Pimiento-stuffed olives, sliced

Slice eggs in half lengthwise, and carefully remove yolks. Mash yolks, and stir in cream cheese, mayonnaise, and bouillon granules; mix until smooth. Stir in horseradish. Stuff egg whites with yolk mixture, and garnish with olive slices. Yield: 12 servings. *Cindy Wilkinson, Sugar Grove, Virginia.*

Make Your Own Ice Cream Sundaes

If you enjoy homemade ice cream sundaes, then read on. You might want to try a combination of two or more toppings for a real treat.

HOT FUDGE SAUCE

1 cup sugar
2 tablespoons cocoa
¼ cup milk
¼ cup whipping cream
2 tablespoons light corn syrup
1 tablespoon butter or margarine
½ tablespoon vanilla extract

Combine sugar and cocoa; gradually stir in milk. Add whipping cream, corn syrup, and butter; mix well. Bring to a boil over medium heat, stirring constantly; reduce heat and simmer 10 minutes without stirring. Remove from heat, and stir in vanilla. Serve warm over vanilla ice cream. Yield: 1 cup. *Sandra Souther, Gainesville, Georgia.*

PRALINE SAUCE

1 cup light corn syrup
½ cup sugar
⅓ cup butter or margarine
1 egg, beaten
1 tablespoon vanilla extract
1 cup coarsely chopped pecans

Combine first 4 ingredients in a heavy saucepan; mix well. Bring to a boil over medium heat, stirring constantly; cook 2 minutes without stirring. Remove from heat; stir in vanilla and pecans. Serve warm or at room temperature over ice cream. Yield: 2 cups. *Mrs. John Rucker, Louisville, Kentucky.*

PEACH SAUCE

6 cups sliced fresh peaches
1 cup water
⅓ cup sugar
⅛ teaspoon ground cinnamon

Combine peaches and water in a large saucepan; cook over medium heat 5 minutes. Cover, reduce heat, and simmer 10 minutes or until tender. Cool.
Combine peaches and remaining ingredients in container of electric blender. Process until smooth. Chill. Serve over ice cream. Yield: 3 cups.
Charlotte A. Pierce,
Greensburg, Kentucky.

STRAWBERRY SAUCE

2 cups fresh strawberries
3 tablespoons sugar
3 tablespoons brandy

Wash and hull strawberries. Place in container of electric blender, and process until smooth. Add sugar and brandy, and process until mixed. Yield: 1½ cups.
Pat Boschen,
Ashland, Virginia.

CRUNCHY GRANOLA

4 cups regular oats, uncooked
1½ cups flaked coconut
1½ cups wheat germ
1 cup firmly packed brown sugar
¾ cup raisins
½ cup coarsely chopped pecans
½ cup whole almonds, coarsely chopped
¼ teaspoon salt
½ cup water
¼ cup vegetable oil
2½ tablespoons vanilla extract

Combine first 8 ingredients in a large bowl; mix well. Combine remaining ingredients; pour over oats mixture, and mix well. Spread mixture evenly in 2 lightly greased 15- x 10- x 1-inch jellyroll pans. Bake at 275° for 1 hour, stirring every 20 minutes. Cool; store in an airtight container. Yield: 9 cups.
Mrs. Kirby Smith,
Clio, Alabama.

Keep The Menu Simple

If your schedule is hectic when company comes for dinner, then be sure to try this menu. It's special enough for guests, but takes only a short time to assemble and cook in the microwave.

Marinated Chicken Kabobs
Chicken-Flavored Rice
Spinach Delight
Cheese-Herb Bread
Pots de Crème

MARINATED CHICKEN KABOBS

3 chicken breast halves, skinned and boned
3 tablespoons soy sauce
3 tablespoons commercial Italian salad dressing
2 teaspoons sesame seeds
2 teaspoons lemon juice
⅛ teaspoon ground ginger
⅛ teaspoon garlic powder
1 small green pepper, cut into eighths
1 small onion, cut into eighths
⅓ cup water
1 (14½-ounce) can artichoke hearts, drained and sliced in half
8 cherry tomatoes

Cut chicken breasts into 1-inch pieces. Place in a shallow container, and set aside. Combine next 6 ingredients in a jar; cover tightly, and shake vigorously. Pour over chicken; cover and marinate in refrigerator at least 2 hours.
Combine green pepper, onion, and water in a large glass bowl. Cover with heavy-duty plastic wrap, and microwave at HIGH for 3 to 4 minutes or until crisp-tender. Drain well.
Remove chicken from marinade, reserving marinade. Alternately thread chicken and vegetables except tomatoes on 12-inch wooden skewers.
Place kabobs in a 12- x 7- x 2-inch baking dish. Brush with reserved marinade. Cover with heavy-duty plastic wrap. Microwave at HIGH for 4 minutes; thread tomatoes on ends and rearrange kabobs. Microwave at HIGH for 4 to 5 minutes or until chicken is done. Yield: 4 servings.

CHICKEN-FLAVORED RICE

1½ cups uncooked instant rice
1½ cups hot water
¼ cup butter or margarine
¼ cup chopped green onions
2 teaspoons chicken-flavored bouillon granules
¼ teaspoon dried whole basil
⅛ teaspoon garlic powder
1 (4-ounce) can mushroom stems and pieces, drained
1 tablespoon minced fresh parsley
1 tablespoon grated Parmesan cheese

Combine first 7 ingredients in a 2-quart casserole. Cover with heavy-duty plastic wrap, and microwave at HIGH for 7 minutes. Stir in mushrooms. Cover and microwave at HIGH for 6 minutes or until the liquid is completely absorbed. Let rice stand 2 to 4 minutes. Add parsley, and fluff rice with a fork; sprinkle with grated Parmesan cheese. Yield: 4 servings.

SPINACH DELIGHT

1 (10-ounce) package frozen chopped spinach
2 eggs, beaten
1 cup herb-seasoned stuffing mix
¼ cup grated Parmesan cheese
¼ cup small-curd cottage cheese
3 tablespoons milk
⅛ teaspoon pepper

Remove wrapper from spinach box; place box in a flat baking dish, and pierce with a fork. Microwave at HIGH for 7 to 11 minutes or until done.
Combine remaining ingredients; add spinach, and mix well. Spoon mixture into a 1-quart casserole; cover with heavy-duty plastic wrap. Microwave at HIGH for 3 to 4 minutes or until casserole is almost set, turning dish once. Let stand 1 minute. Yield: 4 servings.

CHEESE-HERB BREAD

½ cup water
¼ cup shortening
2 tablespoons sugar
¾ teaspoon salt
1 package dry yeast
1 (5-ounce) jar process cheese spread, coarsely chopped
2 cups all-purpose flour, divided
1 egg, beaten
1 tablespoon butter or margarine
2 tablespoons grated Parmesan cheese (optional)
1 teaspoon poppy seeds
½ teaspoon dried whole basil

Combine water, shortening, sugar, and salt in a large glass bowl; microwave at HIGH for 2½ minutes or until shortening melts. Cool to lukewarm (105° to 115°). Add yeast, cheese spread, 1 cup flour, and egg to liquid mixture; beat 30 seconds at low speed of an electric mixer, scraping sides of bowl. Beat 3 minutes at high speed. Stir in remaining 1 cup flour.

Turn dough out onto a lightly floured surface, and knead 1 to 2 minutes. Roll dough into a 9-inch circle. Place dough in a well-greased 9-inch pieplate, and set in a larger, shallow dish; pour about 1 inch hot water in bottom dish. Cover dough loosely with waxed paper. Microwave at MEDIUM LOW (30% power) for 2 minutes; let stand in oven 5 minutes. Repeat microwaving and standing 3 times or until dough is doubled in bulk. Remove from oven, and remove waxed paper.

Place butter in a custard cup; microwave at HIGH for 35 seconds or until butter is melted. Brush over loaf. Combine remaining ingredients, and sprinkle over loaf.

Place pieplate with loaf in microwave oven on an inverted custard cup or saucer. Microwave at MEDIUM (50% power) for 6 to 8 minutes or until surface springs back when touched lightly with finger, giving dish a quarter-turn at 2-minute intervals. Remove from microwave, and place pieplate on foil. Let stand 5 minutes. Remove from pan, and cool. Yield: one 9-inch loaf.

POTS DE CREME

2 (4-ounce) packages sweet baking chocolate
2 tablespoons sugar
1 cup whipping cream
4 egg yolks
1 teaspoon vanilla extract
Whipped cream

Place chocolate in a 4-cup glass measure or a 1-quart mixing bowl. Microwave at HIGH for 3 to 3½ minutes or until chocolate is melted. Stir in sugar. Gradually add 1 cup whipping cream, stirring until smooth. Microwave at HIGH for 2 to 3 minutes, stirring at 1-minute intervals.

Beat yolks with a wire whisk. Gradually stir about one-fourth of chocolate mixture into yolks; quickly add to remaining chocolate mixture, stirring constantly. Stir in vanilla. Spoon into small cordial glasses or custard cups. Chill until set. Garnish with whipped cream. Yield: 4 to 6 servings.

Bake A Garden-Fresh Casserole

Here are some easy-to-fix vegetable casseroles to help you enjoy the season's flavors when fresh summer vegetables are in your garden or grocery store.

GREEN BEAN CASSEROLE

1 (10¾-ounce) can cream of mushroom soup, undiluted
½ cup milk
½ cup (2 ounces) shredded sharp Cheddar cheese
1 tablespoon butter or margarine, melted
½ teaspoon Worcestershire sauce
½ teaspoon garlic salt
4 cups cut fresh green beans, cooked
¼ cup slivered almonds, toasted
¼ cup sliced water chestnuts
2 tablespoons diced pimiento
¼ cup buttered breadcrumbs

Combine first 6 ingredients; stir well. Add next 4 ingredients. Spoon mixture into a lightly greased 1½-quart casserole; top with breadcrumbs. Bake casserole at 350° for 25 minutes or until bubbly. Yield: 6 servings.

Patricia Palmer,
Irving, Texas.

CORN-AND-TOMATO CASSEROLE

6 ears fresh corn
1 medium onion, chopped
1 medium-size green pepper, chopped
2 tablespoons butter or margarine
5 medium tomatoes, sliced ½ inch thick
1 teaspoon salt
½ teaspoon pepper
1 cup soft breadcrumbs
2 tablespoons butter or margarine, melted

Cut corn from cob. Combine corn, onion, and green pepper; sauté in 2 tablespoons butter 5 minutes. Spoon half of corn mixture into a 2-quart casserole; top with half of the tomato slices. Sprinkle with half of salt and pepper. Repeat the layers. Combine breadcrumbs and 2 tablespoons butter; sprinkle evenly over casserole. Bake at 375° for 30 minutes. Yield: 8 servings.

Mary Egland,
Ransom, Illinois.

Tip: Sand and dirt can be removed from fresh vegetables by soaking in warm salted water 5 minutes.

QUICK FRESH ENGLISH PEA CASSEROLE

3 cups fresh English peas
1 (16-ounce) can bean sprouts, drained
1 (10¾-ounce) can cream of mushroom soup, undiluted
1 (8-ounce) can sliced water chestnuts, drained
1 (4-ounce) can mushroom stems and pieces, drained
1 (2.8-ounce) can French-fried onion rings
½ cup (2 ounces) shredded Cheddar cheese

Bring 1 inch salted water to a boil. Add peas; bring to a boil. Cook, uncovered, 5 minutes. Cover and cook 3 to 7 minutes or until tender; drain.

Combine peas and next 4 ingredients; spoon mixture into a lightly greased shallow 2-quart casserole. Bake at 350° for 25 minutes; top with onion rings and cheese. Bake 5 minutes. Yield: 6 servings.

Joan B. Henderson,
Vicksburg, Mississippi.

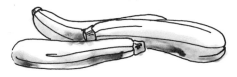

CHEESY ZUCCHINI CASSEROLE

3 medium zucchini, cut into ½-inch cubes
¼ cup (1 ounce) shredded sharp Cheddar cheese
¼ cup (1 ounce) shredded Swiss cheese
¼ cup commercial sour cream
1 tablespoon butter or margarine
½ teaspoon salt
⅛ teaspoon paprika
1 egg yolk, beaten
3 slices bacon, cooked and crumbled
1 tablespoon chopped chives
½ cup soft breadcrumbs
1 tablespoon butter or margarine, melted

Cook squash in a small amount of boiling salted water 5 minutes or until tender; drain well. Place in a lightly greased 1-quart casserole; set aside.

Combine next 6 ingredients in a small saucepan. Cook over low heat, stirring constantly, until cheese melts. Remove from heat. Stir about one-fourth of hot mixture into egg yolk; add to remaining hot mixture, stirring constantly. Stir in bacon and chives. Pour over squash.

Combine breadcrumbs and 1 tablespoon butter; mix well, and sprinkle over top of casserole. Bake at 350° for 25 to 30 minutes. Yield: 4 servings.

Marilyn Garner,
Cape Girardeau, Missouri.

Stretch Summer Flavor With Dried Produce

With the help of electric dehydrators, more and more Southerners are discovering home drying as an excellent way to preserve the fresh taste of seasonal fruit and vegetables.

The drying process is not new. Long before the colonists arrived, Indians were sun-drying corn and berries and storing them for the winter. Over the years, assorted techniques for drying by sun, fire, smoke, and oven have been passed from generation to generation. But until the electric home dehydrator made its way into modern kitchens, most Southerners found home drying to be unsatisfactory, if not impossible.

The drying process was so difficult in the South because of the weather. Traditional drying methods required consecutive days of fairly hot temperatures, low humidity, and no rain. Modern electric dehydrators eliminate these worries; they circulate warm air while exhausting moisture to dry produce quickly and evenly.

Choosing a Dehydrator

A good unit will usually yield better-quality dried food than any other method of drying. Dehydrators are available in a variety of sizes and shapes. Many dehydrators are cabinet models that have sliding trays. Others are modular units with stackable trays. Some convection ovens also include dehydrator racks; these work as well as a regular dehydrator. Just be sure the oven has 140° (the most typical drying temperature) on its thermostat.

A dehydrator should offer a regulated thermostat or dry automatically at 140°. A timer is usually an optional, but helpful, feature.

Look for a dehydrator that has mesh-type trays or racks; mesh openings should be fine enough that small pieces of food do not fall through, but large enough to allow for good airflow. Make sure the trays are easy to remove and clean. In general, plastic trays are easier to clean than metal.

How To Dry Fresh Produce

Start with fresh, high-quality fruit and vegetables. Wash the produce, and prepare it according to the Fruit and Vegetable Dehydration Chart on the following page. Make all slices the same thickness so they will dry in about the same time. Fruit that brown easily after slicing need special treatment. Dilute commercial ascorbic-citric powder according to package directions, and soak the fruit for a few minutes; then gently pat dry.

Some fruit and vegetables require steam blanching before drying to destroy enzyme development and extend their shelf life. The chart will indicate if this is necessary. To blanch, bring several inches of water to a boil in a large saucepan. Place the produce on a rack over the water. Cover and allow the food to steam as directed and pat dry. Arrange food slices or pieces evenly in a single layer on dehydrator trays.

Drying Times

The length of time the food should dry can vary greatly, depending on the amount, type, and size of produce pieces. The times given in the chart are for reference only. It's best to check each batch of food as it dries to determine exact doneness. When fully dried, fruit become leathery and vegetables should be brittle.

Treatment After Drying

As seen in the chart, some produce requires additional treatment after drying to prevent spoilage and to ensure complete dryness.

To condition dried food, loosely pack it into plastic or glass containers, filling two-thirds full. Make sure the containers are airtight, and let them stand 5 to 10 days. Shake the containers each day, and if condensation occurs, return the food to the electric dehydrator for additional drying.

Some foods on the chart require pasteurization to prevent spoilage. After conditioning, place about an inch of the dried food in a roasting pan. Bake at 160° for 30 minutes. Freezing the food may also serve to pasteurize. This method involves placing the containers of dried food in a freezer that's set at 0° up to two weeks.

Storing and Using Dried Produce

One big advantage of dried fruit and vegetables is they take up less space than other preserved foods. After drying, conditioning, and pasteurizing, immediately package the food in plastic bags; then seal inside another container with an airtight lid. Try to package food in small bags so it can be used within several days of opening. Label the containers with the date and contents, and store them in a dark, dry place.

Many dried foods can be rehydrated to look like the fresh, raw product. However, drying sometimes causes a loss of texture. For this reason, dried produce is often used in recipes rather than eating it plain by itself. To rehydrate fruit and vegetables, soak in water and then simmer until tender.

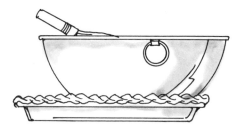

DRIED PEACH CREAM PIE

1¾ cups dried sliced peaches
1½ cups water
¼ cup sugar
1 baked 9-inch pastry shell
¾ cup sugar
2 tablespoons cornstarch
1¾ cups milk
3 eggs, separated
3 tablespoons butter or margarine
1 teaspoon vanilla extract
¼ teaspoon cream of tartar
¼ cup plus 2 tablespoons sugar

Combine peaches and water in a small saucepan; bring to a boil. Reduce heat and simmer, uncovered, 30 minutes or until tender. Stir in ¼ cup sugar; pour into pastry shell.

Combine ¾ cup sugar and cornstarch in a heavy saucepan. Gradually add milk, stirring until blended. Cook over medium heat, stirring constantly, until mixture thickens and comes to a boil; cook 1 minute, stirring constantly. Remove mixture from heat.

Beat egg yolks until thick and lemon colored. Gradually stir about one-fourth of hot mixture into yolks; add to remaining hot mixture, stirring constantly. Cook over medium heat 4 minutes, stirring constantly. Remove from heat; stir in the butter and vanilla. Pour over peaches; bake at 350° for 25 minutes.

Beat egg whites (at room temperature) and cream of tartar until foamy. Gradually add remaining sugar, 1 tablespoon at a time, beating until stiff peaks form. Spread meringue over hot filling, sealing to edge of pastry. Bake at 425° for 6 to 8 minutes or until golden brown. Cool pie to room temperature. Yield: one 9-inch pie. *Dorothy Cox, Snyder, Texas.*

FRUIT AND VEGETABLE DEHYDRATION CHART

Produce	Before Drying	Drying Time At 140°	After Drying
Apples	Peel and core; slice into ⅛-inch-thick rings. Dip in ascorbic-citric solution. Steam blanch 8 minutes, and pat dry.	Dry 4 to 5 hours or until leathery but still pliable. No moistness should remain in center.	Condition. Store up to 6 months.
Bananas	Peel and slice ⅛ inch thick. Dip in ascorbic-citric solution, and pat dry.	Dry 4 to 6 hours or until slightly pliable but crisp.	Store up to 4 months.
Carrots	Wash and scrape; slice ⅛ inch thick. Steam blanch 4 minutes, and pat dry.	Dry 2 to 4 hours or until very tough and brittle.	Condition and pasteurize. Store up to 8 months.
Corn	Husk ears and remove silk; wash and steam blanch whole ears 4 minutes. Slice corn from cobs.	Dry 5 to 7 hours or until brittle, stirring occasionally.	Condition and pasteurize. Store up to 8 months.
English Peas	Shell and wash peas. Steam blanch 3 minutes, and pat dry.	Dry 5 or 6 hours or until shriveled and hard.	Condition. Store up to 6 months.
Grapes	Wash and steam blanch 30 seconds or until skins crack. Gently pat dry.	Dry 32 to 34 hours or until grapes have a raisinlike texture. No moistness should remain in center.	Store up to 6 months.
Green Peppers	Wash, stem, and core. Cut into ½-inch cubes. Steam blanch 3 minutes, and pat dry.	Dry 9 to 11 hours or until brittle.	Condition. Store up to 12 months.
Okra	Wash and steam blanch 4 minutes. Slice ¼ inch thick.	Dry 4 to 6 hours or until tough and brittle.	Condition and pasteurize. Store up to 6 months.
Onions	Wash, trim ends, and remove outer skins. Slice crosswise ⅛ inch thick.	Dry 6 to 9 hours or until brittle.	Condition. Store up to 6 months.
Peaches	Wash, peel, and pit; slice ⅛ inch thick. Dip in ascorbic-citric solution. Steam blanch 8 minutes, and pat dry.	Dry 9 to 11 hours or until leathery but still pliable. No moisture should remain in center.	Condition. Store up to 8 months.
Pineapple	Wash, peel, and remove thorny eyes. Core and slice crosswise ⅛ inch thick.	Dry 7 to 12 hours or until leathery and not sticky.	Store up to 8 months.
Potatoes	Wash, peel, and slice crosswise ⅛ inch thick. Steam blanch 4 to 5 minutes.	Dry 8 to 10 hours or until tough and brittle.	Condition. Store up to 8 months.
Tomatoes	Wash and peel, if desired. To peel, dip in boiling water 30 seconds. Peel away skins. Slice crosswise ⅛ inch thick.	Dry 5 to 7 hours or until tough and crisp.	Condition and pasteurize. Store up to 4 months.

Note: Drying times given here are for reference only. Examine each batch of food carefully to determine exact doneness.

SPICED RAISIN PIE

1⅓ cups dried seedless grapes
3 eggs
1 cup sugar
½ cup butter or margarine, melted
1 tablespoon vinegar
½ teaspoon ground cinnamon
¼ teaspoon ground allspice
¼ teaspoon ground cloves
¼ teaspoon ground nutmeg
1 unbaked 9-inch pastry shell
Whipped cream (optional)

Cover grapes with water in a medium saucepan, and bring to a boil; reduce heat and simmer, uncovered, 8 to 10 minutes or until tender. Drain well, and set aside.

Combine eggs and sugar, beating well. Beat in butter, vinegar, and spices; stir in grapes. Pour into pastry shell. Bake at 375° for 30 to 35 minutes or until browned. Serve with whipped cream, if desired. Yield: one 9-inch pie.

FRUITY GRANOLA

3 cups regular oats, uncooked
½ cup flaked coconut
⅓ cup coarsely chopped almonds
¼ cup salted sunflower kernels
¼ cup firmly packed brown sugar
¼ cup butter or margarine, melted
¼ cup plus 2 tablespoons honey
1 teaspoon ground cinnamon
½ teaspoon vanilla extract
¼ teaspoon salt
½ cup dried seedless grapes
½ cup dried sliced peaches, coarsely
    chopped
½ cup dried sliced apples, coarsely
    chopped
½ cup dried sliced pineapple, coarsely
    chopped
½ cup dried banana slices, coarsely
    chopped

Combine first 4 ingredients in a large bowl; set aside. Combine next 6 ingredients; pour over the oats mixture, and mix well. Spread mixture evenly in a lightly greased 15- x 10- x 1-inch jellyroll pan. Bake at 325° for 15 to 20 minutes or until golden brown, stirring every 5 minutes. Cool completely. Stir in remaining ingredients. Store in an airtight container up to 6 weeks. Serve as a snack or as cereal. Yield: 7 cups.

BANANA-ORANGE MUFFINS

1 cup butter or margarine, softened
1 cup sugar
2 eggs
3 cups all-purpose flour
1 teaspoon baking powder
¾ cup buttermilk
1 teaspoon baking soda
¾ cup dried banana slices, chopped
½ teaspoon grated orange rind
¼ cup orange juice

Cream butter; gradually add sugar, beating until light and fluffy. Add the eggs, one at a time, beating well after each addition.

Combine flour and baking powder; set aside. Combine buttermilk and soda; add to creamed mixture alternately with flour mixture, beginning and ending with flour mixture. Stir in remaining ingredients. Fill greased muffin pans two-thirds full. Bake at 400° for 15 to 20 minutes. Yield: 2 dozen.

VEGETABLE-FLAVORED CROUTONS

2 dried tomato slices
2 dried onion slices
1 tablespoon dried carrot slices
1 tablespoon dried diced green pepper
1 cup butter or margarine, melted
21 slices day-old white bread, cut into
    ½-inch cubes

Combine first 4 ingredients in container of electric blender; blend until powdery. Add butter, and mix well.

Pour butter mixture over bread cubes, and toss gently. Place on a baking sheet in a single layer. Bake at 275° for 1 hour, stirring occasionally. Yield: about 2½ cups.

VEGETABLE SOUP

1½ cups Vegetable Soup Mix
7 cups water
1 tablespoon beef-flavored bouillon
    granules
¼ teaspoon pepper
⅛ teaspoon garlic powder
1 bay leaf

Combine soup mix and water in a large Dutch oven; let soak 1½ hours. Add remaining ingredients, and bring to a boil. Cover, reduce heat, and simmer 1 hour or until vegetables are tender. Remove the bay leaf before serving. Yield: 6 cups.

Vegetable Soup Mix:

¼ cup dried carrot slices
¼ cup dried corn kernels
¼ cup dried English peas
¼ cup dried okra slices
4 to 6 dried tomato slices, coarsely
    chopped
4 to 6 dried potato slices, coarsely
    chopped
3 dried onion slices, coarsely chopped
2 tablespoons dried diced green pepper

Combine all ingredients. Store in an airtight container. Yield: 1½ cups.

From Our Kitchen To Yours

As many visitors tour our *Southern Living* test kitchens, we get a lot of questions about the appliances, cabinets, and especially our counter tops. We have a different counter top in each of our three kitchens, and visitors are often eager to know what they are made of, whether they're durable and practical, and if they're easy to clean.

In our garden kitchen, there is dark-green ceramic tile. It has a glazed surface that acts like a protective coating. This makes it shiny, durable, and easy to clean. The tile can be wiped with hot soapy water, and occasionally the terracotta grout around the tile has to be cleaned with a small brush. The unevenness of the tile is a drawback if you are chopping, kneading dough, or rolling out pastry. To solve this, we keep a cutting board or marble slab handy.

Our gourmet kitchen has an entirely different look and work surface—it's a powdered marble-based surface, and it is great for working with breads and pastries, and doesn't even need a pastry cloth. Because this counter top is able to withstand high heat, hot dishes can be taken from the oven or stove top and placed directly on the counter without a hot pad. This surface may be used to chop on, too. And when it gets scratched, a piece of fine steel wool can be used to erase scratches and knife marks. This surface can be wiped clean in an instant and is one of our favorite work surfaces.

Our homey country kitchen has handmade Mexican tiles covering the counter tops. It is easy to clean with just hot soapy water and with constant use, it has shown no real signs of aging. Since the tiles are handmade and therefore not exactly alike, they create more of an uneven surface than in the garden kitchen. So we always use a cutting board to have a level surface for measuring, and a marble slab for working with breads and pastries.

Side Dishes For Your Cookout

Even if your outdoor cooking skills are limited to hamburgers and steaks, you can turn ordinary barbecues into memorable events by adding a couple of these side dishes.

BEEFY BAKED BEANS

½ pound ground beef
1 (31-ounce) can pork and beans
1 medium onion, chopped
½ green pepper, chopped
½ cup catsup
½ cup dark corn syrup
2 tablespoons prepared mustard
4 slices bacon, cut in half

Cook ground beef until browned, stirring to crumble meat. Drain well.

Combine beef and next 6 ingredients; stir well. Spoon mixture into a lightly greased 12- x 8- x 2-inch baking dish. Arrange bacon on top of beans. Bake at 400° for 40 minutes. Yield: 8 servings.
Beverly Russ Scott,
Morganton, North Carolina.

SPICY CORN-ON-THE-COB

¼ cup butter or margarine,
   melted
1 teaspoon chili powder
¼ teaspoon garlic salt
4 ears fresh corn
1 to 2 quarts water
1 teaspoon sugar

Combine butter, chili powder, and garlic salt; mix well.

Remove husks and silks from corn; discard. Combine water and sugar in a Dutch oven; bring to a boil. Add corn; cover, reduce heat, and simmer 8 to 10 minutes. Drain; brush corn with butter mixture. Yield: 4 servings.
Brenda Gilpatrick,
Albany, Georgia.

OLD-FASHIONED SLAW

1 medium head cabbage, shredded
½ cup chopped celery
½ cup chopped sweet pickle
¼ cup mayonnaise
3 medium carrots, shredded
2 green onions, chopped
1 teaspoon celery seeds
¼ cup butter or margarine
½ cup sweet pickle juice
¼ teaspoon salt
¼ teaspoon pepper
1 egg, beaten

Combine first 7 ingredients in a large bowl; set aside.

Melt butter in a heavy saucepan. Add pickle juice, salt, and pepper; stir well. Gradually stir about one-fourth of hot mixture into egg; add to remaining hot mixture, stirring constantly with a wire whisk. Cook over low heat, stirring constantly, until thickened. Add dressing to cabbage mixture; mix well. Chill 1 to 2 hours before serving. Yield: 8 servings.
Kathleen Pashby,
Memphis, Tennessee.

HERBED ONIONS

3 tablespoons butter or margarine
1 tablespoon brown sugar
¼ teaspoon salt
⅛ teaspoon pepper
2 large onions, cut into ½-inch slices
¼ cup chopped celery
¼ cup chopped fresh parsley
¼ teaspoon dried whole oregano

Melt butter in a large skillet; stir in sugar, salt, and pepper. Arrange onion in skillet; cover, reduce heat, and simmer 10 minutes. Turn onion slices; sprinkle with celery, parsley, and oregano. Cover, and simmer an additional 10 minutes, stirring occasionally. Yield: 4 servings.
Jeannine Allen,
McAllen, Texas.

SOUR CREAM-POTATO SALAD

6 to 8 medium potatoes
2 tablespoons sweet pickle relish
2 tablespoons finely chopped onion
2 tablespoons chopped fresh parsley
1 (2-ounce) jar chopped pimiento, drained
2 tablespoons vinegar
1 tablespoon prepared mustard
1 teaspoon salt
Pepper to taste
1 (8-ounce) carton commercial sour cream
1½ cups chopped celery
2 hard-cooked eggs, chopped

Cook potatoes in boiling water 15 to 20 minutes or until tender. Drain and cool. Peel potatoes, and cut into ½-inch cubes; set aside.

Combine next 8 ingredients in large bowl; fold in sour cream. Add potatoes, celery, and eggs; toss gently. Chill at least 1 hour. Yield: 8 to 10 servings.
Mrs. T. E. Cromer,
Anderson, South Carolina.

LEMON-BUTTERED
NEW POTATOES

2 pounds new potatoes
2 teaspoons sugar
1 teaspoon salt
1 clove garlic, crushed
¼ cup butter or margarine, melted
2 tablespoons lemon juice
½ teaspoon paprika

Wash potatoes, and pare a 1-inch strip around center of each one. Place potatoes, sugar, salt, and garlic in a large saucepan; cover with water, and bring to a boil. Cover, reduce heat, and simmer 15 to 20 minutes or until tender; drain well. Combine butter, lemon juice, and paprika; drizzle over potatoes, and toss gently. Yield: 6 to 8 servings.
Pat Sanders,
Austin, Texas.

Try Bread With A Spicy Spread

If you want a special bread without baking homemade rolls or loaves, use a butter flavored with spices or cheese to spread on slices of commercial bread. It takes just a few minutes to mix up the spread, and less than 20 minutes to bake the bread.

MUSTARD-RYE OVALS

1 (16-ounce) unsliced loaf rye bread
¼ cup butter or margarine, softened
1 tablespoon prepared mustard with
   horseradish

Slice bread into ½-inch slices. Combine butter and mustard, mixing well; spread butter mixture between bread slices. Wrap loaf in foil; bake at 350° for 20 minutes or until thoroughly heated. Yield: 1 loaf. *June Bostick,*
Greenwood, Delaware.

SPICY CHEESE-OLIVE BREAD

1 (16-ounce) loaf unsliced French bread
½ cup butter or margarine, softened
¼ cup mayonnaise
2 cups (8 ounces) shredded mozzarella
  cheese
½ cup finely chopped ripe olives
1 teaspoon garlic powder
1 teaspoon onion powder

Cut French bread in half lengthwise. Combine butter and mayonnaise; stir in remaining ingredients. Spread mixture on cut side of bread. Bake at 350° for 10 to 15 minutes or until cheese melts. Yield: 1 loaf.   *Lucille V. Cheek,*
          Transylvania, Louisiana.

TOASTED HERB LOAF

1 (16-ounce) loaf unsliced French bread
¼ cup butter or margarine, softened
1 small clove garlic, crushed
⅛ teaspoon salt
⅛ teaspoon dry mustard
⅛ teaspoon dried whole thyme
⅛ teaspoon paprika
⅛ teaspoon ground savory

Slice French bread into ½-inch slices. Combine remaining ingredients, mixing well; spread butter mixture between bread slices. Wrap loaf in foil; bake at 400° for 15 minutes or until thoroughly heated. Yield: 1 loaf.   *Diane Butts,*
          Boone, North Carolina.

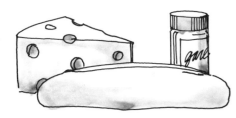

CHEESY GARLIC BREAD

1 (16-ounce) loaf unsliced French bread
1 cup (4 ounces) shredded Swiss cheese
½ cup butter or margarine, softened
¼ teaspoon garlic powder
¼ teaspoon celery seeds
¼ teaspoon parsley flakes

Slice French bread into 1-inch slices. Combine remaining ingredients, mixing well; spread butter mixture between bread slices and on top and sides of loaf. Wrap loaf in foil; bake at 350° for 15 minutes or until thoroughly heated. Yield: 1 loaf.   *Sherry B. Phillips,*
          Knoxville, Tennessee.

Southerners Serve The Best Cakes

From simple sheet cakes to frosted layer cakes, you'll find the recipe you need here. Use a cake mix to bake our moist Quick-and-Easy Carrot Cake. Or bake a sheet cake like our Apple-Orange Cake and Cinnamon Streusel Cake; they're convenient for transporting to family reunions.

MANDARIN-RUM CAKE

1 (18.5-ounce) package yellow cake mix
  with pudding
½ cup ground almonds
1 cup water
⅓ cup vegetable oil
3 eggs
½ cup sugar
¾ cup apricot nectar
1 tablespoon cornstarch
1 tablespoon water
¼ cup rum
1 cup whipping cream
2 tablespoons powdered sugar
2 (8-ounce) cans mandarin oranges,
  drained

Combine first 5 ingredients; beat 2 minutes at high speed of an electric mixer. Pour batter into 2 greased and floured 9-inch round cakepans.

Bake at 350° for 25 to 30 minutes or until a wooden pick inserted in center comes out clean. Cool in pans 10 minutes; remove from pans, and cool completely on wire racks.

Combine sugar and apricot nectar in a saucepan; simmer until sugar dissolves. Combine cornstarch and water; add to nectar mixture. Cook, stirring constantly, until thick and clear. Cool slightly; stir in rum. Cool completely.

Beat whipping cream until foamy; gradually add powdered sugar, beating until soft peaks form. Prick top of cake layers at 1-inch intervals with a wooden pick. Place 1 cake layer on cake platter; spread with half of apricot sauce and half of whipped cream. Top with half of oranges. Repeat procedure with remaining ingredients. Chill at least 2 hours before serving. Store in refrigerator. Yield: one 2-layer cake.

          Patricia Boschen,
          Ashland, Virginia.

Tip: Lower oven temperature 25° when using heat-proof glass dishes to ensure even baking.

QUICK-AND-EASY CARROT CAKE

1 (18.5-ounce) package yellow cake mix
  with pudding
⅓ cup firmly packed brown sugar
2 teaspoons ground cinnamon
½ cup water
⅓ cup vegetable oil
3 eggs
2 cups finely shredded carrots
½ cup raisins
½ cup chopped pecans
Cream Cheese Glaze
Ground cinnamon

Combine first 6 ingredients; beat 2 minutes at medium speed of an electric mixer. Fold in carrots, raisins, and pecans. Spoon batter into a greased and floured 10-inch tube pan. Bake at 350° for 50 to 55 minutes or until a wooden pick inserted in center comes out clean. Cool cake in pan 25 minutes; turn out on a wire rack, and cool completely.

Place cake on a serving plate. Drizzle Cream Cheese Glaze over top, and sprinkle with cinnamon. Yield: one 10-inch cake.

Cream Cheese Glaze:

1 cup sifted powdered sugar
½ (3-ounce) package cream cheese,
  softened
2 tablespoons milk
½ teaspoon vanilla extract

Combine all ingredients; beat well. Yield: ½ cup.   *Judy Cunningham,*
          Roanoke, Virginia.

APPLE-ORANGE CAKE SQUARES

¼ cup plus 2 tablespoons butter or
  margarine, melted
1 cup firmly packed brown sugar
1 egg, beaten
½ cup applesauce
1 teaspoon grated orange rind
1 teaspoon vanilla extract
1¼ cups all-purpose flour
1 teaspoon baking powder
½ teaspoon salt
¼ teaspoon baking soda
½ cup chopped pecans
1½ cups sifted powdered sugar
1½ tablespoons orange juice
½ teaspoon vanilla extract

Combine first 6 ingredients in a large mixing bowl, stirring well.

Combine flour, baking powder, salt, and soda; add to applesauce mixture, mixing well. Stir in pecans.

Spoon the batter into a greased 12- x 8- x 2-inch baking dish. Bake at 350° for 25 minutes.

Combine powdered sugar, orange juice, and vanilla. Spread over cake. Cut into 2½- x 3-inch squares. Yield: 1 dozen.   *Louise E. Lowery, Talbott, Tennessee.*

CINNAMON STREUSEL CAKE

1 (18.5-ounce) package yellow cake mix without pudding
⅔ cup vegetable oil
4 eggs
1 cup buttermilk
¼ cup sugar
⅔ cup firmly packed brown sugar
1 tablespoon plus 1 teaspoon ground cinnamon
¾ cup sifted powdered sugar
2 tablespoons lemon juice

Combine cake mix, oil, eggs, buttermilk, and ¼ cup sugar in a large mixing bowl; beat 2 minutes at medium speed of an electric mixer.

Pour half of batter into a greased and floured 13- x 9- x 2-inch baking pan. Combine brown sugar and cinnamon. Sprinkle half of sugar mixture over batter. Spoon remaining batter evenly over sugar mixture; top with remaining sugar mixture. Draw knife through batter to make a swirl design. Bake at 325° for 40 minutes. Combine powdered sugar and lemon juice; drizzle over cake while warm. Cut cake into squares. Yield: 15 to 18 servings.   *Mary Norman, Whitsett, North Carolina.*

BANANA CAKE

½ cup shortening
1 cup sugar
2 eggs
1 cup mashed bananas
¼ cup plus 1 tablespoon milk
1 teaspoon vanilla extract
1 teaspoon lemon extract
2¼ cups all-purpose flour
2 teaspoons baking powder
¼ teaspoon baking soda
½ teaspoon salt
Frosting (recipe follows)

Cream shortening in a large mixing bowl; gradually add sugar, beating until light and fluffy. Add eggs, one at a time, beating well after each addition.

Add bananas, milk, and flavorings to creamed mixture; beat well. Combine flour, baking powder, soda, and salt; stir into banana mixture.

Pour batter into 3 greased and floured 8-inch cakepans. Bake at 350°

for 25 minutes or until a wooden pick inserted in center comes out clean. Cool in pans 10 minutes; remove from pans, and cool completely on wire racks.

Spread frosting between layers and on top and sides of cake. Yield: one 3-layer cake.

Frosting:

½ cup butter or margarine, softened
1 (16-ounce) package powdered sugar, sifted
3 to 4 tablespoons milk
1 teaspoon vanilla extract
1 teaspoon lemon extract

Cream butter; gradually add sugar, beating well. Add remaining ingredients, beating until smooth. Yield: enough for one 3-layer cake.
Hazel H. Maddox, Lynchburg, Virginia.

Some Cream Cheese Favorites

You can do a lot with cream cheese. Try it in a marbled cheesecake, or even in a fruit salad or an appetizer.

CREAM CHEESE LOAF CAKE

½ cup butter, softened
1 (8-ounce) package cream cheese, softened
1½ cups sugar
4 eggs
1¾ cups all-purpose flour
1½ teaspoons baking powder
2 teaspoons vanilla extract
¼ teaspoon lemon extract

Cream butter and cream cheese; gradually add sugar, beating until light and fluffy. Add eggs, one at a time, beating after each addition.

Combine flour and baking powder; gradually add to creamed mixture, mixing just until blended after each addition. Stir in flavorings.

Pour batter into a greased and floured 9- x 5- x 3-inch loafpan. Bake at 325° for 1 hour and 10 to 15 minutes or until a wooden pick inserted in center comes out clean. Cool cake in pan 10 minutes; remove from pan, and cool completely. Yield: 1 loaf.
Belinda Cesky, Clemmons, North Carolina.

CREAM CHEESE PUFFS

1 (3-ounce) package cream cheese, softened
1 (2-ounce) can sliced mushrooms, drained and chopped
2 tablespoons chopped pimiento
1 teaspoon minced onion
2 drops of hot sauce
1 (8-ounce) can refrigerated crescent dinner rolls
½ cup finely chopped pecans

Combine first 5 ingredients; mix well. Unroll crescent rolls; leave every 2 rolls attached, forming 4 rectangles. Spread each rectangle with one-fourth of mushroom mixture, carefully spreading to edges. Beginning with a long side, roll up each rectangle jellyroll fashion; slice each roll into 6 pieces. Coat with pecans, pressing pecans into dough; place on ungreased baking sheets. Bake at 375° for 20 minutes or until golden brown. Yield: 2 dozen appetizers.   *Gwen Louer, Roswell, Georgia.*

CHEESECAKE SQUARES

1 cup all-purpose flour
⅓ cup firmly packed brown sugar
¼ cup plus 2 tablespoons butter or margarine, softened
1 (8-ounce) package cream cheese, softened
¼ cup sugar
1 egg
2 tablespoons milk
1 tablespoon lemon juice
½ teaspoon vanilla extract
1 tablespoon finely chopped pecans

Combine flour and brown sugar; cut in butter with pastry blender until mixture resembles coarse meal. Reserve 1 cup of crumb mixture; set aside. Press remaining mixture into an ungreased 8-inch square pan. Bake at 350° for 12 to 15 minutes or until lightly browned.

Beat cream cheese with electric mixer until light and fluffy; gradually add ¼ cup sugar, mixing well. Add next 4 ingredients, beating well. Spoon cream cheese mixture over crust. Combine reserved crumb mixture and pecans; sprinkle over cream cheese mixture. Bake at 350° for 25 to 30 minutes. Cool; cut into squares. Yield: 16 squares.

Joy M. Hall, Lucedale, Mississippi.

PEAR-LIME SALAD

1 (16-ounce) can pear halves, undrained
1 (3-ounce) package lime-flavored gelatin
1 (8-ounce) package cream cheese, softened
1 (8-ounce) carton lemon yogurt

Drain pears, reserving juice. Bring juice to a boil, stirring constantly. Remove from heat. Add gelatin, stirring until dissolved. Let cool slightly.

Coarsely chop pear halves. Combine cream cheese and yogurt; beat at medium speed of electric mixer until smooth. Add gelatin mixture, and beat well. Stir in pears. Pour into an oiled 4-cup mold. Chill. Yield: 8 servings.
Ila Ellington,
Greensboro, North Carolina.

MARBLE MINT CHEESECAKE

3 tablespoons graham cracker crumbs
1 (16-ounce) carton cream-style cottage cheese
2 (8-ounce) packages cream cheese, softened
1½ cups sugar
4 eggs, slightly beaten
1 (16-ounce) carton commercial sour cream
½ cup butter, melted
⅓ cup cornstarch
¾ teaspoon peppermint extract
8 (1-ounce) squares semisweet chocolate
1 (8-ounce) carton frozen whipped topping, thawed
1 (8-ounce) jar chocolate fudge topping
2 tablespoons crème de menthe syrup

Grease a 9-inch springform pan. Coat bottom and sides of pan with graham cracker crumbs, and set aside.

Place cottage cheese in container of electric blender, and process until smooth; set aside. Beat cream cheese with electric mixer until smooth; add cottage cheese, mixing well. Gradually add sugar, mixing well. Add eggs, beating well. Add next 4 ingredients, beating at low speed of electric mixer.

Place chocolate squares in top of double boiler; bring water to a boil. Reduce heat to low; cook, stirring constantly, until chocolate melts. Remove from heat, and add 1½ cups of cream cheese mixture; blend thoroughly.

Pour half of remaining cream cheese mixture into prepared pan, and top with half of chocolate mixture. Repeat layers. Gently cut through batter in zigzag fashion in several places. Bake at 325° for 1 hour and 15 to 20 minutes. Turn oven off, and allow cheesecake to cool in oven 2 hours. Remove from oven; let cool to room temperature on a rack; chill several hours.

Remove sides of springform pan. Pipe whipped topping over top of cheesecake. Combine chocolate topping and crème de menthe syrup. To serve, drizzle chocolate topping over each slice. Yield: 10 to 12 servings. *H. W. Asbell,*
Leesburg, Florida.

A Moveable Feast For Two

If you are planning a leisurely hike through the mountains or a stroll in the nearest park, be sure to take this picnic for two along.

Chutney-Cheese Pâté
Crispy Chicken
Simple Carrot Salad
Cool Cucumbers
Stuffed Eggs-and-Tomato Slices
Wine

CHUTNEY-CHEESE PATE

1 (3-ounce) package cream cheese, softened
½ cup (2 ounces) shredded sharp Cheddar cheese
2 teaspoons dry sherry
¼ teaspoon curry powder
⅛ teaspoon salt
½ cup chutney
Finely chopped green onions with tops

Combine first 5 ingredients; beat until smooth. Shape mixture into a ½-inch-thick circle; chill until firm. Spread chutney over top, and sprinkle with onions. Serve with crackers. Yield: 1 cup. *Mrs. Howard B. Vaughn,*
Nashville, Tennessee.

CRISPY CHICKEN

½ cup corn flake crumbs
¼ teaspoon salt
¼ teaspoon celery salt
¼ teaspoon garlic salt
¼ teapoon paprika
⅛ teaspoon ground nutmeg
2 chicken breast halves, skinned
¼ cup skim milk

Combine first 6 ingredients, mixing well. Dip chicken in milk; roll in corn flake crumb mixture, coating well.

Place chicken in a lightly greased baking pan. Bake, uncovered, at 400° for 45 minutes or until the chicken is tender. Yield: 2 servings.
Mrs. H. G. Drawdy,
Spindale, North Carolina.

SIMPLE CARROT SALAD

1½ cups shredded carrots
¼ cup crushed pineapple
2 tablespoons pineapple juice
2 tablespoons flaked coconut
1½ teaspoons sugar
1 tablespoon mayonnaise

Combine carrots and remaining ingredients; stir well. Cover and chill 2 to 3 hours. Yield: 2 servings.
Reba B. Wilson,
Jasper, Alabama.

COOL CUCUMBERS

½ cup commercial sour cream
1 tablespoon lemon juice
2¼ teaspoons prepared horseradish
⅛ teaspoon dried whole dillweed
1 medium cucumber, sliced
Minced fresh parsley

Combine first 4 ingredients, stirring well. Add cucumber; stir gently to coat. Chill several hours. Sprinkle with parsley. Yield: 2 servings. *Cindy Murphy,*
Cleveland, Tennessee.

STUFFED EGGS-AND-TOMATO SLICES

2 hard-cooked eggs
2 teaspoons commercial French salad dressing
1 teaspoon mayonnaise
Pinch of salt
Dash of pepper
Dash of red pepper
Paprika
2 small tomatoes, sliced
Lettuce leaves
Green onion fans (optional)

Slice eggs in half lengthwise, and carefully remove yolks. Mash yolks, and stir in next 5 ingredients. Stuff egg whites with yolk mixture. Sprinkle with paprika. Arrange stuffed eggs and tomato slices on lettuce leaves. Garnish with green onion fans, if desired. Yield: 2 servings. *Julia Manherz,*
Virginia Beach, Virginia.

Bake A Batch Of Bar Cookies

It's fun to raid the cookie jar or sneak a handful of cookies still warm from the oven! Bar cookies are popular because they're easy to make, serve, and store. Whether plain, full of fruit, filled, or frosted, these cookies can be made to suit almost every occasion.

APPLE BUTTER BARS

1½ cups all-purpose flour
1 teaspoon baking soda
1 teaspoon salt
2½ cups quick-cooking oats, uncooked
1½ cups sugar
1 cup butter or margarine, melted
1½ cups apple butter

Combine flour, soda, and salt in a large bowl; add oats and sugar. Stir in butter, and mix well. Press half of mixture into a greased 13- x 9- x 2-inch baking pan; top with apple butter. Sprinkle with remaining crumb mixture, and press in gently with a spoon.

Bake at 350° for 55 minutes or until browned. Cool, and cut into bars. Yield: 3 dozen. *Melody Gourley, Alamo, Tennessee.*

HAWAIIAN BARS

¼ cup butter or margarine, softened
1 cup firmly packed brown sugar
1½ cups flaked coconut
1 cup all-purpose flour
½ teaspoon salt
Pineapple Filling

Cream butter and sugar until mixed well. Add coconut, flour, and salt; mix with a fork until crumbly.

Press half of crumb mixture into a greased 9-inch square pan. Spread Pineapple Filling evenly over crumb mixture. Cover with remaining crumb mixture, and gently press down. Bake at 350° for 30 to 35 minutes. Cut into 1½- x 1-inch bars. Yield: 4½ dozen.

Pineapple Filling:

1 (8-ounce) can crushed pineapple, undrained
¾ cup sugar
3 tablespoons cornstarch
¼ teaspoon salt
1 tablespoon butter or margarine
1 tablespoon lemon juice

Combine pineapple, sugar, cornstarch, and salt in a saucepan, stirring to mix. Bring to a boil; cook stirring constantly, 5 minutes or until thickened. Remove from heat, and stir in butter and lemon juice. Allow to cool slightly. Yield: about ¾ cup. *Harletta Carthel, Gruver, Texas.*

NUTTY DATE BARS

1 cup all-purpose flour
½ cup butter or margarine, softened
½ teaspoon vanilla extract
2 eggs
1 cup firmly packed brown sugar
1 cup chopped dates
1 cup chopped pecans
⅓ cup orange marmalade
2 tablespoons all-purpose flour
½ teaspoon baking powder
½ teaspoon vanilla extract
¼ teaspoon salt

Combine flour, butter, and ½ teaspoon vanilla in a medium bowl; blend with pastry cutter until mixture forms a soft dough. Press into a greased 11- x 7- x 2-inch baking pan. Bake at 350° for 12 to 15 minutes or until lightly browned.

Beat eggs until foamy in a small mixing bowl. Stir in remaining ingredients until mixed well; spread on crust layer. Bake 25 to 30 minutes longer or until top is set and browned. Cool; cut into bars. Yield: 2 dozen.
Mrs. Frances Whitehead, Big Lake, Texas.

PEANUT BUTTER FROSTS

1 cup all-purpose flour
1 cup quick-cooking oats, uncooked
½ cup sugar
½ cup firmly packed brown sugar
½ teaspoon baking soda
½ cup butter or margarine, softened
⅓ cup peanut butter
1 egg, beaten
Peanut Butter Frosting
Chopped peanuts (optional)

Combine flour, oats, sugar, and soda in a large bowl. Add butter, peanut butter, and egg; stir until thoroughly blended. (Mixture will be crumbly.) Press into a greased 9-inch square pan. Bake at 350° for 20 to 25 minutes or until the edges begin to pull away from sides of pan. (Center will be soft.) Cool completely.

Top with Peanut Butter Frosting; sprinkle with chopped peanuts, if desired. Cut into 3- x 1½-inch bars. Yield: 1½ dozen.

Peanut Butter Frosting:
¼ cup butter or margarine, softened
1½ cups sifted powdered sugar
¼ cup peanut butter
1 tablespoon plus 2 teaspoons milk
1 teaspoon vanilla extract

Combine butter and 1 cup sugar in a small mixing bowl; beat until creamy. Add remaining ½ cup sugar, peanut butter, milk, and vanilla; beat until fluffy. Add additional milk, if needed. Yield: about 1¼ cups.
Mrs. Galen Johnson, Transylvania, Louisiana.

This Cornbread Has A Topping

Southerners love cornbread piping hot and spread with butter. But when you bake this cornbread, be prepared to spoon on a thick topping of sour cream, Cheddar cheese, and chopped onions.

ONION-TOPPED CORNBREAD

2½ cups chopped onion
¼ cup butter or margarine
1 (8-ounce) carton commercial sour cream
1 cup (4 ounces) shredded Cheddar cheese, divided
1½ cups self-rising cornmeal
2 tablespoons sugar
¼ teaspoon dried whole dillweed
2 eggs, beaten
1 (8¾-ounce) can cream-style corn
¼ cup milk
¼ cup vegetable oil
Dash of hot sauce

Sauté onion in butter 5 minutes or until tender. Remove from heat; stir in sour cream and ½ cup cheese.

Combine cornmeal, sugar, and dillweed; stir well, and set aside. Combine next 5 ingredients, stirring well; add all at once to cornmeal mixture, stirring until blended. Pour batter into a lightly greased 8-inch square pan. Spread onion mixture evenly over top. Sprinkle with remaining ½ cup cheese. Bake at 400° for 25 to 30 minutes. Yield: 8 to 10 servings.
Lynne Weeks, Midland, Georgia.

Stuff A Summer Vegetable

Nothing could be more natural than serving vegetable side dishes in shells made from the vegetables themselves. When stuffing vegetables, remember to use a gentle touch removing the centers.

BEEF-STUFFED PEPPERS

4 large green peppers
1 medium onion, chopped
2 teaspoons butter or margarine
1 pound ground beef
1 (8-ounce) can tomato sauce
1 (8¾-ounce) can whole kernel corn, drained
2 teaspoons chili powder
½ teaspoon salt
½ cup (2 ounces) shredded Cheddar cheese

Cut off tops of green peppers; remove centers and discard. Cook peppers 5 minutes in boiling water; drain.

Sauté onion in butter until tender; add ground beef, and cook until beef is browned. Drain well. Stir in remaining ingredients, except cheese.

Stuff peppers with meat mixture, and place in an 8-inch square baking dish. Bake at 350° for 15 minutes. Sprinkle tops with Cheddar cheese; bake 5 minutes. Yield: 4 servings. *Sandy Webb, Greenwood, Delaware.*

BROCCOLI-STUFFED ONIONS

6 medium Vidalia or Bermuda onions
1 (1-pound) bunch broccoli
½ cup grated Parmesan cheese
⅓ cup mayonnaise
2 teaspoons lemon juice
2 tablespoons butter or margarine
2 tablespoons all-purpose flour
⅔ cup milk
¼ teaspoon salt
1 (3-ounce) package cream cheese, cubed

Peel onions, cutting a slice from each top. Cook onions in boiling water 15 minutes or until tender but not mushy. Cool; remove centers of onions, leaving shells intact. Set shells aside. Chop centers, and set aside 1 cup (reserve remaining onion for use in other recipes).

Trim off large leaves and tough ends of lower stalks of broccoli, and wash thoroughly. Cook in a small amount of boiling water 10 minutes or until tender. Chop and set aside.

Combine 1 cup of chopped cooked onion, chopped broccoli, Parmesan cheese, mayonnaise, and lemon juice. Fill onion shells with broccoli mixture; place onions in a lightly greased 12- x 8- x 2-inch baking dish.

Melt butter in a heavy saucepan over low heat; add flour, stirring until smooth. Cook 1 minute, stirring constantly. Gradually add milk; cook over medium heat, stirring constantly, until thickened and bubbly. Add salt and cream cheese, stirring until cheese melts. Spoon sauce over onions. Bake at 375° for 20 minutes. Yield: 6 servings. *Elizabeth Ann Davis, Silver Creek, Georgia.*

MUSHROOM-STUFFED YELLOW SQUASH

4 medium-size yellow squash
½ pound fresh mushrooms, chopped
1 small onion, chopped
1 clove garlic, minced
¼ cup butter or margarine
1 cup soft breadcrumbs
½ teaspoon salt
¼ teaspoon pepper
Sliced radishes (optional)

Wash squash thoroughly; cook in boiling water to cover 8 to 10 minutes or until tender but still firm. Drain and cool slightly. Remove and discard stems. Cut each squash in half lengthwise; remove and reserve pulp, leaving a firm shell. Chop pulp, and set aside.

Sauté mushrooms, onion, and garlic in butter in a skillet until tender. Remove from heat; stir in squash pulp, breadcrumbs, salt, and pepper. Place squash shells in a 13- x 9- x 2-inch baking dish. Spoon squash mixture into shells. Bake at 350° for 15 minutes. Garnish with sliced radishes, if desired. Yield: 4 servings. *Mrs. D. M. Smith, Gainesville, Florida.*

Sprout Your Own Beans

More people are eating bean sprouts than ever before—and with good reason. These vegetables are a staple in Oriental cookery, and they add lots of flavor and crispy texture to other foods, such as salads and sandwiches, as well. Within just a few days, you can have tender, fresh bean sprouts growing right in your own kitchen.

Most people grow their own sprouts from either mung beans or alfalfa seeds, both commonly available in health food stores, gourmet shops, or Oriental food stores. While there are many commercial sprouters, the same results can be achieved by using canning jars and a little cheesecloth.

Start growing the sprouts four to six days before you need them. First, remove all foreign material and broken beans; then place the beans in a 1-pint canning jar. (Use about 1 to 2 tablespoons alfalfa seeds or 2 to 4 tablespoons mung beans per jar.) Fill the jar about two-thirds full of water; cover the jar with cheesecloth, and secure it with a plastic canning ring or rubber band. (Metal canning rings might rust with prolonged exposure to water.) Soak beans 8 hours or overnight.

Drain water from beans through the cheesecloth; then cover the jars with a cloth towel to protect the sprouts from light but still let air circulate. Keep the beans you are sprouting in a warm place, about 70°.

Rinse and drain the beans through cheesecloth about three times a day until roots are about 1 inch long, always replacing the towel over them after each rinsing.

Sprouts are ready to harvest when the roots are about 1 inch long. Place sprouts in a large bowl of cool water, and gently agitate them in the water. Strain off any loose seeds that float to the top of the water, but it's not necessary to remove seeds that don't separate from the sprouts. Drain the sprouts, and pat them dry with paper towels. Store sprouts in an airtight container in the refrigerator up to a week.

Tip: Freshen wilted vegetables by letting them stand 10 minutes in cold water to which a few drops of lemon juice have been added; drain, and store in a plastic bag in the refrigerator.

July

Whip Up Meringue, Pipe Out Dessert

Next time you have a dinner party, these piped meringues will provide a lush dessert and a nice bonus—they're pretty enough to be your centerpiece.

Try our recipes for shaping meringue; then experiment with new shapes. You can form simple shells with the back of a spoon, or you can pipe the mixture into elaborate designs like our Summer Berry Basket or smaller individual containers like our Spanish Wind Cakes. You can also make meringue cookies to serve with or without a filling.

Use leftover meringue to pipe pretty flowers to serve as cookies, or to keep on hand in your freezer for garnishing cakes, pies, or dessert trays. One recipe of Piping Meringue makes about two dozen 2-inch flowers.

When experimenting, try folding extracts, finely chopped nuts, or a few drops of liquid food coloring into the prepared meringue before shaping and baking.

Familiarize yourself with the baking directions in the following recipes to help when experimenting. The baking temperatures range from 200° to 225°. (Temperatures are low to keep the meringue from browning during the time it takes to dry out.) Meringues are baked until they are firm and almost dry; then the oven is turned off, and they are left in the oven to cool for several hours or overnight.

Seal baked meringues in an airtight container, and store at room temperature up to two days. For longer storage, freeze up to a month in an airtight container. If the meringues feel softened or sticky after storage, crisp them in a 200° oven about 5 minutes. Then turn the oven off and let cool in the oven until dry. Fill the meringues just before serving to keep them crisp.

When making piped meringues, keep these points in mind:

—For maximum volume in beaten egg whites, separate yolks from the whites while eggs are cold, and let the whites come to room temperature before beating them.

—Make sure bowls for beating egg whites are very clean; the slightest bit of grease can inhibit volume and firmness of the meringue.

—Use superfine sugar when making meringue for piping because it dissolves quicker and better than regular sugar does. Purchase superfine sugar commercially, or make your own by processing regular sugar in an electric blender until finely ground.

—Avoid making meringues in humid weather; extra moisture can make the end product soft and sticky.

—Beat meringue just before piping so it will have maximum volume and be firm enough to hold peaks. After meringue sits a while, it will be firm enough for "gluing" baked meringue pieces together, but not firm enough to pipe new pieces.

—Always pipe meringue shapes on baking sheets lined with foil. Without foil, they will crack upon removal.

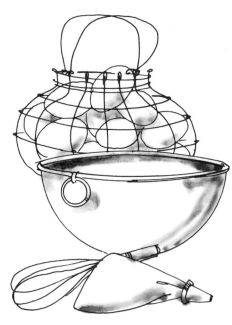

PIPING MERINGUE

6 egg whites
½ teaspoon cream of tartar
¼ teaspoon salt
½ teaspoon vanilla extract
½ teaspoon almond extract
1 cup superfine sugar

Beat egg whites (at room temperature) in a large bowl at high speed of an electric mixer until foamy. Sprinkle cream of tartar, salt, and flavorings over egg whites; continue beating until soft peaks form. Gradually add sugar, 1 tablespoon at a time, beating until stiff peaks form. Pipe or spread meringue into desired shapes; bake as directed. Yield: enough meringue to make 1 Summer Berry Basket or 4 Spanish Wind Cakes.

Note: To make superfine sugar, place granulated sugar in a blender; process until finely ground.

MERINGUE FLOWERS

1 recipe Piping Meringue
Small amount liquid food coloring (optional)

Prepare the Piping Meringue. (For colored flowers, add desired food coloring to meringue just before the sugar is added.) Pipe a dot of meringue onto a metal flower nail; place a 3-inch square of waxed paper on flower nail.

Spoon meringue into a decorating bag fitted with large rose tip No. 127D; holding wide end of tip down, pipe a flower shape onto waxed paper, slowly rotating the nail as you pipe to form the flower. Transfer waxed paper square to a baking sheet; repeat with remaining meringue. Bake at 200° for 1 hour; turn off oven, and cool in oven 1 hour. Remove from oven, and cool completely on wire rack.

Peel the flowers from waxed paper and use immediately, or carefully layer the flowers between waxed paper in an airtight container. Store at room temperature for up to 2 days, or freeze for several weeks. Yield: about 2 dozen.

ORANGE CHANTILLY CREAM

⅔ cup whipping cream
½ cup sifted powdered sugar
⅓ cup commercial sour cream
1½ tablespoons Cointreau or other orange-flavored liqueur
¼ teaspoon grated orange rind
½ teaspoon vanilla extract

Combine whipping cream and sugar in a chilled bowl; beat at low speed of an electric mixer until blended. Increase speed to high, and beat just until stiff peaks begin to form.

Combine sour cream, liqueur, orange rind, and vanilla; fold gently into whipped cream just until blended. Serve with fruit in meringues. Yield: about 1½ cups.

CHOCOLATE BUTTERCREAM

3 (1-ounce) squares unsweetened chocolate
¾ cup butter, softened
¾ cup sugar
⅓ cup water
6 egg yolks
3 tablespoons brandy (optional)

Place chocolate in top of a double boiler; bring water to a boil. Reduce heat to low; cook until chocolate melts. Set aside to cool. Cream butter in a large bowl, and set aside.

Combine sugar and water in a small, heavy saucepan; cook over medium heat, stirring constantly, until mixture boils. Boil, without stirring, until mixture reaches small thread stage (217° to 220°). Remove from heat.

Beat egg yolks in a small bowl at high speed of an electric mixer until thick and lemon colored; gradually add hot syrup to yolks, beating until mixture cools. Add yolk mixture, cooled chocolate, and brandy, if desired, to butter; beat at high speed of electric mixer until blended. Cover and refrigerate until the mixture is thick enough to pipe. Yield: about 2¾ cups.

Note: Buttercream may be stored in a tightly covered container in the refrigerator for up to 1 week. Allow to stand at room temperature until mixture is softened enough to pipe.

SPANISH WIND CAKES

½ recipe Piping Meringue
½ recipe Piping Meringue
½ cup Orange Chantilly Cream or
    sweetened whipped cream
6 to 8 fresh strawberries, sliced
Meringue Flowers (optional)

Line two large baking sheets with aluminum foil; draw six 3-inch circles on each foil-lined baking sheet.

Prepare one-half recipe of Piping Meringue. (Do not make a whole recipe and use half at a time; the reserved meringue would break down before being used in recipe.) Spoon meringue into a decorating bag fitted with No. 2A round or No. 4B star tip.

Pipe a ½-inch-wide ring of meringue just inside 1 circle outline; continue piping rings of meringue within first ring until circle is filled with meringue. Repeat procedure with 3 additional outlines (these are bases for cakes). Pipe ½-inch-wide rings just inside remaining 8 outlines (these are sides for cakes). Bake at 225° for 45 minutes. Turn off oven, and cool meringues in oven at least 1 hour. Carefully peel aluminum foil from meringues, and cool meringues completely on wire racks.

Prepare one-half recipe of Piping Meringue; line baking sheets again with foil. Place the 4 meringue bases on a baking sheet; stack 2 meringue rings on top of each base, using a little meringue

to "glue" layers together. Frost outside of meringue cakes with a thin, smooth layer of meringue. Spoon remaining meringue into a decorating bag fitted with No. 18, 19, or 20 star tip; pipe a border of stars around both the top and bottom edges of the cakes.

Draw four 2-inch circles for lids on second baking sheet. Pipe a ring of meringue shells or stars just inside each outline using same star tip; within each ring, pipe a spiral that ends in center and fills in circle. Bake cakes and lids at

225° for 45 minutes. Turn off oven; cool in oven at least 4 hours or overnight. Carefully peel foil from meringues, and store meringues in airtight container at room temperature up to 2 days.

Just before serving, place meringue cakes on a serving plate; spoon Orange Chantilly Cream evenly into shells, and arrange sliced strawberries on top. Place lids slightly off-center on cakes; serve immediately. Garnish the serving plate with Meringue Flowers, if desired. Yield: 4 servings.

Step 1—For each wind cake, pipe a circle of meringue for the base; pipe 2 rings of meringue for the sides. Bake.

Step 2—Stack rings on bases; spread meringue between layers. Frost sides with meringue. Return to baking sheet.

Step 3—Pipe a border of meringue stars around both the top and bottom edges of each of the wind cakes.

Step 4—Pipe lids on a separate baking sheet. Bake cakes and lids as directed. Cool, peel from foil, and fill.

CHOCOLATE-ALMOND MERINGUE FINGERS

1 recipe Piping Meringue (page 156)
1 tablespoon cornstarch
2 tablespoons unsweetened cocoa
About 1 cup finely chopped, toasted almonds, divided
1 recipe Chocolate Buttercream (page 156)

Line 2 large baking sheets with aluminum foil; prepare Piping Meringue. Combine cornstarch and cocoa, mixing well; fold into meringue just until blended. Spoon mixture into a decorating bag fitted with No. 4B star tip; pipe forty 3- x 1½-inch rectangles using a zigzag motion. Sprinkle lightly with ⅔ cup almonds. Bake at 225° for 1½ hours. Turn off oven; cool in oven at least 2 hours or overnight. Carefully peel foil from meringue fingers. Store meringues in airtight container at room temperature up to 2 days.

Up to 2 hours before serving, pipe Chocolate Buttercream between 2 meringue fingers (flat sides together) using No. 18, 19, or 20 star tip; place on its side in a paper baking cup. Repeat procedure with remaining meringue fingers and buttercream. Sprinkle buttercream filling with remaining toasted almonds. Refrigerate until ready to serve. Yield: 20 meringue fingers.

SUMMER BERRY BASKET

1 recipe Piping Meringue (page 156)
1 small fresh pineapple
1 recipe Orange Chantilly Cream (page 156)
1 cup fresh blueberries
1 large strawberry, sliced in half lengthwise (optional)

Line 2 large baking sheets with aluminum foil. Draw a 12- x 5-inch oval on a piece of paper; cut out oval to make pattern. Trace around pattern 2 times on each foil-lined baking sheet.

Prepare Piping Meringue. Spread about 1⅓ cups meringue evenly inside 1 oval outline. Spoon about ¾ cup meringue into decorating bag fitted with No. 1A or 2A round tip; pipe two ⅝-inch-wide ovals just inside 2 oval outlines. Change to No. 4B, 6B, or 8B star tip; pipe a ⅝-inch-wide oval just inside remaining oval outline, using a shell or star design. To make the handle, pipe two 4-inch-diameter semicircles in a shell or star design. Cover and chill the remaining meringue. Bake the meringue pieces at 200° for 2 hours. Turn off oven; cool meringues in oven at least 4 hours or overnight.

To assemble basket, carefully peel foil from meringue sections. Place filled-in oval on a foil-lined baking sheet. Stack 2 plain ovals, then decorated oval, on top of base, using a little reserved meringue to "glue" layers together. Bake at 225° for 15 minutes; place baking sheet on wire rack to cool completely. Carefully spread small amount of reserved meringue on flat side of 1 handle section; lightly press flat side of other handle section against meringue. Let dry at room temperature 2 hours. Store all meringue pieces in airtight container at room temperature up to 2 days.

Cut off the crown and a slice from bottom of the pineapple; cut off pineapple skin. Cut pineapple crosswise into ½-inch-thick slices, and remove core. Cut slices in half. Set aside 6 pineapple half-moons; reserve remaining pineapple for other uses.

Up to 1 hour before serving time, transfer basket to serving platter. Spread Orange Chantilly Cream evenly in basket. Stand 6 pineapple half-moons around inside edge of basket; arrange blueberries in center. Attach handle across center of basket, just inside basket edges, using more reserved meringue. Attach strawberry halves, if desired, to basket handle using wooden picks. Yield: 4 to 6 servings.

Combine Your Favorite Vegetables

Just about any combination of fresh corn, tomatoes, and okra on the table is a summer treat. Fresh from the garden, these vegetables are best simply seasoned and cooked quickly to retain their flavor and the most nutrients.

OKRA SURPRISE

3 tablespoons butter or margarine
4 to 5 large tomatoes, peeled and chopped
3 cups sliced okra (about ¾ pound)
2 cups fresh corn, cut from cob
¾ teaspoon salt
¼ teaspoon pepper

Melt butter in a large skillet. Stir in remaining ingredients; cover and cook over medium heat 15 minutes or until vegetables are tender. Yield: 8 to 10 servings.
Lillian Moore,
El Paso, Texas.

OLD-FASHIONED OKRA STEW

4 (16-ounce) cans whole tomatoes, undrained and chopped
1 (1-pound) ham hock
3 cups sliced okra (about ¾ pound)
1 cup fresh corn, cut from cob
1 cup fresh lima beans
¾ cup chopped onion
½ cup diced green pepper
1 bay leaf
½ teaspoon salt
¼ teaspoon dried whole oregano
¼ teaspoon pepper
Hot cooked rice

Combine all ingredients except rice in a large Dutch oven; bring to a boil. Cover, reduce heat, and simmer 1½ hours, stirring frequently. Remove bay-leaf and discard. Remove ham hock from stew. Remove meat from the bone and chop. Add meat to stew; stir well. Place rice in bowls, and ladle stew over rice. Yield: about 3 quarts.
Ann Truesdale,
Yonges Island, South Carolina.

SAUTEED CORN AND OKRA

8 slices bacon
2 cups sliced okra (about ½ pound)
2 cups fresh corn, cut from cob
Salt and pepper to taste

Cook bacon in large skillet until crisp; remove bacon and set aside, reserving 3 tablespoons drippings in skillet. Crumble bacon, and set aside. Sauté okra in drippings, stirring frequently, for 5 minutes. Add corn to skillet; cook 5 minutes longer or until vegetables are tender. Stir in crumbled bacon, and season with salt and pepper. Yield: 4 to 6 servings.
Ruth Moffitt,
Smyrna, Delaware.

SUMMER GARDEN MEDLEY

¼ cup chopped onion
2 tablespoons butter or margarine
2 cups fresh corn, cut from cob
3 medium tomatoes, peeled and cubed
4 small yellow squash, sliced
1 teaspoon salt
¾ teaspoon dried whole oregano
½ teaspoon sugar
¼ teaspoon pepper

Sauté onion in butter in a Dutch oven. Add remaining ingredients; cover and cook over medium heat 15 minutes or until the vegetables are tender. Yield: about 8 servings. *Claire Wash,*
Greenwood, South Carolina.

summer Suppers.

This Party Goes Outdoors And Casual

When you think about summer, activities such as swimming, picnicking, and vacationing come to mind. But one of the best things about summer is the delicious food it brings, from tasty barbecued ribs to cool congealed salads and frosty ice cream beverages. Along with our eighth annual "Summer Suppers" special section come these and many other summertime treats.

We begin in Eustis, Florida. Casual is the word in this Central Florida town, where the evenings often center around good food, cool drinks, and a lively group of people.

Among the Florida Citrus Groves

David and Joree Cox enjoy the seclusion of their 90-year-old Colonial-style home, surrounded by towering oaks and citrus groves. A large camphor tree shades most of the front yard from the late afternoon sun. Beneath it, bales of hay are scattered about, each covered with a brightly colored quilt. A buffet table, also dressed in quilts, rests on the patio in the side yard and boasts an assortment of dishes typical of the area.

When the guests arrive, David and Joree greet them with a mug of sparkling Ginger Beer and a selection of appetizers. While everyone mingles, they munch on Homemade Pretzels and vegetables with Green Goddess Dip.

When it's time for dinner, guests select from Apricot Baked Ham or Smoked Turkey, and make their own sandwiches with slices of Easy Beer Bread, piled high in a handmade wicker basket. Succulent melons and berries fill the carved Watermelon Fruit Basket. A creamy strawberry fruit dressing is served alongside. Bright and colorful,

Corn-on-the-Cob With Herb Butter proves to be a favorite.

The refreshing beverage Joree serves is Frosted Mint Tea, garnished with lemon slices and fresh mint sprigs. "To give the best flavor," Joree says, "it's important to dip the rim of each glass in lemon juice and sugar."

Guests enjoy Daffodil Cake for dessert. Light and airy, the cake is flavored with orange rind and makes a most appropriate ending to an evening in Central Florida.

Ginger Beer
Homemade Pretzels
Fresh Vegetables with
Green Goddess Dip
Apricot Baked Ham
Smoked Turkey
Easy Beer Bread
Corn-on-the-Cob With Herb Butter
Crab-Stuffed Mushroom Caps
Stuffed Cherry Tomatoes
Deviled Eggs With Smoked Oysters
Sliced Tomatoes
Watermelon Fruit Basket
Mandarin Orange Salad
Daffodil Cake
Frosted Mint Tea

GINGER BEER

2 (67.6-ounce) bottles ginger ale, chilled
11 (12-ounce) cans beer, chilled

Combine ginger ale and beer in a large container. Serve immediately over ice. Yield: 8 quarts.

HOMEMADE PRETZELS

1 package dry yeast
½ teaspoon sugar
1½ cups warm beer (105° to 115°)
4½ cups all-purpose flour
1 egg, beaten
Kosher salt

Dissolve yeast and sugar in warm beer in a large mixing bowl. Add flour, and mix until blended. Turn dough out onto a lightly floured surface. Knead 8 to 10 minutes until dough is smooth and elastic.

Place dough in a greased bowl, turning to grease top. Cover and let rise in a warm place (85°), free from drafts, 1 hour or until doubled in bulk.

Using kitchen shears dipped in flour, cut dough into 24 pieces; roll each into a ball. With floured hands, roll each ball between hands to form a rope 14 inches long. Twist each into a pretzel shape, placing on greased foil-lined baking sheets, about 1½ inches apart. Brush each pretzel with egg; sprinkle with kosher salt. Bake at 475° for 12 to 15 minutes or until golden brown. Remove pretzels to a wire rack. Serve warm. Yield: about 2 dozen.

Note: Rock or table salt may be substituted for kosher salt.

GREEN GODDESS DIP

1 (16-ounce) carton commercial sour cream
2 cloves garlic, minced
⅔ cup finely chopped fresh parsley
¼ cup plus 2 tablespoons finely chopped fresh chives
¼ cup plus 2 tablespoons tarragon wine vinegar
2 tablespoons anchovy paste
2 teaspoons Worcestershire sauce
1 teaspoon dry mustard
1 teaspoon salt
¼ teaspoon white pepper
Fresh parsley sprigs

Combine first 10 ingredients, stirring until smooth. Chill several hours. Garnish dip with parsley. Serve with assorted raw vegetables or as a salad dressing. Yield: 3 cups.

APRICOT BAKED HAM

1 (10- to 12-pound) fully cooked whole
    ham
⅓ cup dry mustard
1 cup apricot jam
1 cup firmly packed light brown sugar
About 50 whole cloves
2 (15¼-ounce) cans pineapple slices,
    drained
Maraschino cherries

Remove skin and excess fat from ham; place ham on a rack in roasting pan. Combine mustard and jam; spread over ham. Pat brown sugar over jam mixture; insert cloves in ham at 1-inch intervals. Bake at 325° for 2½ to 3 hours (15 to 18 minutes per pound) or until meat thermometer registers 140°. Slice and arrange on serving platter; garnish with pineapple and cherries. Yield: 20 to 25 servings.

SMOKED TURKEY

1 (10- to 15-pound) turkey
1 tablespoon salt
1 tablespoon sugar
1 tablespoon ground cinnamon
1 apple, cored, peeled, and quartered
2 medium onions, quartered
4 stalks celery with leaves, cut into thirds
Lettuce leaves
Cucumber slices (optional)
Ripe olive slices (optional)

Remove giblets and neck from turkey; reserve for other uses, if desired. Rinse turkey with cold water; pat dry. Sprinkle cavity with salt.

Combine sugar and cinnamon; dredge apple in cinnamon-sugar mixture. Stuff apple, onion, and celery into cavity of turkey; close cavity with skewers. Tie ends of legs to tail with cord; lift wing tips up and over back so they are tucked under bird.

Prepare charcoal fire in smoker, and let burn 10 to 15 minutes. Soak hickory chips in water for 15 minutes. Place water pan in smoker, and fill with water. Place hickory chips on coals.

Place turkey on food rack. Cover with smoker lid; cook 8 to 12 hours or until meat thermometer reaches 180° to 185° when inserted in breast or meaty part of thigh, making sure it does not touch bone. Refill water pan, and add charcoal as needed.

Remove turkey from food rack; cover and refrigerate. To serve, thinly slice turkey; serve on lettuce-lined tray. Garnish with cucumber and olive slices, if desired. Yield: 18 to 24 servings.

EASY BEER BREAD

3 cups self-rising flour
3 tablespoons sugar
1 (12-ounce) can beer
2 to 3 tablespoons butter or margarine,
    melted

Combine flour and sugar in a large bowl. Gradually add beer (at room temperature), stirring just until moistened; spoon into a greased and floured 9- x 5- x 3-inch loafpan. Bake at 350° for 55 to 60 minutes or until loaf tests done. Brush top with butter. Cool loaf in pan 10 minutes; remove from pan, and cool completely on wire rack. Slice with electric knife. Yield: 1 loaf.

Note: Three loaves will serve about twenty people.

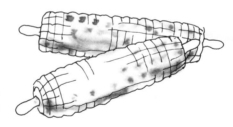

CORN-ON-THE-COB WITH HERB BUTTER

1 cup butter or margarine, softened
¼ cup chopped fresh parsley
¼ cup chopped fresh chives
1 teaspoon dried salad herbs
20 ears fresh corn
About 8 quarts water

Combine butter, parsley, chives, and salad herbs; mix well. Set aside.

Remove husks and silks from corn just before cooking. Bring water to a boil, and add corn. Return to a boil, and cook 8 to 10 minutes. Drain well. Spread the butter mixture over hot corn. Yield: 20 servings.

CRAB-STUFFED MUSHROOM CAPS

About 6 pounds large fresh mushrooms
3 cups finely chopped onion
½ cup butter or margarine
2 pounds fresh crabmeat, drained and
    flaked
Juice of 2 lemons
½ cup chopped fresh parsley
¼ cup capers
2 teaspoons Worcestershire sauce
1 teaspoon salt
½ teaspoon pepper
1 cup mayonnaise
¾ cup dry sherry
Grated Parmesan cheese
1 to 1½ cups butter or margarine, melted

Clean mushrooms with damp paper towels. Remove stems and chop; set aside. Place mushroom caps in a shallow baking pan.

Sauté mushroom stems and onion in ½ cup butter in a skillet until tender. Remove from heat, and set aside.

Sprinkle crabmeat with lemon juice. Add sautéed mushrooms and next 5 ingredients; mix well. Stir in mayonnaise and sherry. Spoon mushroom mixture into mushroom caps; sprinkle with cheese. Drizzle remaining butter over mushrooms. Bake at 350° for 20 minutes. Yield: about 8 dozen.

STUFFED CHERRY TOMATOES

24 cherry tomatoes
1 cup ground smoked turkey
1 (3-ounce) package cream cheese,
    softened
1 tablespoon commercial sour cream
Salt and pepper to taste
Grated Parmesan cheese
Fresh parsley sprigs

Wash tomatoes thoroughly. Cut a thin slice from top of each tomato; carefully scoop out pulp, reserving pulp for other uses. Invert the shells on paper towels to drain.

Combine next 4 ingredients in a mixing bowl; beat at low speed of an electric mixer until smooth. Spoon about 2 teaspoons turkey mixture into tomato shells. Sprinkle with cheese, and garnish with parsley sprigs. Chill. Yield: about 24 appetizer servings.

summer Suppers

DEVILED EGGS WITH SMOKED OYSTERS

10 hard-cooked eggs
¼ cup mayonnaise
1 teaspoon prepared mustard
½ teaspoon salt
½ teaspoon sweet pickle juice
⅛ teaspoon pepper
1 (3.66-ounce) can smoked oysters, drained
Lettuce leaves

Slice hard-cooked eggs in half lengthwise, and carefully remove the yolks. Mash yolks, and add the next 5 ingredients; stir well.

Place a smoked oyster in each egg white. Fit a decorating bag with tip No. 4B, and pipe yolk mixture around the oyster. Serve on a lettuce-lined tray. Yield: 20 servings.

WATERMELON FRUIT BASKET

1 large watermelon
2 medium cantaloupes, peeled and cut into 1-inch cubes
1 medium honeydew, peeled and cut into 1-inch cubes
2 quarts fresh strawberries
2 pints blueberries
1 pound seedless green grapes
Creamy Strawberry Dressing

Mark a line lengthwise around top one-third of watermelon; mark a 2-inch-wide strip across top of watermelon, connecting at the lengthwise line, for handle of basket. Cut out and remove large sections, using a sharp knife, to form basket shape. Cut out watermelon pulp, leaving a 1-inch shell; reserve pulp. Mark a zigzag pattern on edge of watermelon; cut out pattern using a sharp knife.

Cut watermelon pulp into 1-inch cubes. Layer watermelon cubes and next 5 ingredients alternately in watermelon basket. Serve with Creamy Strawberry Dressing. Yield: 20 servings.

Creamy Strawberry Dressing:

3 (8-ounce) cartons strawberry-flavored yogurt
1½ cups commercial sour cream
3 tablespoons honey
1½ tablespoons lemon juice

Combine all ingredients; stir with a wire whisk until well blended. Chill. Yield: 4 cups.

MANDARIN ORANGE SALAD

2 heads iceberg lettuce, torn into bite-size pieces
2 heads Bibb or romaine lettuce, torn into bite-size pieces
2 small purple onions, thinly sliced and separated into rings
2 (8-ounce) cans mandarin oranges, drained
2 (2½-ounce) packages sliced almonds, toasted
Sweet-and-Sour Dressing

Combine first 5 ingredients in a large bowl. Serve with Sweet-and-Sour Dressing. Yield: 20 to 22 servings.

Sweet-and-Sour Dressing:

2 cups vegetable oil
1 cup tarragon wine vinegar
2 tablespoons sugar
2 teaspoons tarragon leaves
1 teaspoon Dijon mustard
1 teaspoon salt
¼ teaspoon white pepper

Combine all ingredients in container of an electric blender. Process on high speed 30 seconds. Yield: 3 cups.

DAFFODIL CAKE

10 egg whites
1 teaspoon cream of tartar
¼ teaspoon salt
1¼ cups sugar
½ teaspoon vanilla extract
2 drops of almond extract
1 cup all-purpose flour
4 egg yolks
2 teaspoons grated orange rind
Orange Glaze

Beat egg whites (at room temperature), cream of tartar, and salt until foamy. Gradually add sugar, 2 tablespoons at a time, beating until stiff peaks form. Fold in flavorings and flour; divide mixture in half. Set aside.

Beat egg yolks until thick and lemon colored. Fold yolks and orange rind into one portion of the egg white mixture.

Spoon one-third of egg white mixture (without yolks) into an ungreased 10-inch tube pan; top with one-third of yolk mixture. Repeat layers twice; cut through batter with a knife, using a swirling motion. Bake at 375° for 30 minutes or until golden. Invert pan on a bottle; let cool. Remove from pan; drizzle with Orange Glaze. Yield: one 10-inch cake.

Orange Glaze:

2 cups sifted powdered sugar
2 to 3 tablespoons orange juice
1 teaspoon sherry
1 tablespoon grated orange rind

Combine sugar, orange juice, and sherry; mix until smooth. Stir in orange rind. Yield: about 1 cup.

FROSTED MINT TEA

3 quarts boiling water
24 regular tea bags
¼ cup mint jelly
¼ cup sugar
Lemon juice
Sugar
3 quarts lemon-lime carbonated beverage or ginger ale, chilled
Lemon or lime slices (optional)
Fresh mint sprigs (optional)

Pour boiling water over tea bags; cover and let stand 5 minutes. Remove tea bags; add mint jelly and ¼ cup sugar, stirring until dissolved. Chill.

Dip rims of glasses in lemon juice and then in sugar; freeze glasses.

To serve, combine tea and lemon-lime carbonated beverage; pour over ice in glasses. Garnish each glass with lemon and mint. Yield: 6 quarts.

Tip: Before trying a new recipe, read through it at least once before beginning; check carefully to see if all ingredients are on hand.

Create an all-American mood by alternating red and blue handkerchiefs at place settings for a barbecue. Use a red bandana to hold the plate, and tuck the silverware inside the blue.

SPICY STEAMED BLUE CRABS

¼ **cup plus 2 tablespoons Old Bay seasoning**
¼ **cup plus 2 tablespoons coarse salt**
3 **tablespoons red pepper**
3 **tablespoons pickling spice**
2 **tablespoons celery seeds**
1 **tablespoon crushed red pepper (optional)**
Vinegar
12 **live blue crabs**

Combine first 6 ingredients; set aside.
Combine water and vinegar in equal amounts to a depth of 1 inch in a very large pot with a lid; bring to a boil. Place a rack in pot over boiling liquid; arrange half of crabs on rack. Sprinkle with half of seasoning mixture. Top with rest of crabs, and sprinkle with remaining seasoning mixture.
Cover tightly, and steam 20 to 25 minutes or until crabs turn bright red. Rinse and drain well, if desired. Serve hot or cold. Yield: 4 servings.
Richard B. Rhodes,
Orange Park, Florida.

Brighten With Bandanas

Once used primarily as a work handkerchief, bandanas also add a bright touch to a summer table setting.

For a colorful barbecue table, feature red and blue bandanas. Fold the red bandanas in quarters to make plate holders, then turn down one corner of each to hold napkins. Self-gripping fastener dots keep the sides together and the corners down. Fold blue bandanas over silverware and slip under the turned-down corners of the red bandanas. During the meal, use the red bandana as a second napkin. Try using a blue bandana to line the bread basket for a coordinating touch of color.

Market baskets lined with pastel bandanas offer a convenient and colorful way for guests to serve themselves at a buffet. Just fit small, rectangular glass casseroles inside bandana-lined baskets. Try using bandanas in different color combinations for each basket; this makes it easy for guests to remember which is theirs.

A bouquet of bandanas and daisies blooming from a clay pot makes an easy and inexpensive centerpiece. To make, put individual daisy stems into rubber-capped plastic tubes filled with water. Then, hold each bandana at its center and shake it so all points fall downward; slide a daisy into the center. Repeat for each bandana. Gather the daisy-filled bandanas into a bunch, and secure with a rubber band. Put the finished bouquet in a pot, and adjust the bandanas and flowers as needed. The number of daisies and bandanas needed depends on the size of the pot.

A Catch Of Seafood Ideas

When summer's seafood catch is in, look forward to lots of shrimp, fish, crab, and scallops. These familiar ocean treasures offer plenty of fresh flavor and make summer cooking easy.

INDIVIDUAL SEAFOOD IMPERIALS

2 **tablespoons finely chopped onion**
1 **tablespoon finely chopped green pepper**
3 **tablespoons butter or margarine**
1 **tablespoon diced pimiento**
1 **teaspoon dry mustard**
⅛ **teaspoon dried whole thyme**
3 **tablespoons all-purpose flour**
1 **cup milk**
1 **teaspoon Worcestershire sauce**
¼ **teaspoon salt**
1 **pound fresh crabmeat, drained and flaked**
3 **tablespoons mayonnaise**
Lemon wedges (optional)
Pimiento strips (optional)

Sauté onion and green pepper in butter until tender. Stir in diced pimiento, mustard, and thyme. Add flour, stirring until smooth; cook 1 minute, stirring constantly. Gradually add milk; cook over medium heat, stirring constantly, until mixture is thickened and bubbly. Stir in Worcestershire sauce and salt. Remove sauce from heat. Stir in the crabmeat and mayonnaise.

Spoon mixture into four 6-ounce lightly greased individual baking shells or dishes. Bake at 375° for 20 minutes. Broil 5 inches from heat for 1 to 2 minutes or until lightly browned. Garnish with lemon wedges and pimiento strips, if desired. Yield: 4 servings.
Claudette Moyers,
Prince George, Virginia.

GROUPER SPECTACULAR

3 pounds grouper fillets
⅓ cup lemon juice
1 medium onion, diced
1 medium-size green pepper, diced
3 tablespoons butter or margarine
2 medium tomatoes, diced
Salt and pepper to taste
2½ cups (10 ounces) shredded mozzarella cheese
½ cup sliced black olives

Place fish fillets in a shallow container. Pour lemon juice over fish, and refrigerate 2 hours. Sauté onion and green pepper in butter 5 minutes. Add tomatoes, and cook an additional 2 minutes; remove from heat, and set aside.

Remove fish from lemon juice; place, skin side down, in a lightly greased 13- x 9- x 2-inch baking dish. Sprinkle with salt and pepper. Bake, uncovered, at 350° for 30 minutes. Spoon vegetable mixture over fish; sprinkle with cheese. Bake at 350° for an additional 15 minutes or until fish flakes easily when tested with a fork. Sprinkle with olives. Yield: 6 servings. *Mary Mostoller,*
Tallahassee, Florida.

SCALLOPS WITH MUSTARD SAUCE

2 pounds fresh scallops
1 pound fresh mushrooms, halved
1 cup chopped onion
2 tablespoons butter or margarine
1 cup mayonnaise
¼ cup prepared mustard
½ cup (2 ounces) shredded Cheddar cheese
Paprika

Arrange scallops in a steaming rack; place over boiling water. Cover and steam 10 minutes. Transfer scallops to lightly greased individual baking dishes; set aside.

Sauté mushrooms and onion in butter until onion is tender; set aside.

Combine mayonnaise and mustard; pour over scallops. Top with onion mixture; sprinkle with cheese and paprika. Broil 5 inches from heat 2 to 3 minutes or until cheese is melted. Yield: 4 to 6 servings. *Laurie C. Beppler,*
Norfolk, Virginia.

SHRIMP IN LEMON BUTTER

1 cup butter
¼ cup lemon juice
1 clove garlic, minced
1 teaspoon dried parsley flakes
1 teaspoon Worcestershire sauce
1 teaspoon soy sauce
½ teaspoon coarsely ground black pepper
¼ teaspoon salt
¼ teaspoon garlic salt
2 pounds large shrimp, peeled and deveined
Lemon wedges (optional)

Melt butter in a large skillet. Add next 8 ingredients; bring to a boil. Add shrimp; cook over medium heat 5 minutes, stirring occasionally. Garnish shrimp with lemon wedges, if desired. Yield: 4 to 6 servings. *Skip Weeks,*
Columbus, Georgia.

Some Cool Molded Salads For Summer

Salads are a favorite year-round, but when the summer heat hits, a cool congealed salad is even more appealing.

These salads can be made in salad molds or most any attractively shaped dish. Measure the amount of water the dish holds to determine the exact size. And be sure to lightly oil dishes or molds before adding salad mixtures. This will help congealed salads to unmold smoothly and easily.

CHICKEN SALAD MOLD

1 envelope unflavored gelatin
½ cup cold water
1 (3-ounce) package lemon-flavored gelatin
1 cup boiling water
½ teaspoon salt
Dash of pepper
⅓ cup mayonnaise
1½ cups finely diced cooked chicken
3 hard-cooked eggs, finely chopped
½ cup finely chopped celery
1 (2-ounce) jar chopped pimiento, drained

Soften unflavored gelatin in cold water. Dissolve lemon gelatin in boiling water. Stir in softened gelatin mixture, salt, and pepper; chill until consistency of unbeaten egg white. Add mayonnaise; stir until blended. Fold in remaining ingredients; pour into a lightly oiled 5-cup mold. Chill until firm. Yield: 6 servings. *Mrs. Arthur L. Barton,*
Marion, Alabama.

CONGEALED TUNA SALAD

1 envelope unflavored gelatin
1 cup cold water
4 hard-cooked eggs, chopped
1 (8½-ounce) can English peas, drained
1 (6½-ounce) can tuna, drained and flaked
1 medium-size green pepper, chopped
1 cup finely chopped celery
1 cup mayonnaise
½ cup pickle relish
2 tablespoons lemon juice
Lettuce leaves (optional)

Sprinkle gelatin over cold water in a saucepan; let stand 1 minute. Cook over low heat, stirring until gelatin dissolves.

Combine next 8 ingredients; stir in gelatin mixture. Pour into a lightly oiled 6-cup mold; chill until firm. Unmold salad on lettuce leaves, if desired. Yield: 6 servings. *Carla C. Hunter,*
Fort Valley, Georgia.

TANGY TOMATO RING

4 cups tomato juice, divided
½ cup chopped onion
¼ cup chopped celery leaves
2 tablespoons brown sugar
1 teaspoon salt
4 whole cloves
2 small bay leaves
1 clove garlic, minced
2 envelopes unflavored gelatin
3½ tablespoons lemon juice
1 tablespoon Worcestershire sauce
1 teaspoon prepared horseradish
1 large green pepper, chopped

Combine 2 cups tomato juice, onion, celery, brown sugar, salt, cloves, bay leaves, and garlic in a heavy saucepan. Bring to a boil; reduce heat and simmer, uncovered, 5 minutes. Strain mixture; discard vegetables and spices.

Soften gelatin in 1¼ cups tomato juice; add to strained hot juice mixture, stirring until gelatin dissolves. Stir in lemon juice, Worcestershire sauce, horseradish, and remaining ¾ cup tomato juice; chill until consistency of unbeaten egg white.

Fold green pepper into gelatin mixture. Pour mixture into a lightly oiled 4-cup mold; chill until firm. Yield: 8 servings.
*Mrs. W. Harold Groce,
Arden, North Carolina.*

CREAMY CUCUMBER MOLD

1 (3-ounce) package lime-flavored gelatin
1 cup boiling water
½ teaspoon salt
1 cup mayonnaise
½ cup commercial sour cream
1 cup finely chopped cucumber
3 tablespoons chopped pimiento
1 tablespoon minced onion
Cucumber slices (optional)

Dissolve gelatin in boiling water; stir in salt. Combine mayonnaise and sour cream; stir into gelatin mixture. Chill until consistency of unbeaten egg white.

Fold cucumber, pimiento, and onion into gelatin. Pour into a lightly oiled 4-cup mold. Chill until firm. Unmold on serving platter; garnish with cucumber slices, if desired. Yield: 8 servings.
*Mrs. John Rucker,
Louisville, Kentucky.*

ORANGE-PEAR SALAD

1 (16-ounce) can pear halves, undrained
1 (6-ounce) package lemon-flavored gelatin
1 cup whipping cream
1 (8-ounce) carton commercial sour cream
1 (11-ounce) can mandarin oranges, drained
2 kiwi, peeled and sliced (optional)
Additional mandarin oranges (optional)

Drain pears, reserving liquid. Add water to liquid to measure 1¾ cups. Slice pear halves lengthwise into 4 slices, and set aside.

Bring pear juice mixture to a boil; add gelatin, stirring until dissolved. Combine whipping cream and sour cream; add to gelatin mixture, blending well. Chill until consistency of unbeaten egg white.

Arrange pear slices and mandarin oranges attractively on bottom of a lightly oiled 9-inch quiche dish; spoon gelatin mixture over fruit. Chill until firm. Unmold on serving platter; garnish with kiwi and additional mandarin oranges, if desired. Yield: 8 servings.
*Michele Zenon,
Alexandria, Virginia.*

PEACH FROST

1 (6-ounce) package peach-flavored gelatin
1½ cups boiling water
1½ cups lemon-lime carbonated beverage or ginger ale
1 (2.8-ounce) envelope whipped topping mix
¾ cup chopped peaches
2 tablespoons piña colada cocktail mix

Dissolve gelatin in boiling water. Add lemon-lime beverage, stirring well. Pour 1 cup gelatin into a lightly oiled 8-inch square dish. Chill until set but not firm.

Prepare whipped topping mix according to package directions; set aside. Add peaches and cocktail mix to remaining gelatin, stirring well; fold in whipped topping. Pour mixture over first layer. Chill until firm. Cut into squares to serve. Yield: 9 servings.
*Mrs. L. H. Carter,
Lexington, Kentucky.*

Chilled Desserts For A Cool Ending

You can't go wrong when you offer Orange Cream Dessert or Creamy Lime Sherbet on a warm summer evening. Both are delightfully refreshing; what's more, they can be made well in advance of your party.

CHILLED STRAWBERRY DESSERT

1 envelope unflavored gelatin
¼ cup orange juice
1 (10¾-ounce) loaf frozen pound cake, thawed
½ cup Cointreau or other orange-flavored liqueur, divided
1 (14-ounce) can sweetened condensed milk
3 tablespoons lemon juice
3 egg whites, stiffly beaten
1 cup whipping cream, whipped
3 cups sliced fresh strawberries
¾ cup slivered almonds, toasted
Additional strawberries (optional)

Sprinkle gelatin over orange juice in a measuring cup; place cup in a bowl of hot water, and stir until gelatin is dissolved. Set aside.

Cut pound cake into ½-inch-thick slices; cut each slice diagonally into 2 triangles. Brush cake slices on both sides with ¼ cup plus 2 tablespoons liqueur. Arrange moistened cake triangles in a 2½-quart round-bottomed bowl, placing narrowest end of triangles in center of bowl, and allowing crustless side of one triangle to meet crust side of another triangle. Make sure the entire surface of bowl is covered; fill gaps with pieces of liqueur-moistened cake.

Combine milk, lemon juice, gelatin mixture, and remaining liqueur in a large bowl; fold in egg whites, whipped cream, strawberries, and almonds. Spoon into prepared bowl. Trim away any protruding cake pieces to level top. Cover; refrigerate overnight.

To serve, invert onto a platter. Spoon into individual serving dishes. Garnish with strawberries, if desired. Yield: 8 to 10 servings.

CREAMY LIME SHERBET

1 cup sugar
1 envelope unflavored gelatin
2 cups milk, scalded
3 cups half-and-half
1 teaspoon grated lime rind
⅔ cup lime juice
Lime slices (optional)

Combine sugar and gelatin in a large bowl. Add scalded milk; stir until sugar and gelatin are dissolved. Add half-and-half, lime rind, and juice; stir well. (Mixture will appear slightly curdled.)

Pour mixture into freezer can of a 1-gallon hand-turned or electric freezer. Freeze according to manufacturer's instructions. Let ripen at least 1 hour before serving. Garnish with lime slices, if desired. Yield: about ½ gallon.

Mrs. A. J. Amador,
Decatur, Alabama.

CHOCOLATE PRALINE TORTE

1½ cups chopped walnuts
1½ cups vanilla wafer crumbs
1 cup firmly packed brown sugar
1 cup butter or margarine, melted
1 (18.5-ounce) package devils food cake mix without pudding
1½ cups whipping cream
3 tablespoons sifted powdered sugar
1 teaspoon vanilla extract

Combine first 4 ingredients. Sprinkle about ¾ cup of walnut mixture in each of 4 ungreased 9-inch round cakepans, pressing lightly into pans.

Prepare cake mix according to package directions; pour batter over walnut mixture in prepared pans. Bake at 350° for 15 to 20 minutes or until a wooden pick inserted in center comes out clean. Remove layers from pans immediately, and let cool completely.

Beat whipping cream until foamy; gradually add powdered sugar, beating until stiff peaks form. Stir in vanilla.

Place 1 layer, nut side up, on serving plate. Spread ¾ cup whipped cream over layer. Repeat with remaining 3 layers, ending with whipped cream; chill. Yield: one 9-inch cake.

Mrs. J. David Stearns,
Mobile, Alabama.

ORANGE CREAM DESSERT

1 envelope unflavored gelatin
¼ cup cold water
½ teaspoon grated orange rind
¾ cup orange juice
2 tablespoons lemon juice
3 tablespoons sugar
1 egg white
3 tablespoons sugar
1 cup whipping cream, whipped
1 orange, sectioned
Mint leaves

Soften gelatin in cold water; set aside.

Combine orange rind, orange juice, lemon juice, and 3 tablespoons sugar in a small saucepan; bring to a boil. Remove from heat, and stir in softened gelatin. Chill mixture until consistency of unbeaten egg white.

Beat egg white (at room temperature) until foamy. Gradually add 3 tablespoons sugar, 1 tablespoon at a time, beating until stiff peaks form.

Fold egg white and whipped cream into juice mixture, blending well. Pour into a lightly oiled 4-cup mold; chill until firm. Unmold; garnish with orange sections and mint. Yield: 6 servings.

Marie Bilbo,
Meadville, Mississippi.

Share A Spread Of Sandwiches

It's easy to see why sandwiches are a favorite during the summer. They're quick to prepare, easy to pack and take with you, and offer endless variety for menus. With the right combination of breads and fillings, you can build a sandwich to suit any occasion, be it a festive luncheon or a hiking trip.

BAKED CHICKEN SANDWICHES

1 (3-ounce) package cream cheese, softened
2 tablespoons milk
2 cups finely chopped cooked chicken
½ teaspoon salt
½ teaspoon pepper
2 (8-ounce) cans refrigerated crescent dinner rolls
¼ cup plus 2 tablespoons butter, melted
1½ cups crushed croutons

Combine cheese and milk; beat on medium speed of electric mixer until mixture is smooth. Stir in chicken, salt, and pepper.

Separate roll dough into triangles. Place 2 to 3 tablespoons chicken mixture on each of eight triangles, spreading to within ½ inch of edges; moisten edges of dough with water. Place remaining eight triangles on top; press edges to seal. Dip each sandwich in butter; coat with crushed croutons. Place on lightly greased baking sheets; bake at 350° for 20 to 25 minutes or until lightly browned. Yield: 8 servings.

Mrs. Otis Jones,
Bude, Mississippi.

ASPARAGUS SPEAR SANDWICHES

1 (16-ounce) loaf whole wheat bread
⅓ cup butter or margarine, softened
¾ cup grated Parmesan cheese
1 (15-ounce) can asparagus spears, drained
3 to 4 tablespoons butter or margarine, melted
Paprika

Trim crusts from bread; spread each slice with softened butter, and sprinkle with Parmesan cheese.

Place an asparagus spear diagonally across each bread slice; fold in opposite corners of bread, securing with a wooden pick. Place sandwiches on a baking sheet. Brush top of each sandwich lightly with butter; sprinkle with paprika. Bake at 400° for 10 minutes. Yield: 20 servings. *Lucile Trent,*
Waverly, Missouri.

PINEAPPLE SANDWICH SPREAD

1 (20-ounce) can crushed pineapple,
  undrained
3 tablespoons sugar
1½ tablespoons all-purpose flour
1 egg, beaten
3 tablespoons lemon juice
2 tablespoons mayonnaise

Drain pineapple, reserving juice; set pineapple aside.

Combine sugar and flour in a small saucepan; add egg, stirring well. Stir in lemon juice and reserved pineapple juice. Cook, stirring constantly, over low heat until thickened. Cool. Add the reserved pineapple and mayonnaise, stirring well. Serve spread on date-nut bread. Yield: about 2 cups.

Nackie F. Hill,
West Columbia, South Carolina.

FRESH RADISH SPREAD

1 cup mayonnaise
1 cup minced radishes
¼ cup commercial sour cream
½ teaspoon salt

Combine all ingredients, mixing well. Chill at least 2 hours. Serve on party rye bread. Yield: about 1½ cups.

Shelley Bennett,
Amarillo, Texas.

VEGETABLE PARTY SPREAD

1 (8-ounce) package cream cheese,
  softened
⅔ cup finely grated carrots
¼ cup minced onion
¼ cup finely chopped celery
¼ cup finely chopped green
  pepper
¼ cup finely chopped cucumber
2 teaspoons lemon juice
1 teaspoon mayonnaise
¼ teaspoon salt
⅛ teaspoon white pepper

Beat cream cheese with an electric mixer until light and fluffy. Stir in remaining ingredients. Serve on party rye bread or onion rolls. Yield: 1¾ cups.

Margaret Clay,
Birmingham, Alabama.

Serve A Super Ice Cream Drink

With just a few scoops of vanilla ice cream and fresh fruit, chocolate, or a favorite liqueur, you can stir up the liveliest ice cream beverage yet. Use ingredients you have on hand and the recipes below to make up a round of these tasty summer coolers.

CHOCOLATE-MINT SMOOTHIE

2 cups milk, divided
¼ cup instant cocoa mix
½ teaspoon vanilla extract
⅛ teaspoon peppermint
  extract
1 pint vanilla ice cream

Heat ½ cup milk just until hot. Combine hot milk and cocoa mix in container of an electric blender; process until smooth. Add remaining 1½ cups milk, vanilla, and peppermint; blend well. Add ice cream, and process until mixture is smooth. Yield: 4 cups.

Lucretia Page,
Birmingham, Alabama.

MOCHA PUNCH

2 cups boiling water
½ cup instant coffee granules
1 (1-ounce) square unsweetened
  chocolate, melted
⅓ cup sugar
½ gallon vanilla ice cream,
  softened
1 quart milk
Sweetened whipped cream
Grated chocolate

Combine water and instant coffee granules, blending well. Stir in chocolate and sugar; mix well and chill. Add ice cream and milk to chocolate mixture just before serving, blending well with a wire whisk. Garnish with whipped cream and grated chocolate. Serve immediately. Yield: 3½ quarts.

Jean Nichol,
Knoxville, Tennessee.

ORANGE MILK SHAKE

2 cups milk
⅓ cup Cointreau or other orange-flavored
  liqueur
3 tablespoons frozen orange juice
  concentrate, thawed and undiluted
1 pint vanilla ice cream
Ground nutmeg or ground cinnamon
Orange slices

Combine the first 3 ingredients, mixing well.

Scoop ice cream into 2 tall glasses; pour milk mixture over ice cream. Sprinkle each serving with nutmeg or cinnamon. Garnish each serving with orange slices. Serve immediately. Yield: about 3 cups.

Carolyn Rosen,
Nashville, Tennessee.

STRAWBERRY-PINEAPPLE SHAKE

2 cups milk
1 (8-ounce) can crushed pineapple,
  undrained
1 cup crushed fresh strawberries
1 cup vanilla ice cream
Pineapple sherbet
Fresh pineapple wedges
Fresh strawberries

Combine milk, crushed pineapple, strawberries, and ice cream in container of an electric blender; process until smooth. Pour into tall glasses; add a scoop of pineapple sherbet to each glass. Garnish each serving with a pineapple wedge and a strawberry. Serve immediately. Yield: about 5 cups.

Lily Jo Drake,
Satellite Beach, Florida.

Right: *Our colorful pastas bear the names of ingredients used to tint the dough: Pimiento Pasta (page 176), Broccoli Pasta (page 176), Orange Noodles (page 177), and Whole Wheat Linguine (page 177). Cut and dry the noodles in different shapes for added interest.*

Above: *Mix up your own soda fountain favorites with our recipes for Strawberry-Pineapple Shake, Mocha Punch, and Orange Milkshake (recipes on page 166).*

Right: *Layer, roll, and scoop ice cream into spectacular desserts. From left to right: Layered Ice Cream Dessert (page 105), Strawberry Ice Cream Roll (page 105), and Easy Ice Cream Balls (page 106).*

Right: *Arrange a variety of fresh fruit around Marshmallow Fruit Dip (page 171) for a refreshing appetizer with plenty of visual appeal.*

Below: *This summer menu is as colorful and attractive as it is delicious. It includes Marinated Pork Tenderloin over Lime-Flavored Rice and Sesame Snow Peas and Red Pepper (recipes on page 175).*

Enjoy Fresh Fruit With A Dressing Or Dip

While fruit is delightful eaten just as is, you can dress it up by serving it as an appetizer or salad.

TANGY COCONUT-FRUIT DRESSING

1 (15-ounce) can cream of coconut
1 (6-ounce) can frozen lemonade
  concentrate, thawed and undiluted

Combine ingredients, stirring until well mixed. Serve over fruit salad. Yield: about 2 cups.   Brenda Clark,
Auburn, Alabama.

COCONUT-HONEY FRUIT DIP

1 (16-ounce) carton cream-style cottage
  cheese
¼ cup plain yogurt
¼ cup honey
¼ cup flaked coconut
1 teaspoon grated orange rind

Combine first 3 ingredients, mixing well; stir in coconut and orange rind. Serve dip with assorted fresh fruit. Yield: 2½ cups.   Eleanor Anderson,
Ludington, Michigan.

MARSHMALLOW FRUIT DIP

1 tablespoon grated orange rind, divided
1 tablespoon orange juice
1 (7-ounce) jar marshmallow creme
½ cup mayonnaise
1 teaspoon grated lemon rind
1 teaspoon lemon juice

Set aside 1 teaspoon orange rind. Combine remaining 2 teaspoons orange rind and next 5 ingredients in a bowl; beat at medium speed of electric mixer until smooth and blended. Spoon into serving container, and sprinkle with reserved orange rind. Serve with assorted fresh fruit. Yield: about 1½ cups.
Martha Martin,
Vardaman, Mississippi.

MARMALADE-FRUIT DRESSING

1 (8-ounce) package cream cheese,
  softened
1 (8-ounce) carton commercial sour cream
⅓ cup orange marmalade
2 tablespoons brown sugar

Beat softened cream cheese at medium speed of electric mixer until fluffy. Add remaining ingredients, and beat until mixture is smooth. Serve dressing over fruit salad. Yield: 2½ cups.
Mary Andrew,
Winston-Salem, North Carolina.

FRUITED YOGURT DIP

1 (8-ounce) package cream cheese,
  softened
2 (8-ounce) cartons orange yogurt
2 tablespoons brown sugar
1 teaspoon lemon juice
1 (8-ounce) can crushed pineapple,
  drained
¾ cup flaked coconut

Beat cream cheese at medium speed of electric mixer until fluffy; add next 3 ingredients, and beat until smooth. Stir in pineapple and coconut. Serve with assorted fresh fruit. Yield: 3½ cups.
Susan Kamer-Shinaberry,
Charleston, West Virginia.

Good Things From The Grill

Make your cookout the best on the block by adding any of these grilled specialties to the menu.

BLUE CHEESE STEAKS

¾ cup unsweetened pineapple juice
⅓ cup teriyaki sauce
1 clove garlic, minced
6 (8-ounce) rib-eye steaks, 1½ inches
  thick
2 cloves garlic, halved
1 (4-ounce) package blue cheese,
  crumbled

Combine first 3 ingredients in a large shallow container; add steaks. Cover and refrigerate 2 hours, turning occasionally. Remove steaks from marinade. Sear steaks on each side over hot coals. Remove from grill, and rub with garlic cloves.

Cut inch-long diagonal slits, ½ inch in depth, into both sides of steaks (making about 4 pockets per side); fill with cheese. Return meat to grill; cook over medium coals to desired degree of doneness (8 minutes per side for rare). Yield: 6 servings.
Lt. Col. R. G. Sigman,
Fort Walton Beach, Florida.

MARINATED FILET MIGNON

½ cup olive oil
¾ teaspoon seasoning salt
¾ teaspoon lemon-pepper seasoning
¾ teaspoon dried whole oregano
½ teaspoon garlic powder
6 (4- to 6-ounce) beef tenderloin steaks

Combine first 5 ingredients in a large shallow container; add steaks. Cover and marinate 3 hours in refrigerator, turning steaks occasionally.

Remove steaks from marinade. Grill over hot coals 5 to 7 minutes on each side or until desired degree of doneness. Yield: 6 servings.   Donna Gershner,
North Little Rock, Arkansas.

MARINATED GRILLED SCALLOPS

1 medium onion, chopped
½ cup vegetable oil
Juice of 1 lemon
½ teaspoon minced garlic
¼ teaspoon salt
½ teaspoon pepper
2 pounds scallops

Combine first 6 ingredients in a large shallow dish. Add scallops, stirring gently to coat; refrigerate 2 hours.

Thread scallops on skewers. Place kabobs 4 to 5 inches from hot coals; grill 10 to 12 minutes, turning and basting occasionally with leftover marinade. Yield: 6 servings.   Alice G. Pahl,
Raleigh, North Carolina.

SMOKY RIBS

3 cups catsup
½ cup firmly packed brown sugar
½ cup molasses
¼ cup prepared mustard
2 tablespoons vinegar
2 tablespoons liquid smoke
2 tablespoons Worcestershire sauce
Red pepper to taste
3 pounds country-style pork ribs
½ teaspoon garlic salt
¼ teaspoon pepper

Combine first 8 ingredients; set aside.
Cut ribs into serving-size pieces; place in a large Dutch oven. Cover ribs with water; add garlic salt and pepper. Bring water to a boil; cover, reduce heat, and simmer 30 minutes. Drain well.
Grill ribs, 5 inches from heat, over slow coals, 45 minutes or until desired degree of doneness, turning frequently. Brush ribs with sauce during last 15 minutes. Serve with remaining sauce. Yield: 3 servings.

Stanley N. Pichon, Jr.,
Slidell, Louisiana.

GRILLED CHICKEN BREASTS

2 teaspoons Dijon mustard
4 chicken breast halves, skinned
¼ teaspoon freshly ground black pepper
⅓ cup butter or margarine
2 teaspoons lemon juice
½ teaspoon garlic salt
1 teaspoon dried whole tarragon

Spread mustard on both sides of chicken, and sprinkle with pepper. Cover and refrigerate 2 to 4 hours.
Melt butter; stir in lemon juice, garlic salt, and tarragon. Cook over low heat 5 minutes, stirring occasionally.
Place chicken on grill over medium coals; baste with sauce, and grill 50 to 55 minutes or until done, turning and basting every 10 minutes. Yield: 4 servings.

JoDell Wright,
Houston, Texas.

GRILLED HERB POTATOES

¼ cup finely chopped celery
¾ cup butter or margarine
1 teaspoon dried whole oregano
½ teaspoon salt
¼ teaspoon garlic powder
⅛ teaspoon pepper
6 medium baking potatoes, unpeeled
1 large onion, thinly sliced

Sauté celery in butter in a small saucepan until tender. Stir in oregano, salt, garlic powder, and pepper.
Wash potatoes; slice each into ½-inch slices, cutting to, but not through bottom peel. Place a slice of onion between each slice of potato. Arrange potatoes on squares of heavy-duty aluminum foil; drizzle about 2 tablespoons of butter mixture over each potato. Fold foil edges over, and wrap each potato securely; cook on grill 1 hour or until done. Yield: 6 servings. *Judy Garrett,*
Lewisville, Texas.

GRILLED VEGETABLES

4 medium tomatoes, quartered
4 yellow squash, sliced
1 medium onion, sliced
1 teaspoon minced fresh basil
½ teaspoon salt
⅛ teaspoon pepper
2 teaspoons butter or margarine

Place vegetables on a large piece of heavy-duty aluminum foil; sprinkle with basil, salt, and pepper and dot with butter. Fold foil edges over, and wrap securely; place on grill. Cook over medium coals 20 to 25 minutes, turning after 10 minutes. Yield: 6 servings.

Annette Peery,
Charlotte, North Carolina.

Flavor The Meat With Barbecue Sauce

Folks in the South stand firm when it comes to their recipe for barbecue sauce—they swear it isn't any good without tomatoes or mustard or some secret ingredient. But since Southerners feel strongly about passing on a good thing, they've shared their treasured recipes here for you to enjoy.

FRESH TOMATO BARBECUE SAUCE

1 cup coarsely chopped onion
2 cloves garlic, minced
2 tablespoons butter or margarine
5 small tomatoes, peeled and chopped
2 tablespoons Worcestershire sauce
2 tablespoons red wine vinegar
2 teaspoons salt
1 teaspoon chili powder
1 teaspoon dry mustard
½ cup dark corn syrup

Sauté onion and garlic in butter in a medium saucepan until tender. Add next 6 ingredients; bring to a boil. Reduce heat; simmer 20 minutes, stirring occasionally. Add corn syrup; simmer 10 minutes. Use to baste beef or ribs when grilling. Yield: 3 cups.

Rita Smith,
Ridgeway, Virginia.

BARBECUE SAUCE

1 medium onion, chopped
½ cup butter or margarine
1 cup vinegar
1 cup chili sauce
⅓ cup firmly packed brown sugar
2 teaspoons lemon juice
1 teaspoon Worcestershire sauce
1 teaspoon red pepper
½ teaspoon dry mustard
½ teaspoon chili powder

Sauté onion in butter until tender; stir in remaining ingredients, and simmer 15 minutes. Use to baste pork when grilling. Yield: 3½ cups. *Louise Pittenger,*
Winchester, Tennessee.

Tip: Store spices in a cool place and away from any direct source of heat as the heat will destroy their flavor. Red spices (chili powder, paprika, and red pepper) will maintain flavor and retain color longer if refrigerated.

MUSTARD BARBECUE SAUCE

2 cups prepared mustard
1 cup mayonnaise
¼ cup plus 2 tablespoons catsup
2 tablespoons sugar
2 tablespoons Worcestershire sauce
1 teaspoon Kitchen Bouquet
½ teaspoon salt
½ teaspoon seasoned salt
¼ teaspoon pepper
¼ cup butter or margarine
½ cup water
¼ teaspoon liquid smoke (optional)

Combine all ingredients in a saucepan; mix well. Bring to a boil; reduce heat and cook, uncovered, 10 minutes, stirring occasionally. Use to baste chicken, pork chops, or ribs when grilling. Yield: 5⅓ cups. *Elizabeth Meetze, Columbia, South Carolina.*

BEER BARBECUE SAUCE

1 cup beer
1 cup catsup
⅓ cup vinegar
⅓ cup firmly packed brown sugar
3 tablespoons Worcestershire sauce
1 teaspoon paprika
1 teaspoon dry mustard
½ teaspoon chili powder
½ teaspoon salt
1 medium onion, thinly sliced
½ lemon, thinly sliced

Combine first 9 ingredients in a saucepan; bring to a boil. Reduce heat and cook, uncovered, 5 minutes, stirring occasionally. Stir in onion and lemon. Use sauce to baste chicken or ribs when grilling. Yield: 3 cups.

DRESSED-UP BARBECUE SAUCE

1 (18-ounce) bottle barbecue sauce with onion bits
⅔ cup firmly packed brown sugar
½ cup red wine
1 teaspoon Worcestershire sauce
Dash of hot sauce

Combine all ingredients, stirring well. Use to baste chicken or other meats when grilling. Heat to serve, if desired. Yield: 2½ cups. *Diane D. Miniard, Aiken, South Carolina.*

Cool Off The Beverages With Style

No party or occasion during the summer is complete without a cooler of iced-down beverages. These coolers range in sizes and styles just right for any occasion.

Baskets: Try lining your favorite wicker basket with several plastic trash bags, using a color that blends with the basket. After pouring in the ice, accent the rim of the basket with summer flowers and foliage. The basket makes a great table decoration as well as being functional.

Galvanized tubs and cans, tin buckets: An unexpected color accent, bold stripes, or polka dots can highlight these ordinary-looking containers. When using a container that isn't galvanized, it would be wise to line it with trash bags, or make sure that the container is completely dry after using.

If time allows, paint the container with a whimsical design or just splash on a design. Before painting, clean with white vinegar. This etches the surface and takes off the protective coating that would keep the paint from sticking. Spray paint or brush with oil-based enamel. (For an extended life, a galvanized primer may be used before applying the enamel, but it is not absolutely necessary.)

Lucite or glass punch bowls: A container like this is seldom used for entertaining, except when serving a punch. Try giving it a new function. Fill the bowl with ice, and add bottles.

Pottery and concrete planters: The best forms of insulation for maintaining cooler temperatures longer are found in these planters. What could be more convenient than to have individual containers by each place setting.

A concrete planter is a natural for keeping beverages cool. Plug up the hole, and add ice.

summer Suppers

COOKING LIGHT

Dining The Light Way

When you've invited guests for dinner, you certainly want the meal to be special. Before, you may have served your favorite recipes with little or no thought of calories. But things are different today since some, if not all of your guests, will likely be dieting. Here are two menus that should appeal to dieting and nondieting guests alike.

Artichokes Stuffed With
Shrimp and Scallops
Carrot-Raisin Salad
Commercial Breadsticks
Strawberry Ice

As your guests enjoy our stuffed artichokes, encourage them to dip the artichoke leaves in Mustard-Vinaigrette Sauce. Serve this entrée with Carrot-Raisin Salad and breadsticks.

ARTICHOKES STUFFED WITH SHRIMP AND SCALLOPS

½ pound small shrimp, peeled, deveined, and cut in half
½ pound bay scallops
½ cup fresh lime juice
½ cup finely chopped celery
¼ cup finely chopped onion
1 tablespoon dried whole cilantro
1 tablespoon olive oil
4 medium artichokes
Lemon wedge
Mustard-Vinaigrette Sauce

Combine first 7 ingredients in a large skillet. Bring to a boil over medium-high heat, stirring occasionally. Remove from heat, and transfer mixture to a large bowl; cover and chill thoroughly.

Wash artichokes by plunging up and down in cold water. Cut off the stem end, and trim about ½ inch from top of each artichoke. Remove any loose bottom leaves. With scissors, trim away about a fourth of each outer leaf. Rub top of artichoke and edges of leaves with a lemon wedge to prevent discoloration. Place artichokes in 2 inches of

water in a large Dutch oven. Cover and bring to a boil; reduce heat, and simmer 30 to 35 minutes or just until outer leaves pull off easily. Place artichokes upside down on a rack to drain; chill thoroughly.

Spread outer leaves of each artichoke apart; scrape out the fuzzy thistle center (choke) with a spoon. Drain shrimp and scallops; spoon mixture into center of each artichoke. Serve with Mustard-Vinaigrette Sauce for dipping. Yield: 4 servings (about 169 calories per serving plus 15 calories per tablespoon sauce).

Mustard-Vinaigrette Sauce:

1 (8-ounce) carton plain low-fat yogurt
2 tablespoons reduced-calorie mayonnaise
1 tablespoon vinegar
2 teaspoons prepared mustard
⅛ teaspoon red pepper

Combine all ingredients in a small bowl; chill thoroughly. Yield: 1 cup.
Judith E. Kosik,
Charlottesville, Virginia.

CARROT-RAISIN SALAD

¼ cup raisins
2 tablespoons cider vinegar
1 (8-ounce) can unsweetened pineapple tidbits, undrained
Dash of ground cinnamon
Dash of ground nutmeg
¾ pound carrots, scraped and coarsely shredded

Combine raisins and vinegar in a small bowl; let stand 30 minutes. Drain, reserving the vinegar; set raisins aside.

Drain pineapple, reserving ¼ cup juice. Combine ¼ cup pineapple juice, reserved vinegar, cinnamon, and nutmeg. Toss with raisins, pineapple, and carrots; chill. Yield: 4 servings (about 90 calories per serving).

Tip: Mix liquid from canned fruit in a jar as you acquire it; use it in a gelatin dessert or as a punch drink.

STRAWBERRY ICE

4 cups fresh strawberries
½ cup unsweetened orange juice
3 tablespoons honey

Combine all ingredients in container of an electric blender; process until smooth. Pour mixture into an 8-inch square baking pan; cover and freeze until slushy. Spoon mixture into container of electric blender; process until smooth. Freeze until firm. Yield: 4 servings (about 114 calories per ⅝-cup serving). *Marsha R. Braunstein, Silver Spring, Maryland.*

**Marinated Pork Tenderloin
Lime-Flavored Rice
Sesame Snow Peas and Red Pepper
Broiled Bananas With Honey**

MARINATED PORK TENDERLOIN

1 (15-ounce) can unsweetened sliced
   pineapple, undrained
2 cloves garlic, minced
2 tablespoons minced fresh gingerroot
2 tablespoons soy sauce
½ teaspoon dry mustard
2 (¾-pound) pork tenderloins
Vegetable cooking spray

Drain pineapple, reserving juice. Combine reserved juice and next 4 ingredients; set aside.

Trim excess fat from tenderloins. Place tenderloins in a large, shallow baking dish; pour marinade over tenderloins. Cover and marinate 24 hours in refrigerator, turning occasionally.

Coat grill rack with cooking spray. Remove tenderloins from marinade; grill over medium coals 50 to 55 minutes, turning tenderloins occasionally. Meat is done when meat thermometer inserted in thickest part of tenderloin registers 170°. Grill pineapple slices 5 minutes or until browned on both sides.

Slice tenderloin, and serve with pineapple slices. Yield: 6 servings (about 206 calories per serving).

LIME-FLAVORED RICE

1 cup uncooked regular rice
½ cup minced fresh parsley
¼ cup minced green onions
Grated rind of 1 small lime

Cook rice according to package directions, omitting salt. Remove from heat, and add remaining ingredients; toss. Transfer rice to a serving dish. Yield: 6 servings (about 117 calories per ½-cup serving). *Leonard G. Amerando, Smyrna, Delaware.*

SESAME SNOW PEAS
AND RED PEPPER

¾ pound fresh snow peas
2 large red peppers, cut into thin strips
½ cup water
1 tablespoon sesame seeds, toasted

Wash snow peas; trim ends, and remove tough strings. Combine snow peas, peppers, and water in a large skillet. Bring to a boil; cover, reduce heat, and simmer 3 to 5 minutes or until crisp-tender. Drain.

Transfer vegetables to a serving bowl; sprinkle with sesame seeds, and toss. Yield: 6 servings (about 44 calories per serving). *Leonard G. Amerando, Smyrna, Delaware.*

BROILED BANANAS
WITH HONEY

6 medium bananas
2 tablespoons honey
2 tablespoons lime juice
Ground cinnamon

Peel bananas, and cut in half lengthwise; arrange bananas, cut side up, in a jellyroll pan. Sprinkle ½ teaspoon each of honey and lime juice over each banana half. Sprinkle lightly with cinnamon. Broil bananas 4 inches from heat for 3 to 4 minutes or until just tender. Serve immediately. Yield: 6 servings (about 122 calories per serving). *Leonard G. Amerando, Smyrna, Delaware.*

Decorate With Summer's Harvest

Summer entertaining is the perfect time to show off the harvest of fruit, vegetables, and flowers that your garden produces or your grocer has available. But there is more to do with fruit and vegetables than just feature them on your menu. Let them be part of your summer table decorations.

A silver basket can be a perfect centerpiece for an afternoon tea. Select a few garden flowers, along with a variety of small fruit and vegetables to fill the basket. Flowers and foliage form the lines of the arrangement; fruit and vegetables complete the design.

Popular as a basket to harvest vegetables and flowers, a garden trug can be filled with a variety of large garden vegetables. The vegetables should be arranged so that the largest ones are massed at the back and the smaller ones placed toward the front.

A silver basket containing flowers, fruit, and vegetables graces this table. Bring out the dominant colors from the arrangement with matching napkins and tablecloths.

Color Means Flavor In These Pastas

Put aside plain pasta—from now on, liven up noodles with shades of brown, orange, green, and gold by stirring vegetables, citrus rind and juice, leafy fresh herbs, and whole wheat flour into pasta dough. Then, enjoy the mild flavor of homemade noodles to the fullest by topping with butter or Parmesan cheese.

In our pasta recipes, you'll note that we've used a food processor for mixing and a pasta machine for rolling the dough. You can prepare any of these pasta recipes by hand, but we found that using the processor and the pasta machine saved time and produced a smoother, more even-textured product.

To mix the dough by hand, combine flour and salt on a smooth surface, forming a mound. Make a well in the center of flour mixture. Break one egg into the well, and draw part of the flour into the egg, using a fork. Repeat with remaining eggs, one at a time. (Add finely chopped vegetables, herbs, or citrus rind to flour with the second egg.) When adding the last egg, work in remaining flour and liquid ingredient (such as wine, oil, water, or juice) to form a soft dough. Knead the dough for 10 minutes.

Always use large eggs. Most pasta recipes call for large eggs as the main liquid ingredient. Using a different size will yield more or less liquid than the recipe needs for the best consistency.

To roll the dough by hand, simply knead the dough until smooth, and roll out on a floured surface to 1/16-inch thickness, turning the dough occasionally. Cut with a knife or fluted pastry cutter into desired shapes.

Homemade pasta dries in about 30 minutes, and it's best eaten as soon after drying as possible. To dry the noodles, simply hang them on a drying rack or wooden dowel, spread them flat on towels, or you can swirl them into a nest of noodles. It will take longer for the nests to dry, so you'll need to place them on a wire rack to dry the bottom evenly. Once you place the nests in boiling water to cook, they will unravel into separate strands.

Freshly made noodles cook faster than commercial noodles, so be certain not to overcook them. After placing in boiling water, the noodles cook in 1 to 4 minutes. They should be cooked just until *al dente,* or "to the tooth," which means the pasta offers a slight resistance when bitten.

BROCCOLI PASTA

1 (10-ounce) package frozen chopped broccoli
4 cups all-purpose flour
3 large eggs
1 tablespoon lemon juice
1 teaspoon salt
3 quarts water
1½ teaspoons salt
1 tablespoon olive or vegetable oil

Cook broccoli according to package directions, and drain well. Place on paper towels, and pat dry until broccoli is barely moist.

Insert stainless steel chopping blade in bowl of food processor. Add broccoli and next 4 ingredients. Process until mixture is well blended.

Turn dough out onto a lightly floured surface, and knead about 5 minutes. Shape dough into a ball, and place in a plastic bag; fasten bag securely. Rest dough in refrigerator at least 1 hour.

Cut dough into 8 pieces, and return 7 pieces to bag. Pat remaining portion into a 4-inch square. Pass each portion of dough through smooth rollers of pasta machine on widest setting. Fold dough crosswise into thirds. Repeat rolling and folding about 10 times or until dough becomes smooth and pliable. Move rollers to the next widest setting; pass dough through rollers. Continue moving width gauge to narrower settings; pass dough through rollers once at each setting until 1/16-inch thickness, dusting lightly with flour, if needed.

Pass dough through desired cutting rollers of machine. Hang pasta over a wooden rack, or spread on a dry towel for 30 minutes or until dry.

Combine 3 quarts water, 1½ teaspoons salt, and oil in a large Dutch oven; bring to a boil. Add pasta, and cook 3 to 4 minutes or until tender. Drain and serve immediately, by itself, or topped with Parmesan cheese or a sauce. Yield: 6 servings.

Note: Substitute one 10-ounce package frozen chopped spinach for broccoli, if desired.

OREGANO PASTA

2 cups firmly packed fresh oregano
3 large eggs
¼ cup water
3 cups all-purpose flour
1 teaspoon salt
3 quarts water
1½ teaspoons salt
1 tablespoon olive or vegetable oil
Pepper to taste

Insert stainless steel chopping blade in bowl of food processor. Combine first 3 ingredients in processor, and process until pureed. Add flour and 1 teaspoon salt, and continue to process until mixture is well blended.

Turn dough out onto a lightly floured surface, and knead until smooth. Shape dough into a ball, and place in a plastic bag; fasten bag securely. Rest dough in refrigerator 1 hour.

Cut dough into 8 pieces, and return 7 pieces to bag. Pat remaining portion into a 4-inch square. Pass each portion of dough through smooth rollers of pasta machine on widest setting. Fold dough crosswise into thirds. Repeat rolling and folding about 10 times or until dough becomes smooth and pliable. Move roller to the next widest setting; pass dough through rollers. Continue moving width gauge to narrower settings; pass dough through rollers once at each setting until it reaches 1/16-inch thickness, dusting with flour, if needed.

Pass dough through desired cutting rollers of machine. Hang pasta over a wooden rack, or spread on a dry towel for 30 minutes or until dry.

Combine 3 quarts water, 1½ teaspoons salt, and oil in a large Dutch oven; bring to a boil. Add pasta, and cook 2 to 4 minutes or until tender; drain. Add pepper to taste; mix well. Serve immediately, by itself, buttered, or with chopped tomatoes and Parmesan cheese, if desired. Yield: 6 servings.

Note: Substitute other fresh leafy herbs for oregano, if desired.

PIMIENTO PASTA

2 (4-ounce) jars sliced pimiento, drained
1 large egg
1 tablespoon dry white wine
3 to 3½ cups all-purpose flour
½ teaspoon salt
3 quarts water
1½ teaspoons salt
1 tablespoon olive oil or vegetable oil

Insert stainless steel chopping blade in bowl of food processor. Combine first 5 ingredients in processor, and process until mixture is well blended.

Turn dough out onto a lightly floured surface, and knead until smooth. Shape dough into a ball, and place in a plastic bag; fasten bag securely. Rest dough in refrigerator 1 hour.

Cut dough into 8 pieces, and return 7 pieces to bag. Pat remaining portion into a 4-inch square. Pass each portion of dough through smooth rollers of pasta machine on widest setting. Fold dough crosswise into thirds. Repeat rolling and folding about 10 times or until dough becomes smooth and pliable. Move rollers to the next widest setting; pass dough through rollers. Continue moving width gauge to narrower settings; pass dough through rollers once at each setting until 1/16-inch thickness, dusting lightly with flour, if needed.

Pass dough through desired cutting rollers of machine. Hang pasta over a wooden rack, shape into nests, or spread on a dry towel for 30 minutes or until dry.

Combine water, 1½ teaspoons salt, and oil in a large Dutch oven; bring to a boil. Add pasta, and cook 1 to 2 minutes or until tender; drain. Serve immediately, by itself, buttered, or with a sauce. Yield: 6 servings.

WHOLE WHEAT LINGUINE

1½ cups whole wheat flour
½ teaspoon salt
2 large eggs
2 tablespoons water
2 tablespoons olive oil
2 quarts water
¾ teaspoon salt
2 teaspoons vegetable oil

Insert stainless steel chopping blade in bowl of food processor. Combine first 5 ingredients in processor, and process until well blended.

Turn dough out onto a lightly floured surface, and knead 1 to 2 minutes. Shape dough into a ball, and place in a plastic bag; fasten bag securely. Rest dough in refrigerator 30 minutes.

Cut dough into 4 pieces, and return 3 pieces to bag. Pat remaining portion into a 4-inch square. Pass each portion of dough through smooth rollers of pasta machine on widest setting. Fold dough crosswise into thirds. Repeat rolling and folding about 10 times or until dough becomes smooth and pliable. Move rollers to the next widest setting; pass dough through rollers. Continue moving width gauge to narrower settings; pass dough through rollers once at each setting until 1/16-inch thickness, dusting lightly with flour, if needed.

Pass dough through linguine cutting rollers of machine. Hang pasta over a wooden rack, or spread on a dry towel for 30 minutes or until dry.

Combine water, ¾ teaspoon salt, and oil in a large Dutch oven; bring to a boil. Add pasta, and cook 1 to 2 minutes or until tender; drain. Serve with fresh tomato sauce or clam sauce. Yield: about 4 servings.

Harris Simpson,
Atlanta, Georgia.

ORANGE NOODLES

3 cups all-purpose flour
½ teaspoon salt
3 large eggs
¼ cup plus 1 tablespoon frozen orange juice concentrate, thawed and undiluted
2 tablespoons grated orange rind
3 quarts water
1 teaspoon salt
1 tablespoon vegetable oil

Insert stainless steel chopping blade in bowl of food processor. Combine first 5 ingredients in processor, and process until mixture is well blended.

Turn dough out onto a lightly floured surface, and knead 8 to 10 minutes. Shape dough into a ball, and place in a plastic bag; fasten bag securely. Rest dough in refrigerator 1 hour.

Cut dough into 8 pieces, and return 7 pieces to bag. Pat remaining portion into a 4-inch square. Pass each portion of dough through smooth rollers of pasta machine on widest setting. Fold dough crosswise into thirds. Repeat rolling and folding about 10 times or until dough becomes smooth and pliable. Move rollers to the next widest setting; pass dough through rollers. Continue moving width gauge to narrower settings; pass dough through rollers once at each setting until 1/16-inch thickness, dusting lightly with flour, if needed.

Pass dough through linguine cutting rollers of machine, or cut with fluted pastry cutter, if desired. Hang pasta over a wooden rack, or spread on a dry towel for 30 minutes or until dry.

Combine water, 1 teaspoon salt, and oil in a large Dutch oven; bring to a boil. Add pasta, and cook 1 to 2 minutes or until tender; drain. Serve immediately, by itself or buttered. Yield: 6 servings.

Note: Substitute lemon or lime rind and juice for orange juice concentrate and orange rind, if desired.

Cobblers And Pies Go Light

Offer a dedicated dieter a bowl of peach or cherry cobbler, and he'll either flatly refuse or guiltily indulge.

Since a single crust of pastry for a 9-inch pie provides about 900 calories, it makes good sense to cut back on the pastry when possible. By making Fresh Apple Pie without a top crust, we cut out about 113 calories per slice. We prepared our two cobblers without bottom crusts and used only small pastry cutouts on the Fresh Cherry Cobbler.

The secret to preparing light fruit fillings is to start with fresh, ripe fruit (the riper fruit has a sweeter flavor). We combined the fruit with unsweetened apple juice or white grape juice and thickened the fruit mixture with cornstarch. Spices such as allspice, nutmeg, and pumpkin pie spice helps cover up the absence of sugar.

BLUEBERRY CRISP

3 cups fresh blueberries
¼ cup white grape juice
½ teaspoon ground allspice
Vegetable cooking spray
⅓ cup quick-cooking oats, uncooked
¼ cup whole wheat flour
2 tablespoons brown sugar
½ teaspoon baking powder
⅛ teaspoon ground nutmeg
3 tablespoons margarine, softened

Combine blueberries, grape juice, and allspice in a medium saucepan. Bring to a boil; reduce heat and simmer 2 minutes, stirring occasionally. Pour mixture into an 8-inch square baking dish coated with cooking spray.

Combine next 5 ingredients in a small bowl; stir in margarine until mixture is crumbly. Sprinkle topping over blueberry mixture; bake at 350° for 25 to 30 minutes. Serve hot or at room temperature. Yield: 6 servings (about 149 calories per serving).

Tip: Quick-cooking oats, browned in a small amount of butter or margarine, make an economical substitute for chopped nuts in cookie recipes.

FRESH APPLE PIE

1 cup all-purpose flour
¼ teaspoon salt
¼ cup shortening
3 to 4 tablespoons cold water
1 tablespoon cornstarch
2 tablespoons unsweetened apple
    juice
5 cups peeled, diced apple
½ cup unsweetened apple juice
1 tablespoon brown sugar
½ teaspoon pumpkin pie spice
1 medium apple, unpeeled and
    thinly sliced
Lemon juice

Combine flour and salt; cut in shortening with pastry blender until mixture resembles coarse meal. Sprinkle cold water, 1 tablespoon at a time, evenly over surface; stir with a fork until all dry ingredients are moistened. Shape into a ball; roll out pastry to ⅛-inch thickness on a lightly floured surface. Place in a 9-inch pieplate; trim and flute edges. Prick bottom and sides of pastry shell with a fork; bake at 425° for 12 to 15 minutes. Set aside to cool.

Combine cornstarch and 2 tablespoons apple juice, mixing well.

Combine next 4 ingredients in a large saucepan. Bring to a boil; cover, reduce heat, and simmer 3 to 4 minutes or until apples are just tender. Stir in cornstarch mixture; cook, stirring constantly, until clear and thickened. Cool; spoon into pastry shell. Dip apple slices in lemon juice; drain. Garnish top of pie with apple slices. Yield: 8 servings (about 164 calories per serving).

FRESH CHERRY COBBLER

2 tablespoons cornstarch
2 tablespoons sugar
⅛ teaspoon ground allspice
1 cup white grape juice
4 cups pitted fresh sweet cherries
½ teaspoon almond extract
Vegetable cooking spray
¼ cup whole wheat flour
¼ cup all-purpose flour
⅛ teaspoon salt
⅛ teaspoon ground cinnamon
2½ tablespoons shortening
1 to 1½ tablespoons cold water

Combine cornstarch, sugar, and allspice in a saucepan; stir in grape juice until blended. Cook over medium heat, stirring constantly, until clear and thickened. Remove from heat; stir in cherries and almond extract. Spoon mixture into a 1½-quart casserole coated with cooking spray; set aside.

Combine flour, salt, and cinnamon; cut in shortening with a pastry blender until mixture resembles coarse meal. Sprinkle cold water evenly over surface; stir with a fork until all dry ingredients are moistened. Roll out pastry to ⅛-inch thickness on a lightly floured surface; cut into decorative shapes.

Place pastry cutouts on top of cherry mixture; bake at 425° for 20 minutes or until lightly browned. Yield: 6 servings (about 202 calories per serving).

PEACH COBBLER

1 tablespoon cornstarch
2 tablespoons unsweetened apple juice
4 cups sliced fresh peaches
½ cup unsweetened apple juice
¼ teaspoon ground nutmeg
½ teaspoon almond extract
½ cup all-purpose flour
⅛ teaspoon salt
⅛ teaspoon ground nutmeg
2 tablespoons shortening
1 to 1½ tablespoons cold water
Vegetable cooking spray

Combine cornstarch and 2 tablespoons apple juice, mixing well.

Combine peaches, ½ cup apple juice, and ¼ teaspoon nutmeg in a saucepan. Bring to a boil; cover, reduce heat, and simmer 8 to 10 minutes or until peaches are tender. Stir in cornstarch mixture; cook, stirring constantly, until clear and thickened. Remove from heat, and stir in almond extract. Cool.

Combine flour, salt, and ⅛ teaspoon nutmeg; cut in shortening with pastry blender until mixture resembles coarse meal. Sprinkle water over surface; stir until dry ingredients are moistened. Shape into a ball. Roll pastry to ⅛-inch thickness on a lightly floured surface; cut into 8- x ½-inch strips.

Spoon cooled peach mixture into an 8-inch square baking dish coated with cooking spray. Arrange pastry strips in lattice design over peaches. Bake at 425° for 20 minutes or until lightly browned. Serve warm. Yield: 6 servings (about 126 calories per serving).

MERINGUE-TOPPED PINEAPPLE

1 small pineapple (about 2¾ pounds)
3 tablespoons kirsch
2 egg whites
¼ cup sugar

Cut pineapple in half lengthwise; remove core. Cut pineapple pulp into ¾-inch cubes; drain. Toss pineapple cubes with kirsch; spoon into pineapple shells, and chill thoroughly.

Beat egg whites (at room temperature) until soft peaks form. Gradually add sugar, 1 tablespoon at a time, beating until stiff peaks form. Spread meringue over fruit, spreading to edge of pineapple shells; bake at 350° for 12 to 15 minutes or until the meringue is golden brown. Yield: 4 servings (about 172 calories per serving).

FRESH FRUIT TART

½ (8-ounce) package Neufchâtel cheese,
    softened
¼ teaspoon grated orange rind
1 tablespoon unsweetened orange juice
1½ teaspoons sugar
Tart crust (recipe follows)
½ cup unsweetened orange juice
2 tablespoons Cointreau or other
    orange-flavored liqueur
2 teaspoons cornstarch
2 medium nectarines, peeled and sliced
Ascorbic-citric powder
1 cup fresh blueberries

Combine first 4 ingredients; beat until fluffy. Spread evenly over tart crust.

Combine ½ cup orange juice, Cointreau, and cornstarch in a small saucepan; stir over low heat until clear and thickened. Set aside to cool slightly.

Dip nectarines in ascorbic-citric solution; drain thoroughly. Arrange nectarines and blueberries on cheese mixture; spoon orange glaze over tart. Chill thoroughly. Yield: 8 servings (about 191 calories per serving).

Tart Crust:

¾ cup quick-cooking oats, uncooked
½ cup whole wheat flour
1 tablespoon brown sugar
1 teaspoon ground cinnamon
¼ cup margarine, melted
2 tablespoons water
Vegetable cooking spray

Combine first 4 ingredients in a small bowl. Sprinkle margarine and water over dry ingredients; stir with a fork until well mixed. Coat an 8½-inch tart pan with cooking spray. With lightly floured hands, press oat mixture evenly over bottom of pan. Bake at 450° for 10 to 12 minutes; cool completely. Yield: pastry for one 8½-inch tart.

Stock Up On Relish And Chutney

Daydreams of Grandma might conjure up memories of a large pantry, shelf after shelf filled with homemade relishes and chutneys. While Grandma may have canned like this to preserve food before the days of refrigeration, her family has probably continued the tradition because of the wonderful taste of those homemade relishes.

Relishes and chutneys are first cousins to the pickle. The major difference is that relishes are chopped, whereas pickles are left whole or in large pieces. Chutneys are similar to relishes, but boast a zippier flavor from spices.

Relishes and chutneys get their smooth texture and rich flavor from simmering over low heat in a sweet-and-sour solution, often as long as two hours. Special pickling salt is not required unless specified in the recipes. The products do need heat treatment, however, to destroy organisms that can cause spoilage. Basic treatment directions are given for each recipe. For a more detailed account of special pickling and canning precautions, don't miss the following article, ''From Our Kitchen to Yours,'' on page 180.

PLUM CHUTNEY

3 pounds plums, pitted and quartered
1 pound tart green apples, peeled, cored, and quartered
1 large onion, chopped
2 cloves garlic, minced
2 cups firmly packed brown sugar
2 cups vinegar (5% acidity)
1 tablespoon salt
1 tablespoon ground ginger
2 teaspoons ground cloves
½ teaspoon red pepper

Combine all ingredients in a large Dutch oven; bring to a boil. Cook, uncovered, over medium heat 2 hours or until thickened, stirring occasionally.

Quickly spoon chutney into hot sterilized jars, leaving ¼-inch headspace; cover at once with metal lids, and screw bands tight. Process in boiling-water bath 10 minutes. Yield: 5 half pints.

Tip: Food cooks just as quickly in gently boiling water as it does in hard boiling water.

PEACH CHUTNEY

4 quarts peeled and finely chopped fresh peaches
1 cup chopped onion
1 cup raisins
1 clove garlic, minced
1 hot red pepper
3 cups firmly packed brown sugar
¼ cup whole mustard seeds
2 tablespoons ground ginger
2 teaspoons salt
5 cups vinegar (5% acidity)

Combine all ingredients in a large Dutch oven; bring to a boil, stirring frequently. Reduce heat and simmer, uncovered, 2 hours or until thickened, stirring often. Remove red pepper.

Quickly spoon chutney into hot sterilized jars, leaving ¼-inch headspace; cover at once with metal lids, and screw bands tight. Process in boiling-water bath 10 minutes. Yield: 6 pints.

INDIA RELISH

3 quarts peeled, chopped tomatoes
3 cups chopped celery
2 cups chopped onion
3 tablespoons salt
4 cups vinegar (5% acidity)
3 cups firmly packed brown sugar
⅓ cup whole mustard seeds
2 hot red peppers, seeded and chopped
1 teaspoon ground cinnamon
¾ teaspoon ground allspice
¾ teaspoon ground cloves

Combine first 4 ingredients in a large Dutch oven; stir gently. Let stand 2 hours. Add remaining ingredients; bring to a boil. Reduce heat and simmer, uncovered, 2 hours or until thickened, stirring occasionally.

Quickly spoon relish into hot sterilized jars, leaving ¼-inch headspace; cover at once with metal lids, and screw bands tight. Process in boiling-water bath 15 minutes. Yield: 4 pints.

BEET RELISH

2½ pounds medium beets
4 cups coarsely chopped cabbage
1 cup chopped onion
1 cup chopped sweet red pepper
1½ cups sugar
3 cups vinegar (5% acidity)
1 tablespoon salt
1 tablespoon prepared horseradish

Leave root and 1 inch of stem on beets; scrub with a brush. Place beets in a large Dutch oven, and add water to cover; bring to a boil. Cover, reduce heat, and simmer 35 to 40 minutes or until tender; drain. Pour cold water over beets, and drain; let cool. Trim off beet stems and roots, and rub off skins. Coarsely chop enough beets to measure 4 cups. Reserve any remaining beets for other uses.

Combine 4 cups beets and next 7 ingredients in a large Dutch oven; cook over low heat for 10 minutes. Bring mixture to a boil.

Quickly spoon relish into hot sterilized jars, leaving ¼-inch headspace; cover at once with metal lids, and screw bands tight. Process in boiling-water bath 15 minutes. Yield: 7 half pints.

Note: Drained and coarsely chopped canned beets may be substituted for fresh beets, if desired.

EIGHT-VEGETABLE RELISH

2 quarts peeled, cored, chopped green tomatoes
1 quart peeled, cored, chopped ripe tomatoes
1 quart coarsely chopped cabbage
3 cups chopped onion
2 cups chopped celery
1 cup peeled and chopped cucumber
1 cup chopped green pepper
1 cup chopped sweet red pepper
½ cup pickling salt
2 quarts vinegar (5% acidity)
4 cups firmly packed brown sugar
1 tablespoon celery seeds
1 tablespoon whole mustard seeds
1 tablespoon ground cinnamon
1 teaspoon ground ginger
½ teaspoon ground cloves
2 cloves garlic, minced

Combine first 8 ingredients in a large mixing bowl; add salt, mixing well. Cover and let stand in a cool place 12 to 18 hours. Drain well, and set aside.

Combine remaining ingredients in a 10-quart Dutch oven; simmer over medium heat 10 minutes. Add the vegetables; simmer over medium heat 30 minutes, stirring occasionally. Bring the mixture to a boil.

Quickly spoon relish into hot sterilized jars, leaving ¼-inch headspace. Cover at once with metal lids, and screw bands tight. Process in boiling-water bath 15 minutes. Yield: 9 pints.

PEPPER-ONION RELISH

2 quarts chopped green pepper
2 quarts chopped sweet red pepper
1½ cups chopped onion
2 teaspoons mixed whole pickling spices
1 hot red pepper
1½ cups vinegar (5% acidity)
¾ cup sugar
2 teaspoons salt

Combine first 3 ingredients in a large bowl. Add enough boiling water to cover; let stand 5 minutes. Drain. Cover again with boiling water; let stand 10 minutes, and drain.

Tie spices and hot pepper in a cheesecloth bag. Combine spice bag, vinegar, sugar, and salt in a Dutch oven; bring to a boil. Reduce heat and simmer, uncovered, 15 minutes. Add vegetables, and simmer 10 minutes. Remove spice bag, and bring mixture to a boil.

Quickly spoon relish into hot sterilized jars, leaving ¼-inch headspace; cover at once with metal lids, and screw bands tight. Process in boiling-water bath 5 minutes. Yield: 9 half pints.

TOMATO-APPLE CHUTNEY

5 cups peeled, cored, chopped tomatoes
2 cups peeled, chopped apple
¾ cup chopped onion
¾ cup chopped sweet red pepper
½ cup raisins, ground
¼ cup peeled, chopped cucumber
1½ cups firmly packed brown sugar
1 small hot red pepper
1 small clove garlic, crushed
1½ teaspoons ground ginger
½ teaspoon salt
½ teaspoon ground cinnamon
1½ cups vinegar (5% acidity)

Combine all ingredients in a large Dutch oven, stirring well. Cook, uncovered, over medium-high heat 2 hours or until thickened, stirring frequently. Remove red pepper.

Quickly spoon chutney into hot sterilized jars, leaving ¼-inch headspace; cover at once with metal lids, and screw bands tight. Process in boiling-water bath 10 minutes. Yield: 5 half pints.

From Our Kitchen To Yours

Take advantage of the abundance of Southern fruit and vegetables when they're in season and capture their freshness in a jar. Since canning is such a precise procedure, here are some basic procedures for safe canning.

Boiling-Water Bath Canning

Remember that the canning method used depends on the type of food you're preserving. If you're working with high-acid foods like fruit, sauerkraut, pickled vegetables, and tomatoes, it's safe to use a boiling-water bath canner. A slightly underripe fruit or tomato will yield the best end product.

If you don't have a water bath canner, you can use any big metal container deep and large enough to allow water to cover the tops and boil freely around all sides of the jars. The container needs a tight-fitting cover and a rack to keep jars in place and off the bottom of the kettle. If your steam-pressure canner is deep enough, it can be used for a water bath canner, but remember to open the steam valve.

Steam-Pressure Canning

Low-acid foods have to be processed at higher temperatures to be safe to eat, so for meats, fish, poultry, and all vegetables other than tomatoes, you need to use a steam-pressure canner. This type of canner is a heavy kettle with a lid that can be locked down to make a tight seal. The lid has a safety valve, a petcock (vent), and a pressure gauge. Accuracy of the pressure gauge is most important. Your county Extension service can usually let you know where to have your dial gauges checked. Keep the stem to the gauge clean, too.

Canning Jars

Standard canning jars with lids should be used for home canning. Canning jars are tougher and are able to withstand higher heats. Lids are especially made to fit tightly to create a seal. Be sure to use only the jars in the best shape, not chipped or cracked, so you won't have problems with jars breaking during processing or not sealing.

Until recently, jelly could be placed in odd jars and sealed with paraffin. However, the new USDA guidelines advise canners to process jelly in the water bath canner for 5 minutes and eliminate the paraffin layer on top; therefore, canning jars are recommended.

Packing Methods

The cold pack method is used when filling jars with raw fruit and vegetables. Most raw fruit and vegetables shrink during processing, so pack them tightly. Corn, lima beans, and peas expand during processing, so pack them loosely. After packing, boiling syrup or water is added before processing.

The hot pack method is usually used for fruit and vegetables that hold their shape well. Fruit is always heated in either syrup, water, or its own juices before packing. The food should be at or near boiling point when packed into the jars. Pack the food loosely.

Whether you're using the hot or cold pack method, be sure to cover the fruit and vegetables completely with liquid. Leave some room between the packed food and the lid to allow for expansion during processing.

Canning Safety

Pounds of pressure and length of processing time are standard, so follow the guidelines for the safest results. Here are some answers to the most common questions about safety.

—Most foods, except pickles and other relish-type products, can be canned without salt. Salt is usually used for flavor and can be cut out or reduced in canning.

—If there's any cloudiness of liquid, mold, or scum in the canned product when you open it, throw it away. Don't try tasting it.

—Most of your canning equipment can be reused except for the flat metal lids. New lids are needed each time because the sealing compound on the lids loses its effectiveness after one use. Oftentimes, the lid gets bent trying to open a jar, and just a slight bend can prevent sealing.

—Processing canned food in the dishwasher, microwave oven, or conventional oven can be dangerous. To can in the microwave, a thermometer has to be placed in each jar to be sure proper internal temperature is reached. And to check temperature, the lid has to be off. So a seal cannot be created, and bacteria can grow. If canning in the oven, the jars may explode. Also, for any high-acid foods, the internal temperature of the canned foods does not become hot enough to kill bacteria.

Tip: Cooking vegetables with the least amount of water possible will preserve vitamins and maintain flavor.

Cool Soups For Summer Dining

Served as an appetizer, these cold soups stimulate taste buds with their light, delicate flavors. And matched with a sandwich or salad, they make a refreshing summer meal.

SHERRIED AVOCADO SOUP

2 large avocados, peeled and quartered
1 cup half-and-half
1 tablespoon lemon juice
¾ teaspoon seasoned salt
2 cups chicken broth
2 tablespoons sherry
Commercial sour cream (optional)
Lime slices (optional)

Combine first 4 ingredients in container of electric blender; process until smooth. Pour into bowl.

Bring chicken broth to a boil; slowly add to avocado puree, stirring constantly. Add sherry, and chill. Garnish with sour cream and lime, if desired. Yield: 5 cups. *Mrs. Farmer L. Burns, New Orleans, Louisiana.*

SUMMER GAZPACHO

2½ cups tomato juice
1 cup finely chopped tomato
½ cup finely chopped celery
½ cup finely chopped green pepper
⅓ cup finely chopped green onions
2 tablespoons wine vinegar
2 tablespoons vegetable oil
2 teaspoons chopped fresh parsley
1 small clove garlic, minced
1 teaspoon salt
¼ teaspoon pepper
½ teaspoon Worcestershire sauce

Combine all ingredients; mix well. Cover and chill 8 hours or overnight. Yield: 4½ cups. *Teddie Hamrick, Quanah, Texas.*

ZUCCHINI SOUP

2 medium zucchini, cut into ½-inch pieces
½ cup water
2 teaspoons dried onion flakes
1 teaspoon dried parsley flakes
½ teaspoon salt
2 cups milk
3 tablespoons butter or margarine
1 (⅞-ounce) package chicken-flavored gravy mix
Sliced zucchini (optional)

Combine first 5 ingredients in a saucepan; bring to a boil. Cover, reduce heat, and simmer 10 minutes or until zucchini is tender. Pour zucchini mixture into container of electric blender; process until smooth.

Combine milk, butter, and gravy mix in a saucepan; cook until thickened. Stir in zucchini mixture. Cover and chill. Garnish with sliced zucchini, if desired. Yield: 4½ cups.
Mrs. Charles De Haven, Owensboro, Kentucky.

CHILLED PEA SOUP

2 cups shelled fresh English peas or 1 (10-ounce) package frozen English peas
2 cups shredded lettuce
1 (10¾-ounce) can chicken broth, undiluted
⅓ cup water
¼ cup tomato juice
¼ cup chopped green onions
1 tablespoon minced fresh parsley
½ teaspoon salt
¼ teaspoon dried whole thyme
¼ teaspoon white pepper
½ cup whipping cream

Combine first 10 ingredients in a saucepan; bring to a boil. Cover, reduce heat, and simmer 20 minutes. Remove from heat, and cool slightly.

Pour pea mixture into container of electric blender; process until smooth. Stir in whipping cream. Cover and chill. Yield: about 4½ cups. *Barbara Davis, Lilburn, Georgia.*

MICROWAVE COOKERY

Shortcuts To Freezer Jams

Fresh tasting, bright-colored freezer jams are easy to make, especially with the help of a microwave oven. Even though these jams are not actually cooked, the microwave still saves time.

With freezer jams, you just combine crushed fruit with sugar and pectin. The pectin must be boiled for 1 full minute, then stirred into the fruit. The jams are stored in airtight jelly glasses or frozen food containers.

The pectin-and-water mixture can be boiled in the microwave without constant stirring. However, the pectin does boil up high, so be sure to use a container that's large enough to prevent any of the mixture from spilling over. We recommend using a 4-cup glass measure or deep mixing bowl.

FREEZER BLACKBERRY JAM

2¾ cups frozen blackberries
3 cups sugar
1 (1¾-ounce) package powdered pectin
¾ cup water

Place blackberries in a 2-quart casserole; microwave at MEDIUM (50% power) for 4 to 5 minutes, stirring after half the defrosting time. Stir again; let stand 5 minutes. Add sugar; let stand 20 minutes, stirring occasionally.

Combine pectin and water in a 4-cup glass measure; stir well. Microwave at HIGH for 2 to 2½ minutes or until boiling. Boil for 1 minute, stirring after 45 seconds. Stir well again, and pour over the fruit. Stir for 3 minutes.

Pour into sterilized jelly glasses or frozen food containers. Cover with lids, and let stand at room temperature 1 to 2 hours or until jelled. Store in freezer up to 1 year or refrigerator up to 3 weeks. To serve, remove and allow to come to room temperature. Yield: about 4¾ cups.

RASPBERRY FREEZER JAM

2 (10-ounce) packages frozen raspberries
3 cups sugar
1 (1¾-ounce) package powdered pectin
¾ cup water

Place raspberries in a 2-quart casserole; microwave at MEDIUM (50% power) for 4 to 5 minutes, stirring after half the defrosting time. Stir again; let stand 5 minutes. Add sugar; let stand 20 minutes, stirring occasionally.

Combine pectin and water in a 4-cup glass measure, stirring well. Microwave at HIGH for 2 to 2½ minutes or until boiling. Boil 1 minute, stirring after 45 seconds. Stir well again; pour over fruit. Stir for 3 minutes.

Pour into sterilized jelly glasses or frozen food containers. Cover with lids, and let stand at room temperature 1 to 2 hours or until jelled. Store in freezer up to 1 year or refrigerator up to 3 weeks. To serve, remove and allow to come to room temperature. Yield: about 4½ cups.

STRAWBERRY FREEZER JAM

2 cups finely mashed fresh strawberries
4 cups sugar
1 (1¾-ounce) package powdered pectin
¾ cup water

Combine strawberries and sugar, stirring well. Let mixture stand 20 minutes, stirring occasionally.

Combine pectin and water in a 4-cup glass measure, stirring well. Microwave at HIGH for 2 to 2½ minutes or until boiling. Boil for 1 minute, stirring after 45 seconds. Stir well again, and pour pectin mixture over the fruit. Stir for 3 minutes.

Pour into sterilized jelly glasses or frozen food containers. Cover with lids, and let stand at room temperature 1 to 2 hours or until jelled. Store in freezer up to 1 year or refrigerator up to 3 weeks. To serve, remove and allow to come to room temperature. Yield: about 5 cups.

FREEZER PEACH JAM

2¼ cups peeled, pitted, and mashed fresh peaches
2 tablespoons lemon juice
1 teaspoon ascorbic-citric powder
4¾ cups sugar
1 (1¾-ounce) package powdered pectin
¾ cup water

Combine first 4 ingredients. Let stand 20 minutes, stirring occasionally.

Combine pectin and water in a 4-cup glass measure, stirring well. Microwave at HIGH for 2 to 2½ minutes or until boiling. Boil 1 minute, stirring after 45 seconds. Stir well again; pour over fruit. Stir for 3 minutes.

Pour into sterilized jelly glasses or frozen food containers. Cover with lids, and let stand at room temperature 1 to 2 hours or until jelled. Store in freezer up to 1 year or refrigerator up to 3 weeks. To serve, remove and allow to come to room temperature. Yield: about 6 cups.

Taste The Lure Of Catfish

Just mentioning catfish brings to mind hot afternoons spent dangling cane poles from a riverbank, hoping for a nibble. That's the way it used to be,

and often still is. But thanks to catfish farms, this Southern delicacy is now widely available, even in supermarkets, and has inspired a host of new recipes.

Probably the most distinctive trait of farm-raised catfish is the absence of any fishy odor or taste. The snowy white fish is easy to prepare, and just as versatile as any other freshwater or saltwater fish. Because of its delicate flavor and texture, farm-raised catfish can be used as a substitute in almost any recipe calling for white, non-oily fish.

That's the idea behind the catfish entrées served in the The Crown at the Antique Mall in Indianola, Mississippi. "We do anything with catfish that you can do with trout or flounder," says owner Evelyn Roughton.

Cock of the Walk in Natchez, Mississippi, takes a much more traditional approach to serving catfish. Crocks of slaw and skillets of cornbread accompany the standard order for each table—a steaming mountain of fried catfish, hush puppies, and French fries.

"I had a dream since I was a kid of opening my own restaurant," says Tom McCalman, "and a year and a half ago I got the chance." That was the start of the Catfish Inn in Metairie, Louisiana. This restaurant, like so many that are springing up across the South, exclusively features catfish.

If you don't seem to be able to get your fill of catfish eating out, try these recipes at home. In addition to the restaurant selections, we've included recipes for some of the winning entries to the National Farm-Raised Catfish Cooking Contest. Held annually, this event is a roundup of some of the best catfish cooks and recipes in the South.

CROWN ROOM'S SHRIMP-STUFFED CATFISH

1 small onion, chopped
3 green onions, chopped
¼ pound fresh mushrooms, chopped
3 tablespoons butter or margarine
½ cup soft breadcrumbs
2 tablespoons chopped fresh parsley
Juice of ½ lemon
6 (7- to 9-ounce) catfish fillets
½ pound medium shrimp, cooked and peeled
Sauce (recipe follows)
¾ cup (3 ounces) shredded Swiss cheese
Paprika

Sauté onions and mushrooms in butter until tender; add breadcrumbs, parsley, and lemon juice, mixing well. Spread about 2 tablespoons of stuffing

mixture down the center of each fillet; top with shrimp. Roll fillets up, securing with a wooden pick. Place each fillet, seam side down, in a lightly greased individual baking dish.

Pour about ½ cup of sauce over each fillet. Bake at 350° for 25 minutes; sprinkle with cheese, and bake an additional 3 minutes or until cheese melts. Sprinkle with paprika. Yield: 6 servings.

Sauce:

⅓ cup butter or margarine
⅓ cup all-purpose flour
2⅔ cups milk
⅓ cup dry white wine
2 egg yolks
½ teaspoon dry mustard
Dash of red pepper

Melt butter in a heavy saucepan over low heat; add flour, stirring until smooth. Cook 1 minute, stirring constantly. Gradually add milk and wine; cook over medium heat, stirring constantly. Beat egg yolks until thick and lemon colored. Gradually stir about one-fourth of hot mixture into yolks; add to remaining hot mixture, stirring constantly. Cook over medium heat, stirring constantly, until thickened and bubbly. Stir in mustard and red pepper. Yield: about 3 cups.

CATFISH INN'S GRILLED FISH WITH HEATHER SAUCE

12 large catfish fillets
Vegetable cooking spray
Heather Sauce

Coat fillets with cooking spray; place in a well-greased wire grill basket.

Grill fish over medium-hot coals for 5 to 8 minutes on each side or until fish flakes easily when tested with a fork. Spoon Heather Sauce over fillets before serving. Yield: 6 servings.

Heather Sauce:

¼ cup minced onion
3 tablespoons butter or margarine
3 tablespoons all-purpose flour
¼ teaspoon dry mustard
1½ cups milk
1¼ cups (5 ounces) shredded process American cheese
½ cup Chablis or other dry white wine
2 tablespoons sliced green onion tops
½ teaspoon salt
¼ teaspoon white pepper

Sauté ¼ cup onion in butter in a heavy saucepan until tender; add flour and mustard, stirring until smooth. Cook 1 minute, stirring constantly.

Gradually add milk; cook over medium heat, stirring constantly, until mixture is thickened and bubbly. Add cheese; stir until cheese melts. Stir in remaining ingredients. Yield: 2¼ cups.

MIDDENDORF'S BROILED MANCHAC CATFISH

½ cup butter or margarine, melted
Garlic salt
8 (5-ounce) catfish fillets
Juice of ½ lemon

Line a shallow baking pan with aluminum foil; lightly brush foil with butter, and sprinkle lightly with garlic salt. Arrange fillets in prepared pan. Brush fish with remaining melted butter; sprinkle lightly with garlic salt and lemon juice. Broil 5 inches from heat for 10 to 15 minutes or until fish flakes easily when tested with a fork. Spoon pan drippings over fish, if desired. Yield: 8 servings.

MANDARIN CATFISH AMANDINE

¼ cup plus 2 tablespoons butter or
    margarine, melted
1 (11-ounce) can mandarin oranges,
    undrained
2 eggs, beaten
1½ cups fine, dry breadcrumbs
1½ teaspoons salt
½ teaspoon grated lemon rind
4 (10- to 12-ounce) pan-dressed catfish
Mandarin-Almond Cream Sauce

Pour melted butter in a 15- x 10- x 1-inch jellyroll pan; set aside. Drain oranges, reserving liquid (reserve oranges for use in sauce recipe). Combine eggs and 2 tablespoons orange liquid in a shallow dish (reserve remaining orange liquid for use in sauce recipe); set aside.
Combine breadcrumbs, salt, and lemon rind in a shallow dish. Dip fish in egg mixture; dredge in breadcrumb mixture. Place in jellyroll pan, turning once to coat with butter. Bake, uncovered, at 350° for 35 minutes or until fish flakes easily when tested with a fork. Serve with Mandarin-Almond Cream Sauce. Yield: 4 servings.

Mandarin-Almond Cream Sauce:

¼ cup sliced almonds
¼ cup butter or margarine
Reserved mandarin orange liquid
1 tablespoon cornstarch
1 tablespoon lemon juice
⅛ teaspoon salt
¼ cup commercial sour cream
Reserved mandarin oranges

Sauté almonds in butter in a medium saucepan until lightly browned. Remove almonds, and set aside. Combine reserved liquid from oranges and cornstarch; mix well, and add to saucepan. Bring to a boil; cook over medium heat 1 minute, stirring constantly. Remove from heat; stir in lemon juice and salt. Allow sauce to cool slightly; add sour cream and reserved oranges, stirring gently. Serve over catfish; sprinkle with almonds. Yield: 1¼ cups.
Prudence Hilburn,
Piedmont, Alabama.

SOUFFLE-STUFFED CATFISH

6 medium catfish fillets
3 tablespoons butter or margarine, melted
1 cup cheese cracker crumbs
½ cup commercial buttermilk salad
    dressing
1 (12-ounce) package frozen spinach
    soufflé
Lemony Cheese Sauce
Lemon slices (optional)
Pimiento strips (optional)

Brush sides of each fillet with butter. Dredge in cracker crumbs; set aside.
Pour salad dressing into a lightly greased 13- x 9- x 2-inch baking dish. Cut frozen soufflé into 6 equal pieces. Roll each fillet around a piece of soufflé; place, seam side down, in baking dish. Cover and bake at 375° for 40 minutes; uncover and bake an additional 15 minutes or until fish flakes easily when tested with a fork.
Spoon Lemony Cheese Sauce into a shallow serving platter; arrange fillets in sauce. Garnish with lemon slices and pimiento, if desired. Yield: 6 servings.

Lemony Cheese Sauce:

1 (8-ounce) package cream cheese, cut
    into cubes
1 egg, beaten
2 tablespoons lemon juice
1 teaspoon sugar
½ teaspoon dry mustard
¼ teaspoon dried whole tarragon
½ to ¾ cup commercial buttermilk salad
    dressing
¼ cup grated Parmesan cheese

Combine first 6 ingredients in a medium saucepan; cook over low heat, stirring frequently, until cream cheese melts. Stir in salad dressing and Parmesan; cook just until thoroughly heated.
Marge Walker,
Indianapolis, Indiana.

CATFISH ELDORADO DE COLORADO

1 medium onion, chopped
1 green pepper, chopped
1 clove garlic, minced
2 tablespoons bacon drippings
1 (28-ounce) can tomatoes, undrained and
    coarsely chopped
⅓ cup beer
1 tablespoon Worcestershire sauce
3 dashes of hot sauce
½ teaspoon dried whole basil
1 bay leaf
½ teaspoon salt
⅛ teaspoon pepper
3 eggs, separated
6 medium pan-dressed catfish
¼ cup plus 2 tablespoons all-purpose flour
2 to 4 tablespoons bacon drippings
2 (4-ounce) cans whole green chiles,
    drained
¾ cup (3 ounces) shredded Monterey Jack
    cheese

Sauté first 3 ingredients in 2 tablespoons bacon drippings in a large skillet until tender. Add tomatoes; reduce heat and simmer, uncovered, 5 minutes. Add next 7 ingredients; cook, uncovered, over low heat 10 to 15 minutes.
Beat egg whites (at room temperature) until soft peaks form; lightly beat yolks. Gently fold yolks into whites. Dredge fish in flour; then dip in egg mixture.
Brown catfish in 2 to 4 tablespoons hot bacon drippings (350°) in an electric skillet, turning once. Transfer fish to an ungreased 13- x 9- x 2-inch baking dish. Slice green chiles lengthwise, and place over catfish; top with tomato mixture. Bake at 350° for 20 minutes or until fish flakes easily; remove bay leaf. Sprinkle fish with cheese, and bake an additional 5 minutes or until cheese melts. Yield: 6 servings.
Karen Spuhler,
Boulder, Colorado.

Tip: Get in the habit of grocery shopping with a list. Watch newspapers for advertised "specials"; then plan a week's menus around bargains in foods the family enjoys.

CATFISH STIR

1½ pounds catfish fillets
3 tablespoons lemon juice
3 tablespoons soy sauce
3 tablespoons vegetable oil, divided
1 cup thinly sliced carrots
1 cup sliced broccoli flowerets
1 cup sliced zucchini
1 cup sliced fresh mushrooms
1 cup sliced cauliflower flowerets
¾ cup green onions, cut into ½-inch pieces
2 medium tomatoes, peeled and cut into eighths
½ cup sliced water chestnuts
2 to 2½ tablespoons cornstarch
¾ cup water
1 teaspoon salt
¼ teaspoon pepper
Hot cooked rice

Cut fillets into 2- x ¾-inch strips. Combine lemon juice and soy sauce, mixing well. Add fish, and let stand 20 minutes.

Pour 2 tablespoons oil around top of preheated wok or large skillet, coating sides; allow to heat at medium high (325°) for 2 minutes. Add carrots; stir-fry 2 minutes. Add next 7 ingredients; stir-fry 2 minutes. Remove vegetables; set aside.

Add 1 tablespoon remaining oil to wok; allow to heat at medium high (325°) for 2 minutes. Drain fish, reserving marinade. Add fish to wok, and stir-fry 2 minutes, or until fish flakes easily when tested with a fork. Return vegetables to wok. Combine cornstarch, water, salt, pepper, and reserved marinade; mix well, and add to wok. Stir-fry over low heat (225°) 2 minutes or until thickened and bubbly. Serve over rice. Yield: 4 servings. *Anne M. Barnes, Tutwiler, Mississippi.*

CATFISH KIEV-STYLE

12 small catfish fillets
1 teaspoon onion salt
1 (3-ounce) package cream cheese with chives, softened
2 tablespoons butter or margarine, softened
1 teaspoon lemon-pepper seasoning
1 (4-ounce) can mushroom stems and pieces, drained and chopped
½ cup butter or margarine, melted
1⅓ cups seasoned crouton crumbs

Sprinkle fillets with onion salt.
Combine cream cheese, softened butter, and lemon-pepper seasoning; mix until blended. Stir in mushrooms. Divide cheese mixture into 12 portions.

Roll each fillet around a portion of cheese mixture, and secure with a wooden pick. Dip fish in butter, and coat with crumbs. Place fish in a lightly greased 13- x 9- x 2-inch baking dish. Drizzle with any remaining butter. Bake at 350° for 25 to 30 minutes or until fish flakes easily. Yield: 6 servings.
Jean W. Sanderson, Leawood, Kansas.

CATFISH FRY

6 (12- to 16-ounce) pan-dressed catfish
1 cup buttermilk
2 tablespoons salt
1 tablespoon pepper
1½ cups self-rising cornmeal
½ cup self-rising flour
Vegetable oil

Score both sides of each fish diagonally, making slits approximately ⅛-inch deep. Place fish in a large shallow dish; set aside. Combine buttermilk, salt, and pepper; stir well. Pour buttermilk mixture over fish. Cover and refrigerate at least 4 hours, turning fish occasionally.

Combine cornmeal and flour in a shallow container; set aside. Remove fish from buttermilk mixture; dredge in cornmeal mixture. Fry fish in deep hot oil (375°) until golden brown. Drain well. Yield: 6 servings.
Mrs. W. F. Burk, Sr., Rome, Georgia.

Favorite Ice Creams And Sherbets

No dessert brings the family running faster than old-fashioned homemade ice cream and sherbet. These cold treats are a delicious way to end a fine meal.

CHERRY ICE CREAM

8 eggs
2½ cups sugar
½ teaspoon salt
3 (13-ounce) cans evaporated milk, chilled
2 (21-ounce) cans cherry pie filling
3¾ cups milk

Beat eggs 3 minutes on high speed of electric mixer in a large mixing bowl; gradually add sugar and salt, beating

well. Add evaporated milk and pie filling, mixing until combined. Stir in milk.

Pour mixture into freezer can of a 1½-gallon hand-turned or electric freezer. Freeze according to manufacturer's instructions. Let ripen at least 1½ hours. Yield: 1½ gallons.
Note: To prepare in a 1-gallon freezer, divide mixture and freeze each half separately. Refrigerate mixture until freezing. *Mary Alice Curl, Miami, Texas.*

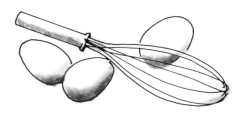

BUTTERMILK SHERBET

2 cups buttermilk
1 cup sugar
1 (8-ounce) can crushed pineapple, undrained
1 tablespoon vanilla extract
2 egg whites

Combine buttermilk, sugar, pineapple, and vanilla; mix well. Place in an airtight container; freeze until slushy.

Beat egg whites (at room temperature) until stiff peaks form. Add buttermilk mixture, and beat well. Pour into airtight freezer container, and return to freezer; freeze until firm. Yield: 1 quart.
Pertie Bickley, Louisa, Virginia.

HOMEMADE STRAWBERRY ICE CREAM

1 (5½-ounce) package vanilla instant pudding mix
2 cups sugar
4 cups milk
1 cup water
1 (13-ounce) can evaporated milk, chilled
2 cups mashed fresh strawberries

Combine pudding mix and sugar in a large bowl; add remaining ingredients, stirring well. Pour mixture into freezer can of a 1-gallon hand-turned or electric freezer. Freeze according to manufacturer's instructions. Let ripen at least 1 hour. Yield: 1 gallon.
Note: Any fresh fruit may be substituted for strawberries. *Nancy Monroe, Elizabethtown, North Carolina.*

Summer Glows With Fruit

Get out your buckets and baskets; August is time to load up on luscious summer fruit. Start with a visit to your local farmers' market and grocery produce bins. If you prefer to pick your own fruit, organize a trip to the family's favorite berry patch or orchard. Once you make your selections, head home to enjoy these fruit-filled delights.

PINEAPPLE-MINT ICE CREAM

3 cups sugar
3 cups water
1 cup light corn syrup
¼ teaspoon peppermint extract
2 cups finely chopped fresh pineapple
2 cups unsweetened pineapple juice
1 quart half-and-half
1 quart whipping cream
½ cup crème de menthe-flavored syrup
Fresh mint sprigs (optional)

Combine sugar and water in a large saucepan; stir well. Place over medium-high heat; cook, stirring constantly, to soft ball stage (235°). Remove from heat; stir in next 7 ingredients.

Pour mixture into freezer can of a 1-gallon hand-turned or electric freezer. Freeze according to manufacturer's instructions. Let ripen 1 hour. Garnish each serving with a sprig of fresh mint, if desired. Yield: 1 gallon.

Note: For firmer ice cream, pack in freezer containers, and let harden 8 hours before serving.

*Harriette Simpkins,
Nashville, Tennessee.*

FRESH PEACH CREPES

2 (8-ounce) packages cream cheese, softened
½ cup sugar
2 teaspoons vanilla extract
8 crêpes (recipe follows)
6 large ripe peaches, peeled, seeded, and sliced
½ cup butter or margarine, softened
½ cup firmly packed light brown sugar
1 cup whipping cream
2 tablespoons powdered sugar

Combine cream cheese, ½ cup sugar, and vanilla; beat until smooth. Spread about 3 tablespoons of cream cheese mixture over each crêpe. Place a row of peach slices down the center of each crêpe, reserving enough slices for garnish. Dot peaches in each crêpe with 1 tablespoon butter, and sprinkle with 1 tablespoon brown sugar. Roll up crêpes, and place in a 13- x 9- x 2-inch baking dish; bake at 325° for 8 to 10 minutes.

Combine whipping cream and powdered sugar; beat until stiff peaks form. Place crêpes on serving dishes; garnish with whipped cream and peach slices. Serve immediately. Yield: 8 servings.

Crêpes:

¾ cup all-purpose flour
¾ cup milk
2 eggs
1 tablespoon light brown sugar
1 tablespoon vegetable oil
Dash of ground cinnamon
Dash of ground nutmeg
Dash of ground ginger
Vegetable oil

Combine first 8 ingredients in container of electric blender; process 1 minute. Scrape down sides of blender with rubber spatula; process an additional 15 seconds. Refrigerate 1 hour. (This allows flour particles to swell and soften so crêpes are light in texture.)

Brush the bottom of a 6-inch crêpe pan or nonstick skillet with vegetable oil; place pan over medium heat until oil is just hot, not smoking.

Pour about 3 tablespoons batter into the hot pan; quickly tilt pan in all directions so that batter covers the pan in a thin film. Cook crêpe 1 minute.

Lift the edge of crêpe to test for doneness. Crêpe is ready for flipping when it can be shaken loose from pan. Flip crêpe, and cook about 30 seconds on other side. (This side is rarely more than spotty brown and is the side on which the filling is placed.)

Place crêpes on a towel to cool. Stack crêpes between layers of waxed paper. Yield: 8 crêpes. *Susan Cheek,
Montgomery, Alabama.*

HONEYDEW FRUIT BOWL

1 medium honeydew melon, halved and seeded
1½ cups cantaloupe balls
1 cup sliced fresh strawberries
1 cup cubed fresh pineapple
⅓ cup fresh blueberries

Carefully scoop out fruit balls from honeydew halves, reserving a 1-inch-thick shell. Combine honeydew balls with the next 4 ingredients; toss gently. Fill each melon half with mixed fruit. Yield: 4 to 6 servings. *Sarah Watson,
Knoxville, Tennessee.*

TROPICAL AMBROSIA

3 large mangoes, peeled, cored, and cubed
3 large papayas, peeled, seeded, and cubed
2½ cups honeydew balls
2½ cups watermelon balls
1 fresh pineapple, peeled, cored, and cubed
6 bananas, sliced
½ cup honey
½ to ¾ cup kirsch or other cherry-flavored brandy
Fresh mint sprig (optional)

Combine fruit and honey, tossing gently. Cover and chill at least 2 hours. Stir in kirsch before serving. Garnish with a sprig of fresh mint, if desired. Yield: 15 to 18 servings.

*Mrs. Earl L. Faulkenberry,
Lancaster, South Carolina.*

From Our Kitchen To Yours

Our test kitchens home economists get a lot of questions about selecting fruit. Judging ripeness is not always easy—color, firmness, fragrance, shape, and weight can vary. Since we shop for large amounts of fruit, we'd like to share some of our tips.

Fruit Selection

Watermelon—Thumping watermelons to judge ripeness is not always accurate because it's hard to tell the difference between ripe and overripe. Color is a better guide. Look for a watermelon that's firm, well proportioned, and has a dull outer skin. The bottom of the melon should be a yellowish color or beginning to turn from a white or pale green to light yellow.

Larger watermelons have more edible flesh per pound than smaller ones, so you usually get more for your money by selecting a larger one.

If you buy a watermelon slice, choose a piece with a bright, deep pink to red-colored flesh. Look for dark brown to black seeds. Don't select a piece with a lot of fibers or hard white streaks in the flesh; this usually means it's old or overripe. A watermelon will not ripen after it's cut, so be choosy.

Cantaloupe—Look for a cantaloupe with no sign of a stem. If the cantaloupe has been picked at the right time, the stem usually breaks cleanly and completely from the vine. Check the netting, shape, and color, too. Choose a cantaloupe with evenly distributed netting and a nice rounded shape. Golden-colored melons are at the peak of ripeness; green ones will ripen in a couple of days if they're kept at room temperature. A mild melon aroma is also a sign of ripeness.

Honeydew—A ripe honeydew has a creamy yellow rind that's soft and velvety. Honeydews are larger than cantaloupes and weigh 5 to 7 pounds. But like the cantaloupe, the best-tasting honeydew smells slightly fruity. It's best to hold a honeydew at room temperature a few days for a tastier product.

Papayas—To select a ripe papaya, look for smooth, unbruised skin that ranges in color from yellow green to yellow orange. Papayas are picked when they are green and unripe; they'll ripen in three to five days when left at room temperature, and may be refrigerated for about a week after they are ripe.

Pineapple—Pineapples are picked ready to eat. They soften and lighten in color as they sit, but they will not ripen once they have been picked.

When selecting a pineapple, choose one that is as fresh and big as possible, to have more edible flesh. The leaves or crown should be fresh looking with a dark green color. Don't pick one with brown leaves or a shriveled-looking shell. If a pineapple is overmature, it will have dark soft spots on the bottom.

Supper Clubs Focus On Food And Fun

The table is set, the flowers are arranged, and the roast is ready—everything is right for a dinner party at the home of Pankey and Tee Kite in Macon, Georgia. You're wondering about the rest of the menu? Well, it comes with the guests and falls into place like a puzzle as each couple arrives. It's the scene of a well-organized supper club where the members share the work and expense of every meal and rotate hosting the party on a regular basis.

When it comes to the food, each menu is carefully planned to offer something new. The hostess of each party plans the entire menu, and finds all the recipes and assigns each couple what she wants them to bring. Past themes

have included foreign menus, holiday spreads, and regional favorites.

Because of the nature of the supper club, the recipes are usually those that can be prepared in one place and transported to another. Last minute reheating or final preparations are done in the hostess' kitchen.

Besides the recipes from the Macon group, we've included some tips from supper clubs around the South.

Flaming Cheese
Fruit   Crackers
French Lettuce Salad
Standing Rib Roast
Broccoli With Wine Sauce
Julienne Carrots With Walnuts
Croissants
Strawberry Meringues
Wine

FLAMING CHEESE

½ pound Kasseri cheese
1 tablespoon butter or margarine, melted
2 tablespoons brandy
Juice of ½ lemon
Grapes
Assorted crackers
Apple wedges

Cut cheese into 3 wedges; place in a shallow heatproof serving dish. Brush cheese with butter; broil 7 to 8 inches from heat about 5 to 6 minutes or until browned and bubbly.

Heat brandy until warm. Ignite with a match, and pour over cheese; add lemon juice. Garnish with grape clusters. Serve immediately with crackers and apple wedges. Yield: about 14 appetizer servings.

Note: Mozzarella cheese may be substituted for Kasseri cheese; decrease broiling time to 4 minutes.

FRENCH LETTUCE SALAD

5 cups torn Boston lettuce
5 cups torn endive
5 cups torn leaf lettuce
5 cups torn romaine lettuce
⅓ cup olive oil
⅓ cup vegetable oil
¼ cup white wine vinegar
½ teaspoon salt
½ teaspoon dry mustard
¼ teaspoon pepper
Radish roses

Combine lettuce in a large bowl; set aside. Combine next 6 ingredients in a jar. Cover tightly, and shake vigorously. Pour over salad greens; toss lightly. Garnish with radish roses. Yield: 14 servings.

STANDING RIB ROAST

1 (8- to 10-pound) standing rib
    roast
Garlic salt
Seasoning salt
Pepper
Spiced crab apples
Fresh parsley sprigs

Sprinkle roast on all sides with garlic salt, seasoning salt, and pepper; place roast, fat side up, on a rack in a roasting pan. Insert a meat thermometer, making sure bulb does not touch fat or bone. Bake, uncovered, at 325° about 3 to 4 hours until meat thermometer reaches 140°. Remove from oven. Trim fat from roast; bake 10 minutes at 400° or until browned. Slice roast and place slices on a serving platter. Garnish with spiced crab apples and parsley. Yield: 16 to 20 servings.

Note: Bake roast to an internal temperature of 150° for medium rare and 160° for medium.

BROCCOLI WITH WINE SAUCE

1 cup mayonnaise
¼ cup Chablis or other dry white wine
1 teaspoon lemon juice
¼ to ½ teaspoon curry powder
2 (1-pound) bunches fresh broccoli
Pimiento strips

Combine first 4 ingredients in a small saucepan. Place over low heat; cook until thoroughly heated. (Do not boil.)

Trim off large leaves of broccoli, and remove tough ends of stalks. Wash broccoli, and separate into spears. Cook, covered, in a small amount of boiling water 10 minutes or until tender.

Arrange spears on a platter with flowerets facing edge of platter. Pour sauce down center of spears. Garnish with pimiento strips. Yield: 14 servings.

JULIENNE CARROTS WITH WALNUTS

3 pounds carrots, cut into 3-inch julienne
  strips
2 tablespoons sliced green onions
⅓ cup butter or margarine, melted
2 (3-ounce) packages walnuts, coarsely
  chopped
Fresh parsley sprigs
Walnut halves

Heat 1 inch salted water in a large Dutch oven to boiling. Add carrots and green onions; return to a boil. Cover and simmer 10 minutes or just until carrots are tender. Add butter and chopped walnuts; toss gently. Transfer to a serving dish; garnish with parsley and walnut halves. Yield: 14 servings.

CROISSANTS

1 cup (2 sticks) butter, chilled
⅔ cup milk
2 packages dry yeast
½ cup warm water (105° to 115°)
¼ cup butter, softened
2 tablespoons sugar
1½ teaspoons salt
2 eggs
4 to 4½ cups all-purpose flour
1 egg yolk
1 tablespoon milk

Cut each stick of chilled butter lengthwise into 3 equal pieces. Place 2 pieces side by side between sheets of waxed paper. Flatten butter into an 8-inch square using a rolling pin. Repeat with remaining butter. Chill butter at least 1½ hours.

Scald ⅔ cup milk; cool to 105° to 115°. Dissolve yeast in warm water in a large bowl. Stir in scalded milk, ¼ cup butter, sugar, salt, eggs, and 2 cups flour. Beat until smooth. Gradually stir in enough of the remaining flour to form a soft dough.

Turn dough out onto a floured surface, and knead 5 to 8 minutes until smooth and elastic. Place in a well-greased bowl, turning to grease top. Cover and let rise in a warm place (85°), free from drafts, 1 hour or until doubled in bulk. Punch dough down. Cover and chill 1 hour.

Punch dough down, and turn out onto a lightly floured surface; roll into a 25- x 10-inch rectangle. Place 1 square of firm butter on center of dough. Fold dough over butter to make 3 layers. Turn dough one quarter turn, and roll out. Repeat twice, placing butter square on center each time. Cut dough crosswise into halves, and cover and refrigerate for 1 hour.

Remove half of dough from refrigerator; roll into a 12- x 8-inch rectangle. Cut in half lengthwise; cut each half crosswise into 3 squares. Cut each square diagonally into 2 triangles. Roll up each triangle tightly, beginning at wide end. Seal points, and place point side down on greased baking sheets; curve into crescent shapes. Repeat with remaining dough. Refrigerate 30 minutes. Combine egg yolk and 1 tablespoon milk; brush over croissants. Bake at 475° for 5 minutes; decrease oven temperature to 400°. Bake 8 to 10 minutes or until golden brown. Yield: about 2 dozen.

STRAWBERRY MERINGUES

6 egg whites
½ teaspoon cream of tartar
1½ cups sugar
1½ cups whipping cream
¾ cup sifted powdered sugar
2¾ cups sliced strawberries
Kiwi slices
Strawberry fans

Beat egg whites (at room temperature) in large bowl at high speed of an electric mixer until foamy; sprinkle cream of tartar over egg whites, and continue beating until soft peaks form. Gradually add sugar, 1 tablespoon at a time, beating until stiff peaks form. (Do not underbeat the mixture.)

Drop meringue by one-fourth cupfuls onto a cookie sheet lined with unglazed brown paper. (Do not use recycled paper.) Shape meringue into 3-inch ovals. Bake at 225° for 1 hour. Turn off oven; cool in oven 1 hour. Carefully remove meringues from paper; cool completely on wire racks.

Beat whipping cream until soft peaks form; gradually add powdered sugar, beating until stiff. Fold strawberries into whipped cream.

Spread the whipped cream mixture between two meringue ovals (flat sides together). Garnish meringues with kiwi slices and strawberry fans. Yield: about 14 servings.

Tip: When food boils over in the oven, sprinkle the burned surface with a little salt. This will stop smoke and odor from forming and make the spot easier to clean. Also, rubbing damp salt on dishes in which food has been baked will remove brown spots.

Start a Supper Club— Here's How

Supper clubs aren't anything new to Southerners. After talking with folks from Texas to Florida, we found that many groups have been gathering for up to 10 years. Each group varies in some way to suit the needs and creative yearnings of the members. Use their ideas and suggestions for starting your own club or for adding a new twist to an existing one.

Rules are essential, says Carter Fitzgerald, initiator of a dinner group in Lakeland, Florida. "Then all members know their obligations to each other." Carter and her supper club enjoy spending extra time planning decorations, costumes, and entertainment, especially for the foreign theme meals. They added sparkle to an Oktoberfest menu by inviting an accordian player to provide authentic German music.

Although most supper clubs operate in the same fashion as the Kites' club in Macon where each person brings food to the party, some clubs prefer to cook together in one kitchen. The Bon Appétit supper club in Columbia, South Carolina, is an example.

One of the most elaborate supper club organizations we found is in Houston. Lucy Hack says that the club grew from a small "new neighbors" club nine years ago to a 20-couple dinner club. To accommodate everyone, all the couples meet the same night with four to five couples gathering in each of three or four homes.

The possibilities are endless for making your own supper club unique. However, some basic problems plague every group. So when drawing up the plans for a new supper club, heed the advice of seasoned club members and keep the following points in mind.

Determine the number of members the group will have—Most of the club members indicated that 8 to 12 people is a convenient number. Dining space and dinnerware of each member should determine the number each person can entertain comfortably.

Decide how the menus will be selected—Whether the menu is a group decision or up to the host and hostess, each member should be aware of his responsibilities. Determine how the menus and recipes will be distributed before the meeting.

Agree on a method for selecting a time to meet—It doesn't need to be a set night, but the deciding process should be consistent enough so members know what to expect.

Discuss expenses—Plan how to fairly distribute the cost of the food, whether it's rotating who provides the most expensive item at each meeting or dividing the cost of each meal.

Make plans for cancellations—Have a procedure for members to follow if they must bow out of a scheduled meeting. Some groups suggest inviting an alternate. If cancellation is last-minute, the member might be asked to make arrangements for getting his assigned dish to the meeting.

Entrées Glisten With Aspic

The next time you're looking for recipes that are cool and refreshing, try one of these aspic-and-entrée combinations.

Aspic is always served chilled, and its unique jelling properties open up endless ways to use it. As a bonus to the pretty appearance and great flavors of aspic entrées, you can make them ahead of time, and they'll wait patiently in your refrigerator until the dinner bell rings. In fact, these recipes require that you make them early to give the aspic time to jell. While refrigerated, the aspic keeps the food moist and fresh.

Working With Gelatin

These recipes depend on unflavored gelatin for their jelling properties. Always soften this type of gelatin in cold liquid, letting it stand one minute; then cook and stir the gelatin mixture over low heat until the gelatin dissolves. If you don't let the entire dissolving process take place, the gelatin will be lumpy and won't have as much jelling ability. Then set the mixture aside at room temperature to cool to the consistency specified in the recipe.

Embedding Entrées in Aspic

Setting entrées in aspic is one of the easiest ways to team the two foods. Cook the meat beforehand, and chill it thoroughly before adding aspic.

Aspic mixtures for embedding need to be more concentrated than you may be used to—about one cup of liquid to one envelope gelatin. Dissolve the gelatin, and let the mixture sit at room temperature until cooled and syrupy.

Arrange the meat on a luncheon-size plate, and pour the aspic around the meat. Arrange individual garnishes around the meat, actually embedding them in the aspic, too. Cover and chill until firm.

Molding With Aspic

Aspics for molding keep the same proportion of liquid to gelatin as for traditional molded vegetable salads. In our recipe for Fish 'n Aspic, the aspic mixture cools slightly at room temperature; then a chilling and layering process begins, which builds the mold. As you layer the fish and aspic mixture, leave the unused aspic at room temperature to keep it pourable.

Chill the molded mixture thoroughly—at least six hours—before trying to unmold it. To help break the suction, carefully run a knife around the edge of the mold. If the mold has very curved or fluted sides, then press the edge of the congealed mixture lightly with your finger, and gently pull away from the sides of the mold. Then invert the mold on the serving platter.

Garnishing With Aspic

Setting garnishes with aspic, as in our Snapper With Dill, makes a dramatic presentation for company. The aspic mixture for drizzling over garnishes is more concentrated than for most other techniques—three-fourths cup liquid to one envelope gelatin. Dissolve the gelatin, and let sit at room temperature until cooled and syrupy. Cook the fish and prepare garnishes ahead of time; chill fish and garnishes until ready to add the aspic.

Place fish on a wire rack set in a larger pan, and drizzle a thin coating of aspic over fish. Arrange garnishes on fish as desired; then drizzle a thin layer of aspic over the top of fish and garnishes. Chill 10 minutes; then continue the drizzling and chilling process several times until you've built up a thin, smooth layer of aspic. Don't worry if the first couple of layers aren't smooth; the coating will smooth out with subsequent layers.

Leave the aspic at room temperature throughout the entire drizzling period. If aspic sets too much before you've finished drizzling, just reheat it over very low heat, stirring constantly, until it's melted. Let cool again, if necessary.

When drizzling is complete, chill the food until firm, and transfer to a serving platter. Insert wooden picks in several places around food; then cover with plastic wrap. Chill until ready to serve.

Selecting Garnishes

Plan garnishes for these aspics with an eye to color, texture, and flavor.

For our entrées, we made simple vegetable flowers out of turnips, carrots, and yellow squash, and leaves out of carrots and cucumber. To make flowers and leaves, simply cut ⅛-inch slices of the vegetables (crosswise if you want the inside color of the vegetable, like turnips, and lengthwise along the outside if you want the skin color, like green from cucumbers and yellow from squash). Then cut the slices into flowers or leaves using small canapé cutters, or carve them with a paring knife. Ripe olive slices and small pieces of pimiento make good flower centers.

Other garnishes that work nicely are snow peas, lemon slices, green onion or chive stems, and sprigs of fresh herbs.

Be Creative With Aspic

After trying these entrée recipes, keep in mind that almost any smooth surface can be glazed and garnished, including chilled pâtés and terrines, cheese with edible rinds, even molded gelatin dishes themselves. For experimenting with aspic on your own, our recipe for Basic Aspic for Garnishing will be a good guide.

The aspic coating you use for experimentation can be varied, depending on your taste preferences. It can be flavored with chicken, beef, or vegetable-flavored bouillon granules (which color the gelatin pale gold) or tomato juice (which colors it bright red). You can also use no flavoring at all for a clear glaze when the purpose is simply to embed garnishes or add shine. Our one basic recipe includes variations for each of these flavors. Use the larger amount of liquid for embedding foods on top of aspic, and the smaller amount for drizzling over garnishes.

BASIC ASPIC FOR GARNISHING

1 envelope unflavored gelatin
¾ to 1 cup water or tomato juice
½ to 1 teaspoon beef, chicken, or
vegetable-flavored bouillon granules
(optional)

Soften gelatin in water in a small saucepan. Add bouillon granules to saucepan, if desired; bring mixture to a boil, stirring until gelatin and bouillon granules dissolve. Remove mixture from heat. Use aspic when cooled and syrupy, and before the mixture begins to set. Yield: ¾ to 1 cup.

CHICKEN IN TOMATO ASPIC

½ cup commercial Italian salad
    dressing
2 tablespoons tarragon vinegar
1 teaspoon dried whole basil
1 clove garlic, minced
4 chicken breast halves, skinned and
    boned
1 cup tomato juice
1 tablespoon tarragon vinegar
1 teaspoon Worcestershire sauce
1 envelope unflavored gelatin
12 snow peas
4 turnip flowers
4 black olive slices
8 carrot leaves

Combine first 4 ingredients in a jar; cover tightly, and shake vigorously. Pour over chicken in a shallow dish; cover and refrigerate at least 6 hours.

Remove chicken from marinade, reserving marinade. Place chicken on rack in a broiler pan. Broil 6 inches from heat source 4 minutes on each side, basting occasionally with marinade. Transfer chicken to a platter; cool completely. Cover, and chill thoroughly.

Combine tomato juice, 1 tablespoon vinegar, and Worcestershire sauce in a small saucepan; sprinkle gelatin over mixture, and let stand 1 minute. Cook over low heat, stirring until gelatin dissolves. Remove from heat; let stand until mixture is cooled and syrupy (this is just before mixture begins to set).

For each serving, arrange a chicken breast half on a luncheon-size serving plate. Pour ¼ cup aspic mixture around each piece of chicken; carefully arrange vegetables in aspic as desired. Cover and chill until firm. Yield: 4 servings.

SNAPPER WITH DILL

1½ cups Chablis or other dry white
    wine
1½ cups water
½ teaspoon salt
8 peppercorns
1 (2-pound) dressed red snapper
Fish Aspic
Optional garnishes: minced fresh dillweed,
    pimiento-stuffed olive slices, fresh dill
    stalk, carrot flowers, turnip flowers,
    yellow squash flowers, radish flowers,
    cucumber leaves, ripe olive slices
Sprigs of fresh dill (optional)
Horseradish Sauce

Combine first 4 ingredients in a fish poacher or electric skillet; bring to a boil, and add snapper. Cover, reduce heat, and simmer 20 minutes or until snapper flakes easily. Carefully transfer fish to a wire rack; place rack in a jelly-roll pan. Cover and chill thoroughly. Discard cooking liquid.

Drizzle a thin coating of Fish Aspic over fish, spreading smoothly with the back of a spoon, if necessary. Chill 10 to 15 minutes or until aspic sets. Sprinkle snapper head with minced dillweed; place a pimiento-stuffed olive slice over eye. Place dill stalk down center of snapper; arrange remaining vegetable garnishes in place as desired. Drizzle a thin coating of aspic over snapper; chill 10 to 15 minutes or until aspic sets. Repeat drizzling and chilling process until fish is coated with aspic; chill until firm. Transfer to serving platter, and garnish with sprigs of dill, if desired. Serve snapper with Horseradish Sauce. Yield: 4 to 6 servings.

Fish Aspic:

1 envelope unflavored gelatin
¾ cup Chablis or other dry white wine
½ teaspoon vegetable-flavored bouillon
    granules

Sprinkle gelatin over wine in a small saucepan, and let stand 1 minute. Add bouillon granules to saucepan; cook over low heat, stirring until gelatin and bouillon granules dissolve. Remove from heat; use when mixture is just cooled and syrupy (just before mixture begins to set). Yield: ¾ cup.

Horseradish Sauce:

¾ cup whipping cream, whipped
2 teaspoons prepared horseradish
1 teaspoon minced fresh dillweed
¼ teaspoon garlic salt
Minced fresh dillweed

Combine first 4 ingredients; mix well. Spoon into serving container; sprinkle with dillweed. Yield: about 1½ cups.

FISH 'N ASPIC

2 cups water
¼ cup lemon juice
½ teaspoon salt
5 peppercorns
2 bay leaves
12 ounces sole or flounder fillets
2 (8-ounce) cans tomato sauce
2 cups tomato juice
2 tablespoons lemon juice
½ teaspoon celery salt
2 envelopes unflavored gelatin
½ medium cucumber, peeled, seeded, and
    finely diced
Quartered lemon slices
Chives
Fresh parsley sprigs
Tarragon Sauce

Combine first 5 ingredients in a medium saucepan; bring to a boil. Add fish; reduce heat and simmer, uncovered, 4 to 5 minutes or until fish flakes easily. Gently remove fish using a slotted spatula; cool completely. Flake into large pieces, and chill. Discard liquid.

Combine tomato sauce, tomato juice, 2 tablespoons lemon juice, and celery salt in a medium saucepan; sprinkle gelatin over mixture, and let stand 1 minute. Cook over low heat, stirring until gelatin dissolves. Remove from heat; let mixture cool slightly.

Pour 1 cup gelatin mixture in a lightly oiled 6-cup fish mold; refrigerate 20 to 30 minutes or until just set, but not firm. Arrange half of fish pieces down center of mold, leaving a ½-inch border at sides; sprinkle cucumber evenly over fish. Spoon 1 cup gelatin mixture evenly over cucumber; refrigerate 15 minutes or until just set, but not firm. Arrange remaining fish down center of mold, leaving a ½-inch border at sides; cover with remaining gelatin. Cover and refrigerate 6 hours or until firm.

Unmold onto a serving platter; garnish with lemon slices, chives, and parsley as desired. Serve with Tarragon Sauce. Yield: 6 to 8 servings.

Tarragon Sauce:

½ cup mayonnaise
½ cup commercial sour cream
2 teaspoons lemon juice
1 teaspoon dried whole tarragon, crushed
¼ teaspoon salt
Paprika

Combine first 5 ingredients in a small bowl; cover and refrigerate at least 1 hour. Spoon into a serving dish, and sprinkle with paprika. Yield: 1 cup.

Try A Juicy Melon

Nothing cools you off on a hot summer afternoon like cool, juicy melon. Refreshing is the word for a bowl of cold Fresh Cantaloupe Soup or a stemmed glass full of chilled Honeydew Salad With Apricot Cream Dressing.

FRESH CANTALOUPE SOUP

1 medium cantaloupe, halved and
    seeded
3 cups orange juice
½ teaspoon ground cinnamon
2 tablespoons lime juice

Scoop pulp from cantaloupe. Place cantaloupe pulp and remaining ingredients in container of electric blender; process until smooth. Chill before serving. Yield: 4⅓ cups. *Connie Burgess, Knoxville, Tennessee.*

HONEYDEW SALAD WITH APRICOT CREAM DRESSING

1 (8-ounce) carton commercial sour cream
¼ cup chopped pecans or walnuts
¼ cup flaked coconut
2 tablespoons apricot preserves
3 to 4 cups honeydew balls, chilled

Combine first 4 ingredients; stir well. Spoon melon balls into sherbet or champagne glasses. Top with dressing. Yield: 4 servings. *Veleda Boyd, Conway, Arkansas.*

WATERMELON SPARKLE

½ cup sugar
⅓ cup light rum
3 tablespoons lime juice
6 cups cubed watermelon

Combine first 3 ingredients; stir well. Pour over cubed melon; cover and chill 2 to 3 hours. Yield: 6 servings.
Mrs. Bruce Fowler, Woodruff, South Carolina.

A Few Quick Snack Ideas

The next time you want a snack and want it in a hurry, whip up one of our quick snack ideas. All are made from ingredients kept on-hand, and take only minutes to prepare.

CONFETTI APPETIZERS

1 cup chopped pimiento-stuffed olives
3 green onions with tops, chopped
¾ cup (3 ounces) shredded Monterey Jack cheese
¾ cup (3 ounces) shredded Cheddar cheese
½ teaspoon chili powder
½ cup mayonnaise
8 whole wheat English muffins, split

Combine first 6 ingredients; cover and chill 2 to 3 hours. Spread cut side of each muffin half with 2 tablespoons of the cheese mixture.
Place muffins on cookie sheet, and bake at 400° for 10 to 15 minutes or until bubbly. Cut each muffin half into 4 wedges, and serve warm. Yield: about 5 dozen. *Kathy Hunt, Dallas, Texas.*

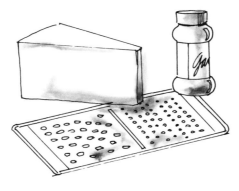

QUICK CHEESE SQUARES

7 slices white bread
1 cup (4 ounces) shredded sharp Cheddar cheese
3 slices bacon, cooked and crumbled
Dash of garlic powder
About ¼ cup grated Parmesan cheese

Trim crust from bread, if desired; reserve for other uses. Cut bread slices into fourths; set aside.
Combine next 3 ingredients. Top each piece of bread with cheese mixture; sprinkle with Parmesan cheese. Broil about 3 inches from heat 1 minute or until bubbly. Serve squares immediately. Yield: about 2 dozen.
John L. Wood, Memphis, Tennessee.

PUFF NIBBLES

6 cups puffed wheat cereal
2 cups unsalted roasted peanuts
½ cup firmly packed brown sugar
¼ cup unsalted butter or margarine, melted
¼ cup honey

Combine cereal, peanuts, and sugar in a large bowl. Combine butter and honey; pour over cereal mixture, tossing gently. Pour into a lightly greased 15- x 10- x 1-inch jellyroll pan. Bake at 275° for 30 to 35 minutes, stirring mixture once. Let cool in pan, stirring occasionally. Yield: 2 quarts.
Mrs. Ross H. Sachs, Lancaster, Pennsylvania.

OLIVE-RYE SNACK CRACKERS

1 (3-ounce) package thinly sliced smoked beef, chopped
1 cup (4 ounces) shredded Cheddar cheese
1 cup sliced ripe olives
½ cup mayonnaise
2½ dozen whole grain rye crackers

Combine first 4 ingredients; spread 1 tablespoon mixture on each cracker. Place on baking sheet; bake at 375° for 5 to 7 minutes or until cheese melts. Yield: 2½ dozen.
Mrs. Ronald D. Smith, Houston, Texas.

Serve An Enticing Summer Dessert

Give a special summer menu a perfect finale with one of our light and airy warm-weather desserts.

MOCHA ALASKA DESSERT

¾ cup vanilla wafer crumbs
¾ cup cinnamon graham cracker crumbs
½ cup finely chopped pecans
½ cup butter or margarine, melted
2 tablespoons cocoa
½ gallon coffee ice cream, softened
6 (1-1/16-ounce) English toffee-flavored candy bars, crushed
1 (7-ounce) jar marshmallow creme
1 tablespoon Kahlúa or other coffee-flavored liqueur
3 egg whites

Combine first 5 ingredients, mixing well. Press mixture evenly into bottom of a 9-inch baking pan. Bake at 350° for 8 minutes. Cool.
Combine softened ice cream and crushed candy bars. Spoon over cooled crust; cover and freeze until firm.
Combine marshmallow creme and liqueur, mixing with wire whisk until blended. Beat egg whites (at room temperature) until foamy. Gradually add marshmallow creme mixture, 1 tablespoon at a time, beating until stiff peaks form. Spread meringue over top of ice cream mixture, making sure edges are sealed. Bake at 475° for 3 minutes or until lightly browned. Yield: 9 servings. *Mary Andrew, Winston-Salem, North Carolina.*

LEMON CHARLOTTE RUSSE

1 envelope unflavored gelatin
½ cup water
4 eggs, separated
1 cup sugar
1 teaspoon grated lemon rind
1½ tablespoons lemon juice
¼ cup sugar
2 cups whipping cream
18 to 24 ladyfingers
2 to 3 tablespoons sliced almonds, toasted

Soften gelatin in water in top of a double boiler; place over boiling water and cook, stirring constantly, until gelatin dissolves.

Beat egg yolks in a large bowl until thick and lemon colored. Gradually add 1 cup sugar, lemon rind, juice, and gelatin mixture, beating well.

Beat egg whites (at room temperature) until foamy. Gradually add ¼ cup sugar, 1 tablespoon at a time, beating until stiff peaks form; gently fold into yolk mixture. Beat whipping cream until stiff peaks form; gently fold into egg mixture. Line sides and bottom of a 3-quart soufflé dish with ladyfingers; pour in half the filling. Layer remaining ladyfingers on top; cover with remaining filling. Sprinkle almonds over top; cover and chill until firm. Yield: 12 to 14 servings.
Sharon Elder,
Phenix City, Alabama.

WALNUT CREAM ROLL

Vegetable oil
2 tablespoons sugar
4 eggs, separated
½ cup plus 2 teaspoons sifted powdered
    sugar
2 tablespoons all-purpose flour
1 cup ground walnuts
½ teaspoon vanilla extract
¼ teaspoon salt
2 tablespoons sifted powdered sugar
Additional powdered sugar
1½ cups whipping cream
¼ cup sifted powdered sugar
½ teaspoon peppermint extract (optional)
Walnut halves (optional)

Grease bottom and sides of a 15- x 10- x 1-inch jellyroll pan with vegetable oil; line with waxed paper. Grease waxed paper with vegetable oil. Sprinkle 2 tablespoons sugar over pan.

Beat egg yolks in a medium bowl at high speed of electric mixer until foamy; gradually add ½ cup plus 2 teaspoons powdered sugar, beating until mixture is thick and lemon colored. Gradually add flour, ground walnuts, and vanilla; mix just until blended.

Beat egg whites (at room temperature) and salt at high speed of electric mixer until foamy. Gradually add 2 tablespoons powdered sugar, 1 tablespoon at a time, beating until stiff peaks form. Gently fold egg whites into yolk mixture. Pour into jellyroll pan, spreading evenly. Bake at 350° for 18 minutes.

Sift powdered sugar in a 15- x 10-inch rectangle on a linen towel. When cake is done, immediately loosen from sides of pan, and turn out on sugar. Peel off waxed paper. Starting at long side, roll up cake and towel together; let cool completely on a wire rack.

Beat whipping cream until foamy; gradually add ¼ cup powdered sugar and peppermint extract, if desired, beating until soft peaks form.

Unroll cake; remove towel. Spread cake with two-thirds of whipped cream mixture, and reroll. Place on serving plate, seam side down. Pipe remaining whipped cream mixture down center of cake, and garnish with walnut halves, if desired. Chill until serving time. Yield: 8 to 10 servings. *Shirley Schlessmann,*
Rockledge, Florida.

FROZEN RASPBERRY DESSERT

1 cup all-purpose flour
½ cup firmly packed light brown sugar
½ cup chopped walnuts
½ cup butter or margarine, melted
2 egg whites
½ cup sugar
1 (10-ounce) package frozen raspberries,
    thawed and drained
2 teaspoons lemon juice
1 (12-ounce) carton frozen whipped
    topping, thawed

Combine first 4 ingredients; mix well. Spread to ¼-inch thickness on an ungreased cookie sheet; bake at 350° for 20 minutes, stirring with a fork every 5 minutes to crumble. Let cool; sprinkle half of crumb mixture in a 13- x 9- x 2-inch baking pan. Set aside; reserve remaining crumb mixture.

Beat egg whites (at room temperature) until foamy. Gradually add ½ cup sugar, 1 tablespoon at a time, beating until stiff peaks form. Gradually stir in raspberries and lemon juice; fold in whipped topping. Spread evenly in pan; sprinkle with reserved crumb mixture. Freeze until firm. Yield: 15 servings.
Ranae Phelps,
Balch Springs, Texas.

COOKING LIGHT

Packing A Lunch? Make It Light

Do daily lunches at the office pose a threat to your low-calorie diet? Here's a variety of lunchbox recipes to help you count calories, yet enjoy a meal that's satisfying enough to get you through a busy day.

For our first menu, freeze individual serving-size cans of orange juice ahead of time. The frozen juice helps keep the sandwich chilled but will still be thawed or slushy by lunchtime. We suggest wrapping lettuce leaves for the sandwich separately to prevent wilting. Carry Crispy Marinated Vegetable Salad in an individual plastic or insulated container. And instead of those high-calorie chips, why not take along a variety of raw, crisp vegetables.

For our second menu, keep Whole Wheat-Macaroni Tuna Salad cold by packing it in a widemouthed vacuum bottle. An Apple Muffin or a few breadsticks (about 25 calories each) taste good with the salad. An orange or other fresh fruit is a convenient, nutritious dessert.

If you're packing our lunch with Vegetarian Pita Sandwiches, we suggest carrying the vegetable filling separately from the bread and assembling the sandwich at mealtime. A widemouthed vacuum bottle will keep Summer Squash Soup hot or cold. Again, fresh fruit is just right for dessert.

Add variety and fiber to your lunchbox by experimenting with different whole grain breads. You can purchase very thinly sliced bread (2 slices contain about the same number of calories as 1 regular slice). Use reduced-calorie margarine or mayonnaise instead of the regular 100-calorie-per-tablespoon kind. Remember that mustard contains only 5 to 10 calories per teaspoon.

A chef's salad is a good lunchtime choice, especially if there's a refrigerator in your office. If one is not available, drop some ice cubes in a watertight bag to pack along with the salad greens. This will help keep them cool and crisp. A low-calorie dressing can be packed in a separate container.

Whenever packing a lunch to eat away from home, be very cautious about food safety. First, be careful that your hands are clean before handling the food, and place the food only in very clean containers.

Store your meal in a refrigerator if possible. Or purchase commercial freezing gels to pack with your lunch. A widemouthed vacuum bottle is excellent for carrying cottage cheese, meat salads, and chilled canned fruit.

A lunchbox tends to keep foods cold longer than a paper bag. But if you prefer the traditional brown bag, purchase bags for that purpose.

Tasty Chicken Spread Sandwiches
Crispy Marinated Vegetable Salad
Fresh Vegetables
Orange Juice

TASTY CHICKEN SPREAD

2 cups minced cooked chicken breast
¼ cup minced dill pickle
3 hard-cooked eggs, finely chopped
½ cup minced celery
½ cup minced apple
1 (4-ounce) jar diced pimiento, drained
¾ cup reduced-calorie mayonnaise
¼ teaspoon salt
¼ teaspoon pepper

Combine all ingredients; cover and chill at least 1 hour. Use as a sandwich filling or to stuff celery. Yield: 3½ cups (about 22 calories per tablespoon).

CRISPY MARINATED VEGETABLE SALAD

1 cup cider vinegar
1⅓ cups unsweetened apple juice
1 teaspoon pepper
1 (10-ounce) package frozen French-style green beans, thawed and drained
1 (10-ounce) package frozen tiny English peas, thawed and drained
1 (12-ounce) can shoe peg whole kernel corn, drained
1 (2-ounce) jar diced pimiento, drained
½ cup diagonally sliced celery
1 small green pepper, finely chopped
½ cup chopped green onions

Combine first 3 ingredients; set aside. Combine remaining ingredients; pour marinade over vegetables, stirring gently. Cover and refrigerate overnight, stirring occasionally. Yield: 12 servings (about 58 calories per ½-cup serving).

Tip: Plastic bags that have been used to wrap dry foods, vegetables, and fruit can often be washed and reused.

Whole Wheat Macaroni-Tuna Salad
Commercial Breadsticks
or
Apple Muffin
Fresh Orange
Skim Milk

WHOLE WHEAT MACARONI-TUNA SALAD

1⅔ cups uncooked whole wheat seashell macaroni
¾ pound fresh broccoli
1 large tomato, unpeeled and coarsely chopped
2 small green onions with tops, thinly sliced
1 (6½-ounce) can water-packed tuna, drained
1 tablespoon chopped fresh basil or 1 teaspoon dried whole basil
½ tablespoon chopped fresh oregano or ½ teaspoon dried whole oregano
2 tablespoons red wine vinegar
1 tablespoon olive oil
⅛ teaspoon salt
Freshly ground black pepper

Cook macaroni according to package directions, omitting salt. Drain and rinse with cold water.

Trim off large outer leaves of broccoli, and remove tough ends of lower stalks. Wash broccoli thoroughly; cut flowerets into bite-size pieces, and slice stalks thinly. Steam broccoli 4 to 6 minutes or until crisp-tender; cool.

Combine macaroni, broccoli, tomato, green onions, and tuna in a large bowl; toss gently. Combine remaining ingredients in a jar; cover tightly, and shake vigorously. Pour dressing over salad, and toss to coat. Chill several hours, stirring occasionally. Yield: 6 servings (about 153 calories per serving).
Ruby Kirkes,
Tuskahoma, Oklahoma.

APPLE MUFFINS

1 cup peeled, finely chopped apple
1 tablespoon honey
1⅔ cups all-purpose flour
¼ cup sugar
2 teaspoons baking powder
1 teaspoon ground cinnamon
¼ teaspoon salt
1 egg, beaten
⅔ cup skim milk
3 tablespoons margarine, melted
Vegetable cooking spray

Combine apple and honey; set aside.
Combine next 5 ingredients in a medium bowl; make a well in center of mixture. Combine egg, milk, and margarine. Add to dry ingredients; stir just until moistened. Stir in apple mixture.

Place paper liners in muffin pans; coat liners with cooking spray. Spoon batter into liners, filling two-thirds full. Bake at 400° for 18 minutes. Yield: 1 dozen (about 118 calories each).
Ruth Moffitt,
Smyrna, Delaware.

Vegetarian Pita Sandwiches
Summer Squash Soup
Fresh Apple
Water

VEGETARIAN PITA SANDWICHES

1 (16-ounce) can garbanzo beans, drained
2 cups shredded romaine lettuce
2 green onions, thinly sliced
½ cup chopped celery
½ cup chopped green pepper
½ cup crumbled feta cheese
½ cup Italian reduced-calorie salad dressing
¼ cup thinly sliced ripe olives
4 (6-inch) whole wheat pita bread rounds

Combine first 8 ingredients, tossing gently; cover and chill overnight.

Cut bread rounds in half; spoon sandwich mixture into bread, and serve immediately. Yield: 4 servings (about 332 calories per serving).

Note: For lunchbox, place filling in a covered plastic container or a widemouthed vacuum bottle; assemble sandwich at mealtime.

SUMMER SQUASH SOUP

2 cups water
2 beef-flavored bouillon cubes
2 medium zucchini, sliced
2 medium onions, sliced
⅛ teaspoon hot sauce
Freshly ground pepper to taste
¼ cup plus 2 tablespoons plain yogurt

Combine first 4 ingredients in a medium saucepan; bring to a boil. Cover, reduce heat, and simmer 10 to 15 minutes. Add hot sauce and pepper.

Spoon squash mixture into container of electric blender; add yogurt. Process until smooth. Serve hot or cold. Yield: 4 cups (about 50 calories per 1-cup serving). *Mrs. Donald C. Kiscaden,*
Staunton, Virginia.

Fill yellow squash shells with a spicy shrimp mixture for Shrimp-Stuffed Yellow Squash, or cut zucchini into julienne strips for a cheese-flavored Zucchini Pesto.

Summer Squash At Its Best

Bright yellow squash and slender zucchini fill produce stands in August, and our readers have discovered some delicious ways to prepare them.

SHRIMP-STUFFED YELLOW SQUASH

6 medium-size yellow squash
1½ cups water
½ pound unpeeled medium shrimp
1 large onion, finely chopped
1 clove garlic, crushed
3 tablespoons butter or margarine
½ teaspoon salt
⅛ teaspoon pepper
1 cup soft breadcrumbs
1 egg, beaten
1 teaspoon chopped fresh parsley
½ teaspoon dried whole thyme
½ cup crumbled, cooked bacon
½ cup fine, dry breadcrumbs
1 tablespoon butter or margarine, melted

Wash squash; cook in boiling salted water to cover 8 minutes or until tender, but still firm. Drain and cool slightly. Trim off stems. Cut squash in half lengthwise, and remove the pulp, leaving a firm shell. Coarsely chop pulp, and set aside.

Bring 1½ cups water to a boil; add shrimp, and return to a boil. Reduce heat and simmer 3 to 5 minutes. Drain shrimp well, and rinse with cold water. Cool. Peel and devein shrimp; chop and set aside.

Sauté onion and garlic in 3 tablespoons butter until tender. Stir in salt, pepper, soft breadcrumbs, and reserved squash pulp. Cook over medium heat 5 minutes, stirring frequently. Remove from heat; cool. Stir in egg, parsley, thyme, bacon, and shrimp; mix well.

Place squash shells in a 13- x 9- x 2-inch baking dish. Spoon shrimp mixture into shells. Combine dry breadcrumbs and 1 tablespoon butter. Sprinkle over each squash half. Bake at 375° for 25 minutes. Yield: 6 servings.
Frances Gray,
Fort Worth, Texas.

ZUCCHINI PESTO

6 small zucchini, cut into julienne strips
Salt
1½ cups fresh basil leaves, chopped
2 tablespoons olive oil
3 tablespoons pine nuts
2 cloves garlic
1 cup grated Parmesan cheese
½ teaspoon salt
3 tablespoons butter or margarine, divided

Lightly sprinkle zucchini with salt; set aside to drain.

Position knife blade in processor bowl; add basil, olive oil, pine nuts, and garlic. Process until smooth. Add Parmesan cheese, ½ teaspoon salt, and 2 tablespoons butter; process 10 seconds or until well blended.

Sauté zucchini in remaining 1 tablespoon butter about 3 minutes or until crisp-tender. Stir in basil mixture, tossing gently to coat. Serve immediately. Yield: 6 to 8 servings. *Lynette Walther,*
East Palatka, Florida.

ZUCCHINI MANICOTTI

10 to 12 uncooked manicotti shells
1 large zucchini, diced
2 tablespoons butter or margarine
1 (12-ounce) carton cottage cheese
1½ cups (6 ounces) shredded Cheddar cheese, divided
1 (6-ounce) can tomato paste
1¼ cups boiling water
1 (1.5-ounce) envelope sloppy joe seasoning mix

Cook manicotti shells according to package directions; drain and set aside.

Sauté zucchini in butter in a large skillet 6 to 8 minutes. Remove from heat; add cottage cheese and 1 cup Cheddar cheese, mixing well. Stuff manicotti shells with cheese mixture; arrange in a lightly greased 12- x 8- x 2-inch baking dish.

Combine tomato paste, water, and sloppy joe mix, stirring well; pour over manicotti. Cover with foil, and bake at 350° for 30 minutes. Remove foil; sprinkle with remaining Cheddar cheese, and bake an additional 10 minutes. Yield: 6 servings.
Mary Kay Menees,
White Pine, Tennessee.

Tip: Check foods closely as you are shopping to be sure they are not spoiled before you purchase them. Do not buy cans that are badly dented, leaking, or bulging at the ends. Do not select presealed packages which have broken seals.

Choose An Entrée And Salad For Two

If you're looking for salads and entrées sized just for two, here are recipes for you to try.

STUFFED PORK CHOPS

½ small onion, chopped
1 tablespoon butter or margarine
¼ cup chopped, cooked ham
½ cup sliced fresh mushrooms
¼ teaspoon dried whole oregano
Dash of pepper
2 (1-inch-thick) pork chops
2 tablespoons butter or margarine
½ cup dry sherry
Fresh parsley sprigs
Fresh mushroom slices

Sauté onion in 1 tablespoon butter until tender; remove from heat. Add ham, mushrooms, oregano, and pepper; mix well, and set aside.

Make pockets in pork chops, cutting from rib side just to beginning of fat edge of each chop. Stuff pockets of pork chops with ham mixture.

Brown pork chops in 2 tablespoons butter in a medium skillet over medium-low heat about 5 minutes on each side. Add sherry; cover, reduce heat, and simmer 45 to 50 minutes or until pork chops are tender. Remove to serving platter; garnish with parsley and mushroom slices. Yield: 2 servings.
Mrs. B. K. Davisson,
Montgomery, Alabama.

STIR-FRY VEGETABLES WITH CHICKEN

¼ cup vegetable oil, divided
2 small boneless chicken breast halves, skinned and cut into 1-inch pieces
1 medium zucchini, sliced
1 medium-size green pepper, cut into strips
1 small onion, cut into eighths
1 cup sliced fresh mushrooms
2 tablespoons dry sherry
1 tablespoon cornstarch
3 tablespoons water
1 tablespoon soy sauce
1 cup hot cooked rice
Additional soy sauce (optional)

Pour 3 tablespoons oil into a preheated wok or large skillet; heat at medium high (325°) for 2 minutes. Add chicken, and stir-fry 2 to 3 minutes or until lightly browned. Remove chicken; set aside.

Pour remaining tablespoon of oil in wok; heat at medium high 2 minutes. Add vegetables and sherry; cover and cook 2 to 3 minutes or until vegetables are crisp-tender. Combine cornstarch, water, and 1 tablespoon soy sauce; stir well. Add mixture and chicken to vegetables. Reduce heat; simmer, stirring constantly, until thickened. Serve over rice with additional soy sauce, if desired. Yield: 2 servings.
Laura D. Hare,
Bahama, North Carolina.

CHICKEN BRANDADO

2 chicken breast halves, skinned and boned
1 clove garlic, minced
2 tablespoons butter or margarine
½ cup Chablis or other dry white wine
¼ cup brandy
½ cup whipping cream
1 egg yolk, slightly beaten
⅛ teaspoon salt
⅛ teaspoon ground nutmeg
Dash of pepper

Cook chicken and garlic in butter in a medium skillet 15 minutes or until chicken is golden, turning once. Add wine and brandy (do not stir). With a long match, ignite brandy mixture; shake pan until flame goes out. Cover, reduce heat, and simmer 15 minutes or until chicken is tender. Remove chicken to a serving platter, and set aside.

Combine remaining ingredients, stirring well; add to pan juices. Cook over medium heat, stirring constantly, until thickened and bubbly. Pour sauce over chicken. Yield: 2 servings.
Susie Lavenue,
Ridgely, Tennessee.

BLUE CHEESE TOSSED SALAD

¼ cup vegetable oil
2 tablespoons vinegar
½ teaspoon sugar
¼ teaspoon salt
⅛ teaspoon paprika
1 cup sliced cauliflower
1 small onion, sliced and separated into rings
2 tablespoons sliced pimiento-stuffed olives
2 cups torn lettuce
1 ounce blue cheese, crumbled

Combine first 5 ingredients; mix well. Combine cauliflower, onion, and olives in a small bowl; pour dressing over top,

and mix well. Cover and chill at least 1 hour. Add lettuce and cheese; toss gently to coat. Serve salad immediately. Yield: 2 servings. *Mrs. Roy Sweeney,*
Louisville, Tennessee.

HAM COLESLAW

1 cup shredded cabbage
½ cup cubed, cooked ham
2 tablespoons chopped green pepper
1 tablespoon chopped pimiento, drained
2 tablespoons vegetable oil
1 tablespoon vinegar
½ teaspoon sugar
½ teaspoon celery seeds
¼ teaspoon salt
¼ teaspoon dry mustard
⅛ teaspoon pepper
⅛ teaspoon paprika

Combine first 4 ingredients; mix well. Combine remaining ingredients; mix well. Pour over cabbage mixture, and toss gently. Serve immediately. Yield: 2 servings. *Reba B. Wilson,*
Jasper, Alabama.

SUMMERTIME SALAD

½ small head lettuce, torn
2 hard-cooked eggs, chopped
½ cup frozen English peas, thawed
4 slices bacon, cooked and crumbled
½ cup (2 ounces) shredded Swiss cheese
½ teaspoon finely chopped onion
½ cup finely chopped celery
¼ cup mayonnaise
⅛ teaspoon salt
⅛ teaspoon pepper
Hard-cooked egg slices

Combine all ingredients except egg slices in a salad bowl; toss gently. Garnish each serving with hard-cooked egg slices. Serve the salad immediately. Yield: 2 servings. *Angela B. Arnold,*
Tullahoma, Tennessee.

Three Ways With Peas And Beans

Warm, sunny days bring an abundance of freshly shelled black-eyed peas, lima beans, and English peas. They're delicious cooked and eaten by themselves, but they offer even more menu possibilities when they're combined in dishes with other vegetables.

CREAMY PEAS WITH MUSHROOMS

6 cups shelled fresh English peas
½ cup finely chopped onion
¼ cup butter or margarine
1 (4½-ounce) jar sliced mushrooms, drained
1 (8-ounce) carton commercial sour cream
2 tablespoons slivered almonds, toasted

Cover peas with water, and bring to a boil. Cover, reduce heat, and simmer 10 to 15 minutes or until peas are tender. Drain and set aside.

Sauté onion in butter in a large skillet for 2 minutes. Add mushrooms; cook, stirring occasionally, 1 minute. Add peas; fold in sour cream and almonds. Cook just until thoroughly heated (do not boil). Yield: 8 to 10 servings.

Mrs. Ed Stetz, Jr.,
Johnstown, Pennsylvania.

TOMATO-PEA DELIGHT

2 cups shelled fresh black-eyed peas
3 slices bacon
2 tablespoons chopped fresh mushrooms
2 tablespoons chopped green pepper
2 tablespoons finely chopped onion
1 (14½-ounce) can tomatoes, drained and chopped
¼ cup tomato sauce
¼ to ½ teaspoon salt
¼ teaspoon chili powder
¼ teaspoon pepper

Cover peas with water, and bring to a boil. Cover, reduce heat, and simmer 15 to 18 minutes or until peas are tender. Drain and set aside.

Fry bacon until crisp; remove bacon, reserving drippings in skillet. Crumble bacon, and set aside. Sauté mushrooms, green pepper, and onion in drippings until tender. Combine sautéed mixture with peas, bacon, and remaining ingredients, stirring well. Cook over low heat just until thoroughly heated. Serve immediately. Yield: 6 to 8 servings.

Gay Evaldi,
East Windsor, New Jersey.

LIMA BEANS AND CARROTS WITH SAVORY SAUCE

2 cups shelled fresh baby lima beans
½ pound baby carrots
1 tablespoon butter or margarine, melted
Savory Sauce

Cover beans with water, and bring to a boil. Cover, reduce heat, and simmer 20 minutes or until tender. Cover carrots with water, and bring to a boil. Cover, reduce heat, and simmer 15 minutes or until tender. Drain vegetables well. Combine vegetables, and toss with butter; place in a 2-quart casserole. Pour Savory Sauce over vegetables, and toss to coat. Serve immediately. Yield: 6 servings.

Savory Sauce:

2 tablespoons butter or margarine
2 tablespoons all-purpose flour
1½ cups chicken broth
3 tablespoons whipping cream
1 egg yolk, beaten
1 tablespoon chopped fresh parsley
½ teaspoon ground savory
⅛ teaspoon pepper

Melt butter in a heavy saucepan over low heat. Add flour, stirring until smooth. Cook 1 minute, stirring constantly. Gradually add broth; cook over medium heat, stirring constantly.

Combine cream and egg yolk, mixing well. Gradually stir about one-fourth of hot mixture into yolk mixture; add to remaining hot mixture, stirring constantly. Stir in remaining ingredients. Cook over medium heat 2 minutes, stirring constantly. Yield: about 1¾ cups.

Mike Singleton,
Scotts Hill, Tennessee.

Rice That's Ready For Company

You may think of rice as rather dull and uninteresting. But Fruit-and-Vegetable Rice Pilaf won't have that reputation. Raisins, carrots, apple, celery, and almonds give this dish excitement.

BROWN RICE PARMESAN

1 cup uncooked brown rice
½ cup chopped onion
2 tablespoons butter or margarine
½ cup grated Parmesan cheese
4 slices bacon, cooked and crumbled

Cook rice according to package directions, reducing salt to ½ teaspoon; set aside. Sauté onion in butter until tender. Add onion and Parmesan cheese to cooked rice; mix well. Sprinkle with bacon. Yield: 4 servings.

Betty Matteson,
Beverly, Massachusetts.

SPANISH BROWN RICE

1½ cups uncooked brown rice
¼ pound fresh mushrooms, sliced
2 small sweet red peppers, chopped
1 large onion, chopped
1 clove garlic, minced
2 tablespoons butter or margarine
2 cups peeled, chopped tomato
1 tablespoon minced fresh cilantro or parsley
2 tablespoons soy sauce
⅛ teaspoon pepper

Cook brown rice according to directions on the package, and set aside.

Sauté mushrooms, red peppers, onion, and garlic in butter in a large skillet 5 to 7 minutes or until vegetables are tender. Stir in the rice and remaining ingredients; cook until thoroughly heated. Yield: 6 servings.

Lisa Robinson,
Little Rock, Arkansas.

FRUIT-AND-VEGETABLE RICE PILAF

¼ cup raisins
½ cup water
2 cups chicken broth
1 cup uncooked regular rice
1 tablespoon butter or margarine
½ teaspoon salt
½ teaspoon poultry seasoning
⅛ teaspoon pepper
1 carrot, scraped and diced
1 cooking apple, chopped
1 stalk celery, thinly sliced
¼ cup slivered almonds, toasted
Thin apple wedges (optional)

Combine raisins and water in a small saucepan; cover and cook over medium heat 5 minutes or until raisins are soft. Drain, and set aside.

Combine next 6 ingredients in a medium saucepan. Cover and bring to a boil; reduce heat and simmer 15 minutes. Remove from heat, and stir in carrot, apple, celery, almonds, and raisins. Cover pan, and let stand 5 minutes. Garnish with thin apple wedges, if desired.

Mrs. Robert H. Kirk,
Winchester, Virginia.

PARSLEY RICE

¾ cup thinly sliced green onions
2 to 3 tablespoons vegetable oil
1 cup uncooked regular rice
½ cup minced green pepper
¼ cup minced fresh parsley
2 cups chicken broth
½ teaspoon salt
¼ teaspoon pepper

Sauté onions in hot oil in a large skillet until tender. Add remaining ingredients; cover and simmer 20 minutes or until liquid is absorbed and rice is tender. Yield: 6 servings.
Mrs. Joe E. Payne,
Midland, Texas.

FRIED RICE

1 cup uncooked regular rice
1 teaspoon vegetable oil
1 egg, beaten
½ cup diced pork
2 strips bacon, diced
1 tablespoon vegetable oil
½ cup chopped fresh mushrooms
2 green onions, sliced
2 tablespoons soy sauce

Cook rice according to package directions, omitting salt; set aside.
Heat 1 teaspoon oil in a small skillet; add egg and cook, stirring constantly, until firm but still moist. Set aside.
Cook pork and bacon in 1 tablespoon hot oil in a large skillet until bacon is crisp. Add mushrooms; stir-fry over medium heat 2 minutes. Stir in rice, onions, and soy sauce; stir-fry at medium high 3 minutes. Stir in egg; serve immediately. Yield: 4 servings.
Lisette L. Helveston,
Kannapolis, North Carolina.

No-Cook Recipes Take The Heat Off

When it's too hot to cook, don't bother to turn on your oven. Just head for the refrigerator or the pantry. There you'll find fresh vegetables, juices, and canned products that will help you put a meal on the table without cooking.

FRUITFUL TURKEY SALAD

2 cups chopped, cooked turkey
1 cup finely chopped celery
1 (8-ounce) can pineapple chunks, well drained
1 small banana, sliced
½ cup seedless green grapes
½ cup sliced almonds, toasted
½ cup mayonnaise
¼ cup commercial sour cream
⅛ teaspoon curry powder
Lettuce leaves
Paprika
Cantaloupe slices (optional)

Combine first 6 ingredients, tossing gently. Combine mayonnaise, sour cream, and curry powder; add to turkey mixture, and toss gently. Chill.
Serve on lettuce leaves, and sprinkle with paprika. Serve with cantaloupe slices, if desired. Yield: 6 servings.
Gloria Different,
Harvey, Louisiana.

ORANGE-SHRIMP SALAD

3 cups torn iceberg lettuce
1 cup torn romaine
2 (4¼-ounce) cans shrimp, rinsed and drained
2 (11-ounce) cans mandarin oranges, drained
½ cup slivered almonds, toasted
1 medium onion, thinly sliced
2 tablespoons vinegar
¼ cup vegetable oil
2 teaspoons sesame seeds
2 teaspoons soy sauce
2 teaspoons lemon juice
2 teaspoons dry sherry

Combine first 6 ingredients in a large bowl. Combine remaining ingredients; mix well. Pour over salad mixture just before serving; toss gently to coat. Serve immediately. Yield: about 6 servings. *Kay Castleman Cooper,*
Burke, Virginia.

CHEESE-AND-WINE MOLD

2½ cups (10 ounces) shredded sharp Cheddar cheese
¼ cup dry white wine
⅛ teaspoon ground nutmeg
⅛ teaspoon white pepper
¼ cup butter, softened
Apple wedges
Pear wedges
Assorted crackers

Combine cheese, wine, nutmeg, and pepper; beat at medium speed of an electric mixer about 10 minutes or until

almost smooth. Add butter, and beat well. Spoon into a greased 1½-cup mold; pack well. Cover and chill overnight. Unmold onto a serving platter; serve with apple and pear wedges or assorted crackers. Yield: 1½ cups.
Betty Hornsby,
Columbia, Maryland.

CRUNCHY MARINATED BEAN SALAD

4 stalks celery, sliced
1 (17-ounce) can small English peas, drained
1 (16-ounce) can cut green beans, drained
1 (8½-ounce) can baby lima beans, drained
1 (4-ounce) jar diced pimiento, drained
1 medium-size green pepper, chopped
1 medium onion, chopped
1 cup vegetable oil
1 cup vinegar
½ cup sugar
1 teaspoon paprika
¼ teaspoon garlic powder
¼ teaspoon salt
¼ teaspoon pepper

Combine first 7 ingredients in a large bowl; set aside.
Combine remaining ingredients in a jar. Cover tightly, and shake vigorously. Pour over vegetable mixture; cover and chill overnight. Yield: 8 to 10 servings.
Pat Graham,
Wallace, North Carolina.

COLD GARDEN VEGETABLE SOUP

1 beef-flavored bouillon cube
½ cup hot water
2 cups tomato juice
¼ cup plus 2 tablespoons herb-seasoned stuffing mix
¼ cup olive oil
3 medium tomatoes, coarsely chopped
4 stalks celery, finely chopped
½ large cucumber, chopped
1 small onion, grated
Juice of 1 lemon
½ teaspoon commercial steak sauce
½ teaspoon pepper
¼ teaspoon salt
Lemon slices
Fresh parsley sprigs

Dissolve bouillon cube in ½ cup hot water. Add next 11 ingredients, stirring well. Cover and chill at least 2 hours. Garnish each serving with lemon slices and parsley. Yield: about 7 cups.
Debra Leckie,
Shreveport, Louisiana.

STRAWBERRY-LEMON PARFAITS

1 (16-ounce) carton commercial sour
   cream
1 (3¾-ounce) package lemon instant
   pudding mix
1 quart fresh strawberries, sliced
2 tablespoons sugar
1 cup vanilla wafer crumbs

Combine sour cream and pudding mix; beat at medium speed of electric mixer for 1 minute. Set aside. Combine strawberries and sugar; toss lightly.

Layer half each of wafer crumbs, pudding mixture, and strawberries equally in 6 parfait glasses. Repeat layers of wafer crumbs and pudding mixture. Reserve remaining strawberries for topping; cover and set aside in refrigerator. Cover parfaits, and chill 1 hour. Top each parfait with reserved strawberries just before serving. Yield: 6 servings.   *Faye Poole,*
                              Moneta, Virginia.

MICROWAVE COOKERY

Faster Ways To Yeast Rolls And More

Saving time is what microwave cooking is all about. And when you take advantage of convenience products to speed preparation, you can save yourself hours in the kitchen.

OPEN-FACE PIZZA SANDWICHES

1 pound ground beef
1 (1.5-ounce) package spaghetti sauce mix
¼ teaspoon dried whole oregano
1 (6-ounce) can tomato paste
4 English muffins, split and toasted
32 slices pepperoni
1 cup (4 ounces) shredded mozzarella
   cheese

Crumble beef into a 2-quart casserole. Cover with heavy-duty plastic wrap, and microwave at HIGH for 5 to 7 minutes or until browned, stirring at 2-minute intervals. Drain off excess drippings.

Combine spaghetti sauce mix, oregano, and tomato paste; add to beef,
stirring well. Cover and microwave at HIGH for 2 to 3 minutes or until hot, stirring once.

Place 4 muffin halves on a paper napkin-lined plate. Spoon meat mixture over muffin halves; top each with 4 pepperoni slices. Microwave at MEDIUM HIGH (70% power) for 2 minutes, giving plate one-half turn after 1 minute. Sprinkle shredded cheese on top. Microwave at MEDIUM HIGH for 30 seconds or until cheese melts. Repeat procedure with remaining ingredients. Yield: 8 servings.

QUICK CURRIED SHRIMP

1 (10¾-ounce) can cream of chicken
   soup, undiluted
¼ cup milk
1 teaspoon curry powder
1 (8-ounce) package frozen cooked
   shrimp, unthawed
1 (10-ounce) package frozen English
   peas, unthawed
Hot cooked rice

Combine first 5 ingredients in a 1½-quart casserole. Cover and microwave at HIGH for 11 to 13 minutes or until bubbly, stirring mixture every 4 minutes. Serve over hot cooked rice. Yield: 6 servings.

CHERRY-ALMOND ROLLS

1 (13.75-ounce) package hot roll mix
2 tablespoons butter or margarine
3 tablespoons sugar
1½ teaspoons ground cinnamon
½ cup cherry preserves
¼ cup firmly packed brown sugar
3 tablespoons chopped, toasted
   almonds

Prepare roll mix according to package directions up to the first rising. Place dough in a well-greased bowl, turning once to grease top. Set bowl in a larger, shallow dish; pour 1 inch hot water into bottom dish. Cover dough loosely with waxed paper. Microwave at MEDIUM LOW (30% power) for 2 minutes; let stand in oven 5 minutes. Repeat microwaving and standing 2 times or until doubled in bulk. Carefully turn dough over in bowl if surface appears to be drying out during rising period. Punch dough down.

Place the butter in a 2-cup glass measure. Microwave at HIGH for 45 seconds or until melted; set aside.

Turn dough out onto a lightly floured surface; roll out into an 18- x 16-inch rectangle. Brush with melted butter. Combine sugar and cinnamon; sprinkle evenly over dough. Roll up dough, jellyroll fashion, beginning with the long side. Pinch edges of seam together. Cut roll into 1½-inch slices.

Combine preserves, brown sugar, and almonds. Spread preserves mixture in a greased 8-inch square baking dish. Place rolls, cut side down, in baking dish.

Set baking dish in a 13- x 9- x 2-inch baking dish containing 1 inch hot water. Cover dough loosely with waxed paper. Microwave at MEDIUM LOW for 2 minutes; let stand 5 minutes. Repeat microwaving and standing 2 times or until doubled in bulk. Remove baking dishes from oven.

Place an inverted saucer in microwave oven, and place baking dish with rolls on top of saucer. Microwave at MEDIUM HIGH (70% power) for 6 to 9 minutes or until firm to touch, giving dish a one-quarter turn every 2 minutes. Let stand 3 minutes, and invert onto a serving platter. Yield: 1 dozen.

APPLE-PECAN COBBLER

1 (21-ounce) can apple pie filling
¼ cup chopped pecans
½ cup biscuit mix
1 tablespoon brown sugar
3 tablespoons buttermilk
1 tablespoon sugar
¼ teaspoon ground cinnamon
Dash of nutmeg

Combine pie filling and pecans in a 1½-quart casserole. Microwave at HIGH for 4 to 5 minutes, stirring after 2 minutes, until hot and bubbly.

Combine biscuit mix and brown sugar in a bowl. Stir in buttermilk, mixing well. Drop biscuit dough in 6 spoonfuls into hot pie filling. Combine sugar, cinnamon, and nutmeg; sprinkle over dough. Microwave, uncovered, at HIGH for 3 to 4½ minutes, giving dish one-half turn after 1½ minutes. Yield: 4 servings.

Tip: Properly canned foods have been sterilized and won't spoil as long as the container remains airtight. However, most canned foods have a "shelf life" of approximately one year—they then may begin to slowly lose flavor and nutrients. If you use large amounts of canned foods, date them at time of purchase and use the oldest first.

Cocoa Makes It Rich And Chocolate

The one ingredient that makes the following recipes so chocolaty is cocoa, the most concentrated form of chocolate available. About three-fourths of the cocoa butter (fat) remaining in solid chocolate products is squeezed out during the process used to make cocoa powder. And since cocoa butter contributes nothing to the chocolate flavor, all that's left is rich chocolate flavor.

Even though cocoa appears lighter in color than other chocolate products, the color changes to black-brown as soon as it's mixed with a liquid. Besides the extra flavor, cocoa needs no melting and blends easily with other ingredients.

It's easy to use cocoa in place of other chocolate cooking products. For unsweetened chocolate squares, just add extra shortening to replace the cocoa butter; and for semisweet chocolate, add some sugar, as well. To substitute, stir the cocoa in with the flour, and add shortening and sugar in with similar ingredients in the recipe. The following list will help you determine the amount of cocoa, shortening, and sugar to use for various chocolate products.
—One 1-ounce square unsweetened chocolate equals 3 tablespoons cocoa and 1 tablespoon shortening
—One 1-ounce envelope liquid baking chocolate equals 3 tablespoons cocoa and 1 tablespoon of vegetable oil or melted shortening
—One 4-ounce bar sweet baking chocolate equals ¼ cup cocoa, 2 tablespoons plus 2 teaspoons shortening, and ¼ cup plus 2 teaspoons sugar
—One 6-ounce package semisweet chocolate morsels (1 cup) or six 1-ounce squares semisweet chocolate equals ¼ cup plus 2 tablespoons cocoa, ¼ cup shortening, and ¼ cup plus 3 tablespoons sugar

CHOCO-NUT SANDWICH COOKIES

½ cup butter or margarine, softened
1 cup sugar
1 egg
2 cups all-purpose flour
1½ teaspoons baking soda
½ teaspoon baking powder
½ teaspoon salt
½ cup cocoa
½ cup milk
1 teaspoon vanilla extract
Coconut Cream Filling

Cream butter; gradually add sugar, beating until light and fluffy. Add egg, blending well. Combine flour, soda, baking powder, salt, and cocoa. Add to creamed mixture alternately with milk, beginning and ending with flour mixture; mix well after each addition. Stir in vanilla extract. Drop dough by rounded teaspoonfuls onto greased cookie sheets. Bake at 400° for 6 to 8 minutes. Cool on wire racks.

Spread about 2 tablespoons Coconut Cream Filling on bottom side of half the cookies. Place remaining cookies, bottom side down, on top of filling. Yield: about 1½ dozen.

Coconut Cream Filling:

½ cup butter or margarine, softened
1 cup sifted powdered sugar
1 cup flaked coconut
1 (7-ounce) jar marshmallow creme
⅓ cup chopped pecans
1 teaspoon vanilla extract

Combine butter and powdered sugar; beat at medium speed of electric mixer until smooth. Add remaining ingredients, blending well. Yield: 2¼ cups.
Roxanne Menees,
White Pine, Tennessee.

CHOCOLATE-FROSTED ICE CREAM ROLL

½ cup all-purpose flour
⅓ cup cocoa
1 teaspoon baking powder
¼ teaspoon salt
4 eggs, separated
¾ cup sugar
½ teaspoon vanilla extract
¼ teaspoon almond extract
1 quart vanilla ice cream, softened
Chocolate frosting (recipe follows)
Finely chopped dry-roasted pistachios
Whole dry-roasted pistachios

Grease a 15- x 10- x 1-inch jellyroll pan. Line pan with paper; grease paper, and set pan aside.

Sift first 4 ingredients together; set mixture aside.

Beat egg whites (at room temperature) at high speed of an electric mixer until foamy. Gradually add sugar, beating until soft peaks form. Set aside.

Beat egg yolks until thick and lemon colored; stir in flavorings. Fold yolk mixture into egg white mixture; then gently fold in flour mixture. Spread batter evenly in the prepared pan. Bake at 350° for 12 minutes.

When cake is done, immediately loosen from sides of pan and turn out onto a damp towel. Peel off waxed paper. Starting at wide end, roll up cake and towel together; cool on wire rack, seam side down, 30 minutes.

Unroll cake; remove towel. Spread ice cream evenly over cake. Gently roll cake back up; carefully place on a large baking sheet, seam side down. Freeze until ice cream is firm.

Frost cake with chocolate frosting; freeze until serving time. Garnish with pistachios. Yield: 8 to 10 servings.

Chocolate Frosting:

¼ cup butter or margarine, softened
3 tablespoons milk
3 tablespoons cocoa
2 cups sifted powdered sugar
1 teaspoon vanilla extract

Combine all ingredients; beat until smooth. Yield: enough frosting for one cake roll. *Mrs. Charles L. Poteet, Little Rock, Arkansas.*

CHOCOLATE-CHERRY CAKE

½ cup butter or margarine, softened
1 cup sugar
1 egg
1 (10-ounce) jar maraschino cherries, undrained
2 cups all-purpose flour
¼ cup cocoa
1 teaspoon baking soda
¼ teaspoon salt
1 cup buttermilk
1 teaspoon vanilla extract
½ cup chopped pecans
Cream Cheese Frosting
Sifted cocoa

Cream butter; gradually add sugar, beating until fluffy. Add egg; beat well.

Drain cherries, reserving juice; slice cherries and set aside. Combine flour, cocoa, soda, and salt; add to creamed mixture alternately with buttermilk and cherry juice, beginning and ending with flour mixture. Mix just until blended after each addition. Fold in vanilla, pecans, and cherries.

Pour batter into a greased and floured 9-inch tube pan. Bake at 350° for 45 to 50 minutes or until cake tests done. Cool in pan 10 to 15 minutes; remove from pan, and cool completely.

Frost top and sides of cake with Cream Cheese Frosting. Place a paper doily on top, and sift cocoa over it. Carefully remove doily. Yield: one 9-inch cake.

Cream Cheese Frosting:
1 (3-ounce) package cream cheese, softened
½ cup butter or margarine, softened
2 cups sifted powdered sugar
2 teaspoons lemon juice
2 teaspoons vanilla extract

Combine cream cheese and butter; beat until light and fluffy. Add remaining ingredients; beat until smooth. Yield: enough for one 9-inch cake.
Marcella R. White,
Pensacola, Florida.

COOKING LIGHT

Main Dishes Minus The Meat

To most people, the word protein is synonymous with red meat, poultry, or fish. But what about kidney beans, brown rice, sunflower seeds, and tofu? You can get all the protein you need (along with vitamins, minerals, and fiber) by eating these and other plant sources of protein.

Each of us needs protein to build, maintain, and repair body tissue. Different protein foods are made up of specific combinations of amino acids, the building blocks of protein. A total of twenty-two amino acids are known—eight of which are considered essential since they cannot be manufactured within the body. The body can produce any of the remaining nonessential amino acids from the protein in the food we eat. In order for protein to perform its building activities properly, all eight of the essential amino acids must be present in the body at the same time.

Animal products, such as meat, fish, poultry, milk, cheese, and eggs, are considered "complete proteins" since they contain the eight essential amino acids in proportions needed by humans. However, plant sources of protein, such as dried beans and peas, rice, sunflower seeds, and peanuts, are considered "incomplete" since they contain only some of the essential amino acids.

Plant sources of protein can equal the quality of animal protein only when combined with another type of plant protein or with an animal source of protein. By eating together two incomplete proteins in which different essential amino acids are missing, you end up with a complete protein. The combined two plant sources are called "complementary proteins."

Black-eyed peas with cornbread and red beans and rice are two examples of the complementary protein combination between legumes and grains. When legumes are served with seeds or nuts, the proteins are also complementary.

Another way to improve the quality of plant sources of protein is by eating an animal source of protein (egg, milk, cheese, or yogurt) at the same meal. When you prepare macaroni and cheese, you're combining pasta (a grain product) with cheese (an animal product) to improve the protein quality of the pasta. Cheese pizza or a bowl of cereal with milk are two other complementary combinations of protein.

Black-eyed peas and cornbread are starchy foods you may have avoided. Actually, it's not the starches that are high in calories, but the butter on rice, the bacon drippings in black-eyed peas, and the cream on fettuccine. In fact, most plant sources of protein provide carbohydrate and protein but little, if any, fat. Animal products contain substantial amounts of fat along with the protein and may be high in calories. For example, one ounce of cooked brown rice is much lower in calories than an equal amount of cooked steak.

Here are several recipes that show how plant foods can be prepared to make a protein-rich main dish appropriate for a low-calorie diet.

VEGETABLE LASAGNA

2 tablespoons chopped onion
1 clove garlic, minced
1 teaspoon olive oil
1½ cups peeled diced tomato
2 cups peeled diced eggplant
½ cup chopped green pepper
1 small zucchini, diced
¼ pound fresh mushrooms, chopped
1 teaspoon dried whole oregano
1 bay leaf
¼ teaspoon salt
¼ teaspoon pepper
6 uncooked lasagna noodles
⅛ teaspoon salt
2 eggs, beaten
1 cup low-fat cottage cheese
1 tablespoon chopped fresh parsley
Vegetable cooking spray
½ cup (2 ounces) shredded mozzarella cheese
1 tablespoon grated Parmesan cheese

Sauté onion and garlic in hot oil in a large skillet 2 minutes. Stir in next 9 ingredients; cover, reduce heat, and simmer 10 minutes. Remove bay leaf; set vegetable mixture aside.

Cook lasagna according to package directions, reducing salt to ⅛ teaspoon. Drain noodles, and cut in half crosswise; set aside.

Combine eggs, cottage cheese, and parsley; set aside.

Coat an 8-inch square baking dish with cooking spray. Place 4 noodle halves in dish. Spoon half of cottage cheese mixture over noodles. Spread half of vegetable mixture over cottage cheese mixture; sprinkle with half of mozzarella. Repeat layers, ending with noodles. Cover and bake at 350° for 20 minutes. Sprinkle with Parmesan; cover and bake 5 minutes. Yield: 6 servings (about 245 calories per serving).
Mrs. David S. Wilson,
Tyler, Texas.

PASTA VERDE

1 pound fresh spinach, torn
½ cup chopped onion
1 tablespoon vegetable oil
1 (8-ounce) carton plain low-fat yogurt
1 large clove garlic, crushed
1½ teaspoons dried whole basil
1½ teaspoons dried whole oregano
7 ounces uncooked linguine
1 cup (4 ounces) shredded Monterey Jack cheese
¼ cup grated Parmesan cheese

Sauté spinach and onion in hot oil in a large skillet 4 minutes. Stir in next 4 ingredients; set aside, and keep warm.

Cook linguine according to package directions; drain well. Add cheese to hot linguine; toss gently. Add to spinach mixture; cook over low heat until thoroughly heated, stirring constantly. Serve immediately. Yield: 6 servings (about 280 calories per serving).
Clarine Spetzler,
Salem, Virginia.

Tip: Burned food can be removed from an enamel saucepan by using the following procedure: Fill the pan with cold water containing 2 to 3 tablespoons salt, and let stand overnight. The next day, cover and bring water to a boil; rinse and scrub clean.

STROGANOFF TOFU

1 pound tofu
1 tablespoon vegetable oil
3 cups sliced fresh mushrooms
1 clove garlic, crushed
2 tablespoons all-purpose flour
1½ teaspoons chicken-flavored bouillon
    granules
½ teaspoon dried whole chervil
¼ teaspoon pepper
¾ cup skim milk
1 (8-ounce) carton plain low-fat yogurt
3 cups hot cooked spinach noodles
½ tomato, sliced
½ hard-cooked egg, sliced
Fresh dill

Wrap tofu with several layers of cheesecloth or paper towel; press lightly to extract excess liquid. Remove cheesecloth; cut tofu into ¾-inch cubes.

Sauté tofu in hot oil in a large skillet 3 to 4 minutes; remove tofu, and set aside. Add mushrooms and garlic to skillet, and sauté 2 to 3 minutes; remove and set aside.

Combine flour, bouillon granules, chervil, and pepper; gradually add milk, stirring until blended. Add milk mixture to skillet; bring to a boil. Cook 1 minute, stirring constantly. Stir yogurt into milk mixture. Add sautéed ingredients, and cook until thoroughly heated (do not boil). Serve over spinach noodles. Garnish with tomato slices, egg slices, and dill. Yield: 6 servings (about 140 calories per serving plus 100 calories per ½ cup cooked noodles). *Kathy Henry, Jefferson City, Tennessee.*

MINESTRONE SOUP

Vegetable cooking spray
1 cup finely chopped onion
½ cup chopped celery
6 cups beef broth
2 medium zucchini, cubed
1 (16-ounce) can tomatoes, undrained
1 (20-ounce) can cannellini beans,
    undrained
1 cup uncooked elbow macaroni
1 cup finely chopped cabbage
½ cup chopped fresh parsley
1 clove garlic, minced
½ teaspoon pepper

Coat a Dutch oven with cooking spray; place over medium-high heat until hot. Add onion and celery; sauté until tender. Add remaining ingredients; bring to a boil. Reduce heat and simmer, uncovered, 30 minutes. Yield: 3 quarts (about 123 calories per 1-cup serving). *Ruth Rowley, Orlando, Florida.*

STUFFED PEPPERS

4 medium-size sweet red or green peppers
½ cup chopped onion
4 large mushrooms, sliced
2 tablespoons Chablis or other dry white
    wine
2 tablespoons wheat germ
¾ cup cooked brown rice
1 (8-ounce) can whole kernel corn,
    drained
½ cup (2 ounces) shredded sharp Cheddar
    cheese
1 teaspoon garlic powder
1½ teaspoons dried whole rosemary
1½ teaspoons dried parsley flakes
2 teaspoons wheat germ

Cut off tops of peppers, and remove seeds. Chop pepper tops; reserve ⅓ cup chopped pepper.

Combine ⅓ cup chopped pepper, onion, mushrooms, and wine in a medium skillet; cook, uncovered, over medium heat until tender. Remove from heat, and add next 7 ingredients; mix well. Stuff peppers with mixture; place in a shallow baking dish. Top each pepper with ½ teaspoon wheat germ. Bake at 350° for 30 minutes. Yield: 4 servings (about 181 calories per serving).
Traci Myers, Boca Raton, Florida.

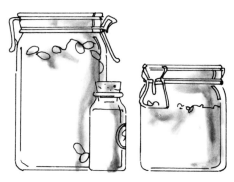

LENTIL-AND-RICE SUPPER

6 cups water
1¾ cups uncooked lentils
½ teaspoon ground turmeric
3 tablespoons chopped fresh coriander or
    1 tablespoon dried whole coriander
2 medium-size yellow squash, sliced
½ pound fresh mushrooms, sliced
1 medium-size green pepper, chopped
1 medium onion, chopped
1 tablespoon Worcestershire sauce
2 teaspoons salt
1 tablespoon vegetable oil
½ teaspoon cumin seeds
¼ teaspoon coarsely ground pepper
¼ to ½ teaspoon hot sauce
4 cups hot cooked rice

Combine first 4 ingredients; bring to a boil. Cover, reduce heat, and simmer 1 hour or until lentils are done. Add next 6 ingredients; cover and simmer 15 to 20 minutes or until vegetables are tender, stirring occasionally.

Heat oil in a small skillet; add cumin seeds and pepper. Cook over medium heat, stirring constantly, 1 to 2 minutes. Add to lentil mixture; stir in hot sauce. Serve over rice. Yield: 8 servings (about 183 calories per serving plus 90 calories per ½ cup cooked rice).
Mrs. R. E. Allen, Daphne, Alabama.

BROWN RICE-AND-VEGETABLE SALAD

1 cup uncooked brown rice
½ cup chopped carrot
1 cup cut fresh green beans
1 cup frozen English peas
1 cucumber, peeled and chopped
1 medium-size sweet red pepper,
    chopped
1 large tomato, unpeeled and
    chopped
⅓ cup unsalted sunflower kernels,
    toasted
1 cup (4 ounces) shredded Monterey
    Jack cheese
¼ cup Italian reduced-calorie salad
    dressing
3 tablespoons tarragon vinegar
2 tablespoons olive oil
¼ to ½ teaspoon freshly ground
    pepper
Lettuce leaves (optional)

Cook the rice according to the package directions, omitting the salt and butter, and chill.

Combine carrot, beans, and peas in a medium saucepan; cover with water, and cook 5 to 10 minutes or until crisp-tender. Drain and cool.

Combine rice, carrot, beans, peas, cucumber, red pepper, tomato, sunflower kernels, and cheese in a large bowl. Combine next 4 ingredients, stirring well; pour over salad, and toss gently. Chill. Serve on lettuce leaves, if desired. Yield: 8 servings (about 244 calories per serving).

Right: *Cocoa makes Chocolate-Frosted Ice Cream Roll and Choco-Nut Sandwich Cookies rich with chocolate. Use it to make Chocolate-Cherry Cake, too; then sift cocoa over a doily for an attractive pattern on top of the cream cheese frosting (recipes on page 200).*

Above: *Our wine-flavored aspic mixture is just the right consistency for jelling colorful herb and vegetable garnishes on Snapper With Dill (page 190).*

Right: *Chicken in Tomato Aspic (page 190) embeds the meat and garnishes in a colorful gelatin mixture that's flavored and meant to be eaten right along with the chicken.*

Kick Off With A Tailgate Party

One good way to kick off an afternoon of football is to gather friends for a tailgate party.

Preparation for the tailgate begins the night before by tossing together Spaghetti Salad and mixing up Olive-Relish Dip. Both can be made and taken to the game in plastic containers. Zesty Deviled Eggs can also be stuffed the night before. Save the egg carton, and place the stuffed eggs in it for safekeeping while traveling to the game.

The dough for Orange Crispies can be prepared ahead, shaped into rolls, and chilled. Bake a batch of the citrus-sweet cookies, and let them cool before packing in airtight containers. A lemon juice and soy sauce marinade gives Zippy Chicken Strips tangy flavor. Dipped in a light batter and fried until crisp, these thin strips of chicken are the ideal finger food.

Olive-Relish Dip
Tortilla Chips
Zippy Chicken Strips
Spaghetti Salad
Zesty Deviled Eggs
Orange Crispies
Beer

ZIPPY CHICKEN STRIPS

3 pounds boneless chicken breast
   halves
½ cup lemon juice
2 tablespoons soy sauce
¾ teaspoon salt
1 cup all-purpose flour
1 teaspoon pepper
½ teaspoon salt
½ teaspoon paprika
Vegetable oil

Cut chicken into 3- x 1-inch strips, and place in a shallow dish. Combine the lemon juice, soy sauce, and salt; pour over chicken strips. Cover and marinate at least 30 minutes.

Combine flour, pepper, salt, and paprika. Dredge chicken pieces in flour mixture, and fry in hot oil (375°) until golden brown. Drain on paper towels. Yield: 8 to 10 servings.
Mrs. H. E. Taylor,
Pittsburg, Texas.

SPAGHETTI SALAD

1 (16-ounce) package spaghetti
1 medium-size red onion, finely diced
4 green onions, finely chopped
1 cup Italian salad dressing
2 tablespoons salad seasoning
2 tomatoes, diced
1 cucumber, diced

Cook spaghetti according to package directions; drain. Rinse with cold water, and drain again.

Combine spaghetti and next 4 ingredients; toss gently. Cover and chill overnight. Add tomatoes and cucumber, tossing gently before serving. Yield: 10 to 12 servings. *Barbara Burrows,*
Livonia, Michigan.

OLIVE-RELISH DIP

1 (12-ounce) jar chile peppers, drained, seeded, and finely chopped
1 (4.2-ounce) can chopped ripe olives, drained
1 (3.25-ounce) jar pimiento-stuffed olives, drained and finely chopped
4 green onions and tops, finely chopped
3 tomatoes, finely chopped
¼ cup vegetable oil
2 tablespoons vinegar

Combine the first 5 ingredients; mix well. Combine oil and vinegar; stir into vegetable mixture. Chill overnight.

Serve dip with tortilla chips. Yield: about 4½ cups. *Linda Keeton,*
Memphis, Tennessee.

ZESTY DEVILED EGGS

6 hard-cooked eggs
3 tablespoons mayonnaise
2 teaspoons lemon juice
1 teaspoon Worcestershire sauce
¼ teaspoon dry mustard
⅛ teaspoon salt
⅛ teaspoon pepper
Paprika
Fresh parsley sprigs

Slice eggs in half lengthwise, and carefully remove yolks. Mash yolks; add next 6 ingredients, mixing well. Stuff egg whites with yolk mixture. Garnish with paprika and parsley sprigs. Yield: 6 to 8 servings. *Mrs. Roy G. Johnson,*
Ozark, Arkansas.

ORANGE CRISPIES

1 cup butter or margarine, softened
½ cup sugar
½ cup firmly packed brown sugar
1 egg
1 tablespoon grated orange rind
2 tablespoons orange juice
¼ teaspoon vanilla extract
2½ cups all-purpose flour
¼ teaspoon salt
¼ teaspoon baking soda
½ cup finely chopped pecans

Cream butter; gradually add sugar, beating until light and fluffy. Add egg, orange rind, juice, and vanilla; beat well. Combine flour, salt, and soda; gradually add to creamed mixture. Stir in pecans.

Shape dough into 2 long rolls, 1½ inches in diameter; wrap each in waxed paper, and chill 3 hours or until firm.

Unwrap rolls, and cut into ¼-inch slices. Place cookies 2 inches apart on ungreased cookie sheets. Bake at 375° for 8 to 10 minutes or until edges are lightly browned. Yield: about 6 dozen.
Lynette L. Walther,
East Palatka, Florida.

Start A Party With Winning Appetizers

What better way to begin or end an afternoon of football than with this winning assortment of appetizers. Whether you're planning a casual get-together in front of the television or a tailgate party at the stadium, this selection of tempting appetizers will get your party going.

CHICKEN LIVER PATE

⅓ cup finely chopped onion
2 tablespoons butter or margarine
½ pound chicken livers
¼ teaspoon salt
2 tablespoons dry sherry
½ cup butter, softened

Sauté onion in butter until tender; add chicken livers and cook 10 to 15 minutes, stirring often. Pour livers into container of electric blender. Add salt and sherry; process until smooth. Cool.

Combine liver mixture and softened butter; place in a small bowl or crock, and serve with crackers. Yield: about 1½ cups. *Betty Joyce Mills,*
Birmingham, Alabama.

TOSTADA DIP

2 pounds ground beef
1 large onion, chopped
2 (15-ounce) cans tomato sauce with
    tomato pieces
1 (12-ounce) jar mild picante sauce
1 (8-ounce) jar hot taco sauce
2 (4-ounce) cans chopped green chiles,
    undrained
2 tablespoons chili powder
1 cup (4 ounces) shredded sharp Cheddar
    cheese

Cook ground beef and onion until meat is browned, stirring to crumble; drain well. Stir in next 5 ingredients; cover, reduce heat, and simmer 1 hour, stirring occasionally. Transfer mixture to a chafing dish; sprinkle with cheese. Serve with tortilla chips. Yield: about 6 cups.   *Sheree Garvin,*
Wilkesboro, North Carolina.

FLAVORFUL MEATBALLS

1 pound lean ground beef
½ teaspoon salt
¼ teaspoon pepper
¼ cup shortening
½ cup beer
½ cup catsup
2 tablespoons sugar
2 tablespoons wine vinegar
2 tablespoons Worcestershire sauce
¼ teaspoon garlic salt
Chopped green onions (optional)

Combine ground beef, salt, and pepper; mix well. Shape into 1-inch meatballs. Cook in hot shortening over medium heat 10 to 15 minutes or until browned. Drain well on paper towels.
Combine next 6 ingredients in a medium saucepan; stir well. Add meatballs; simmer 30 minutes, stirring occasionally. Garnish with green onions, if desired. Serve warm. Yield: about 2 dozen.   *Linda Wilson,*
Little Rock, Arkansas.

FAST GOODIES

2 cups biscuit mix
½ cup butter or margarine, melted
1 (8-ounce) carton commercial sour cream
½ cup (2 ounces) shredded Cheddar
    cheese

Combine all ingredients, mixing well; spoon into greased miniature muffin pans, filling one-half full. Bake at 450° for 10 to 12 minutes. Yield: 4 dozen.
Susan A. Houston,
Tucker, Georgia.

MUSHROOM LOGS

2 (8-ounce) cans refrigerated crescent
    dinner rolls
1 (8-ounce) package cream cheese,
    softened
1 (4-ounce) can mushroom stems and
    pieces, drained and chopped
1 teaspoon seasoned salt
1 egg, beaten
1 to 2 tablespoons poppy seeds

Separate crescent dough into 8 rectangles; press perforations to seal.
Combine cream cheese, mushrooms, and salt, mixing well. Spread mushroom mixture in equal portions over each rectangle of dough. Starting at long sides, roll up each rectangle jellyroll fashion; pinch seams to seal. Slice logs into 1-inch pieces; place seam side down on an ungreased baking sheet.
Brush each log with beaten egg, and sprinkle with poppy seeds. Bake at 375° for 10 to 12 minutes. Yield: 4 dozen.
Yvonne M. Bennett,
Greenville, South Carolina.

SEASONED STUFFED MUSHROOMS

24 large fresh mushrooms
½ cup soft breadcrumbs
⅓ cup grated Parmesan cheese
⅓ cup melted butter or olive oil
¼ cup grated onion
2 tablespoons fresh minced parsley
1 clove garlic, minced
½ teaspoon dried whole oregano
¼ teaspoon pepper

Clean mushrooms with damp paper towels. Remove mushroom stems, and finely chop; set caps aside.
Combine mushroom stems and remaining ingredients, stirring well; spoon into mushroom caps. Place on a lightly greased baking sheet. Bake at 350° for 25 to 30 minutes. Yield: 2 dozen.
Jill Rorex,
Arlington, Texas.

FRIED DILL PICKLES

1 egg, beaten
1 cup milk
1 tablespoon all-purpose flour
1 tablespoon Worcestershire sauce
6 drops of hot sauce
3½ cups all-purpose flour
¾ teaspoon salt
¾ teaspoon pepper
1 quart sliced dill pickles, drained
Vegetable oil

Combine first 5 ingredients, stirring well; set aside. Combine 3½ cups flour, salt, and pepper, stirring well.
Dip pickles into milk mixture, and dredge in flour mixture; repeat procedure. Deep fry in hot oil (350°) until pickles float to surface and are golden brown. Drain on paper towels; serve immediately. Yield: about 8½ dozen.
Louise Holmes,
Winchester, Tennessee.

CREAMY CURRY DIP

2 cups mayonnaise
1½ teaspoons celery seeds
1 teaspoon garlic powder
1 teaspoon dry mustard
½ teaspoon curry powder
¼ teaspoon instant minced onion
2 teaspoons Worcestershire sauce
1 teaspoon prepared horseradish
Dash of hot sauce

Combine all ingredients, mixing well. Chill. Serve with fresh vegetables. Yield: 2 cups.   *Glenda Boudreaux,*
Birmingham, Alabama.

OLIVE-CHEESE BALLS

¼ cup butter or margarine, softened
1½ cups (6 ounces) shredded Monterey
    Jack cheese
¾ cup all-purpose flour
About 1 cup small pimiento-stuffed olives
¼ cup plus 2 tablespoons fine, dry
    breadcrumbs
Paprika

Cream butter and cheese; add flour, mixing well. Shape a small amount of dough around each olive, covering it completely; coat with breadcrumbs. Sprinkle lightly with paprika. Place on ungreased baking sheets; bake at 350° for 20 to 25 minutes. Serve warm. Yield: about 3 dozen. *Patsy M. Smith,*
Lampasas, Texas.

LAYERED TACO APPETIZER

1 (16-ounce) can refried beans
1 (4¼-ounce) can chopped ripe olives,
    drained
1 (4-ounce) can chopped green chiles,
    drained
1 (6-ounce) carton avocado dip
8 green onions, chopped
2 medium tomatoes, diced
1 cup (4 ounces) shredded Cheddar cheese

Layer ingredients on a 12-inch pizza plate in order listed. Serve with tortilla or corn chips. Yield: 8 cups.
Earlene Ramay,
Englewood, Colorado.

This Architect Builds Some Showy Desserts

When he talks about his favorite recipes, Charles Wolf of Macon, Georgia, rolls out their French names like a native. But the Georgia architect lapses back into his soft Southern drawl when he starts describing them and the flavors he delights in blending.

Fruit tarts are the most fun to prepare and serve, he says. "They're tasty and a very pretty dessert—the kind that gets a lot of 'oohs' and 'aahs.' "

Another of Charles's specialties is a showy pyramid of Profiteroles (page 208)—filled cream puffs stacked like cannonballs and drizzled with chocolate glaze. "The first time I ate that was in a restaurant in Florence, Italy," he recalls. "It was the centerpiece of the food cart and a beautiful dessert. I just enjoyed it so much that when I got back, I tried to find a recipe for it." When he couldn't find the recipe, Charles says he just experimented and figured one out for himself.

How does he come up with his creative recipes? "I improvise," says Charles. "I don't know of too many original recipes. They're variations of something someone else has done." Reading cookbooks spurs him on to new ideas and techniques, he says.

APPLE CREAM TART

1 cup all-purpose flour
¼ teaspoon salt
½ cup butter
7 to 8 tablespoons commercial sour cream
2 medium Golden Delicious apples
¾ cup sugar
¼ cup all-purpose flour
Pinch of salt
3 egg yolks, beaten
⅓ cup commercial sour cream
2 tablespoons apple jelly, melted

Combine 1 cup flour and ¼ teaspoon salt; cut in butter with a pastry blender until mixture resembles coarse meal. Add 7 tablespoons sour cream, 1 tablespoon at a time; stir with a fork until dry ingredients are moistened. Stir in an additional tablespoon sour cream, if mixture seems too dry. Shape into a ball, and chill 30 minutes.

Roll dough to ⅛-inch thickness on a lightly floured surface. Fit pastry into a 9-inch round tart pan; trim edges.

Peel and core apples; slice each into 16 wedges. Arrange wedges in tart shell. Combine sugar, ¼ cup flour, pinch of salt, egg yolks, and ⅓ cup sour cream; mix well. Pour evenly over apples; bake at 350° for 55 to 60 minutes or until set. Let cool; brush with apple jelly. Yield: one 9-inch tart.

QUICK PUFF PASTRY

1 cup butter, chilled
1¼ cups plus 2½ tablespoons all-purpose flour
½ cup cake flour
¼ teaspoon salt
½ cup ice water

Cut butter into ⅜-inch cubes. Freeze 10 minutes.

Combine flour and salt; mound on a smooth surface, and make a well in center. Place chilled butter in well. Working quickly, cut butter coarsely into flour using a pastry scraper, until cubes of butter are halved or quartered. Sprinkle water evenly over mixture; stir with a fork until dry ingredients are moistened. Quickly shape into a ball, and wrap in waxed paper. (Dough will be very lumpy, with pieces of butter showing.) Chill 15 minutes.

Working quickly, roll dough into a ⅜-inch-thick rectangle (about 14 x 9 inches) on floured surface. Fold short sides inward to meet in center; fold in half along center where the two sides meet. Lightly flour surface, and roll dough out again into ⅜-inch-thick rectangle; fold as before. Repeat rolling and folding process 1 additional time. Chill 15 minutes. Yield: enough pastry for one tart shell.

CREME PATISSIERE

3 egg yolks
¼ cup plus 2 tablespoons sugar
¼ cup all-purpose flour
1 cup milk
1½ teaspoons butter or margarine, softened
1 teaspoon vanilla extract

Whisk egg yolks and sugar in a heavy saucepan; add flour, and stir until blended. Gradually stir in milk; cook over medium heat, stirring constantly, just until mixture comes to a boil. Reduce heat, and cook 1 minute. Cool to lukewarm; stir in butter and vanilla. Cover and chill. Yield: 1⅓ cups.

Note: When doubling recipe for Profiteroles (page 208), use 5 egg yolks and exactly double of all other ingredients.

To make Open-Face Fruit Tart, spread Crème Pâtissière into a puff pastry shell.

OPEN-FACE FRUIT TART

1 recipe Quick Puff Pastry
1 egg, slightly beaten
1 recipe Crème Pâtissière
1 kiwi, peeled and sliced
About 5 large strawberries, halved
About 5 seedless green grapes, halved
About 5 purple grapes, halved and seeded
2 tablespoons apple jelly, melted
1 tablespoon amaretto liqueur
Fresh mint sprigs (optional)

Roll puff pastry dough to ⅛-inch thickness; trim edges to form a 13- x 8-inch rectangle. Place dough on a waxed paper-lined baking sheet. Chill 15 minutes.

Cut a ¾-inch strip from each side of pastry. Brush strips with egg, and lay them, egg side down, on top of each side of pastry rectangle, edges flush together, overlapping corners to form a border. Prick pastry generously with a fork, excluding border. Brush top of border with egg. Chill 30 minutes.

Bake at 400° for 15 to 20 minutes or until puffed and golden brown. Reduce oven temperature to 300°. Open oven, and prick bottom of pastry with a knife in several places to allow steam to escape and bottom to collapse. Bake an additional 15 minutes at 300°. Gently remove pastry from baking sheet with spatulas, and let cool on a wire rack. Transfer to serving platter.

Spread Crème Pâtissière evenly in pastry shell, and arrange fruit in alternating rows over filling.

Melt apple jelly in saucepan; stir in amaretto. Brush fruit with jelly glaze. Garnish with mint sprigs, if desired. Yield: 8 servings.

PROFITEROLES

1 cup water
½ cup butter
1 cup all-purpose flour
4 eggs
2 recipes Crème Pâtissière (page 207),
    using 5 egg yolks
Chocolate sauce (recipe follows)

Combine water and butter in a medium saucepan; bring to a boil. Add flour to butter mixture all at once, stirring vigorously over low heat until mixture leaves sides of pan and forms a smooth ball. Remove from heat, and cool about 5 minutes.

Add eggs, one at a time, beating with a wooden spoon after each addition; beat until batter is smooth.

Drop batter by rounded teaspoonfuls 2 inches apart on ungreased baking sheets. Bake at 400° for 25 minutes or until golden brown and puffed. Cool away from drafts.

Cut top off cream puffs; pull out, and discard soft dough inside. Fill bottom halves with about 1½ tablespoons Crème Pâtissière, and cover with top halves. Arrange cream puffs in a mound on serving platter, and drizzle with chocolate sauce. Serve immediately or refrigerate. Yield: 2½ dozen.

Chocolate Sauce:

½ cup whipping cream
1 (4-ounce) package sweet baking
    chocolate
¼ teaspoon vanilla extract

Heat cream in a heavy saucepan until hot (do not boil); remove from heat. Add chocolate; stir until melted. Stir in vanilla. Yield: ¾ cup.

Plain Potatoes? Not These

Most cooks can mash, French-fry, or bake and dress a great-tasting potato without even a recipe. But when the occasion calls for something more than these favorite standbys, you'll want to try one of our fancy potato recipes.

Have you ever tried piping this versatile vegetable? Potatoes Duchesse starts out like a basic mashed potato, but a little extra seasoning and just the right amount of liquid ingredients give it a good piping consistency. The potato mixture needs to be somewhat firm so it

Take plain potatoes and bake, fry, or mash them into an array of fancy side dishes: (from front) Potatoes Anna With Rosemary, Potato Nests With Savory Shavings, Potatoes Duchesse, and Parmesan Potato Croquettes. Recipes on pages 209 and 210.

will hold its shape during baking. Use the large-size fabric or plastic decorating bags to make the mixture easier to pipe.

Potatoes Anna With Rosemary features thin slices in a graceful petal arrangement that looks almost like a flower. Be sure to layer the slices in the center of the pan, working outward, otherwise, there won't be a petaled effect. We arranged a simple garnish of sliced zucchini, carrot, and olive to carry out the flower theme. Slice the round into wedges to serve.

You can also mold potato mixtures into almost any shape you want—we chose small brioche pans for our Parmesan Potato Croquettes. (Custard cups work, too.) Just grease the molds well, sprinkle them with ground pecans, and add the potato mixture. Once baked, the layer of pecans helps unmold the potato mounds without marring their shape. Crown them with the Sherried Cream Sauce and a pecan half.

Since fried potatoes are always a favorite, we've included a variation for that, too—Potato Nests With Savory Shavings. Slice potatoes into waffle-like rounds using a mandoline (other smaller, similar cutting tools will make

the same cut); then arrange and fry them in a special "birds nest" frying basket. Most kitchen specialty shops have both gadgets. If you don't have access to a mandoline, simply cutting the potatoes into julienne strips will produce a similar basket.

The fried baskets are just the right size to hold individual servings of sautéed or creamed vegetables, even mashed or fried potatoes. We found that the leftover potato peel shavings would fry into crispy, little nibbles. They're great plain or tossed with our herb seasoning mixture included with the recipe for fried baskets.

Try These Ideas, Too

Whenever you scoop cooked potatoes from the shells, keep the shells. Cut them into bite-size pieces, fry them until crisp, and add your favorite toppings to make a tasty appetizer served in many restaurants—fried potato skins.

Homemade potato chips are also easy to fry. Cut peeled or unpeeled potatoes into very thin slices—the thinner the better. Deep fry them as you would any other potato, and surprise your family with the freshest tasting chips they've ever eaten. Add salt if you like, or omit it if that better suits your diet.

For information on choosing what type of potato you need for the style of cooking planned, see "From Our Kitchen to Yours" on page 210.

Slice potatoes for Potato Nests into waffle cuts using a mandoline. Rotating the potato 90 degrees after each cut with the special blade produces the waffled shape.

Layer waffled potato slices in the larger basket of a "bird's nest" frying basket; secure with smaller basket and clip. Deep fry in hot oil until browned.

POTATOES ANNA WITH ROSEMARY

¼ cup plus 3 tablespoons butter or margarine, melted and divided
2 pounds round red or long white potatoes, scrubbed and peeled
½ teaspoon dried whole rosemary, finely crushed
Salt
Red pepper (optional)
5 to 6 zucchini slices, blanched
5 carrot slices, blanched
Ripe olive half
Curly endive (optional)

Coat a nonstick 9-inch cakepan with 2 tablespoons melted butter.

Cut potatoes crosswise into ⅛-inch-thick slices; pat dry with paper towels. Starting in center of pan, arrange a thin layer of potato slices (using about one-fifth of the slices), overlapping, on bottom of cakepan. Drizzle 2 tablespoons butter over slices; sprinkle lightly with rosemary, salt, and red pepper, if desired. Repeat layering potatoes, rosemary, salt, and red pepper 4 times; drizzle remaining 3 tablespoons butter over top. Place a piece of buttered foil on top layer of potatoes, and weight down using a cakepan filled with pie weights or any other suitable ovenproof weight.

Cook over medium heat 7 minutes. Transfer to a 450° oven, and bake, covered, 30 minutes. Remove top cakepan and foil; bake 20 to 30 additional minutes or until golden brown.

Carefully pour off excess butter in pan; invert potatoes onto a serving platter. Arrange zucchini slices, carrot slices, and olive half in center of potatoes to resemble a flower. Garnish with endive, if desired. Yield: 6 servings.

Tip: Avoid purchasing green-tinted potatoes. The term used for this condition is "light burn," which causes a bitter flavor. To keep potatoes from turning green once you have bought them, store in a cool, dark, dry place.

POTATO NESTS WITH SAVORY SHAVINGS

3 large baking potatoes (about 2¼ to 2¾ pounds), scrubbed
Vegetable oil
Savory Shavings
Fresh parsley sprigs

Remove potato skins by paring each potato lengthwise into long, thin shavings using a vegetable peeler. Let shavings drop into a bowl of cold water. Pare 1 whole potato into shavings, and drop into bowl of water; reserve for use in Savory Shavings.

Cut remaining 2 potatoes crosswise in half. Using the corrugated slicing blade of a mandoline or similar slicing device, slide the cut side of a potato half down the mandoline; discard first potato slice. Rotate the potato 90 degrees, and slide it down the mandoline to produce a thin slice with a waffle cut. Repeat slicing procedure using remaining potato halves, rotating the potato 90 degrees after each waffle-cut slice. Drop slices into a large bowl of cold water as they are cut; let stand at least 15 minutes. Drain and dry thoroughly.

Dip both layers of a "bird's nest" frying basket separately in oil to coat (this will help prevent potatoes from sticking to basket); arrange potato slices, overlapping, in the larger bottom basket, covering completely. (You will need about 16 to 22 slices for each basket, depending on the size of the slices.) Place the smaller wire basket on top, and secure with clip.

Completely immerse the basket nest in hot oil (350°), and deep fry about 1 to 2 minutes until golden brown. Remove the basket nest from oil, and unclip; let stand 2 minutes on paper towel.

Lift out smaller basket; tip larger basket to turn out potatoes. Drain. If potatoes stick to wire basket, tap basket lightly on countertop, and gently pry out with a knife. Repeat procedure with remaining potatoes. Fill potato nests with Savory Shavings; garnish with parsley. Yield: 4 potato nests.

Note: If a mandoline is unavailable, pare the potatoes as directed. Cut the 2 pared whole potatoes into very thin julienne strips (about 1/16 inch thick). Soak in cold water 15 minutes; drain and dry thoroughly on paper towels. For each potato nest, dip the wire basket in oil as directed above; fill the larger bottom basket with about 1½ cups potato strips. Make a well in center, and place smaller top basket over potato strips; secure firmly with clip. Deep fry as directed above for 1 to 2 minutes; remove from oil, and trim potato strips that stick out from bottom of basket. Remove clip, and let potato basket stand 2 minutes; unmold as directed above.

Savory Shavings:

¼ cup grated Parmesan cheese
¼ teaspoon garlic salt
½ teaspoon paprika
½ teaspoon dried whole thyme
Reserved potato shavings
Vegetable oil

Combine first 4 ingredients; set aside.

Drain potato shavings, and dry thoroughly with paper towels. Deep fry shavings, a small batch at a time, in hot oil (375°) about 2 minutes or until golden brown. Drain on paper towels. Toss potato shavings with cheese mixture; serve in potato nests. Yield: enough to fill 4 potato nests.

PARMESAN POTATO CROQUETTES

4 large baking potatoes (about 3 to 3¼ pounds), scrubbed
¼ cup butter or margarine, melted
1 egg, beaten
2 egg yolks
¾ cup freshly grated Parmesan cheese
¼ teaspoon salt
¼ teaspoon white pepper
¼ teaspoon ground nutmeg
¾ cup ground pecans, divided
Sherried Cream Sauce
6 to 8 pecan halves

Pierce potatoes several times with a fork; bake at 400° for 1 hour. Let stand until cool enough to handle. Cut in half lengthwise, and scoop out pulp; reserve skins for other uses. Force potato pulp through a ricer or food mill into a large bowl; add next 7 ingredients, and blend.

Generously butter eight ½-cup brioche molds or six 6-ounce custard cups. Sprinkle molds with ½ cup pecans, coating well.

Shape potato mixture into 8 or 6 equal balls; place each in a mold, and press mixture to fill sides of molds. Level tops, and sprinkle with remaining ¼ cup pecans; press in lightly. Place molds on a baking sheet; bake at 375° for 25 to 30 minutes. Let stand 5 minutes; loosen edge of molds with a sharp knife, and unmold onto individual serving plates. Drizzle with Sherried Cream Sauce, and garnish each with a pecan half. Yield: 6 to 8 servings.

Sherried Cream Sauce:

1 small clove garlic, crushed
1½ tablespoons butter or margarine
1 tablespoon all-purpose flour
¾ cup half-and-half
1 bay leaf
2 tablespoons freshly grated Parmesan cheese
3 tablespoons dry sherry
⅛ teaspoon salt
⅛ teaspoon white pepper

Sauté garlic in butter in a heavy saucepan over low heat 1 minute. Add flour, stirring until smooth; cook 1 minute, stirring constantly. Gradually add half-and-half; add bay leaf, and cook over medium heat, stirring constantly, until mixture is thickened and bubbly. Stir in cheese, sherry, salt, and pepper. Remove from heat; cover and let stand 5 minutes. Remove bay leaf. Yield: about 1 cup.

POTATOES DUCHESSE

3 cups mashed, unseasoned potatoes
2 egg yolks
¼ cup whipping cream
½ teaspoon salt
¼ teaspoon white pepper
¼ teaspoon curry powder
Egg glaze (recipe follows)
¼ cup sliced almonds, lightly toasted (optional)

Combine first 6 ingredients in a large mixing bowl; beat at low speed of an electric mixer until smooth and blended. (Mixture will be stiff.)

Lightly grease a large baking sheet. Spoon potato mixture into a decorating bag fitted with a No. 6B or 8B star tip; pipe into eight to ten 4½-inch spiral shapes. Brush lightly with egg glaze using a small, soft-bristled brush (a small art brush will help prevent disturbing the potato shapes' edges); arrange almonds on potato spirals, if desired. Bake at 400° for 25 to 30 minutes or until edges are lightly browned. Carefully transfer to a serving platter. Yield: 4 to 5 servings.

Egg Glaze:

1 egg
1 tablespoon olive oil
¼ teaspoon salt

Combine all ingredients; beat well. Yield: glaze for 8 to 10 potato shapes.

From Our Kitchen To Yours

No matter how you serve potatoes—baked, fried, boiled, or mashed—they'll fit into any meal. In addition to recipes, our test kitchens would like to pass on some information about the most common types of potatoes and how to choose the right one for your purpose, along with storing and cooking tips.

About Potatoes

You can usually choose from four basic types of potatoes at the market—the russet, round white, long white, and round red. New potatoes are any type that comes straight from the field to the market without being stored, so they're not mature.

Russet potatoes, which are long and brownish-red in color, are best for baking; they are rather mealy and fall apart easily if you try boiling them. Round and long white potatoes are slightly mealy and can be used for boiling, baking, mashing, and frying; so they're considered all-purpose potatoes. Round red potatoes, on the other hand, are waxy, making them best for boiling.

Selection and Preparation

Whatever type you choose, look for potatoes that are firm, smooth, and have clean skins. Those with wrinkled,

Mold Parmesan Potato Croquettes in brioche pans lined with ground pecans. Once baked, invert croquettes onto serving plates and top with Sherried Cream Sauce.

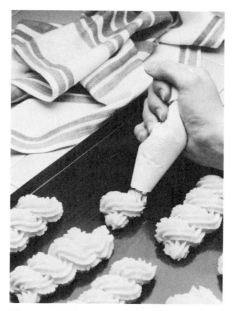

Pipe spiraled Potatoes Duchesse onto baking sheets using a decorating bag fitted with a large star tip. Top with egg glaze and almonds; bake until golden brown.

wilted skins or dark spots are overmature. Green potatoes may be bitter.

When baking potatoes it's best to leave them unpeeled. The skin is full of nutrients and also keeps the potato from drying out when cooked. You can rub the outer skin with oil to give it a softer texture and shiny look.

Before baking, the peel should be punctured by pricking with a fork; this will allow steam to escape and prevent the potato from exploding. Bake at 400° about 45 minutes or until the potato is soft when pierced with a fork.

A good way to cut back on baking time is to use your microwave. The potatoes should be pricked and placed on a paper towel. If you're baking more than one, leave some space between potatoes, just as in oven baking. The total baking time will vary, depending on the number and size of potatoes. If baking more than five, rearrange potatoes halfway through so they'll bake evenly.

To boil potatoes, you can peel them or leave the skin on. If you prefer to peel them, keep the peelings as thin as possible because some of the potatoes' nutrients are found close to the skin.

Potatoes can be boiled whole, sliced, or diced in just a small amount of water. Whole boiled potatoes take about 30 minutes to cook. If they're diced, cooking time is shortened to about 20 minutes.

If you do boil whole potatoes unpeeled, the skins will easily slip off after they're punctured.

When frying potatoes, the temperature of the oil is the most important variable. Oil should be heated to 375°. Hotter oil can cause potatoes to brown too fast before cooking, whereas oil that's too cool can make potatoes soggy and oily.

To prevent uncooked, sliced potatoes from browning, drop the cut portions in ice water for a short time. If they soak too long, they may become soggy. You can also toss them with a little lemon juice to keep them white.

Storage Tips

Potatoes chosen carefully should keep for several weeks when kept in a cool, dark, humid place, about 50 to 75 degrees. If potatoes are refrigerated or exposed to cold temperatures for a long period, the starch in them will turn to sugar, causing darkening during cooking and a sweet taste. A storage temperature that's too warm can make the potatoes sprout and shrivel up. Long exposure to light will make potatoes turn green and taste bitter. Don't wash potatoes before storing.

Quick Breakfasts Just For Two

Morning meals are fast to fix when you use our recipes selected just for households of two.

CINNAMON FRENCH TOAST

½ cup skim milk
2 eggs, beaten
2 tablespoons honey
1 teaspoon ground cinnamon
½ teaspoon vanilla extract
Dash of salt
Vegetable cooking spray
4 slices whole wheat bread

Combine first 6 ingredients, beating well. Set aside. Coat a large skillet with cooking spray, and place over medium heat. Dip both sides of bread slices into egg mixture. Cook slices 3 minutes on each side or until lightly browned. Yield: 2 servings.   *Lisa Robinson,*
Little Rock, Arkansas.

BRAN MUFFINS FOR TWO

½ cup shreds of wheat bran cereal
½ cup milk
½ cup all-purpose flour
1½ teaspoons baking powder
¼ teaspoon salt
2 tablespoons sugar
2 tablespoons shortening, melted

Combine bran cereal and milk in medium bowl; let stand 2 minutes.

Combine next 4 ingredients; set aside. Stir shortening into cereal mixture, mixing well. Add flour mixture, stirring just until dry ingredients are moistened. Spoon the batter evenly into 4 greased muffin cups. Bake at 400° for 20 minutes. Yield: 4 muffins.   *Ella Stivers,*
Abilene, Texas.

FRESH VEGETABLE OMELET

2 tablespoons butter or margarine, divided
1 small onion, sliced
¼ cup chopped green pepper
1 small zucchini, sliced
1 medium tomato, chopped
¼ teaspoon salt
¼ teaspoon dried whole oregano
⅛ teaspoon pepper
4 eggs, separated
¼ cup water
¼ teaspoon cream of tartar
⅓ cup (1.3 ounces) shredded sharp Cheddar cheese

Melt 1 tablespoon butter in a large skillet; add onion and green pepper, cooking until slightly tender. Add zucchini, tomato, salt, oregano, and pepper; cook until vegetables are tender and liquid evaporates. Keep warm.

Beat egg whites (at room temperature), ¼ cup water, and cream of tartar until stiff but not dry; set aside. Beat egg yolks in a medium bowl until thick and lemon colored. Fold egg white mixture into yolks.

Heat an ovenproof 10-inch omelet pan or heavy skillet over medium heat until hot enough to sizzle a drop of water. Add remaining 1 tablespoon butter; rotate pan to coat bottom. Pour egg mixture into skillet, and gently smooth surface. Reduce heat and cook omelet about 5 minutes or until puffy and lightly browned on bottom, gently lifting omelet at edge to judge color. Bake at 350° for 8 to 10 minutes or until knife inserted in center comes out clean.

Spoon vegetable mixture over half of omelet. Loosen omelet with a spatula, and fold in half. Slide omelet onto a warm serving plate; sprinkle with cheese. Yield: 2 servings.
Wanda Bishop,
Little Rock, Arkansas.

Lunchbox Treats For Kids

For many families, back to school means back to fixing lunches. Send the kids off this fall with something special tucked inside those lunchboxes.

NO-BAKE PEANUT BUTTER LOGS

1¾ cups sifted powdered sugar
¼ cup butter or margarine, melted
1 cup crunchy peanut butter
2 cups crisp rice cereal
Commercial chocolate frosting

Combine powdered sugar and butter in a large mixing bowl, and beat with an electric mixer until smooth. Stir in peanut butter and cereal, mixing with hands, if needed. Shape dough into 1½- x ½-inch logs. Chill. Spread tops of cookies with chocolate frosting. Yield: 7½ dozen.   *Sally Gress,*
Royal Palm Beach, Florida.

RASPBERRY BARS

½ cup butter, softened
½ cup margarine, softened
1 cup sugar
2 egg yolks
2 cups all-purpose flour
1 cup chopped walnuts
½ cup raspberry preserves

Cream butter and margarine; gradually add sugar, beating until light and fluffy. Add egg yolks; blend well. Add flour; mix thoroughly. Stir in walnuts.

Spread one-third of batter in a greased 9-inch square pan. Drop preserves by spoonfuls over batter, and spread almost to edges of pan. Completely cover preserves with remaining batter. Bake at 325° for 50 minutes or until golden. Cool and cut into bars. Yield: 2 dozen. *Mrs. Robert Taylor, Largo, Florida.*

BY-CRACKY BARS

¾ cup shortening
1 cup sugar
2 eggs
1¾ cups all-purpose flour
1 teaspoon salt
¼ teaspoon baking soda
⅓ cup milk
1 teaspoon vanilla extract
1 (1-ounce) square unsweetened chocolate, melted
¾ cup chopped walnuts
8 to 9 double graham crackers
1 (6-ounce) package semisweet chocolate morsels

Cream shortening and sugar. Add eggs, beating well.

Combine flour, salt, and soda; add to creamed mixture alternately with milk, mixing well after each addition. Stir in the vanilla.

Place one-third of batter in another bowl, and add unsweetened chocolate and walnuts to this mixture. Spread chocolate mixture in a greased 13- x 9- x 2-inch pan. Arrange 8 to 9 double graham crackers over batter.

Add chocolate morsels to remaining two-thirds batter, and drop by spoonfuls over graham crackers. Spread batter to cover. Bake at 375° for 25 minutes. Cool and cut into bars. Yield: 3 dozen. *Hazel Boschen, Ashland, Virginia.*

Tip: Use baking soda on a damp cloth to shine up your kitchen appliances.

SUNNY ORANGE GRANOLA

2 cups regular oats, uncooked
1 cup wheat germ
½ cup flaked coconut
½ cup sliced almonds
½ cup dry-roasted sunflower kernels
½ cup chopped dates
2 tablespoons sesame seeds
2 teaspoons grated orange rind (optional)
½ cup firmly packed brown sugar
⅓ cup vegetable oil
¼ cup frozen orange juice concentrate, thawed and undiluted
½ teaspoon vanilla extract
¾ cup raisins

Combine first 7 ingredients in a large bowl; mix well. Combine remaining ingredients except raisins; pour over oats mixture, and mix well.

Spread mixture evenly in a lightly greased 15- x 10- x 1-inch jellyroll pan. Bake at 300° for 40 minutes, stirring every 10 minutes. Add raisins, and mix well; cool. Store granola in an airtight container. Yield: 6¾ cups.
Candice Gardner, Fort Walton Beach, Florida.

Entertain With An Easy Menu

If you have a career and a family, and there never seems to be enough time to cook for guests, here's a menu that will help.

Begin the night before by poaching the pears. You can also make the Raspberry Sauce and plan to reheat it just before serving. Another "night before" step is to prepare the dressing for the lettuce wedges.

The remainder of the menu is fairly uncomplicated. Put the potatoes on to boil, place the pork chops under the broiler, and start the sauce for the potatoes. Zucchini With Walnuts should be prepared last to prevent overcooking.

**Lettuce Wedges With
Pimiento Dressing
Apple-Glazed Pork Chops
New Potatoes With
Parsley-Chive Sauce
Zucchini With Walnuts
Poached Pears With
Raspberry Sauce**

LETTUCE WEDGES WITH PIMIENTO DRESSING

3 tablespoons olive or vegetable oil
3 tablespoons red wine vinegar
1 tablespoon diced pimiento
1 teaspoon sugar
¼ teaspoon salt
¼ teaspoon pepper
1 medium head Boston lettuce, quartered

Combine first 6 ingredients in a jar. Cover tightly, and shake vigorously. Serve dressing over lettuce quarters. Yield: 4 servings. *Mrs. John H. Kolek, Lakeland, Florida.*

APPLE-GLAZED PORK CHOPS

½ cup apple jelly
1 teaspoon ground cinnamon
¼ teaspoon ground allspice
⅛ teaspoon ground cloves
4 (1-inch-thick) pork chops
2 small baking apples, cored and sliced

Combine first 4 ingredients in saucepan; cook over low heat, stirring occasionally, until jelly melts. Keep warm.

Place pork chops on rack in broiler pan. Broil 5 inches from heat, 7 minutes on each side. Remove from oven; brush one side with jelly glaze, and broil 3 minutes. Brush other side with glaze; top with apple slices, and drizzle with remaining glaze. Broil 3 minutes. Yield: 4 servings. *Audrey Bledsoe, Smyrna, Georgia.*

NEW POTATOES WITH PARSLEY-CHIVE SAUCE

12 small new potatoes
Parsley-Chive Sauce

Wash potatoes; peel a ½-inch strip around center of each potato. Cook potatoes in boiling water 15 to 20 minutes or until tender; drain. Serve with Parsley-Chive Sauce. Yield: 4 servings.

Parsley-Chive Sauce:

2 tablespoons butter or margarine
2 tablespoons all-purpose flour
¼ teaspoon dry mustard
1¼ cups milk
⅓ cup (1.3 ounces) shredded sharp Cheddar cheese
2 tablespoons chopped fresh parsley or 2 teaspoons dried parsley flakes
2 tablespoons chopped fresh chives or 2 teaspoons freeze-dried chives
¼ teaspoon salt

Melt butter in a heavy saucepan over low heat. Add flour and mustard; cook 1 minute, stirring constantly. Gradually add milk; stir over medium heat until thickened. Add remaining ingredients; stir until cheese melts. Yield: about 1½ cups. *Zola Messick Powell, Adams, Tennessee.*

ZUCCHINI WITH WALNUTS

½ cup coarsely chopped walnuts
¼ cup butter or margarine, divided
3 to 4 medium zucchini, cut into ¼-inch thick slices
Salt and pepper to taste

Sauté walnuts in 2 tablespoons butter until lightly browned. Remove walnuts from skillet; drain and set aside.

Melt 2 tablespoons butter in skillet; add zucchini and cook over medium heat, stirring often, 4 to 5 minutes or until crisp-tender. Add walnuts; toss gently. Sprinkle with salt and pepper. Yield: 4 servings. *Sherri D. Medley, Greensboro, North Carolina.*

POACHED PEARS WITH RASPBERRY SAUCE

4 small pears
Lemon juice
4 cups water
2 cups sugar
1 teaspoon grated lemon rind
Juice of ½ lemon
1 (3-inch) stick cinnamon
3 whole cloves
Vanilla ice cream (optional)
Raspberry Sauce
Mint leaves (optional)

Peel pears, removing core from bottom end, leaving stems intact. Brush with lemon juice to prevent browning.

Combine next 6 ingredients in a Dutch oven; bring to a boil over medium heat, stirring constantly, until sugar dissolves. Place pears in Dutch oven in an upright position. Cover, reduce heat, and simmer 20 to 25 minutes. Let the pears cool in poaching syrup; chill, spooning the syrup over pears occasionally.

Transfer pears to serving dish, using a slotted spoon. Strain syrup, reserving 1 cup for use in Raspberry Sauce. Serve pears on ice cream, if desired. Spoon sauce over pears before serving, and garnish with mint leaves, if desired. Yield: 4 servings.

Raspberry Sauce:

¼ cup butter or margarine
¼ cup raspberry preserves
Pinch of ground cinnamon
1 cup reserved poaching syrup

Melt butter in a small saucepan. Add raspberry preserves, cinnamon, and 1 cup reserved poaching syrup; simmer, uncovered, 15 to 20 minutes. Yield: about 1 cup. *Carolyn Rosen, Nashville, Tennessee.*

Oysters Are At Their Best

Some oyster fans like to eat this delicately flavored shellfish raw. But if you prefer your oysters cooked, try combining them with spinach, cheese, bacon, or mushrooms.

OYSTER-CHEESE SOUP

1 (12-ounce) container fresh Standard oysters, undrained
½ cup chopped carrots
½ cup chopped celery
3½ cups chicken broth, undiluted
½ cup chopped onion
¼ cup butter
½ cup all-purpose flour
4 cups milk
1 cup (4 ounces) sharp Cheddar cheese
½ to 1 teaspoon pepper

Drain oysters, reserving ½ cup liquid. Coarsely chop oysters; set aside.

Combine carrots, celery, chicken broth, and reserved oyster liquid in a large saucepan. Bring mixture to a boil; reduce heat and simmer about 5 minutes or until vegetables are crisp-tender.

Sauté onion in butter in a Dutch oven until tender. Add flour, stirring until smooth. Cook 1 minute, stirring constantly. Gradually add milk; cook over medium heat, stirring constantly, until thickened. Stir in broth mixture, cheese, and pepper; stir over low heat until cheese melts. Add oysters, and simmer 5 to 8 minutes or until edges of oysters curl. Yield: 9½ cups. *Helen Way, Baton Rouge, Louisiana.*

SCALLOPED OYSTERS

3 cups cracker crumbs
2 (12-ounce) containers fresh Standard oysters, drained
Salt and pepper to taste
½ cup butter
1⅓ cups half-and-half
2 eggs, beaten
⅛ teaspoon Worcestershire sauce

Sprinkle ½ cup cracker crumbs in a lightly greased 8-inch square baking dish. Cover with half the oysters; sprinkle with salt and pepper. Dot with half the butter and cover with half the remaining cracker crumbs. Repeat layers with the remaining oysters, salt, pepper, butter, and cracker crumbs.

Combine half-and-half, eggs, and Worcestershire sauce; beat well. Pour over oysters. Bake at 350° for 40 minutes or until bubbly and lightly browned. Yield: 6 servings. *Mrs. M. Dykes Barber, Birmingham, Alabama.*

SPINACH-OYSTER LOAVES

1 (10-ounce) package frozen leaf spinach
½ cup sliced fresh mushrooms
1½ tablespoons butter or margarine
1 (3-ounce) package cream cheese
⅛ teaspoon salt
⅛ teaspoon pepper
4 slices French bread
1 tablespoon plus 1 teaspoon butter or margarine
⅛ teaspoon garlic powder
16 large raw oysters, undrained (about 1¼ pounds)
¼ cup cream sherry
8 slices bacon, cooked and crumbled

Cook spinach according to package directions, omitting salt; drain well.

Sauté mushrooms in 1½ tablespoons butter until tender. Reduce heat to low; add cream cheese, salt, and pepper, stirring until cheese melts. Add spinach, mixing well. Set aside, and keep warm.

Spread each slice of bread with 1 teaspoon butter, and sprinkle with garlic powder; toast.

Drain oysters, reserving 1 tablespoon liquid. Combine oyster liquid and sherry in a large skillet; add oysters and cook over medium heat 8 to 10 minutes or until edges of oysters begin to curl.

Divide spinach mixture equally over toasted bread slices. Place 4 oysters on each loaf, and sprinkle with bacon. Serve immediately. Yield: 4 servings. *Gloria Different, Harvey, Louisiana.*

CREOLE OYSTER PIE

6 slices bacon
2 cups sliced fresh mushrooms
½ cup chopped onion
½ cup chopped green onions
¼ cup chopped celery
¼ cup chopped green pepper
1 clove garlic, minced
¼ cup all-purpose flour
½ teaspoon salt
⅛ to ¼ teaspoon red pepper
1 (12-ounce) container fresh Standard
    oysters, drained
1 tablespoon chopped fresh parsley
1 tablespoon lemon juice
1 cup water
1 cup biscuit mix
⅓ cup milk

Cook bacon in a large skillet until crisp; remove bacon, reserving drippings in skillet. Crumble bacon, and set aside.

Stir next 6 ingredients into drippings; cover and simmer 5 minutes or until vegetables are tender. Add flour, salt, and red pepper, stirring well. Stir in bacon, oysters, parsley, lemon juice, and water. Spoon mixture into a lightly greased 9-inch square baking pan.

Combine biscuit mix and milk, stirring well. Roll dough out on a lightly floured surface to fit baking pan. Carefully place pastry over oyster mixture; cut slits in pastry to allow steam to escape. Bake at 400° for 20 minutes or until crust is golden brown. Yield: 4 to 6 servings.
Geneva Giuffre,
New Orleans, Louisiana.

BAKED OYSTERS OVER TOAST POINTS

6 slices bacon
½ cup chopped onion
½ cup chopped green pepper
¼ cup chopped celery
2 teaspoons lemon juice
1 teaspoon Worcestershire sauce
⅛ teaspoon hot sauce
Dash of pepper
2 (12-ounce) containers fresh Standard
    oysters, drained
Buttered toast points

Cook bacon until crisp; remove bacon, reserving 1 tablespoon drippings in skillet. Crumble bacon, and set aside.

Add vegetables to bacon drippings; cook until tender. Stir in the next 4 ingredients. Arrange oysters in a lightly greased 12- x 8- x 2-inch baking dish.

Spoon vegetable mixture over oysters. Bake at 400° for 10 to 12 minutes or until edges of oysters begin to curl. Using a slotted spoon, serve oysters on toast points. Yield: 4 to 6 servings.
Mrs. Herbert W. Rutherford,
Baltimore, Maryland.

Pass The Mushrooms

Mushrooms are known for their versatility with other foods, but these delicacies can stand on their own as well. Served whole, sliced, or quartered, they add an interesting touch to an ordinary meal. And their delicate flavor and texture will enhance your favorite entrées.

CURRIED MUSHROOMS

½ pound fresh mushrooms, quartered
¾ cup finely chopped onion
¼ cup butter or margarine
1 small clove garlic, crushed
1 teaspoon curry powder
¼ teaspoon salt
⅓ cup beef broth
Cooked rice or noodles

Sauté mushrooms and onion in butter in a skillet about 5 minutes. Add garlic and curry powder; cook 2 minutes or until curry powder is darkened. Stir in salt and broth; simmer over low heat 8 to 10 minutes. Serve over cooked rice. Yield: 4 servings.
Susan Kamer-Shinaberry,
Charleston, West Virginia.

HERBED MUSHROOMS

1 pound fresh mushrooms, sliced
1 tablespoon lemon juice
5 green onions, chopped
2 teaspoons chopped fresh parsley
½ teaspoon dried whole thyme
½ teaspoon dried whole marjoram
½ teaspoon seasoned salt
½ teaspoon freshly ground pepper
¼ cup butter or margarine, melted

Toss mushrooms with lemon juice in a medium mixing bowl. Add remaining ingredients, and mix well.

Divide mixture in half, and place each portion on a large sheet of heavy-duty aluminum foil. Fold foil into packets. Grill over medium-hot coals 8 to 10 minutes. Yield: 4 servings.
Jill Rorex,
Arlington, Texas.

MUSHROOMS SUPREME

1½ pounds fresh mushrooms, quartered
1 tablespoon butter or margarine
1 beef-flavored bouillon cube
½ cup hot water
¼ cup butter or margarine
2 tablespoons all-purpose flour
Dash of pepper
½ cup whipping cream
¼ cup fine, dry breadcrumbs
¼ cup grated Parmesan cheese

Sauté mushrooms in 1 tablespoon butter in a large skillet over medium heat 8 to 10 minutes. Drain well. Dissolve bouillon cube in hot water, and set aside.

Melt ¼ cup butter in a small saucepan; add flour, and stir until smooth. Blend in pepper, whipping cream, and bouillon. Stir into mushrooms; pour mixture into a greased 1-quart casserole. Top with breadcrumbs and cheese. Bake, uncovered, at 350° for 30 minutes. Yield: 4 to 6 servings.
Ann Copley,
Lynchburg, Virginia.

MUSHROOM FILLING IN A PEEL

4 large baking potatoes
Vegetable oil
1 (1.25-ounce) package sour cream
    sauce mix
1 pound fresh mushrooms, sliced
6 green onions with tops, chopped
1 teaspoon seasoned salt
¼ teaspoon dried whole tarragon
¼ teaspoon dried whole marjoram
¼ teaspoon chives
¼ cup plus 2 tablespoons butter or
    margarine

Wash potatoes, and rub with oil. Bake at 400° for 1 hour or until soft when pierced with a fork.

Prepare sour cream sauce according to package directions, and set aside.

Sauté mushrooms, green onions, and seasonings in butter over medium heat about 10 minutes. Stir in sour cream sauce, and heat thoroughly.

Split tops of potatoes lengthwise, and fluff pulp with a fork. Spoon topping over potatoes. Yield: 4 servings.
Mrs. Ben M. Beasley,
Orlando, Florida.

Tip: Wash most vegetables; trim any wilted parts or excess leaves before storing in crisper compartment of refrigerator. Keep potatoes and onions in a cool, dark place with plenty of air circulation to prevent sprouting.

MUSHROOMS IN SOUR CREAM-DILL SAUCE

1 pound small fresh mushrooms
2½ tablespoons butter or margarine
1 small clove garlic, crushed
1½ tablespoons butter or margarine
2 teaspoons all-purpose flour
½ cup beef broth
⅛ teaspoon pepper
½ teaspoon dried whole dillweed
1½ teaspoons lemon juice
1 tablespoon dry sherry
½ cup commercial sour cream

Sauté mushrooms in 2½ tablespoons butter in a large skillet. Remove mushrooms with slotted spoon, and set aside. Reserve liquid, and set aside.

Sauté garlic in 1½ tablespoons butter until golden. Stir in flour, and cook until bubbly. Add broth, pepper, dillweed, lemon juice, sherry, and reserved liquid from mushrooms. Continue to cook over medium heat until sauce thickens, stirring often.

Gradually stir about one-fourth of sauce into sour cream; add to remaining sauce mixture, stirring constantly. Stir in mushrooms. Heat thoroughly, and serve immediately. Yield: 4 servings.
Grace Bravos,
Timonium, Maryland.

Surround Shrimp With Icy Shells

Try Icy Marinated Shrimp for a tasty addition to your seafood dinners. By arranging seashells in an ice ring, you can create an unusual, but practical way to keep the spicy shrimp cold.

ICY MARINATED SHRIMP

3 pounds unpeeled fresh shrimp
1 (3-ounce) package crab and shrimp boil
1 teaspoon salt
1¼ cups vegetable oil
⅓ cup catsup
⅓ cup vinegar
2 cloves garlic, crushed
2 teaspoons sugar
2 teaspoons Worcestershire sauce
1½ teaspoons dry mustard
¼ teaspoon pepper
⅛ teaspoon hot sauce
1 large onion, sliced
4 bay leaves
Fresh parsley sprigs

Prepare shrimp according to package directions on crab boil, adding 1 teaspoon salt. Drain well; cool completely. Peel and devein shrimp.

Combine next 9 ingredients in container of electric blender; process until smooth. Layer half of shrimp, onion, and bay leaves in a large bowl; pour half of marinade over shrimp mixture. Repeat procedure with remaining ingredients. Cover and refrigerate 2 days.

Arrange seashells in the bottom of a 6-cup ring mold; fill with water, and freeze overnight.

Unmold ice ring onto a large serving platter. Using a slotted spoon, fill ice ring with shrimp; pile remaining shrimp around ring. Garnish with parsley. Yield: 12 appetizer servings.
Rita W. Cook,
Corpus Christi, Texas.

Eggplant—Bake It In A Casserole

Eggplant Parmesan, Italian Eggplant, and Eggplant-Sausage Casserole are some of the best ways we know to make the most of satiny eggplant. Oregano, Italian seasoning, and Parmesan cheese give these dishes a spicy flavor.

When buying an eggplant, look for one with purple to purple-black skin that is glossy and free of dark spots. Some people insist on removing the eggplant skin while others prefer to leave it on. This depends on individual taste and the particular recipe. If you prefer the skin, be sure the eggplant is young and tender; otherwise the skin will be tough and hard to chew.

EGGPLANT-SAUSAGE CASSEROLE

2 medium eggplants
¾ teaspoon salt
3 tablespoons vegetable oil
1 pound bulk pork sausage
½ cup sliced onion
¾ cup grated Parmesan cheese, divided
2 tablespoons chopped fresh parsley
½ teaspoon dried whole oregano
3 large tomatoes, peeled and sliced
¼ teaspoon salt
⅛ teaspoon pepper
2 tablespoons fine, dry breadcrumbs
2 tablespoons butter or margarine

Peel eggplant, and cut crosswise into ⅓-inch slices. Sprinkle slices with ¾ teaspoon salt, and let drain on paper towels for 30 minutes; pat dry. Sauté eggplant slices in hot oil in a large skillet over medium heat until slightly tender and brown. Drain.

Cook sausage and onion in skillet until meat is browned; drain off drippings. Combine ½ cup Parmesan cheese, parsley, and oregano; set aside. Sprinkle tomato slices with ¼ teaspoon salt and pepper. Layer eggplant, sausage mixture, cheese mixture, and tomato slices in a greased 2-quart casserole. Sprinkle with remaining ¼ cup Parmesan cheese and breadcrumbs; dot with butter. Bake, uncovered, at 375° for 45 minutes. Yield: 4 to 6 servings.
Jackie Myers,
Engelhard, North Carolina.

EGGPLANT PARMESAN

1 cup chopped onion
1 clove garlic, minced
2 tablespoons vegetable oil
1 (16-ounce) can whole tomatoes, undrained and chopped
1 (8-ounce) can tomato sauce
½ teaspoon salt
½ teaspoon dried whole basil
½ teaspoon dried whole oregano
1 large eggplant
1 cup wheat germ
⅔ cup dry whole wheat breadcrumbs
½ teaspoon salt
2 eggs, beaten
½ cup vegetable oil
1 (8-ounce) package sliced mozzarella cheese
½ cup grated Parmesan cheese

Sauté onion and garlic in 2 tablespoons hot oil in a skillet until tender. Stir in tomatoes, tomato sauce, ½ teaspoon salt, basil, and oregano. Cover and bring to a boil. Reduce heat and simmer 20 minutes, stirring the mixture occasionally.

Peel eggplant, if desired. Cut eggplant crosswise into ½-inch slices. Combine wheat germ, breadcrumbs, and ½ teaspoon salt. Dip eggplant slices in eggs; coat with breadcrumb mixture. Sauté in hot oil (375°) until golden brown, turning once. Drain.

Spoon half of tomato sauce mixture into a 13- x 9- x 2-inch baking dish. Arrange eggplant over sauce; top with cheese slices and remaining sauce. Sprinkle with Parmesan cheese. Bake at 400° for 10 minutes. Yield: 6 servings.
Anita McLemore,
Knoxville, Tennessee.

ITALIAN EGGPLANT

1 large eggplant, peeled and cut into
   1-inch cubes
½ cup chopped onion
¼ cup chopped green pepper
1 tablespoon vegetable oil
1 medium tomato, peeled
2 tablespoons grated Parmesan cheese
¾ teaspoon Italian seasoning
¼ teaspoon garlic powder
¼ teaspoon lemon-pepper seasoning
8 saltine crackers, crumbled
¼ cup (1 ounce) shredded sharp Cheddar
   cheese
Paprika

Cook eggplant in a small amount of boiling water 10 minutes or until tender. Drain well.

Sauté onion and green pepper in oil in a large skillet until tender; add eggplant and next 6 ingredients, mixing well. Spoon mixture into a lightly greased 1-quart casserole; bake at 350° for 20 minutes. Sprinkle with Cheddar cheese and paprika; bake 10 minutes. Yield: 4 to 6 servings.

Josephine Steiner,
Memphis, Tennessee.

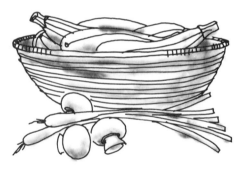

MICROWAVE COOKERY

Appetizers With Ease

Giving a cocktail party is one of the easiest ways to entertain, especially when you use your microwave oven. Some of these appealing appetizers can be assembled ahead and microwaved as needed. Others can be completely prepared a day in advance.

Our recipes recommend cooking only a certain amount of appetizers at a time. If the number is increased, the time required in the microwave will also increase, and cooking may become uneven. The best solution to this problem is to prepare the recipes again or to add additional recipes to your menu.

HOT BEEF SPREAD

1 tablespoon butter or margarine
½ cup chopped green onions
2 tablespoons Chablis or other dry white
   wine
1 (8-ounce) package cream cheese,
   softened
½ cup commercial sour cream
½ cup mayonnaise
1 (2½-ounce) jar dried beef, finely
   chopped
½ cup chopped pecans

Place butter in a 1-quart casserole; microwave at HIGH for 35 seconds or until melted. Add onions; cover and microwave at HIGH 2 minutes or until tender. Stir in wine; microwave at HIGH for 1 minute. Add next 4 ingredients, mixing well. Sprinkle with pecans. Microwave at HIGH for 4 minutes. Serve with crackers. Yield: 4 cups.

CRAB-ZUCCHINI BITES

4 small zucchini, cut into ¾-inch-thick
   pieces
¼ cup chopped fresh mushrooms
1½ tablespoons butter or margarine
1 tablespoon all-purpose flour
¼ cup milk
¼ cup chopped green onions
¼ teaspoon paprika
⅛ teaspoon salt
⅛ teaspoon white pepper
2 to 3 dashes of hot sauce
1 (6-ounce) can crabmeat, drained and
   rinsed

Scoop out each zucchini center about halfway down on one end; set aside. Reserve the zucchini centers for use in other recipes.

Combine mushrooms and butter in a 1-quart casserole. Microwave at HIGH for 1½ to 2 minutes. Stir in flour. Blend in milk, stirring until smooth. Stir in next 5 ingredients. Microwave at HIGH for 1 minute or until thick. Stir in crabmeat, and let stand for 1 minute.

Spoon 1 to 1½ teaspoons crabmeat mixture into each zucchini piece. Place half of stuffed zucchini pieces around outer edge of a paper towel-lined plate. Microwave at MEDIUM HIGH (70% power) for 2 to 2½ minutes or until heated, rotating plate after 1 minute. Repeat with remaining zucchini. Yield: about 20 appetizer servings.

Tip: Reheat single servings in a microwave or toaster oven; these use less energy than a standard range.

BACON-CHESTNUT WRAPS

8 slices bacon, cut in half
1 (8-ounce) can water chestnuts, drained
1 large green pepper, cut into 16 pieces
2 tablespoons water
2 tablespoons soy sauce
2 tablespoons chili sauce
2 tablespoons plum or grape jelly

Place half of bacon on a microwave roasting rack set inside a 12- x 8- x 2-inch baking dish. Cover with paper towels, and microwave at HIGH for 1½ to 2 minutes or until bacon is slightly brown, but not crisp. Repeat with remaining bacon slices.

Wrap each piece of bacon around a water chestnut and a piece of green pepper; secure with a wooden pick. Place in an 8-inch square baking dish.

Stir together remaining ingredients; mix well. Pour over wrapped chestnuts; refrigerate 2 hours. Microwave at HIGH for 6 to 9 minutes or until done. Yield: 16 appetizer servings.

TIPSY MUSHROOMS

2 small onions, thinly sliced
⅔ cup water
⅓ cup vinegar
¼ cup Chablis or other dry white wine
1 teaspoon salt
½ teaspoon butter or margarine
½ teaspoon celery seeds
½ teaspoon mustard seeds
¼ teaspoon whole cloves
½ pound fresh mushrooms
¼ cup vegetable oil

Combine first 9 ingredients in a 1-quart casserole; microwave at HIGH for 6 minutes. Add mushrooms; microwave at HIGH for 3 minutes.

Remove mushrooms with a slotted spoon, and place in a medium bowl. Strain liquid, discarding onions. Add oil to reserved liquid; pour over mushrooms, and toss gently. Cover and chill overnight. Drain before serving. Yield: about 16 appetizer servings.

GREEN ONION CANAPES

½ pound bacon
1 bunch green onions, chopped
¼ cup plus 2 tablespoons mayonnaise
¼ cup grated Parmesan cheese
Dash of pepper
1½ dozen melba cracker rounds

Place half of bacon on a microwave roasting rack set inside a 12- x 8- x 2-inch baking dish. Cover with paper towels; microwave at HIGH for 5 to 6 minutes or until done. Drain; crumble bacon, and set aside. Repeat with remaining bacon.

Combine bacon and next 4 ingredients; stir well. Spread about 1 teaspoon mixture on each cracker. Place half of crackers around outer edge of a paper towel-lined plate. Microwave at HIGH for 1 minute or until hot. Repeat with remaining crackers. Yield: 1½ dozen appetizer servings.

Dress Up Everyday Vegetables

In the recipes listed here, you'll find some tasty ways to liven up the simplest vegetables. Mix them with spices, tomato sauce, or cheese for some flavorful fresh vegetable variations.

DEVILED BEETS

2 tablespoons vinegar
1 tablespoon brown sugar
1 tablespoon butter or margarine
1 teaspoon Worcestershire sauce
½ teaspoon salt
½ teaspoon paprika
¼ teaspoon dry mustard
¼ teaspoon ground cloves
3 cups diced, cooked beets

Combine all ingredients except beets in a medium saucepan; cook over low heat about 2 minutes, stirring constantly. Stir in beets; cook 4 minutes or until heated. Yield: 6 servings.
Sarah Dickerson,
Senatobia, Mississippi.

STUFFED CABBAGE ROLLS

10 large cabbage leaves
1¼ pounds ground beef
1 egg
1 cup minced onion
½ cup uncooked regular rice
2 tablespoons butter or margarine, melted
2 teaspoons salt
½ teaspoon pepper
½ cup grated Parmesan cheese
1 (28-ounce) can whole tomatoes, undrained

Cook cabbage leaves in boiling, salted water 5 to 8 minutes or until just tender; drain leaves.

Combine ground beef, egg, onion, rice, butter, salt, and pepper; mix well. Place equal portions of meat mixture in center of each cabbage leaf; fold ends over, and roll up. Place cabbage rolls, seam side down, in a large greased skillet. Sprinkle cheese over cabbage rolls.

Drain tomatoes, reserving 1 cup juice. Arrange tomatoes on top of cabbage rolls in skillet. Pour reserved tomato juice over cabbage rolls. Bring mixture to a boil; cover, reduce heat, and simmer 1 hour. Yield: 10 servings.
Penny Petty,
Burlington, North Carolina.

EGGPLANT CASSEROLE

1 large eggplant, peeled and cut into ½-inch-thick slices
¼ cup butter or margarine, melted
Salt and pepper
1 medium onion, chopped
2 tablespoons vegetable oil
2 (8-ounce) cans tomato sauce
⅓ cup tomato paste
½ teaspoon dried whole oregano
1 tablespoon chopped fresh parsley
1 egg, beaten
¼ cup grated Parmesan cheese, divided
1 cup cottage cheese

Place eggplant slices on a cookie sheet; brush with melted butter, and sprinkle with salt and pepper. Broil 6 inches from heat 5 minutes or until golden brown; turn slices over and broil until brown. Set eggplant aside.

Sauté onion in oil in a medium skillet until tender. Add tomato sauce, tomato paste, oregano, and parsley; stir well, and set aside.

Combine egg, 2 tablespoons Parmesan cheese, and cottage cheese. Stir well, and set aside.

Spoon half of tomato sauce mixture into a lightly greased 12- x 8- x 2-inch casserole dish. Arrange half of eggplant slices over tomato sauce. Spread cottage cheese mixture over eggplant. Top with remaining eggplant and remaining tomato sauce mixture. Sprinkle remaining 2 tablespoons Parmesan cheese over top of casserole. Bake at 350° for 40 minutes. Yield: 6 to 8 servings.
Anna Weber,
Atmore, Alabama.

SPINACH-MUSHROOM CASSEROLE

2 pounds fresh spinach
½ cup chopped onion
¼ cup butter or margarine, divided
½ teaspoon salt
1 cup (4 ounces) shredded Cheddar cheese, divided
¼ pound small fresh mushrooms

Remove stems from spinach; wash leaves thoroughly, and pat dry. Place in a Dutch oven (do not add water); cover and cook over high heat 3 to 5 minutes. Drain spinach well; chop and set aside.

Sauté onion in 2 tablespoons butter until tender; add spinach and salt, tossing gently. Spoon into a lightly greased 1-quart casserole; sprinkle with ½ cup Cheddar cheese.

Sauté mushrooms in 2 tablespoons butter; place over cheese layer. Sprinkle with remaining ½ cup cheese. Bake at 350° for 20 minutes. Yield: 6 servings.
Dolly Rivard,
Petersburg, Kentucky.

Make The Entrée Sweet-And-Sour

Mix a dash of sweet, such as molasses, with a dash of sour, such as vinegar, and you've got the beginnings of a sweet-and-sour meal. Here are some of our favorite sweet-and-sour dishes.

PLANTATION RIBS

½ cup molasses
¼ cup vinegar
¼ cup prepared mustard
2 tablespoons Worcestershire sauce
½ teaspoon hot sauce
½ teaspoon salt
4 pounds spareribs

Combine first 6 ingredients in a saucepan; bring mixture to a boil. Remove from heat, and set aside.

Cut ribs into serving-size pieces; place meaty side down in a large shallow baking pan. Bake, uncovered, at 450° for 30 minutes. Drain off excess drippings. Reduce heat to 350°. Turn ribs over, and bake an additional 50 to 60 minutes. Brush ribs with sauce during last 30 minutes of cooking. Yield: 6 to 8 servings.
Mary Kay Menees,
White Pine, Tennessee.

SWEET-AND-SOUR CHICKEN

1 egg, beaten
2 tablespoons cornstarch
2 tablespoons vegetable oil
1 teaspoon soy sauce
¼ teaspoon white pepper
1½ pounds boneless chicken breast,
  skinned and cut into ¾-inch pieces
¾ cup all-purpose flour
¾ cup water
2 tablespoons cornstarch
1 teaspoon baking soda
½ teaspoon salt
Vegetable oil
1 cup sugar
1 cup chicken broth
1 (8-ounce) can pineapple chunks,
  undrained
¾ cup vinegar
¼ cup catsup
2 teaspoons soy sauce
1 clove garlic, crushed
¼ teaspoon ground ginger
¼ cup cornstarch
¼ cup water
2 tomatoes, cut into wedges
1 green pepper, cut into 1-inch squares
Hot cooked rice

Combine first 5 ingredients in a large bowl; mix well. Stir in chicken; cover and refrigerate 20 minutes.

Combine flour, ¾ cup water, 2 tablespoons cornstarch, baking soda, and salt; mix well. Drain chicken pieces; add to batter, stirring to coat. Heat 1 inch of oil in an electric skillet to 375°; add chicken, and cook about 6 minutes or until golden brown. Drain well.

Combine sugar and chicken broth in a large saucepan. Drain pineapple, reserving juice; set pineapple aside. Add reserved juice to chicken broth mixture, stirring well. Stir in next 5 ingredients; bring mixture to a boil. Combine ¼ cup cornstarch and ¼ cup water, stirring well. Stir into chicken broth mixture. Cook over medium heat, stirring constantly, until thickened. Stir in the tomatoes, green pepper, and pineapple. Bring to a boil; then remove from heat.

To serve, arrange chicken pieces over rice on a platter. Pour sauce over chicken, and serve immediately. Yield: 6 to 8 servings.   *Susan Sessions,*
Birmingham, Alabama.

Tip: Always measure accurately. Level dry ingredients in a cup with a knife edge or a spoon handle. Measure liquids in a cup so that the fluid is level with the top of the measuring line. Measure solid shortening by packing it firmly in a graduated measuring cup.

SWEET-AND-SOUR PORK

2 eggs, beaten
¼ cup plus 2 tablespoons all-purpose
  flour
2 tablespoons milk
1 teaspoon salt
1½ pounds boneless pork shoulder, cut
  into ¾-inch cubes
Vegetable oil
1 (20-ounce) can pineapple chunks,
  undrained
¼ cup firmly packed brown sugar
2 tablespoons cornstarch
1 (8-ounce) can tomato sauce
¼ cup cider vinegar
¼ cup light corn syrup
¼ teaspoon garlic salt
⅛ teaspoon pepper
1 medium-size green pepper, cut into
  1-inch squares
½ cup thinly sliced onion
Hot cooked rice

Combine eggs, flour, milk, and salt; mix well. Add pork cubes, stirring to coat. Heat 1 inch of oil in a large skillet to 375°; add pork, and fry 6 minutes or until golden brown. Drain well.

Drain pineapple, reserving ½ cup liquid; set pineapple aside. Combine reserved pineapple liquid and next 7 ingredients in a Dutch oven; stir well. Cook over medium heat, stirring constantly, until thickened. Stir in pork, pineapple chunks, green pepper, and onion. Cover and simmer 10 minutes. Serve over hot cooked rice. Yield: 6 to 8 servings.   *Cindy Murphy,*
Cleveland, Tennessee.

Breads And Pastry From The Processor

The food processor saves time, there's no doubt about it. See for yourself when you mix up these recipes for muffins, biscuits, piecrust, and pancakes in your processor.

Start by using the processor to combine the dry ingredients for bread doughs and batters. Just place flour and other dry ingredients in the processor bowl fitted with the knife blade, attach the lid, and pulse one or two times.

Be sure to add liquid to dry ingredients slowly, and check the consistency as you mix. The amount of moisture the dough will need varies with the type of flour used and the humidity in the air, so remember that it's easier to use less liquid in the beginning than to add more flour to already mixed dough.

It's important to be careful with processing time when mixing any bread doughs and batters; overmixing results in tough bread products. Using the pulsing method (a series of quick on/off turns of the machine) helps prevent this problem. Mix pie or biscuit dough by processing only until the mixture begins to form a ball. This occurs in just a few seconds, so pay close attention during the last mixing step.

EASY PROCESSOR BISCUITS

2½ cups self-rising flour
½ cup cold butter, cut into 1-inch pieces
¾ cup buttermilk

Position knife blade in food processor bowl. Add flour and butter. Top with cover, and process pulsing 6 or 7 times until mixture resembles coarse meal. With processor running, slowly add buttermilk through food chute until the dough forms a ball leaving sides of bowl. Turn dough out onto a floured surface, and knead lightly 3 to 4 times.

Roll dough to ½-inch thickness; cut into rounds with a 2½-inch biscuit cutter. Place biscuits on an ungreased baking sheet; bake at 450° for 10 minutes. Yield: 1 dozen.   *Susie Lavenue,*
Ridgely, Tennessee.

The key to fluffy, tender biscuits from the processor is to avoid overmixing.

Step 1—Use the knife blade for Easy Processor Biscuits. Place the flour in the processor bowl; add 1-inch chunks of cold or frozen butter. Pulse 6 or 7 times until it resembles coarse meal.

Step 2—Let the processor do the mixing for you by adding buttermilk to the butter and flour mixture while the machine is running.

Step 3—Stop processing as soon as the dough forms a ball. Remove dough, roll out on a floured surface, and cut out biscuits.

QUICK FOOD PROCESSOR PIE DOUGH

1 cup all-purpose flour
1 teaspoon salt
¼ cup plus 2 tablespoons butter, frozen
2 to 2½ tablespoons ice water

Position knife blade in food processor bowl; add flour and salt. Top with cover, and process pulsing 3 or 4 times or until combined. Cut butter into 6 pieces; add to flour mixture. Process pulsing 5 or 6 times or until mixture resembles coarse meal. With processor running, slowly add water, a teaspoon at a time, until dough forms a ball leaving sides of bowl. Cover and chill dough 30 minutes.

Roll dough to ⅛-inch thickness, and fit into a 9-inch pieplate. Prick bottom and sides of the pastry; bake at 425° for 10 to 12 minutes. Yield: one 9-inch pastry shell.
Joanne Champagne,
Covington, Louisiana.

CINNAMON-PECAN MUFFINS

1½ cups all-purpose flour
½ cup sugar
2 teaspoons baking powder
½ teaspoon ground cinnamon
½ teaspoon salt
⅔ cup pecan halves
1 egg
½ cup milk
¼ cup vegetable oil

Position knife blade in food processor bowl; add first 5 ingredients to processor. Top with cover, and pulse 3 or 4 times to combine ingredients. Add pecans, pulsing 2 or 3 times until chopped. Add remaining ingredients; pulse 4 or 5 times just until mixed. Do not overmix batter.

Fill greased muffin pans two-thirds full. Bake muffins at 400° for 20 to 25 minutes. Yield: 1 dozen.

STRAWBERRY PANCAKES

1 cup all-purpose flour
1 tablespoon sugar
1 teaspoon baking soda
½ teaspoon salt
1 cup buttermilk
1 egg
1 tablespoon vegetable oil
Strawberry preserves
Sifted powdered sugar

Position plastic mixing blade in food processor bowl. Add first 4 ingredients. Top with cover, and process pulsing 3 or 4 times until combined. Add buttermilk, egg, and oil; process 10 seconds or until smooth.

For each pancake, pour about ¼ cup batter onto a hot, lightly greased griddle. Turn pancakes when tops are covered with bubbles and edges are browned. Immediately spread each pancake with strawberry preserves, roll up, and secure with a wooden pick. Sprinkle pancakes with the powdered sugar. Yield: eight 4-inch pancakes.
Jan Lewis,
Simpsonville, South Carolina.

Chicken—It's Always A Bargain

Chicken is low in cost, calories, and cholesterol and high in protein and flavor—which makes it a bargain anytime. These recipes combine the delicate taste of tender boneless chicken breasts with a variety of sauces and seasonings.

You'll save money by boning regular chicken breast halves yourself. The process is simple—just use a small, sharp knife and your thumbs to help loosen the meat from the bones.

CHICKEN SUPREME CASSEROLE

1 cup uncooked instant rice
1 carrot, scraped and shredded
1 stalk celery, finely chopped
1 tablespoon minced fresh parsley
1 (15-ounce) can cut asparagus, undrained
6 chicken breast halves, skinned and boned
1 tablespoon soy sauce
⅛ teaspoon salt
⅛ teaspoon pepper
1 (10¾-ounce) can cream of celery soup, undiluted
1 cup water
1 cup herb-seasoned stuffing mix

Layer first 5 ingredients in a lightly greased 12- x 8- x 2-inch baking dish. Arrange chicken on top; sprinkle with soy sauce, salt, and pepper. Cover and bake at 350° for 45 minutes.

Combine celery soup and water, mixing well. Uncover chicken, and pour soup over top. Sprinkle with the stuffing mix. Bake, uncovered, 15 minutes or until lightly browned. Yield: 6 servings.
Mrs. Melville Hicks,
Warrenton, North Carolina.

CHICKEN MILANO

½ cup fine, dry breadcrumbs
¼ cup grated Parmesan cheese
¼ teaspoon dried whole basil
¼ teaspoon dried whole oregano
6 chicken breast halves, skinned
1 egg, beaten
3 tablespoons vegetable oil
1 (8-ounce) can tomato sauce
1 (1.5-ounce) package spaghetti sauce mix
6 (1-ounce) slices mozzarella cheese

Combine first 4 ingredients in a medium bowl. Dip chicken in egg, and dredge in breadcrumb mixture.

Heat oil in a large skillet to 325°; brown chicken in oil on both sides. Remove chicken from skillet, and drain well on paper towels.

Arrange chicken in a lightly greased 12- x 8- x 2-inch baking dish. Combine tomato sauce and spaghetti sauce mix; stir well, and spoon over chicken. Cover and bake at 350° for 25 minutes.

Remove chicken from oven. Place 1 slice mozzarella cheese over each breast half. Bake, uncovered, an additional 5 to 10 minutes or until cheese melts. Yield: 6 servings.
*Quala Matocha,
El Campo, Texas.*

SAUCY CHICKEN BAKE

6 chicken breast halves, skinned and boned
½ cup all-purpose flour
¼ cup vegetable oil
1 cup orange juice
½ cup chili sauce
2 tablespoons soy sauce
1 tablespoon dark corn syrup
1 teaspoon prepared mustard
1 or 2 cloves garlic, crushed
1 large green pepper, cut into strips
Orange slices
Fresh parsley sprigs

Dredge chicken in flour; brown in oil in a heavy skillet over medium heat, turning once. Transfer chicken to a lightly greased 12- x 8- x 2-inch baking dish; set aside. Drain off drippings.

Combine next 7 ingredients in skillet, mixing well; bring to a boil. Reduce heat and simmer 5 minutes, stirring occasionally. Pour over chicken; cover and bake at 350° for 30 to 35 minutes or until tender. Garnish with orange slices and parsley. Yield: 6 servings.
*Marie Greiner,
Baltimore, Maryland.*

Choose A Cheesy Entrée

You won't need to prepare a separate meat dish when you serve Saucy Cheese Enchiladas—it provides plenty of protein for eight people.

QUICK LASAGNA

1 pound ground beef
1 (15½-ounce) jar spaghetti sauce with mushrooms
1 (15½-ounce) jar meatless spaghetti sauce
1 (3-ounce) can sliced mushrooms, drained
1½ teaspoons minced onion
¼ teaspoon garlic salt
1 (8-ounce) package lasagna noodles
1 teaspoon salt
1 teaspoon vegetable oil
1 (16-ounce) carton cream-style cottage cheese
2 cups (8 ounces) shredded mozzarella cheese

Brown meat in a large skillet; drain well. Stir in next 5 ingredients; simmer 10 minutes, stirring occasionally.

Cook noodles according to package directions using 1 teaspoon each of salt and oil; drain. Layer half of noodles, cottage cheese, mozzarella, and meat sauce in a lightly greased 13- x 9- x 2-inch baking dish; repeat layers. Bake at 350° for 30 minutes. Let stand 10 minutes. Yield: 6 servings.
*Janice C. Dishman,
Danville, Virginia.*

SAUCY CHEESE ENCHILADAS

2 large onions, chopped
4 cloves garlic, minced
2 tablespoons olive oil
1 (28-ounce) can tomatoes, undrained and chopped
1 (15-ounce) can tomato sauce
1 to 2 tablespoons chili powder
1 teaspoon salt
2 teaspoons ground oregano
½ teaspoon ground cumin
1 (12-ounce) carton cream-style cottage cheese
2 cups (8 ounces) shredded Monterey Jack cheese, divided
1 (4-ounce) can chopped green chiles, drained
12 corn tortillas
½ cup olive oil
1 (15-ounce) can pinto beans, drained and rinsed
1 (7-ounce) can whole kernel corn, drained

Sauté onion and garlic in 2 tablespoons oil in a large skillet until tender. Stir in tomatoes, tomato sauce, chili powder, salt, oregano, and cumin. Simmer, uncovered, 20 minutes, stirring occasionally. Set aside 2 cups enchilada sauce in a shallow bowl. Spoon 1 cup sauce into a lightly greased 13- x 9- x 2-inch baking dish; set aside. Reserve remaining sauce in skillet.

Combine cottage cheese, 1 cup Monterey Jack cheese, and chiles; stir well, and set aside. Fry tortillas, one at a time, in ½ cup olive oil for 1 second on each side or just until tortillas are softened. Drain on paper towels; dip each tortilla in the reserved enchilada sauce.

Add beans and corn to remaining sauce in skillet; stir well. Spread about 2 tablespoons cottage cheese mixture on each tortilla. Spoon about ½ cup bean mixture over half of each tortilla; fold tortilla in half. Transfer each enchilada to reserved baking dish. Top with remaining sauce and cheese. Bake at 350° for 20 minutes or until bubbly. Yield: 8 to 10 servings.
*Lorine Kramer,
Needville, Texas.*

MACARONI CASSEROLE

1 (8-ounce) package elbow macaroni
1 (10¾-ounce) can cream of mushroom soup, undiluted
1 small onion, grated
4 cups (16 ounces) shredded Cheddar cheese
1 (2-ounce) jar chopped pimiento, drained
1 cup mayonnaise
3 tablespoons butter or margarine, melted
1 cup cracker crumbs

Cook macaroni according to package directions; drain. Combine macaroni and next 5 ingredients; pour into a greased 12- x 8- x 2-inch baking dish.

Combine butter and cracker crumbs; sprinkle evenly over macaroni mixture. Bake at 350° for 30 minutes. Yield: 6 to 8 servings.
*Mrs. Lewis Self,
Sylvania, Georgia.*

Tip: Keep butter, margarine, and fat drippings tightly covered in the refrigerator. Vegetable shortening can be kept covered at room temperature. Homemade salad dressing should be kept in the refrigerator; mayonnaise and commercial salad dressings should be refrigerated after opening. Foods mixed with mayonnaise, such as potato salad or egg salad, should be refrigerated and used within a couple of days.

Make A Meal Of Salad

If you're looking for a light, satisfying meal that requires little time to prepare, try a main dish salad.

TACO SALAD

2 pounds ground beef
2 (1½-ounce) packages taco seasoning mix
2 large tomatoes, chopped
1 avocado, peeled and chopped
1 medium head lettuce, shredded
1½ cups corn chips, crushed
1 cup (4 ounces) shredded Cheddar cheese

Prepare ground beef and taco seasoning mix according to package directions. Set aside, and keep warm.

Combine tomatoes and avocado in a large salad bowl; toss gently. Just before serving, add lettuce and chips; toss gently. Place salad on individual serving plates; top with ground beef mixture and cheese. Yield: 8 servings.

Ella Rae Poehls,
Houston, Texas.

SHRIMP SALAD

3 cups water
1 pound unpeeled medium-size fresh shrimp
2 envelopes unflavored gelatin
½ cup water
1 (10¾-ounce) can tomato soup, undiluted
1 (8-ounce) package cream cheese, softened
1 cup mayonnaise
1 tablespoon lemon juice
Dash of Worcestershire sauce
Dash of hot sauce
1 cup chopped celery
1 tablespoon grated onion

Bring 3 cups water to a boil; add shrimp, and return to a boil. Reduce heat and simmer 3 to 5 minutes. Drain well; rinse with cold water. Peel shrimp; cut each in half. Cool.

Soften gelatin in ½ cup water, and set aside.

Place soup in a heavy saucepan; bring to a boil over medium heat, stirring constantly. Remove from heat, and add unflavored gelatin, stirring until gelatin is dissolved. Cool mixture completely.

Beat cream cheese; add soup mixture, and beat until blended. Stir in shrimp and remaining ingredients. Pour into an oiled 5-cup mold; chill until firm. Yield: 6 servings.

Marjorie Smith,
Turkey, North Carolina.

CHICKEN SALAD WITH A TWIST

1 (8-ounce) package corkscrew macaroni
½ cup mayonnaise
½ cup commercial Italian salad dressing
3 tablespoons lemon juice
1 tablespoon prepared mustard
1 teaspoon pepper
½ teaspoon salt
3 cups chopped cooked chicken
1 cup chopped cucumber
1 cup chopped celery
¾ cup sliced ripe olives
1 medium onion, chopped
Leafy lettuce (optional)

Cook macaroni according to package directions; drain and cool. Combine next 6 ingredients; stir until blended. Add to macaroni, stirring well. Stir in chicken, cucumber, celery, olives, and onion. Chill at least 2 hours. Serve salad in a lettuce-lined bowl, if desired. Yield: about 8 servings.

Mrs. Robert Burgess,
Fort Smith, Arkansas.

LAYERED TUNA SALAD

2 (6½-ounce) cans tuna, drained and flaked
¾ cup prepared buttermilk salad dressing
3 tablespoons sliced green onions
2 cups shredded lettuce
2 medium tomatoes, coarsely chopped
1 (3.2-ounce) can black olives, drained and sliced
1 avocado, peeled and thinly sliced
½ pound bacon, cooked and crumbled

Combine tuna, dressing, and green onions, stirring well.

Layer 1 cup lettuce, tomatoes, and olives in a serving bowl. Spoon half of tuna mixture over salad ingredients. Top with a layer each of avocado, bacon, remaining lettuce, and remaining tuna mixture. Yield: 6 servings.

Margot Foster,
Hubbard, Texas.

Cheese Starts A Party

Whether you're planning a casual get-together or dinner party, start by offering guests some cheesy appetizers. The rich flavors of Parmesan, Cheddar, and blue cheese are always popular, so these snacks are sure to be a hit.

FRIED HAM-AND-CHEESE BALLS

2 cups fine, dry breadcrumbs, divided
2 cups ground cooked ham
1 cup grated Parmesan cheese
4 eggs, slightly beaten
1 small onion, finely chopped
¼ cup finely chopped fresh parsley
Vegetable oil

Combine 1½ cups breadcrumbs with next 5 ingredients, mixing well; shape into 1-inch balls. Roll balls in remaining ½ cup breadcrumbs. Chill 30 minutes.

Deep fry ham-and-cheese balls in hot oil (375°) for 2 to 3 minutes or until golden brown. Drain on paper towels. Serve immediately with prepared mustard or a sweet-and-sour sauce. Yield: 4 dozen appetizer servings. *Linda Sutton,*
Winston-Salem, North Carolina.

HOT CHEESY SEAFOOD DIP

1 pound process cheese, cut into 1-inch cubes
1 (3-ounce) package cream cheese
¼ cup butter or margarine
⅛ teaspoon hot sauce
1 (4½-ounce) can small shrimp, drained, rinsed, and chopped
1 (4-ounce) can chopped green chiles, drained
Chopped green onions with tops (optional)

Combine first 3 ingredients in top of a double boiler; bring water to a boil. Reduce heat to low; cook, stirring frequently, until cheese melts. Stir in next 3 ingredients. Transfer mixture to a chafing dish; sprinkle with onions, if desired. Serve warm with tortilla chips. Yield: about 4 cups. *Susan Pajcic,*
Jacksonville, Florida.

BLUE CHEESE BALL

1 (8-ounce) package cream cheese, softened
½ pound blue cheese, crumbled
½ cup butter or margarine, softened
½ cup pimiento-stuffed olives, sliced
1 tablespoon minced onion
⅛ teaspoon garlic powder
⅛ teaspoon coarsely ground pepper
1 cup chopped pecans

Combine cheese and butter in container of an electric blender; process until smooth. Add olives, onion, garlic powder, and pepper; mix well. Chill mixture at least 1 hour. Shape into a ball, and roll in pecans. Chill at least 3 hours. Yield: one 5-inch cheese ball.

Lynne T. Weeks,
Columbus, Georgia.

QUICHE SQUARES

2 (6-ounce) jars marinated artichoke
   hearts, undrained
½ cup finely chopped onion
1 clove garlic, minced
4 eggs, beaten
2 cups (8 ounces) shredded sharp
   Cheddar cheese
¼ cup fine, dry breadcrumbs
2 tablespoons minced fresh
   parsley
⅛ teaspoon dried whole oregano
⅛ teaspoon pepper
⅛ teaspoon hot sauce

Drain 1 jar artichoke hearts, reserving marinade. Drain remaining jar, discarding marinade. Chop artichoke hearts, and set aside.

Pour reserved artichoke marinade into a skillet. Add onion and garlic; cook over medium heat until tender. Cool slightly. Combine onion mixture, artichoke hearts, and remaining ingredients, mixing well; spoon into a lightly greased 10- x 6- x 2-inch baking dish. Bake at 325° for 35 to 40 minutes or until set. Let stand 10 minutes before serving. Cut into 1-inch squares. Quiche may be served warm or cool. Yield: 5 dozen.
Mrs. R. D. Leake,
Memphis, Tennessee.

CHEESE-HORSERADISH SPREAD

2 pounds process cheese, cut into
   cubes
1 cup mayonnaise
1 (6-ounce) jar prepared horseradish
½ teaspoon hot sauce

Melt cheese over low heat, stirring occasionally. Stir in remaining ingredients; mix well. Cover and refrigerate. Serve with crackers. Yield: 3½ cups.
Mrs. E. W. Hanley
Palm Harbor, Florida.

Take A New Look
At Chicken Livers

Chicken Livers en Brochette is one of the tastiest and most attractive ways we've seen to prepare chicken livers. Another way to serve livers is in Pâté Maison. Plan to make this recipe at least 8 hours before serving so it will be chilled and unmold properly.

CHICKEN LIVERS
EN BROCHETTE

1½ pounds chicken livers
⅓ cup vegetable oil
3 tablespoons wine vinegar
1 teaspoon salt
¾ to 1 teaspoon dried whole tarragon
⅛ teaspoon pepper
1 bay leaf
6 pearl onions
2 green peppers, cut into 1-inch cubes
12 cherry tomatoes
Hot cooked rice (optional)

Place chicken livers in a shallow container; set aside. Combine next 6 ingredients in a jar; cover tightly, and shake vigorously. Pour marinade over chicken livers; cover and chill at least 2 hours.

Cook onions in boiling water 8 to 10 minutes or until just tender; drain.

Drain livers, reserving marinade; discard bay leaf. Arrange livers, onions, green pepper, and tomatoes on skewers; brush with marinade. Broil 6 to 8 inches from heat 10 to 12 minutes, turning and brushing occasionally with marinade. Serve over rice, if desired. Yield: 6 servings.
Patricia Boschen,
Ashland, Virginia.

CHICKEN BITS AND LIVERS

4 chicken breast halves, skinned and
   boned
1½ cups all-purpose flour, divided
¼ cup butter or margarine
1 pound chicken livers
¼ cup butter or margarine

Cut chicken breasts into 1-inch cubes; dredge in ¾ cup flour. Melt ¼ cup butter in a heavy skillet over medium heat; add chicken, and cook until browned. Drain; arrange on platter. Drain off drippings from skillet.

Dredge chicken livers in remaining flour. Melt ¼ cup butter in skillet; add livers and cook until browned. Drain on paper towels; arrange over chicken. Yield: 6 servings.
Helen Nicholas,
Grantsville, West Virginia.

PATE MAISON

1 medium onion, chopped
1 clove garlic, minced
¼ cup butter
½ pound chicken livers
1 bay leaf
¼ teaspoon salt
¼ teaspoon pepper
¼ teaspoon dried whole thyme
¼ cup butter, softened
1 tablespoon brandy

Sauté onion and garlic in ¼ cup butter in a large skillet until tender. Add next 5 ingredients; cook over medium heat 5 to 8 minutes, stirring often. Cool. Discard bay leaf. Spoon liver mixture, softened butter, and brandy into container of electric blender or food processor; process until smooth. Spoon mixture into a well-oiled 1-cup mold; cover and chill 8 hours or overnight.

Unmold pâté, and garnish as desired. Serve with melba toast or crackers. Yield: 1 cup.
Carolyn M. Howe,
Shippensburg, Pennsylvania.

Is It Chili Or
Spaghetti?

Spicy and thick is the way to describe Herbed Chili-Spaghetti, because it's flavored with herbs and spices and a package of spaghetti is stirred in.

HERBED CHILI-SPAGHETTI

2 pounds ground beef
2 medium onions, chopped
2 cloves garlic, minced
1 green pepper, chopped
4 (16-ounce) cans whole tomatoes,
   undrained
1 (20-ounce) can tomato sauce
1 (15½-ounce) can kidney beans,
   undrained
1 (12-ounce) package spaghetti
¼ cup chopped fresh parsley
2 to 3 tablespoons chili powder
1 tablespoon minced fresh marjoram or 1
   teaspoon dried whole marjoram
1 tablespoon minced fresh oregano or 1
   teaspoon dried whole oregano
2 teaspoons salt
1 teaspoon ground cumin
1 teaspoon red pepper

Cook ground beef, onion, garlic, and green pepper in a Dutch oven until browned, stirring to crumble meat. Drain off drippings. Add remaining ingredients; mix well. Cover, reduce heat, and simmer 2 hours, stirring occasionally. Yield: 10 to 12 servings.
Bettye McClure,
Bardstown, Kentucky.

These inviting cakes show off a few new tricks that give home-baked cakes the professional look: (from front) Sugar 'n Spice Cake, Stately Fruit-and-Nut Cake, Chocolate-Almond Cake With Cherry Filling. Recipes on pages 225 and 226.

Cakes For Show And Eating Too

Most Southern hostesses aim for dessert to be the hit of their supper club or covered dish dinner. If you do too, you can enjoy all the "oohs and aahs" when you bake one of these cakes.

The beauty of these cakes lies in the fact that they're simple to make. They need no elaborate equipment or special piping tools to make them. Together, these three cakes boast the use of five easy decorating ideas. Reproduce the exact designs on these cakes, or adapt the designs to a favorite cake of your own. But be prepared—everyone will probably ask, "How'd you do that?" Here's what to tell them.

Coat the Cake With Nuts

The South is noted for its nuts, especially pecans and peanuts. You can jazz up cakes with these and other nuts by just gently patting them onto the frosting. Cover the entire cake, or cover just the sides with nuts; swirl the top frosting into a pretty design, coat the top with fruit, or add any other eye-catching decoration.

When choosing what type of nut, consider the form in which you'll use it. Pecans, peanuts, walnuts, macadamias, and almost any other nut work well coarsely chopped. (Finely chopped nuts won't look as pretty and may not adhere to the frosting as well.) Halves of pecans and sliced or slivered almonds add even more visual interest than the chopped form.

Toast the nuts lightly before patting them onto the cake; this will bring out their full flavor and color.

Add a Fancy Touch With Fruit

It's easy to coat the top of any cake with fruit and a glaze without even having a recipe. Just use whatever fresh fruit is in season or whatever canned fruit you have on hand in your pantry. Vary the color, size, and shape of the fruit to add visual interest. Be sure to select soft fruit so that the cake will slice more easily.

Arrange the fruit on top of the cake. (You can frost the top beforehand if you want the added sweetness, or leave the top unfrosted to cut calories.) Remember that some fruit darkens upon slicing, so dip them in orange or lemon juice before arranging on the cake.

Once the fruit is in place, cook and stir about ½ cup jam over low heat until melted. Sieve the jam if it's very thick; then brush over the fruit to add a glaze and to hold the fruit together.

Wrap It in Almond Paste

Almond paste right out of the can is of near perfect consistency for rolling into sheets to wrap around the sides of a cake. To one 8-ounce can of almond paste, add 1 cup sifted powdered sugar, 1 tablespoon liquid (our recipe calls for brandy or milk), and 1 teaspoon almond extract; mix well, and knead the mixture until it is the consistency of craft dough.

Roll the mixture on waxed paper into a 3/16-inch-thick strip long enough to wind around the sides of the cake. Brush the sides of the cake with melted sieved preserves or jam to help the almond paste strip adhere; then wind the strip around the cake, gently pressing it onto cake. We rolled the strip about ½ inch taller than the cake, clipped ½-inch slits at ½-inch intervals around the

Dress up any plain frosted cake with a coating of nuts—in this case, sliced almonds.

For a fancy design, arrange assorted fruit on top; then brush with a glaze.

Wrap a strip of almond paste mixture around the sides; clip and flute the top edges.

top edge, then gently curved the "fingers" back and forth to create a herringbone effect. (If a finger breaks, just moisten it lightly with water, and gently press it back into place.)

You can create several other cake decorations with the same almond paste mixture. Try making cutouts with cookie or canapé cutters and pressing them into icing on the top or sides of a cake. Or take the same mixture and hand shape flowers or other figures to garnish the top of a cake, working with the mixture just as you would with craft dough. You can even color the mixture by kneading in paste food coloring.

Keep the almond paste mixture covered when not working with it. This keeps it from drying out.

Comb the Frosting

The process is done just like it sounds—comb the frosting into either straight, curvy, or zigzag lines using a very inexpensive gadget known as a frosting comb. The tool is available in most kitchen specialty shops. If you can't locate one, comb with the tines of a fork (although the process will take longer and a little more care) or a regular wide-toothed hair comb (buy one just for cake decorating purposes).

Make waves on a smoothly frosted cake with a frosting comb.

Roll dried apricots to ⅛-inch thickness; then press several together for apricot roses.

Before combing, spread the frosting smoothly using a metal spatula. Comb the sides of the cake first, then the top. Periodically wipe off any excess frosting that accumulates on the comb.

This design is especially pretty used in combination with other simple designs, such as an arrangement of nuts or fruit.

Roll Pretty Apricot Roses

Many cooks bake spice cakes or fruitcakes about this time of year, and roses made from dried apricots make a pretty and unusual garnish that will complement either cake.

A cluster of several roses looks best, and each rose will take 6 to 8 dried apricot halves to make. Roll each apricot half with a rolling pin—shiny, sticky side down—to about ⅛-inch thickness on a wooden cutting board. Gently peel the apricot from the board after each roll to keep it from sticking to the board. (If the apricots are especially sticky, roll them on thick paper towels to absorb excess moisture. But remember, they need to be somewhat sticky to make the roses hold together.)

Roll one small flattened apricot half jellyroll fashion, sticky side in, to make it adhere to itself and to make it look like the tight center bud of a rose. Wrap several larger apricot halves, one at a time, around the outside of the bud, sticky sides to the bud, pressing gently to adhere. Peel the top of each apricot half outward slightly to look like rose petals. Pinch firmly at the bottom to make a stem end.

Cluster several apricot roses together on a cake, and arrange pecan halves, mint leaves, or chocolate leaves around the base of the roses.

CHOCOLATE-ALMOND CAKE WITH CHERRY FILLING

4 (1-ounce) squares semisweet chocolate
2 (8-ounce) cans almond paste
1 cup sugar
1 egg
⅔ cup butter, softened
4 eggs
2 teaspoons vanilla extract
1½ teaspoons almond extract
2 cups cake flour, sifted
Cherry Filling
¼ cup cherry or strawberry preserves
1 cup sifted powdered sugar
1 tablespoon brandy or milk
1 teaspoon almond extract

Place chocolate in top of double boiler; bring water to a boil. Reduce heat and cook until chocolate melts. Cool slightly.

Crumble 1 can almond paste into a large mixing bowl. Add 1 cup sugar and 1 egg; beat at medium speed of an electric mixer until well blended. Add butter, and beat until blended. Add 4 eggs, one at a time, beating well after each addition. Beat in melted chocolate, vanilla, and 1½ teaspoons almond extract. Gradually add flour, beating at low speed just until blended.

Pour batter into 2 greased and floured 9-inch round cakepans; bake at 325° for 35 minutes or until a wooden pick inserted in center comes out clean. Cool in pans 10 minutes on a wire rack; remove from pans, and cool completely.

Place one cake layer on a serving plate; place waxed paper strips under edge of cake, covering plate. Spread half of Cherry Filling on cake layer, and top with second cake layer. Melt cherry preserves; press through a fine-meshed sieve to remove lumps of fruit. Brush sieved preserves on sides of cake. Spoon remaining Cherry Filling on top of cake, spreading just to the edge.

Combine remaining can of almond paste, powdered sugar, brandy, and 1 teaspoon almond extract in a large mixing bowl; mix at low to medium speed until crumbly. Knead until well blended (mixture will be soft and pliable). Roll out almond paste mixture on a piece of waxed paper into a strip 28 inches long and 3 inches wide, trimming to make strip even. Using waxed paper to help lift and guide almond paste strip, wind strip around side of cake, pressing edges firmly together to adhere. Lightly press strip onto side of cake. Cut ½-inch slits at ½-inch intervals around top edge of almond paste strip; gently bend alternating "fingers" back and forth to create a herringbone effect. If a "finger" breaks off from cake, moisten the almond paste lightly with water, and gently press back onto cake. Cover until serving time. Yield: one 9-inch cake.

Cherry Filling:

2 (16½-ounce) cans pitted tart cherries,
undrained
¼ cup brandy
3 tablespoons cornstarch

Drain cherries, reserving 1⅓ cups liquid. Set cherries aside.

Combine reserved cherry liquid, brandy, and cornstarch in a small saucepan, stirring until smooth. Cook over medium heat, stirring occasionally, until mixture thickens. Cool slightly. Stir in cherries; cool to room temperature. Yield: 3 cups.

SUGAR 'N SPICE CAKE

¾ cup shortening
¾ cup firmly packed brown sugar
1 cup sugar
3 eggs
1 teaspoon vanilla extract
2¼ cups all-purpose flour
1 teaspoon baking powder
¾ teaspoon baking soda
1 teaspoon salt
¾ teaspoon ground cinnamon
¾ teaspoon ground cloves
1 cup buttermilk
Spiced Buttercream
1 (6-ounce) package dried apricots
Chocolate leaves or pecan halves (optional)

Cream shortening; beat in brown sugar. Gradually add 1 cup sugar, beating well. Add eggs, one at a time, beating well after each addition; stir in vanilla.

Combine dry ingredients; add to creamed mixture alternately with buttermilk, beginning and ending with dry ingredients. Mix well after each addition.

Grease two 9-inch round cakepans, and line with waxed paper; grease waxed paper. Pour batter into prepared pans; bake at 325° for 40 to 45 minutes or until a wooden pick inserted in center comes out clean. Cool in pans 10 minutes; remove from pans, and cool completely on wire racks. Spread Spiced Buttercream between layers and on top and sides of cake, spreading it smoothly. Rake frosting on sides of cake, swirling it back and forth, using a metal frosting comb. Rake top of cake in zigzag lines.

Make about 5 apricot roses. To make apricot roses, roll apricots to ⅛-inch thickness using a rolling pin. (Cut side of apricots will be somewhat sticky.) For each rose, roll one round of apricot, jellyroll fashion, sticky side in, into a bud. Roll 5 to 7 remaining rounds around bud, pressing sticky side inward, and curling upper edges outward for a petal effect; pinch rose at bottom to make stem end.

Arrange roses in center of cake, and nestle chocolate leaves or pecan halves under and around roses, if desired. Yield: one 9-inch cake.

Spiced Buttercream:

1½ cups butter or margarine, softened
4½ cups sifted powdered sugar
2 tablespoons orange juice
¾ teaspoon ground cinnamon
¼ teaspoon ground cloves

Combine butter and powdered sugar, creaming until light and fluffy. Add orange juice; beat until spreading consistency. Beat in spices. Yield: 3¼ cups.

STATELY FRUIT-AND-NUT CAKE

1 cup shortening
2 cups sugar
4 eggs
3 cups sifted cake flour
2½ teaspoons baking powder
½ teaspoon salt
1 cup milk
1 teaspoon almond extract
1 teaspoon vanilla extract
Frosting (recipe follows)
1 cup sliced almonds, toasted
1 small banana
2 teaspoons lemon juice
½ cup peach or apricot jam
1 (8½-ounce) can sliced peaches, drained
1 (6-ounce) jar maraschino cherries, drained and halved
½ cup green grapes, halved

Cream shortening; gradually add sugar, beating until light and fluffy. Add eggs, one at a time, beating well after each addition.

Combine flour, baking powder, and salt; add to creamed mixture alternately with milk, beginning and ending with flour mixture. Mix well after each addition. Stir in flavorings.

Pour batter into 3 greased and floured 9-inch round cakepans. Bake at 375° for 20 to 25 minutes or until a wooden pick inserted in center comes out clean. Cool in pans 10 minutes; remove from pans, and let cool completely. Spread frosting between layers and on sides of cake. Press almonds onto sides of cake.

Slice banana; toss with lemon juice. Melt jam; press through a sieve to remove lumps. Arrange fruit on top of cake; brush fruit with melted jam. Yield: one 9-inch cake.

Frosting:

¼ cup butter or margarine, softened
4 cups sifted powdered sugar
¼ cup milk
1 teaspoon almond extract
½ teaspoon vanilla extract

Cream butter; add remaining ingredients, beating until light and fluffy. Yield: 2½ cups.

Tip: When squeezing fresh lemons or oranges for juice, first grate the rind by rubbing the washed fruit against surface of grater, taking care to remove only the outer colored portion of the rind. Wrap in plastic in teaspoon portions and freeze for future use.

Cooking Up The Apple Harvest

With their glowing crimsons, lemony yellows, and dramatically splashed pinks and greens, apples capture the essence of fall color. Bite into them and find that they vary in flavor as significantly as fine wines—some are tart with a sweet aftertaste; others are spicy. Some are mild and subtle; others fairly burst with flavor.

Apple orchards started filling Southern hillsides soon after the Jamestown Colony was established in 1607. George Washington at Mount Vernon and Thomas Jefferson at Monticello were two of the earliest apple growers. Many kinds of apples are being produced in the South today: Red Delicious, Golden Delicious, Stayman, York Imperial, Rome Beauty, and Jonathan provide the major volume, but Winesap, Rambo, Granny Smith, and Lodi are also grown.

When selecting apples, consider how they are going to be used. There are three basic types—eating, all-purpose, and cooking. Red Delicious is the sweetest eating apple, and Golden Delicious is an all-purpose apple. It's not too tart or too sweet—just juicy and full-flavored.

Stayman and Winesap are also good all-purpose apples. We particularly recommend Stayman for pies. You'll find Jonathans are good in salads while the Rome Beauties and York Imperials are better for cooking. For more information on apples, see "From Our Kitchen to Yours" on the following page.

OLD-FASHIONED APPLE DUMPLINGS

3 cups all-purpose flour
2 teaspoons baking powder
1 teaspoon salt
1 cup shortening
¾ cup milk
3 large Winesap, York, or other cooking apples
2 tablespoons butter or margarine, divided
1 tablespoon sugar, divided
½ teaspoon ground cinnamon, divided
1½ cups sugar
1½ cups water
1 tablespoon butter or margarine
¼ teaspoon ground nutmeg
¼ teaspoon ground cinnamon

Combine first 3 ingredients; cut in shortening with pastry blender until mixture resembles coarse meal. Gradually add milk, stirring to make a soft dough. Roll dough out on a lightly floured surface to ¼-inch thickness, shaping into a 21- x 14-inch rectangle; cut dough with a pastry cutter into six 7-inch squares.

Peel and core apples. Cut in half. Place one apple half on each pastry square; dot each with 1 teaspoon butter. Sprinkle each with ½ teaspoon sugar and ¼ teaspoon cinnamon. Moisten edges of each dumpling with water; bring corners to center, pinching edges to seal. Place the dumplings in a lightly greased 12- x 8- x 2-inch baking dish. Bake at 375° for 35 minutes.

Combine 1½ cups sugar, 1½ cups water, 1 tablespoon butter, nutmeg, and ¼ teaspoon cinnamon in a medium saucepan; bring to a boil. Reduce heat and simmer 4 minutes, stirring occasionally until butter melts and sugar dissolves. Pour the syrup over cooked dumplings; serve immediately. Yield: 6 servings.
Mrs. G. Pedersen,
Brandon, Mississippi.

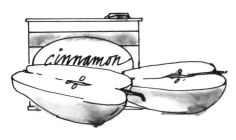

DELUXE APPLE TART

1½ cups all-purpose flour
½ teaspoon baking powder
½ teaspoon salt
¼ cup cold butter
¼ cup shortening
3½ to 4 tablespoons milk
½ cup plus 2 tablespoons blanched, slivered almonds
½ cup sugar
1 egg
1 tablespoon butter, melted
2 cups water
2 tablespoons lemon juice
5 medium Golden Delicious or other cooking apples
¼ cup sugar
¼ cup butter
½ teaspoon ground cinnamon
½ cup peach preserves
2 tablespoons water
2 tablespoons apricot brandy

Combine flour, baking powder, and salt; cut in ¼ cup cold butter and shortening with pastry blender until mixture resembles coarse meal. Sprinkle milk over surface; stir with a fork until dry

ingredients are moistened. Shape into a ball; chill at least 1 hour.

Roll dough to ⅛-inch thickness on a lightly floured surface. Fit pastry into an 11- x 7½- x 1-inch tart pan. Set aside.

Position knife blade in food processor bowl. Add almonds; process 40 to 50 seconds or until finely ground. Add ½ cup sugar, egg, and 1 tablespoon melted butter; process until well mixed. Spread mixture evenly over bottom of pastry; set aside.

Combine 2 cups water and lemon juice. Peel and core apples; cut into ¼-inch-thick vertical slices. Dip apples in lemon juice mixture; drain well. Arrange apples so slices are overlapping, curved side up, in rows on top of almond mixture. Sprinkle with ¼ cup sugar, dot with ¼ cup butter, and sprinkle with cinnamon. Bake at 400° for 1 hour. Combine peach preserves and 2 tablespoons water; cook over low heat, stirring constantly, until melted. Press mixture through a sieve, reserving syrup. Discard preserves. Stir in brandy. Carefully brush syrup over the tart. Remove tart from pan before serving. Yield: 16 servings.

APPLE CIDER PIE

Pastry for double-crust 9-inch pie
1 cup apple cider
⅔ cup sugar
6½ cups peeled, sliced Stayman, Winesap, or other cooking apples
2 tablespoons cornstarch
2 tablespoons water
½ teaspoon ground cinnamon
1 tablespoon butter or margarine

Line a 9-inch pieplate with half of pastry; set aside.

Combine cider and sugar in a large saucepan; bring to a boil. Add apples; cook, uncovered, 8 minutes or until apples are tender. Drain, reserving syrup. Add enough water to syrup to measure 1⅓ cups liquid; return syrup mixture and apples to saucepan. Combine cornstarch and 2 tablespoons water, stirring well; add to apple mixture. Stir in cinnamon; cook, stirring constantly, until thickened. Stir in butter. Spoon mixture into pastry-lined pieplate. Cover with top crust. Trim edges of pastry; seal and flute edges. Cut slits in top of crust to allow steam to escape.

Bake at 375° for 45 to 50 minutes (cover edges with foil to prevent overbrowning, if necessary). Serve warm or cool. Yield: one 9-inch pie.
Agnes Kolk,
Arlington, Texas.

DOUBLE APPLE SALAD

1 large Red Delicious or other variety eating apple, unpeeled and diced
1 large Golden Delicious apple, unpeeled and diced
½ teaspoon ascorbic-citric powder
1 (8-ounce) can pineapple chunks, drained
1 cup miniature marshmallows
⅔ cup flaked coconut
½ cup chopped pecans
¼ cup raisins
2 tablespoons chopped celery
¼ cup mayonnaise

Combine apples and sprinkle with ascorbic-citric powder. Add remaining ingredients; mix well. Cover salad, and chill. Yield: 6 to 8 servings.
Jacquelyn Christopher,
Asheville, North Carolina.

From Our Kitchen To Yours

Apples may be red, yellow, or green; round or tapered; tart or sweet. We get lots of letters from readers asking about apples—how they're best used, the amounts needed, and storage tips. Here are some answers to the more common questions.

Which of the Southern apples are best for eating and which are best for cooking? The Red Delicious, Golden Delicious, and Jonathan apples are all good eating apples because they're crisp and juicy. The Red Delicious has a tapered shape, a big top, smaller base, and a deep red color. The Golden Delicious apple has a rounder shape than the Red Delicious and is yellow-green to bright yellow in color. It will stay white longer after being cut than other varieties. The Golden Delicious is really an all-purpose apple and works well for both snacking and cooking. The Jonathan apple is rounded and has a bright red color. Its taste is a little tart.

Stayman, Rome Beauty, and York Imperial apples are best for cooking because they hold their shape and retain their flavor while cooking. A Stayman apple has a definite round shape, with a deep red skin and purplish undertones. A Rome Beauty apple is round, rather than tapered, and bright red in color. These varieties have a mildly tart flavor. The York Imperial apple is easy to spot with its lopsided shape and green skin with varying degrees of red. It has a distinct, winelike taste.

Why do apples look waxy? You'll find many apples look shiny and polished on the fruit stand. All apples produce a natural wax that helps hold in moisture and protects them from diseases and insects. But before they're packed and distributed, every apple is washed, removing the natural wax, then sprayed with a new coating of wax. This wax is like that on medicine tablets, without odor and taste, and is completely safe.

How do you know how many apples to buy? These tips should help.

—One pound of apples will usually equal 4 small apples, 3 medium apples, or 2 large apples.

—Two medium apples usually yield 1 cup grated apple.

—You'll need about 2 pounds of apples for one 9-inch pie.

—One pound of apples will yield about 3 cups of diced apples or about 2¾ cups sliced apples.

—A bushel of apples weighs about 42 pounds and will usually yield 16 to 20 quarts of apple slices.

How can I keep apples from turning brown when they're cut? After you cut apples, dip them in lemon juice or ascorbic-citric powder to keep them from browning. They should be drained and patted dry before they're used.

What's the best way to store apples? It's best to store apples in a plastic bag or the vegetable crisper area in the refrigerator. If left at room temperature, apples will ripen 10 times faster than when refrigerated. Apples that become too cold (colder than 32 degrees) will ruin, so it's best to keep them away from your freezer section.

COOKING LIGHT

Good Reasons To Serve These Breads

Bread is probably one of the first foods you give up when starting a low-calorie diet. Actually, bread *isn't* one of the non-nutritious foods you should avoid. Bread is a source of complex carbohydrate, protein, and some important vitamins. And when enriched with fiber, bread contributes even more to a sensible diet plan.

Why all this talk lately about fiber? For years, fiber has been known to aid in relieving or preventing constipation. But today, scientists and nutritionists credit fiber as a possible reducer of blood cholesterol, preventer of colon cancer, and aid in controlling diabetes. Whether or not all of these claims are true, we are yet to know. But the consensus among nutritionists is that eating foods high in fiber makes sense not only because of fiber itself, but also because of the trace vitamins and minerals that are provided by fiber-rich foods.

WHOLE WHEAT WAFFLES

1¼ cups whole wheat flour
1 tablespoon baking powder
2 tablespoons brown sugar
¼ teaspoon salt
2 eggs, separated
1¼ cups skim milk
Vegetable cooking spray

Combine first 4 ingredients in a medium bowl. Combine egg yolks and milk; add to dry ingredients, stirring until mixture is smooth.

Beat egg whites (at room temperature) until stiff peaks form, and gently fold into batter.

Coat an 8-inch square waffle iron with cooking spray; allow to preheat. Pour about 1 cup batter into hot waffle iron. Bake about 5 minutes or until steaming stops. Repeat procedure until all the batter is used. Yield: sixteen 4-inch waffles (about 54 calories and 101 milligrams sodium each). *Jackie Dane, Farmington, Missouri.*

FLAKY BISCUITS

2 cups all-purpose flour
1 tablespoon baking powder
½ teaspoon salt
⅔ cup skim milk
¼ cup vegetable oil

Combine first 3 ingredients; stir well. Combine milk and oil; add to dry ingredients, stirring quickly with a fork until dry ingredients are moistened. Turn dough out onto a lightly floured surface, and knead lightly 4 or 5 times.

Roll dough to ½-inch thickness, and cut with a 2-inch biscuit cutter. Place biscuits on an ungreased baking sheet; bake at 450° for 8 to 10 minutes. Yield: 1 dozen (about 113 calories and 160 milligrams sodium each).

Margie Livengood, Georgetown, Kentucky.

LOW-SODIUM YEAST ROLLS

1 package dry yeast
¼ cup warm water (105° to 115°)
2 egg whites, slightly beaten
1 cup warm water (105° to 115°)
½ cup vegetable oil
½ cup sugar
5 to 5½ cups all-purpose flour, divided

Dissolve yeast in ¼ cup water. Add egg whites, 1 cup water, oil, sugar, and 2 cups flour. Beat 2 minutes at medium speed of electric mixer until smooth. Stir in 2½ cups flour (dough will be sticky). Cover and chill overnight.

Remove from refrigerator, and stir in enough remaining flour to make a soft dough. Turn dough out onto a floured surface, and knead 10 to 12 times.

Divide dough into four parts. Shape each part into 8 rolls. Place on greased baking sheets. Cover and let rise in a warm place (85°), free from drafts, 1 hour or until doubled in bulk. Bake at 375° for 10 to 12 minutes or until browned. Yield: 32 rolls (about 110 calories and 4 milligrams sodium each).

Mary Kay Meyer, Mobile, Alabama.

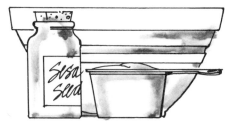

WHOLE WHEAT BREADSTICKS

1½ cups whole wheat flour
1½ cups all-purpose flour
1 package dry yeast
1 tablespoon sugar
¾ teaspoon salt
1 cup warm water (105° to 115°)
1 tablespoon vegetable oil
¼ cup sesame seeds
Vegetable cooking spray

Combine flour; combine 1½ cups flour mixture, yeast, sugar, and salt in a large bowl. Add water and oil; beat at medium speed of an electric mixer 3 to 4 minutes or until smooth. Stir in enough remaining flour mixture to make a stiff dough; turn out onto a lightly floured surface, and knead 4 to 5 times or until smooth and elastic.

Divide dough into fourths; shape each fourth into a ball. Cut each ball into ten pieces. Shape each piece into an 8-inch rope. (Cover remaining dough while working to prevent drying.) Roll ropes in sesame seeds.

Place ropes 2 inches apart on baking sheets coated with cooking spray. Cover and let rise in a warm place (85°), free from drafts, for 50 minutes. (Dough will not double in bulk.) Bake at 400° for 10 to 13 minutes or until lightly browned. Yield: 40 breadsticks (about 40 calories and 38 milligrams sodium each).

BRAN-APPLESAUCE BREAD

1½ cups shreds of wheat bran cereal
½ cup all-purpose flour
½ cup whole wheat flour
2 tablespoons brown sugar
1 teaspoon baking powder
1 teaspoon baking soda
1 teaspoon ground cinnamon
½ teaspoon salt
1 cup unsweetened applesauce
¼ cup vegetable oil
2 eggs
¾ cup raisins
Vegetable cooking spray

Combine first 8 ingredients in a large mixing bowl; stir well. Add applesauce, oil, and eggs; mix well. Stir in raisins. Pour into an 8½- x 4½- x 3-inch loaf-pan coated with cooking spray; bake at 350° for 40 to 45 minutes or until a wooden pick inserted in center comes out clean.

Cool loaf in pan 10 minutes; remove from pan, and cool completely on a wire rack. Yield: 1 loaf (about 113 calories and 184 milligrams sodium per ½-inch slice). *Gayle A. Gibson,*
Slidell, Louisiana.

SPICED BRAN MUFFINS

1½ cups whole wheat flour
¾ cup wheat bran
2 teaspoons baking powder
½ teaspoon salt
¾ teaspoon ground cinnamon
⅛ teaspoon ground nutmeg
1 teaspoon grated lemon rind
2 eggs, slightly beaten
1¼ cups skim milk
¼ cup vegetable oil
2 tablespoons honey
Vegetable cooking spray

Combine first 7 ingredients in a large bowl; make a well in center of mixture. Combine eggs, milk, oil, and honey; add to dry ingredients, stirring just until moistened. Spoon into muffin pans coated with cooking spray, filling two-thirds full. Bake at 350° for 25 minutes. Yield: 1 dozen (about 119 calories and 144 milligrams sodium each).

HONEY-OATMEAL MUFFINS

1 cup quick-cooking oats, uncooked
¾ cup bread flour
¾ cup whole wheat flour
1 tablespoon baking powder
⅛ teaspoon salt
1 egg, beaten
3 tablespoons honey
2 tablespoons vegetable oil
1 cup skim milk
Vegetable cooking spray

Combine first 5 ingredients in a mixing bowl. Make a well in center of mixture; set aside. Combine egg, honey, oil, and milk; mix well. Add liquid mixture to dry ingredients; stir just until moistened. Spoon into muffin pans coated with cooking spray, filling two-thirds full. Bake at 350° for 18 minutes. Yield: 14 muffins (about 106 calories and 91 milligrams sodium each).
Lynn Symonette,
Georgetown, Delaware.

Take A Fresh Look At Turnips

From October through March, there should be a good supply of turnips available in markets. You can buy turnips with or without their tops. Store the roots in a cool, well-ventilated place or in the refrigerator. They will last as long as a month.

TURNIP CASSEROLE

6 to 7 medium turnips, peeled and cut into 2- x ⅜-inch strips
2 large carrots, scraped and cut into 2- x ⅜-inch strips
1 small onion, chopped
½ teaspoon salt
1 cup frozen English peas, thawed
1 (4-ounce) jar chopped pimiento, drained
1 (10¾-ounce) can cream of chicken soup, undiluted
1 (8-ounce) carton commercial sour cream
¼ teaspoon dried whole basil
1¾ cups herb-seasoned stuffing mix
¼ cup butter or margarine, melted

Place first 4 ingredients in a Dutch oven; cover with water, and bring to a boil. Cover and cook 5 to 10 minutes or until vegetables are tender; drain. Add peas and pimiento; set aside.

Combine soup, sour cream, and basil; stir into vegetable mixture. Spoon into a greased 9-inch square baking dish. Combine stuffing mix and butter; spread mixture over casserole. Bake at 350° for 25 to 30 minutes. Yield: 8 servings.
Fran Allison,
Hixson, Tennessee.

TURNIPS AU GRATIN

2 pounds turnips, peeled and sliced ¼ inch thick
½ teaspoon salt
1 cup whipping cream
1 teaspoon dried whole savory
½ teaspoon pepper
1 cup cooked ham, cut into julienne strips and divided
1½ cups (6 ounces) shredded Swiss cheese
½ cup soft breadcrumbs
2 tablespoons butter or margarine

Place turnips and salt in a saucepan; cover with water, and bring to a boil. Cover and cook over medium-high heat 5 minutes; drain and set aside.

Combine whipping cream, savory, and pepper; set aside. Place one-third of turnips in a greased 2-quart casserole. Top with ⅓ cup ham and ⅓ cup whipping cream mixture. Repeat procedure with remaining turnips, ham, and whipping cream mixture. Top with cheese and breadcrumbs; dot with butter. Bake at 375° for 40 to 45 minutes. Yield: 6 servings. *Betty R. Butts,*
Kensington, Maryland.

TURNIPS IN CHEESE SAUCE

4 medium turnips, peeled and sliced
¼ cup butter or margarine
¼ cup all-purpose flour
1½ cups half-and-half
1 cup (4 ounces) shredded process American cheese
1 tablespoon minced chives

Place turnips in a saucepan; cover with water, and bring to a boil. Cover and cook 8 to 10 minutes or until crisp-tender; drain well.

Melt butter in a heavy saucepan over low heat; add flour, stirring until smooth. Cook 1 minute, stirring constantly. Gradually add half-and-half; cook over medium heat, stirring constantly, until thickened and bubbly. Add cheese; stir until cheese melts. Pour over the turnips; stir gently. Sprinkle with chives. Yield: 6 servings.
Mrs. Ernest Harmon,
Elk Park, North Carolina.

TURNIP GREENS WITH TURNIPS

2 pounds turnip greens
8 slices bacon
3 medium turnips, peeled and sliced
1 teaspoon sugar
¼ teaspoon salt

Wash turnip greens thoroughly; drain. Tear into bite-size pieces.

Combine greens and bacon in a Dutch oven; cover with water, and bring to a boil. Cover, reduce heat, and simmer 20 minutes. Stir in turnips, sugar, and salt. Cover and cook an additional 30 minutes or until the turnips are tender. Yield: 6 to 8 servings.
Mrs. J. C. Graham,
Athens, Texas.

PARTY TURNIPS

6 medium turnips, peeled and cubed
1 cup English peas, cooked and drained
1 cup cubed carrots, cooked and drained
2 tablespoons butter or margarine
½ teaspoon salt
⅛ teaspoon pepper

Place turnips in a saucepan; cover with water, and bring to a boil. Cover and cook 15 to 20 minutes or until tender; drain.

Combine turnips, peas, and carrots; stir in butter, salt, and pepper. Cook over low heat until vegetables are thoroughly heated, stirring constantly. Yield: 6 servings. *Roberta E. McGrath,*
Hopkinsville, Kentucky.

These Entrées Are Ready In Minutes

When you need a special entrée for company but are running short on time, try one of the following recipes. Any one of these dishes featuring chicken, beef, seafood, or turkey is sure to be a crowd pleaser.

SEASONED HAMBURGERS

1 pound ground chuck
1 tablespoon plus 1 teaspoon soy sauce
1 teaspoon grated lemon rind
1 tablespoon lemon juice
¼ teaspoon salt
¼ teaspoon ground ginger

Combine all ingredients; mix well. Shape mixture into 4 patties about ½ inch thick. Broil 4 to 5 inches from heat 5 to 6 minutes on each side or until desired degree of doneness. Yield: 4 servings.
Mrs. Vaiden P. Hiner,
Abilene, Texas.

HAMBURGER STEAKS WITH MUSTARD SAUCE

1 pound ground beef
2 tablespoons finely chopped onion
2 tablespoons finely chopped green pepper
2 tablespoons butter or margarine
¼ cup plus 2 tablespoons undiluted consommé
¼ cup prepared mustard
4 (½-inch-thick) slices French bread

Shape ground beef into 4 patties about ½ inch thick. Cook patties in a large skillet over medium heat 5 to 7 minutes on each side or until desired degree of doneness; drain.

Sauté vegetables in butter until tender, stirring occasionally. Stir in consommé and mustard; bring to a boil. Reduce heat to low; simmer, uncovered, 20 minutes, stirring occasionally.

Place hamburger patties on French bread; serve with mustard sauce. Yield: 4 servings.
Mrs. James Schutte,
Kingsland, Texas.

CHICKEN PICCATA

6 chicken breast halves, skinned and boned
⅓ cup all-purpose flour
1½ teaspoons salt
¼ teaspoon pepper
¼ cup butter or margarine
¼ cup lemon juice
1 lemon, thinly sliced
2 tablespoons chopped fresh parsley
Fresh parsley sprigs (optional)

Place each piece of chicken between 2 sheets of waxed paper, and flatten to ¼-inch thickness using a meat mallet or rolling pin. Combine flour, salt, and pepper; dredge chicken in flour mixture.

Melt butter in a large skillet over medium heat. Add chicken, and cook 3 to 4 minutes on each side or until golden brown. Remove chicken, and drain on paper towels; keep warm. Add lemon juice and lemon slices to pan drippings in skillet; cook until thoroughly heated. Pour lemon mixture over chicken, and sprinkle with chopped parsley. Garnish with parsley sprigs, if desired. Yield: 6 servings.
Noreen W. Herward,
Pittsburgh, Pennsylvania.

SCRUMPTIOUS CHICKEN LIVERS

1 pound chicken livers
⅓ cup Chablis or other dry white wine
2½ tablespoons lemon juice
Salt and pepper to taste
½ to ¾ cup all-purpose flour
3 to 4 tablespoons vegetable oil

Cut chicken livers in half; set aside. Combine wine and lemon juice in a medium bowl; add livers and toss. Cover and marinate in refrigerator 30 minutes.

Drain livers. Sprinkle with salt and pepper; dredge in flour. Sauté in hot oil about 5 minutes or until done. Drain well, and serve immediately. Yield: 4 servings.
Pat Boschen,
Ashland, Virginia.

TURKEY SCHNITZEL

1 pound boneless turkey breast, skinned
¼ cup all-purpose flour
2 eggs, beaten
¾ cup fine, dry breadcrumbs
⅓ cup butter or margarine
Salt and pepper to taste

Slice turkey breast crosswise into ½-inch-thick slices. Place each slice between 2 sheets of waxed paper, and flatten to ¼-inch thickness using a meat mallet or rolling pin.

Dredge turkey in flour, dip in eggs, and coat with breadcrumbs, pressing in crumbs firmly. Melt butter in a heavy skillet over medium heat. Add turkey; cook 2 minutes on each side or until golden brown. Sprinkle with salt and pepper. Yield: 4 servings.
Jacquelyn Christopher,
Asheville, North Carolina.

SHRIMP SCAMPI

2½ pounds large fresh shrimp, unpeeled
1 cup butter, melted
¼ cup olive oil
1 tablespoon dried parsley flakes
1 tablespoon lemon juice
¾ teaspoon salt
¾ teaspoon garlic powder
¾ teaspoon dried whole basil
½ teaspoon dried whole oregano
Hot cooked rice

Peel and devein shrimp; place in a single layer in a 15- x 10- x 1-inch jelly-roll pan. Set aside.

Combine next 8 ingredients; pour over shrimp. Bake at 450° for 5 minutes. Broil 4 inches from heat 5 minutes or until shrimp are done. Serve over rice. Yield: 6 servings. *Betsy Rose,*
Greensboro, North Carolina.

FISH SURPRISE

1 pound whitefish fillets
Vegetable cooking spray
1½ tablespoons lemon juice
¼ teaspoon lemon pepper
1 small onion, sliced
½ medium-size green pepper, cut
  into thin strips
1 tomato, peeled and sliced
¼ to ½ teaspoon salt
Dash of pepper
2 teaspoons Worcestershire sauce
1 tablespoon butter or margarine
3 (1-ounce) slices provolone cheese

Wash fish and pat dry. Place fish, skin side down, on an 18- x 12-inch piece of aluminum foil coated with cooking spray. Sprinkle fish with lemon juice and lemon pepper. Top fish with sliced onion, green pepper strips, and tomato slices. Sprinkle with salt, pepper, and Worcestershire sauce; dot with 1 tablespoon butter. Bring edges of foil up around fish and seal; bake at 350° for 20 to 25 minutes or until fish flakes easily when tested with a fork.

Open foil; top fish with a layer of cheese. Reseal foil, and bake an additional 1 to 2 minutes or until cheese melts. Yield: 3 to 4 servings.

Mrs. J. K. Garrett, Jr.,
Jonesboro, Georgia.

Sweet Potato Treats

Fall brings the sweet potato harvest, and with the first one plucked from the ground, there's a pot ready for boiling or an oven ready for baking it. Use these recipes for a variety of ways to enjoy the sweet flavor of this Southern vegetable—try it seasoned with rum in a casserole or mashed and stuffed back into the original shell.

SWEET POTATO-RUM CASSEROLE

3 large sweet potatoes, peeled, cooked,
  and mashed
¼ cup plus 2 tablespoons butter or
  margarine, melted
½ cup firmly packed dark brown sugar
½ cup flaked coconut
½ cup coarsely chopped pecans
¼ cup dark rum
1½ teaspoons vanilla extract
About 6 large marshmallows
Pecan halves

Combine first 7 ingredients, mixing well. Spoon into a lightly greased 1½-quart casserole. Bake, uncovered, at 325° for 45 minutes. Arrange marshmallows and pecan halves on top; continue baking until marshmallows are lightly browned. Yield: 6 servings.

Mary Elizabeth Johnson,
Sheffield, Alabama.

SWEET POTATOES-AND-BERRIES CASSEROLE

2 pounds sweet potatoes
1 (16-ounce) can whole berry cranberry
  sauce
½ teaspoon ground cinnamon
⅔ cup self-rising flour
⅔ cup firmly packed brown sugar
⅔ cup quick-cooking oats, uncooked
¼ cup plus 2 tablespoons butter or
  margarine
1 cup miniature marshmallows

Cook potatoes in boiling water to cover 20 minutes or until tender. Let cool to the touch; peel and mash potatoes. Stir in cranberry sauce and cinnamon. Spoon into a lightly greased 2-quart casserole.

Combine flour, sugar, and oats; cut in butter until mixture resembles coarse crumbs. Spoon over sweet potato mixture. Bake at 375° for 20 minutes. Top with marshmallows, and bake until golden brown. Yield: 8 servings.

Dana Peck,
Clinton, Tennessee.

COCONUT-BROILED SWEET POTATOES

8 medium-size sweet potatoes
1¼ cups flaked coconut, divided
½ cup firmly packed brown sugar
¼ cup butter or margarine, melted
¼ cup whipping cream
8 maraschino cherries, halved

Cook sweet potatoes in boiling water 20 to 25 minutes or until tender. Let cool to touch; peel and cut in half lengthwise. Arrange the potatoes in a greased 13- x 9- x 2-inch baking dish; sprinkle with 1 cup coconut.

Combine brown sugar, butter, and whipping cream; pour mixture over sweet potatoes. Top with remaining ¼ cup coconut and cherries. Broil 5 inches from heat for 2 to 3 minutes or until lightly browned. Yield: 10 to 12 servings.

Mrs. John Shoemaker,
Louisville, Kentucky.

STUFFED BAKED SWEET POTATOES

6 medium-size sweet potatoes
Vegetable oil
1 teaspoon salt
3 tablespoons butter or margarine,
  softened
1 (6-ounce) can frozen orange
  juice concentrate, thawed
  and undiluted
1 cup crushed pineapple, drained
½ cup chopped pecans
12 large marshmallows

Wash potatoes, and rub with vegetable oil. Bake at 400° for 1 hour or until done. Split potatoes in half lengthwise. Carefully scoop out pulp, leaving shells intact; mash pulp. Add salt, butter, orange juice concentrate, and pineapple to mashed pulp; mix well.

Stuff potato shells with pulp mixture; sprinkle with pecans. Cut each marshmallow in half; place 2 marshmallow halves, cut side down, on each potato half. Place potato shells on a baking sheet; bake at 400° until lightly browned on top. Yield: 6 servings.

Ann Elsie Schmetzer,
Madisonville, Kentucky.

Accent Meals With Salad

Add some excitement to everyday fall meals by including Salad Mandarin or Marinated Cauliflower Salad. If congealed salads are your favorite, be sure to try Apple Crunch Salad.

SALAD MANDARIN

1 medium head Bibb or Boston lettuce,
  torn
1 (11-ounce) can mandarin oranges,
  chilled and drained
½ medium avocado, peeled and
  thinly sliced
½ cup coarsely chopped pecans,
  toasted
2 green onions, thinly sliced
Freshly ground pepper to taste
⅓ cup Italian salad dressing

Combine first 6 ingredients in a medium bowl. Add Italian dressing, tossing gently. Yield: 6 servings.

Susan S. K. Menetrey,
Fort Myer, Virginia.

MARINATED CAULIFLOWER SALAD

4 cups thinly sliced cauliflower
1 cup sliced ripe olives
⅔ cup chopped green pepper
1 (4-ounce) jar diced pimiento, drained
½ cup chopped onion
½ cup vegetable oil
3 tablespoons wine vinegar
3 tablespoons lemon juice
1 teaspoon sugar
½ teaspoon salt
¼ teaspoon pepper

Combine first 5 ingredients in a salad bowl; toss gently.

Combine remaining ingredients in a jar. Cover tightly, and shake vigorously. Pour dressing over vegetables, tossing gently. Cover salad, and chill 8 hours or overnight, stirring occasionally. Yield: 6 to 8 servings.　*Joyce Andrews, Washington, Virginia.*

APPLE CRUNCH SALAD

1 (6-ounce) package strawberry-flavored gelatin
1¾ cups boiling water
1½ cups apple juice
¼ teaspoon ground cinnamon
1 cup peeled, finely chopped apple
½ cup finely chopped celery
¼ cup finely chopped pecans

Dissolve gelatin in boiling water. Stir in apple juice and cinnamon; chill until consistency of unbeaten egg white. Stir in remaining ingredients. Pour into an oiled 8-inch square dish; chill until firm. Yield: 9 servings.　*Bettye Cortner, Cerulean, Kentucky.*

PINEAPPLE DAIQUIRI SALAD

1 (15½-ounce) can crushed pineapple, undrained
2 envelopes unflavored gelatin
½ cup light rum
1 (6-ounce) can frozen limeade concentrate, thawed and undiluted
8 to 10 ice cubes

Drain pineapple, reserving juice. Add enough water to juice to make 1 cup; set aside ½ cup liquid. Combine remaining ½ cup liquid and gelatin in container of an electric blender. Process 30 seconds; let stand 1 minute. Bring remaining ½ cup liquid to a boil; add to gelatin mixture. Process 30 seconds or until gelatin dissolves. Add rum, limeade, and ice cubes, processing until smooth. Stir in pineapple; pour into an oiled 4-cup mold. Chill until firm. Yield: 8 servings.　*Marietta Marx, Louisville, Kentucky.*

MARINATED VEGETABLE PATCH SALAD

1 (16-ounce) can cut green beans, drained
1 (16-ounce) can kidney beans, drained
1 (7-ounce) can pitted ripe olives, drained
1 (6-ounce) jar sliced mushrooms, drained
1 (4-ounce) jar sliced pimientos, drained
1 (14-ounce) can artichoke hearts, drained and quartered
1 small red onion, thinly sliced
1½ cups sliced celery
¼ cup tarragon vinegar
¼ cup vegetable oil
1 tablespoon capers
1 teaspoon sugar
1 teaspoon fines herbes
½ teaspoon salt
½ teaspoon pepper
¼ teaspoon hot sauce

Combine first 8 ingredients in a large bowl; toss lightly, and set aside.

Combine remaining ingredients in a jar. Cover jar tightly, and shake vigorously; pour marinade over vegetables. Cover salad and chill overnight, stirring occasionally. Yield: 12 servings.　*Nell H. Amador, Guntersville, Alabama.*

LUNCHEON SALAD

½ cup Italian salad dressing, divided
¾ cup water
1 cup uncooked instant rice
1 (17-ounce) can English peas, drained
4 green onions with tops, thinly sliced
¼ cup sliced pimiento-stuffed olives
¼ cup peeled, diced cucumber
1 cup (4 ounces) shredded Cheddar cheese
Lettuce leaves
1 hard-cooked egg, sliced

Combine ¼ cup dressing and water in a medium saucepan; bring to a boil. Stir in rice; cover and remove from heat. Let stand 5 minutes. Combine rice, remaining ¼ cup dressing, and next 5 ingredients. Cover and chill. Serve salad on lettuce; garnish with egg slices. Yield: 4 to 6 servings.

Mrs. George Lance, Madison, Tennessee.

Stretch The Flavor Of Southern Seafood

If you live far from the coast, the sea's harvest may be a costly and savored treat. But with the following seafood-stretching recipes, you'll find ways to extend your budget and the flavor of fresh shrimp, crab, scallops, and smoked fish.

Fortunately, the mild flavor of most seafood permits an unlimited variety of flavor combinations. Vegetables and seafood teamed in soups or sauces or served over pasta or rice can make the servings go farther.

Crabmeat is ideal for casseroles since the flaky meat separates easily. You'll probably find it most economical to use claw meat, instead of white lump crabmeat. There's no difference in taste, but claw meat has a brownish tint that you'll never notice mixed in a casserole.

Try experimenting with your own recipes by substituting seafood for the meat in your favorite casseroles or stirring it into dips, spreads, soups, sauces, and salads. There's no limit to the tasty ways you can stretch seafood to fit your budget and your serving needs.

CRABMEAT-BROCCOLI CASSEROLE

12 slices bread
2½ cups milk
1 cup mayonnaise
7 hard-cooked eggs, finely chopped
1 pound fresh crabmeat
¼ cup chopped onion
1 tablespoon plus 1 teaspoon minced fresh parsley
2 (10-ounce) packages frozen broccoli
1 cup (4 ounces) shredded sharp Cheddar cheese

Remove crust from bread, reserving crust for use in other recipes. Cut bread into ½-inch cubes. Combine bread cubes, milk, and mayonnaise; stir well. Cover and refrigerate 30 minutes. Remove mixture from refrigerator; stir in eggs, crabmeat, onion, and parsley.

Cook broccoli according to package directions; drain well. Arrange broccoli in a lightly greased 13- x 9- x 2-inch baking dish. Spoon crabmeat mixture evenly over broccoli. Bake, uncovered, at 325° for 40 minutes. Sprinkle with cheese, and bake an additional 5 minutes or until cheese melts. Yield: 8 servings.　*Mrs. Ronald D. Smith, Houston, Texas.*

SHRIMP MARINARA

1 medium onion, chopped
¼ cup olive oil
1 medium-size green pepper, chopped
1 carrot, scraped and finely chopped
1 cup sliced fresh mushrooms
2 cloves garlic, crushed
⅓ cup frozen English peas,
    unthawed
½ cup red wine
1 (6-ounce) can tomato paste
1½ teaspoons dried whole basil
1 teaspoon dried whole oregano
Pinch of sugar
¼ to ½ teaspoon pepper
½ to 1 cup water
1 pound fresh large shrimp, peeled
    and deveined
Hot cooked linguine
Grated Romano cheese (optional)

Sauté onion in hot oil in a large skillet 1 or 2 minutes; add next 4 ingredients, and sauté until vegetables are tender. Add peas, wine, tomato paste, and seasonings, stirring well. Thin mixture with ½ to 1 cup water to reach desired consistency. Bring to a boil, reduce heat, and simmer 5 minutes.

Add shrimp; cook 3 to 5 minutes or until shrimp are done. Serve over linguine. Serve with grated Romano cheese, if desired. Yield: 4 to 6 servings.
Charles Walton,
Birmingham, Alabama.

BAY SCALLOPS WITH VEGETABLES

½ cup water
½ cup dry white wine
½ teaspoon salt
1½ pounds fresh bay scallops
½ pound fresh mushrooms, sliced
½ cup sliced green onions
½ cup sliced celery
3 tablespoons butter or margarine
1 (6-ounce) package frozen Chinese pea
    pods, thawed and drained
1 tablespoon soy sauce
2 teaspoons lemon juice
2 teaspoons cornstarch
¼ teaspoon white pepper
3 dashes of hot sauce
1 (2-ounce) jar diced pimiento, drained
Hot cooked rice

Combine first 3 ingredients in a large saucepan; bring to a boil. Add scallops; reduce heat and simmer 2 minutes, stirring occasionally, or until done. Drain scallops, reserving ½ cup liquid. Set scallops aside.

Sauté mushrooms, onions, and celery in butter until tender; stir in pea pods.

Combine reserved liquid and next 5 ingredients; mix well, and stir into vegetables. Cook over medium heat, stirring constantly, until smooth and thickened. Stir in scallops and pimiento; cook just until thoroughly heated. Serve over rice. Yield: 4 to 6 servings.

SMOKED FISH-POTATO SALAD

2 to 2½ cups flaked, smoked fish
2 cups diced, cooked potatoes
1 cup chopped celery
½ cup peeled, chopped cucumber
½ cup sliced ripe olives
¼ cup shredded carrot
¼ cup chopped onion
2 tablespoons chopped fresh parsley
½ cup mayonnaise
1 tablespoon prepared mustard
1 teaspoon lemon juice
1 teaspoon vinegar
¼ teaspoon celery seeds
Dash of pepper
Lettuce leaves (optional)
Tomato wedges (optional)

Combine first 8 ingredients in a large bowl; set aside.

Combine mayonnaise, mustard, lemon juice, vinegar, celery seeds, and pepper; add to fish mixture, tossing gently. Cover salad, and chill. Serve on lettuce leaves, and garnish with tomato wedges, if desired. Yield: 6 servings.
Vicky Murphy,
Atlanta, Georgia.

Fajitas Lead These Tex-Mex Entrées

The delights of Tex-Mex cooking—enchiladas, tacos, tostadas, chalupas, burritos, chiles rellenos—have been popular with our readers for many years. Now it's time to add another winning recipe to the list. People across the South have discovered fajitas (pronounced fa-**hee**-tuhs), a dish that's rapidly becoming a favorite with Tex-Mex aficionados everywhere.

Like other dishes in this once-regional cuisine, fajitas originated in Mexico and crossed the border into Texas, receiving adaptations along the way. The basic fajita consists of thin strips of marinated and grilled skirt or flank steak wrapped in a soft flour tortilla. The marinade usually contains a generous amount of lime juice and garlic. Fajitas may be served with any number of different toppings, but purists insist that picante sauce or a spicy tomato relish is a mandatory ingredient. Other toppings include sautéed onion and green pepper rings, guacamole, sour cream, salsa verde, chopped tomatoes, lettuce, and shredded cheese. Whatever you put on fajitas, they're best rolled up and eaten with your hands.

Another essential ingredient, according to many Texans, is mesquite wood for grilling the meat. We used mesquite in our test kitchens and felt that it really did add a unique flavor. But if you don't have access to mesquite, regular charcoal will do.

FAJITAS

½ cup olive oil
¼ cup red wine vinegar
⅓ cup lime juice
⅓ cup finely chopped onion
1 teaspoon sugar
1 teaspoon dried whole oregano
½ teaspoon salt
½ teaspoon pepper
¼ teaspoon ground cumin
3 cloves minced garlic
2 pounds skirt or flank steak
6 flour tortillas

Combine first 10 ingredients in a shallow container, and mix well.

Pound steak to ¼-inch thickness. Add steak to marinade, turning to coat each side thoroughly. Cover and refrigerate 8 hours or overnight.

Remove steak from marinade, and drain well. Grill steak over medium coals 6 to 7 minutes on each side or until desired degree of doneness. Slice steak across the grain into thin slices.

Wrap tortillas in aluminum foil, and heat in a 325° oven about 15 minutes. Wrap tortillas around meat and choice of toppings: picante sauce, guacamole, chopped tomatoes, salsa verde, and sour cream. Yield: 4 to 6 servings.
Gloria Patrick,
Sweeny, Texas.

CHILES RELLENOS CASSEROLE

1 pound ground beef
½ cup chopped onion
½ teaspoon salt
¼ teaspoon pepper
2 (4-ounce) cans whole green chiles, cut in half lengthwise and seeded
1½ cups (6 ounces) shredded medium Cheddar cheese
¼ cup all-purpose flour
¼ cup milk
4 eggs, beaten
1¼ cups milk
4 dashes of hot sauce
½ teaspoon salt
Dash of pepper

Brown ground beef and onion in a skillet, stirring to crumble beef; drain well. Stir in ½ teaspoon salt and ¼ teaspoon pepper, and set aside.

Arrange half of chiles in a lightly greased 10- x 6- x 1½-inch baking dish. Sprinkle with cheese; top with meat mixture. Arrange remaining chiles over meat mixture.

Combine flour and ¼ cup milk, blending until smooth. Add eggs, 1¼ cups milk, hot sauce, salt, and pepper, and mix well. Pour over casserole.

Bake at 350° for 45 to 50 minutes. Let stand 5 minutes before serving. Cut into squares. Yield: 6 servings.

Janine Kuykendall,
Cedar Park, Texas.

SPICY FIESTA CHICKEN

4 eggs, beaten
¼ cup commercial green chile salsa
¼ teaspoon salt
2 cups fine, dry breadcrumbs
2 teaspoons chili powder
2 teaspoons ground cumin
1½ teaspoons garlic salt
½ teaspoon ground oregano
6 chicken breast halves, boned and skinned
¼ cup butter or margarine
Shredded lettuce
1 (8-ounce) carton commercial sour cream
¼ cup plus 2 tablespoons chopped green onions
12 cherry tomatoes
1 avocado, sliced (optional)
6 lime wedges (optional)
Additional salsa (optional)

Combine eggs, ¼ cup salsa, and salt in a shallow bowl; set aside.

Combine the next 5 ingredients in a shallow pan, and mix well.

Dip chicken in egg mixture, and dredge in the breadcrumb mixture; repeat and set aside.

Melt butter in a 13- x 9- x 2-inch pan. Place chicken in pan, turning once to coat with butter. Bake, uncovered, at 375° for 30 to 35 minutes.

Arrange chicken on a bed of shredded lettuce on a large platter. Garnish each piece with a dollop of sour cream and 1 tablespoon green onions; arrange cherry tomatoes on platter. Garnish with avocado slices and lime wedges, and serve with additional salsa, if desired. Yield: 6 servings.

Dorothy M. Maxwell,
Morrilton, Arkansas.

GREEN CHILE-CHEESE PIE

Pastry for 9-inch pie
1½ cups (6 ounces) shredded Monterey Jack cheese
1 cup (4 ounces) shredded mild Cheddar cheese, divided
3 eggs, slightly beaten
1 cup half-and-half
1 (4-ounce) can chopped green chiles, drained well
¼ teaspoon salt
½ teaspoon ground cumin

Line a 9-inch pieplate with pastry; trim excess pastry around edges. Prick bottom and sides of pastry shell with a fork; bake at 375° for 10 minutes. Let cool on a rack.

Spread 1½ cups Monterey Jack cheese and ½ cup Cheddar cheese in the pastry shell.

Combine eggs, half-and-half, chiles, salt, and cumin; beat until blended. Pour mixture into pastry shell; sprinkle with remaining ½ cup Cheddar cheese. Bake at 325° for 40 minutes or until set. Let stand 15 minutes before serving. Yield: one 9-inch pie.

Mrs. Karl Koenig,
Dallas, Texas.

GREEN CHILE-SOUR CREAM ENCHILADAS

4 to 6 whole fresh green chiles
12 corn tortillas
⅓ cup vegetable oil
1 medium onion, finely chopped
2 cups (8 ounces) shredded Monterey Jack cheese
¼ cup butter or margarine
¼ cup all-purpose flour
1 cup chicken broth
1 (8-ounce) carton commercial sour cream

Place chiles on a baking sheet; broil 5 to 6 inches from heat, turning often with tongs until blistered on all sides.

Immediately place chiles in a plastic bag, fasten securely, and let steam 15 minutes. Remove and discard stem and peel of each chile, and rinse under cold water to remove seeds. Chop chiles, and set aside.

Fry tortillas, one at a time, in a small skillet in hot oil 3 to 5 seconds on each side or just until tortillas are softened.

Combine onion and cheese; place about 3 tablespoons cheese mixture on each tortilla. Roll tortillas up, and place in a greased 13- x 9- x 2-inch baking dish, seam side down.

Melt butter in a heavy saucepan over low heat; add flour, stirring until smooth. Cook 1 minute, stirring constantly. Gradually add chicken broth; cook over medium heat, stirring constantly, until mixture thickens. Remove from heat.

Stir in sour cream and chiles. Pour sauce over tortillas, and bake at 375° for 10 to 15 minutes or until bubbly. Yield: 6 servings.

Note: Two 4-ounce cans chopped green chiles may be substituted for the fresh chiles. *Lee Ann Sutherland,*
Abilene, Texas.

It's Autumn—Soup's On!

There's something about the first hint of cool weather that makes us think about putting on a pot of soup. A big pot of homemade soup bubbling on the back burner is a good way to mark the beginning of the season. And the delicious aroma while it's cooking is almost as wonderful as the soup itself.

MEXICAN CHICKEN SOUP

1 (3- to 3½-pound) broiler-fryer, cut up
6 cups water
3 stalks celery
1 medium onion, sliced
1 teaspoon salt
⅛ teaspoon pepper
1 tablespoon plus 1 teaspoon chicken-flavored bouillon granules
3 medium carrots, thinly sliced
1 medium onion, chopped
1 (16-ounce) can tomatoes, undrained and chopped
1 small zucchini, thinly sliced
1 cup frozen English peas

Combine first 6 ingredients in a Dutch oven; bring to a boil. Cover, reduce heat, and simmer 1 hour or until tender. Drain chicken, reserving broth. Remove skin, bone chicken, and chop. Set aside.

Strain broth, discarding vegetables. Return broth to Dutch oven. Add bouillon granules, carrots, chopped onion, and tomatoes; cover and simmer 30 minutes. Add chicken, zucchini, and peas; cover and simmer an additional 10 to 15 minutes or until vegetables are tender. Yield: 6 cups. *Joanne Land, Round Rock, Texas.*

CHICKEN CHOWDER SAUTERNE

1 (3½- to 4-pound) broiler-fryer, cut up
1 quart water
1 large carrot, scraped and sliced
1 teaspoon salt
1 cup milk
½ cup chopped green onions
½ cup chopped green pepper
½ cup chopped fresh parsley
½ cup chopped celery
¼ cup plus 1 tablespoon butter or margarine, divided
⅓ cup all-purpose flour
1 egg yolk, beaten
½ cup Sauterne or other dry white wine
½ teaspoon salt
¼ teaspoon pepper

Combine first 4 ingredients in a large Dutch oven; bring to a boil. Cover, reduce heat, and simmer 30 to 35 minutes or until tender. Drain chicken, reserving broth. Remove skin, bone chicken, and chop. Set aside. Strain broth, reserving 3 cups. Add milk to the reserved broth; set aside.

Sauté onions, green pepper, parsley, and celery in 2 tablespoons butter in a heavy skillet until tender; set aside.

Melt 3 tablespoons butter in a heavy Dutch oven over low heat; add flour, stirring well. Cook 1 minute, stirring constantly. Gradually add reserved broth mixture; cook over medium heat, stirring constantly, until thickened and bubbly. Combine egg yolk and Sauterne; mix well. Stir into the broth mixture. Add chicken, vegetables, ½ teaspoon salt, and pepper; cook, stirring constantly, until thoroughly heated. Yield: 2 quarts. *Jill T. Flournoy, Memphis, Tennessee.*

ITALIAN SAUSAGE SOUP

1½ pounds Italian sausage, cut into ¼-inch slices
½ cup chopped onion
1 (28-ounce) can Italian-style tomatoes, undrained and chopped
4 small potatoes, peeled and cubed
1 cup chopped celery
2 tablespoons chopped celery leaves
¼ cup chopped fresh parsley
7 cups water
1 beef-flavored bouillon cube
2 tablespoons sugar
1 tablespoon lemon juice
1 bay leaf
½ teaspoon dried whole thyme
¼ teaspoon pepper

Brown sausage in a large Dutch oven; add onion and cook, stirring constantly, until tender. Add remaining ingredients. Bring to a boil; cover, reduce heat, and simmer 45 minutes. Remove bay leaf. Yield: about 2½ quarts. *Sugar Strauss, Kansas City, Missouri.*

These Pies Make Their Own Crust

Looking for a way to cut preparation time without serving the same old fare? Make a crustless pie. We've rounded up several for you to choose from, including some in the main-dish, dessert, and vegetable categories.

CRUSTLESS HAM QUICHE

½ pound fresh mushrooms, sliced
2 tablespoons butter or margarine, melted
4 eggs
1 (8-ounce) carton commercial sour cream
1 (8-ounce) carton small curd cottage cheese
½ cup grated Parmesan cheese
¼ cup all-purpose flour
1 teaspoon onion powder
6 to 8 drops of hot sauce
2 cups (8 ounces) shredded Monterey Jack cheese
½ cup chopped cooked ham

Sauté mushrooms in butter in a medium skillet until lightly browned; drain well, and set aside.

Combine next 7 ingredients in container of electric blender; process until well blended.

Combine egg mixture, mushrooms, cheese, and ham. Pour into a greased 10-inch quiche dish. Bake at 350° for 45 minutes or until set. Quiche should be puffed and golden brown. Let stand 10 minutes before serving. Yield: one 10-inch quiche. *Rublelene Singleton, Scotts Hill, Tennessee.*

BROCCOLI-CHEESE PIE

1 (1-pound) bunch broccoli
⅔ cup chopped onion
¼ cup water
4 eggs, slightly beaten
1¼ cups milk
4 to 6 drops of hot sauce
½ teaspoon salt
⅛ teaspoon freshly ground pepper
⅛ teaspoon ground nutmeg
1 tablespoon minced fresh parsley
⅔ cup fresh shredded Swiss cheese
⅓ cup grated Parmesan cheese

Trim off large leaves of broccoli. Remove tough ends of lower stalks, and wash broccoli thoroughly; cut flowerets and stems into thin slices.

Combine broccoli, onion, and ¼ cup water in a saucepan; cover and cook over medium heat 6 to 8 minutes. Drain thoroughly, pressing out moisture with paper towels.

Combine next 8 ingredients. Stir in vegetables, and pour mixture into a greased 10-inch pieplate. Sprinkle with Parmesan cheese; bake at 350° about 30 minutes or until set. Let stand 10 minutes. Yield: one 10-inch pie.
Esther Dick, Crown Point, Indiana.

CRUSTLESS SPINACH QUICHE

1 large onion, chopped
1 tablespoon vegetable oil
1 (10-ounce) package frozen chopped spinach, thawed and pressed dry
5 eggs, beaten
3 cups (12 ounces) shredded Muenster cheese
¼ teaspoon salt
⅛ teaspoon pepper

Sauté onion in oil in a large skillet until tender. Add spinach, and cook until excess moisture evaporates; cool.

Combine eggs, cheese, salt, and pepper; stir into spinach mixture. Pour into a greased 9-inch pieplate. Bake at 350° for 30 minutes or until set. Yield: one 9-inch quiche. *Mrs. James L. Hastings, Madisonville, Kentucky.*

NO-CRUST SWEET POTATO PIE

4 medium-size sweet potatoes, peeled,
  cooked, and mashed
1 cup sugar
½ cup all-purpose flour
½ cup butter or margarine,
  softened
1 egg
½ to 1 teaspoon almond extract
Whipped cream

Combine all the ingredients except
whipped cream in a large mixing bowl;
beat at medium speed of electric mixer
until well blended. Spoon mixture into a
9-inch pieplate. Bake at 450° for 25
minutes or until lightly browned. Serve
warm or cool with a dollop of whipped
cream. Yield: one 9-inch pie.

Niki Bolls,
Largo, Florida.

BLENDER COCONUT PIE

1 (13-ounce) can evaporated milk
3 eggs
1 cup sugar
1 cup flaked coconut
3 tablespoons all-purpose flour
3 tablespoons vegetable oil
½ teaspoon vanilla extract
Ground nutmeg

Combine all ingredients except nutmeg in container of electric blender.
Process mixture until well blended.
Pour into a greased and floured 10-inch
pieplate (mixture will be thin). Sprinkle
top of mixture with nutmeg; bake at
325° for 40 minutes or until pie is set.
Let pie stand 10 minutes before serving.
Yield: one 10-inch pie.

Mrs. Bill Duncan,
Vicksburg, Mississippi.

Homemade Crackers—Crisp And Delicious

Want to try your hand at making
homemade crackers? It's not as difficult
as you might think. Oatmeal-Wheat
Germ Crackers are rolled directly onto
a baking sheet and cut into squares before baking; they separate easily after-
wards. These crackers keep well, so
save some for snacking later.

OATMEAL-WHEAT GERM CRACKERS

3 cups quick-cooking oats, uncooked
2 cups unbleached all-purpose flour
1 cup wheat germ
3 tablespoons sugar
1 teaspoon salt
¾ cup vegetable oil
1 cup water

Combine first 5 ingredients in a large
mixing bowl; mix well. Add oil and
water, stirring until dry ingredients are
moistened.

Divide mixture onto 2 ungreased
cookie sheets. Roll mixture directly on
cookie sheets to ⅛-inch thickness, and
cut into 2-inch squares or diamonds.
Bake at 350° for 20 to 25 minutes. Separate crackers, and let cool on a wire
rack. Store in a tightly covered container. Yield: 6½ dozen.

Mary Belle Purvis,
Greeneville, Tennessee.

CHEDDAR CRACKERS

½ cup butter, softened
2 cups (8 ounces) shredded sharp Cheddar
  cheese
1½ cups all-purpose flour
½ teaspoon salt
1 tablespoon chopped chives

Cream butter and cheese until
smooth. Combine flour, salt, and
chives; add to creamed mixture, blending well.

Shape dough into 1-inch balls; place 2
inches apart on ungreased cookie
sheets. Flatten each ball to ⅛-inch
thickness with the bottom of a glass
dipped in flour. Prick top with a fork.
Bake at 350° for 12 to 15 minutes; let
cool on a wire rack. Store in a tightly
covered container. Yield: 4 dozen
crackers. *Sharon M. Crider,*
Evansville, Wisconsin.

Fry Crisp Chicken Nuggets

Give fried chicken a new twist that
everyone will like: batter bite-size
pieces of chicken and fry them into
crisp, golden nuggets. We suggest serving them with Pineapple Sauce.

CHICKEN NUGGETS WITH PINEAPPLE SAUCE

2 eggs, beaten
2 tablespoons water
¼ cup all-purpose flour
1 teaspoon salt
6 chicken breast halves, skinned and
  boned
1 cup all-purpose flour
¾ cup peanut oil
Pineapple Sauce

Combine eggs, water, flour, and salt,
mixing well. Chill 1 hour.

Cut chicken into 1-inch pieces. Dip
chicken pieces into batter, and dredge
in 1 cup flour.

Pour oil around top of preheated
wok; allow to heat to 375°. Fry 4 to 5
pieces of chicken at a time until golden
brown. Drain well on paper towels.
Serve with Pineapple Sauce. Yield:
about 3 dozen appetizer servings.

Pineapple Sauce:

1 cup pineapple juice
2 tablespoons sugar
1 tablespoon cornstarch
¼ cup pineapple juice
1 (8-ounce) can crushed pineapple,
  drained
2 tablespoons cider vinegar
2 teaspoons prepared mustard
Sliced fresh pineapple (optional)
Sliced kiwi (optional)

Combine 1 cup pineapple juice and
sugar in a small saucepan; cook over
medium heat, stirring constantly until
sugar dissolves.

Combine cornstarch and ¼ cup pineapple juice; stir into pineapple juice
mixture in saucepan. Bring mixture to a
boil; cook 1 minute, stirring constantly.
Stir in pineapple, vinegar, and mustard.

Serve sauce warm, and garnish with
fresh pineapple and kiwi, if desired.
Yield: 1¾ cups. *John Riggins,*
Nashville, Tennessee.

Right: *Add fiber and texture to your*
low-calorie diet with these whole grain
breads. From left to right: Whole Wheat
Breadsticks (page 228), Spiced Bran
Muffins (page 229), Honey-Oatmeal Muffins
(page 229), and Bran-Applesauce Bread
(page 229).

Page 238: *Apples flavor an assortment of*
fall treats: Apple Cider Pie (page 227),
Double Apple Salad (page 227), and
Old-Fashioned Apple Dumplings (page 226).

Cook Potatoes In Only Minutes

Bake a potato the conventional way, and it takes an hour. Bake it in the microwave, and it cooks in about 5 minutes. Of course, if you bake more than one, the cooking time must be increased, but you'll certainly agree that it's a considerable timesaver.

When baking potatoes or any skin-covered vegetable in the microwave, it's important to prick the skin with a fork in several places to allow steam to escape. Potatoes will cook more evenly if you select firm, well-shaped potatoes of the same size. To bake, arrange in a circle end to end, and rearrange after half the cooking time. If you have more than four potatoes, you may find it easier to arrange them like spokes on a wheel.

The potatoes will continue to cook after they are removed from the microwave, so check for doneness after standing about 5 minutes. If necessary, microwave again for a couple of minutes; then let stand 2 minutes.

STUFFED POTATOES WITH BECHAMEL SAUCE

4 medium baking potatoes
1 (3-ounce) package cream cheese with chives
¼ cup milk
1 tablespoon chopped fresh parsley
Béchamel Sauce

Wash potatoes and pat dry; prick each potato several times with a fork. Arrange potatoes end to end in a circle on paper towels in microwave oven, leaving at least 1 inch between each potato. Microwave at HIGH for 12 to 14 minutes, turning and rearranging potatoes after 6 minutes. Let potatoes stand 5 minutes. (If potatoes are not done after standing, microwave briefly, and let stand an additional 2 minutes.)

Slice away skin from top of each potato; carefully scoop out pulp, leaving shells intact. Mash pulp, and set aside.

Place cream cheese in a medium-size glass mixing bowl. Microwave at MEDIUM LOW (30% power) for 1 minute or until softened. Add potato pulp, milk, and parsley; mix well. Stuff shells

with potato mixture, and place on a microwave-safe serving platter. Microwave at HIGH 5 minutes or until thoroughly heated, giving dish one half-turn after 3 minutes. Serve with Béchamel Sauce. Yield: 4 servings.

Béchamel Sauce:

2 tablespoons butter or margarine
2 tablespoons all-purpose flour
½ cup chicken broth
½ cup half-and-half
½ teaspoon salt
¼ teaspoon paprika
⅛ teaspoon pepper

Place butter in a 4-cup glass measure; microwave at HIGH for 45 seconds or until melted. Add flour; stirring until smooth. Combine broth and half-and-half; gradually add to flour mixture, stirring well. Microwave at HIGH for 3½ to 4 minutes, stirring at 1-minute intervals until thickened and bubbly. Stir in seasonings. Yield: 1 cup.

CHEESE POTATO SKINS

6 slices bacon
3 medium baking potatoes
¼ cup butter or margarine
⅛ teaspoon hot sauce
1 cup (4 ounces) shredded Cheddar cheese
Commercial sour cream

Place bacon on a rack in a 12- x 8- x 2-inch baking dish; cover with paper towels. Microwave at HIGH for 5 to 7 minutes or until bacon is crisp. Drain bacon; crumble and set aside.

Wash potatoes and pat dry; prick several times with a fork. Arrange potatoes end to end in a circle on paper towels in microwave oven, leaving at least 1 inch between each potato. Microwave at HIGH for 9 to 11 minutes, turning and rearranging potatoes after 5 minutes. Let potatoes stand 5 minutes. (If potatoes are not done after standing, microwave briefly and let stand 2 minutes.)

Cut potatoes in half lengthwise; carefully scoop out pulp, leaving ¼-inch shells. (Reserve pulp for other recipes.) Cut shells in half crosswise.

Place butter in a 1-cup glass measure; microwave at HIGH for 55 seconds or until melted. Stir hot sauce into butter. Brush butter mixture on both sides of potato quarters. Place potatoes skin side up in a paper towel-lined baking dish. Microwave at HIGH for 2 minutes, giving dish one half-turn after 1 minute.

Sprinkle inside of potato skins with bacon, and top with cheese. Microwave at HIGH for 50 seconds or until cheese melts. Serve with sour cream. Yield: 12 appetizer servings.

PEAS IN A POTATO NEST

3 medium-size red potatoes, peeled and quartered
¼ cup salted water
¼ cup commercial sour cream
2 tablespoons butter or margarine, melted
2 tablespoons grated Parmesan cheese
¼ teaspoon salt
½ cup milk
Paprika
2 tablespoons water
½ teaspoon salt
1 (10-ounce) package frozen English peas
¼ cup chopped pecans
¼ teaspoon celery salt
Dash of garlic powder

Place potatoes in a 1½-quart casserole; add ¼ cup salted water. Cover and microwave at HIGH for 9 to 11 minutes or until potatoes are tender, stirring after 3 minutes. Drain.

Mash potatoes; stir in sour cream, butter, cheese, and ¼ teaspoon salt. Gradually add milk, beating at high speed of an electric mixer until smooth. Spoon or pipe potatoes in a 9-inch circle on a microwave-safe serving plate. Make an indentation in the center of the potato mound using the back of a spoon. Sprinkle outside edge of potatoes with paprika. Set aside.

Place 2 tablespoons water and ½ teaspoon salt in a 1-quart casserole. Add peas; cover and microwave at HIGH 5 to 6 minutes, stirring after 3 minutes. Drain well.

Stir remaining ingredients into peas. Let stand 1 minute. Spoon pea mixture into center of potato mound. Cover with waxed paper and microwave at MEDIUM HIGH (70% power) for 6 to 8 minutes or until thoroughly heated, giving dish one half-turn after 3 minutes. Yield: 6 to 8 servings.

October 239

PARMESAN POTATO FANS

6 medium baking potatoes
¼ cup butter or margarine, divided
⅓ cup grated Parmesan cheese
½ teaspoon dried parsley flakes
¼ teaspoon garlic powder
¼ teaspoon onion salt
¼ teaspoon paprika

Wash potatoes, and pat dry. Cut each potato into ¼-inch slices, cutting crosswise and to, but not through, bottom of potato. Cut potato should resemble a fan. Allow potatoes to stand in ice water for 5 minutes to open slices.

Place butter in a 1-cup glass measure; microwave at HIGH for 55 seconds or until melted.

Drain potatoes well, and arrange cut side up in a 13- x 9- x 2-inch baking dish. Brush tops and sides of potatoes with 2 tablespoons butter. Cover with waxed paper, and microwave at HIGH for 10 minutes, rearranging potatoes after 5 minutes.

Combine remaining butter and remaining ingredients. Sprinkle evenly over potatoes. Cover potatoes with waxed paper; microwave at HIGH for 8 to 10 minutes or until potatoes are tender, rearranging potatoes after 4 minutes. Yield: 6 servings.

You'll Love These Nut Desserts

Many of our readers' favorite recipes call for nuts, especially pecans and peanuts. In fact, since we use so many pecans for recipe testing, we order a large shipment in the fall, and freeze the nuts until needed.

WALNUT-CREAM CHEESE BROWNIES

4 (1-ounce) squares unsweetened chocolate
¾ cup butter or margarine, softened
2 cups sugar
3 eggs
1 cup all-purpose flour
½ teaspoon salt
1 cup chopped walnuts or pecans
1 teaspoon vanilla extract
1 (8-ounce) package cream cheese, softened
½ cup sugar
1 egg
1 teaspoon vanilla extract

Melt chocolate in top of a double boiler over hot water; set aside to cool.

Cream butter; gradually add 2 cups sugar, beating well. Add 3 eggs, one at a time, beating well after each addition. Stir melted chocolate into butter mixture. Add flour, salt, walnuts, and 1 teaspoon vanilla, stirring well. Pour batter into a greased and floured 13- x 9- x 2-inch baking pan; set aside.

Beat cream cheese until smooth; gradually add ½ cup sugar, beating well. Add 1 egg and 1 teaspoon vanilla, beating well. Drop mixture by heaping tablespoonfuls over chocolate mixture. Swirl cream cheese mixture into chocolate mixture with a knife. Bake at 350° for 45 minutes. Cool and cut into squares. Yield: 3½ dozen.

Elizabeth M. Haney,
Dublin, Virginia.

TOASTED ALMOND CHIP BALLS

1 cup all-purpose flour
½ cup miniature semisweet chocolate morsels
½ cup chopped almonds, toasted
½ cup butter or margarine, softened
2 tablespoons sugar
1 tablespoon brown sugar
1 teaspoon vanilla extract
Sifted powdered sugar (optional)

Combine first 7 ingredients; mix well. Shape into ¾-inch balls. Place on ungreased cookie sheets; bake at 350° for 12 to 15 minutes. Remove cookies to wire racks to cool. Coat warm cookies with powdered sugar, if desired. Yield: about 2½ dozen.   *Lois Kelly,*
St. Petersburg, Florida.

CHOCOLATE-PEANUT BUTTER CAKE

3¼ cups all-purpose flour
2¼ cups sugar
1 tablespoon plus 1 teaspoon baking powder
½ teaspoon salt
½ cup butter or margarine, softened
½ cup creamy peanut butter
1½ cups milk
3 eggs
1⅓ cups finely chopped unsalted roasted peanuts
Chocolate-Peanut Butter Frosting
1 (6-ounce) package semisweet chocolate morsels
2 to 4 tablespoons chopped unsalted roasted peanuts

Combine first 4 ingredients in a large mixing bowl; mix well. Add butter, peanut butter, and milk; beat 2 minutes on medium speed of electric mixer. Add eggs; beat 2 minutes on medium speed. Fold in 1⅓ cups chopped peanuts.

Pour batter into 3 greased and floured 9-inch cakepans. Bake at 350° for 25 to 30 minutes or until a wooden pick inserted in center comes out clean (do not overbake). Cool in pans 10 minutes; remove layers from pans, and cool completely.

Spread Chocolate-Peanut Butter Frosting between layers and on top and sides of cake; chill 1 hour or until firm.

Melt chocolate morsels in top of a double boiler over hot water. Drizzle around top edge and down sides of cake. Sprinkle 2 to 4 tablespoons chopped peanuts on top. Chill until ready to serve. Yield: one 3-layer cake.

Chocolate-Peanut Butter Frosting:

1 (6-ounce) package semisweet chocolate morsels
½ cup butter or margarine, softened
½ cup sifted powdered sugar
1⅓ cups creamy peanut butter

Melt chocolate morsels in top of a double boiler over hot water; set aside. Combine remaining ingredients in a small mixing bowl; beat on medium speed of electric mixer until smooth. Add melted chocolate to peanut butter mixture; beat until smooth. Chill 15 minutes or until spreading consistency. Yield: enough for one 3-layer cake.

Marilyne Hubert,
Tifton, Georgia.

SPICY PECAN PIE

3 eggs, beaten
1 cup light corn syrup
¾ cup sugar
2 tablespoons butter or margarine, melted
¼ teaspoon salt
1 teaspoon freshly grated nutmeg
½ teaspoon ground cinnamon
¼ teaspoon ground cloves
1 teaspoon vanilla extract
1 cup chopped pecans
1 unbaked 9-inch pastry shell
½ cup pecan halves
Whipped cream

Combine first 9 ingredients; beat with an electric mixer until blended. Stir in chopped pecans. Pour mixture into pastry shell; arrange pecan halves on top. Bake at 375° for 35 to 40 minutes. Serve with whipped cream. Yield: one 9-inch pie.   *Rublelene Singleton,*
Scotts Hill, Tennessee.

Make It Tonight, Serve It Tomorrow

Save yourself from last-minute hurry by preparing a main-dish casserole ahead of time. Each of these recipes was assembled one day, refrigerated overnight, and cooked the next day.

SPAGHETTI CASSEROLE

1 (8-ounce) package thin spaghetti
1 pound ground beef
½ cup chopped green pepper
1 large onion, chopped
1 (10¾-ounce) can tomato soup, undiluted
⅔ cup water
1 (8-ounce) can whole kernel corn, drained
½ cup sliced ripe olives
2 cups (8 ounces) shredded Cheddar cheese
½ teaspoon salt
1½ teaspoons dried Italian seasoning

Cook spaghetti according to package directions; drain and set aside.

Cook ground beef, chopped green pepper, and onion in a large skillet until meat is browned, stirring to crumble meat. Drain off drippings. Add remaining ingredients to beef mixture, mixing well. Combine beef mixture and drained spaghetti; spoon into a lightly greased 13- x 9- x 2-inch baking dish. Cover and refrigerate several hours or overnight.

Remove casserole from refrigerator; let stand at room temperature 30 minutes. Bake, covered, at 350° for 45 minutes. Yield: 6 to 8 servings.
Camilla C. Hudson,
Denton, Texas.

HAM TETRAZZINI

1 (8-ounce) package thin spaghetti
1 (6-ounce) jar sliced mushrooms, undrained
1 small onion, chopped
¼ cup butter or margarine
¼ cup all-purpose flour
½ teaspoon dry mustard
1½ cups milk
1 teaspoon chicken-flavored bouillon granules
1 teaspoon Worcestershire sauce
2 cups diced cooked ham
½ cup grated Parmesan cheese

Cook spaghetti according to package directions; drain and set aside.

Drain mushrooms, reserving liquid. Add enough water to mushroom liquid to equal 1 cup; set aside.

Sauté onion in butter in a medium saucepan until tender. Add flour and mustard, stirring until smooth; cook 1 minute, stirring constantly. Gradually add 1 cup mushroom liquid, milk, bouillon granules, and Worcestershire sauce; cook, stirring constantly, until thickened and bubbly.

Combine spaghetti, mushrooms, onion sauce, and ham; mix well. Spoon mixture into a greased shallow 2-quart baking dish; cover and refrigerate several hours or overnight.

Remove from refrigerator; let stand 30 minutes. Bake, covered, at 350° for 30 minutes. Uncover and bake 5 minutes; sprinkle with cheese, and bake 10 minutes. Yield: 6 to 8 servings.
Mrs. Richard L. Brownell,
Salisbury, North Carolina.

NIPPY TUNA CASSEROLE

¼ cup chopped green pepper
3 tablespoons butter or margarine
2 tablespoons all-purpose flour
1 cup milk
1 tablespoon grated onion
2 teaspoons prepared mustard
1 teaspoon prepared horseradish
1 teaspoon lemon juice
¼ teaspoon salt
¼ teaspoon pepper
1 (17-ounce) can whole kernel corn, drained
2 hard-cooked eggs, sliced
1 (7-ounce) can tuna, drained and flaked
1 cup (4 ounces) shredded Cheddar cheese, divided

Sauté green pepper in butter in a heavy saucepan over low heat until tender. Add flour, stirring until smooth. Cook 1 minute, stirring constantly. Gradually stir in milk; cook over medium heat, stirring constantly, until mixture is thickened and bubbly. Stir in next 6 ingredients.

Spoon half each of corn, eggs, tuna, sauce, and cheese into a greased 1-quart casserole. Repeat layers of corn, eggs, tuna, and sauce, reserving ½ cup cheese. Cover and refrigerate for several hours or overnight.

Remove casserole from refrigerator; let stand at room temperature 30 minutes. Remove cover, and bake at 350° for 25 minutes. Sprinkle with remaining ½ cup cheese; bake an additional 5 minutes or until cheese melts. Yield: 4 servings.
Martha E. Sheard,
Orlando, Florida.

CHICKEN-WILD RICE CASSEROLE

1 (6-ounce) package long grain and wild rice
¼ cup butter or margarine
¼ cup all-purpose flour
1 (13-ounce) can evaporated milk
½ cup chicken broth
2½ cups chopped cooked chicken
1 (3-ounce) can sliced mushrooms, drained
⅓ cup chopped green pepper
¼ cup chopped pimiento
¼ cup slivered almonds, lightly toasted

Prepare rice according to package directions; set aside.

Melt butter in a heavy saucepan over low heat; add flour, stirring until smooth. Cook 1 minute, stirring constantly. Gradually add milk and broth; cook over medium heat, stirring constantly, until thickened and bubbly.

Combine sauce, rice, chicken, mushrooms, green pepper, and pimiento. Pour into a lightly greased 2-quart casserole. Sprinkle with almonds. Cover and refrigerate overnight.

Remove casserole from refrigerator; let stand at room temperature 30 minutes. Remove cover, and bake at 350° for 35 minutes. Yield: 6 to 8 servings.
Anita McLemore,
Knoxville, Tennessee.

MAKE-AHEAD CHICKEN CASSEROLE

1 (7-ounce) package elbow macaroni
3 cups chopped cooked chicken
1 small onion, chopped
1 (2½-ounce) jar sliced mushrooms, drained
2 cups (8 ounces) shredded American cheese
2 cups milk
1 (10¾-ounce) can cream of celery soup, undiluted
½ teaspoon salt

Cook macaroni according to package directions; drain. Add remaining ingredients to macaroni, mixing well. Spoon into a lightly greased 3-quart baking dish; cover and refrigerate for several hours or overnight.

Remove from refrigerator; let stand at room temperature 30 minutes. Bake, uncovered, at 350° for 45 minutes. Yield: 6 to 8 servings. *Cindy Murphy,*
Cleveland, Tennessee.

Flavor Breads With Buttermilk

Southerners have found a variety of ways to stir buttermilk into breads for the richest flavor. You'll love the taste it brings to muffins, pancakes, cornbread, and coffee cake.

If you run out of buttermilk, a combination of lemon juice or vinegar and sweet milk will make a handy substitution. For 1 cup buttermilk, add 1 tablespoon of lemon juice or vinegar to a measuring cup, and fill it to the 1 cup mark with milk. Mix well, and let the milk stand about 5 minutes to thicken.

APPLE-PECAN COFFEE CAKE

½ cup shortening
½ cup butter or margarine, softened
2 cups sugar
2 eggs
3 cups all-purpose flour
2 teaspoons baking powder
1 teaspoon baking soda
¼ teaspoon salt
1¾ cups buttermilk
2 medium cooking apples, peeled and
    thinly sliced
½ cup all-purpose flour
½ cup sugar
1½ teaspoons ground cinnamon
3 tablespoons butter or margarine
½ cup finely chopped pecans

Cream shortening and ½ cup butter; gradually add 2 cups sugar, beating until light and fluffy. Add eggs, one at a time, beating well after each addition.

Combine 3 cups flour, baking powder, soda, and salt; add to creamed mixture alternately with buttermilk, beginning and ending with flour mixture. Spoon half of batter into a greased and floured 13- x 9- x 2-inch baking pan. Arrange apple slices over batter. Spread remaining cake batter evenly over top.

Combine ½ cup flour, ½ cup sugar, and cinnamon, mixing well. Cut in 3 tablespoons butter with a pastry blender until mixture resembles coarse meal; stir in chopped pecans. Sprinkle mixture evenly over batter. Bake at 350° for 45 minutes. Cool completely. Cut cake into squares to serve. Yield: 15 servings.
Dee Buchfink,
Lufkin, Texas.

BROWN BREAD

1 cup whole wheat flour
1 cup cornmeal
1 cup all-purpose flour
2 teaspoons baking powder
1½ teaspoons baking soda
1 teaspoon salt
2 cups buttermilk
¾ cup molasses
2 tablespoons shortening, melted
¾ cup raisins

Combine first 6 ingredients in a large mixing bowl; add buttermilk, molasses, and shortening; beat until well mixed. Stir in raisins.

Pour batter into two well-greased 13-ounce coffee cans. Cover the cans with a double thickness of foil; tie securely with string.

Place cans on a shallow rack in a large, deep kettle; add water to a 1-inch depth. Cover kettle; steam bread 3 hours with water boiling continuously (replace water as needed). Remove bread from cans; let cool 10 minutes on wire racks. Serve warm. Yield: 2 loaves.
Betty R. Butts,
Kensington, Maryland.

GINGERBREAD PANCAKES

2½ cups all-purpose flour
1 teaspoon baking powder
1 teaspoon baking soda
½ teaspoon salt
1½ teaspoons ground cinnamon
1½ teaspoons ground ginger
1½ teaspoons ground nutmeg
⅛ to ¼ teaspoon ground cloves
3 eggs
¼ cup firmly packed brown sugar
1 cup buttermilk
1 cup water
¼ cup brewed coffee
¼ cup butter or margarine, melted
Applesauce (optional)
Maple syrup (optional)

Combine first 8 ingredients; mix well, and set aside. Combine eggs and sugar, beating well. Add buttermilk, water, coffee, and butter; mix well. Add buttermilk mixture to dry ingredients, stirring just until moistened (batter will be slightly lumpy).

For each pancake, pour about ¼ cup batter onto a hot, lightly greased griddle or skillet. Turn pancakes over when the tops are covered with bubbles and edges appear slightly dry. Serve with warm applesauce or maple syrup, if desired. Yield: 16 pancakes.
Eileen Wehling,
Austin, Texas.

MEXICAN CORNBREAD

1 tablespoon vegetable oil
1½ cups self-rising cornmeal
1 cup buttermilk
2 eggs, beaten
3 tablespoons vegetable oil
1 (8¾-ounce) can cream-style corn
½ cup chopped green pepper
6 slices bacon, cooked and crumbled
¼ cup chopped canned jalapeño peppers
Dash of garlic powder
2 cups (8 ounces) shredded sharp Cheddar
    cheese, divided

Grease a 10½-inch cast-iron skillet with 1 tablespoon oil. Heat skillet at 350° for 10 minutes.

Combine next 9 ingredients in a bowl, stirring well. Pour half of cornmeal mixture into skillet. Sprinkle with 1 cup cheese. Top with remaining cornmeal mixture. Bake at 350° for 45 minutes. Sprinkle with remaining cheese, and bake an additional 10 minutes. Yield: 10 to 12 servings. *Mary Nell Brandel,*
Marco Island, Florida.

BEST-EVER OATMEAL MUFFINS

1 cup quick-cooking oats, uncooked
1 cup buttermilk
1 egg, beaten
½ cup firmly packed brown sugar
½ cup vegetable oil
1 cup all-purpose flour
1 teaspoon baking powder
½ teaspoon baking soda
½ teaspoon salt
½ cup raisins

Combine oats and buttermilk in a large bowl; let stand 1 hour. Add egg, sugar, and oil, stirring well.

Combine remaining ingredients, except raisins, in a medium bowl; add to oats mixture, stirring just until moistened. Stir in raisins.

Spoon into greased muffin pans, filling three-fourths full. Bake at 400° about 18 minutes. Yield: 18 muffins.
Mrs. Marion Gilmore,
Lake Placid, Florida.

Tip: Always measure ingredients accurately. For liquids, use a glass measuring cup; this allows you to see that you are measuring correctly. Use metal or plastic dry measuring cups for solids; fill cups to overflowing, and level with a knife or metal spatula.

Treats For A Halloween Carnival

Caramel Corn Candy and Crisp Sugar Cookies are perfect goblin food. The spooks in our test kitchens especially enjoyed the Caramel Corn Candy. Since the recipe makes a large amount, we stored some of the mixture in an airtight container for 4 weeks. It was still crunchy and fresh.

CANDY APPLES

6 medium-size Red Delicious apples
6 wooden skewers
3 cups sugar
⅔ cup light corn syrup
⅔ cup water
1 teaspoon vinegar
6 to 8 drops red food coloring

Wash and dry apples; remove stems. Insert wooden skewers into stem end of each apple; set aside.

Combine next 4 ingredients in a heavy saucepan; mix well. Cook over medium heat until mixture reaches 295°, stirring occasionally. Remove from heat; stir in food coloring. Quickly dip apples into mixture; allow excess to drip off. Place apples on a buttered baking sheet to cool. Yield: 6 servings.
Marlo Maria Little,
Greenville, North Carolina.

CRISP SUGAR COOKIES

1 cup shortening
½ cup sugar
½ cup firmly packed brown sugar
1 egg, beaten
3 tablespoons milk
2 teaspoons vanilla extract
2⅔ cups all-purpose flour
2 teaspoons cream of tartar
1 teaspoon baking soda
½ teaspoon salt
Colored sugar (optional)
Raisins (optional)
Chocolate-flavored decorator candies
  (optional)

Cream shortening and sugar, beating until light and fluffy. Add egg, milk, and vanilla; beat well. Combine next 4 ingredients; add to creamed mixture, stirring well. Cover and refrigerate overnight. (Dough will be soft.)

Work with one-fourth of dough at a time; store remainder in refrigerator. Place dough on a lightly greased cookie sheet; roll out to ¼-inch thickness. Cut dough with floured cookie cutters, leaving 1 inch between each cookie. Remove excess dough; combine with remaining dough in refrigerator.

Decorate cookies with colored sugar, raisins, and decorator candies, if desired. Bake at 350° for 7 to 10 minutes or until lightly browned. Cool on cookie sheets 3 to 5 minutes; remove from cookie sheets, and cool completely. Repeat procedure with remaining dough. Yield: 5 dozen. *Theada Witherspoon,*
Kingsport, Tennessee.

CARAMEL CORN CANDY

8 quarts popped corn
2 cups salted peanuts
1 cup butter or margarine
½ cup light corn syrup
1 cup sugar
1 cup firmly packed brown sugar
1 teaspoon salt
1 teaspoon baking soda
1 teaspoon vanilla extract
1 teaspoon maple flavoring

Combine popped corn and peanuts in a large mixing bowl; set aside.

Combine butter, corn syrup, sugar, and salt in a saucepan; bring to a boil. Reduce heat and simmer 5 minutes, stirring occasionally. Remove from heat; quickly stir in soda and flavorings. Pour over popcorn mixture; mix well.

Spoon mixture onto three 15- x 10- x 1-inch jellyroll pans. Bake at 250° for 1 hour, stirring occasionally. Remove from oven; stir occasionally while mixture cools. Store in an airtight container. Yield: 8½ quarts.
Sherry Baynes,
North Wilkesboro, North Carolina.

PEANUT BUTTER BARS

1 (6-ounce) package semisweet chocolate
  morsels
½ cup butter or margarine, softened
⅔ cup peanut butter
1 cup firmly packed brown sugar
1 egg
1 teaspoon vanilla extract
1¼ cups all-purpose flour
½ teaspoon baking soda
½ teaspoon salt
1½ cups quick-cooking oats, uncooked

Melt chocolate in top of a double boiler over hot water; set aside.

Cream butter and peanut butter. Add sugar, egg, and vanilla, mixing well. Combine flour, soda, and salt; stir into creamed mixture. Stir in oats.

Press three-fourths of peanut butter mixture into a greased 13- x 9- x 2-inch baking pan. Spread chocolate over top. Crumble remaining peanut butter mixture over chocolate. Bake at 350° for 18 to 20 minutes. Cool and cut into bars. Yield: 2 dozen. *Mrs. V. O. Walker,*
Pennington, Texas.

You'll Want Seconds Of Ratatouille

Who needs meat when you can achieve the tasty blend of vegetables and spices you'll find in our hearty Ratatouille? Tomato, onion, eggplant, zucchini, and green pepper are simmered in a tomato-wine mixture.

RATATOUILLE

1 medium onion, chopped
2 cloves garlic, crushed
1 bay leaf
¼ cup olive oil
1 medium eggplant, peeled and cubed
¾ cup tomato juice
3 tablespoons Burgundy or other dry
  red wine
2 tablespoons tomato paste
½ teaspoon dried whole basil
½ teaspoon dried marjoram leaves
½ teaspoon dried whole oregano
½ teaspoon salt
⅛ teaspoon dried whole rosemary, crushed
⅛ teaspoon pepper
2 medium-size green peppers, cut into
  strips
1 medium zucchini, cubed
2 medium tomatoes, coarsely chopped
2 tablespoons chopped fresh parsley
Hot cooked rice
Grated Parmesan cheese
Sliced black olives

Sauté onion, garlic, and bay leaf in oil in a Dutch oven 3 to 5 minutes. Add eggplant, tomato juice, wine, tomato paste, and seasonings; cover and cook 10 minutes. Add green pepper and zucchini; cover and cook 10 minutes. Add tomatoes, and cook just until thoroughly heated; stir in parsley. Discard bay leaf. Serve over rice. Top with cheese and olives. Yield: 6 servings.
Michele Poynton,
Huntington Woods, Michigan.

Try These Recipes For Fall Fruit

When pears and apples are ripe and juicy in the fall, they're ready for enjoying in a fresh fruit salad, dessert, or side dish. In the following recipes, our readers share some tempting ways to use them cooked or fresh.

TURKEY FRUIT SALAD

4 cups chopped cooked turkey
1 cup pineapple tidbits, drained
1 cup seedless green grapes, halved
1 cup chopped red apple
1 cup chopped walnuts
1½ cups mayonnaise

Combine all ingredients; mix well. Cover and chill for 2 to 3 hours. Yield: 8 servings. *Mrs. Randall L. Wilson, Louisville, Kentucky.*

HONEY BAKED APPLES

6 large baking apples
3 tablespoons chopped walnuts
3 tablespoons raisins
1 cup water
⅓ cup honey
1 (3-inch) stick cinnamon
1 tablespoon lemon juice

Core apples; peel top third of each. Place apples in a shallow baking dish. Combine walnuts and raisins; stuff cavities of apples with nut mixture.

Combine water, honey, and cinnamon in a small saucepan; bring to a boil. Reduce heat and simmer 5 minutes. Remove from heat, and stir in lemon juice. Remove cinnamon stick; pour liquid over apples. Cover and bake at 350° for 45 to 50 minutes or until apples are tender, basting occasionally. Yield: 6 servings. *Deborah Smith, Salem, Missouri.*

SKILLET SPICED APPLES

1 tablespoon vegetable oil
½ teaspoon ground cloves
4 medium cooking apples, peeled, cored, and sliced into wedges
2 tablespoons orange marmalade

Combine vegetable oil and cloves in a medium bowl; add apples, stirring well to coat slices. Fry apples, covered, in a large skillet over medium heat 10 minutes, stirring occasionally. Remove cover; stir in marmalade and continue cooking, uncovered, 3 to 5 minutes. Yield: 4 servings. *Shirley W. Hodge, Delray Beach, Florida.*

CRUNCHY PEAR SALAD

3 ripe pears, peeled, halved, and cored
2 teaspoons lemon juice
1 (3-ounce) package cream cheese, softened
3 tablespoons milk
¼ teaspoon dried whole tarragon
½ cup sliced celery
½ cup chopped dates
Lettuce leaves
¼ cup chopped walnuts or pecans

Sprinkle pear halves with lemon juice. Combine cream cheese, milk, and tarragon; beat until smooth. Stir in celery and dates. Spoon one-sixth of cheese mixture on each pear half. Arrange on a lettuce-lined platter; sprinkle with walnuts. Cover and chill 1 to 2 hours. Yield: 6 servings.
Susan Buckmaster, Charlotte, North Carolina.

PEAR STREUSEL PIE

½ cup all-purpose flour
¾ cup firmly packed brown sugar
¾ cup flaked coconut
⅓ cup butter, melted
4 large pears, peeled and cubed
1 unbaked 9-inch pastry shell

Combine flour, brown sugar, and coconut; gradually add butter, stirring with a fork. Set aside.

Place 1 cup pears in pastry shell; top with half of coconut mixture. Repeat layers with remaining pears and coconut mixture. Cover pie with foil, and bake at 450° for 10 minutes. Remove foil; reduce oven to 350°, and bake an additional 30 minutes or until pears are tender. Yield: one 9-inch pie.
Mrs. Clayton J. Turner, De Funiak Springs, Florida.

Another Way To Serve Nachos

Chicken Nachos are a great appetizer to serve to company. Whip a batch up and watch these nachos become the hit of your party.

CHICKEN NACHOS

4 chicken breast halves, boned and skinned
1 teaspoon salt
1½ teaspoons ground cumin
½ cup diced onion
¼ cup diced green pepper
2 tablespoons butter or margarine
1 (4-ounce) can chopped green chiles, undrained
⅔ cup chopped tomato
1 teaspoon ground cumin
¼ teaspoon salt
⅛ teaspoon pepper
About 3 dozen round tortilla chips
3 cups (12 ounces) shredded Monterey Jack cheese
¾ cup commercial sour cream
About 3 dozen jalapeño pepper slices
Paprika (optional)

Combine chicken and 1 teaspoon salt in a large saucepan; cover with water. Bring to a boil; cover, reduce heat, and simmer 5 to 8 minutes. Drain chicken, reserving ⅔ cup broth.

Place chicken and 1½ teaspoons cumin in container of food processor; process until coarsely ground. Set aside.

Sauté onion and green pepper in butter in a large skillet until tender. Add chicken, reserved broth, and next 5 ingredients; simmer, uncovered, about 10 minutes or until the liquid evaporates.

Place tortilla chips on baking sheets, and spoon about 1 tablespoon chicken mixture on each. Top each nacho with 1 heaping tablespoon cheese; broil until cheese melts. Remove from oven, and top each nacho with 1 teaspoon sour cream and a jalapeño pepper slice. Sprinkle with paprika, if desired, and broil 30 seconds. Serve immediately. Yield: about 3 dozen. *Brent Berry, Dewey, Oklahoma.*

Tip: Refrigerate cheese in its original wrap until opened. After opening, rewrap tightly in plastic wrap, plastic bags, or aluminum foil, or place in airtight containers.

Enjoy cooked pears in this elegant dessert of Pears in Orange Cream.

Let's Have Limas

Lima beans are popular all over the South. Your grandmother probably called them butter beans and seasoned them richly with salt pork or bacon. But there's much more you can do.

Don't shell limas until you're ready to cook them. Refrigerate unshelled limas in a moisture-proof container or plastic bag; they should keep about 3 or 4 days. If you can't find fresh limas, substitute frozen ones for any of these recipes, and cook according to package directions.

LIMA BEANS WITH CANADIAN BACON

4 cups shelled fresh lima beans
6 slices Canadian bacon, coarsely
  chopped
2 tablespoons chopped onion
2 tablespoons butter or margarine
2 tablespoons all-purpose flour
2 teaspoons brown sugar
¼ teaspoon salt
¼ teaspoon ground turmeric
⅛ teaspoon pepper
3 medium tomatoes, peeled and coarsely
  chopped

Cook lima beans, covered, in boiling salted water 20 minutes or until tender; drain, reserving liquid. Add enough water to reserved liquid to equal 1 cup; set beans and liquid aside.

Fry Canadian bacon in a large skillet about 3 minutes; remove from skillet, and set aside.

Sauté onion in butter in a skillet until tender. Combine flour, brown sugar, salt, turmeric, and pepper; add to onion, stirring until well blended. Cook 1 minute, stirring constantly. Gradually add reserved liquid; cook over medium heat, stirring constantly, until thickened and bubbly. Stir in beans; cook until thoroughly heated.

Spoon half of bean mixture into a lightly greased 1½-quart casserole. Layer tomatoes and bacon over beans; top with remaining beans. Cover and bake at 350° for 20 minutes. Yield: 6 servings.
Allison Whiteside,
Hinsdale, Illinois.

A New Twist For Pears

A ripe juicy pear makes a great snack for eating out of hand. It's also the basis of a fancy dessert called Pears in Orange Cream.

PEARS IN ORANGE CREAM

¾ cup milk
2 egg yolks
3 tablespoons sugar
1 teaspoon arrowroot
¼ cup sugar
1½ cups water
6 medium pears, peeled, halved,
  and cored
1 large orange
1 tablespoon plus 2 teaspoons
  sugar
¾ cup whipping cream

Scald milk in a small saucepan. Beat egg yolks, 3 tablespoons sugar, and arrowroot until thick and lemon colored. Gradually stir about one-fourth of hot milk into yolk mixture; add to remaining milk, stirring constantly. Cook over low heat, stirring constantly, until thickened; cool. Cover and refrigerate custard 1 to 2 hours.

Combine ¼ cup sugar and water in a large saucepan; bring to a boil, stirring constantly. Add pears; cover, reduce heat, and simmer 15 to 20 minutes or until tender. Remove from heat.

Thinly peel rind from half of orange; cut into 2- x ⅛-inch strips. Place in a small amount of boiling water; remove from heat. Cover and let stand 5 minutes. Drain and set aside.

Grate ½ teaspoon rind from remaining half of orange. Squeeze orange, reserving ⅓ cup juice. Combine juice, grated orange rind, and 1 tablespoon plus 2 teaspoons sugar; stir until sugar dissolves.

Beat whipping cream until stiff peaks form. Combine custard and orange syrup; fold into whipped cream.

Drain pears, and place in serving dish; spoon orange-whipped cream mixture over top. Garnish with orange rind strips. Yield: 6 servings.
Rublelene Singleton,
Scotts Hill, Tennessee.

Tip: Compare costs of fresh, frozen, canned, and dried foods. To compute the best buy, divide the price by the number of servings. The lower price per serving will be the thriftiest buy.

LIMA BEAN GARDEN CASSEROLE

2 cups shelled fresh lima beans
1 cup fresh corn cut from cob
2 tablespoons butter or margarine
2 tablespoons all-purpose flour
1 cup milk
1 teaspoon minced fresh dillweed or ¼
   teaspoon dried whole dillweed
½ teaspoon salt
Dash of freshly ground black pepper
1 cup shredded carrots
¼ cup grated Parmesan cheese

Cook lima beans, covered, in boiling salted water 20 minutes or until tender; drain and set aside.

Cook corn, covered, in boiling salted water 10 minutes; drain and set aside.

Melt butter in a heavy saucepan over low heat; add flour, stirring until smooth. Cook 1 minute, stirring constantly. Gradually add milk; cook over medium heat, stirring constantly, until thickened and bubbly. Stir in dillweed, salt, pepper, and vegetables. Pour into a lightly greased 2-quart casserole; cover and bake at 350° for 25 minutes. Sprinkle with cheese; bake, uncovered, an additional 5 minutes. Yield: 6 servings.   *Jan Thompson,*
Highland, Maryland.

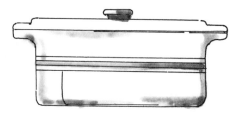

SAVORY LIMA BEANS

2 cups shelled fresh lima beans
2 slices bacon
½ cup water
1 tablespoon all-purpose flour
2 tablespoons chopped onion
1 tablespoon brown sugar
¼ teaspoon salt
¼ teaspoon celery salt
¼ teaspoon paprika

Cook lima beans, covered, in boiling salted water 20 minutes or until tender; drain well.

Cook bacon until almost crisp; drain and set aside.

Gradually add water to flour, stirring until smooth. Combine lima beans, flour mixture, onion, and next 4 ingredients, mixing well. Pour into a lightly greased 1-quart baking dish. Place bacon on top. Bake, uncovered, at 375° for 20 minutes. Yield: 4 servings.
Rublelene Singleton,
Scotts Hill, Tennessee.

Try Navajo Tacos

Outdoor craft fairs and art festivals are popular throughout the Southwest during the fall, and food booths that offer local specialties are among the main attractions. One of the hottest-selling items is Navajo Tacos, a Southwestern specialty that uses Navajo fry bread as a base. Layered with various toppings, it's really more like a chalupa than a taco.

NAVAJO TACOS

4½ cups all-purpose flour
2 tablespoons instant nonfat dry milk
   powder
1 tablespoon baking powder
1 teaspoon salt
1½ cups warm water
Vegetable oil
Chili Topping
3 cups shredded lettuce
2 large tomatoes, chopped
1 small onion, finely chopped

Combine first 4 ingredients in a mixing bowl, and blend thoroughly. Gradually add water, stirring to form a stiff dough. Turn dough out onto a floured surface; knead 5 minutes or until elastic. Divide dough into 8 equal portions; let rest 10 minutes. Roll each portion into a circle about 8 inches in diameter and ⅛ inch thick.

Fry dough rounds, one at a time, in 1 inch hot oil (400° to 450°) about 1 minute on each side or until puffed and golden brown. Drain rounds on paper towels. Keep warm while frying remaining dough.

Spoon an equal amount of Chili Topping on each piece of fry bread. Top with lettuce, tomatoes, and onion. Serve immediately. Yield: 8 servings.

Chili Topping:
1 cup dried pinto beans
5½ cups water
1½ pounds uncooked turkey, ground
1 tablespoon vegetable oil
1½ to 2 tablespoons chili powder
2 cups (8 ounces) shredded process
   American cheese

Sort and wash beans; place in a Dutch oven. Cover with water 2 inches above beans; let soak overnight. Drain beans. Add 5½ cups water, and bring to a boil; reduce heat and simmer, uncovered, 45 minutes to 1 hour or until beans are tender. Drain beans, reserving ¼ cup cooking liquid; set aside.

Sauté turkey in hot oil in a large skillet over medium heat until pink color

disappears. Add beans, reserved cooking liquid, and chili powder; cook 2 to 3 minutes or until beans are thoroughly heated. Add cheese; stir until melted. Yield: 5½ cups.   *Mrs. Darrell Cox,*
Houston, Texas.

Flavor Soup With Beer And Cheese

Over the years we've received numerous requests from readers for Beer-Cheese Soup. It seems that there are many Southerners who have sampled a similar creamy-smooth soup in restaurants and would like to serve it at home. Our test kitchens staff reviewed several versions of the soup and decided this recipe was most like the one we had tried in restaurants. It's thick with the flavor of process cheese spread and has the added punch of two cans of beer. Of course, if you prefer a milder taste, you may add less beer.

BEER-CHEESE SOUP

6 cups milk
2 (12-ounce) cans beer, divided
2 (16-ounce) jars plus 1 (8-ounce) jar
   process cheese spread
1 (10¾-ounce) can chicken broth,
   undiluted
1 teaspoon Worcestershire sauce
3 dashes of hot sauce
¼ cup plus 2 tablespoons cornstarch

Combine milk and 2½ cups beer in a large Dutch oven. Cook over low heat until thoroughly heated, stirring constantly. Add cheese spread, broth, Worcestershire sauce, and hot sauce. Cook over low heat until thoroughly heated, stirring constantly.

Combine cornstarch and remaining beer, mixing well. Add to cheese mixture; simmer, stirring constantly, until thickened (do not boil). Yield: 4 quarts.
George Barr,
Birmingham, Alabama.

Tip: Bent or dented measuring utensils give inaccurate measures. Use only standard measuring cups and spoons that are in good condition.

These Vegetables Are Freshest In The Fall

If you love the taste of broccoli, brussels sprouts, and cauliflower, fall is the season to enjoy them fresh. Harvested during the late fall and winter months in most of the South, these vegetables provide hearty side dishes for cooler days. As with all produce in the peak of flavor, look for recipes with simple seasonings and sauces to present the fullest vegetable flavor.

When purchasing vegetables by the bunch or head, weigh them to get a measurement of your expected yield. You'll get 4 cups of brussels sprouts or 1½ cups of cauliflower flowerets per pound of vegetable for use in recipes. Use the vegetables as soon after harvest as possible for the best flavor. But if you must store them, broccoli, brussels sprouts, and cauliflower will keep a week if refrigerated. For more information on buying and preparing cool-weather vegetables, see "From Our Kitchen to Yours" on page 249.

BROCCOLI AND CAULIFLOWER WITH SHRIMP SAUCE

1 (1-pound) bunch broccoli
1 medium head cauliflower, broken into flowerets
1 (3-ounce) package cream cheese with chives, cubed
1 (10¾-ounce) can cream of shrimp soup, undiluted
1 tablespoon lemon juice
1 (4¼-ounce) can shrimp, rinsed and drained
½ cup slivered almonds, toasted

Trim off large leaves of broccoli. Wash broccoli, and break off flowerets; reserve stalks for use in other recipes.

Place the cauliflower and broccoli flowerets in a small amount of boiling salted water; return to a boil. Cover, reduce heat, and simmer 8 minutes; drain well. Set aside.

Combine cream cheese, soup, and lemon juice in a heavy saucepan; cook over medium heat, stirring constantly, until cream cheese melts. Remove from heat; stir in shrimp.

Place cauliflower in center of serving platter; arrange broccoli around edges. Spoon sauce on top; sprinkle with almonds. Yield: 10 servings.
*Renee Wells,
Columbia, South Carolina.*

BROCCOLI WITH SUNSHINE SAUCE

1 (1-pound) bunch broccoli
3 egg yolks, beaten
2 tablespoons tarragon vinegar
1 tablespoon half-and-half
¼ teaspoon salt
⅛ teaspoon paprika
¼ cup butter or margarine, melted
¼ teaspoon grated onion
2 hard-cooked eggs, finely chopped
Pimiento strips

Trim off large leaves of broccoli. Remove tough ends of stalks, and wash broccoli thoroughly. Make lengthwise slits in thick stalks. Arrange broccoli spears in a steaming rack with stalks to center of rack. Place over boiling water; cover and steam 10 to 15 minutes or until tender. Arrange broccoli in a serving dish; keep warm.

Combine next 5 ingredients in top of a double boiler; mix well. Stir in 2 tablespoons butter; cook, stirring constantly, until smooth and thickened. Add remaining butter, 1 tablespoon at a time, stirring constantly, until smooth. Remove from heat; stir in onion. Spoon sauce over broccoli. Sprinkle with chopped egg, and garnish with pimiento strips. Yield: 4 to 6 servings.
*Alice McNamara,
Eucha, Oklahoma.*

FRIED CAULIFLOWER

1 medium head cauliflower, broken into flowerets
⅔ cup fine, dry breadcrumbs
1 teaspoon grated Parmesan cheese
¼ teaspoon salt
¼ teaspoon pepper
2 eggs, beaten
¼ cup milk
Vegetable oil

Place cauliflower in a small amount of boiling water; return to a boil. Cover, reduce heat, and simmer 10 minutes or until tender. Drain and cool.

Combine next 4 ingredients; mix well. Combine eggs and milk; mix well. Dip flowerets in egg mixture; roll in crumb mixture. Fry in deep hot oil (375°) until golden. Drain on paper towels. Serve hot. Yield: 4 servings. *Audrey Bledsoe,
Smyrna, Georgia.*

BRUSSELS SPROUTS PIERRE

About ¾ pound brussels sprouts
1 cup diced celery
2 tablespoons butter or margarine
2 tablespoons all-purpose flour
1 cup milk
½ cup (2 ounces) shredded process American cheese
⅛ teaspoon pepper

Wash brussels sprouts thoroughly, and remove discolored leaves. Cut off stem ends, and slash bottom of each sprout with a shallow X. Place in a small amount of boiling salted water. Cover, reduce heat, and simmer 10 minutes or until tender; drain and set aside. Cook celery in a small amount of boiling water 5 minutes or until tender; drain and set aside.

Melt butter in a heavy saucepan over low heat; add flour, stirring until smooth. Cook 1 minute, stirring constantly. Gradually add milk; cook over medium heat, stirring constantly, until thickened and bubbly. Add cheese and pepper, stirring constantly until cheese melts. Combine cheese sauce, sprouts, and celery, tossing lightly. Cook until thoroughly heated. Yield: 6 servings.
*Daisy Cotton,
Edcouch, Texas.*

DEVILED BRUSSELS SPROUTS

1 pound fresh brussels sprouts
⅔ cup butter or margarine, melted
2 tablespoons prepared mustard
1 teaspoon Worcestershire sauce
½ teaspoon salt
¼ teaspoon red pepper

Wash brussels sprouts thoroughly, and remove discolored leaves. Cut off stem ends, and slash bottom of each sprout with a shallow X. Place sprouts in a small amount of boiling salted water. Cover, reduce heat, and simmer 7 minutes or until tender. Drain well, and place in a serving dish.

Combine remaining ingredients, and pour over warm brussels sprouts. Yield: 6 servings. *Georgia F. Chapman,
Bedford, Virginia.*

Tip: A special topping for cooked vegetables or casseroles can be made by crushing ½ cup herb-seasoned stuffing mix with 2 tablespoons melted butter or margarine; top dish with this mixture and sprinkle with 1 cup shredded cheese.

From Our Kitchen To Yours

Broccoli, brussels sprouts, and cauliflower are all at their best during the winter—they're tastier, more widely available, and less expensive. Along with the recipes featured in "These Vegetables Are Freshest in the Fall" on page 248, we'd like to share some buying tips and preparation techniques.

Broccoli grows best and keeps longest in cool temperatures. When buying, look for a firm bunch, one with dark green, tight-clustered flowerets. If the flowerets are spread and yellowish-green or wilted, or if the stem is slippery, the broccoli is overmature.

In our *Southern Living* recipes, we often call for a pound of broccoli, which is roughly equivalent to one bunch. We always suggest that you cut off the large leaves and remove tough ends of the lower stalk. If the stalks are more than a half inch in diameter, make some lengthwise cuts in the stem up to the flowerets to help the stalks cook evenly.

We usually steam broccoli or cook it in a small amount of water just until it is crisp-tender. This helps preserve the color and nutritive value. To keep from destroying vitamins found in broccoli, use stainless steel or aluminum cookware; avoid using copper. Do not add baking soda because this may also destroy nutrients.

Just as with broccoli, look for **brussels sprouts** that are firm with a nice green color, not yellow. Each sprout should be a tight cluster of leaves, unwrinkled, and free of black spots. Before cooking brussels sprouts, pull off any discolored leaves, cut off the stem end, and wash the sprouts. Fresh brussels sprouts are best cooked in a small amount of water or steamed about 5 minutes or until tender. Cutting a crisscross into the stem end speeds up cooking time.

When choosing **cauliflower**, look for one with tight flowerets, white or creamy in color. Brown bruises or specks and loosely spread flowerets indicate an old cauliflower. The size of the vegetable doesn't affect the flavor. To prepare a cauliflower, wash it and remove the leaves and core; it can be cooked whole or broken into flowerets. Cauliflower cooks best in a small amount of water or steamed.

All of these vegetables are very perishable and need to be refrigerated and used soon after they're bought. It's best to keep them in a plastic bag and stored in the fruit-and-vegetable compartment of your refrigerator.

Let Sausage Add Spice

Just mention sausage and visions of quaint delis and country stores overflowing with tangy, smoky aromas come to mind. Sausage became popular when people had to preserve meat because food supplies were scarce. Records reveal that some 3,500 years ago, the Babylonians and Chinese were making and eating different types of sausage. And the Romans liked sausage so much that no festive occasion was considered complete without it.

In this country, the Indians were the first to make sausage, and when immigrants arrived, they brought their sausage-making skills with them. Over the years, Southerners have blended the old sausage-making techniques with new ones to become experts in their own right. Today, most sausage is commercially prepared, but some folks still like to make their own.

Of course, most Southerners are fond of frying sausage for breakfast and serving it along with grits and biscuits. But the truth of the matter is that sausage can be served at any meal in a variety of dishes.

PASTA WITH SAUSAGE AND MIXED VEGETABLES

1 (5-ounce) package medium egg noodles
½ pound fresh mushrooms, sliced
1 cup fresh broccoli flowerets
½ cup chopped zucchini
¼ cup chopped onion
¼ cup chopped green pepper
1 teaspoon dried whole oregano
¼ teaspoon garlic powder
3 tablespoons butter or margarine
1 pound smoked sausage, cut into ½-inch slices
6 large cherry tomatoes, halved
½ cup grated Parmesan cheese, divided

Cook noodles according to package directions; drain well.

Sauté next 7 ingredients in butter in a large skillet 3 to 5 minutes or until vegetables are crisp-tender. Add sausage; cover and cook over medium heat 2 minutes. Stir in tomatoes; heat thoroughly. Stir in ¼ cup Parmesan cheese; spoon the sausage mixture over the noodles. Sprinkle with remaining ¼ cup cheese. Yield: 6 to 8 servings.
Mildred Sheppard,
Crawfordville, Florida.

SAUSAGE JAMBALAYA

1 cup uncooked regular rice
1 medium onion, sliced
¾ cup chopped celery
2 tablespoons vegetable oil
2 cloves garlic, chopped
1 pound smoked sausage, cut into ¼-inch slices
1⅓ cups diced cooked ham
1 (14½-ounce) can beef broth, undiluted
½ teaspoon pepper
½ teaspoon red pepper

Cook rice according to package directions; set aside.

Sauté onion and celery in oil in a large skillet until crisp-tender. Stir in garlic, sausage, and ham; cook 2 to 3 minutes. Add remaining ingredients, and bring to a boil; reduce heat and simmer, uncovered, 15 minutes. Stir in rice; cook until heated. Yield: 6 to 8 servings.
Charlene Broussard,
Port Neches, Texas.

HOT-AND-SPICY CABBAGE ROLLS

1 medium cabbage
2 medium onions, chopped
2 stalks celery, chopped
2 tablespoons butter or margarine
1 tablespoon salt
¼ teaspoon pepper
1 pound hot bulk sausage
1½ cups cooked regular rice
Paprika
2 tablespoons butter or margarine
2 tablespoons all-purpose flour
1 (28-ounce) can whole tomatoes, undrained
1 teaspoon ground nutmeg
½ teaspoon sugar

Remove large outer leaves of cabbage; cook in boiling water 3 to 5 minutes or until tender. Drain.

Sauté onion and celery in 2 tablespoons butter in a large skillet until tender. Stir in next 4 ingredients.

Sprinkle each cabbage leaf with paprika; place 2 tablespoons meat mixture in center of each leaf. Roll each leaf up over meat mixture, and place in lightly greased 13- x 9- x 2-inch baking dish.

Melt 2 tablespoons butter over low heat; add flour, stirring until smooth. Cook 1 minute, stirring constantly. Gradually add tomatoes; cook over medium heat, stirring constantly, until thickened. Stir in ground nutmeg and sugar. Pour mixture over cabbage rolls. Cover and bake at 350° for 1 hour. Yield: 8 to 10 servings. *Karen Young,*
Princeton, Texas.

SAUSAGE-WILD RICE CASSEROLE

1 (6-ounce) package long-grain and wild rice mix
1 pound bulk pork sausage
1 (10¾-ounce) can cream of mushroom soup, undiluted
1 cup chopped fresh mushrooms
½ cup chopped onion
½ cup chopped green pepper
½ cup (2 ounces) shredded sharp Cheddar cheese
½ cup chicken broth
¼ cup minced celery
1 teaspoon dried parsley flakes
½ teaspoon coarsely ground pepper

Cook rice according to package directions; set aside.

Brown sausage in a skillet, stirring to crumble; drain well. Combine cooked rice, sausage, and remaining ingredients in a large bowl; mix well. Spoon into a lightly greased 2-quart casserole. Bake at 350° for 1 hour. Yield: 6 servings.
*Susan Kamer-Shinaberry,
Charleston, West Virginia.*

SAUSAGE SANDWICHES WITH MUSTARD SAUCE

2 tablespoons butter or margarine
2 large onions, sliced
1 clove garlic, minced
1½ tablespoons all-purpose flour
¾ cup chicken broth
2 tablespoons catsup
2 tablespoons Dijon mustard
1 tablespoon prepared horseradish
1½ pounds Italian or Polish sausage, cut into ¼-inch slices
2 tablespoons vegetable oil
4 (8- to 10-inch) French rolls

Melt butter in a large skillet. Add onion and garlic; cover and cook over medium heat 10 minutes, stirring often. Remove cover and cook an additional 20 minutes, stirring occasionally. Stir in flour; cook 1 minute, stirring occasionally. Gradually add broth; cook over medium heat, stirring constantly, until thickened and bubbly. Stir in catsup, mustard, and horseradish. Remove from heat; set aside.

Brown sausage in oil in a medium skillet over medium heat; remove from skillet, and drain well. Stir sausage into mustard sauce.

Split French rolls; spoon sausage mixture over roll bottoms. Cover with roll tops; cut rolls in half, and serve. Yield: 8 servings.
*Carol Forcum,
Marion, Illinois.*

ITALIAN SAUCE WITH NOODLES

1¼ pounds Italian sausage
1 large onion, chopped
1 medium-size green pepper, chopped
1 clove garlic, minced
1 (4-ounce) can sliced mushrooms, drained
1 (16-ounce) can whole tomatoes, undrained and chopped
1 (8-ounce) can tomato sauce
1 teaspoon dried whole thyme
½ teaspoon dried whole oregano
¼ teaspoon pepper
Hot cooked noodles

Remove casings from sausage. Brown sausage in a large skillet, stirring to crumble. Remove sausage from skillet, and drain on paper towels; reserve drippings in skillet.

Sauté onion, green pepper, and garlic in drippings until tender. Add next 6 ingredients and sausage, and bring to a boil; reduce heat and simmer, uncovered, 10 minutes. Serve over noodles. Yield: 4 to 6 servings. *Helen Klicher,
Jacksonville, Florida.*

SAUSAGE-VEGETABLE DINNER

¾ pound Polish sausage
4 medium baking potatoes
1 medium-size green pepper, cut into strips
4 medium carrots, cut into 3- x ¼-inch strips
1 (16-ounce) can French-style green beans, drained
1 medium onion, quartered
1 medium head cabbage, cored and quartered
½ teaspoon salt
¼ teaspoon pepper
1 cup water

Cut sausage diagonally into ½-inch slices. Wash potatoes; cut into ⅓-inch crosswise slices. Layer sausage, potatoes, and next 5 ingredients in order given in a large Dutch oven, sprinkling each vegetable layer with salt and pepper. Add 1 cup water, and bring to a boil. Cover, reduce heat, and simmer 35 to 45 minutes or until the vegetables are tender. Yield: 4 to 6 servings.

*Thelma Bradley,
Alvarado, Texas.*

BRATWURST AND SAUERKRAUT

¾ pound fully-cooked bratwurst sausage
¼ cup butter or margarine, melted and divided
⅓ cup coarsely chopped onion
1 (16-ounce) can sauerkraut, drained
1 (14½-ounce) can whole tomatoes, undrained and coarsely chopped
2 tablespoons brown sugar

Cook sausage in 2 tablespoons butter in a large skillet until browned; remove from skillet, and drain well.

Sauté onion in remaining 2 tablespoons butter in skillet until tender; stir in sauerkraut, tomatoes, and brown sugar. Cook until thoroughly heated. Arrange sausage over sauerkraut mixture; cover, reduce heat, and simmer 15 minutes or until sausage is heated. Yield: 4 servings. *Peggy Fowler Revels,
Woodruff, South Carolina.*

SUPERB SUBMARINE SANDWICHES

2 (1-pound) loaves French bread
1 (3-ounce) package cream cheese, softened
⅔ cup mayonnaise
2 tablespoons chopped chives
8 (⅛-inch-thick) slices fully-cooked ham
8 (⅛-inch-thick) slices Genoa salami
8 (⅛-inch-thick) slices pickle and pimiento loaf
8 (⅛-inch-thick) slices summer sausage
8 (⅛-inch-thick) slices pepper loaf
4 cups torn romaine lettuce
1 medium tomato, chopped and drained
⅓ cup sliced pimiento-stuffed olives
2 tablespoons commercial Italian dressing

Cut bread loaves in half crosswise; split each half lengthwise. Set aside.

Combine next 3 ingredients; mix well. Spread about 1 tablespoon on inside cut surface of each piece of bread. Fold the meat slices in half; arrange 2 folded slices of each type of meat on bread bottoms; set aside.

Combine lettuce, tomato, olives, and dressing; toss gently to coat. Spoon over meat slices; cover with bread tops. Serve immediately. Yield: 8 servings.
*Sara A. McCullough,
Broaddus, Texas.*

Tip: Use the store's comparative pricing information for good buys. The unit-price data allows you to compare the cost of similar products of different sizes by weight, measure, or count.

Share In The Holiday Spirit

The holidays are the busiest time of the year. There are gifts to wrap, friends and family to visit, parties to attend. Through it all, food plays a very special part. The holidays just wouldn't be complete without the aromas of festive entrées and baked goods drifting from the kitchen. On the following pages you'll find all the recipes you need to make this one of the most delicious seasons ever.

We begin our holiday season at Janie and Tom Wood's vacation home, Mulberry Hill, overlooking Albemarle Sound near Edenton, North Carolina. You can see Mulberry Hill even when you're a mile away; it stands tall and erect, a fine four-story Georgian manor house that was built around 1780. Several times a year, friends and family are invited down from Raleigh for hunting trips or oyster roasts. When the holiday season arrives, they look forward to one of Janie's lavish dinners.

As guests arrive, they gather in the spacious hallway around a silver punchbowl filled with Edenton Eggnog. Then everyone gradually drifts toward the drawing room to relax and enjoy Skewered Pineapple and Strawberries.

Upon entering the dining room, the candles are lighted, leaving a soft glow surrounding a beautiful fruit-and-greenery centerpiece. Steaming bowls of Tomato-Clam Chowder are ladled up.

Pheasants With Port Wine Sauce and Sunshine-Glazed Ham are the featured entrées. A simple dressing, filled with apples, pecans, and raisins, is just right with the pheasants.

Shad roe, familiar to those living along Albemarle Sound, is also served. Green beans, a raspberry congealed salad, and a sweet potato casserole round out the Woods' holiday feast.

Guests choose between two desserts—Port Wine Jelly With Whipped Cream and a Sachertorte. The wine jelly has a light, spicy flavor while the Sachertorte is rich with chocolate. Both desserts are delicious ways to end a lovely holiday evening.

Edenton Eggnog
Skewered Pineapple and Strawberries
Tomato-Clam Chowder
Pheasants With Port Wine Sauce
Fruit-and-Pecan Dressing
Sunshine-Glazed Ham
Baked Shad Roe With
Lemon-Butter Sauce
Coconut-Orange Sweet Potatoes
Green Beans With Almonds
Raspberry Holiday Mold
Soft Batter Bread
Sachertorte
Port Wine Jelly With Whipped Cream

EDENTON EGGNOG

12 eggs, separated
1 (16-ounce) package powdered sugar, sifted
1½ to 2 cups dark rum, divided
1½ to 2 cups bourbon, divided
1 quart milk
1½ quarts whipping cream
Freshly grated nutmeg

Beat egg yolks until foamy. Gradually add sugar, beating until thick and lemon colored. Stir in 1 cup of rum and 1 cup of bourbon, mixing well. Chill 1 hour.

Stir in the remaining rum and bourbon. Add milk and whipping cream, stirring well.

Beat egg whites (at room temperature) until soft peaks form. Gently fold into yolk mixture. Chill thoroughly. Sprinkle eggnog with nutmeg. Yield: about 6 quarts.

SKEWERED PINEAPPLE AND STRAWBERRIES

2 fresh pineapples
4 cups fresh strawberries
½ cup Kirsch or Cointreau

Peel and trim eyes from 1 pineapple; remove core. Cut pineapple into 1-inch pieces. Combine pineapple pieces, strawberries, and Kirsch in a large bowl. Chill at least 30 minutes, stirring occasionally. Place pineapple and strawberries alternately on wooden picks; insert wooden picks into whole pineapple. Yield: 12 to 14 appetizer servings.

TOMATO-CLAM CHOWDER

4 slices bacon
3 medium onions, chopped
4 medium potatoes, peeled and diced
6 cups water
4 (8-ounce) bottles clam juice
1 (28-ounce) can tomatoes, undrained and chopped
2 (6½-ounce) cans minced clams, undrained
¼ teaspoon pepper
⅛ teaspoon red pepper

Cook bacon until crisp; remove bacon, reserving drippings. Crumble bacon, and set aside. Add onion to drippings; sauté until tender.

Combine potatoes, onion, bacon, and remaining ingredients in a Dutch oven. Bring to a boil; reduce heat and simmer, uncovered, for 2 hours. Yield: about 4 quarts.

PHEASANTS WITH PORT WINE SAUCE

4 (2-pound) pheasants, dressed
¼ cup butter or margarine,
　melted
½ teaspoon salt
½ teaspoon pepper
½ teaspoon onion powder
½ teaspoon dried whole thyme
½ teaspoon ground nutmeg
½ teaspoon dried parsley flakes
4 slices bacon
½ cup chicken broth
½ cup port wine
Fresh parsley sprigs (optional)
Grapes (optional)
Port Wine Sauce

Brush pheasants with butter; place breast side up on a rack in a large roasting pan, and broil 5 minutes. Remove from oven; rub each pheasant with ⅛ teaspoon each of salt, pepper, onion powder, thyme, nutmeg, and parsley. Place a strip of bacon lengthwise over each pheasant. Insert meat thermometer in breast or thigh of one bird, making sure it does not touch bone. Cover and bake pheasants at 375° for 1 hour.

Combine broth and port wine, stirring well. Remove bacon from pheasants. Continue to bake 30 to 40 minutes, uncovered, until meat thermometer registers 185°, basting frequently with broth mixture. Garnish with parsley and grapes, if desired. Serve with Port Wine Sauce. Yield: 12 servings.

Port Wine Sauce:

½ cup red currant jelly
½ cup port wine
¼ cup catsup
½ teaspoon Worcestershire sauce

Combine all ingredients in a saucepan; cook over low heat, stirring until smooth. Yield: 1¼ cups.

Tip: Fresh meat, poultry, and fish should be loosely wrapped and refrigerated; use in a few days. Loosely wrap fresh ground meat, liver, and kidneys; use in one or two days. Wieners, bacon, and sliced sandwich meats can be stored in original wrappings in the refrigerator. Store all meat in the coldest part of the refrigerator.

FRUIT-AND-PECAN DRESSING

2 cups water
½ cup butter or margarine
2 (8-ounce) packages herb-seasoned
　stuffing mix
2 large apples, unpeeled, cored, and
　minced
1 cup coarsely chopped pecans
½ cup raisins or currants
2 tablespoons grated orange rind
Fresh parsley sprigs (optional)
Cherry tomatoes (optional)

Combine water and butter in a large Dutch oven; heat until butter melts. Stir in next 5 ingredients. Spoon into a lightly greased 13- x 9- x 2-inch baking dish; bake at 350° for 30 minutes. Garnish with parsley and cherry tomatoes, if desired. Yield: 10 to 12 servings.

SUNSHINE-GLAZED HAM

1 (10- to 12-pound) uncooked ham
Whole cloves
1 (6-ounce) can frozen orange juice
　concentrate, thawed and undiluted
½ cup molasses
¼ cup prepared mustard
1 tablespoon grated orange rind
Peach halves (optional)
Fresh parsley sprigs (optional)

Remove skin from ham. Score fat in a diamond design, and stud with cloves. Place ham in a shallow baking pan, fat side up. Insert meat thermometer, making sure it does not touch fat or bone.

Combine next 4 ingredients, stirring well; brush on ham. Bake, uncovered, at 325° for 3 to 4 hours or until meat thermometer registers 160°; baste every 30 minutes with juice mixture. Garnish with peach halves and parsley, if desired. Yield: 20 servings.

BAKED SHAD ROE WITH LEMON-BUTTER SAUCE

¾ pound shad roe
2 tablespoons lemon juice
Endive (optional)
Dried whole dillweed
Lemon slices (optional)
Cherry tomato (optional)
Lemon-Butter Sauce

Place shad roe in a lightly greased 10- x 6- x 2-inch baking dish; brush with lemon juice. Bake at 350° for 15 minutes, basting with lemon juice every 5 minutes. Serve shad roe over endive, if desired; sprinkle with dillweed. Garnish with lemon slices and a cherry tomato, if desired. Serve with Lemon-Butter Sauce. Yield: 4 servings.

Lemon-Butter Sauce:

½ cup butter
½ teaspoon grated lemon rind
Juice of 1 lemon
⅛ teaspoon dried parsley flakes
Dash of paprika

Melt butter over low heat; stir in remaining ingredients. Yield: ½ cup.

COCONUT-ORANGE SWEET POTATOES

4 (17-ounce) cans sweet potatoes, drained
　and mashed
4 eggs
1 cup firmly packed brown sugar
¼ cup butter or margarine, melted
¾ teaspoon salt
½ teaspoon ground cinnamon
3 tablespoons rum
1 cup chopped pecans
1 cup flaked coconut
2 tablespoons butter or margarine, melted
Orange slices

Combine first 7 ingredients; beat with electric mixer 1 to 2 minutes or until light and fluffy. Stir in pecans; spoon into a lightly greased 2½-quart casserole. Bake at 325° for about 35 minutes.

Combine coconut and 2 tablespoons butter, stirring well. Sprinkle around edge of casserole; top with orange slices. Bake an additional 10 to 15 minutes or until coconut is lightly browned. Yield: 10 to 12 servings.

GREEN BEANS WITH ALMONDS

2 pounds fresh green beans
2 quarts water
1 teaspoon salt
¼ cup butter or margarine
Salt and pepper to taste
⅔ cup sliced almonds, toasted

Wash beans; trim ends, and remove strings. Cut diagonally into 3-inch pieces. Combine water and 1 teaspoon salt; bring to a boil. Add beans. Cook, uncovered, 4 to 5 minutes, or just until crisp tender. Drain beans, and plunge into cold water; drain again.

Melt butter in a large skillet; add the beans, and sauté 2 to 3 minutes or until thoroughly heated. Sprinkle with salt, pepper, and almonds. Yield: 8 to 10 servings.

RASPBERRY HOLIDAY MOLD

1 (20-ounce) can pineapple chunks,
    undrained
2 (10-ounce) packages frozen raspberries,
    thawed
2 (6-ounce) packages raspberry-flavored
    gelatin
3½ cups boiling water
2 tablespoons lemon juice
1 teaspoon hot sauce
½ teaspoon salt
1 cup chopped celery
1 cup chopped walnuts
1 (8-ounce) package cream cheese,
    softened
½ cup mayonnaise
Finely chopped walnuts

Drain pineapple chunks and raspberries, reserving liquid; set liquid aside. Press raspberries through a sieve or food mill. Set the puree aside, and discard seeds.

Dissolve gelatin in 3½ cups boiling water. Stir in pineapple juice, raspberry juice, lemon juice, hot sauce and salt; chill until the consistency of unbeaten egg white. Fold in pineapple, raspberry puree, celery, and 1 cup chopped walnuts. Pour gelatin mixture into a lightly oiled 10-cup ring mold. Chill until firm.

Combine cream cheese and mayonnaise; beat until smooth. Spoon into center of raspberry mold; sprinkle with walnuts. Yield: 16 servings.

SOFT BATTER BREAD

2 cups milk
1 cup cornmeal
2 tablespoons butter or margarine
1 teaspoon salt
2 eggs, separated
1½ teaspoons baking powder

Combine first 4 ingredients in a saucepan; cook over medium heat until thickened, stirring constantly. Remove pan from heat.

Beat egg yolks until thick and lemon colored. Gradually stir about one-fourth of hot mixture into yolks; add to remaining hot mixture, stirring constantly. Stir in baking powder.

Beat egg whites (at room temperature) until stiff peaks form; fold into cornmeal mixture. Pour into a lightly greased 1-quart loaf baking dish.

Bake at 350° for 30 minutes or until a knife inserted in center comes out clean. Yield: 1 loaf.

Note: Bread will not rise very high and should appear dense and moist.

SACHERTORTE

6 (1-ounce) squares bittersweet chocolate
¾ cup butter, softened
1 cup sugar
6 eggs, separated
1 cup sifted cake flour
¼ cup apricot preserves
Chocolate glaze (recipe follows)
Whole cranberries
Slivered almonds

Grease an 8-inch springform pan; line bottom with greased waxed paper. Lightly flour pan.

Place chocolate in top of a double boiler; bring water to boil. Reduce heat to low; cook, stirring occasionally, until chocolate melts. Remove from heat, and let cool slightly.

Cream butter; gradually add sugar, beating until light and fluffy. Add egg yolks, beating well.

Gradually add chocolate to creamed mixture, beating at low speed of an electric mixer. Add flour, beating just until mixed. Set aside.

Beat egg whites (at room temperature) at high speed of electric mixer until soft peaks form. Gently fold one-fourth of egg whites into chocolate mixture (do not fold in completely). Repeat procedure with one-fourth additional egg whites. Gently fold in remaining egg whites.

Spoon batter into pan. Shake pan slightly to level batter. Bake at 350° for 40 to 45 minutes or until a wooden pick inserted in center comes out clean. Cool in pan 10 minutes; remove from pan and peel off waxed paper. Cool completely. (Cake should be about 1½ inches high.) Chill several hours.

Carefully split cake in half horizontally to make 2 layers. Press apricot preserves through a sieve into a small saucepan; bring to a boil. Pour over bottom cake layer, spreading evenly. Place remaining cake layer on top. Pour three-fourths of chocolate glaze over cake; spread evenly over top and sides. Let cake stand 20 minutes. Use remaining glaze to drizzle designs over top. Garnish with cranberries and almonds. Yield: 10 servings.

Chocolate Glaze:

¼ cup light corn syrup
3 tablespoons water
2 tablespoons butter
8 (1-ounce) squares semisweet chocolate,
    coarsely chopped

Combine syrup, water, and butter in a small saucepan over medium heat; bring to a boil. Remove from heat and add chocolate; stir until chocolate melts and mixture is smooth. Let stand until glaze reaches room temperature before pouring over cake. Yield: about 1 cup.

Tip: To keep cake layers from sticking in pan, grease the bottom and sides of pan and line bottom with waxed paper. (Trace outline of pan on waxed paper and cut out.) Pour batter in pan and bake. Invert cake layer on rack to cool; gently peel off waxed paper while cake is still warm.

PORT WINE JELLY WITH WHIPPED CREAM

1 cup sugar
1 cup water
Grated rind of ½ medium lemon
Juice of ½ medium lemon
1 (3-inch) stick cinnamon
8 whole cloves
2 envelopes unflavored gelatin
1 cup cold water
1 cup port wine
Whipped cream
Sliced red grapes

Combine first 6 ingredients in a medium saucepan; bring to a boil. Reduce heat, and simmer 5 minutes.

Soften gelatin in 1 cup cold water; let stand 5 minutes.

Add gelatin mixture to hot mixture, stirring until dissolved. Strain into a 1-quart serving bowl; add port wine, and stir well. Chill until firm. Garnish with whipped cream and red grapes. Yield: 8 to 10 servings.

Dress Up The Season's Vegetables

It takes a delicious variety of vegetable side dishes to make holiday menus complete. You'll want your selections to be tasty, look attractive, and go well with the main course. We suggest trying Carrots and Celery With Pecans and Peas Continental. Mushrooms and sherry give the peas a dressy look and special flavor. The carrots and celery are sliced diagonally and glazed with buttered pecans and dillweed.

CARROTS AND CELERY WITH PECANS

2½ cups water
¼ teaspoon salt
4 medium carrots, sliced diagonally
6 stalks celery, sliced diagonally
1 cup chopped pecans
½ teaspoon dried whole dillweed
¼ cup butter or margarine

Combine water and salt; bring to a boil. Add carrots; cover, reduce heat, and simmer 10 minutes. Add celery; cover and simmer an additional 5 minutes or until celery is crisp-tender. Drain well.

Sauté pecans and dillweed in butter until pecans are golden; toss with carrots and celery. Yield: 6 servings.
Tony Jones,
Atlanta, Georgia.

PEAS CONTINENTAL

2 (10-ounce) packages frozen English peas
¼ cup chopped onion
2 tablespoons butter or margarine
1 (4-ounce) can sliced mushrooms, drained
2 tablespoons dry sherry
¼ teaspoon salt
¼ teaspoon ground nutmeg
⅛ teaspoon ground marjoram
Dash of pepper

Cook peas according to package directions, omitting salt. Drain; set aside.

Sauté onion in butter in a medium saucepan until tender. Add peas and remaining ingredients; cook, stirring occasionally, just until thoroughly heated. Yield: 6 servings. *Donna Weselius,*
Helena, Alabama.

GREEN BEANS AND BRAISED CELERY

2 pounds fresh green beans
4 cups water
1 bunch celery hearts
¼ cup butter or margarine
3 to 5 tablespoons chicken broth
Salt and pepper to taste
3 tablespoons butter or margarine
1 teaspoon lemon juice
1 (4-ounce) jar whole pimientos, drained and diced

Wash beans, trim ends, and remove strings. Bring 4 cups water to a boil in a Dutch oven. Add beans; cook, uncovered, 10 minutes or until crisp-tender. Drain, and plunge beans into cold water. Drain again, and set aside.

Cut celery into 4- to 5-inch-long pieces. Melt ¼ cup butter in a large

skillet; add broth, and bring to a boil. Add celery, salt, and pepper; cover and cook 5 minutes or until tender. Drain.

Melt 3 tablespoons butter; add green beans, lemon juice, salt, and pepper. Heat beans thoroughly, stirring gently.

Arrange green beans and celery on a serving platter. Garnish with pimiento. Yield: 8 servings. *Jeanette Guess,*
Edinburg, Virginia.

CRUNCHY VEGETABLE MEDLEY

1 small onion, sliced and separated into rings
3 cloves garlic, minced
2 tablespoons butter or margarine
1 cup water
1 teaspoon beef-flavored bouillon granules
2 cups broccoli flowerets
1 cup cauliflower flowerets
1 cup brussels sprouts, halved
¾ cup sliced carrots
½ cup sliced fresh mushrooms
¼ cup chopped green pepper
½ cup slivered almonds, toasted
¼ cup chopped walnuts
3 tablespoons sesame seeds, toasted
1 teaspoon poppy seeds
½ teaspoon soy sauce
⅛ teaspoon dried whole basil
Cherry tomatoes (optional)

Sauté onion and garlic in butter in a large skillet until onion is tender. Add water and bouillon granules, stirring until bouillon is dissolved. Add next 6 ingredients; bring to a boil. Cover, reduce heat to low, and cook 5 minutes. Drain well. Combine vegetables and next 6 ingredients, tossing gently. Garnish with cherry tomatoes, if desired. Yield: 6 to 8 servings. *Kathy Nelson,*
El Paso, Texas.

HOLIDAY SWEET POTATO SURPRISE

6 medium-size sweet potatoes
1 (15-ounce) can coconut-almond frosting
1 teaspoon vanilla extract
½ teaspoon ground cinnamon
2 cups miniature marshmallows

Cook sweet potatoes in boiling water 20 to 25 minutes or until tender. Drain and cool. Peel potatoes and mash.

Combine mashed sweet potatoes, frosting, vanilla, and cinnamon; mix well. Spoon into a greased 12- x 8- x 2-inch baking dish. Bake, uncovered, at 350° for 18 minutes. Sprinkle with marshmallows; continue baking 5 minutes or until thoroughly heated. Yield: 6 to 8 servings. *Diana L. Troxell, Mannford, Oklahoma.*

PINEAPPLE-STUFFED ACORN SQUASH

3 medium acorn squash
1 (8-ounce) can crushed pineapple, drained
⅓ cup firmly packed brown sugar
3 tablespoons butter or margarine, softened
¼ cup chopped pecans or walnuts
½ teaspoon ground cinnamon
¾ cup water
Lemon twists (optional)

Cut squash in half lengthwise, and remove seeds. Set aside.

Combine next 5 ingredients in a medium bowl; mix well. Spoon pineapple mixture into each squash half. Arrange squash in a 13- x 9- x 2-inch baking dish; pour water into dish. Cover and bake at 375° for 50 minutes. Uncover and bake an additional 10 minutes. Garnish with lemon twists, if desired. Yield: 6 servings. *Edith Askins, Greenville, Texas.*

SNOW-CAPPED POTATOES

8 medium-size new potatoes
¼ cup butter or margarine, melted
¼ cup chopped green onions with tops
1 teaspoon salt
½ to 1 teaspoon pepper
4 eggs, separated
2 tablespoons mayonnaise
1 teaspoon lemon juice

Cook potatoes in boiling water 30 minutes or until tender; drain and cool. Peel potatoes and mash. Stir in next 4 ingredients. Beat egg yolks until thick

and lemon colored; gradually stir into potato mixture. Drop mixture by spoonfuls in 3-inch round mounds onto a lightly greased cookie sheet, or pipe mixture using a decorator tube and tip.

Beat egg whites (at room temperature) until stiff but not dry; fold in mayonnaise and lemon juice. Frost each potato mound with meringue mixture. Bake at 350° for 15 to 18 minutes or until lightly browned. Yield: 8 to 10 servings. *Mildred Sherrer, Bay City, Texas.*

Coconut—A Sweet Finale

The holidays aren't complete unless there's at least one dessert laden with coconut. The sweet crunchy flavor adds a richness unequaled by any other fruit. And with its creamy-white color and texture, coconut lends itself to a variety of holiday trimmings.

COCONUT-SPICE CAKE

1 cup vegetable oil
1 cup firmly packed brown sugar
1 cup sugar
2 eggs
2½ cups all-purpose flour
½ teaspoon salt
1 teaspoon baking soda
1 teaspoon ground cinnamon
1 teaspoon ground nutmeg
1 cup buttermilk
1 teaspoon vanilla extract
1 cup flaked coconut
1 cup chopped pecans
Cream Cheese Frosting
1 cup flaked coconut
Pecan halves

Combine first 3 ingredients; beat well. Add eggs, one at a time, beating well after each addition. Combine flour and next 4 ingredients; add to creamed mixture alternately with buttermilk, beginning and ending with the flour mixture.

Stir in vanilla, 1 cup coconut, and chopped pecans.

Pour batter into 2 greased and floured 9-inch round cakepans. Bake at 350° for about 25 minutes or until a wooden pick inserted in the center comes out clean. Cool cake layers in pans 10 minutes. Remove layers from pans, and cool on wire racks.

Spread Cream Cheese Frosting between layers and on top and sides of cake. Sprinkle top and sides with 1 cup coconut, and gently press into frosting. Garnish with pecan halves. Yield: one 2-layer cake.

Cream Cheese Frosting:

1 (8-ounce) package cream cheese, softened
¼ cup butter or margarine, softened
1 (16-ounce) package powdered sugar, sifted
1 cup chopped pecans

Combine cream cheese and butter, beating until light and fluffy. Add powdered sugar; beat until smooth. Stir in chopped pecans. Yield: enough for one 2-layer cake. *Cathy L. Toler, Glen Fork, West Virginia.*

GOLDEN BARS

1½ cups all-purpose flour
½ cup firmly packed brown sugar
½ cup butter or margarine, softened
2 eggs, beaten
1 cup firmly packed brown sugar
2 tablespoons all-purpose flour
½ teaspoon baking powder
¼ teaspoon salt
½ teaspoon vanilla extract
1¼ cups flaked coconut
½ cup chopped pecans

Combine flour and ½ cup brown sugar; cut in butter until mixture resembles coarse meal. Press mixture into a lightly greased 9-inch square pan. Bake at 350° for 15 minutes.

Combine eggs and next 5 ingredients, mixing well. Stir in flaked coconut and chopped pecans. Pour egg mixture over crust. Bake at 350° for 20 minutes. Cool and cut into bars. Yield: 3 dozen. *Amy T. Brown, Fort Bragg, North Carolina.*

BANANAS SUPREME

4 ripe bananas, sliced in half lengthwise
2 tablespoons butter or margarine
¼ cup flaked coconut
½ cup whipped cream or whipped topping
¼ cup coarsely chopped pecans
¼ cup amaretto

Sauté bananas in butter over medium heat 1 to 2 minutes on each side or until bananas are soft. Carefully remove bananas to four serving dishes, and sprinkle each serving with a tablespoon of coconut. Top coconut with a dollop of whipped cream; sprinkle with a tablespoon of chopped pecans and a tablespoon of amaretto. Serve immediately. Yield: 4 servings. *Junetta Davis, Norman, Oklahoma.*

COCONUT-PINEAPPLE PIE

3 eggs
¼ cup plus 2 tablespoons butter or margarine, melted
1½ cups sugar
3 tablespoons all-purpose flour
1 cup crushed pineapple, drained
1 cup flaked coconut
1 unbaked 9-inch pastry shell

Beat eggs until thick and lemon colored. Stir in next 5 ingredients, mixing well. Pour mixture into pastry shell. Bake at 350° for 50 minutes or until filling is set. Yield: one 9-inch pie. *Vi Jensen, Grand Prairie, Texas.*

COCONUT-ALMOND BALLS

1 (14-ounce) package flaked coconut
1 (14-ounce) can sweetened condensed milk
2 cups chopped almonds, toasted
1 tablespoon almond extract
2 (12-ounce) packages semisweet chocolate morsels
2 tablespoons shortening

Combine first 4 ingredients; mix well. Let stand at least 30 minutes; shape into ¾-inch balls (mixture will be moist). Place balls on waxed paper; cover with an additional sheet of waxed paper. Let stand 8 hours or overnight.

Place chocolate and shortening in top of a double boiler; bring water to a boil. Reduce heat to low; cook just until chocolate melts. Remove from heat. Using 2 forks, quickly dip candy balls into chocolate mixture, covering completely. Place on waxed paper, and chill until firm. Transfer candy balls to an airtight container; store in refrigerator. Yield: about 6½ dozen.
Mrs. Kenneth W. Clemmer, Fairfield, Virginia.

CUSTARD SAUCE AMBROSIA

2 egg yolks, beaten
¼ cup sugar
½ cup milk
½ cup whipping cream
1½ teaspoons rum
4 cups orange sections, drained
2 cups flaked coconut

Combine egg yolks and sugar in a saucepan. Gradually stir in milk and whipping cream; cook over low heat until slightly thickened. Cool. Stir in rum, and chill.

Stir orange sections and coconut into custard sauce. Yield: 6 servings.
Mrs. A. T. Knight, Sulphur Springs, Texas.

Showy, Delicious Dips And Spreads

The secret to making holiday guests feel welcome is to serve lots of delicious appetizers. One favorite is Caviar-Cream Cheese Spread, made by layering a cream cheese mixture with black caviar, chopped, hard-cooked eggs, and lots of fresh parsley.

Make sure your appetizer table looks great when guests arrive. An assortment of fresh vegetables arranged around Zippy Vegetable Dip makes a colorful appetizer.

CAVIAR-CREAM CHEESE SPREAD

2 (8-ounce) packages cream cheese, softened
1 (3-ounce) package cream cheese, softened
1 cup mayonnaise
1 small onion, grated
1 tablespoon Worcestershire sauce
1 tablespoon lemon juice
Dash of hot sauce
1 (3½-ounce) jar black caviar
4 hard-cooked eggs, finely chopped
1 cup chopped fresh parsley

Beat cream cheese with an electric mixer until smooth. Add mayonnaise, onion, Worcestershire sauce, lemon juice, and hot sauce; beat well.

Spoon cream cheese mixture into a shallow serving dish; top with caviar, eggs, and parsley. Serve spread with assorted crackers. Yield: 24 to 30 appetizer servings. *Becky Patterson, Birmingham, Alabama.*

ZIPPY VEGETABLE DIP

1 cup mayonnaise
1 (8-ounce) carton cream-style cottage cheese
¼ cup grated onion
1 teaspoon Worcestershire sauce
½ teaspoon caraway seeds
½ teaspoon dry mustard
½ teaspoon pepper
¼ teaspoon salt
⅛ teaspoon garlic salt
¼ teaspoon celery seeds
⅛ teaspoon hot sauce

Combine all ingredients; mix well. Chill 1 to 2 hours; serve with fresh vegetables. Yield: about 2¼ cups. *Daphne K. Harbinson, Arden, North Carolina.*

CONFETTI CHEESE SPREAD

1 (8-ounce) package process cheese, shredded
½ cup chopped almonds, toasted
4 slices bacon, cooked and crumbled
2 green onions, chopped
3 tablespoons mayonnaise
Dash of garlic powder

Combine all ingredients, and mix well. Serve with assorted crackers. Yield: about 2 cups. *Jean Voan, Shepherd, Texas.*

EDAM-SHERRY SPREAD

1 (2-pound) whole Edam cheese (at room temperature)
¼ cup butter or margarine, softened
½ teaspoon dry mustard
Dash of Worcestershire sauce
½ cup finely chopped pimiento-stuffed olives
¼ cup finely chopped onion
2 tablespoons dry sherry
Fresh parsley sprigs (optional)

Carefully cut off top quarter of Edam cheese; cut out cheese from both sections, leaving a ½-inch shell in bottom section. Discard top shell of wax.

Cut cheese into small pieces. Position knife blade in processor bowl, and add cheese. Process until cheese is smooth and forms a ball. Add butter, mustard, and Worcestershire sauce. Process until mixture is blended. Knead in olives, onion, and sherry until blended. Pack cheese spread into cavity of cheese. Garnish with parsley, if desired; serve with crackers. Yield: about 3 cups.
Lenah Miller Elliott, Destin, Florida.

Everyone's Invited To An Open House

When you want to invite all your friends over for the holidays but space in your home is at a premium, try an open house party. List the party hours on the invitation, and guests can drop in at the most convenient hour. This will give you more time to spend with each guest and keep from crowding your house. Replenish the food during lulls.

Carefully planning the food to serve can make the time you spend in the kitchen less frantic and help the party go smoothly. In our menu, make-ahead recipes will leave you with time for last-minute details. And since the food can be eaten easily, guests won't need to use a fork or sit down while eating.

CHUNKY ONION DIP

1 (8-ounce) package cream cheese, softened
⅓ cup chili sauce
3 tablespoons mayonnaise
¼ teaspoon Worcestershire sauce
⅓ cup finely chopped onion
Fresh parsley sprigs

Combine first 4 ingredients; beat at medium speed of electric mixer until smooth. Stir in onion, blending well. Chill dip. Garnish with parsley. Serve with raw vegetables. Yield: 1⅔ cups.
Note: Chunky Onion Dip is a good accompaniment to Christmas Relish Tree (below). *Mary Linda Brooks, Hayes, Virginia.*

CHRISTMAS RELISH TREE

2 bunches curly endive
Florist picks
1 (9-inch) plastic foam cone, about 1½ feet tall
1 carton cherry tomatoes
1 zucchini, sliced
½ head cauliflower, separated into flowerets
4 carrots, cut into 2-inch sticks
Radish roses
Wooden picks

Wash and separate endive, and remove the tough ends of each leaf. Begin to form the tree by attaching leaves to the bottom of the cone with florist picks, and move upward, completely covering cone with endive.

Attach vegetables to endive-covered cone with wooden picks, arranging in desired pattern to resemble a decorated Christmas tree.

Place tree on a tray or cake stand; arrange extra vegetables around the base, if desired. Yield: about 8 dozen appetizer servings.
Note: Serve Chunky Onion Dip with Christmas Relish Tree. *Margaret Long, Forsyth, Georgia.*

CHICKEN SALAD TARTS

2¼ cups all-purpose flour
½ teaspoon salt
½ cup shortening
¼ cup butter or margarine
½ to ⅔ cup milk
4 cups finely chopped cooked chicken
2 stalks celery, finely chopped
½ cup slivered almonds, toasted
⅔ cup mayonnaise
2 tablespoons steak sauce
½ teaspoon curry powder
½ teaspoon seasoned salt
¼ teaspoon garlic salt
Pimiento strips

Combine flour and salt; cut in shortening and butter with a pastry blender until mixture resembles coarse meal. Sprinkle milk, 1 tablespoon at a time, evenly over surface; stir with a fork just until dry ingredients are moistened. Shape dough into about sixty ¾-inch balls. Place in ungreased 1¾-inch muffin pans, and shape each ball into a shell. Bake at 400° for 10 to 12 minutes. Cool completely.

Combine next 8 ingredients; mix well. Cover and chill at least 1 hour; spoon into tart shells. Garnish with pimiento strips. Yield: about 5 dozen appetizers.
Omagene C. Cooper, Mobile, Alabama.

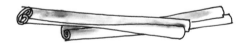

SPICED NUTS

1 cup sugar
½ teaspoon ground cloves
½ teaspoon ground nutmeg
2 teaspoons ground cinnamon
¼ teaspoon salt
¼ cup water
2 cups mixed salted nuts

Combine first 6 ingredients in a saucepan; stir well. Place over medium heat, stirring constantly, until sugar dissolves; then cook to soft ball stage (232°). Remove from heat; add nuts, stirring until well coated.

Spread nuts on waxed paper, and separate with a fork. Cool. Yield: 2 cups.
Sharon McClatchey, Muskogee, Oklahoma.

PARTY CHEESE BALL

1 (3-ounce) package cream cheese,
   softened
1 (8-ounce) package cream cheese,
   softened
1 (4½-ounce) can deviled ham
2 cups (8 ounces) shredded sharp Cheddar
   cheese
2 tablespoons finely chopped
   pimiento-stuffed olives
1 tablespoon prepared mustard
¾ teaspoon chopped chives
¼ teaspoon dry mustard
¼ teaspoon ground celery seeds
¼ teaspoon red pepper
⅛ teaspoon salt
½ cup chopped pecans

Combine all ingredients except
pecans; mix well. Shape into a ball, and
roll in the chopped pecans. Chill well.
Serve with assorted crackers. Yield: one
5-inch cheese ball.
Note: Make the cheese ball several
days in advance for full flavor. It freezes
well, too. *Mrs. J. D. McMullen,*
Georgetown, Kentucky.

FRUITCAKE FONDUE

1 (14-ounce) package date bar mix
⅔ cup hot water
3 eggs, beaten
¼ cup orange marmalade
¼ cup all-purpose flour
¾ teaspoon baking powder
1 teaspoon ground cinnamon
¼ teaspoon ground nutmeg
¼ teaspoon ground allspice
1 cup chopped pecans
1 cup raisins
1 cup chopped candied red cherries
Lemon Sauce

Combine filling mix from date bar
package and hot water in a large mixing
bowl; mix well. Add remaining date bar
mix, eggs, marmalade, flour, baking
powder, and spices; mix well. Stir in
pecans, raisins, and candied cherries.
Spoon batter into a brown paper-lined
and greased 9- x 5- x 3-inch loafpan.
Bake at 325° for 1 hour and 15 minutes
or until a wooden pick inserted in center comes out clean. Cool 10 minutes in
pan. Remove from pan, and cool completely on a wire rack. Chill overnight.

Cut fruitcake into ¾-inch cubes with
an electric knife. Serve with warm
Lemon Sauce. Yield: 1 loaf.

Lemon Sauce:

2 tablespoons cornstarch
½ cup sugar
¼ teaspoon salt
2 cups water
¼ cup butter or margarine
1 tablespoon grated lemon rind
3 tablespoons lemon juice
3 thin lemon slices

Combine cornstarch, sugar, and salt
in a small saucepan. Gradually add
water, and cook over medium heat, stirring constantly, until mixture thickens
and comes to a boil. Boil 1 minute,
stirring constantly. Remove sauce from
heat; stir in the remaining ingredients
except lemon slices.
Serve sauce warm in a chafing dish or
fondue pot. Float lemon slices on top.
Yield: about 2 cups. *Carolyn McCue,*
Oklahoma City, Oklahoma.

CHOCOLATE-TIPPED
BUTTER COOKIES

1 cup butter or margarine, softened
½ cup sifted powdered sugar
1 teaspoon vanilla extract
2 cups all-purpose flour
1 (6-ounce) package semisweet chocolate
   morsels
1 tablespoon shortening
½ cup finely chopped pecans

Cream butter; gradually add sugar,
beating until light and fluffy. Stir in vanilla. Gradually add flour to butter mixture; mix well.
Shape dough into 2½- x ½-inch
sticks. Place on ungreased cookie
sheets. Flatten three-quarters of each
cookie lengthwise with a fork to ¼-inch
thickness. Bake at 350° for 12 to 14
minutes. Remove to wire racks to cool.
Combine chocolate morsels and shortening in top of a double boiler; bring
water to a boil. Reduce heat to low;
cook until chocolate melts, stirring occasionally. Remove double boiler from
heat, leaving chocolate mixture over hot
water. Dip unflattened tips of cookies in
warm chocolate to coat both sides; roll

tips in finely chopped pecans. Place
cookies on wire racks until the chocolate is firm.
Arrange cookies between layers of
waxed paper in an airtight container;
store in a cool place. Yield: 5 dozen.

SPICED CIDER PUNCH

2 quarts apple cider
2 (3-inch) sticks cinnamon
12 whole cloves
2 cups pineapple juice, chilled
1½ quarts orange juice, chilled
2 cups lemon juice, chilled
1½ quarts ginger ale, chilled

Combine cider, cinnamon, and cloves
in a Dutch oven; bring to a boil. Cover,
reduce heat, and simmer 15 minutes.
Strain cider to remove cinnamon and
cloves; chill. Combine cider and juice.
Just before serving, combine juice
mixture and ginger ale in a punch bowl.
Yield: 6 quarts. *Cathy Allen,*
Staunton, Virginia.

Celebrate With
Seasonal Beverages

Whether it's a treasured family recipe
or created just for the occasion, beverages served in Southern homes are always special. Scents of simmering spices
from a pot of wassail or a cool drink
with a seasonal flavor welcome guests.

IRISH COFFEE NOG

1 quart eggnog
1¼ cups brewed coffee, cooled
⅔ cup Irish Cream liqueur
½ cup brandy
½ cup sugar

Combine all ingredients, stirring to
dissolve sugar. Chill several hours before serving. Yield: about 6½ cups.
Vivian Levine,
Oak Ridge, Tennessee.

CRANBERRY-RUM SLUSH

1 (12-ounce) can frozen cranberry juice
    cocktail concentrate, undiluted
1½ cups rum
Juice of 1 lemon
About 8 cups crushed ice

Combine half of first 3 ingredients in container of an electric blender; process until smooth. Gradually add half of ice; process until mixture reaches desired consistency. Repeat with remaining ingredients. Yield: about 7 cups.

Mrs. Paul E. Kline,
Palm Beach Gardens, Florida.

REFRESHING CHAMPAGNE PUNCH

1 quart water
1 quart-size tea bag
2 cups sugar
2 cups lemon juice
2 cups lime juice
1 quart club soda, chilled
3 (25.4-ounce) bottles champagne,
    chilled

Bring water to a boil in a large saucepan; add tea bag. Remove from heat; cover and let stand 3 to 4 minutes. Remove tea bag. Add sugar, lemon juice, and lime juice to tea, stirring until the sugar dissolves. Chill.

Stir in the club soda and champagne just before serving. Yield: about 5½ quarts. *Susan Laubacher,*
Marietta, Georgia.

CHRISTMAS PUNCH

2 cups boiling water
¾ cup sugar
½ teaspoon ground cinnamon
1 (46-ounce) can pineapple juice, chilled
1 (32-ounce) bottle cranberry juice, chilled
1 (28-ounce) bottle ginger ale, chilled

Combine water, sugar, and cinnamon in a saucepan; bring to a boil, and stir until sugar dissolves. Chill.

Combine sugar syrup, fruit juice, and ginger ale. Serve over ice. Yield: about 3¾ quarts. *Gayle Beckham,*
Carthage, Mississippi.

WASSAIL

2 quarts apple juice
2¼ cups pineapple juice
2 cups orange juice
1 cup lemon juice
½ cup sugar
1 (3-inch) stick cinnamon
1 teaspoon whole cloves

Combine all ingredients in a Dutch oven; bring to a boil. Cover, reduce heat, and simmer 30 minutes. Uncover and simmer an additional 30 minutes. Strain and discard the spices. Serve hot. Yield: about 11 cups. *Marie Bilbo,*
Meadville, Mississippi.

Present A Distinctive Entrée

Holiday entrées call for something a little extra. It might be a special cut of meat or maybe just an unusual way of preparing the same basic fare. For those with a hunter in the family, it might be wild game saved for the occasion. No matter what your preference, you want something special for the holiday table.

CRAB-STUFFED SHRIMP

1 dozen jumbo fresh shrimp
1 medium onion, finely chopped
½ medium-size green pepper, finely
    chopped
½ cup finely chopped celery
¼ cup butter or margarine
1 pound fresh crabmeat
2 teaspoons Worcestershire sauce
⅛ teaspoon red pepper
1 tablespoon prepared mustard
1 egg, beaten
½ cup mayonnaise
¾ cup cracker crumbs
Paprika
¼ cup butter or margarine, melted

Peel shrimp, leaving tails on; devein and butterfly. Cook shrimp in boiling water 1 minute. Drain and place in a shallow baking dish.

Sauté onion, green pepper, and celery in ¼ cup butter in a heavy skillet until tender. Set aside.

Combine crabmeat and the next 6 ingredients, mixing lightly. Stir in sautéed vegetables.

Top each shrimp with 3 tablespoons crabmeat mixture. Sprinkle with paprika, and drizzle ¼ cup butter over shrimp. Bake at 350° for 20 minutes. Broil 6 minutes, basting occasionally with butter in bottom of baking dish. Yield: 4 to 6 servings. *Rheda Meekins,*
North East, Maryland.

SPICY RIB-EYE BEEF

1 (6-pound) boneless beef rib-eye roast
⅓ to ½ cup coarse or cracked pepper
½ teaspoon ground cardamom
1 cup soy sauce
¾ cup red wine vinegar
1 tablespoon tomato paste
1 teaspoon paprika
½ teaspoon garlic powder
Apricot halves (optional)
Hot pepper jelly (optional)
Fresh parsley sprigs (optional)

Trim excess fat from roast. Combine pepper and cardamom; pat onto roast.

Combine next 5 ingredients; pour over roast. Cover; marinate overnight in refrigerator, turning occasionally.

Remove roast from marinade; discard marinade. Wrap roast in foil, and place in a shallow baking pan. Insert meat thermometer, making an opening so that thermometer does not touch foil. Bake at 325° for 2 hours or until thermometer registers 140° (rare) or 160° (medium). Garnish with apricot halves, hot pepper jelly, and parsley, if desired. Yield: 16 to 18 servings. *Jeanette Korn,*
Louisville, Kentucky.

VEAL BIRDS

8 veal cutlets (about 1½ pounds)
½ cup chopped onion
½ cup chopped celery
¼ cup chopped green pepper
½ cup butter or margarine
6 cups bread cubes
¼ cup white wine
½ teaspoon salt
⅛ teaspoon pepper
1 teaspoon poultry seasoning
8 slices bacon, cut in half
¼ cup water

Remove and discard any excess fat from cutlets. Place cutlets on waxed paper, and flatten to ⅛-inch thickness with a meat mallet or rolling pin. Slice cutlets in half; set aside.

Sauté onion, celery, and green pepper in butter. Combine vegetables, bread cubes, and next 4 ingredients. Place 1 heaping tablespoon stuffing on each half of cutlet. Roll up each piece jellyroll fashion; wrap with bacon, and secure with wooden picks. Place seam side down in a 13- x 9- x 2-inch baking pan; add water. Cover and bake at 325° for 30 minutes. Yield: 8 servings.
Mrs. R. P. Hotaling,
Martinez, Georgia.

MARINATED PORK ROAST

3 tablespoons vegetable oil
1 clove garlic, crushed
1 teaspoon dry mustard
1 teaspoon dried whole thyme
1 teaspoon dried rosemary
1 teaspoon minced fresh parsley
½ teaspoon salt
½ teaspoon pepper
1 (4- to 5-pound) rolled boneless pork
  loin roast
1 cup white wine

Combine first 8 ingredients. Score roast; rub on seasonings. Wrap roast in foil, and refrigerate overnight.

Remove roast from foil. Place roast, fat side up, on a rack in a shallow baking pan. Insert meat thermometer (not touching fat). Bake, uncovered, at 325°

for 2½ to 3 hours or until thermometer reaches 170°, basting frequently with wine. Let stand 10 to 15 minutes; slice and serve. Yield: 12 to 15 servings.
Nelda G. Sawyer,
Chouteau, Oklahoma.

HAM ROYALE

¾ cup orange juice
½ cup dry sherry
1 cup firmly packed brown sugar
2 tablespoons prepared mustard
¼ teaspoon ground cloves
1 (5- to 6-pound) fully cooked ham half
1 tablespoon cornstarch
1 tablespoon water

Combine first 5 ingredients in a small bowl, stirring well. Place ham in a shallow baking pan; prick thoroughly with a fork. Pour orange juice mixture over ham; marinate 2 hours in refrigerator, turning ham occasionally.

Place ham, fat side up, in baking pan along with marinade; insert meat thermometer, making sure it does not touch fat or bone. Bake, uncovered, at 325° for 1½ to 2 hours or until meat thermometer registers 140°, basting every 30 minutes with marinade.

Remove ham from baking pan; reserve 1 cup marinade.

Combine cornstarch and water in a small saucepan, mixing well. Add the reserved marinade, and bring to a boil. Boil 1 minute, and remove from heat. Serve sauce with sliced ham. Yield: 10 to 12 servings.
Diane Butts,
Boone, North Carolina.

BRAISED TURKEY BREAST

1 (5- to 5½-pound) boneless turkey breast
2 tablespoons vegetable oil
1½ teaspoons salt
1 teaspoon ground sage
½ teaspoon paprika
¼ teaspoon white pepper
1 medium onion, sliced
1 small clove garlic, crushed
½ cup apple juice

Rub turkey breast with oil; sprinkle with salt, sage, paprika, and pepper.

Place onion and garlic in a lightly greased 13- x 9- x 2-inch baking pan; place turkey breast on onion. Bake at 450° for 30 minutes; remove from oven.

Pour apple juice over turkey; cover pan with foil. Insert meat thermometer through foil into thickest portion of breast, making an opening so that thermometer does not touch foil. Bake at 325° for 2 hours or until thermometer registers 185°. Transfer turkey to serving platter; serve with drippings. Yield: 14 to 16 servings. *Barbara E. Bach,*
Clearwater, Florida.

CHICKEN VERONIQUE

¼ cup all-purpose flour
1 teaspoon salt
½ teaspoon pepper
8 chicken breast halves, skinned and
  boned
½ cup butter or margarine
1 tablespoon currant jelly
⅔ cup Madeira wine
1½ cups seedless green grapes
Additional grapes (optional)

Combine flour, salt, and pepper; dredge chicken in flour mixture.

Sauté chicken in butter in a large skillet until golden brown on each side. Cover, reduce heat, and cook 15 minutes or until tender. Remove chicken to serving platter, reserving pan drippings.

Stir jelly and wine into pan drippings; cook until heated. Stir in grapes; cook until thoroughly heated. Spoon sauce and grapes over chicken. Garnish with additional grapes, if desired. Yield: 8 servings.
Betty Beske,
Arlington, Virginia.

Here's A Menu For Six

It's fun to entertain casually for a few close friends, especially if your holiday schedule is filled with large parties. Invite a few friends to your home for a

simple evening meal. We chose from our readers' favorite recipes to come up with this menu for six.

Spiced Cranberry Cider
Pecan-Stuffed Mushrooms
Cheesy Chicken-and-Ham Bundles
or
Crab-and-Egg Delight
Carrots and Zucchini
Southern-Style Citrus Salad
Apple Cake
Iced Tea   Coffee

SPICED CRANBERRY CIDER

1 quart apple cider
3 cups cranberry juice cocktail
1 tablespoon brown sugar
2 (3-inch) sticks cinnamon
¾ teaspoon whole cloves
½ lemon, thinly sliced
Additional cinnamon sticks (optional)

Combine first 6 ingredients in a Dutch oven; bring to a boil. Reduce heat and simmer 15 to 20 minutes. Strain cider, discarding spices and lemon. Serve hot with additional cinnamon sticks, if desired. Yield: 7 cups.
Shirley E. Flynn,
Charleston, West Virginia.

PECAN-STUFFED MUSHROOMS

16 to 18 large fresh mushrooms
¼ cup butter or margarine, divided
2 tablespoons vegetable oil
2 tablespoons minced onion
5 slices bacon, cooked and crumbled
1 cup soft breadcrumbs
2 tablespoons minced pecans
2 tablespoons dry sherry
2 tablespoons commercial sour cream
2 teaspoons minced chives
Fresh parsley sprigs (optional)

Clean mushrooms with damp towels. Remove mushroom stems, and reserve for other uses.

Heat 2 tablespoons butter and oil in a large skillet. Add mushroom caps; sauté 3 minutes on each side. Remove caps with a slotted spoon; place on a baking sheet. Reserve drippings in skillet.

Melt 2 tablespoons butter in skillet; add onion, and sauté until tender. Stir in next 6 ingredients; spoon mixture into mushroom caps.

Broil 5 inches from heat for 2 to 3 minutes. Garnish with parsley, if desired. Yield: 6 to 8 servings.
Mrs. E. W. Hanley,
Palm Harbor, Florida.

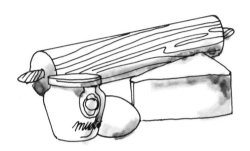

CHEESY CHICKEN-AND-HAM BUNDLES

2½ cups water
3 chicken-flavored bouillon cubes
6 chicken breast halves
½ cup dry sherry
1 (10-ounce) package frozen patty shells
¼ cup plus 2 tablespoons prepared mustard
¾ teaspoon fines herbes
⅛ teaspoon garlic powder
6 (1-ounce) slices Monterey Jack cheese
6 (1-ounce) slices cooked ham
1 egg white, beaten
Sesame seeds (optional)

Combine water and bouillon cubes in a Dutch oven; bring to a boil, stirring until bouillon is dissolved. Add chicken and sherry; return to a boil. Cover, reduce heat, and simmer 20 minutes or until tender. Let chicken cool in broth 30 minutes. Remove chicken, and let cool completely. (Reserve broth for other uses.) Remove skin; bone chicken.

Let patty shells stand at room temperature 30 minutes.

Combine mustard, fines herbes, and garlic powder. Spread about 1 tablespoon mustard mixture over each chicken piece. Wrap a cheese slice and a ham slice around each chicken piece, and set aside.

Roll out each patty shell to an 8-inch circle. Place a chicken piece, seam side down, in the center of each pastry circle. Bring sides of pastry to overlap in center; moisten with water, and pinch together. Fold up ends of pastry; moisten and pinch together. Place pastry-wrapped piece, seam side down, on an ungreased baking sheet. Brush with egg white, and sprinkle with sesame seeds, if desired. Repeat procedure with remaining ingredients. Chill 30 minutes.

Preheat oven to 450°. Place chicken in oven, and reduce heat to 400°. Bake for 30 minutes or until golden brown. Yield: 6 servings.   *Marie Berry,*
Louisville, Kentucky.

CRAB-AND-EGG DELIGHT

1½ tablespoons butter or margarine
1½ tablespoons all-purpose flour
½ cup half-and-half
½ cup chicken broth
1 tablespoon dry sherry
1 (6-ounce) package frozen crabmeat, thawed, drained, and flaked
3 English muffins, split and toasted
6 poached eggs
1 cup (4 ounces) shredded Cheddar cheese

Melt butter in a heavy saucepan over low heat; add flour, stirring until mixture is smooth. Cook 1 minute, stirring constantly. Gradually add half-and-half and chicken broth; cook over medium heat, stirring constantly, until thickened and bubbly. Stir in 1 tablespoon sherry and crabmeat; cook until thoroughly heated.

Top each muffin half with a poached egg; spoon crabmeat sauce over eggs. Sprinkle with Cheddar cheese; broil 1 to 2 minutes or until cheese melts. Serve immediately. Yield: 6 servings.
Mrs. E. L. Warstler,
Kill Devil Hills, North Carolina.

Tip: Always try to match pan size with the burner. A pan that is smaller in diameter than its accompanying burner will allow heat to escape.

CARROTS AND ZUCCHINI

4 medium carrots, scraped and cut
  into thin strips
2 medium zucchini, cut into thin
  strips
3 tablespoons butter or margarine,
  melted
⅛ to ¼ teaspoon salt
⅛ teaspoon freshly ground pepper
2 tablespoons chopped fresh parsley

Arrange carrots on a steaming rack, and place over boiling water; cover and steam 1½ minutes. Add zucchini to steaming rack, and steam an additional 3 to 4 minutes. Place vegetables in a serving bowl; add butter, salt, pepper, and parsley, tossing gently. Serve immediately. Yield: 6 servings.

Loy Witherspoon,
Charlotte, North Carolina.

SOUTHERN-STYLE
CITRUS SALAD

3 cups torn spinach leaves
3 cups torn leaf lettuce
3 cups torn iceberg lettuce
1 grapefruit, peeled and sectioned
2 oranges, peeled and sectioned
1 avocado, peeled and sliced
½ cup sliced celery
½ cup sliced green pepper
¼ cup slivered almonds, toasted
Grapefruit Salad Dressing

Combine spinach and lettuce in a large bowl; toss lightly. Arrange next 6 ingredients over salad greens. Serve with Grapefruit Salad Dressing. Yield: 6 to 8 servings.

Grapefruit Salad Dressing:

1 (.75-ounce) package Italian salad
  dressing mix
⅔ cup vegetable oil, divided
1½ teaspoons grated grapefruit rind
½ cup grapefruit juice

Combine salad dressing mix and ⅓ cup oil in a jar. Cover tightly, and shake vigorously. Add remaining ⅓ cup oil and remaining ingredients; cover tightly, and shake vigorously. Refrigerate. Yield: about 1¼ cups.

Margot Foster,
Hubbard, Texas.

APPLE CAKE

3 medium apples, peeled and thinly
  sliced
¼ cup plus 1 tablespoon sugar
1 tablespoon plus 2 teaspoons ground
  cinnamon
3 cups all-purpose flour
2 cups sugar
1 tablespoon baking powder
1 teaspoon salt
4 eggs, beaten
1 cup vegetable oil
¼ cup orange juice
1 tablespoon vanilla extract
Sifted powdered sugar (optional)
Additional apple slices (optional)

Combine first 3 ingredients, tossing well; set aside.

Combine flour, 2 cups sugar, baking powder, and salt in a large mixing bowl. Combine next 4 ingredients; add to flour mixture, mixing well.

Pour one-third of batter into a greased and floured 10-inch tube pan. Top with half of thinly sliced apples, leaving a ½-inch margin around center and sides. Repeat layering, ending with batter on top. Bake at 350° for 1 hour and 20 minutes or until a wooden pick inserted in center comes out clean. Cool in pan 10 to 15 minutes; then remove from pan, and cool completely. Sprinkle with powdered sugar, and garnish with additional apple slices, if desired. Yield: one 10-inch cake. *Charlotte Watkins, Lakeland, Florida.*

Let Spices Scent
The Air

It's time to go through your spice cabinet and pull out all the holiday flavors. Cinnamon, cloves, ginger, allspice, and more are baked into cakes, pies, and breads, or preserved in chutneys for the seasonal treats you'll find here.

You'll find the flavor of spices lasts longer if you store them in a cool place away from any source of heat or light. Here at *Southern Living,* we keep spices in the freezer to preserve flavor.

BANANA CREPES FLAMBE

1 tablespoon lemon juice
2 cups chopped bananas (about 3 medium
  bananas)
½ cup flaked coconut, toasted and divided
1 teaspoon ground cinnamon
Spicy Dessert Crêpes
2 tablespoons butter or margarine
1 tablespoon light corn syrup
1 (7.15-ounce) package creamy white
  frosting mix
1 cup evaporated milk
¼ cup light rum

Sprinkle lemon juice over bananas. Add ¼ cup coconut and cinnamon; toss gently. Spoon about 2 tablespoons banana mixture into center of each crêpe; roll up, leaving ends open. Set aside.

Melt butter in a medium saucepan over low heat until golden brown; remove from heat. Stir in syrup; gradually add frosting mix, beating until smooth. Stir in milk; cook over low heat, stirring constantly, until thoroughly heated.

Place sauce in a lightly greased 13- x 9- x 2-inch baking dish; place filled crêpes in sauce. Sprinkle remaining ¼ cup coconut on top. Heat rum in a saucepan over medium heat (do not boil). Ignite and pour over crêpes. After flames die down, serve immediately. Yield: 7 servings.

Spicy Dessert Crêpes:

1⅓ cups milk
1 cup plus 1 tablespoon all-purpose flour
2 eggs
2 tablespoons brown sugar
2 tablespoons vegetable oil
1 tablespoon molasses
½ teaspoon ground cinnamon
¼ teaspoon ground ginger
⅛ teaspoon ground nutmeg

Combine all ingredients in container of electric blender; process 1 minute. Scrape down sides of blender container with rubber spatula; process an additional 25 seconds. Refrigerate 1 hour. (This allows flour particles to swell and soften so crêpes are light in texture.)

Brush the bottom of a 6-inch crêpe pan with oil; place pan over medium heat until oil is just hot, not smoking.

Pour 3 tablespoons batter into pan; quickly tilt pan in all directions so batter covers the pan in a thin film. Cook crêpe about 1 minute.

Lift edge of crêpe to test for doneness. Crêpe is ready for flipping when it can be shaken loose from pan. Flip crêpe, and cook about 30 seconds on other side. (This side is rarely more than spotty brown.) Place on a towel to cool. Stack crêpes between layers of waxed paper to prevent sticking. Repeat procedure until all batter is used. Yield: about 14 crêpes. *Mary Ann Bryant, Franklin, Virginia.*

KENTUCKY PECAN CAKE

2½ cups self-rising flour
2 cups sugar
1½ cups vegetable oil
1 cup applesauce
2½ tablespoons ground cinnamon
4 egg yolks
2 tablespoons hot water
1 cup chopped pecans
4 egg whites
Sifted powdered sugar

Combine first 7 ingredients in order listed; beat until smooth. Stir in pecans.

Beat egg whites (at room temperature) until stiff; fold into batter. Pour mixture into an ungreased 10-inch tube pan. Bake at 350° for 1½ hours. Invert pan, and cool cake completely; remove from pan. Sprinkle top of cake with sifted powdered sugar. Yield: one 10-inch cake. *Sherlon Page, Spring Hope, North Carolina.*

OLD SOUTH SPICE CAKE

1 cup butter or margarine, softened
2 cups sugar
5 eggs
2 cups all-purpose flour
½ cup cocoa
2 teaspoons ground allspice
2 teaspoons ground cinnamon
½ to 1 teaspoon ground cloves
½ teaspoon salt
1 teaspoon baking soda
1 cup buttermilk
Nut-and-Fruit Filling
Caramel Frosting
Pecan halves
About ½ cup semisweet chocolate morsels, melted

Cream butter; gradually add sugar, beating well. Add eggs, one at a time, beating well after each addition.

Combine flour, cocoa, allspice, cinnamon, cloves, and salt. Dissolve soda in buttermilk. Add flour mixture to creamed mixture alternately with buttermilk mixture, beginning and ending with flour mixture.

Pour batter into 3 greased and floured 9-inch cakepans. Bake at 375° for 20 minutes or until a wooden pick inserted in center comes out clean. Cool in pans 10 minutes. Remove layers from pans; cool completely on wire racks.

Spread Nut-and-Fruit Filling between layers; frost top and sides of cake with Caramel Frosting.

Arrange pecan halves around base of cake. Fill a pastry bag with the melted chocolate; pipe desired designs with chocolate over the pecans and on top of cake. Yield: one 3-layer cake.

Nut-and-Fruit Filling:

1 (14-ounce) can sweetened condensed milk
1½ cups sifted powdered sugar
1 teaspoon ground allspice
1 teaspoon ground cinnamon
¼ teaspoon ground cloves
1½ cups raisins, ground
1 cup chopped pecans

Combine all ingredients, mixing well. Yield: about 4 cups.

Caramel Frosting:

2 cups sugar
½ cup firmly packed brown sugar
½ cup butter
½ teaspoon baking soda
1 cup buttermilk
2 tablespoons light corn syrup

Combine all ingredients in a large heavy saucepan; cook over medium heat, stirring until sugar dissolves. Cook until a candy thermometer reaches soft ball stage (236°). Cool mixture slightly. Beat until mixture reaches spreading consistency; frost top and sides of cake, working rapidly. Yield: enough frosting for top and sides of one 3-layer cake.
Mrs. C. B. Glenn, Scottsboro, Alabama.

SPICY GINGERBREAD

1 cup firmly packed brown sugar
1 cup molasses
½ cup butter or margarine, melted
2 eggs
1 cup milk
1 tablespoon lemon juice
3 cups all-purpose flour
1 teaspoon baking soda
2 teaspoons ground ginger
1½ teaspoons ground cinnamon
1 teaspoon ground cloves

Combine sugar, molasses, and butter; beat well. Add eggs, beating mixture well; set aside.

Combine milk and lemon juice, stirring well; set aside. Combine remaining dry ingredients; add to egg mixture alternately with milk mixture, beginning and ending with flour mixture. Mix well after each addition.

Pour batter into a greased and floured 13- x 9- x 2-inch baking pan; bake at 350° for 25 to 30 minutes or until a wooden pick inserted in the center comes out clean. Yield: 15 to 18 servings. *Mrs. Lewis R. Carroll, Easton, Maryland.*

SOUR CREAM-PUMPKIN PIE

1 cup sugar
¼ teaspoon salt
½ teaspoon ground ginger
1 teaspoon ground cinnamon
¼ teaspoon ground nutmeg
¼ teaspoon ground cloves
1 (16-ounce) can pumpkin
1 (8-ounce) carton commercial sour cream
3 eggs, separated
1 unbaked 9-inch pastry shell

Combine first 6 ingredients; add pumpkin and sour cream, stirring well.

Beat egg yolks until thick and lemon colored; stir into pumpkin mixture. Beat egg whites (at room temperature) until stiff peaks form; fold into pumpkin mixture. Pour into pastry shell. Bake at 450° for 10 minutes; reduce heat to 350°, and bake 55 minutes or until set. Yield: one 9-inch pie.
Mrs. W. J. Wallace, Orlando, Florida.

PEAR MINCEMEAT

7 pounds pears, peeled, cored, and cut
    into eighths
2 lemons, unpeeled and cut into eighths
2 oranges, unpeeled and cut into eighths
2 cups raisins
6 cups sugar
1 tablespoon salt
1 tablespoon ground allspice
1 tablespoon ground cinnamon
1 tablespoon ground nutmeg
1 tablespoon ground cloves
½ cup vinegar

Position knife blade in food processor
bowl. Add about 1 cup pears; process
until finely chopped. Repeat with remaining fruit.

Combine chopped fruit and remaining
ingredients in a Dutch oven. Bring to a
boil; reduce heat and simmer, uncovered, 30 minutes.

Pour hot mixture into hot sterilized
jars, leaving ¼-inch headspace. Cover
at once with metal lids, and screw bands
tight. Process in boiling-water bath for
25 minutes. Serve as a relish, or use to
make Pear Mincemeat Pie and Pear
Mincemeat Cookies. Yield 7½ pints.
Billie Campbell,
Marlin, Texas.

PEAR MINCEMEAT PIE

Pastry for a double-crust 9-inch pie
2 cups prepared pear mincemeat
¼ cup firmly packed brown sugar
2 tablespoons all-purpose flour
½ cup chopped pecans

Roll half of pastry onto a lightly
floured surface to ⅛-inch thickness; fit
into a 9-inch pieplate. Set aside. Chill
remaining pastry.

Combine mincemeat, brown sugar,
flour, and pecans; spoon mixture evenly
into prepared pastry shell.

Roll out remaining pastry to ⅛-inch
thickness, and place over filling. Trim
edges; seal and flute. Cut slits in top
pastry to allow steam to escape, making
a decorative pattern with slits, if desired. Bake at 375° for 35 to 40 minutes.
(Cover edges of pie with aluminum foil
to prevent overbrowning, if necessary.)
Yield: one 9-inch pie. *Billie Campbell,*
Marlin, Texas.

PEAR MINCEMEAT COOKIES

½ cup shortening
1 cup sugar
2 eggs
2 teaspoons half-and-half
1 teaspoon vanilla extract
2½ cups all-purpose flour
½ teaspoon salt
¼ teaspoon baking soda
½ cup prepared pear mincemeat
1 egg yolk, beaten (optional)
2 tablespoons water (optional)
Melted butter or margarine (optional)

Cream shortening; gradually add 1
cup sugar, beating well. Add eggs, one
at a time, beating well after each addition. Add half-and-half and vanilla,
beating well. Combine flour, salt, and
baking soda. Add to creamed mixture,
stirring well. Cover dough and chill for
at least 1 hour.

Roll dough to ⅛-inch thickness on a
lightly floured surface; cut with a 2-inch
round cookie cutter. Place half the
cookies on a greased cookie sheet;
spoon 1 teaspoon mincemeat onto center of each. Top with remaining cookies; press edges together with a fork.

Combine egg yolk and water; brush
tops of cookies with egg yolk mixture or
with melted butter, if desired. Bake at
375° for 12 to 15 minutes. Yield: about
4 dozen. *Billie Campbell,*
Marlin, Texas.

PUMPKIN BREAD WITH
CREAM CHEESE AND
PRESERVES

2 cups sugar
¾ cup vegetable oil
4 eggs
1 (16-ounce) can pumpkin
3⅓ cups all-purpose flour
2 teaspoons baking soda
½ teaspoon baking powder
1 teaspoon salt
2 teaspoons pumpkin pie spice
1 teaspoon ground cinnamon
1 teaspoon ground nutmeg
⅔ cup water
2 teaspoons vanilla extract
1 cup chopped pecans
Cream Cheese and Peach Preserves

Combine sugar and oil, stirring well.
Add eggs, one at a time, mixing well
after each addition. Stir in pumpkin.

Combine next 7 ingredients; add to
pumpkin mixture alternately with water,
beginning and ending with flour mixture. Stir in vanilla and pecans. Spoon
batter into 2 lightly greased 9- x 5- x
3-inch loafpans; bake at 325° for 1 hour
and 10 minutes or until a wooden pick
inserted in center comes out clean. Cool
bread in pans 10 minutes; remove from
pans and cool on wire racks. Serve with
Cream Cheese and Peach Preserves.
Yield: 2 loaves.

Cream Cheese and Peach Preserves:

¼ cup peach preserves
¼ teaspoon ground ginger
1 (8-ounce) package cream cheese,
    softened

Combine peach preserves and ginger;
spoon preserves over block of softened
cream cheese. *Mrs. Harry H. Lay, Jr.*
Fairmount, Georgia.

FRESH APPLE MUFFINS

2 cups all-purpose flour
½ cup sugar
1 tablespoon baking powder
½ teaspoon salt
½ teaspoon ground cinnamon
½ teaspoon ground nutmeg
1½ cups peeled, chopped cooking apple,
    divided
1 cup milk
¼ cup vegetable oil
1 egg, beaten
¼ cup sugar
½ teaspoon ground cinnamon

Combine first 6 ingredients in a large
mixing bowl; stir in 1 cup apples, and
make a well in center of mixture. Combine milk, oil, and egg; add to dry ingredients, stirring just until moistened.
Spoon batter into greased muffin pans,
filling two-thirds full.

Combine remaining ½ cup apple, ¼
cup sugar, and ½ teaspoon cinnamon;
sprinkle over muffin batter. Bake at
350° for 20 to 25 minutes. Yield: 1
dozen. *Marie Jefferson,*
Danville, Virginia.

PICKLED REFRIGERATOR ONION RINGS

1 cup water
1 cup vinegar
¼ cup sugar
3 (2-inch) sticks cinnamon, broken
½ teaspoon salt
½ teaspoon whole cloves
1 small white onion, thinly sliced and separated into rings
1 small red onion, thinly sliced and separated into rings

Combine first 6 ingredients in a small saucepan; bring to a boil. Cover, reduce heat, and simmer 10 minutes. Remove from heat; strain mixture, and discard spices. Pour strained hot mixture over onion; cover and chill overnight. Drain before serving. Yield: about 1⅔ cups.
Margaret L. Hunter,
Princeton, Kentucky.

CRANBERRY CHUTNEY

1 cup water
½ cup sugar
¾ cup firmly packed dark brown sugar
¼ cup grated orange rind
¾ cup cider vinegar
1 small onion, thinly sliced
2 medium apples, peeled and finely chopped
½ teaspoon salt
1 teaspoon ground ginger
½ teaspoon mace
½ teaspoon curry powder
1 quart fresh cranberries
½ cup raisins or currants
¾ cup orange juice

Combine first 4 ingredients in a large saucepan. Bring mixture to a boil; reduce heat and simmer 30 minutes.

Add next 7 ingredients; return mixture to a boil. Reduce heat and simmer 30 minutes, stirring occasionally.

Add remaining ingredients, stirring well; simmer 10 minutes or until cranberries pop. Serve with pork or poultry. Yield: 2 quarts.
Rebecca Benhard,
Palmetto, Louisiana.

Tip: Roll lemons, oranges, and grapefruits on a counter before cutting to soften; you will get more juice.

HOT SPICY CIDER

1 gallon apple cider
½ cup firmly packed brown sugar
½ teaspoon ground nutmeg
4 (4-inch) sticks cinnamon
20 whole cloves
1 (6-ounce) can frozen orange juice concentrate, undiluted
½ cup lemon juice
Additional sticks cinnamon (optional)

Combine first 5 ingredients in a large saucepan. Bring to a boil; cover, reduce heat, and simmer 10 minutes. Strain spices from cider. Add orange juice concentrate and lemon juice; stir until thoroughly heated.

Serve hot with cinnamon stick, if desired. Yield: about 1 gallon.
Paula Sprinkle,
Troutville, Virginia.

Salads Spruce Up The Menu

A distinctive entrée, a sumptuous dessert—two important ingredients of any holiday meal. But don't forget a fresh and sparkling salad when you're planning holiday menus.

FESTIVE CHERRY SALAD

1 (3-ounce) package lemon-flavored gelatin
1 (3-ounce) package apricot-flavored gelatin
1½ cups boiling water
1½ cups orange juice
1 (16½-ounce) can pitted dark cherries, drained and chopped
1 (15½-ounce) can crushed pineapple, drained
1 cup finely chopped celery
¾ cup finely chopped pecans

Dissolve gelatin in boiling water; stir in orange juice. Chill until consistency of unbeaten egg white. Fold in remaining ingredients; spoon into a lightly oiled 5-cup mold. Chill until set. Yield: 8 to 10 servings. *Mrs. Henry Derby,*
Onancock, Virginia.

ROYAL PEAR SALAD

1 (6-ounce) package raspberry-flavored gelatin
1 cup boiling water
2 cups cold water
½ teaspoon lemon juice
1 (16-ounce) can whole cranberry sauce
1 (29-ounce) can pear halves, drained and chopped
½ cup chopped pecans

Dissolve gelatin in boiling water; stir in cold water, lemon juice, and cranberry sauce. Chill until consistency of unbeaten egg white. Fold in pears and pecans. Spoon into a 7-cup mold. Chill until firm. Yield: 10 servings.
Betty Williams,
Knoxville, Tennessee.

CREAMY FRUIT SALAD

1 (15¼-ounce) can pineapple chunks
2 tablespoons lemon juice
1 cup sugar
1 tablespoon all-purpose flour
2 egg yolks
2 oranges, sectioned
2 bananas, sliced
2 apples, cubed
½ pound seedless grapes, halved
½ cup whipping cream, whipped

Drain pineapple, reserving the juice; set aside.

Add enough water to pineapple juice to make 1 cup of liquid. Combine with next 4 ingredients in a heavy saucepan; mix well. Cook over medium heat, stirring constantly, until dressing is smooth and thickened; remove from heat, and cool completely.

Combine pineapple and remaining fruit in a large bowl. Add whipped cream to dressing mixture; fold into fruit. Chill. Yield: 8 to 10 servings.
Jane Green,
Loris, South Carolina.

CONGEALED AVOCADO SALAD

2 ripe avocados, peeled, seeded, and
  coarsely chopped
1 (8-ounce) package cream cheese,
  softened
½ cup mayonnaise
1 (6-ounce) package lime-flavored gelatin
2 cups boiling water
1½ cups cold water
1 (2-ounce) jar diced pimiento, drained
¼ cup chopped green pepper
2 teaspoons grated onion
Dash of hot sauce
Dash of Worcestershire sauce
Lettuce leaves (optional)

Combine first 3 ingredients in container of an electric blender; process
until smooth. Set aside.

Combine gelatin and boiling water in
a large bowl, stirring until dissolved.
Stir in cold water. Add avocado mixture, diced pimiento, and the next 4
ingredients; mix well.

Pour mixture into a lightly oiled 8-cup
mold; chill until firm. Unmold on lettuce leaves. Yield: 10 to 12 servings.
Carol Barclay,
Portland, Texas.

LAYERED SPINACH-LETTUCE SALAD

½ pound fresh spinach, torn into bite-size
  pieces
2 small heads iceberg lettuce, torn into
  bite-size pieces
½ cup chopped celery
1 (17-ounce) can English peas, drained
10 green onions, chopped
6 hard-cooked eggs, sliced
1 pound bacon, cooked and crumbled
½ cup sliced water chestnuts
2 cups mayonnaise
1 (8-ounce) carton commercial sour cream
1 (0.4-ounce) package buttermilk salad
  dressing mix

Layer first 8 ingredients in order
listed in a large salad bowl.

Combine remaining ingredients; mix
well. Spread over top of salad, sealing
to edge of bowl. Cover salad tightly,
and refrigerate for several hours or
overnight. Yield: 12 to 15 servings.
Mary Nelson,
Richardson, Texas.

GRECIAN GREEN SALAD

2 large heads romaine lettuce, torn into
  bite-size pieces
2 medium cucumbers, thinly sliced
2 green peppers, chopped
1 cup thinly sliced radishes
¾ cup crumbled feta cheese
Olive Oil Dressing

Combine first 5 ingredients in a large
bowl; toss well. Toss salad with Olive
Oil Dressing just before serving. Yield:
12 servings.

Olive Oil Dressing:

½ cup olive oil
3 tablespoons lemon juice
¼ teaspoon salt
¼ teaspoon pepper

Combine all ingredients in a jar.
Cover tightly, and shake vigorously.
Chill several hours. Yield: ⅔ cup.
Rita Hastings,
Edgewater, Maryland.

TOSSED VEGETABLE MARINADE

½ pound fresh green beans
1 cup water
1 (1-pound) bunch broccoli
1 medium head cauliflower, broken into
  flowerets
½ pound carrots, cut into 3-inch strips
1 (14-ounce) can artichoke hearts, drained
  and halved
¼ pound fresh mushrooms, sliced
10 cherry tomatoes
1 cup vegetable oil
1 cup dry white wine
½ cup lemon juice
2 cloves garlic, crushed
2 teaspoons salt
½ teaspoon ground oregano
2 teaspoons honey

Wash beans; trim ends, and remove
strings. Cut beans into 3-inch pieces.
Bring 1 cup water to a boil; add beans.
Return to a boil; reduce heat and simmer, uncovered, 5 minutes. Drain
beans, and cool.

Trim off large leaves of broccoli, and
remove tough ends of lower stalks.
Wash broccoli thoroughly. Cut off
flowerets (reserve stems for another
use), and place in a large mixing bowl.

Add the beans, cauliflower, carrots, artichoke hearts, mushrooms, and cherry
tomatoes; set aside.

Combine remaining ingredients; mix
well, and pour over vegetables. Toss
gently. Cover salad, and chill for 8
hours or overnight. Toss again before
serving. Yield: 12 servings.
Anita McLemore,
Knoxville, Tennessee.

This Fruitcake Is A Tradition

Every Christmas for the past two dec-
ades, Alice R. Robertson of Warrenton,
North Carolina, has served Sherry-Nut
Fruitcake—an old family recipe that originated with her grandmother. She
makes the cake several weeks before
Christmas so it will mellow.

SHERRY-NUT FRUITCAKE

¾ cup dry sherry
2 cups golden raisins
¾ pound candied red cherries
¾ pound candied green cherries
¾ pound candied red pineapple, chopped
¾ pound candied green pineapple,
  chopped
4 cups chopped pecans
3 cups all-purpose flour, divided
¾ cup butter, softened
¾ cup sugar
¾ cup firmly packed light brown sugar
6 eggs
¼ teaspoon salt
¾ teaspoon ground mace
¾ teaspoon ground cinnamon
¾ teaspoon ground allspice
¾ cup whipping cream
1 (10-ounce) jar strawberry preserves
¾ teaspoon almond extract
¾ teaspoon orange extract
¾ teaspoon vanilla extract
Light corn syrup
Pecan halves (optional)
Additional candied red and green cherries
  (optional)

Pour sherry over raisins, and let them soak overnight. Combine next 5 ingredients; dredge in 1 cup flour, stirring to coat. Set aside.

Cream butter in a large mixing bowl; gradually add sugar, beating until light and fluffy. Add eggs, one at a time, beating well after each addition.

Combine remaining 2 cups flour, salt, mace, cinnamon, and allspice. Add to creamed mixture alternately with whipping cream, beginning and ending with flour mixture. Add strawberry preserves and flavorings, mixing well. Stir in fruit-nut mixture and raisins.

Spoon batter into a greased and waxed paper-lined 10-inch tube pan. Bake at 275° for 3 hours or until a wooden pick inserted in center comes out clean. Cool cake completely in pan. Remove from pan, and remove waxed paper. Place on serving plate. Brush top with corn syrup; garnish with pecans and candied cherries, if desired. Yield: one 10-inch cake.

Note: To store, wrap with cheesecloth soaked in sherry, if desired; store in an airtight container. A cut apple may be placed in container with cake.

Alice R. Robertson,
Warrenton, North Carolina.

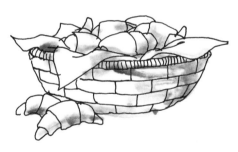

There's Something Special About Homemade Bread

While commercial rolls will certainly fill the space in your holiday bread basket, they're just not the same as homemade. The dough for our Crescent Rolls is prepared and refrigerated a day ahead of time; kneading is not required. And the finished rolls are delicious.

CRESCENT ROLLS

1 package dry yeast
¼ cup warm water (105° to 115°)
4½ cups all-purpose flour
½ cup sugar
1 teaspoon salt
¾ cup butter or margarine, softened
2 eggs, slightly beaten
¾ cup warm milk (105° to 115°)
Melted butter or margarine

Dissolve yeast in warm water; let stand 5 minutes.

Combine flour, sugar, and salt in a large mixing bowl. Cut in ¾ cup butter with pastry blender until mixture resembles coarse meal. Combine eggs, milk, and yeast mixture; add to the flour mixture, stirring well (dough will be sticky). Cover and refrigerate overnight.

Punch dough down, and divide in half. Roll each half into a 12-inch circle on a floured surface; cut each circle into 12 wedges. Roll up each wedge tightly, beginning at wide end. Seal points and place rolls, point side down, on greased baking sheets. Curve rolls into crescent shape. Brush with melted butter.

Cover and let rise in a warm place (85°), free from drafts, about 1 hour or until doubled in bulk. Bake at 400° for 8 minutes. Yield: 2 dozen.

Paula Patterson,
Houston, Texas.

BUTTERHORNS

1 package dry yeast
¼ cup warm water (105° to 115°)
¾ cup milk, scalded
½ cup sugar
½ cup shortening
2 teaspoons salt
3 eggs, beaten
4 to 4½ cups all-purpose flour, divided
¼ cup butter or margarine, melted

Dissolve yeast in warm water; let stand 5 minutes.

Combine milk, sugar, shortening, and salt in a large mixing bowl, stirring until shortening melts; cool to 105° to 115°. Add eggs, 1 cup flour, and yeast mixture, mixing well. Gradually stir in enough of the remaining flour to make a soft dough.

Turn dough out onto a floured surface, and knead 8 to 10 minutes until smooth and elastic. Place in a well-greased bowl, turning to grease top. Cover and let rise in a warm place (85°), free from drafts, 2 hours.

Punch dough down, and divide into thirds; roll each third into a 9-inch circle on a lightly floured surface.

Brush with melted butter; cut each circle into 12 wedges. Roll up each wedge tightly, beginning at wide end. Seal points, and place rolls, point side down, on lightly greased baking sheets.

Cover and let rise in a warm place (85°), free from drafts, 45 minutes. Bake at 400° for 10 to 12 minutes or until browned. Yield: 3 dozen.

Claire Phillips,
Valdosta, Georgia.

QUICK YEAST ROLLS

1¼ cups water
¼ cup shortening
3 tablespoons sugar
1 teaspoon salt
1 package dry yeast
1 egg, beaten
3½ cups all-purpose flour

Combine water, shortening, sugar, and salt in a small saucepan; cook, stirring constantly, until shortening melts. Let cool to lukewarm (105° to 115°). Dissolve yeast in mixture. Add egg; mix well. Stir in flour.

Spoon dough into greased muffin pans, filling half full. Cover and let rise in a warm place (85°), free from drafts, 1 hour or until doubled. Bake at 425° for 12 to 14 minutes or until golden brown. Yield: 15 rolls.

Lorene Dinwiddie,
Shallowater, Texas.

Tip: Use an instant-registering thermometer to judge the liquid temperature used in bread baking. If the temperature is too low, the yeast will not dissolve and grow; if too high, the yeast will be killed and the bread will not rise.

WHOLE WHEAT BISCUITS

1 package dry yeast
2 teaspoons warm water (105° to 115°)
2½ cups whole wheat flour
½ cup all-purpose flour
2 teaspoons baking powder
½ teaspoon salt
½ teaspoon baking soda
¼ cup margarine, softened
1 tablespoon honey
1 cup buttermilk
Melted butter or margarine

Dissolve yeast in warm water, and set aside.

Combine dry ingredients; cut in margarine until mixture resembles coarse meal. Add yeast mixture, honey, and buttermilk, mixing well. Turn dough out onto a floured surface. Roll dough to ½-inch thickness; cut into rounds with a 2-inch cutter. Place biscuits on lightly greased baking sheets. Brush with melted butter. Bake at 400° for 12 to 15 minutes. Yield: about 1 dozen.
Mrs. W. P. Chambers,
Jeffersonville, Indiana.

CHEDDAR CHEESE BREAD

2 packages dry yeast
1 cup warm water (105° to 115°)
1 cup milk, scalded
3 tablespoons sugar
1 tablespoon salt
2 tablespoons shortening
1 egg, slightly beaten
7 cups all-purpose flour, divided
2 cups (8 ounces) shredded sharp Cheddar cheese

Dissolve yeast in warm water in a large mixing bowl; let stand 10 minutes.

Combine milk, sugar, salt, and shortening, stirring until shortening melts; cool to 105° to 115°. Add milk mixture, egg, and 2 cups flour to yeast mixture; stir until smooth. Stir in cheese; gradually stir in enough of the remaining flour to make a soft dough.

Turn dough out onto a floured surface; cover and let rest 10 to 15 minutes. Knead dough 8 to 10 minutes until smooth and elastic. Place in a well-greased bowl, turning to grease top. Cover and let rise in a warm place

(85°), free from drafts, 1 hour or until doubled in bulk.

Punch dough down; turn out onto a lightly floured surface. Divide and shape into 2 loaves; place in 2 greased 9- x 5- x 3-inch loafpans. Cover and let rise in a warm place, free from drafts, 45 minutes or until doubled in bulk. Bake at 375° for 30 minutes. Remove loaves from pans, and cool on wire racks. Yield: 2 loaves. *Pat MacDermott, Fort Benning, Georgia.*

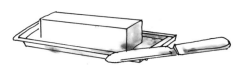

LIGHT-BROWN BREAD

2 packages dry yeast
½ cup warm water (105° to 115°)
2 cups milk, scalded
¼ cup plus 1 tablespoon sugar
1 tablespoon salt
3 tablespoons shortening
2 cups whole wheat flour
4 cups bread flour

Dissolve yeast in warm water; let stand 5 minutes. Combine next 4 ingredients in a large mixing bowl; stir until shortening melts. Cool to 105° to 115°. Add yeast mixture to milk mixture. Add 1 cup whole wheat flour and 2 cups bread flour. Beat at medium speed of electric mixer 3 minutes. Stir in remaining 1 cup whole wheat flour and enough remaining bread flour to make a soft dough.

Turn dough out onto a lightly floured surface, and knead 8 to 10 minutes until smooth and elastic. Place in a greased bowl, turning to grease top. Cover and let rise in a warm place (85°), free from drafts, 1 hour or until doubled in bulk.

Punch dough down; let rest 20 minutes. Divide dough in half; shape each half into a loaf. Place in 2 greased 9- x 5- x 3-inch loafpans. Cover and let rise in a warm place, 45 minutes or until almost doubled in bulk.

Bake at 375° for 35 minutes or until loaves sound hollow when tapped. Remove loaves from pans, and cool on wire racks. Yield: 2 loaves.
Mildred P. Johnson,
Pfafftown, North Carolina.

HERB BREAD

2 packages dry yeast
½ cup warm water (105° to 115°)
1 tablespoon honey
3 cups milk
¼ cup plus 1 tablespoon olive oil
¼ cup honey
2 tablespoons butter or margarine
1 teaspoon dried parsley flakes
1 teaspoon dried whole basil
1 teaspoon dried whole oregano
1 teaspoon celery flakes
½ teaspoon onion flakes
¼ teaspoon dried whole thyme
8 to 8½ cups unbleached flour
1 cup whole wheat flour
1½ teaspoons salt

Dissolve yeast in warm water; stir in 1 tablespoon honey, and set aside.

Combine next 10 ingredients in a medium saucepan; heat slowly to 105°. Stir in yeast mixture.

Combine flour and salt in a large mixing bowl; add milk mixture. Stir until all dry ingredients are moistened. (Dough will be sticky.)

Turn dough out onto a heavily floured surface, and knead 4 to 5 minutes or until smooth and elastic. Place dough in a well-greased bowl, turning to grease top. Cover and let rise in a warm place (85°), free from drafts, 50 minutes or until doubled in bulk.

Punch dough down, and turn out onto a floured surface. Let dough rest 5 minutes. Knead dough 3 or 4 times. Divide dough into thirds, and shape each third into a loaf. Place loaves in three greased 9- x 5- x 3-inch loafpans. Cover and let rise in a warm place (85°), free from drafts, 30 minutes or until doubled in bulk.

Bake at 350° for 45 minutes or until loaves sound hollow when tapped. Remove loaves from pans, and cool on wire racks. Yield: 3 loaves.
Mrs. Russell Rehkemper,
Tampa, Florida.

Tip: When preparing a recipe, follow directions carefully. Avoid substituting items, for example, soft margarine for butter or margarine, or whipped cream cheese for cream cheese.

GOLDEN CAKE BREAD

1 cup milk, scalded
½ cup butter or margarine
½ cup sugar
1 teaspoon salt
1 package dry yeast
¼ cup warm water (105° to 115°)
2 eggs
2 teaspoons vanilla extract
4 to 4½ cups all-purpose flour

Heat milk and butter in a saucepan until butter melts; stir in sugar and salt. Cool to 105° to 115°.

Dissolve yeast in warm water; add to milk mixture. Beat eggs lightly with a fork in a small bowl; set aside 1 tablespoon egg. Add remaining egg and vanilla to milk mixture, mixing well.

Stir in flour; beat with a wooden spoon 2 minutes or until mixture is smooth (dough will be sticky).

Spoon dough into a greased bowl. Cover and let rise in a warm place (85°), free from drafts, 1 hour or until doubled in bulk. Punch dough down, and beat with a wooden spoon 1 minute (dough will be stiff). Cover and let rise in a warm place (85°), free from drafts, 45 minutes or until doubled in bulk.

Divide dough in half; shape each half into a loaf, and place in 2 greased 8½- x 4½- x 3-inch loafpans. Let rise in a warm place (85°), free from drafts, 45 minutes or until almost doubled in bulk.

Brush loaves with reserved egg. Bake at 325° for 25 to 30 minutes. Remove from pans; cool on wire racks. Yield: 2 loaves.
*Robbin Dorrier,
Charlotte, North Carolina.*

CRANBERRY-PECAN MUFFINS

1½ cups coarsely chopped fresh
   cranberries
¼ cup sugar
3 cups all-purpose flour
1 cup sugar
1 tablespoon plus 1½ teaspoons baking
   powder
½ teaspoon salt
½ cup shortening
1 cup chopped pecans
2 teaspoons grated lemon rind
2 eggs
1 cup milk

Combine cranberries and ¼ cup sugar; set aside.

Combine next 4 ingredients, mixing well. Cut in shortening with a pastry blender until mixture resembles coarse meal. Stir in pecans and lemon rind; make a well in center of mixture. Beat eggs until light and lemon colored; stir in milk. Add egg mixture to dry ingredients, stirring just until moistened; gently stir in cranberry mixture.

Spoon batter into greased muffin pans, filling two-thirds full. Bake at 400° for 20 minutes. Yield: about 2½ dozen.
*Mildred Bickley,
Bristol, Virginia.*

Snacks From The Freezer

Take a tip from some savvy *Southern Living* readers, and get a headstart on the holidays. Stock your freezer with these tasty appetizers, and they'll be ready for drop-in guests or holiday entertaining. Friends and family appreciate the welcoming touch; and with most of the preparation out of the way, you'll spend less time in the kitchen and more time visiting with your guests.

CRAB PUFFS

1 (6-ounce) can crabmeat, drained and
   flaked
½ cup (2 ounces) shredded sharp Cheddar
   cheese
3 green onions, chopped
1 teaspoon dry mustard
1 teaspoon Worcestershire sauce
1 cup water
½ cup butter or margarine
¼ teaspoon salt
1 cup all-purpose flour
4 eggs

Combine first 5 ingredients, stirring well; set aside.

Combine water, butter, and salt in a medium saucepan; bring mixture to a boil. Reduce heat to low; add flour, and stir vigorously until mixture leaves sides of pan and forms a smooth ball. Remove saucepan from heat, and allow mixture to cool slightly.

Add eggs, one at a time, beating with a wooden spoon after each addition; beat until batter is smooth. Add crab mixture; stir well.

Drop batter by heaping teaspoonfuls onto ungreased baking sheets. Bake at 400° for 15 minutes; reduce heat to 350°, and bake an additional 10 minutes. Serve puffs warm.

To freeze before baking, cover baking sheets with foil before dropping batter onto them. Place unbaked puffs on baking sheets in freezer until hard. Remove from sheets, and store in an airtight container in freezer. To serve, remove from freezer, and bake, unthawed, at 375° for 35 minutes.

To freeze after baking, place crab puffs in an airtight container in freezer. To serve, remove from freezer, let thaw completely, and bake at 350° for 8 to 10 minutes. Yield: about 4½ dozen.
*Eileen Wehling,
Austin, Texas.*

PIZZA SLICES

1 pound bulk pork sausage
1 pound process American cheese
2 tablespoons catsup
1 teaspoon Worcestershire sauce
½ teaspoon dried whole oregano
⅛ teaspoon garlic powder
2 (8-ounce) loaves party rye bread

Brown sausage in a heavy skillet; drain well.

Place cheese in top of a double boiler; bring water to a boil. Reduce heat to low; cook until cheese melts. Add sausage, catsup, and next 3 ingredients; blend well.

Spread about a teaspoon of cheese mixture on each bread slice; bake on an ungreased baking sheet at 375° about 5 minutes. Serve warm.

To freeze, place unbaked slices in an airtight container in freezer. To serve, remove from freezer; place on an ungreased baking sheet. Bake at 375° for 10 to 15 minutes. Yield: about 5 dozen appetizers.
*Nancy Eisele,
Valrico, Florida.*

BACON ROLLS

¼ cup butter or margarine
½ cup water
1½ cups herb-seasoned stuffing mix
¼ pound bulk pork sausage
1 egg, slightly beaten
12 slices bacon, cut in half

Melt butter in a medium saucepan. Add water, and bring to a boil. Remove from heat; stir in stuffing mix. Add sausage and egg; mix well. Cover and chill 30 minutes.

Shape chilled mixture into twenty-four 2- x ¾-inch logs; wrap a piece of bacon around each log, and fasten securely with wooden picks. Place on a 15- x 10- x 1-inch jellyroll pan; bake at 375° for 20 minutes. Turn logs, and bake an additional 15 minutes or until lightly browned. Drain well on paper towels; serve warm.

To freeze, place baked rolls in an airtight container in freezer. To serve, let thaw completely. Place on jellyroll pan, cover with foil, and bake at 375° for 10 minutes. Yield: 24 appetizers.

Mildred Bickley,
Bristol, Virginia.

CHEESE-BACON CRISPIES

½ cup butter or margarine, softened
2 cups (8 ounces) shredded sharp Cheddar cheese
¼ teaspoon salt
¼ teaspoon dry mustard
1 teaspoon Worcestershire sauce
3 drops of hot sauce
1¼ cups all-purpose flour
10 slices cooked bacon, crumbled

Combine first 6 ingredients in a large mixing bowl; mix well. Stir in flour and bacon. Shape dough into 2 rolls, 1½ inches in diameter; wrap in waxed paper, and chill overnight.

Unwrap rolls, and cut into ¼-inch-thick slices. Place slices on a lightly greased baking sheet; bake at 375° for 8 to 10 minutes or until lightly browned. Cool on wire rack.

To freeze before baking, place unbaked slices on baking sheets in freezer until hard. Remove from baking sheets; store in an airtight container in freezer. To serve, remove from freezer, place on lightly greased baking sheets, and bake at 375° for 10 to 12 minutes or until lightly browned.

To freeze after baking, let wafers cool completely on wire rack. Transfer to an airtight container, and freeze. To serve, thaw wafers at room temperature for 1 hour. Yield: about 3 dozen.

Lynn Bartlett,
Jacksonville, Florida.

ASPARAGUS ROLL-UPS

½ cup butter or margarine, softened
1 tablespoon minced onion
1 tablespoon lemon juice
22 to 24 slices white bread
1 (15-ounce) can asparagus spears, well drained
¼ cup butter or margarine, melted
Black olive slices
Pimiento slices

Combine first 3 ingredients, mixing well; set aside.

Trim crusts from bread; press each slice to ⅛-inch thickness with fingertips or a rolling pin. Spread each slice with a slightly rounded teaspoonful of butter mixture. Place an asparagus spear on each slice with the tip extending over one edge, and roll up tightly; secure with a wooden pick. Brush rolls with melted butter, and place on ungreased baking sheets. Bake at 350° for 30 minutes. Remove picks, and serve warm. Garnish with olives and pimiento.

To freeze, do not brush with melted butter. Place unbaked rolls in an airtight container in freezer. To serve, remove from freezer, brush with melted butter, and bake at 350° for 30 minutes. Yield: about 2 dozen.

Mrs. John R. Allen,
Dallas, Texas.

A Fresh, New Look For Holiday Flowers

Southerners love parties, but never so much as during the holidays. And most of these occasions call for flowers. Following are several arrangement ideas that may help to update traditional designs with a contemporary flair.

Mix spring flowers with those traditionally used during the holidays to give seasonal arrangements a fresh, new look. Dutch iris, lilies, and alstroemeria are popular and always available during the holiday season.

Feature a centerpiece using a glass hat filled with fresh rubrum lilies and miniature carnations. Use florist foam to hold the flowers for this arrangement. Sprigs of ivy and rich, dark begonia leaves complete the arrangement.

A lavish fruit bowl is a holiday tradition, but when it sprouts bare branches and fresh flowers, the look becomes upbeat and new. Use florist foam to support the weight of the arrangement. Wire fruit onto florist picks, and complete the arrangement with white and red gladiolus and miniature carnations.

And what could be more festive than a glass top hat filled with iced champagne and bright-red flowers? An arrangement like this is designed for a party and generally has a short vase life (just a day or two). If you choose to use the champagne bottle as a decorative feature only, then the arrangement can literally use the ice to support the flowers and foliage. However, if you plan to use the champagne for the party, arrange the flowers in florist foam. Be sure to select a bottle shape that can be easily removed.

After placing the champagne and ice in the top hat, create a dramatic line with dried branches of Chinese tallow (also known as popcorn tree). Once this is done, add Burford holly.

Right: *At only 12 calories each, Shrimp Dippers are the perfect accompaniment for Dilled Garden Dip. Offer a bowl of fresh vegetables as another low-calorie dipping choice (recipes on page 324).*

Far left: *Garnished with apricots and hot pepper jelly, Spicy Rib-Eye Beef (page 259) makes a memorable entrée.*

Above left: *Peas Continental and Carrots and Celery With Pecans are appealing vegetable combinations that will complement most any entrée (recipes on page 254).*

Above: *A few butter curls on the side make homemade Crescent Rolls (page 267) even more attractive and elegant.*

Left: *Showy and colorful, Tossed Vegetable Marinade (page 266) goes with many different entrées; artichoke hearts are a surprise ingredient.*

Right: *Although Squash Bisque and Navy Bean Soup are thick and satisfying, each provides less than 160 calories per cup. Serve either with a sandwich or main dish salad for a nutritious cold-weather meal (recipes on page 280).*

Below: *Most of the vegetables in Light Vegetable Soup (page 280) are high in vitamins but low in calories. That's why this soup is excellent for low-calorie diets.*

Top It With A Fruit Sauce

Just 5 to 15 minutes is all it takes to whip up one of these fruit-flavored sauces and turn plain food into a festive treat. Use whole fruit, juice, and rind.

BANANA SUNDAE SAUCE

½ cup butter or margarine, melted
1½ cups sifted powdered sugar
¼ teaspoon ground cinnamon
1 tablespoon water
1 teaspoon lemon juice
1 teaspoon vanilla extract
2 cups sliced bananas

Combine all ingredients except bananas in a medium saucepan; cook over medium heat for 5 minutes or until smooth, stirring occasionally. Stir in bananas. Serve warm over vanilla ice cream or pound cake. Yield: 2 cups.

Kitty Lawson,
Taylorsville, Kentucky.

PINEAPPLE-RUM SAUCE

1 cup firmly packed brown sugar
2 tablespoons cornstarch
1⅓ cups pineapple juice
2 tablespoons butter or margarine
1¼ teaspoons rum flavoring

Combine sugar and cornstarch in a medium saucepan; mix well. Stir in pineapple juice; cook over medium heat, stirring constantly, until thickened. Remove from heat; stir in butter and rum flavoring. Serve warm or chilled over ice cream or pound cake. Yield: 1⅔ cups.

Mrs. Thomas Lee Adams,
Kingsport, Tennessee.

HONEY-LEMON MUSTARD SAUCE

¼ cup butter or margarine
2 tablespoons honey
1 teaspoon grated lemon rind
1 tablespoon plus 1 teaspoon lemon juice
1 teaspoon prepared mustard

Combine all ingredients in a small saucepan. Cook over low heat until thoroughly heated. Serve with vegetables. Yield: about ½ cup.

Mrs. Thomas R. Cherry,
Birmingham, Alabama.

FRESH CRANBERRY SAUCE

4 cups fresh cranberries
2 cups sugar
2 cups water
2 tablespoons grated orange rind

Wash cranberries and drain. Combine cranberries, sugar, and water in a medium saucepan; bring to a boil, and cook 7 to 10 minutes or until cranberry skins pop. Stir in orange rind. Mash berries slightly. Cool. Serve with pork or poultry. Yield: 4 cups.

Marilyn Salinas,
Fort Worth, Texas.

RAISIN SAUCE

½ cup firmly packed brown sugar
1½ tablespoons all-purpose flour
1½ teaspoons dry mustard
1½ cups water
½ cup vinegar
½ cup raisins

Combine first 3 ingredients in a medium saucepan, stirring well. Add remaining ingredients; cook over low heat, stirring constantly, until thickened. Serve warm over pork. Yield: about 2⅓ cups.

Virginia Mathews,
Jacksonville, Florida.

Ever Steamed A Pudding?

For many families, steamed plum puddings are a long-standing holiday tradition. But if you've never made one, we've got two to try—Steamed Holiday Pudding and Flamed Plum Pudding.

Even though numerous ingredients are required, both puddings are simple to prepare. You will probably get better results if a true steamed pudding mold with a locking top is used. However, some readers tell us they often use heat-proof bowls, covered with a double thickness of buttered aluminum foil secured with string.

Plum puddings used to be made with plums, but over the years dried fruits, figs, and prunes have been substituted.

STEAMED HOLIDAY PUDDING

2⅓ cups all-purpose flour
1⅓ cups finely chopped suet
1⅓ cups firmly packed brown sugar
½ teaspoon salt
¼ teaspoon ground cinnamon
¼ teaspoon ground cloves
¼ teaspoon ground ginger
¼ teaspoon ground nutmeg
2 eggs, well beaten
⅔ cup orange juice
⅔ cup water
1⅓ cups chopped raisins
1⅓ cups chopped mixed candied fruit
1⅓ cups currants
⅔ cup finely chopped dried figs
Commercial hard sauce

Combine first 8 ingredients in a large bowl; mix well. Add eggs, orange juice, and water; stir well. Combine raisins, candied fruit, currants, and figs; add to flour mixture, stirring well. Spoon mixture into a greased 1½-quart steamed pudding mold; cover tightly.

Place mold on a shallow rack in a large, deep kettle with enough boiling water to come two-thirds up the mold. Cover kettle; steam pudding about 5 hours in continuously boiling water (replace water as needed). Let pudding stand 5 minutes; unmold and serve with hard sauce. Yield: 10 to 12 servings.

Jeanne Wood,
New Orleans, Louisiana.

FLAMED PLUM PUDDING

½ cup butter, softened
1½ cups firmly packed brown sugar
2 eggs, beaten
1 teaspoon vanilla extract
1 cup scraped, grated carrots
1 cup raisins
1 cup dried figs, chopped
1 cup pecans, chopped
½ cup currants
1 cup all-purpose flour
1 teaspoon baking soda
½ teaspoon salt
1 teaspoon ground cinnamon
1 teaspoon ground ginger
½ teaspoon ground allspice
¼ teaspoon ground nutmeg
1 cup fine, dry breadcrumbs
⅛ cup brandy
⅛ cup sherry
¼ cup plus 2 tablespoons brandy,
    divided

Cream butter, gradually add sugar, beating well. Add eggs and vanilla; beat well. Stir in the next 5 ingredients, mixing well. Combine flour, soda, salt, and spices; add to creamed mixture. Stir in breadcrumbs, ⅛ cup brandy, and sherry. Stir until all ingredients are combined.

Spoon mixture into a well-greased 1½-quart steamed pudding mold; cover mold tightly.

Place mold on a shallow rack in a large, deep kettle with enough boiling water to come halfway up mold. Cover kettle; steam pudding 3 hours in continuously boiling water (replace water as needed).

Let pudding stand 5 minutes; unmold onto serving plate. Pour 2 tablespoons brandy over hot pudding. Heat remaining ¼ cup brandy in a small saucepan to produce fumes (do not boil); ignite and pour over pudding. Chill overnight. Yield: 10 to 12 servings.

Aline C. Poythress,
Port Republic, Virginia.

Tip: Keep staples such as sugar, flour, and spices in tightly covered containers at room temperature. Staples that are frequently replenished should be rotated so that the oldest is always used first.

COOKING LIGHT

Feast On These Light Entrées

If you're on a low-sodium or low-calorie diet, you may be disheartened at the idea of planning a special dinner for the holidays. The first question you'll probably face is "What do I serve for the entrée?" Don't despair. Here's a collection of outstanding entrées—some low in calories, others low in sodium, but all suited for a company dinner.

VEAL SPAGHETTI

2 medium-size green peppers, cut into
    strips
1 tablespoon vegetable oil
1 pound veal cutlets or boneless steaks,
    cut into bite-size pieces
Pepper
1 (14½-ounce) can low-sodium whole
    tomatoes, undrained
¼ pound fresh mushrooms, sliced
¼ cup dry red wine
1 small clove garlic, crushed
2 cups hot cooked spaghetti (no salt
    added)

Sauté green pepper in oil in a heavy skillet until tender; remove from skillet, and set aside.

Season veal with pepper; place in skillet. Cook over medium heat until lightly browned on both sides. Add green pepper and remaining ingredients except spaghetti. Simmer, uncovered, 1 hour or until veal is tender. Serve over hot cooked spaghetti. Yield: 4 servings (about 342 calories and 100 milligrams sodium per serving).

ROAST LOIN OF PORK

1 cup dry red wine
1 clove garlic, crushed
¼ teaspoon dried whole rosemary, crushed
¼ teaspoon dried whole dillweed
5 pounds lean center loin pork roast
1 clove garlic, cut in half
Freshly ground pepper

Combine first 4 ingredients; set aside. Trim excess fat from roast; rub with garlic and pepper. Place roast on rack of a roasting pan; insert meat thermometer, being careful not to touch fat or bone. Baste with about one-sixth of wine mixture. Cover with foil, and bake at 325° about 30 to 35 minutes per pound or until meat thermometer registers 170°, basting every 20 to 30 minutes with remaining wine mixture. Yield: 10 servings (about 235 calories and 66 milligrams sodium per 3-ounce serving).

Lois Schlatter,
Rochester, Michigan.

MARINATED SHRIMP KABOBS

1 pound large fresh shrimp
1 (8-ounce) can unsweetened
    pineapple chunks, undrained
2 tablespoons sesame oil
2 tablespoons soy sauce
¼ teaspoon white pepper
⅛ teaspoon garlic powder
⅛ teaspoon ground ginger
6 pearl onions
6 cherry tomatoes
1 green pepper, cut into 1-inch
    pieces
Hot cooked rice (optional)

Peel shrimp, leaving tails on; devein shrimp. Set aside.

Drain pineapple, reserving juice; set pineapple aside. Combine reserved pineapple juice and next 5 ingredients in a shallow dish; mix well. Add shrimp, tossing gently to coat. Cover and marinate at least 1 hour in the refrigerator, stirring occasionally.

Cook onions in boiling water to cover 4 to 5 minutes or just until crisp-tender, and drain.

Remove shrimp from marinade, reserving marinade. Alternate vegetables, pineapple, and shrimp on 6 skewers. Broil 4 to 5 inches from heat 2 to 3 minutes on each side or until shrimp are done, basting frequently with marinade. Serve over hot cooked rice, if desired. Yield: 6 servings (about 158 calories and 437 milligrams sodium per serving without rice).

Joe Maugans,
Birmingham, Alabama.

DIJON LAMB CHOPS

4 lamb chops (about 1½ pounds)
1 lemon, cut in half
Garlic powder
Freshly ground pepper
1 cup chopped fresh parsley
⅓ cup Dijon mustard
1 tablespoon plus 1 teaspoon wheat
    bran
Vegetable cooking spray
Lemon slices (optional)
Lime slices (optional)

Trim fat from lamb chops. Rub both sides with lemon; sprinkle lightly with garlic powder and pepper.

Combine next 3 ingredients; mix well, and press on all sides of chops. Place chops in a 12- x 8- x 2-inch baking dish coated with cooking spray; insert meat thermometer into one chop, being careful not to touch fat or bone. Bake, uncovered, at 500° for 4 minutes. Reduce heat to 350°, and bake an additional 15 minutes or until thermometer registers 180°. Garnish with lemon and lime slices, if desired. Yield: 4 servings (about 177 calories and 575 milligrams sodium per serving).
Patra Collins Sullivan,
Columbia, South Carolina.

BAKED CHICKEN WITH WINE-SOAKED VEGETABLES

1 tablespoon chopped onion
¼ cup diced carrots
¼ cup diced yellow squash
¼ cup sliced mushrooms
¼ cup English peas
2 tablespoons diced celery
1 tablespoon chopped fresh parsley
½ cup Chablis or other dry white wine
1 (3½-pound) broiler-fryer, skinned
½ cup unsalted margarine, melted
¼ cup lemon juice
½ teaspoon paprika

Combine first 7 ingredients in a small bowl. Pour wine over vegetables, and toss lightly. Set aside.

Remove giblets and neck from chicken; reserve for other uses. Rinse chicken with cold water; pat dry.

Stuff vegetable mixture into cavity of chicken, and close cavity with skewers.

Keep calories low in your holiday dinner by planning the menu around Dijon Lamb Chops.

Tie leg ends together with string or cord; tuck wing tips under bird securely.

Combine margarine, lemon juice, and paprika. Brush entire bird with mixture; place chicken, breast side up, on a rack in roasting pan. Bake at 375° for 1¼ to 1½ hours or until drumsticks move up and down easily; baste often with remaining margarine mixture. Yield: 6 servings (about 310 calories and 92 milligrams sodium per serving).
Mrs. James L. Stellhorn,
Oviedo, Florida.

CHICKEN A L'ORANGE

1 orange
6 chicken breast halves (about 3 pounds),
    skinned and boned
½ teaspoon paprika
¼ cup reduced-calorie margarine
1 cup unsweetened orange juice
1 teaspoon dried whole tarragon
1 teaspoon cornstarch
1 tablespoon water
2 tablespoons slivered almonds,
    toasted

Peel orange, and cut the rind into thin strips; set aside. Reserve orange for other uses.

Sprinkle chicken with paprika; sauté chicken in margarine 2 minutes on each side or until lightly browned. Transfer to a 13- x 9- x 2-inch baking dish; add orange juice, tarragon, and orange rind strips. Cover and bake at 350° for 25 minutes or until done. Remove chicken; set aside, and keep warm.

Pour orange juice mixture into a small saucepan. Combine cornstarch and water, stirring until blended; add to orange juice mixture. Cook, stirring constantly, until mixture comes to a boil; cook 1 minute, stirring constantly. Sprinkle chicken with almonds; serve with sauce. Yield: 6 servings (about 207 calories and 177 milligrams sodium per serving).
Beth R. McClain,
Grand Prairie, Texas.

Tip: Freeze small portions of leftover meat or fowl till you have enough for a pot pie, curry, or rice casserole.

Weave A Holiday Bread

One look at Sweet Christmas Loaf will tell you it was meant for the holidays. Sweet yeast bread is wrapped around a spicy fruit filling and topped with a powdered-sugar glaze. A garnish of almond slices and candied cherries offers a wonderful touch.

SWEET CHRISTMAS LOAF

1 package dry yeast
¾ cup warm water (105° to 115°), divided
¼ cup butter or margarine, melted
1 egg, beaten
¼ cup sugar
½ teaspoon salt
3 to 3½ cups all-purpose flour
¼ cup chopped pecans
2 tablespoons raisins
2 tablespoons chopped candied citron
2 tablespoons butter or margarine, melted
2 tablespoons sugar
1½ teaspoons ground cinnamon
1 egg white
1 tablespoon water
1 cup sifted powdered sugar
1½ tablespoons milk
½ teaspoon vegetable oil
½ teaspoon vanilla extract
¼ teaspoon almond extract
Candied cherries
Sliced almonds, toasted

Dissolve yeast in ¼ cup warm water. Combine remaining ½ cup water, butter, egg, ¼ cup sugar, and salt in a large bowl. Add yeast mixture, stirring well. Gradually add 1 cup flour; beat at medium speed of electric mixer 2 minutes. Stir in enough remaining flour to make a soft dough.

Turn dough out onto a floured surface, and let rest 10 minutes. Knead 8 to 10 minutes or until smooth and elastic. Place dough in a well-greased bowl,

turning to grease top. Cover and let rise in a warm place (85°), free from drafts, 1 hour or until doubled in bulk.

Punch dough down; turn out on a lightly floured surface. Roll into a 10- x 14-inch rectangle, and place on a lightly greased baking sheet. Combine next 6 ingredients; spread filling down the center of the rectangle, leaving a 1-inch margin at each end. Using kitchen shears, make 3-inch diagonal cuts 1 inch apart on each long side of rectangle.

Starting at one end, bring corresponding dough strips to center at an angle; overlap opposite sides. Fold next set of dough strips so that they cover the overlap of first folded strips. Repeat with remaining strips, alternating top strip to resemble braiding. Fold end of rectangle up and tuck under. (One end will be left open with filling showing.) Cover and let rise in a warm place (85°), free from drafts, for 1 hour or until doubled.

Combine egg white and 1 tablespoon water; brush over loaf. Bake at 375° for 18 to 20 minutes or until golden brown. Remove from baking sheet, and place on wire rack to cool.

Combine powdered sugar, milk, oil, and flavorings; drizzle over bread while bread is warm. Garnish with candied cherries and almonds. Yield: 1 loaf.

Susie Dent,
Saltillo, Mississippi.

Votive Lights For Holiday Nights

There's nothing quite like candlelight to set the mood for holiday entertaining. And using tiny votive candles instead of long tapers opens up a whole new range of decorating possibilities.

Easy to find and inexpensive, votive candles are dramatic in a grouping—or you can use them alone to call subtle attention to a certain spot.

A number of holders are available for votive candles. Use your imagination to come up with different kinds of glassware and other odds and ends to use as containers.

This lacy basket is made from a doily and holds a small candle. Potpourri and baby's-breath are sprinkled around the outside for a delicate addition.

If you're using glassware, the heat of the candles shouldn't harm the glass, even if the flames briefly touch the sides. Pouring a small amount of water in the glass first lessens the chance of breakage and makes the wax easier to remove later. If the wax sticks to the glass, a little hot water will release it.

Place a single votive candle in a lace basket to keep it from getting lost in a room. Make a lace basket from an 8-inch-diameter paper doily molded around the candle container. To shape the doily, dip it into a solution of white glue diluted with water to the consistency of cream. Center it on the container (turned upside down) and arrange in loose, even folds. (Spread a light coat of petroleum jelly or cooking oil on the glass to keep the glue from sticking to it.) Elevate the container slightly to keep the edges of the doily from dragging. Let dry overnight.

Votive candles are also good to use with cut greenery. The container keeps the flame away from leaves and branches and holds the wax as it runs down the sides. (This gives votive candles a longer burning life, too.)

When you replace a votive candle, remove the piece of metal that held the previous wick. If you don't, it will get hot and could break the container.

To prolong the life of any candle, wrap it in plastic, and store it in the refrigerator the day before it is used. (Make sure it's wrapped; this keeps the wick from absorbing moisture.)

Set The Mood With Soup

These elegant soups will set the tone for festive food to follow. Each creamy spoonful is filled with vegetables or seafood. You'll find they offer a refreshing contrast to main courses and add color to your meals.

QUICK CRAB SOUP

1 medium onion, finely chopped
2 tablespoons butter or margarine
1 tablespoon all-purpose flour
2 cups water
1 (6-ounce) package frozen crabmeat, thawed and drained
¼ cup finely chopped celery
2 tablespoons chopped fresh parsley
½ teaspoon salt
¼ teaspoon pepper
⅛ teaspoon hot sauce
3 cups milk

Sauté onion in butter in a heavy skillet until tender; add flour, stirring until smooth. Cook 1 minute, stirring constantly. Gradually add water; cook over medium heat, stirring constantly, until mixture is thickened and bubbly.

Add remaining ingredients, stirring well. Cook mixture over low heat, stirring constantly, just until thoroughly heated. Serve soup immediately. Yield: about 1½ quarts.

Mrs. C. Robert Bauer,
Charlottesville, Virginia.

CELERY-AND-POTATO SOUP

4 cups chopped celery
1 cup chopped onion
½ cup butter or margarine
1 clove garlic, minced
1¼ cups peeled, diced potatoes
¼ cup chopped fresh parsley
4 cups chicken broth
½ teaspoon Beau Monde seasoning
¼ teaspoon white pepper

Sauté celery and onion in butter in a Dutch oven for 5 minutes or until tender. Add garlic, and sauté an additional minute. Stir in potatoes, parsley, and broth. Bring to a boil; cover, reduce heat, and simmer 20 minutes or until the potatoes are tender.

Pour half of celery mixture into container of electric blender; process 45 seconds. Repeat with remaining celery mixture. Stir in seasonings. Serve immediately. Yield: 7 cups. *Vivian Gregory,*
Naples, Florida.

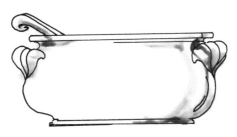

FRESH CAULIFLOWER SOUP

2½ cups water
½ teaspoon salt
2 tablespoons lemon juice
1 medium head cauliflower, quartered
2 tablespoons butter or margarine
2 tablespoons all-purpose flour
3 cups half-and-half
1 bay leaf
½ teaspoon dried whole thyme
½ teaspoon white pepper
2 tablespoons chopped fresh parsley

Combine water, salt, and lemon juice in a large saucepan; bring to a boil. Add cauliflower; cover and cook 10 to 15 minutes or until tender.

Drain cauliflower, reserving liquid; break into flowerets, and set aside.

Melt butter in a heavy saucepan over low heat; add flour, stirring until smooth. Cook 1 minute, stirring constantly. Gradually add reserved cauliflower liquid; cook over medium heat, stirring constantly, until thickened and bubbly.

Stir in half-and-half, bay leaf, thyme, and pepper. Cook over low heat, stirring occasionally, 5 to 10 minutes or until thickened. Add cauliflower, and cook 5 minutes or just until thoroughly heated. Remove and discard bay leaf. Sprinkle each serving with chopped fresh parsley. Yield: about 7 cups.
Ruth Horomanski,
Satellite Beach, Florida.

CREAMY TURNIP SOUP

4 cups peeled and thinly sliced turnips
2 medium onions, sliced
1 large carrot, sliced
1 stalk celery, chopped
1½ teaspoons salt
1 teaspoon sugar
⅛ teaspoon pepper
1 cup water
3 cups milk
1 cup half-and-half

Combine first 8 ingredients in a Dutch oven. Bring to a boil; reduce heat and simmer 15 to 20 minutes or until vegetables are tender. Spoon vegetable mixture into container of electric blender; process until smooth.

Return vegetable mixture to Dutch oven; stir in milk and half-and-half. Cook over low heat, stirring constantly, just until thoroughly heated. Serve immediately. Yield: 6 cups. *Joe Whitten,*
Odenville, Alabama.

Tip: Remember that deep green, yellow, and orange fruits and vegetables are good sources of vitamin A. Sources of vitamin C are citrus fruits, deep green vegetables, and potatoes.

COOKING LIGHT

Ladle Up A Light Soup

On a cool evening, nothing satisfies quite like a steaming bowl of soup or stew. But all too often extra fat and calories are part of those hearty mixtures. Protect your low-calorie diet and still enjoy soups and stews by choosing low-fat ingredients and following low-fat methods of cooking.

Fatty ham bones, beef bones, or stew meat are common ingredients in many soups and stews. Add a half cup of chopped lean ham to Navy Bean Soup to get a meaty flavor without excess calories from fat.

Another way to capture the flavor of ham at a minimal cost of calories is to make a stock by cooking ham bones or ham hock in boiling water for 40 to 50 minutes. Discard the bones, and refrigerate the broth—the dispersed fat will harden and float to the top. You'll throw away 100 calories with every tablespoon of hardened fat you remove. You can do the same with beef and poultry bones, as well.

SEAFOOD STEW

Vegetable cooking spray
1 teaspoon vegetable oil
¼ cup chopped green pepper
2 tablespoons chopped onion
1 clove garlic, minced
1 (16-ounce) can tomatoes, undrained
1 (8-ounce) can tomato sauce
½ cup Burgundy or other dry red wine
3 tablespoons chopped fresh parsley
¼ teaspoon salt
¼ teaspoon dried whole oregano
¼ teaspoon dried whole basil
Dash of pepper
1 (16-ounce) package frozen perch fillets
1 (4½-ounce) can shrimp, rinsed and drained
1 (6½-ounce) can minced clams, undrained

Coat a Dutch oven with cooking spray; add oil, and place over medium heat until hot. Add green pepper, onion, and garlic; sauté until tender. Add next 8 ingredients; bring mixture to a boil. Cover, reduce heat, and simmer 20 minutes.

Cook perch according to package directions; cut into small pieces. Add perch, shrimp, and clams to tomato mixture; cover and simmer an additional 3 minutes. Yield: 6 cups (about 149 calories per 1-cup serving).
Clarine Spetzler,
Salem, Virginia.

LIGHT VEGETABLE SOUP

1 (46-ounce) can vegetable cocktail juice
1 (12-ounce) can carrot juice
2 medium potatoes, peeled and diced
1 medium onion, chopped
3 stalks celery, sliced
1 cup broccoli flowerets
1 cup cauliflower flowerets
2 medium zucchini, sliced
1 cup sliced fresh mushrooms
2 carrots, scraped and sliced
½ teaspoon pepper
4 cups torn spinach

Combine first 11 ingredients in a large Dutch oven. Bring to a boil; cover, reduce heat, and simmer 20 minutes or until vegetables are tender. Add spinach, and simmer an additional 5 minutes. Yield: about 3½ quarts (about 64 calories per 1-cup serving).
Deborah Neydon,
New Iberia, Louisiana.

NAVY BEAN SOUP

1 cup dried navy beans
5 cups water
½ cup chopped celery
½ cup chopped onion
½ cup chopped carrot
1 tablespoon chopped fresh parsley
1 chicken-flavored bouillon cube
½ cup diced lean cooked ham
1 bay leaf
1 tablespoon catsup
1 teaspoon Worcestershire sauce
½ teaspoon dried whole basil
½ teaspoon dried whole oregano
Grated Romano cheese (optional)

Sort and wash beans; place in a large Dutch oven. Cover with water 2 inches above beans; let soak overnight. Drain beans; combine beans, 5 cups water, celery, onion, carrot, parsley, and bouillon cube; bring to a boil. Cover, reduce heat, and simmer 45 minutes.

Add next 6 ingredients; cover and simmer an additional 30 minutes. Remove bay leaf. Sprinkle each serving with Romano cheese, if desired. Yield: about 6 cups (about 155 calories per 1-cup serving plus 21 calories per tablespoon grated Romano cheese).
Martha McKenna,
Paducah, Kentucky.

SQUASH BISQUE

1 small butternut squash (about 1 pound), peeled, seeded, and sliced
1 stalk celery, sliced
1 medium apple, peeled and sliced
1 small potato, peeled and sliced
1 small onion, sliced
1 medium carrot, scraped and sliced
¼ teaspoon dried whole oregano
¼ teaspoon dried whole rosemary
1 (14½-ounce) can chicken broth, undiluted
¾ cup skim milk

Combine first 9 ingredients in a large Dutch oven; cover and simmer 20 to 30 minutes or until vegetables are tender.

Spoon half of vegetable mixture into container of electric blender, and process until smooth. Repeat procedure with remaining vegetable mixture. Return pureed mixture to Dutch oven; stir in skim milk. Cook over low heat, stirring constantly, until mixture is thoroughly heated. Yield: 4 cups (about 126 calories per serving). *Cynda A. Spoon,*
Broken Arrow, Oklahoma.

VEGETARIAN CHILI

1 (16-ounce) package dried kidney beans
7 cups water, divided
1 cup tomato juice
1 cup bulgur or cracked wheat
Vegetable cooking spray
2 cloves garlic, crushed
1½ cups chopped onion
2 cups chopped tomatoes
2 cups water
1 cup chopped carrot
1 cup chopped celery
1 cup chopped green pepper
1 (6-ounce) can tomato paste
½ cup dry red wine
2 tablespoons lemon juice
1½ teaspoons ground cumin
1½ teaspoons chili powder
1 teaspoon dried whole basil
¼ to ½ teaspoon salt
¼ teaspoon pepper

Sort and wash beans. Place beans and 3 cups water in a large Dutch oven; bring to a boil, and cook 3 minutes. Remove from heat; cover and let soak 1 hour. Add remaining 4 cups water; bring to a boil. Cover, reduce heat, and simmer 1 hour. Set aside.

Bring tomato juice to a boil; pour over bulgur. Stir well, and set aside.

Coat a medium Dutch oven with cooking spray; place over medium heat until hot. Add garlic and onion; sauté until onion is tender. Add remaining ingredients; cover and simmer 15 to 20 minutes. Add vegetable mixture and bulgur mixture to beans. Cook until thoroughly heated. Yield: about 3 quarts (about 223 calories per 1-cup serving).

Gwen Louer,
Roswell, Georgia.

Wholesome Grains Fit Any Meal

We're all familiar with cereals and grains at breakfast and appreciate their nutritional value, but you can benefit from these foods at other meals, too.

BARLEY CASSEROLE

1 cup pearl barley
¼ cup butter or margarine
1 (1⅜-ounce) envelope onion soup mix
2⅔ cups water
1 (4-ounce) can sliced mushrooms, drained

Sauté barley in butter in a medium skillet over medium heat, stirring constantly, until barley is browned. Remove from heat; stir in soup mix and water. Pour into a lightly greased 1½-quart casserole. Bake, uncovered, at 350° for 1 hour or until liquid is absorbed. Add mushrooms; bake an additional 15 minutes. Yield: 6 servings.

Velma Bryant,
Johnson City, Tennessee.

WALDORF RICE

½ cup chopped onion
2 tablespoons butter or margarine
2 cups apple juice
⅓ cup water
½ teaspoon salt
1 cup uncooked regular rice
2 medium apples, chopped
1 cup sliced celery
½ cup coarsely chopped walnuts
½ teaspoon rum extract

Sauté onion in butter in a Dutch oven until tender. Add apple juice, water, and salt; bring to a boil. Stir in rice; cover, reduce heat, and simmer 20 minutes. Add remaining ingredients; remove from heat, and let stand 5 minutes. Yield: 6 to 8 servings.

Gwen Louer,
Roswell, Georgia.

GRITS 'N GREENS DINNER BAKE

4 cups water
½ teaspoon salt
1 cup uncooked regular grits
1 (10-ounce) package frozen chopped spinach, thawed and well drained
2 cups (8 ounces) shredded Swiss cheese
1½ cups chopped cooked ham
2 eggs, beaten
1 tablespoon prepared mustard
¼ cup grated Parmesan cheese

Bring water and salt to a boil in a large saucepan; gradually add grits, stirring constantly. Cover, reduce heat, and cook 5 minutes. Add spinach, Swiss cheese, and ham, stirring until cheese melts. Stir in eggs and mustard. Pour into a lightly greased 8-inch square baking dish. Sprinkle with grated Parmesan cheese. Bake at 325° for 45 minutes or until a knife inserted in the center comes out clean. Yield: 6 servings.

Sherry Hilliard,
Rhine, Georgia.

Invite Company For Sandwiches

Getting tired of typical sandwiches? Then give them extra flavor by using a different filling, topping, or bread. You'll find these suggestions are special enough for company.

BIG WHEEL LOAF

1 (8-inch) round loaf sourdough bread
2 teaspoons prepared horseradish
¼ pound thinly sliced roast beef
2 tablespoons mayonnaise
4 (1-ounce) slices Swiss cheese
2 tablespoons prepared mustard
¼ pound thinly sliced fully cooked ham
1 medium tomato, thinly sliced
4 slices bacon, cooked and drained
4 (1-ounce) slices American cheese
½ medium-size red onion, thinly sliced
¼ cup butter or margarine, softened
1 tablespoon sesame seeds, toasted
½ teaspoon onion salt

Slice bread horizontally into 6 equal layers using an electric or serrated knife. Spread first layer with horseradish, and top with roast beef and second bread layer. Spread second layer with mayonnaise, and top with Swiss cheese and third bread layer. Spread mustard

over third layer, and top with ham and fourth bread layer. Cover fourth layer with tomato slices, bacon, and fifth bread layer. Top fifth bread layer with American cheese, onion, and remaining bread layer.

Combine remaining ingredients in a small mixing bowl; spread over top and sides of loaf. Place loaf on a baking sheet; bake, uncovered, at 400° for 15 to 20 minutes. Slice into wedges with an electric knife. Yield: 8 servings.

Mary Lou Vaughn,
Dallas, Texas.

NEPTUNE HEROES

3 tablespoons mayonnaise
2 tablespoons drained sweet pickle relish
2 teaspoons prepared mustard
¼ teaspoon dried whole dillweed
2 (8-ounce) packages frozen fish portions
4 French rolls, split lengthwise
1 large tomato, thinly sliced
2 cups shredded lettuce

Combine first 4 ingredients; mix well, and set aside. Cook fish portions according to package directions. Place one fish portion on bottom half of each roll. Top with tomato slices, lettuce, and a heaping tablespoonful of mayonnaise mixture. Cover with roll tops, and serve immediately. Yield: 4 servings.

Ruth G. Newman,
Galax, Virginia.

HOT TUNA SALAD ROLLS

1 (12-ounce) can tuna, drained and flaked
1 cup chopped celery
1 cup frozen English peas, thawed and drained
1 cup (4 ounces) shredded Swiss cheese
¾ cup mayonnaise
¼ cup chopped fresh parsley
6 hoagie rolls
¼ cup butter or margarine, melted
1 lemon, cut into 6 wedges (optional)
12 pimiento-stuffed olives (optional)

Combine first 6 ingredients; mix well.
Cut a thin slice from top of each roll; set tops aside. Hollow out roll bottoms, leaving a thick shell. Brush inside of roll bottoms with butter; fill with tuna mixture, and cover with roll tops. Wrap each roll separately in aluminum foil. Bake at 400° for 15 minutes. Remove foil, and secure each sandwich with a wooden pick skewered with a lemon wedge and 2 olives, if desired. Yield: 6 servings.

Alberta Pinkston,
Corryton, Tennessee.

SOUTH SEAS CLUB SANDWICH

3 cups water
¾ pound medium shrimp, unpeeled
1 (8¾-ounce) can pineapple tidbits,
    drained
½ cup chopped celery
2 tablespoons finely chopped green
    onions
2 tablespoons mayonnaise
8 slices whole wheat bread, toasted
    and buttered
4 slices white bread, toasted and buttered
8 slices bacon, cooked and drained
8 slices tomato

Bring water to a boil; add shrimp, and return to a boil. Reduce heat and simmer 3 to 5 minutes. Drain well; rinse with cold water. Chill. Peel, devein, and coarsely chop shrimp.

Combine chopped shrimp and next 4 ingredients; toss lightly. Spread shrimp mixture on 4 slices whole wheat toast; top with white toast. Place 2 slices of bacon and 2 slices of tomato on each. Top with remaining toast. Secure sandwiches with wooden picks; cut into triangles to serve. Yield: 4 servings.

Doris Garton,
Shenandoah, Virginia.

Tidewater Cook Has A Cajun Flair

Chuck Spacek's favorite food to prepare is whatever specialties are native to the area in which he's living. Since his engineering job demands frequent moves, Chuck says this has helped him add to his repertoire. Of course, he carries all his favorites with him wherever he goes. His recipe for Jambalaya is an example. Now that he's settled in Portsmouth, Virginia, Chuck still yearns for the taste of the Cajun specialty he learned to love when he lived in Baton Rouge. Chuck says he enjoys Cajun food so much that he even tries to add the hot, spicy flavor to his other recipes.

Moving to the Virginia Tidewater area turned Chuck's attention to seafood. After learning the local specialties, he experimented with a recipe for Bluefish Chowder.

Frequenting the local restaurants with his wife, Dianne, helps Chuck decide what new regional recipes he wants to try. He suggests skipping the main restaurants and heading to the lesser-known ones.

Below you'll find some of the regional recipes Chuck lists as his favorites. We've also included recipes from other Southern men who love to cook.

STUFFED CABBAGE

½ cup uncooked regular rice
½ pound ground beef
½ pound bulk pork sausage
1 medium onion, chopped
1 egg, slightly beaten
1 tablespoon Worcestershire sauce
¼ teaspoon salt
¼ teaspoon pepper
½ teaspoon dried whole thyme
¼ teaspoon dried whole oregano
¼ teaspoon dried whole tarragon
¼ teaspoon garlic powder
16 large cabbage leaves
2 (10½-ounce) cans tomato soup, undiluted
1 (6-ounce) can tomato paste
2 bay leaves

Cook rice according to package directions. Combine rice and next 11 ingredients, mixing well; cook over medium heat in skillet until meat is brown and onion is tender. Set aside.

Cook cabbage leaves in boiling salted water 5 to 8 minutes or until just tender; drain. Place 3 tablespoons of meat mixture in center of each cabbage leaf; fold sides over meat mixture, and roll ends over, forming a rectangular roll. Fasten the cabbage rolls with wooden picks. Set aside.

Combine tomato soup, tomato paste, and bay leaves in a Dutch oven, stirring well. Bring to a boil over medium heat. Reduce heat to low; place cabbage rolls in tomato mixture, spooning mixture over rolls. Cover and simmer 1½ to 2 hours. Remove bay leaves from mixture. Yield: 8 servings.

BLUEFISH CHOWDER

3 slices bacon, cut into 1-inch pieces
2 medium onions, chopped
1 pound bluefish fillets, cut into 1-inch
    pieces
2 large potatoes, peeled and cubed
1 cup chopped celery
3 cups water
2 tablespoons chopped fresh parsley
1½ teaspoons salt
¼ teaspoon pepper
¾ teaspoon dried whole tarragon
½ teaspoon dried whole basil
½ teaspoon dried whole rosemary, crushed
3 tablespoons butter or margarine
3 tablespoons all-purpose flour
1 (13-ounce) can evaporated milk

Partially cook bacon in a large Dutch oven over medium heat until slightly browned; add onion, and cook until onion is tender and bacon is crisp. Add bluefish and cook, stirring occasionally, 4 to 5 minutes or until fish begins to brown. Add next 9 ingredients, and simmer 20 minutes or until potatoes are tender.

Melt 3 tablespoons butter in a heavy saucepan over low heat; add flour, stirring until smooth. Cook 1 minute, stirring constantly. Gradually add milk; cook over medium heat, stirring constantly, until thickened and bubbly.

Stir white sauce into fish mixture; simmer, stirring occasionally, for 20 minutes or until thickened. Yield: about 9 cups.

JAMBALAYA

3 tablespoons bacon drippings
3 tablespoons all-purpose flour
2 medium onions, chopped
1 bunch green onions, chopped
2 tablespoons minced fresh parsley
1 clove garlic, minced
½ pound boneless lean pork, cubed
½ pound boneless chicken breasts, cubed
6 to 8 chicken wings
½ pound mild Italian sausage links, cut
    into bite-size pieces
3 to 4 tablespoons bacon drippings
5 cups water
2 cups uncooked regular rice
1 teaspoon salt
¼ to ½ teaspoon red pepper
¼ to ½ teaspoon black pepper
Fresh parsley sprigs

Combine 3 tablespoons bacon drippings and flour in a large Dutch oven; cook over medium heat, stirring constantly, 10 minutes or until roux is the color of a copper penny. Stir in onions, parsley, and garlic. Cook 10 to 15 minutes or until onions are tender, stirring mixture occasionally.

Cook pork, chicken, and sausage in 3 to 4 tablespoons bacon drippings until brown. Add meat and next 5 ingredients to vegetable mixture; bring to a boil. Cover and simmer over low heat 25 to 30 minutes. Remove chicken wings, and transfer rice mixture to platter. Arrange chicken wings around rice mixture; garnish with parsley. Yield: 8 servings.

Tip: If soups, stews, or other foods are too salty, add 1 teaspoon of vinegar, 1 teaspoon of sugar, and reheat.

GOLDEN BROCCOLI SOUFFLE

5 cups finely chopped fresh broccoli
   (about 1½ pounds)
⅓ cup butter or margarine
½ cup all-purpose flour
2 cups milk
2 cups (8 ounces) shredded Cheddar
   cheese
8 eggs, separated
½ teaspoon salt
1 teaspoon chili powder
Dash of black pepper
Dash of red pepper

Cut a piece of aluminum foil long enough to fit around a 2-quart soufflé dish, allowing a 1-inch overlap; fold foil lengthwise into thirds. Lightly oil one side of foil and bottom of dish; wrap foil around dish, oiled side against dish, allowing it to extend 3 inches above rim to form a collar. Secure foil with string.

Cook broccoli, covered, in a small amount of boiling water 8 to 10 minutes or until crisp-tender; drain well, and set aside.

Melt butter in a heavy saucepan over low heat; add flour, stirring until smooth. Cook 1 minute, stirring constantly. Gradually add milk; cook over medium heat, stirring constantly, until thickened and bubbly. Add cheese; stir until melted.

Beat egg yolks until thick and lemon colored. Gradually stir about one-fourth of hot mixture into yolks; add to remaining hot mixture, stirring constantly. Stir in reserved broccoli, salt, chili powder, and pepper.

Beat egg whites (at room temperature) until stiff but not dry. Gently fold into broccoli mixture. Spoon into prepared soufflé dish. Bake at 425° for 10 minutes. Reduce oven temperature to 400° and bake 30 to 35 minutes or until puffed and golden. Yield: 8 servings.
Craig R. McNees,
Sarasota, Florida.

ONION-FRENCH DRESSING

½ cup sugar
½ cup cider vinegar
½ cup vegetable oil
2 tablespoons catsup
1 tablespoon lemon juice
1 teaspoon paprika
½ teaspoon salt
1 medium onion, minced

Combine all ingredients except onion in container of electric blender; blend until smooth. Stir in onion. Chill. Yield: 1⅔ cups.
David L. Nickel,
Irvington, Virginia.

SPEEDY GREEN BEAN SALAD

2 (9-ounce) packages frozen cut green
   beans
1 cup cauliflower flowerets
½ cup French dressing
8 slices bacon, cooked and crumbled

Cook green beans according to package directions; drain and cool. Add cauliflower and French dressing; chill well. Sprinkle with bacon just before serving. Yield: 8 servings.
Jeff Leonard,
Manassas, Virginia.

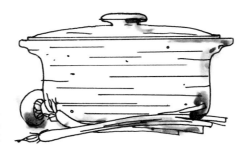

Traditional Dressings Take On New Flavor

Dressing for the holiday turkey is usually as traditional as the season. But the recipe used can be as creative as the cook who prepares it. Whether you prefer to stuff the bird or cook the dressing separately as a side dish, you're sure to enjoy these variations.

WHOLE WHEAT-MUSHROOM DRESSING

2 tablespoons butter or margarine
⅓ cup dry white wine
1 pound small fresh mushrooms, halved
⅓ cup chopped green onions
2¼ cups whole wheat bread cubes, toasted
½ cup slivered almonds, toasted
¼ to ½ teaspoon salt
½ teaspoon dried whole thyme
¼ teaspoon dried whole marjoram
¼ to ½ cup chicken broth (optional)

Combine butter, wine, mushrooms, and green onions in a medium saucepan; cook over low heat 10 minutes or until mushrooms are tender.

Add next 5 ingredients to mushroom mixture, stirring well. Add chicken broth, if desired, for a moister consistency. Stuff turkey lightly with dressing, or spoon dressing into a lightly greased 1-quart casserole. Bake at 325° for 25 to 30 minutes. Yield: 4 to 6 servings.
Peggy Fowler Revels,
Woodruff, South Carolina.

SAGE-CORNBREAD DRESSING

3 cups crumbled cornbread
2 cups coarsely crumbled day-old bread
2 cups chicken broth
2 hard-cooked eggs, chopped
2 large onions, finely chopped
1 cup finely chopped celery
½ cup butter or margarine, melted
1 tablespoon dried whole sage, crushed

Combine all ingredients; stir well. Spoon mixture into a lightly greased 13- x 9- x 2-inch baking dish. Bake, uncovered, at 325° for 1 hour or until golden brown. Yield: 8 to 10 servings.
Lana W. Fuller,
Martinsville, Virginia.

These Breads Are Easy

Following are some ways our readers have dressed up convenience breads. Twist refrigerator roll dough and sesame seeds for fancy Sesame Bread Twists, or take a short cut with biscuit mix and mincemeat for a coffee cake.

SESAME BREAD TWISTS

1 (8-ounce) can refrigerator crescent
   dinner rolls
1 egg
⅓ cup sesame seeds

Unroll dough and separate into 4 rectangles. Press 2 rectangles together end to end, making 1 long rectangle. Cut each long rectangle lengthwise into 6 strips.

Beat egg slightly with a fork in a pie-plate; set aside. Sprinkle sesame seeds onto a 15- x 12-inch piece of waxed paper. Twist each strip of dough several times; dip in egg, and roll in sesame seeds. Place each strip, 1 inch apart, on a greased baking sheet. Repeat procedure with remaining ingredients. Bake at 400° for 8 to 10 minutes or until golden brown. Yield: 1 dozen.
Cheryl Knight,
Greensboro, North Carolina.

Tip: If breads, cakes, or pies are browning too fast, put a piece of aluminum foil over the top and finish baking.

CHEESY TWISTS

½ cup grated Parmesan cheese
3 tablespoons butter or margarine,
   softened
½ teaspoon Dijon mustard
1 (7.5-ounce) can refrigerator biscuits

Combine cheese, butter, and mustard; set aside.

Roll each biscuit into a 5- x 2-inch rectangle; spread with 1 heaping teaspoonful cheese mixture, and cut in half lengthwise. Twist each strip 2 or 3 times, and place on lightly greased baking sheets. Bake at 400° for 8 to 10 minutes or until golden. Yield: 1⅔ dozen.
Abby Moore,
Ballwin, Missouri.

ONION-PARMESAN BREAD

1 (14-ounce) loaf unsliced French bread
½ cup mayonnaise or salad dressing
½ cup grated Parmesan cheese
¼ cup finely chopped onion

Slice bread lengthwise; place on a baking sheet. Combine remaining ingredients; spread cheese mixture over cut sides of bread. Bake at 375° for 15 to 18 minutes or until bread is golden brown. Yield: 1 loaf.
June Bostick,
Greenwood, Delaware.

BISCUIT BREAD

2 cups self-rising flour
1 cup milk
½ cup vegetable oil

Combine all ingredients; mix well. Pour batter into a hot, well-greased cast-iron skillet. Bake at 400° for 18 to 20 minutes or until golden brown. Yield: 8 to 10 servings.
Ruth Henry,
Maggie Valley, North Carolina.

APPLESAUCE MUFFINS

2 cups biscuit mix
¼ cup sugar
1 teaspoon ground cinnamon
1 egg, slightly beaten
½ cup applesauce
¼ cup milk
2 tablespoons vegetable oil
¼ cup sugar
½ teaspoon ground cinnamon
2 tablespoons butter or margarine, melted

Combine biscuit mix, ¼ cup sugar, and 1 teaspoon cinnamon in a large bowl; make a well in center of mixture. Combine egg, applesauce, milk, and oil in a small bowl; add applesauce mixture to dry ingredients, stirring just until moistened.

Spoon batter into greased muffin pans filling two-thirds full. Bake at 400° for 12 minutes. Combine ¼ cup sugar and ½ teaspoon cinnamon in a small bowl; dip tops of warm muffins in butter and then in sugar mixture. Yield: 1 dozen.
Nancy Swinney,
Tallahassee, Florida.

HOLIDAY COFFEE CAKE

2 cups biscuit mix
¼ cup sugar
¾ cup prepared mincemeat
½ cup milk
1 egg
2 tablespoons butter or margarine,
   melted
Glaze (recipe follows)
3 tablespoons chopped pecans

Combine first 6 ingredients, mixing well. Pour batter into a greased and floured 6½-cup ring mold. Bake at 400° for 20 to 25 minutes. Remove from mold and pour glaze over coffee cake while still warm. Sprinkle with chopped pecans. Yield: 10 servings.

Glaze:

1½ cups sifted powdered sugar
1 teaspoon grated orange rind
2 tablespoons orange juice

Combine all ingredients, stirring until smooth. Yield: about ¾ cup.
Bobbie Collins,
Shelbyville, Tennessee.

Give Coffee A Flavor Boost

There's more than one way to make good coffee. Some like it hot and steaming while others prefer it cold with ice. And, of course, there are more flavored coffees available on the market today than ever before.

SPECIAL SPICED COFFEE

½ cup whole Colombian coffee
   beans
½ teaspoon ground cardamom
½ teaspoon almond extract
½ teaspoon vanilla extract
4½ cups water
Cream to taste
Sugar to taste

Place coffee beans in container of a coffee grinder, and process to a medium grind. Assemble drip coffeemaker according to manufacturer's instructions. Place ground coffee beans in the paper filter or filter basket; sprinkle with ground cardamom. Pour flavorings over the coffee mixture. Add water to coffeemaker and brew. Serve coffee immediately with cream and sugar to taste. Yield: 4½ cups.

PEACH-COFFEE MILK SHAKE

3 cups softened vanilla ice cream
2 cups milk
1 (16-ounce) can sliced peaches,
   undrained
½ cup orange juice
2 teaspoons instant coffee granules
¼ teaspoon almond extract

Combine half of all ingredients in container of electric blender; process until smooth. Pour mixture into a pitcher. Repeat procedure with remaining half of ingredients; stir mixture well. Pour into individual glasses, and serve immediately. Yield: about 7 cups.
Lily Jo Drake,
Satellite Beach, Florida.

Fix A Quick Entrée For Two

Wouldn't it be great to have dinner ready for two in just 10 minutes? With the recipes here, you can do just that.

Chilled Salmon With Dill Sauce is simple to prepare, and can be made ahead of time. Just poach the salmon, mix up the no-cook sauce, and chill until you're ready to serve.

Spiced Beef and Rice takes a little longer to bake, but since it requires only a few minutes to assemble the ingredients and put them in a casserole, you can tend to other tasks while the entrée bakes.

SPICED BEEF AND RICE

½ pound lean ground beef
1 small green pepper, chopped
1 small onion, chopped
1 (8-ounce) can stewed tomatoes
½ teaspoon chili powder
½ teaspoon dry mustard
½ teaspoon dried whole oregano
½ teaspoon salt
½ teaspoon hot sauce
1½ cups cooked regular rice
¼ cup (1 ounce) shredded Cheddar cheese

Brown ground beef, green pepper, and onion in a large skillet; drain.

Combine all ingredients except cheese in a lightly greased 1½-quart casserole. Cover and bake at 350° for 20 minutes; add cheese and bake, uncovered, an additional 10 minutes. Yield: 2 servings.
Patrick I. Greer,
Meridian, Mississippi.

CHILLED SALMON WITH DILL SAUCE

1 (10¾-ounce) can chicken broth, undiluted
½ cup dry white wine
½ cup chopped onion
2 (¾-inch thick) salmon steaks
¼ cup commercial sour cream
¼ cup peeled, seeded, and thinly sliced cucumber
⅛ teaspoon dried whole dillweed
Lemon wedges

Combine first 3 ingredients in a fish poacher or large skillet; bring to a boil, and add salmon. Cover, reduce heat, and simmer 8 to 10 minutes or until fish flakes easily when tested with a fork. Reserve 1 tablespoon poaching liquid; set aside. Refrigerate salmon in poaching liquid until thoroughly chilled.

Combine 1 tablespoon reserved liquid with sour cream, cucumber, and dillweed, mixing well; chill.

Remove salmon from poaching liquid; drain on paper towels. Serve salmon with dill sauce. Garnish with lemon. Yield: 2 servings.
Mrs. Randall L. Wilson,
Louisville, Kentucky.

CRABMEAT SANDWICHES

1 (6-ounce) can crabmeat, rinsed, drained, and flaked
½ cup mayonnaise
2 small green onions, finely chopped
1 teaspoon Worcestershire sauce
2 English muffins, split
1 tablespoon butter or margarine
4 slices Longhorn cheese

Combine first 4 ingredients in a medium bowl; mix well.

Lightly toast English muffin halves; spread with butter. Top each muffin half with a heaping ¼ cup of crabmeat mixture. Place sandwiches on baking sheet, and broil 6 to 7 inches from heat for 2 to 3 minutes or until hot. Top each with a slice of cheese; broil until cheese melts. Yield: 2 servings.
Anna Mack,
Santa Fe, New Mexico.

Do Something Different With Winter Squash

For a change of taste, why not fill an acorn squash with a fruit or meat stuffing, or whip butternut squash into a sweet pie for dessert? During the fall and winter months, hard-rinded squash are colorful additions to many meals. Try these recipes and sample their rich, warm flavors.

SAUSAGE-STUFFED ACORN SQUASH

2 medium acorn squash
Salt
½ pound bulk pork sausage
1 small onion, chopped
¾ cup breadcrumbs

Cut squash in half lengthwise, and remove seeds. Place cut side down in a shallow baking dish, and add ½ inch boiling water. Bake at 375° for 35 minutes. Turn cut side up, and sprinkle with salt; set aside.

Cook sausage and onion until browned, stirring to crumble meat; drain well. Stir in breadcrumbs; spoon into squash cavities. Bake at 375° for 20 minutes. Yield: 4 servings.
Pat Stratford,
Burlington, North Carolina.

BUTTERNUT SQUASH CHIFFON PIE

1 envelope unflavored gelatin
¼ cup water
3 eggs, separated
1½ cups cooked, mashed butternut squash
¾ cup firmly packed brown sugar
½ teaspoon salt
½ teaspoon ground nutmeg
1 teaspoon ground cinnamon
½ cup milk
¼ cup sugar
1 baked 9-inch pastry shell
Whipped cream (optional)

Soften gelatin in water; set aside. Beat egg yolks. Combine squash, softened gelatin, egg yolks, brown sugar, salt, nutmeg, cinnamon, and milk in top of a double boiler. Cook over boiling water, stirring occasionally, about 10 minutes or until mixture is thoroughly heated. Chill until mixture mounds when dropped from a spoon.

Beat egg whites (at room temperature) until foamy. Gradually add sugar, beating until stiff peaks form. Fold into squash mixture; spoon into pastry shell. Chill pie several hours until firm. Garnish with whipped cream, if desired. Yield: one 9-inch pie. *Dora Farrar,*
Gadsden, Alabama.

APPLE-STUFFED ACORN SQUASH

3 medium acorn squash
2 tablespoons butter or margarine, melted
Salt
Ground cinnamon
3 apples, peeled, cored, and chopped
1 tablespoon grated lemon rind
1 tablespoon lemon juice
2 tablespoons butter or margarine, melted
½ cup honey

Cut squash in half lengthwise, and remove seeds. Place cut side down in a shallow baking dish, and add ½ inch boiling water. Bake, uncovered, at 375° for 35 minutes. Turn cut side up; brush cut surfaces and cavities with 2 tablespoons butter. Sprinkle lightly with salt and cinnamon.

Combine apples, lemon rind, lemon juice, 2 tablespoons butter, and honey; mix well and spoon into squash cavities. Bake, uncovered, at 350° for 30 minutes. Yield: 6 servings.
Debra S. Petersen,
Slidell, Louisiana.

Tip: For just a squirt of lemon juice, poke a hole in one end and squeeze.

Seafood Entrées Made Easy

Microwaving is an excellent way of preparing fish and shellfish. One reason is because minimal handling is required; this helps prevent fragile fish fillets from breaking apart. Another reason is that rapid cooking in the microwave preserves the moist texture and delicate flavor of fresh shrimp, crabmeat, and fish.

Cooking seafood can be tricky. The least amount of overcooking can leave you with a dry, tough, tasteless product. Fish is done when it turns from translucent to opaque and flakes easily if tested with a fork. Don't forget that standing time after the seafood is taken out of the microwave must also be taken into consideration.

If fish does not appear done when tested with a fork, we have found it is better to microwave briefly, a few seconds at a time, checking as you go. You may want to remove the seafood from the oven as it approaches doneness, and let it stand, covered, for several minutes to complete cooking.

Since most seafood is tender, it can be microwaved successfully at HIGH. If it needs to be defrosted, we suggest using LOW (10% power). Most seafood defrosts rapidly, so be careful not to toughen it by overdefrosting in the microwave oven. Best results will be achieved by allowing 6 to 9 minutes per pound on LOW (10% power), rotating after half the time. If the food is still icy, continue to microwave, checking every 30 seconds.

SHRIMP IN CREAM SAUCE

¼ cup chopped green onions with tops
¼ cup butter or margarine
1 pound medium shrimp, peeled and deveined
1 (6-ounce) can sliced mushrooms, drained
1 tablespoon all-purpose flour
¼ teaspoon salt
Dash of red pepper
1 (8-ounce) carton commercial sour cream
1 tablespoon lemon juice
Hot cooked rice
Chopped fresh parsley

Combine onions and butter in a 1½-quart casserole. Arrange shrimp over onions around outer edge of casserole. Place mushrooms in center of shrimp; sprinkle with flour, salt, and pepper. Cover with heavy-duty plastic wrap and microwave at HIGH for 4 minutes. Stir well. Cover and microwave at HIGH an additional 2 minutes. Stir in sour cream and lemon juice. Microwave, uncovered, at HIGH for 35 to 40 seconds or just until thoroughly heated (do not boil). Serve over rice; sprinkle with fresh parsley. Yield: 4 servings.

PINEAPPLE-CRAB IMPERIAL

1 pound fresh crabmeat, drained and flaked
¼ cup mayonnaise
3 tablespoons finely chopped celery
1 tablespoon chopped pimiento
2 teaspoons chopped fresh parsley
½ teaspoon prepared mustard
¼ teaspoon salt
3 to 4 drops hot sauce
6 pineapple slices, drained
¾ cup corn flake crumbs, divided
Pimiento strips
Sliced pimiento-stuffed olives

Combine first 8 ingredients in a large bowl; mix well.

Dredge both sides of each pineapple slice in ½ cup corn flake crumbs. Arrange in a lightly greased 10- x 6- x 2-inch baking dish. Place a rounded scoop of crab mixture on top of each pineapple slice. Sprinkle with remaining ¼ cup corn flake crumbs. Microwave, uncovered, at HIGH for 5 to 6 minutes. Garnish with pimiento strips and olive slices. Yield: 6 servings.

SOLE WITH CUCUMBER SAUCE

¼ cup fine, dry breadcrumbs
¼ cup chopped green onions with tops
1 (6½-ounce) can crabmeat, drained and flaked
1 egg, beaten
2 tablespoons chopped pimiento
6 (4- to 5-ounce) sole fillets
2 tablespoons butter or margarine
Cucumber Sauce

Combine first 5 ingredients, mixing well. Divide crabmeat mixture among fillets, spreading evenly. Roll up each fillet, and secure with a wooden pick. Arrange in an 8-inch square baking dish. Place butter in a 1-cup glass measure. Microwave at HIGH for 45 seconds or until melted; brush over fillets. Cover dish with heavy-duty plastic wrap; microwave at HIGH for 4 to 5 minutes, rotating dish after 2 minutes. Serve with Cucumber Sauce. Yield: 6 servings.

Cucumber Sauce:

½ cup peeled, seeded, and chopped cucumber
½ cup mayonnaise
½ cup commercial sour cream
1 tablespoon chopped green onions with tops
½ teaspoon chopped fresh parsley
⅛ to ¼ teaspoon salt
¼ teaspoon dried whole dillweed

Combine all ingredients, stirring well. Yield: 1½ cups.

SUNSHINE TROUT

4 (5- to 6-ounce) trout fillets
½ cup orange juice
1 teaspoon salt
Dash of lemon-pepper seasoning
1 cup fine, dry breadcrumbs
3 tablespoons butter or margarine
Orange Sauce

Remove skin from fillets. Combine orange juice, salt, and lemon-pepper seasoning. Dip fillets in juice mixture, and dredge in breadcrumbs.

Place fillets in a lightly greased 12- x 8- x 2-inch baking dish with thicker portions to outside (thinner portions may overlap if necessary); dot fish with butter. Microwave at HIGH, uncovered, for 7 to 8 minutes, turning dish after 4 minutes, or until fish flakes easily when tested with a fork. Serve Orange Sauce over fish. Yield: 4 servings.

Orange Sauce:

¼ cup plus 2 tablespoons chicken broth
1 tablespoon grated orange rind
¼ cup orange juice
3 tablespoons dry white wine
3 tablespoons water
1½ tablespoons sugar
1 tablespoon white wine vinegar
1 tablespoon cornstarch

Combine all ingredients in a 4-cup glass measure. Microwave at HIGH for 5 to 6 minutes, stirring after 3 minutes, or until thickened. Yield: 1¼ cups.

OCEAN PAPILLOTE

4 (5- to 6-ounce) flounder fillets
2 tablespoons brandy
1 tablespoon lemon juice
3 tablespoons butter or margarine
1 cup sliced fresh mushrooms
1 (5-ounce) can shrimp, drained and
    rinsed
1 small onion, sliced into rings
¼ cup chopped green onions with tops
Salt to taste
White pepper to taste
Paprika

Cut four 18- x 12-inch pieces of parchment paper; fold each piece in half diagonally. Lay parchment flat; place a fillet diagonally next to center fold on each sheet of paper. Sprinkle fillets with brandy and lemon juice; set aside.

Place butter in a 1-quart casserole. Microwave at HIGH for 50 seconds or until melted. Add mushrooms; microwave at HIGH for 2 to 3 minutes, stirring well.

Top each fillet with mushroom mixture, shrimp, and sliced onion. Sprinkle with green onion, salt, pepper, and paprika. Bring opposite corners of parchment together; fold edges over twice to seal securely. Fold pointed ends underneath. Place pouches on a 12-inch platter. Microwave at HIGH for 7 to 9 minutes. Cut an opening in pouches before serving. Yield: 4 servings.

Serve Baked Fruit As A Side Dish

Looking for something to spruce up a buffet or round out a special meal? Include a fruit casserole as a side dish.

APPLE-CHEESE CASSEROLE

½ cup all-purpose flour
½ cup sugar
¼ teaspoon salt
¼ cup butter or margarine
7 medium apples, peeled, cored, and
    sliced
¼ cup plus 2 tablespoons water
1 tablespoon lemon juice
1 cup (4 ounces) shredded sharp Cheddar
    cheese

Combine flour, sugar, and salt; mix well. Cut in butter with pastry blender until mixture resembles coarse meal.

Toss apples with water and lemon juice. Spoon into a lightly greased 8-inch square baking dish. Sprinkle flour mixture over apples. Bake, uncovered, at 350° for 35 minutes. Top with cheese; bake an additional 5 minutes. Yield: 8 servings.
Mary Andrew,
Winston-Salem, North Carolina.

BAKED PINEAPPLE

2 tablespoons cornstarch
¼ cup water
2 eggs, beaten
1 (15¼-ounce) can crushed pineapple,
    undrained
½ cup sugar
1 teaspoon vanilla extract
Butter or margarine
Ground cinnamon

Combine cornstarch and water; stir until smooth. Add to eggs, and blend well. Add pineapple, sugar, and vanilla; mix well. Pour into a lightly greased 1½-quart casserole; dot with butter, and sprinkle with cinnamon. Bake at 350° for 1 hour. Yield: 6 servings.
Bobbie Collins,
Shelbyville, Tennessee.

HOT CURRIED FRUIT

½ cup golden raisins
1 (29-ounce) can pear halves, undrained
1 (29-ounce) can peach halves, undrained
1 (20-ounce) can pineapple chunks,
    undrained
1 (17-ounce) can pitted Royal Anne
    cherries, undrained
1 (16-ounce) can apricot halves, undrained
1 (11-ounce) can mandarin oranges,
    undrained
¼ cup sugar
3 tablespoons all-purpose flour
¼ teaspoon salt
3 tablespoons butter or margarine
½ cup white wine
½ to 1 teaspoon curry powder

Cover raisins with boiling water; soak 10 minutes. Drain and set aside.

Drain fruit, reserving all juice. Stir reserved juice well, and measure ¾ cup; set aside. (Save the remaining juice for other uses.) Combine fruit and raisins in a 13- x 9- x 2-inch baking dish, stirring well. Set aside.

Combine sugar, flour, and salt in a medium saucepan, blending well. Gradually stir in reserved ¾ cup fruit juice. Add butter, and cook over medium heat, stirring constantly, until mixture comes to a boil. Boil 1 minute, stirring

constantly; remove from heat. Gradually stir in wine and curry powder.

Fold sauce into fruit, mixing well. Cover fruit mixture, and let stand 3 hours. Bake at 350° for 30 minutes. Yield: 8 to 10 servings.
Mrs. Fred A. Ludwig,
Ennis, Texas.

These Eggs Are In A Pickle

Tuck a jar of pickled eggs in the cooler to take on your next picnic. Pickled eggs can also replace regular hard-cooked eggs if making deviled eggs or tossing a salad.

For best results, start with eggs that are a few days old because they will peel better than those that are extremely fresh. To cook the eggs, cover them completely with water, and bring to a gentle boil. Turn the heat off, cover the container, and let the eggs stand for 15 to 20 minutes.

Quick cooling also makes eggs easier to shell. This can be done by running cold tap water over the hot eggs. Crack the shells by tapping the eggs all over and rolling between your hands. Gradually peel off the shells starting at the large end of each egg.

BEET PICKLED EGGS

12 hard-cooked eggs
1¾ cups vinegar
1 cup beet juice
⅓ cup dry white wine
8 peppercorns
3 whole cloves
3 cloves garlic
1 bay leaf
1 tablespoon sugar
½ teaspoon salt
⅛ teaspoon ground allspice
2 sprigs fresh dillweed

Peel eggs, and place loosely in a jar; set aside.

Combine next 10 ingredients in a saucepan; bring to a boil. Reduce heat to low; simmer 3 minutes. Pour hot mixture over eggs; add dillweed. Seal with airtight lids. Refrigerate 2 days before serving. Store in refrigerator up to two weeks. Yield: 12 servings.
Madeline Gibbons,
Little Rock, Arkansas.

SPICED PICKLED EGGS

12 hard-cooked eggs
2 cups vinegar
1 medium onion, sliced and separated into rings
2 tablespoons sugar
1½ teaspoons pickling spice
1 teaspoon salt

Peel eggs, and place loosely in a jar; set aside.

Combine remaining ingredients in a saucepan; bring to a boil. Reduce heat to low; simmer 5 minutes. Pour hot mixture over eggs; seal with airtight lids. Refrigerate two days before serving. Store in refrigerator for up to two weeks. Yield: 12 servings.

Mrs. J. E. Sypher,
Charlotte, North Carolina.

Chicken's Always A Favorite

Over the years we've received hundreds of chicken recipes from readers who serve chicken often in their homes because of its price, leanness, and versatility. Here are just a few of our readers' favorites that we tested and enjoyed in our kitchens, too.

CRISPY CHICKEN ROLLS

6 chicken breast halves, skinned and boned
1¼ cups chopped, cooked shrimp
¾ cup butter or margarine, softened
¼ cup chopped onion
¾ teaspoon salt
1 cup all-purpose flour
1¼ teaspoons baking powder
½ teaspoon salt
¾ cup water
Additional all-purpose flour
Vegetable oil

Place each chicken breast half on a sheet of waxed paper. Flatten chicken to ¼-inch thickness using a meat mallet or rolling pin.

Combine shrimp, butter, onion, and ¾ teaspoon salt; spoon about ¼ cup shrimp mixture in center of each piece of chicken. Roll up lengthwise, and secure with a wooden pick. Cover and refrigerate 15 minutes.

Combine 1 cup flour, baking powder, salt, and water. Dredge each chicken roll in flour, and coat with batter. Fry in 1 inch hot oil (375°) in a large skillet about 15 minutes or until golden brown. Drain thoroughly on paper towels; serve immediately. Yield: 6 servings.

Mrs. W. H. Burnside,
Newport, North Carolina.

ISLAND BROILED CHICKEN

½ cup vegetable oil
3 tablespoons lemon juice
1½ tablespoons soy sauce
1 clove garlic, minced
½ teaspoon dried whole oregano
¼ teaspoon salt
⅛ teaspoon pepper
1 (2½- to 3-pound) broiler-fryer, halved

Combine first 7 ingredients in a heavy-duty plastic bag. Add chicken and seal; marinate in refrigerator overnight, turning occasionally.

Remove chicken from marinade, reserving marinade. Place chicken, skin side down, on a broiling rack. Broil 7 inches from heat for 25 minutes, basting often with the marinade. Turn chicken over; broil an additional 15 minutes or until chicken is tender. Yield: 4 servings.

Marcy Hart,
Killeen, Texas.

ORIENTAL PINEAPPLE CHICKEN

6 chicken breast halves, skinned and boned
2 tablespoons soy sauce
2 eggs, beaten
¾ cup all-purpose flour
Vegetable oil
2 carrots, scraped and cut into 2-inch strips
2 stalks celery, cut into 2-inch strips
1 green pepper, cut into 2-inch strips
1 onion, thinly sliced and separated into rings
2 tablespoons butter or margarine
1 (15¼-ounce) can pineapple chunks, undrained
2 tablespoons cornstarch
1 teaspoon beef-flavored bouillon granules
1 cup water
Dash of pepper
Hot cooked rice

Cut chicken into 1-inch pieces; combine chicken and soy sauce. Let stand 20 minutes. Dip chicken into eggs, and dredge in flour. Fry in hot oil (375°) until golden brown. Drain on paper towels, and set aside.

Sauté carrots, celery, green pepper, and onion in butter until crisp-tender; set aside.

Drain pineapple, reserving liquid; set pineapple aside. Combine reserved liquid and cornstarch in a saucepan, stirring well; add bouillon granules and water. Bring mixture to a boil; cook 1 minute, stirring constantly. Stir in dash of pepper and the pineapple chunks.

To serve, place chicken pieces on a serving platter; arrange sautéed vegetables over chicken, and top with pineapple sauce. Serve with hot cooked rice. Yield: 6 servings.

Mrs. Charles Hellem,
Columbia, Missouri.

OVEN-FRIED PECAN CHICKEN

½ cup biscuit mix
½ cup ground pecans
1 teaspoon paprika
½ teaspoon salt
¼ teaspoon pepper
3 tablespoons butter or margarine
1 (2½- to 3-pound) broiler-fryer, cut up

Combine first 5 ingredients, mixing well; set aside.

Melt butter in a 13- x 9- x 2-inch baking dish. Dredge chicken pieces in pecan mixture, and place chicken in melted butter. Bake, uncovered, at 350° for 30 minutes. Turn chicken over; cover and bake an additional 30 minutes or until done. Yield: 4 servings.

Mae McClaugherty,
Marble Falls, Texas.

Shrimp Decorate This Tree

This shrimp tree is not just a decorative centerpiece; it's a delicious appetizer as well. The tree is made of plastic foam covered with endive, and it can be assembled quickly and easily.

To completely cover the tree, you'll need about 4 bunches of endive. Wash and separate each bunch, and remove the tough ends of each leaf. Begin by attaching leaves to the bottom of the cone, and move upward. Then cover the plastic foam base, and fill in any holes. After decorating the tree with shrimp, crown it with a bow. Place the bowls of Mustard Sauce and Holiday Dip on the endive-covered base, and then arrange cherry tomatoes or other raw vegetables between them.

Our shrimp tree is great for holiday entertaining. Let guests remove Spicy Boiled Shrimp from the endive-covered tree and dip them in Mustard Sauce or Holiday Dip.

SPICY BOILED SHRIMP

10 peppercorns
4 whole cloves
3 bay leaves
½ teaspoon mustard seeds
½ teaspoon dried whole oregano
½ teaspoon dried whole basil
½ teaspoon crushed red pepper
⅛ teaspoon celery seeds
Dash of dried whole thyme
2½ quarts water
½ teaspoon salt
1 lime, halved
1 lemon, halved
1 clove garlic, crushed
3 pounds fresh large or jumbo shrimp, unpeeled

Combine the first 9 ingredients in a doubled cheesecloth bag; tie securely with a string.

Bring 2½ quarts water to a boil in a large Dutch oven. Add salt, lime, lemon, garlic, and herb bag; return to a boil, and boil 2 to 3 minutes. Add shrimp, and return to a boil. Reduce heat and simmer, uncovered, 3 to 5 minutes. Drain well; rinse with cold water. Chill. Peel and devein shrimp, leaving tails on, if desired. Yield: 12 appetizer servings.

Tip: Use kitchen shears to cut shells from shrimp, to snip parsley, to trim pastry shells, and to cut many other foods. This saves time and gives a neat-looking cut.

HOLIDAY DIP

1 cup mayonnaise
⅓ cup minced onion
¼ cup catsup
¼ cup chili sauce
2 cloves garlic, minced
1 teaspoon dry mustard
1 teaspoon pepper
Dash of paprika
Dash of hot sauce

Combine all ingredients in a medium mixing bowl, stirring well. Cover and chill 2 to 3 hours. Serve dip with boiled shrimp. Yield: 2 cups.
Mrs. R. L. Bryant,
Franklin, Virginia.

MUSTARD SAUCE

1½ cups mayonnaise
½ cup prepared Creole mustard
1 to 2 tablespoons prepared horseradish
2 tablespoons lemon juice

Combine all ingredients in a medium mixing bowl; stir well. Cover and chill 2 to 3 hours. Serve sauce with boiled shrimp. Yield: about 2¼ cups.
Patrick I. Greer,
Meridian, Mississippi.

Make-Ahead Salads For Convenience

While they may be served first, salads usually take last place when it comes to meal planning. By the time the entrée and a couple of side dishes are made, there's often little time left over to prepare anything very imaginative. As a solution, we've come up with several salads you can make ahead that offer both variety and convenience.

SALMON-RICE SALAD

3 cups cooked rice
1 (15½-ounce) can salmon, drained
1 (10-ounce) package frozen English peas, thawed
2 carrots, diced
2 green onions, chopped
¼ cup chopped fresh parsley
½ cup Italian salad dressing
Green pepper rings
Lettuce leaves (optional)
Tomato quarters (optional)

Combine first 7 ingredients in a large bowl. Cover and refrigerate overnight. Garnish with green pepper rings. Serve on lettuce leaves, and garnish with tomato quarters, if desired. Yield: 6 to 8 servings.
Katherine Edwards,
Nashville, Tennessee.

TUNA-POTATO SALAD

1 (6½-ounce) can tuna, drained and flaked
1 medium-size cooked potato, peeled and cubed
1 hard-cooked egg, chopped
½ cup chopped celery
3 green onions, finely chopped
2 to 3 tablespoons sweet pickle relish
3 tablespoons mayonnaise
Salt and pepper to taste

Combine all ingredients in a medium bowl, and toss well. Chill thoroughly before serving. Yield: 6 servings.
Frances Edwards,
Tampa, Florida.

TASTY CORN SALAD

1 (12-ounce) can whole kernel yellow corn, drained
1 (12-ounce) can whole kernel white corn, drained
½ cup finely chopped onion
½ cup finely chopped celery
½ cup finely chopped green pepper
1 (2-ounce) jar chopped pimiento, drained
½ cup sugar
½ cup white wine vinegar
⅛ teaspoon garlic powder

Combine first 6 ingredients; mix well, and set aside.

Combine sugar, vinegar, and garlic powder; stir until sugar dissolves. Pour over vegetables, tossing gently. Cover tightly, and chill 8 hours or overnight. Yield: 6 to 8 servings. *Margaret Corn,*
Lonoke, Arkansas.

ORIENTAL VEGETABLE SALAD

1 (16-ounce) can green beans, drained
1 (16-ounce) can tiny English peas, drained
1 (16-ounce) can Chinese vegetables, drained
1 (8-ounce) can sliced water chestnuts, drained
1 small purple onion, thinly sliced
1½ cups thinly sliced celery
¾ cup vinegar
½ cup sugar

Combine first 6 ingredients in a large bowl, and toss gently. Combine vinegar and sugar in a small saucepan. Bring to a boil, and cook until sugar dissolves, stirring constantly. Cool mixture slightly. Pour over vegetables; stir gently. Cover and refrigerate overnight. Yield: 10 servings.
Tassie Bradley,
Sparta, Tennessee.

THREE PEA SALAD

1 (19-ounce) can chick-peas or garbanzo beans, drained and rinsed
1 (16-ounce) can black-eyed peas, drained and rinsed
1 (17-ounce) can English peas, drained
1 (8-ounce) jar cocktail onions, undrained
½ cup thinly sliced onion
1 medium green pepper, chopped
½ cup sugar
½ cup vegetable oil
½ teaspoon salt
¼ teaspoon pepper
Lettuce leaves (optional)

Combine all ingredients except lettuce in a medium bowl, and toss well. Cover and chill several hours or overnight. Serve on lettuce leaves, if desired. Yield: 10 servings.
Jean Jordan,
Oviedo, Florida.

GLAZED FRUIT SALAD

1 (21-ounce) can peach pie filling
1 (20-ounce) can chunk pineapple, drained
1 (16-ounce) package frozen whole strawberries, thawed and drained
1 (11-ounce) can mandarin oranges, drained
4 bananas, sliced
2 tablespoons lemon juice

Combine first 4 ingredients in a large bowl; chill well. Coat bananas with lemon juice, and add to mixture. Serve immediately. Yield: 10 servings.
Carolyn Sutton,
Savannah, Georgia.

LAYERED FRUIT SALAD

2 cups shredded lettuce
2 apples, chopped
½ teaspoon ascorbic-citric powder
2 oranges, peeled and sliced crosswise
2 cups seedless green grapes
⅓ cup mayonnaise
⅓ cup commercial sour cream
1 cup (4 ounces) shredded Cheddar cheese

Spread lettuce in a 2-quart bowl. Sprinkle apples with ascorbic-citric powder. Layer apples, oranges, and grapes over lettuce. Combine mayonnaise and sour cream; spread evenly over top, sealing to edge of bowl. Sprinkle with cheese. Cover salad, and refrigerate overnight. Yield: 6 to 8 servings.
Nancy Siekman,
Beaver Crossing, Nebraska.

Give Menus A Lift With Salad

A fresh, pretty salad may be exactly what's needed to spruce up your menus. Here, we suggest combining fruit, vegetables, meats, eggs, and macaroni into some refreshing creations.

For the best salads, start with a base of in-season produce and add canned fruit and vegetables. Remember to place freshly washed greens in a plastic bag or bowl and refrigerate. Potatoes, dry onions, and tomatoes retain more flavor and better texture if stored at room temperature.

FRUITED CHICKEN SALAD

4 cups diced, cooked chicken
1 (15¼-ounce) can pineapple chunks, drained
1 (11-ounce) can mandarin oranges, drained
1 cup chopped celery
½ cup sliced ripe olives
½ cup chopped green pepper
2 tablespoons grated onion
1 cup mayonnaise
1 tablespoon prepared mustard
¼ teaspoon salt
1 (0.3-ounce) can chow mein noodles
Lettuce leaves

Combine first 7 ingredients in a large bowl; mix well. Combine mayonnaise, mustard, and salt; toss with chicken mixture. Cover and chill. Stir in noodles just before serving. Serve on lettuce leaves. Yield: 8 servings.
Cynthia W. Faircloth,
Lexington, North Carolina.

PEACH PARTY SALAD

1 (6-ounce) package orange-flavored gelatin
2 cups boiling water
1 (15¼-ounce) can crushed pineapple, undrained
1 (28-ounce) can sliced peaches, drained
1 egg, beaten
¼ cup sugar
1½ tablespoons all-purpose flour
1½ teaspoons butter or margarine, softened
½ cup whipping cream, whipped
½ cup miniature marshmallows
½ cup (2 ounces) shredded Cheddar cheese

Dissolve gelatin in boiling water; set aside. Drain pineapple, reserving juice; set pineapple aside. Add enough water to juice to make 1 cup. Add ¾ cup of juice mixture to gelatin mixture; chill until mixture is the consistency of unbeaten egg white. Set remaining ¼ cup of juice mixture aside.

Arrange peach slices in a lightly oiled 12- x 8- x 2-inch dish. Pour gelatin mixture over peaches; chill mixture until almost firm.

Combine egg, sugar, flour, butter, and remaining ¼ cup of juice mixture in a small saucepan; cook over low heat, stirring constantly, until smooth and thickened. Cool.

Combine pineapple, whipped cream, marshmallows, and cheese; fold in egg mixture. Spread evenly over salad. Cover and chill overnight. Yield: 12 servings.
Miriam Brenneman,
Montezuma, Georgia.

GARDEN MACARONI SALAD

1 (8-ounce) package elbow macaroni
1 cup diced cucumber
1 cup sliced celery
¼ cup chopped green pepper
¼ cup sliced radishes
2 teaspoons chopped green onions
2 medium tomatoes, diced
¾ cup mayonnaise
1 teaspoon salt
¼ teaspoon dried whole basil
Radishes (optional)
Fresh parsley sprigs (optional)

Cook macaroni according to package directions, omitting salt; drain well.

Combine macaroni and next 6 ingredients, tossing well. Combine mayonnaise, salt, and basil; toss with macaroni mixture. Cover and chill at least 3 hours. Garnish with radishes and parsley, if desired. Yield: about 8 servings.
Mrs. Jack Hampton,
Elizabethton, Tennessee.

CAULIFLOWER SALAD

1 medium cauliflower, broken into flowerets
1 medium tomato, coarsely chopped
1 medium cucumber, peeled and coarsely chopped
3 green onions with tops, chopped
1 stalk celery, finely chopped
½ cup chopped green pepper
2 hard-cooked eggs, chopped
2 tablespoons sweet pickle relish, drained
½ cup mayonnaise
½ teaspoon salt
¼ teaspoon pepper
1 tablespoon lemon juice
4 slices bacon, cooked and crumbled

Cook cauliflower, covered, in a small amount of boiling water 10 minutes; drain well. Add next 11 ingredients; toss gently. Cover and refrigerate several hours. Spoon salad into serving container, and sprinkle with bacon. Yield: 8 servings.
Irene Smith,
Fayetteville, Arkansas.

Flavor It With Garlic

True garlic fans can't get enough of this flavorful herb. That's why they go for San Antonio Hot Sauce; it's filled with the pungent taste of crushed garlic. If you like garlic flavor but prefer a milder taste, then try our Easy Scampi. In this recipe, the garlic is sautéed, leaving a definite, but subtle flavor.

When buying garlic, select firm, plump bulbs that have dry skins. Store the garlic in a cool, dry place that is well ventilated. The flavor should remain sharp for up to four months.

EASY SCAMPI

¼ cup finely chopped onion
4 cloves garlic, crushed
4 sprigs fresh parsley, chopped
¾ cup butter
2 pounds fresh medium shrimp, peeled and deveined
¼ cup dry white wine
2 tablespoons lemon juice
Salt to taste
Freshly ground pepper to taste

Sauté onion, garlic, and parsley in butter until onion is tender. Reduce heat to low; add shrimp. Cook, stirring frequently, about 5 minutes. Remove shrimp with a slotted spoon to a serving dish; keep warm. Add remaining ingredients to butter mixture; simmer 2 minutes. Pour butter mixture over shrimp. Serve immediately with French bread. Yield: 4 servings.
Betty Rabe,
Plano, Texas.

PASTA WITH CLAM SAUCE

4 cloves garlic, minced
¼ cup butter or margarine
¼ cup olive oil
¼ cup chopped fresh parsley
3 tablespoons grated Parmesan cheese
1 tablespoon dried whole oregano
1 tablespoon finely chopped green pepper
Pinch of red pepper
2 (6½-ounce) cans chopped clams, undrained
1 (8-ounce) can tomato sauce
1 (7-ounce) package vermicelli or thin spaghetti, cooked and drained

Sauté garlic in butter and oil 1 minute. Reduce heat to low; add next 5 ingredients, and heat until bubbly. Stir in clams and tomato sauce. Cover and simmer 1 hour, stirring occasionally. Pour clam sauce over hot vermicelli; toss well. Yield: 6 servings.
Carolyn Rosen,
Nashville, Tennessee.

SAN ANTONIO HOT SAUCE

1 (29-ounce) can whole tomatoes, drained and chopped
1 medium onion, finely chopped
2 to 3 jalapeño peppers, finely chopped
3 cloves garlic, crushed
2 tablespoons vegetable oil
1 tablespoon vinegar
1 teaspoon salt
2 teaspoons crushed red pepper
1 teaspoon dried whole oregano
¼ teaspoon ground cumin

Combine all ingredients in a medium bowl, mixing well. Refrigerate for 2 to 3 hours. Serve the hot sauce with taco chips. Store any leftover sauce in the refrigerator. Yield: about 3 cups.
Vicki R. Helton,
San Antonio, Texas.

Serve Dinner In Just One Dish

After a long, busy day it's hard to think about a meal that requires a lot of time and effort. The one-dish dinners featured here require little preparation and even less cleanup as a solution to the problem. Each recipe teams a good source of protein, either meat or seafood, with a starch and a variety of vegetables. The results are tasty and nutritious combinations that can be ready in minutes.

BEEF-AND-EGGPLANT SUPPER

1 pound ground beef
¾ cup chopped onion
1 clove garlic, minced
¼ cup vegetable oil
2 tablespoons butter or margarine
1 small eggplant, peeled and cubed
2 cups cooked elbow macaroni
1 (16-ounce) can whole tomatoes, undrained and coarsely chopped, or 3 large tomatoes, peeled and coarsely chopped
¼ teaspoon dried whole oregano
¼ teaspoon dried whole thyme
¼ to ½ teaspoon salt
⅛ teaspoon pepper
1 cup (4 ounces) shredded Monterey Jack cheese

Brown ground beef in a large skillet, stirring often to crumble beef. Drain; remove meat, and set aside.

Sauté onion and garlic in oil and butter in a large skillet until tender. Add eggplant, and cook 5 to 7 minutes over medium heat, stirring often. Stir in ground beef and next 6 ingredients. Cover, reduce heat, and simmer 20 minutes, stirring occasionally. Sprinkle with cheese, and cook just until cheese melts. Yield: 4 to 6 servings.
Marie Elrod,
Warner Robins, Georgia.

BEEF-AND-LIMA BEAN DINNER

1 pound ground beef
1 medium onion, chopped
1 (16-ounce) can lima beans, undrained
¾ cup barbecue sauce
1 cup (4 ounces) shredded sharp Cheddar
    cheese
1 (5-ounce) can refrigerated buttermilk
    biscuits

Brown ground beef and onion in a large skillet, stirring often to crumble beef; drain. Stir in lima beans and barbecue sauce; heat until bubbly.

Spoon meat mixture into a lightly greased shallow 2-quart casserole; sprinkle with cheese. Separate each biscuit into 2 halves, making 10 biscuit rounds. Place rounds on top of casserole, overlapping edges if necessary. Bake, uncovered, at 375° for 25 minutes or until biscuits are golden brown. Yield: 4 to 6 servings.   *Mrs. Howard Freeman,*
Lynchburg, Virginia.

CHICKEN LIVERS WITH RICE

1½ to 2 pounds chicken livers
¼ cup vegetable oil
1 cup coarsely shredded carrots
1 cup coarsely chopped onion
½ cup chopped fresh parsley
1 clove garlic, minced
4 cups water
1½ cups uncooked regular rice
2 tablespoons chicken-flavored bouillon
    granules
¼ teaspoon salt
¼ teaspoon pepper
½ teaspoon ground turmeric
2 cups peeled, coarsely chopped tomatoes

Sauté chicken livers in oil in a Dutch oven 5 minutes or until browned. Remove livers, and drain on paper towels; reserve skillet drippings. Cut livers into quarters; set aside.

Sauté carrots, onion, parsley, and garlic in reserved drippings until onion is tender. Add chicken livers and next 6 ingredients; bring to a boil.

Cover, reduce heat, and simmer 20 minutes or until rice is tender. Stir in tomatoes, and cook until thoroughly heated. Yield: 6 to 8 servings.
Janis Moyer,
Farmersville, Texas.

WILD RICE-AND-SHRIMP CREOLE

½ cup chopped onion
⅓ cup chopped green pepper
¼ cup butter or margarine
1 (28-ounce) can whole tomatoes,
    undrained and coarsely chopped
1 cup water
¼ teaspoon garlic salt
¼ teaspoon dried whole rosemary, crushed
¼ teaspoon paprika
¼ teaspoon pepper
1 (6-ounce) package long-grain and wild
    rice mix
1 pound fresh shrimp, peeled and
    deveined

Sauté onion and green pepper in butter in a large saucepan until tender. Stir in next 7 ingredients; bring to a boil. Cover, reduce heat, and simmer 20 to 25 minutes. Stir in shrimp; cover and simmer 10 minutes, adding water if necessary. Yield: 6 to 8 servings.
Teresa Wilson,
Gordo, Alabama.

Give Jack Cheese A Try

Monterey Jack cheese adds mellow flavor to these recipes, turning them into satisfying main dishes.

When storing Jack cheese, it should be wrapped tightly in plastic wrap to stay moist and fresh. If mold appears on the surface, simply scrape or cut it off; the remaining cheese is safe to eat.

MONTEREY BURRITOS

1 pound ground beef
1 small onion, chopped
1 medium-size green pepper, chopped
2 cups (8 ounces) shredded Monterey Jack
    cheese, divided
½ cup wheat germ
1 to 2 jalapeño peppers, finely chopped
1 teaspoon dried whole basil
1 teaspoon dried whole oregano
½ teaspoon ground cumin
8 (6-inch) flour tortillas
1 (16-ounce) can tomato sauce
1¼ teaspoons chili powder
1 teaspoon ground cumin
Sour cream (optional)

Cook ground beef, onion, and green pepper in a skillet until beef is browned, stirring to crumble. Drain; stir

in 1 cup shredded cheese and next 5 ingredients, mixing well.

Wrap tortillas tightly in aluminum foil; bake at 350° for 15 minutes.

Place a heaping ⅓ cup of meat mixture on center of each tortilla. Fold bottom edge of tortilla up and over filling just until mixture is covered. Fold in one side of tortilla to center; roll up. Repeat with remaining tortillas.

Place burritos in a greased 13- x 9- x 2-inch baking dish; set aside. Combine tomato sauce, chili powder, and 1 teaspoon cumin. Bring mixture to a boil; reduce heat and simmer 5 minutes. Spoon sauce mixture over burritos. Cover and bake at 375° for 15 minutes. Sprinkle remaining 1 cup cheese over top, and bake an additional 5 minutes. Serve with sour cream, if desired. Yield: 4 servings.   *Mrs. Robert Pierce,*
Germantown, Tennessee.

CHICKEN ROMANOFF

1 (6-ounce) package egg noodles
1 (12-ounce) carton small-curd cottage
    cheese
1 (8-ounce) carton commercial sour cream
¾ cup chopped green onions with tops
2 tablespoons butter or margarine, melted
1 clove garlic, crushed
⅛ teaspoon pepper
6 chicken breast halves, skinned and
    boned
4 ounces Monterey Jack cheese, sliced
2 eggs, beaten
1 cup fine, dry breadcrumbs
⅓ cup butter or margarine
1 chicken-flavored bouillon cube
1 cup boiling water
½ cup chopped onion
½ cup chopped green pepper
2 tablespoons butter or margarine
2 tablespoons all-purpose flour
¼ teaspoon salt
¼ teaspoon pepper
1 (4-ounce) can sliced mushrooms, drained
2 tablespoons chopped pimiento

Cook egg noodles according to package directions; drain. Rinse with cold water, and drain again. Combine next 6 ingredients; mix well. Add noodles, and toss lightly; set aside.

Place each piece of chicken on waxed paper; flatten to ¼-inch thickness using a meat mallet or rolling pin. Place a slice of cheese over each piece of chicken, and top with 1 to 2 tablespoons of noodle mixture. Fold sides and ends of chicken over noodles and cheese, and secure with wooden picks. Spoon remaining noodle mixture into a lightly

greased 12- x 8- x 2-inch baking dish;
set aside.

Dip each piece of chicken in egg; coat
with breadcrumbs. Melt ⅓ cup butter in
a heavy skillet; brown chicken on all
sides. Place chicken over noodles in
baking dish.

Dissolve bouillon cube in boiling
water. Sauté onion and green pepper in
2 tablespoons butter until tender. Add
flour, stirring until smooth; cook 1 minute, stirring constantly. Gradually add
bouillon mixture; cook over medium
heat, stirring constantly, until thickened. Stir in next 4 ingredients, and
pour over chicken. Bake, uncovered, at
400° for 20 to 30 minutes. Yield: 6
servings. *Ardis O. Rea,*
Kansas City, Missouri.

GUACAMOLE SUBS

1 small avocado, peeled and mashed
1 tablespoon lemon juice
1 tablespoon mayonnaise
¼ teaspoon hot sauce
1 clove garlic, minced
1 (1-pound) loaf Italian bread
8 (1-ounce) slices cooked turkey
1 large tomato, sliced
¼ cup chopped green onions with tops
1 (8-ounce) package sliced Monterey Jack
   cheese
12 ripe olives, sliced

Combine first 5 ingredients; mix well,
and set aside.

Cut bread in half crosswise; slice each
piece in half horizontally. Lightly toast
bread; spread with avocado mixture.
Top each piece with 2 slices each of
turkey and tomato. Sprinkle with
onions; top each with 2 slices of cheese.

Place sandwiches on a baking sheet,
and broil just until cheese melts. Garnish with sliced olives. Yield: 4 to 6
servings. *Jill Rorex,*
Arlington, Texas.

FISH MONTEREY

1½ pounds flounder fillets
2 tablespoons butter, melted
White pepper to taste
Monterey Jack Sauce

Place fillets in a greased 13- x 9- x
2-inch baking dish; brush with butter,
and sprinkle with pepper. Bake, uncovered, at 400° for 12 to 15 minutes or
until fish flakes easily when tested with
a fork. Serve Monterey Jack Sauce over
fish. Yield: 4 servings.

Monterey Jack Sauce:

2 cups (8 ounces) cubed Monterey Jack
   cheese
2 teaspoons cornstarch
1 tablespoon water
6 to 7 medium-size cooked shrimp,
   chopped or 1 (4½-ounce) can small
   shrimp, drained and rinsed
⅓ cup sliced fresh mushrooms
¼ cup dry white wine

Place cheese in top of a double
boiler; bring water to a boil. Reduce
heat to low; cook, stirring constantly,
until cheese melts. Combine cornstarch
and water, stirring well; stir into cheese.
Cook, stirring constantly, 1 minute.
Add remaining ingredients, and stir
until thoroughly heated. Yield: about
2½ cups. *John Riggins,*
Nashville, Tennessee.

EGG-AND-CHEESE CASSEROLE

8 eggs, beaten
½ cup all-purpose flour
1 teaspoon baking powder
1 (16-ounce) carton small-curd cottage
   cheese
2 cups (8 ounces) shredded Monterey Jack
   cheese
2 cups (8 ounces) shredded Cheddar
   cheese
2 (4-ounce) cans chopped green chiles,
   drained
¼ cup butter or margarine, melted
½ teaspoon garlic powder
½ teaspoon chili powder

Combine eggs, flour, and baking powder, stirring well. Stir in remaining ingredients. Pour into a lightly greased
13- x 9- x 2-inch baking dish. Bake at
325° for 35 minutes. Yield: 10 to 12
servings. *Mrs. Bill Anthony,*
Poteau, Oklahoma.

Fill Casseroles With Frozen Vegetables

Frozen vegetables are a good alternative when fresh produce is out of season. Here you'll find some tasty
vegetable casseroles to put on the table
without much fuss. For each recipe,
allow time to cook the vegetables according to package directions; then assemble the casserole, and bake less than
30 minutes.

Since most vegetable casseroles are
topped with a layer of cheese or breadcrumbs, make them look as good as
they taste with garnishes. Use items
such as pimiento strips, parsley, or
some ingredient in the casserole.
Cheese-topped casseroles are usually
best if you sprinkle on the cheese during the last few minutes of baking.

CRUNCHY SQUASH CASSEROLE

2 (10-ounce) packages frozen sliced yellow
   squash
1 cup chopped onion
1 tablespoon butter or margarine
1 (8-ounce) carton commercial sour cream
1 (10¾-ounce) can cream of chicken soup,
   undiluted
1 (8-ounce) can water chestnuts, drained
1 (6-ounce) package chicken-flavored
   stuffing mix
¼ cup plus 2 tablespoons butter, melted
Squash slices (optional)
Celery leaves (optional)

Cook the squash according to package directions; drain well. Sauté onion
in 1 tablespoon butter. Combine the
squash, onion, sour cream, soup, and
water chestnuts.

Combine stuffing mix and ¼ cup plus
2 tablespoons melted butter; stir well.
Add three-fourths of stuffing mixture to
squash mixture; spoon into a lightly
greased 2-quart casserole. Sprinkle remaining stuffing mixture over casserole.
Bake at 350° for 20 minutes or until
bubbly. Garnish casserole with thawed
squash slices and celery leaves, if desired. Yield: 8 servings. *Edith Roberts,*
Brookport, Illinois.

CHEESY BROCCOLI CASSEROLE

2 (10-ounce) packages frozen chopped
   broccoli
1 (8-ounce) carton commercial sour cream
1 (10¾-ounce) can cream of mushroom
   soup, undiluted
1 cup chopped celery
1 (2-ounce) jar chopped pimiento, drained
1 cup (4 ounces) shredded Cheddar cheese

Cook broccoli according to package
directions; drain well. Place in a lightly
greased 2-quart casserole. Combine next
4 ingredients, and spoon over broccoli.
Bake at 350° for 15 minutes. Sprinkle
with cheese, and bake an additional 5
minutes. Yield: 8 servings.
Kathryn Watkins,
Justin, Texas.

SPINACH-AND-CELERY CASSEROLE

2 (10-ounce) packages frozen
    chopped spinach
2½ cups thinly sliced celery
1 cup water
1 teaspoon salt
3 tablespoons butter or margarine
1 tablespoon all-purpose flour
½ cup half-and-half
¼ teaspoon pepper
2 teaspoons prepared horseradish
1 tablespoon grated Parmesan
    cheese

Cook spinach according to package directions; drain well, and set aside.

Combine celery, water, and salt in a medium saucepan; bring to a boil. Reduce heat to medium; cook, uncovered, 10 minutes or until celery is tender. Drain celery well.

Add butter to celery; cook over low heat until butter melts. Add flour, stirring until smooth. Cook 1 minute, stirring constantly. Gradually add half-and-half; cook over medium heat, stirring constantly, just until mixture is thickened and bubbly. Stir in pepper, horseradish, and drained spinach. Spoon mixture into a lightly greased 1½-quart baking dish; sprinkle with grated Parmesan cheese. Bake at 375° for 20 minutes. Yield: 6 servings.

Edna Chadsey,
Corpus Christi, Texas.

Create A Spectacular Entrée

These entrées may take a little more time to prepare, but they are worth it. Select from showy gourmet dishes such as our flaky Phyllo Sausage Log or Italian Stuffed Cabbage.

PHYLLO SAUSAGE LOG

¾ pound bulk pork sausage
½ cup chopped onion
1 (8-ounce) carton large curd cottage
    cheese
1 (10-ounce) package frozen chopped
    spinach, thawed and pressed dry
1½ cups (6 ounces) shredded mozzarella
    cheese
8 sheets commercial frozen phyllo pastry,
    thawed
⅓ cup butter or margarine, melted

Cook sausage and onion in a large skillet until meat is browned, stirring to crumble. Drain off pan drippings. Stir in cottage cheese, spinach, and mozzarella cheese; set aside.

Working one at a time, and keeping remaining phyllo covered, brush 1 sheet of phyllo with melted butter; place on a lightly greased baking sheet. Brush remaining sheets of phyllo with additional butter, stacking sheets evenly after brushing. Spoon sausage mixture on phyllo in a 2-inch strip about 3 inches from one lengthwise edge, and to within 2 inches of crosswise edges. Fold the 3-inch edge of dough over filling; roll up phyllo log, jellyroll fashion.

Place log, seam side down, on baking sheet; tuck ends under. Brush with additional butter, and bake at 350° for 45 minutes or until golden brown. Cool 5 minutes. Cut into slices to serve. Yield: 4 to 6 servings.

ITALIAN STUFFED CABBAGE

1 green or savoy cabbage
½ pound ground beef
½ pound hot or mild bulk sausage
1 small onion, finely chopped
1 clove garlic, minced
2 eggs, beaten
¼ cup catsup
½ teaspoon salt
¼ teaspoon dried whole oregano
⅛ teaspoon pepper
¼ cup grated Parmesan cheese
¼ cup soft breadcrumbs
1½ cups beef broth
Spicy Tomato Sauce

Remove 10 large outer leaves of cabbage; reserve remaining cabbage for other uses. Steam 2 to 3 minutes, and set aside. Combine next 11 ingredients; mix well, and set aside.

Pare down the outside of thick ribs of cabbage leaves until thin. Arrange 4 or 5 cabbage leaves in a lightly greased 2-quart ovenproof bowl, placing leaf tips toward center with rib ends extending beyond edge of bowl. (The leaves should overlap.)

Spoon one-third of meat mixture into bowl, and spread evenly over cabbage. Cover with 2 to 3 cabbage leaves and press gently; repeat. Spread with remaining meat mixture, and fold over cabbage ends. Top with the remaining cabbage leaves, and press down.

Bring broth to a boil; slowly pour over cabbage mixture, easing a knife between leaves and inside of bowl so liquid will flow down.

Cover and bake at 400° for 30 minutes. Reduce heat to 350°, and bake an additional hour. Tilt bowl carefully, and drain off liquid; let stand 5 minutes, and drain again. Invert onto a serving plate; cut into wedges. Serve with Spicy Tomato Sauce. Yield: 4 to 6 servings.

Spicy Tomato Sauce:

1 clove garlic, minced
1 tablespoon vegetable oil
1 (14½-ounce) can whole tomatoes,
    undrained and chopped
1 (8-ounce) can tomato sauce
1 teaspoon dried Italian seasoning
½ teaspoon sugar

Sauté garlic in hot oil in a heavy skillet until tender. Stir in remaining ingredients; bring to a boil. Reduce heat and simmer, uncovered, 25 minutes or until thickened, stirring occasionally. Yield: 1½ cups.

FISH IN A CRUST

½ cup uncooked brown rice
3 slices bacon
½ cup sliced fresh mushrooms
⅓ cup thinly sliced celery
¼ cup sliced green onions
¼ cup slivered almonds
1 teaspoon soy sauce
1 (11-ounce) package pie crust mix
4 (6-ounce) flounder fillets
Mornay Sauce
1 egg
1 teaspoon cold water
Watercress
Lemon wedges

Cook brown rice according to the package directions.

Cook bacon in a large skillet until crisp; remove bacon, reserving 2 tablespoons drippings in skillet. Drain bacon well; crumble and set aside. Sauté mushrooms, celery, onions, and almonds in drippings until almonds are golden brown. Stir rice, bacon, and soy sauce into vegetable mixture. Set aside.

Prepare pie crust mix according to package directions for a double-crust pie. Divide pastry in half. Roll out 1 portion of pastry diagonally across a lightly greased large baking sheet, making a large oval about ⅛ inch thick. Make a fish pattern (about 16½ inches long and 7 inches at widest point) out of brown paper. Lay pattern on pastry, and cut around pattern using a sharp knife; lift off pattern and pastry scraps. Add scraps to remaining pastry.

Spread about two-thirds of rice mixture over pastry, spreading to within 1 inch of edges. Arrange fillets to cover rice, dividing fillets as necessary to ensure coverage. Spoon Mornay Sauce over fish, and top with remaining rice mixture.

Roll out remaining pastry on a lightly floured surface to ⅛-inch thickness. Drape pastry over filling; trim edges of pastry to extend ½ inch beyond bottom pastry, and reserve scraps. Tuck top pastry under bottom pastry.

Roll out pastry scraps to ⅛-inch thickness, and cut out eye, mouth, gill, and fins. Beat egg and water until frothy. Brush back of eye, mouth, gill, and fins with egg, and attach to fish. Press edges of fish with the tines of a fork to seal. Snip through pastry on body of fish with sharp scissors to make scales. Brush pastry with egg mixture, being careful not to let egg drip onto baking sheet. Bake at 425° for 25 to 30 minutes or until golden brown. If edges of fish brown too quickly; cover with strips of foil. Let stand 10 minutes before slicing. Carefully transfer to serving platter, and garnish with watercress and lemon wedges. Yield: 6 servings.

Mornay Sauce:

2 tablespoons butter or
    margarine
2 tablespoons all-purpose flour
1 cup milk
¼ teaspoon salt
⅛ teaspoon white pepper
1 egg yolk
1½ teaspoons whipping cream
¼ cup (1 ounce) shredded Swiss
    cheese

Melt butter in a heavy 2-quart saucepan over low heat; add flour, stirring until smooth. Cook 1 minute, stirring constantly. Gradually add milk; cook over medium heat, stirring constantly, until mixture is thickened and bubbly. Stir in salt and pepper.

Beat egg yolk until thick and lemon colored; stir in whipping cream. Gradually stir about one-fourth of hot mixture into yolk; add to remaining hot mixture, stirring constantly. Cook over medium heat about 2 to 3 minutes, stirring constantly, until mixture is thickened. Add cheese, and stir until melted. Remove sauce from heat. Yield: about 1 cup.

Tip: Do not thaw fish at room temperature or in warm water; it will lose moisture and flavor. Instead, place in the refrigerator to thaw; allow 18 to 24 hours for thawing a 1-pound package. Do not refreeze thawed fish.

A Cheesecake Swirled With Chocolate

For a special dessert to serve company, choose Chocolate Swirl Cheesecake. Swirl melted chocolate through the cheesecake before baking for a rich, eye-catching dessert—enough to serve at least 10 people.

CHOCOLATE SWIRL CHEESECAKE

2 cups graham cracker crumbs
1½ teaspoons ground cinnamon
½ cup butter or margarine, melted
2 (1-ounce) squares semisweet chocolate
2 (8-ounce) packages cream cheese,
    softened
1 cup sugar
6 eggs
¼ cup plus 1 tablespoon all-purpose flour
1½ teaspoons grated lemon rind
3 tablespoons lemon juice
1 teaspoon vanilla extract
1 cup whipping cream, whipped
Grated chocolate (optional)

Combine graham cracker crumbs, cinnamon, and butter, mixing well; firmly press into bottom and up sides of a 9-inch springform pan. Refrigerate.

Place chocolate in top of a double boiler; bring water to a boil. Reduce heat to low; cook until chocolate melts. Set aside to cool slightly.

Beat cream cheese with electric mixer until light and fluffy; gradually add sugar, mixing well. Add eggs, one at a time, beating after each addition; stir in flour, lemon rind, lemon juice, and vanilla. Fold whipped cream into the cream cheese mixture.

Combine 1 cup cheesecake mixture and melted chocolate; set aside. Pour remaining cheesecake mixture into prepared crust. Pour chocolate mixture over top of cheesecake mixture; gently swirl with a knife.

Bake at 300° for 1 hour. Turn off oven, and let cheesecake stand in closed oven 1 hour. Open oven door, and allow cheesecake to stand in oven 2 to 3 hours or until completely cooled. Chill several hours. Garnish with grated chocolate, if desired. Yield: one 9-inch cheesecake.   *Lynn Koenig,*
Charleston, South Carolina.

Potatoes Can Be A Dinner Favorite

You may think of potatoes as just an everyday vegetable, but add a few extra ingredients, and suddenly they're fancy fare. Rather than reserving them as a standby, try these recipes and they may become your favorite side dish.

SOUFFLE POTATOES

1 (2.7-ounce) package mashed potato
    flakes
1 (8-ounce) carton commercial sour cream
1 cup cream-style cottage cheese
3 tablespoons minced onion
1 teaspoon dried parsley flakes
¼ teaspoon garlic salt
¼ teaspoon pepper
3 eggs, separated

Prepare potatoes according to package directions, using 1 cup water.

Combine mashed potatoes and next 6 ingredients, stirring well.

Beat egg yolks until thick and lemon colored; stir into potato mixture.

Beat egg whites (at room temperature) until stiff but not dry. Gently fold into potato mixture. Spoon into a lightly greased 1½-quart casserole. Bake at 350° for 1 hour and 5 minutes or until puffed and lightly browned. Serve immediately. Yield: 6 servings.
Mrs. W. J. Nichol,
Knoxville, Tennessee.

POTATOES WITH FETA CHEESE

5 medium-size baking potatoes
10 pimiento-stuffed olives, thinly sliced
1¼ cups crumbled feta cheese
⅓ cup half-and-half
2 tablespoons butter or margarine, melted
¼ teaspoon white pepper
⅛ teaspoon garlic salt
1 medium-size green pepper, cut into
    rings
2 tablespoons butter or margarine

Cook potatoes in boiling salted water 25 to 30 minutes or until tender; drain well, and cool. Peel potatoes, and cut into 1-inch cubes.

Combine potatoes and next 6 ingredients; toss gently. Spoon into a lightly greased 10- x 6- x 2-inch baking dish.

Sauté green pepper in 2 tablespoons butter; arrange around edge of baking dish. Bake at 350° for 20 minutes. Yield: 6 servings.   *Ella C. Stivers,*
Abilene, Texas.

GARLIC POTATOES

4 large baking potatoes, peeled and cubed
2 stalks celery, finely chopped
1 small onion, finely chopped
2 to 3 cloves garlic, minced
½ cup butter or margarine, melted
3 tablespoons chopped fresh parsley
½ teaspoon salt
½ teaspoon pepper

Combine all ingredients; place in a lightly greased 12- x 8- x 2-inch baking dish. Bake at 350° for 1 hour and 15 minutes or until potatoes are tender. Yield: 6 to 8 servings.
Charlotte Watkins,
Lakeland, Florida.

HOT DEVILED POTATOES

4 medium-size red potatoes peeled and cubed
1 (8-ounce) carton commercial sour cream
2 tablespoons chopped green onions
2 to 3 teaspoons prepared mustard
¼ teaspoon salt
¼ teaspoon white pepper
Paprika

Cook potatoes in boiling salted water 20 minutes or until tender. Drain well, and mash.
Combine potatoes and next 5 ingredients, mixing well. Spoon mixture into a lightly greased 1-quart casserole; sprinkle with paprika. Cover and bake at 350° for 15 minutes. Yield: 4 servings.
Michele Zenon,
Alexandria, Virginia.

FLUFFY POTATOES

2 cups mashed potatoes
½ cup milk
2 tablespoons butter or margarine, softened
1 teaspoon salt
Dash of pepper
2 eggs, separated
½ cup (2 ounces) shredded sharp Cheddar cheese

Combine potatoes, milk, butter, salt, and pepper; beat at medium speed of electric mixer until smooth. Beat egg yolks until thick and lemon colored; stir yolks and cheese into potato mixture. Beat egg whites (at room temperature) until stiff but not dry; gently fold into potato mixture. Spoon mixture into a lightly greased 1-quart casserole. Cover and bake at 350° for 20 to 25 minutes. Yield: 4 servings.
Margot Foster,
Hubbard, Texas.

Make Pork The Main Dish

The next time you're planning a menu, take a look at these tasty pork recipes. Orange-Glazed Spareribs bake right in your oven. Or if you're hungry for a barbecue sandwich, try our easy Spicy Barbecued Pork. You don't have to set up the grill to enjoy this flavorful entrée; the meat is cooked in a Dutch oven, shredded, and then simmered in smoke-flavored barbecue sauce.

ORANGE-GLAZED SPARERIBS

4 pounds spareribs
1 (6-ounce) can frozen orange juice concentrate, thawed and undiluted
1½ teaspoons Worcestershire sauce
½ teaspoon garlic salt
⅛ teaspoon pepper

Cut ribs into serving-size pieces; place in a large Dutch oven. Add enough water to cover ribs; bring to a boil. Cover, reduce heat, and simmer 1 hour. Drain ribs, and place in a large shallow roasting pan; set aside.
Combine remaining ingredients; mix well. Brush ribs with sauce. Bake, uncovered, at 325° for 30 to 40 minutes, basting and turning occasionally. Yield: about 4 servings.
De Lea Lonadier,
Montgomery, Louisiana.

SPICY BARBECUED PORK

1 (5- to 6-pound) Boston butt
2 medium onions, sliced
4 to 5 whole cloves
1 (18-ounce) bottle hickory smoke-flavored barbecue sauce
⅛ teaspoon hot sauce
Hamburger buns

Cover roast with water in a large Dutch oven. Add onion and cloves; cover and cook over medium heat 2 to 2½ hours or until pork is tender. Drain and shred with a fork. Combine shredded pork, barbecue sauce, and hot sauce in a Dutch oven. Cover and cook over low heat 15 to 20 minutes, stirring occasionally. Serve on buns. Yield: 10 to 12 servings.
Liz Wilson,
Marietta, Georgia.

RIO GRANDE PORK ROAST

½ teaspoon salt
½ teaspoon garlic salt
½ teaspoon chili powder
1 (4-pound) boneless pork loin roast
½ cup apple jelly
½ cup catsup
1 tablespoon vinegar
½ teaspoon chili powder

Combine first 3 ingredients; rub on all sides of roast. Place roast, fat side up, on rack in a roasting pan. Insert meat thermometer (not touching bone or fat). Bake, uncovered, at 325° for 2 hours.
Combine remaining ingredients in a small saucepan; bring to a boil. Reduce heat and simmer, uncovered, 2 minutes, stirring occasionally. Baste roast with sauce. Bake an additional 20 to 25 minutes or until thermometer reaches 170°, basting occasionally.
Place roast on a serving platter. Add enough water to pan drippings to make 1 cup; place in saucepan, and bring to a boil. Serve sauce with the roast. Yield: 12 servings.
Mrs. Jack Davis,
Morganton, North Carolina.

TEXAS SAUSAGE, BEANS, AND RICE

1 pound dried kidney beans
1 ham bone
2 large onions, chopped
1 medium-size green pepper, chopped
2 stalks celery, chopped
3 cloves garlic, crushed
1 bay leaf
½ teaspoon salt
¼ teaspoon pepper
1 pound hot bulk sausage
1 pound mild bulk sausage
¼ cup chopped fresh parsley
Hot cooked rice

Sort and wash beans; place in a large Dutch oven. Cover with water 2 inches above beans; let soak overnight. Drain beans; cover with water. Stir in next 8 ingredients; bring to a boil. Cover, reduce heat, and simmer 1 hour.
Brown sausage in a large skillet, stirring to crumble; drain well. Stir into bean mixture. Cook, uncovered, an additional 15 minutes. Remove bay leaf and ham bone; stir in parsley. Serve over cooked rice. Yield: 8 to 10 servings.
Carol Barclay,
Portland, Texas.

Tip: Use a bulb baster to remove fat from broth, stew, or soup.

December

Homemade Candy For A Sweeter Season

Candy seems to have more appeal at Christmas than at other times of the year. Many folks prepare large batches early in the season so they'll have plenty for their families and drop-in guests. These treats can also be packed into festive gift boxes and given to friends and relatives.

After the initial testing of these candy recipes we kept some of the candies around for several days to make sure they would hold up if packed into holiday gift boxes. Notice that refrigeration is recommended for some of the recipes, and it's usually best to store the candy in an airtight container.

CHOCOLATE BOURBON BALLS

1 (6-ounce) package semisweet chocolate morsels
½ cup bourbon
3 tablespoons light corn syrup
2½ cups vanilla wafer crumbs
½ cup sifted powdered sugar
1 cup finely chopped pecans
Sugar

Place chocolate morsels in top of a double boiler; bring water to a boil. Reduce heat to low; cook until chocolate melts, stirring occasionally. Remove from heat; stir in bourbon and corn syrup. Set aside.

Combine crumbs, powdered sugar, and pecans; mix well. Stir into chocolate mixture; let stand 30 minutes. Shape into 1-inch balls; roll in sugar. Store in an airtight container in refrigerator. Yield: about 5 dozen.
*Mary B. Quesenberry,
Dugspur, Virginia.*

CHOCOLATE-COVERED CHERRIES

1 (16-ounce) jar plus 1 (10-ounce) jar maraschino cherries with stems, undrained
3 tablespoons butter or margarine, softened
3 tablespoons light corn syrup
¼ teaspoon salt
2 cups sifted powdered sugar
1 (12-ounce) package semisweet chocolate morsels
1 tablespoon shortening

Drain 50 cherries; pat dry on absorbent paper towels, and set aside. Reserve remaining cherries for other uses.

Combine butter, syrup, and salt in a medium mixing bowl, stirring well; stir in powdered sugar, and knead in bowl until smooth.

Shape ½ teaspoon sugar mixture around each cherry. Place on a waxed paper-lined baking sheet; chill about 2 hours or until firm.

Combine chocolate and shortening in top of a double boiler; bring water to a boil. Reduce heat to low; cook until chocolate melts. Dip each cherry by the stem into chocolate. Place on a waxed paper-lined baking sheet; chill until firm. Store in an airtight container in the refrigerator. Yield: 50 cherries.
*Mrs. Jack Martin,
Courtland, Virginia.*

HOLIDAY MOCHA FUDGE

1 (5.33-ounce) can evaporated milk
1⅔ cups sugar
2 tablespoons butter or margarine
½ teaspoon salt
2 cups miniature marshmallows
1 (6-ounce) package semisweet chocolate morsels
½ cup butterscotch morsels
1 tablespoon instant coffee granules
1 teaspoon vanilla extract
½ cup chopped pecans
Candied red and green cherries (optional)

Combine milk, sugar, butter, and salt in a Dutch oven. Cook over medium heat, stirring constantly, until sugar dissolves. Bring to a boil; cook 3 minutes or until mixture reaches 225°, stirring occasionally.

Remove from heat, and add next 6 ingredients, stirring until marshmallows melt. Pour into a buttered 8-inch square pan. Cool and cut into squares. Garnish with candied cherries, if desired. Yield: 3 dozen.
*Gail Dormon,
Anniston, Alabama.*

ROCKY ROAD

1 (12-ounce) package semisweet chocolate morsels
1 (14-ounce) can sweetened condensed milk
2 tablespoons butter or margarine
2 cups dry-roasted peanuts
1 (10½-ounce) package miniature marshmallows

Place chocolate morsels, milk, and butter in top of a double boiler; bring to a boil. Reduce heat to low; cook until chocolate and butter melt, stirring constantly. Remove from heat, and stir in peanuts and marshmallows. Spread mixture into a waxed paper-lined 13- x 9- x 2-inch baking pan. Chill at least 2 hours. Cut into 1½-inch squares. Store in refrigerator. Yield: about 4 dozen.
*Rebecca Conkling,
Northville, Michigan.*

CHOCOLATE VELVETS

12 ounces milk chocolate candy
¼ cup unsalted butter
¾ cup whipping cream, scalded
1½ tablespoons crème de cacao or Kahlúa
Chocolate-flavored dècors or finely chopped pecans

Position knife blade in food processor bowl. Break chocolate into pieces, and place in bowl; process until finely chopped.

Heat butter to 110°. With processor running, add butter and hot whipping cream through feed chute; continue processing 1 minute. Stir in crème de cacao. Pour mixture into a bowl, and chill overnight.

Shape mixture into ¾-inch balls, and roll in chocolate-flavored dècors or chopped pecans. Freeze 1 hour or until firm. Refrigerate until serving time. Yield: 3 dozen. *Cynthia Kannenberg,
Brown Deer, Wisconsin.*

PEANUT BRITTLE

2 cups shelled raw peanuts
2 cups sugar
1 cup light corn syrup
⅓ cup water
2 tablespoons butter or margarine
¼ teaspoon salt
1 teaspoon baking soda
1 teaspoon vanilla extract

Spread peanuts evenly in a 15- x 10- x 1-inch jellyroll pan; bake at 350° for 15 minutes, stirring once. Set aside.

Combine next 5 ingredients in a Dutch oven; cook over medium heat, stirring constantly, until sugar dissolves. Continue cooking, stirring occasionally, until mixture reaches hard crack stage (300°). Remove from heat; stir in peanuts, soda, and vanilla.

Working rapidly, spread mixture thinly onto a buttered 15- x 10- x 1-inch jellyroll pan. Let cool; break into pieces. Yield: about 2 pounds.
*Mary Jane Highland,
Carbondale, Illinois.*

SPICY PRALINE DELIGHTS

1 cup evaporated milk
1 (16-ounce) package brown sugar
¼ cup butter or margarine
12 large marshmallows
1 teaspoon ground cinnamon
½ teaspoon ground nutmeg
2 cups coarsely chopped pecans

Combine milk and sugar in a Dutch oven; bring to a boil, stirring constantly. Cook over medium heat, stirring constantly, until mixture reaches soft ball stage (234°). Remove from heat; stir in butter, marshmallows, cinnamon, and nutmeg. Beat with a wooden spoon until mixture is creamy and begins to thicken. Quickly stir in pecans. Working rapidly, drop by rounded tablespoonfuls onto waxed paper; let cool. Yield: about 2¼ dozen. *Fern Henriksen, Shreveport, Louisiana.*

ORANGE PECANS

1 cup sugar
1 tablespoon light corn syrup
⅓ cup orange juice
1 tablespoon butter or margarine
2¼ cups pecan halves
½ teaspoon grated orange rind

Combine sugar, corn syrup, and orange juice in a saucepan; mix well. Cook over medium heat, stirring occasionally, until mixture reaches soft ball stage (240°). Remove from heat; stir in butter. Beat with a wooden spoon until mixture just begins to thicken. Stir in pecans and orange rind. Working rapidly, drop by heaping teaspoonfuls onto waxed paper, and let cool. Yield: about 1¼ dozen. *Romanza Johnson, Bowling Green, Kentucky.*

FRUIT BALLS

2 cups chopped, mixed dried fruit
1 cup raisins
1 cup flaked coconut
½ cup sifted powdered sugar
¼ cup cocoa
2 tablespoons orange juice
Additional sifted powdered sugar

Position steel blade in food processor bowl; add mixed fruit, raisins, and coconut. Process about 1 minute or until finely ground. Stir in ½ cup powdered sugar, cocoa, and orange juice. Chill 2 or 3 hours. Shape into 1-inch balls; roll in powdered sugar. Chill. Yield: about 2⅔ dozen. *Bettye Cortner, Cerulean, Kentucky.*

CRYSTAL CANDY

4 cups sugar
1 cup water
1 cup light corn syrup
5 drops red food coloring
¾ teaspoon oil of cinnamon

Combine sugar, water, and syrup in a large Dutch oven. Bring to a boil over medium heat, stirring constantly. Stir in food coloring. Continue to cook, without stirring, until mixture reaches hard crack stage (300°). Remove from heat, and stir in oil of cinnamon.

Working rapidly, spread mixture onto an oiled 15- x 10- x 1-inch jellyroll pan. Let cool; break into pieces. Yield: about 4 dozen pieces.

Note: Oil of cinnamon may be purchased at drug stores.

EASY HOLIDAY MINTS

1 (16-ounce) package powdered sugar
3 tablespoons butter or margarine, softened
3½ tablespoons evaporated milk
¼ to ½ teaspoon peppermint or almond extract
Few drops of desired food coloring

Combine all ingredients in a large mixing bowl; knead in bowl until smooth. Shape mints in rubber candy molds, and place on baking sheets; cover with a paper towel, and let dry. Remove candy from molds, and store in an airtight container. Yield: 6 dozen.
Evelyn Milam, Knoxville, Tennessee.

Cook Up A Gift Idea

Most of us like to follow the pleasure of cooking with the fun of sharing the results. That's why the holiday season will find cooks preparing some delicious food gifts. A bag of cookies or a jar of jam bearing your personal touch will be a welcome sign of friendship to neighbors or coworkers. Besides being fun to make and share, our selection of baked goods, snacks, and other savory items are attractive and often cost less than those that are store-bought.

GINGERBREAD MEN

1 cup shortening
1 cup sugar
1 cup molasses
1 egg
2 tablespoons vinegar
5 cups all-purpose flour
1½ teaspoons baking soda
½ teaspoon salt
2 to 3 teaspoons ground ginger
1 teaspoon ground cinnamon
1 teaspoon ground cloves
Raisins
Cinnamon-flavored candies

Cream shortening; gradually add sugar, beating until light and fluffy. Add molasses, egg, and vinegar; mix well.

Combine flour, soda, salt, and spices; stir well. Add to molasses mixture, mixing well. Shape dough into a ball; knead until smooth. Chill overnight.

Divide dough in half; place one portion in refrigerator. Roll half of dough to ¼- to ⅛-inch thickness on a lightly floured surface. Cut with a 4-inch gingerbread man cutter, and place on ungreased cookie sheets. Press raisins into dough for eyes, nose, and mouth. Use cinnamon-flavored candies or additional raisins for buttons.

Bake at 375° for 6 to 7 minutes. Cool 2 minutes; remove cookies to wire racks, and cool completely. Repeat procedure with remaining dough. Yield: about 2 dozen. *Mildred Edwards, Hamburg, Arkansas.*

TROPICAL MUFFINS

1¾ cups all-purpose flour
½ cup sugar
2 teaspoons baking powder
¼ teaspoon baking soda
½ cup flaked coconut
1 cup mashed ripe banana
1 teaspoon grated orange rind
⅓ cup orange juice
⅓ cup shortening, melted
1 egg, beaten

Combine first 4 ingredients in a large bowl; stir in coconut. Make a well in center of mixture. Combine remaining ingredients; add to dry ingredients, stirring just until moistened. Spoon into lightly greased muffin pans, filling two-thirds full. Bake at 375° for 25 minutes. Yield: 1 dozen. *Mrs. Albert F. Roddy, Chattanooga, Tennessee.*

Tip: To thaw frozen bread or rolls, wrap in aluminum foil and heat at 325° for 5 minutes.

PARADISE PEAR JAM

2 pounds pears, unpeeled, cored, and ground
1 medium orange, unpeeled, seeded, and ground
1 medium lemon, unpeeled, seeded, and ground
1 (8½-ounce) can crushed pineapple, undrained
¼ cup maraschino cherries, coarsely chopped
1 (1¾-ounce) package powdered fruit pectin
5 cups sugar

Combine first 6 ingredients in a large Dutch oven, stirring well; bring to a boil over high heat, stirring frequently. Add sugar, and return to a boil; boil 1 minute, stirring constantly. Remove from heat, and skim off foam with a metal spoon.

Quickly ladle jam into hot jars, leaving ¼-inch headspace; cover at once with metal lids, and screw bands tight. Process in boiling-water bath 15 minutes. Yield: 7 half pints.
Dorothy Grant,
Pensacola, Florida.

CRAN-APPLE RELISH

4 cups fresh cranberries, ground
2½ cups sugar
2 medium apples, unpeeled, cored, and ground
2 small oranges, unpeeled, seeded, and ground
1 small lemon, unpeeled, seeded, and ground
½ cup currants
½ cup finely chopped pecans or walnuts
2 tablespoons Grand Marnier or other orange-flavored liqueur

Combine all ingredients in a large mixing bowl; mix well. Chill several hours or overnight. Store in an airtight container in the refrigerator. Yield: about 1 quart.
Jeanne Wood,
New Orleans, Louisiana.

HONEYCOMB PECANS

2 cups sugar
½ cup water
2 tablespoons honey
2 teaspoons vanilla extract
1 teaspoon rum flavoring
3 cups pecans

Combine sugar, water, and honey in a heavy saucepan, stirring to mix. Bring mixture to a boil (do not stir), and cook to soft ball stage (240°). Remove from heat; add flavorings, and cool to lukewarm. Beat with an electric mixer 2 to 3 minutes or until mixture turns creamy. Add pecans, stirring until coated. Drop by heaping teaspoonfuls onto waxed paper. Let cool. Yield: 3¼ cups.
Dorsella Utter,
Louisville, Kentucky.

HERBED CHEESE ROUND

1 (8-ounce) package cream cheese, softened
1 teaspoon dried whole basil
1 teaspoon caraway seeds
1 teaspoon chopped fresh chives
1 teaspoon dillseeds
1 clove garlic, crushed
Lemon-pepper seasoning

Combine first 6 ingredients. Shape into a 5- x 1-inch patty; coat top and sides with lemon-pepper seasoning. Cover and chill 10 to 12 hours; serve with crackers. Yield: one 5-inch round.
Mrs. E. W. Hanley,
Palm Harbor, Florida.

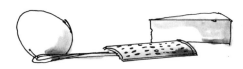

ONION TWIST LOAVES

1 package dry yeast
¼ cup warm water (105° to 115°)
¼ cup sugar
½ cup milk
½ cup warm water (105° to 115°)
¼ cup butter or margarine, softened
1 egg, beaten
1½ teaspoons salt
4 cups all-purpose flour, divided
¼ cup butter or margarine, melted
2 tablespoons instant minced onion
1 tablespoon grated Parmesan cheese
1 tablespoon poppy seeds
1 teaspoon garlic salt
1 teaspoon paprika

Dissolve yeast in ¼ cup warm water in a large bowl. Add next 6 ingredients. Gradually add 2 cups flour, beating at medium speed of an electric mixer until smooth. Gradually stir in enough remaining flour to make a soft dough.

Turn dough out onto a well-floured surface, and knead 5 minutes until smooth and elastic. Place dough in a well-greased bowl, turning to grease top. Cover and let rise in a warm place (85°), free from drafts, 1 hour or until doubled in bulk.

Punch dough down; turn out onto a floured surface, and knead 1 minute. Roll into an 18- x 12-inch rectangle. Combine ¼ cup melted butter and remaining ingredients, stirring well; spread evenly over dough. Cut dough lengthwise into three 18- x 4-inch strips. Roll each strip up, jellyroll fashion, beginning with long side. Cut each strip in half crosswise. Place 3 halves, side by side, on a greased baking sheet; braid. Tuck ends under to seal. Repeat with remaining dough.

Cover and let rise in a warm place (85°), free from drafts, 1 hour or until doubled in bulk. Bake at 350° for 30 to 35 minutes or until golden brown. Remove from baking sheets, and place on wire racks to cool. Yield: 2 loaves.
Betty Rabe,
Plano, Texas.

DILL-AND-CHIVE VINEGAR

3 large sprigs fresh dill or 2 teaspoons dried whole dillweed
8 to 10 sprigs fresh chives or 2 teaspoons freeze-dried chives
1¼ cups white vinegar (5% acidity)
Additional fresh dill sprigs (optional)
Additional fresh chive sprigs (optional)

Place dill and chives in a wide-mouth glass jar. Pour vinegar over herbs, and cover. Let stand at room temperature for 3 to 4 weeks.

Strain vinegar into a decorative jar, discarding herb residue; add additional sprigs of fresh dill and chives, if desired. Seal jar with a cork or other airtight lid. Yield: 1¼ cups.
Linda Askey,
Birmingham, Alabama.

HARVEST POPCORN

2 quarts freshly popped popcorn, unsalted
2 (1½-ounce) cans potato sticks
1 cup salted mixed nuts
½ cup unsalted butter, melted
1 teaspoon lemon-pepper seasoning
1 teaspoon dried whole dillweed
1 teaspoon Worcestershire sauce
½ teaspoon garlic powder
½ teaspoon onion powder

Combine popcorn, potato sticks, and nuts in a 15- x 10- x 1-inch jellyroll pan.

Combine remaining ingredients; pour over popcorn mixture, stirring until evenly coated. Bake at 350° for 6 to 8 minutes, stirring mixture once. Yield: 2½ quarts.
Joyce Andrews,
Washington, Virginia.

Holiday Desserts™

The Holidays Are Here—Bring On Dessert!

In late November and early December, people begin to stock up on flour, sugar, candied fruit, and nuts. Across the South, visions of rich pecan pies, towering chocolate cakes, and luscious fruit desserts fill the air. Yes, Christmas is traditionally celebrated with an abundance of desserts. So to help make those sweet visions a reality, we've put together one of our favorite special sections, "Holiday Desserts."

In the following pages, you'll find spectacular cakes, pies, soufflés, and confections. And lest you think we forgot the calorie-conscious, we also prepared a collection of "Cooking Light" recipes just for you.

Many people bake cookies during the holiday season too. But this year try a different type of cookie—shape it like a Christmas card. Decorate the top with icing and candy; when the recipient opens the card tied together with ribbon, he'll find the holiday message inscribed just for him.

Fashion personalized holiday greeting cards using cookies, candies, and icing. One recipe yields four assorted cards for special family and friends.

Lift the top cookie to reveal a message. Satin ribbon ties the two cookies together.

The cookies are totally edible, but since they will keep for several years, we suggest that the recipients save them for display. At the end of each season, wrap the cookie cards tightly in plastic wrap and store them in a cool dry place. Send along a gift box of extra cookie-cutter cookies so your friends can sample how good the cookies taste.

One batch of the dough will make four cookie cards. You can easily make two or three recipes and set up an assembly line for baking and decorating them. Once the icing is made and colored, the decorating won't take long. The icing requires overnight drying time, however, so start the cookies several days before you need them.

Holiday Desserts

Tips for Piping Icing

If you've never piped icing before, don't let that stop you from making these novel Christmas cookie cards. Invest in a starter set of cake decorating tips or borrow the equipment from a friend. With a little practice, you'll have all the experience needed to pipe the simple decorations on these cookies.

Before decorating the cookies, mix up a batch of icing to practice the borders and decorations you'll use. Pipe them on a waxed paper-lined cookie sheet just as if it were the real thing. Practice until you develop the pressure control necessary to make the decorations.

When you're ready to decorate the cookies, color the icing with paste food coloring, adding a very small amount at a time; a little goes a long way. Remember also that the icing will darken in color slightly as it dries. Always mix enough of each icing color in the beginning, because it is difficult to duplicate any tint exactly.

For decorating the cookies, you'll need bags to hold icing, metal decorating tips to define the icing shapes you'll make, and couplers to allow you to change tubes without refilling bags.

You can buy reusable plastic bags, disposable bags, or you can make your own from parchment paper.

To assemble the decorating bag, drop coupler into bag and push as far down into bag as possible. Insert metal tip over tip of coupler, and screw coupler ring over metal tip. Spoon icing into decorating bag, filling it about half full; fold corners of bag over and crease until all air is pressed out. To change tips, simply unscrew the coupler ring and replace the tip.

Metal decorating tips can be categorized into five basic groups that determine the type of decorations they produce. The size and shape of the opening on a decorating tip determines the group to which it belongs.

The types of tips include smooth round tips that produce dots, lines, stems, stringwork, and writing; rose tips that make an assortment of flowers, as well as bows and ruffled borders; notched leaf tips that produce several types of leaves, as well as decorative borders; fluted star tips that pipe stars, shells, drop flowers, and zigzag and other borders; and special drop flower tips that produce flowers of all shapes and sizes.

Remember that when piping, the amount of pressure and the steadiness with which it is applied to the decorating bag will determine the size and uniformity of any icing design. Some decorations require even pressure, others a varying application of light, medium, or heavy pressure. The more pressure is controlled, the more exact the decoration will be. If icing ripples, you are squeezing the bag too hard. If icing breaks, you are moving the bag too quickly or icing is too thick.

If you are left-handed, hold the decorating bag in your left hand and guide decorating tube with the fingers of your right hand. If instructions say to hold decorating bag over to the right, you should hold it over to the left. Most right-handed people decorate from left to right; left-handed people might find it easier to decorate from right to left, except when writing.

There are five decorating techniques that require different pressure and tip positions. Follow these basic instructions for each technique, and you can make almost any type of decoration.

Dots, stars, and drop flowers: Hold the bag at a 90-degree angle with tip almost touching the surface. Steadily squeeze out icing. Lift bag slightly as icing builds up in desired design, keeping tip buried in icing; then stop pressure and pull tip away.

Straight lines: To pipe a straight line, touch the tip to the surface at a 45-degree angle, letting a small amount of icing flow. Continue squeezing bag and draw tip across surface, about ½ inch from surface. Touch surface with tip, and release pressure to end line. Literally pulling the line of icing through the air rather than against the surface keeps line straight.

Leaves: Hold bag at a 45-degree angle to surface. Squeeze bag to build up a base; then pull bag away as you relax pressure, stop squeezing, and lift away.

Borders: For most borders, hold bag at a 45-degree angle. Touch tip to the surface, and squeeze out icing as you pull tip in desired border design, such as zigzag, push-pull, interlooping "e" shape, etc.

Writing: Use small round tip, holding tip at 45-degree angle to surface; move tip with motion of arm, not wrist, to form desired letters. The tip should lightly touch the surface as you write.

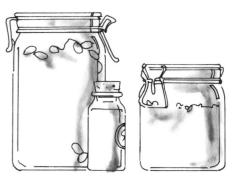

CHRISTMAS COOKIE CARDS

1 cup shortening
1½ cups sugar
2 eggs, beaten
1 teaspoon vanilla extract
½ cup plus 2 tablespoons orange juice
5¼ cups all-purpose flour
⅛ teaspoon salt
1 teaspoon baking powder
1 teaspoon baking soda
1 to 2 recipes Royal Icing
Red and green paste food coloring
Assorted candies and sprinkles

Cut a 6½- x 4½-inch paper pattern to use as a guide in cutting rectangles for cookie cards. (Do not use recycled paper.) Draw 2 small circles on top and on one side of pattern to indicate holes for placement of ribbon to tie cookies together for horizontal and vertical cookie cards. Set aside.

Cream shortening; gradually add sugar, beating at medium speed of an electric mixer until fluffy. Beat in eggs, vanilla, and orange juice, mixing well. Combine dry ingredients; add to creamed mixture, mixing well.

Divide dough into thirds, wrap in foil, and chill. Working with one portion at a time, roll to ⅛-inch thickness on lightly greased and floured cookie sheets. Cut 8 rectangles using pattern, and cut 4 assorted shapes for top design of cards

302   December

Holiday Desserts

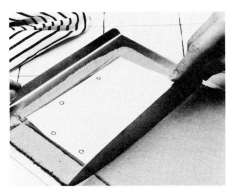

Step 1—Roll dough directly on cookie sheets; cut out cookies following patterns you make. Remove scraps.

Step 2—Inscribe messages in half the cookie rectangles, pressing deeply into the dough. Bake at 350° for 10 minutes.

Step 3—Make cookies from cutters as desired for tops of cookie cards; decorate them with icing and candies.

Step 4—Decorate remaining rectangles for tops as directed, contrasting the color with that of the cutter-shaped cookie.

using cookie cutters. (Make sure your cookie cutters will fit size of cards.) Remove and reroll scraps of dough. Cut any leftover dough into extra cookie cutter shapes as desired.

With a drinking straw, punch holes in top or side of cookie rectangles for cards, following holes in paper pattern. Write desired message in dough on half of rectangular cookies using the point of a wooden pick or other pointed instrument and pressing almost through dough. Bake all cookies at 350° for 10 to 12 minutes. Cool cookies on wire racks. Set aside cookies with inscribed messages. Remaining cookies will be decorated with Royal Icing.

Color one-third of Royal Icing bright green and one-third red, leaving remaining one-third white. Keep Royal

Icing covered with plastic wrap when not in use.

Spoon white icing into decorating bag fitted with No. 16 star tip. Pipe a zigzag border around edges of 4 plain rectangle cookies; pipe a small zigzag circle around holes for ribbons, and set aside.

Decorate cookie cutter shapes for tops of cards as desired. For a boot, pipe a white zigzag border around boot, and pipe fluffy white icing (overlapping zigzag lines) as a boot cuff. For a striped boot, pipe plain diagonal lines across boot using No. 3 or 4 round tip. Remaining icing for boot will be completed later. For a tree, we pipe green icing into fluffy greenery, starting at bottom of cookie, using No. 233 specialty tip. Attach candies as decorations on tree, and set aside to dry.

Dilute red and green icing with a few drops of water to make icing a smooth flowing consistency. (When stirred, icing should gradually settle into a smooth top surface. If icing is too watery, it will not dry properly and may run under outline into other color areas.) Spoon icing into decorating bags fitted with No. 4, 5, 6, 7, or 8 round tips. Let diluted icing flow from bag within piped outlines of rectangles and boot or other cookie cutouts as desired, smoothing icing into corners using a wooden pick. For good contrast, pipe red diluted icing on rectangle that will have a green top cookie, and green diluted icing where top cookie will be red. Let dry overnight. Cover leftover icing with plastic wrap, and chill.

Carefully attach decorated top cookies onto rectangles using leftover icing. (If icing is too dry, make a new batch.) Attach assorted candies around cookie cutouts with icing as desired. Let icing dry thoroughly.

Match decorated cookie rectangles with inscribed cookies. Tie cookies together loosely with ribbon. Yield: 4 cookie cards.

Royal Icing:

3 egg whites
½ teaspoon cream of tartar
1 (16-ounce) package powdered sugar, sifted

Combine egg whites (at room temperature) and cream of tartar in a large mixing bowl. Beat at medium speed of an electric mixer until frothy. Gradually add powdered sugar, mixing well. Beat 5 to 7 minutes. Yield: about 2 cups.

Note: Icing dries very quickly; keep covered at all times with plastic wrap. Do not double recipe. If additional icing is needed, make another batch.

Tip: Use odd pieces of candy to make a topping for ice cream. Plain chocolate, mints, or cream candies may be placed in top of a double boiler with a little cream and heated until well blended. Serve hot over ice cream or cake, or store in refrigerator and use later cold.

Cake Rolls Are Filled With Flavor

You can fill your dessert plates with swirls of flavor and color by serving these luscious cake rolls. They won't take long to prepare since you only bake one thin layer of cake; but it may take some practice to roll them up. Just use extra care during the rolling process to keep the tender layer from cracking. Even if the cake cracks, you can use frosting to cover it up.

If you'd rather skip the frosting, cake rolls can look just as elegant with powdered sugar sifted over the top. If the cake is light colored, try sifting cocoa over the top for a pretty contrast. Piping sweetened whipped cream on the cake is another simple way to dress up the dessert.

BUCHE DE NOEL

5 eggs, separated
⅓ cup sugar
½ teaspoon vanilla extract
1 cup ground walnuts
¼ cup all-purpose flour
¼ cup cocoa
½ teaspoon salt
¼ teaspoon cream of tartar
⅓ cup sugar
Powdered sugar
1 cup whipping cream
½ teaspoon vanilla extract
¼ cup sifted powdered sugar
¼ cup chopped candied cherries
Rich Chocolate Frosting

Grease a 15- x 10- x 1-inch jellyroll pan with vegetable oil, and line with waxed paper. Grease waxed paper lightly; set aside.

Beat egg yolks at high speed of an electric mixer until thick. Gradually add ⅓ cup sugar, beating well. Stir in ½ teaspoon vanilla. Combine walnuts, flour, and cocoa; fold into yolk mixture.

Beat egg whites (at room temperature), salt, and cream of tartar until foamy; gradually add ⅓ cup sugar, beating until peaks are stiff, but not dry. Gradually fold yolk mixture into whites. Spread batter evenly in prepared pan. Bake at 350° for 15 minutes.

Sift powdered sugar in a 15- x 10-inch rectangle on a towel. When cake is done, immediately loosen from sides of pan, and turn out onto sugar. Peel off waxed paper. Starting at long side, roll up cake and towel together; cool on a wire rack, seam side down.

Beat whipping cream and ½ teaspoon vanilla until foamy; gradually add ¼ cup powdered sugar, beating until peaks hold their shape. Fold in cherries.

Unroll cake, and remove towel. Spread cake with whipped cream mixture and reroll. Place on serving plate, seam side down. Spread Rich Chocolate Frosting over top and sides of cake roll. Yield: 10 to 12 servings.

Rich Chocolate Frosting:

¼ cup butter or margarine, softened
1¾ cups sifted powdered sugar
1 tablespoon cocoa
1 tablespoon hot water
½ teaspoon vanilla extract

Cream butter. Combine sugar and cocoa; gradually add to butter alternately with water, beating well. Add vanilla; beat until smooth. Yield: enough frosting for one cake roll.

Peggy H. Amos,
Martinsville, Virginia.

COCONUT-PINEAPPLE CAKE ROLL

4 eggs
¾ cup sugar
1 teaspoon vanilla extract
¾ cup biscuit mix
1 cup flaked coconut
Powdered sugar
1 (3½-ounce) package vanilla instant
    pudding mix
1½ cups milk
1 (8-ounce) can crushed pineapple,
    drained
1 (4-ounce) carton frozen whipped
    topping, thawed
1 cup flaked coconut
Red and green maraschino cherries
Pineapple tidbits

Grease a 15- x 10- x 1-inch jellyroll pan, and line with waxed paper. Grease and flour waxed paper; set aside.

Beat eggs until light and lemon colored; gradually add ¾ cup sugar and

vanilla, beating well. Gradually add biscuit mix; stir well. Stir in 1 cup coconut. Spread batter evenly in prepared pan. Bake at 400° for 10 to 12 minutes.

Sift powdered sugar in a 15- x 10- x 1-inch rectangle on a towel. When cake is done, immediately loosen from sides of pan, and turn out onto powdered sugar. Peel off waxed paper. Starting at narrow end, roll up cake and towel together. Place seam side down on a wire rack, and cool.

Combine pudding mix and milk in a medium mixing bowl. Beat on low speed of an electric mixer until thickened. Let stand 3 minutes.

Unroll cake, and remove towel. Spread cake with pudding, leaving a 1-inch margin around edges; sprinkle with crushed pineapple. Reroll cake. Place on serving plate, seam side down. Frost top and sides with whipped topping. Sprinkle top and sides with 1 cup coconut. Chill until serving time. Garnish cake roll with cherries and pineapple tidbits. Yield: 8 to 10 servings.

Sandra Russell,
Gainesville, Florida.

CHOCOLATE-MOCHA CREAM ROLL

6 eggs, separated
½ cup sugar
½ cup cocoa
½ teaspoon vanilla extract
Dash of salt
¼ cup sugar
Powdered sugar
Mocha Cream Filling

Grease a 15- x 10- x 1-inch jellyroll pan with vegetable oil, and line with waxed paper. Grease waxed paper lightly; set aside.

Beat egg yolks in a large bowl, and beat until foamy at high speed of electric mixer; gradually add ½ cup sugar, beating until mixture is thick and lemon colored. Add cocoa, vanilla, and salt; beat at low speed of electric mixer until blended.

Beat egg whites (at room temperature) at high speed of electric mixer until foamy. Gradually add ¼ cup sugar, 1 tablespoon at a time, beating until stiff peaks form. Fold egg whites into chocolate mixture. Spread batter evenly in prepared pan. Bake at 375° for 15 minutes.

Sift powdered sugar in a 15- x 10-inch rectangle on a towel. When cake is done, immediately loosen from sides of pan, and turn out onto sugar. Peel off waxed paper. Starting at long side, roll up cake and towel together; cool on a wire rack, seam side down.

Unroll cake, and remove towel. Spread Mocha Cream Filling over cake, and reroll. Place on a serving plate, seam side down. Chill. Before serving, sift additional powdered sugar over roll. Yield: 10 servings.

Mocha Cream Filling:

1½ cups whipping cream
½ cup sifted powdered sugar
¼ cup cocoa
2 teaspoons instant coffee granules
1 teaspoon vanilla extract

Beat whipping cream until foamy; gradually add powdered sugar, cocoa, and coffee granules, beating until soft peaks form. Stir in vanilla. Yield: about 3¼ cups.   *Mrs. Harland J. Stone,*
Ocala, Florida.

STRAWBERRY CAKE ROLL

4 eggs, separated
¾ cup sugar
1 teaspoon vanilla extract
¾ cup sifted cake flour
¾ teaspoon baking powder
¼ teaspoon salt
Powdered sugar
1 cup whipping cream
3 tablespoons sugar
¼ teaspoon vanilla extract
1 (10-ounce) package frozen sliced
    strawberries, thawed and drained
¼ cup strawberry jam
¼ cup light corn syrup

Grease a 15- x 10- x 1-inch jellyroll pan, and line with waxed paper. Grease and flour waxed paper; set aside.

Beat egg yolks until thick and lemon colored; gradually add ¾ cup sugar, beating well. Stir in 1 teaspoon vanilla. Combine flour and baking powder; gradually add to sugar mixture, beating just until blended. Beat egg whites (at room temperature) and salt until stiff peaks form; stir one-fourth of egg white mixture into flour mixture. Repeat with remaining egg white mixture, stirring in one-fourth of mixture at a time.

Spread batter evenly in prepared pan. Bake at 375° for 10 to 12 minutes.

Sift powdered sugar in a 15- x 10-inch rectangle on a towel. When cake is done, immediately loosen from sides of pan and turn out onto sugar. Peel off waxed paper. Starting at narrow end, roll up cake and towel together; cool on a wire rack, seam side down.

Beat whipping cream until foamy; gradually add 3 tablespoons sugar, beating until soft peaks form. Add ¼ teaspoon vanilla; beat until mixed. Fold in strawberries. Unroll cake, and remove towel. Spread cake with strawberry filling, and reroll. Place on serving plate, seam side down.

Combine jam and corn syrup in a small saucepan; bring to a boil, stirring constantly. Remove from heat; brush mixture over cake roll. Chill until serving time. Yield: 8 to 10 servings.
Derrell H. Sears,
Anderson, South Carolina.

Crazy About Cranberries!

Cranberries add flavor and color to holiday desserts whether they're chilled in a tart, baked with apples in a cobbler, or whipped into a creamy soufflé. You'll find these tangy, tasty berries most plentiful during December.

TASTY CRANBERRY JUBILEE

1 cup sugar
1½ cups water
2 cups fresh cranberries
¼ cup brandy
Vanilla ice cream

Combine sugar and water in a saucepan. Bring mixture to a boil, stirring occasionally; boil 5 minutes. Add cranberries, and return to a boil; cook 5 minutes, stirring occasionally.

Heat brandy in a saucepan over medium heat. (Do not boil.) Ignite and pour over cranberries. After flames die, spoon over ice cream. Yield: 2 cups.
Alice McNamara,
Eucha, Oklahoma.

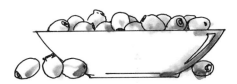

CRANBERRY-NUT TART

1 cup plus 2 tablespoons finely chopped
    walnuts
¼ cup sugar
1½ cups all-purpose flour
½ cup butter or margarine
1 egg, slightly beaten
1 teaspoon vanilla extract
1 envelope unflavored gelatin
¼ cup cold water
3 cups fresh cranberries
1 cup sugar
½ cup red currant jelly
½ cup whipping cream, whipped

Combine first 3 ingredients in a medium mixing bowl; cut in butter with a pastry blender until mixture resembles coarse meal. Add egg and vanilla, and stir with a fork until dry ingredients are moistened. Press mixture on bottom and sides of a lightly greased 9-inch springform pan; chill 30 minutes. Bake at 350° for 15 to 20 minutes or until golden brown. Cool completely.

Sprinkle gelatin over water in small bowl; set aside. Combine cranberries, 1 cup sugar, and jelly in a medium saucepan; cook 10 minutes over low heat or until cranberry skins pop. Remove cranberry mixture from heat, and let cool 5 minutes; add softened gelatin, and stir until dissolved. Cool completely.

Pour cranberry mixture into tart shell. Chill several hours. Place tart on a serving platter, and remove rim from springform pan. Garnish with whipped cream. Yield: one 9-inch tart.
Mrs. Joseph D. Brown,
Towson, Maryland.

FESTIVE CRANBERRY FREEZER PIE

1½ cups graham cracker crumbs
½ cup chopped pecans
¼ cup sugar
¼ cup plus 2 tablespoons butter or
    margarine, melted
2 cups fresh cranberries
1 cup sugar
2 egg whites
1 tablespoon frozen orange juice
    concentrate
1 teaspoon vanilla extract
⅛ teaspoon salt
1 cup whipping cream
Cranberry Glaze

Combine first 4 ingredients; mix well. Press mixture on bottom and sides of an ungreased 8-inch springform pan. Chill.

Combine cranberries and 1 cup sugar in a large mixing bowl; let stand 5 minutes. Add egg whites, orange juice concentrate, vanilla, and salt. Beat on low speed of an electric mixer until frothy; continue to beat at high speed 5 to 8 minutes or until stiff peaks form.

Beat whipping cream in a mixing bowl until soft peaks form; fold into cranberry mixture. Spoon mixture into prepared crust. Freeze overnight or until firm. Place dessert on a serving platter, and remove rim from springform pan. Serve with Cranberry Glaze. Yield: one 8-inch pie.

Cranberry Glaze:

½ cup sugar
1 tablespoon cornstarch
¾ cup fresh cranberries
⅔ cup water

Combine sugar and cornstarch in a small saucepan; stir well. Add cranberries and water; cook and stir until thickened and bubbly. Cool. Yield: about 1½ cups.   *Pearl T. Raines,*
Fort Valley, Georgia.

Tip: Most fruits are best stored in the refrigerator. Allow melons, avocados, and pears to ripen at room temperature; then refrigerate. Berries should be sorted to remove imperfect fruit before refrigerating; wash and hull just before serving.

CRANBERRY-TOPPED HOLIDAY SOUFFLE

2 envelopes unflavored gelatin
2 cups milk
4 eggs, separated
⅓ cup sugar
⅓ cup Grand Marnier or other
    orange-flavored liqueur
⅓ cup sugar
2 cups whipping cream, whipped
2 (16-ounce) cans whole berry cranberry
    sauce
1 cup chopped walnuts
2 tablespoons grated orange rind

Soften gelatin in milk in a saucepan; let stand 1 minute. Beat egg yolks, and add to gelatin mixture. Stir in ⅓ cup sugar; bring to a boil over low heat, stirring constantly. Remove mixture from heat, and cool; stir in liqueur. Chill until mixture is the consistency of unbeaten egg whites.

Beat egg whites (at room temperature) until foamy. Gradually add ⅓ cup sugar, 1 tablespoon at a time, beating until soft peaks form; fold into gelatin mixture. Fold whipped cream into gelatin mixture; spoon into a 3-quart soufflé dish. Chill until firm.

Combine cranberry sauce, chopped walnuts, and orange rind, stirring well; chill. Spoon soufflé into individual serving dishes; top each serving with cranberry mixture. Yield: 12 to 14 servings.   *Susie M. E. Dent,*
Saltillo, Mississippi.

CRANBERRY PUDDING

½ cup molasses
½ cup boiling water
2 teaspoons baking soda
1⅓ cups all-purpose flour
½ teaspoon salt
2 cups fresh cranberries
Lemon Sauce

Combine molasses and water in a large mixing bowl; stir in soda. Combine flour and salt; add molasses mixture, and stir until smooth. Add cranberries; stir gently.

Grease the top of a double boiler; pour in cranberry mixture. Cover and cook over boiling water 2 hours or until done. Cool pudding in pan 10 minutes;

invert onto a wire rack. Cool completely; serve with Lemon Sauce. Yield: 8 servings.

Lemon Sauce:

1 cup sugar
½ cup lightly salted butter
½ cup half-and-half
¼ teaspoon lemon extract

Combine all ingredients in a small saucepan; cook over medium heat, stirring constantly, until mixture boils. Remove from heat; serve warm. Yield: about 2 cups.   *Carol L. Bowling,*
Aiken, South Carolina.

CRANBERRY-AND-APPLE COBBLER

2 cups fresh cranberries
5 cups peeled, sliced cooking apples
1¼ cups sugar
2½ tablespoons quick-cooking tapioca
1 teaspoon vanilla extract
2 tablespoons butter or margarine
1 cup all-purpose flour
½ teaspoon salt
⅓ cup plus 1 tablespoon shortening
2 to 3 tablespoons cold water

Combine cranberries, apples, sugar, tapioca, and vanilla, tossing gently. Spoon fruit mixture into a lightly greased 12- x 8- x 2-inch baking dish. Dot with butter; set aside.

Combine flour and salt; cut in shortening with a pastry blender until mixture resembles coarse meal. Sprinkle water evenly over flour mixture, and stir with a fork until all ingredients are moistened. Shape pastry into a ball.

Roll out pastry to ⅛-inch thickness on a lightly floured board; cut into ½-inch strips, and arrange in lattice design over fruit. Bake at 425° for 15 minutes. Reduce oven temperature to 350°, and bake an additional 30 minutes. Yield: 6 servings.   *Jennie B. Hall,*
Winterville, North Carolina.

Right: You can make something to please everyone on your gift list. From bottom left clockwise: Herbed Cheese Round, Gingerbread Men, Tropical Muffins, Dill-and-Chive Vinegar, Paradise Pear Jam, Cran-Apple Relish, and Honeycomb Pecans (recipes begin on page 299).

Right: *Turn your kitchen into a candy shop for preparing a delightful assortment of Christmas sweets. In the center, colorful foil and paper give Chocolate Velvets and Chocolate Bourbon Balls a festive look. Other seasonal candies shown clockwise from the top left include: Peanut Brittle, Crystal Candy, commercial peppermint candy, Easy Holiday Mints, Chocolate-Covered Cherries, Holiday Mocha Fudge, and Spicy Praline Delights (recipes begin on page 298).*

Below: *Fashion holiday greeting cards using cookies, candies, and icing. One recipe yields four assorted cards for special friends (instructions begin on page 301).*

Far right: *Cranberry-Nut Tart (page 305) is an elegant way to end the meal or to start a dessert party. The walnut-flavored crust is filled with a congealed mixture of fresh cranberries and red currant jelly.*

Left: *Beaten egg whites and whipped cream help make Chilled Orange Soufflé (page 317) a light and airy dessert.*

Below: *Strips of orange rind in an apple juice sauce give Fruit Dessert Orange (page 314) an interesting look. To make eating easier, the oranges are first sliced crosswise, and restacked into their original shape.*

Holiday Desserts

Coffee Adds An Exotic Touch

Coffee—dark, rich, and flavorful—makes these desserts special. The mocha flavor is paired with chocolate for an extra bonus.

FROZEN MOCHA DESSERT

2 (3-ounce) packages ladyfingers, split
1 cup water
1 tablespoon instant coffee granules
1 (16-ounce) package marshmallows
2 tablespoons cream sherry
3 cups whipping cream
2 (1-ounce) squares semisweet chocolate, grated

Line the bottom and sides of a 10-inch springform pan with ladyfingers, placing the rounded sides of ladyfingers toward pan. Set aside.

Combine water and coffee in top of a double boiler; bring water to a boil. Reduce heat to low; add marshmallows, and cook until marshmallows are melted. Remove from heat; add sherry. Set aside to cool.

Beat whipping cream until soft peaks form. Fold whipped cream into cooled marshmallow mixture; pour into prepared pan. Cover and freeze overnight.

Place dessert on a serving plate, and remove rim from springform pan. Cover top with grated chocolate. Yield: 14 to 16 servings.
Mrs. Bernie Benigno,
Gulfport, Mississippi.

DOUBLE MOCHA CAKE

1 cup shortening
2½ cups sugar
5 eggs, separated
3 cups all-purpose flour
¼ cup cocoa
1 teaspoon baking soda
½ teaspoon salt
1 cup buttermilk
¼ cup plus 1 tablespoon brewed cold coffee
2 teaspoons vanilla extract
Creamy Mocha Frosting
Chocolate leaves or chocolate curls (optional)

Cream shortening; gradually add sugar, beating well. Beat egg yolks; add to creamed mixture, and beat well. Combine flour, cocoa, soda, and salt; add to creamed mixture alternately with buttermilk, beginning and ending with flour mixture. Stir in coffee and vanilla.

Beat egg whites (at room temperature) until stiff peaks form; gently fold into batter.

Pour batter into 3 greased and floured 9-inch round cakepans. Bake at 350° for 23 to 25 minutes or until a wooden pick inserted in center comes out clean. Cool in pans 10 minutes; remove layers from pans, and cool completely. Spread Creamy Mocha Frosting between layers and on top and sides of cake. Garnish with chocolate leaves, if desired. Yield: one 3-layer cake.

Creamy Mocha Frosting:

¾ cup butter or margarine, softened
6 cups sifted powdered sugar
1 tablespoon cocoa
1 egg yolk, beaten
¼ cup plus 1½ teaspoons brewed cold coffee
1½ teaspoons vanilla extract

Cream butter. Combine powdered sugar and cocoa; gradually add to butter, beating until smooth. Add remaining ingredients, and beat until frosting is light and fluffy. Yield: enough for one 3-layer cake.
Clonelle G. Jones,
Nashville, Tennessee.

QUICK-AS-A-WINK MOUSSE

¾ cup hot milk
3 tablespoons brewed hot coffee
2 tablespoons Cointreau or other orange-flavored liqueur
1 (6-ounce) package semisweet chocolate morsels
2 eggs
Sweetened whipped cream

Combine first 5 ingredients in container of an electric blender; process 2 minutes or until smooth. Spoon into stemmed glasses or individual serving dishes; chill until set. Top with whipped cream. Yield: 4 servings.
Mrs. John Rucker,
Louisville, Kentucky.

DARK MOCHA-CHOCOLATE CAKE

1 tablespoon butter or margarine
2 tablespoons fine, dry breadcrumbs
4 (1-ounce) squares unsweetened chocolate
½ cup water
¼ cup instant coffee granules
½ cup butter or margarine, softened
1 cup sugar
2 eggs
1¾ cups all-purpose flour
2 teaspoons baking powder
1 teaspoon ground cinnamon
¼ teaspoon ground cloves
½ cup milk
1 teaspoon vanilla extract
Cinnamon-Cream Frosting

Grease two 8-inch cakepans with 1 tablespoon butter; sprinkle breadcrumbs on bottom and sides of pans. Set aside.

Combine chocolate, water, and coffee granules in top of a double boiler; bring water to a boil. Reduce heat to low; cook until chocolate melts.

Cream ½ cup butter; gradually add sugar, beating well. Add eggs, one at a time, beating well after each addition. Add chocolate mixture, and beat well.

Combine flour and next 3 ingredients. Add to creamed mixture alternately with milk, beating at low speed of electric mixer, beginning and ending with flour mixture. Do not overbeat.

Pour batter into prepared cakepans. Bake at 350° for 20 to 25 minutes or until a wooden pick inserted in center comes out clean. Cool in pans 10 minutes; remove layers from pans, and let cool completely.

Spread Cinnamon-Cream Frosting between layers and on top of cake only. Serve at once, or refrigerate until ready to serve. Yield: one 2-layer cake.

Cinnamon-Cream Frosting:

1 cup whipping cream
2 tablespoons sugar
1 tablespoon coffee granules
¼ teaspoon ground cinnamon

Beat whipping cream until foamy; gradually add sugar, coffee granules, and cinnamon, beating until stiff peaks form. Yield: 2 about cups.
Grace Bravos,
Timonium, Maryland.

Spike Desserts With Flavor

Just a spoonful of liqueur, an ounce or two of brandy, or a few tablespoons of bourbon can turn an ordinary dessert into something fancy. You'll enjoy the recipes here—most can be prepared ahead of time or in just a few minutes.

BRANDY CREAM

1 quart vanilla ice cream
¼ cup plus 2 tablespoons brandy
2 tablespoons anisette
Ground nutmeg

Combine ice cream, brandy, and anisette in container of electric blender; process until smooth. Pour into serving glasses, and sprinkle cream with nutmeg. Yield: about 3½ cups.
Peggy Blackburn,
Winston-Salem, North Carolina.

CHERRY CORDIAL DESSERT

½ gallon vanilla ice cream, softened
4 (1.45-ounce) milk chocolate bars, finely chopped
1 cup maraschino cherries, halved
½ cup coarsely chopped pecans
Sweetened whipped cream
Grated semisweet chocolate
Maraschino cherries
¼ cup créme de cacao

Gently combine first 4 ingredients; spoon into a 9-inch springform pan. Cover and freeze until firm.

Place dessert on a serving platter, and remove rim from springform pan. Garnish with whipped cream, grated chocolate, and cherries. To serve, spoon about 1 teaspoon créme de cacao over each slice. Serve immediately. Yield: 8 to 10 servings. *Linda Nay,*
Herndon, Virginia.

Tip: For a great dessert, pour cream sherry over a chilled grapefruit.

GRAND MARNIER CREAM

¾ cup sugar
1 teaspoon grated orange rind
¼ cup orange juice
½ cup water
8 egg yolks
¼ cup Grand Marnier or other orange-flavored liqueur
1 cup whipping cream, whipped

Combine first 4 ingredients in a small saucepan. Bring to a boil, stirring constantly. Cook 5 minutes without stirring; set aside.

Beat egg yolks at high speed of an electric mixer until thick and lemon colored. Gradually stir about one-fourth of hot mixture into yolks. Add remaining hot mixture to yolk mixture, beating at high speed of an electric mixer. Continue beating until mixture thickens and cools. Stir in liqueur. Fold in whipped cream. Spoon into a 9-inch square pan. Cover and freeze until firm. Yield: 9 servings. *Mrs. A. J. Amador,*
Decatur, Alabama.

ICE CREAM PIE WITH RUM-FRUIT SAUCE

¾ cup vanilla wafer crumbs
½ cup wheat germ
2 tablespoons sugar
½ teaspoon ground nutmeg
¼ cup butter or margarine, melted
½ cup diced mixed candied fruit
2 tablespoons rum
1 quart vanilla ice cream, softened
Rum-Fruit Sauce

Combine first 5 ingredients; mix well. Firmly press crumb mixture evenly over bottom and sides of a buttered 9-inch pieplate. Bake at 350° for 5 minutes. Cool completely.

Combine fruit and rum; fold into ice cream. Spread ice cream mixture evenly over crust; cover and freeze until ice cream is firm. To serve, spoon Rum-Fruit Sauce over each slice of pie. Yield: one 9-inch pie.

Rum-Fruit Sauce

½ cup apricot preserves
½ cup diced mixed candied fruit
¼ cup light corn syrup
¼ cup rum, divided

Combine all ingredients except 2 tablespoons rum in a small saucepan. Stir over low heat until mixture is hot.

Rapidly heat remaining 2 tablespoons rum in a small saucepan to produce fumes (do not boil). Ignite; pour over rum fruit mixture. Stir until flames die down. Serve immediately. Yield: about 1 cup. *Mrs. H. C. Clinton,*
Orlando, Florida.

PUMPKIN CHIFFON PIE

1 envelope unflavored gelatin
¼ cup bourbon
3 eggs, separated
1 (16-ounce) can pumpkin
¾ cup firmly packed brown sugar
½ teaspoon salt
2 teaspoons pumpkin pie spice
½ cup milk
¼ teaspoon cream of tartar
¼ cup plus 2 tablespoons sugar
1 baked 9-inch pastry shell
Ginger Cream Topping

Soften gelatin in bourbon; let stand 5 minutes. Beat egg yolks slightly. Combine gelatin mixture, egg yolks, pumpkin, brown sugar, salt, pumpkin pie spice, and milk in top of a double boiler. Cook over boiling water, stirring occasionally, about 10 minutes or until thoroughly heated. Chill until mixture mounds when dropped from a spoon.

Beat egg whites (at room temperature) and cream of tarter until foamy. Gradually add sugar, beating until stiff peaks form. Fold into pumpkin mixture; spoon into prepared pastry shell. Chill several hours or until firm. To serve, top with Ginger Cream Topping. Yield: one 9-inch pie.

Ginger Cream Topping:

½ teaspoon ground ginger
1 tablespoon sugar
1 cup whipping cream

Combine all ingredients; beat at medium-high speed of electric mixer until stiff peaks form. Yield: 2 cups.
Loy Witherspoon,
Charlotte, North Carolina.

Holiday Desserts

Fancy A Quick Dessert

Although these easy desserts require little preparation time, they offer glamorous endings for your fanciest meals.

PRALINE BANANAS

5 large bananas
1 (15-ounce) can ready-to-spread coconut pecan frosting
¼ teaspoon ground cinnamon
2 tablespoons rum
Vanilla ice cream

Peel bananas; slice in half crosswise, then slice in half lengthwise. Set aside.

Combine frosting and cinnamon in a large skillet; cook over medium heat 3 to 5 minutes or until frosting melts. Add bananas; cook 3 minutes, stirring occasionally.

Place rum in a small, long-handled saucepan; heat just until warm (do not boil). Ignite rum, and pour over bananas; stir until flames die down. Serve immediately over ice cream. Yield: 10 servings.
Cathy Darling,
Grafton, West Virginia.

FLAMING PEARS

2 tablespoons butter or margarine
¼ cup firmly packed light brown sugar
½ cup orange juice
1 (29-ounce) can pear halves, drained and quartered
¼ cup slivered almonds, toasted
2 tablespoons brandy
Vanilla ice cream

Melt butter in a large skillet; add brown sugar and orange juice. Cook over medium heat, stirring until sugar dissolves. Add pears and almonds; cook until thoroughly heated.

Place brandy in a small, long-handled saucepan; heat just until warm (do not boil). Ignite brandy, and pour over pears; stir until flames die down. Serve immediately over ice cream. Yield: 6 to 8 servings.
Pat Boschen,
Ashland, Virginia.

DATE BARS

2 eggs, beaten
1 cup sifted powdered sugar
1 tablespoon butter or margarine, melted
¼ cup cake flour
¼ teaspoon salt
½ teaspoon baking powder
1 cup chopped dates
¾ cup chopped pecans or walnuts
1 teaspoon vanilla extract
Additional powdered sugar

Combine first 3 ingredients, beating well. Sift dry ingredients; add to egg mixture. Mix well, and stir in dates, pecans, and vanilla. Pour into a greased 8-inch square pan, and bake at 325° for 25 to 30 minutes. Cool and cut into bars. Dust with additional powdered sugar. Yield: about 2 dozen.
Thomas Farmer,
Richmond, Virginia.

AMBROSIA BOWL

2 (8-ounce) cans unsweetened pineapple chunks, undrained
3 tablespoons Cointreau or other orange-flavored liqueur
4 large oranges
4 medium bananas
2 tablespoons powdered sugar, divided
1 (3½-ounce) can flaked coconut
6 maraschino cherries, halved

Drain pineapple, reserving juice; set aside. Combine Cointreau and pineapple juice; set aside.

Peel oranges removing white membrane; cut into ⅛-inch-thick slices. Peel bananas, and cut diagonally into ⅛-inch thick slices. Dip banana slices into reserved pineapple juice mixture to prevent browning.

Arrange half the orange slices in a 2½-quart serving bowl. Sprinkle with 1 tablespoon powdered sugar. Top with half the banana slices and half the pineapple chunks; sprinkle with half the coconut. Repeat layers of fruit and powdered sugar. Pour reserved pineapple juice mixture over fruit; sprinkle with remaining coconut and garnish with cherries. Refrigerate until serving time. Yield: 10 servings.
Carolyn Brantley,
Greenville, Mississippi.

HOT FUDGE SUNDAE DESSERT

1 (12-ounce) package vanilla wafers, crushed
½ cup finely chopped pecans
¾ cup butter or margarine, melted
½ gallon vanilla ice cream, softened
Chocolate sauce (recipe follows)

Combine vanilla wafer crumbs, pecans, and butter, mixing well. Press half of crumb mixture into a 13- x 9- x 2-inch baking dish. Spread ice cream evenly over crust. Press remaining crumb mixture over ice cream. Cover and freeze until firm. To serve, cut into squares and top each serving with chocolate sauce. Yield: 15 servings.

Chocolate Sauce:

1 cup sugar
¼ cup plus 1 tablespoon cocoa
3 tablespoons all-purpose flour
1 cup milk
2 tablespoons butter or margarine
1 teaspoon vanilla extract

Combine first 4 ingredients in a medium saucepan. Cook over medium heat until slightly thickened, stirring constantly. Remove from heat, and stir in butter and vanilla. Yield: 2 cups.
Dana L. Bryant,
Shreveport, Louisiana.

EASY PECAN TARTS

2 eggs
1 cup firmly packed light brown sugar
2 tablespoons butter or margarine, melted
1 tablespoon water
1 teaspoon vanilla extract
Pinch of salt
1 cup chopped pecans
8 (2-inch) unbaked commercial tart shells
Whipped cream (optional)
Pecan halves (optional)

Combine first 6 ingredients in a medium mixing bowl; beat well. Stir in chopped pecans. Spoon pecan mixture into tart shells. Bake at 425° for 15 to 17 minutes. Garnish with whipped cream and pecan halves, if desired. Yield: 8 servings.
Evelyn M. Wilson,
Burnsville, North Carolina.

Holiday Desserts

STRAWBERRY SAUCE WITH DUMPLINGS

2 (16-ounce) packages frozen whole
  strawberries, thawed
1 cup water
2 tablespoons sugar
2 tablespoons butter or margarine
⅛ teaspoon salt
1 cup all-purpose flour
1½ teaspoons baking powder
Dash of salt
¼ cup sugar
2 tablespoons butter or margarine
⅓ cup milk
½ teaspoon vanilla extract
Ice cream (optional)

Combine first 5 ingredients in a saucepan; bring to a boil.

Combine flour, baking powder, dash of salt, and ¼ cup sugar; cut in 2 tablespoons butter until mixture resembles coarse meal. Stir in milk and vanilla; mix well. Drop mixture by teaspoonfuls into boiling strawberry mixture; cook, uncovered, 5 minutes. Cover, reduce heat, and simmer 15 minutes. Serve over ice cream, if desired. Yield: 8 servings.

Vivian Carter,
Pisgah, Alabama.

COOKING LIGHT

Light Desserts Make Dieting Fun

Who ever heard of low-calorie desserts for the holidays? We have, and here they are. Our "Cooking Light" readers don't let the holidays interrupt their efforts at losing weight. They dress up nutritious, calorie-wise fruit in some fancy ways to make special desserts.

We've found that unsweetened apple juice and white grape juice are both excellent for sweetening fruit desserts naturally. Either juice adds almost no color to a finished dish, and their flavors seem to complement, not cover, that of other fruits.

DELUXE LIGHT BANANA CAKE

1 (10¾-ounce) loaf commercial pound cake
1 (16-ounce) carton vanilla low-fat yogurt
2 medium-size ripe bananas, sliced
2 tablespoons chopped pecans

Slice cake horizontally into 3 layers. Spread bottom layer with ⅓ cup yogurt. Layer half of banana slices over yogurt; spread with additional ⅓ cup yogurt. Repeat layers, ending with cake layer. Spread remaining yogurt over top of cake; sprinkle with pecans. Cover and chill overnight. Yield: 10 servings (about 195 calories per serving).

Doris S. Shortt,
Leesburg, Florida.

CARIBBEAN FRUIT DESSERT

2 medium bananas
1 (16-ounce) can unsweetened sliced
  peaches, undrained
½ cup unsweetened white grape juice
2 teaspoons grated lime rind
2 tablespoons lime juice
¼ cup vanilla low-fat yogurt
2 tablespoons shredded coconut
Lime slices

Peel bananas; cut in half crosswise, and slice each half lengthwise, and set aside.

Drain peaches, reserving ½ cup juice. Combine reserved juice, peaches, and next 3 ingredients in a skillet. Bring to a boil and reduce heat. Add bananas to peach mixture; cook over medium-low heat 3 minutes or just until bananas are thoroughly heated.

Spoon fruit mixture into 4 serving dishes; top each with 1 tablespoon yogurt and ½ tablespoon coconut. Garnish with lime slices. Yield: 4 servings (about 142 calories per serving).

Helene Guest,
Trenton, Florida.

FRUIT DESSERT ORANGE

6 medium oranges
1 (12-ounce) can frozen apple juice
  concentrate, thawed and undiluted
6 slices unsweetened pineapple
Fresh mint sprigs

Remove thin strips of rind from 4 oranges; set aside. Peel remainder of membrane from oranges. Peel remaining 2 oranges; cover oranges and chill.

Combine reserved rind strips and apple juice concentrate in a small saucepan; bring to a boil. Reduce heat to medium and cook 7 minutes, stirring occasionally. Remove from heat; cool.

Place a pineapple slice on each individual serving dish. Cut oranges crosswise into ½-inch slices; stack each orange in original shape, and secure with wooden picks. Place an orange on each pineapple slice. Spoon one-sixth of the syrup mixture over each orange. Garnish with mint. Yield: 6 servings (about 206 calories per serving).

Deborah Newman,
Haymarket, Virginia.

BAKED FRUIT COMPOTE

1 (16-ounce) can unsweetened apricot
  halves, undrained
1 (16-ounce) can unsweetened pear halves,
  undrained
1 (16-ounce) can unsweetened peach
  halves, undrained
1 (8-ounce) can unsweetened sliced
  pineapple, undrained
1 large orange, peeled and sliced
½ cup dry sherry
½ teaspoon grated lemon rind
2 tablespoons flaked coconut

Drain fruit, reserving liquid. Set aside ½ cup liquid; reserve remaining liquid for other uses. Arrange fruit in a 12- x 8- x 2-inch baking dish; set aside.

Combine ½ cup liquid, sherry, and lemon rind; pour over fruit. Sprinkle coconut over fruit. Bake at 425° for 15 minutes. Yield: 8 servings (about 105 calories per serving).

BAKED APPLES WITH ORANGE SAUCE

3 medium-size Golden Delicious apples
¾ cup unsweetened orange juice
1 tablespoon lemon juice
2 (3-inch) sticks cinnamon
6 whole cloves
1 teaspoon cornstarch
1 tablespoon water
1½ cups vanilla ice milk

Peel apples, and cut in half lengthwise; remove core. Arrange apples in a single layer in a 10- x 6- x 2-inch baking dish. Combine next 4 ingredients in a small saucepan; bring to a boil, and pour over apples. Cover and bake at 350° for 30 minutes or until just tender.

Transfer liquid in baking dish to saucepan; set apples aside, and keep warm. Combine cornstarch and water; stir into liquid in saucepan. Cook over medium heat, stirring constantly, until smooth and thickened. Remove cinnamon stick and cloves.

Place each apple half in an individual serving dish; spoon ¼ cup ice milk on each. Top with sauce. Yield: 6 servings (about 97 calories per serving).

RAISIN-PUMPKIN PUDDING

4 eggs
2 cups low-fat cottage cheese
1 (16-ounce) can pumpkin
¼ cup sugar
¾ cup raisins
¼ cup chopped pecans
Ground cinnamon

Place eggs in container of electric blender; process until beaten. Add next 3 ingredients, and process until smooth. Fold in raisins and pecans. Pour mixture into an ungreased 12- x 8- x 2-inch baking dish. Sprinkle with cinnamon.

Place baking dish in a larger pan; add warm water to larger pan to measure ¾ inch. Bake at 350° for 45 minutes or until knife inserted in center comes out clean. Yield: 12 servings (about 127 calories per serving). *Mrs. D. R. Heun, Louisville, Kentucky.*

KIWI ICE

4 kiwi, peeled and cubed
2 cups unsweetened apple juice
1 tablespoon lemon juice
½ teaspoon grated orange rind
Orange slices (optional)

Combine kiwi, apple juice, and lemon juice in container of an electric blender; process until smooth. Stir in orange rind. Pour mixture into an 8-inch square baking pan; freeze until almost firm.

Spoon frozen mixture into a mixing bowl; beat with an electric mixer until fluffy. Return to pan, and freeze until firm. Let stand at room temperature 10 minutes before serving. Garnish with orange slices, if desired. Yield: 4 cups (about 58 calories per ½-cup serving).

For Christmas, Only The Best

Southerners usually spend a lot of time planning recipes for their Christmas dinner. Only the best will do—the lightest homemade rolls, a favorite dressing for the turkey, and the prettiest garnishes for all the dishes. Rest assured that your choice of that special dessert will be easy. Take your pick of these cake recipes, all reprinted from past issues of *Southern Living*.

DAFFODIL SPONGE CAKE

1 cup sifted cake flour
½ cup sugar
4 egg yolks
½ teaspoon lemon extract
10 egg whites
1 teaspoon cream of tartar
½ teaspoon salt
¾ cup sugar
½ teaspoon vanilla extract

Sift flour and ½ cup sugar together 3 times; set aside.

Beat egg yolks at high speed of an electric mixer 4 minutes or until thick and lemon colored. Add lemon extract; beat at medium speed an additional 5 minutes or until thickened. Set aside.

Beat egg whites (at room temperature) until foamy. Add cream of tartar and salt; beat until soft peaks form. Add ¾ cup sugar, 2 tablespoons at a time; continue beating 5 minutes or until stiff peaks form.

Sprinkle one-fourth of flour mixture over egg whites; gently fold in with a rubber spatula. Repeat procedure with remaining flour, adding one-fourth of

the mixture at a time. Divide egg white mixture in half.

Fold vanilla extract into half of the egg white mixture. Gently fold the beaten egg yolks into the remaining egg white mixture.

Pour half of the yellow mixture into an ungreased 10-inch tube pan. Then gently add half of the white mixture; repeat procedure.

Bake at 350° for 55 to 60 minutes or until cake springs back when touched lightly with fingers. Invert cake; cool about 40 minutes. Loosen cake from sides of pan, using a small metal spatula. Remove cake from pan; place on a serving platter. Yield: one 10-inch cake. *Mabel B. Couch, Chelsea, Oklahoma.*

CARROT CAKE

3 cups grated carrots
2 cups all-purpose flour
2 cups sugar
2 teaspoons baking soda
1 teaspoon baking powder
½ teaspoon salt
1 teaspoon ground cinnamon
4 eggs, well beaten
1¼ cups vegetable oil
1 teaspoon vanilla extract
Cream Cheese Frosting

Combine first 7 ingredients; stir in eggs, oil, and vanilla, mixing well. Spoon batter into 3 greased and floured 9-inch round cakepans. Bake at 350° for 30 minutes or until a wooden pick inserted in center comes out clean.

Spread Cream Cheese Frosting between layers and on top of cake while still warm. Yield: one 3-layer cake.

Cream Cheese Frosting:

1 (16-ounce) package powdered sugar
1 (8-ounce) package cream cheese, softened
½ cup butter or margarine, softened
1 teaspoon vanilla extract
1 cup chopped pecans

Cream first 4 ingredients until well blended; stir in pecans. Yield: enough for one 3-layer cake. *Mrs. Paul B. Keith, McAllen, Texas.*

BELGIAN MOCHA CAKE

½ cup sugar
3 tablespoons water
2 (1-ounce) squares unsweetened chocolate
¾ cup butter or margarine, softened
2 cups sugar
1 teaspoon vanilla extract
4 eggs, separated
2¼ cups cake flour
½ teaspoon baking soda
½ teaspoon salt
1 cup milk
1 teaspoon cream of tartar
Mocha frosting (recipe follows)
Chocolate curls or grated chocolate
    (optional)

Combine ½ cup sugar, water, and chocolate in a heavy saucepan; cook over low heat, stirring until chocolate melts. Remove from heat; cool.

Cream butter; gradually add sugar, beating well. Stir in vanilla. Add egg yolks, one at a time, beating well after each addition. Stir in chocolate mixture.

Combine flour, soda, and salt; add to creamed mixture alternately with milk, beginning and ending with flour mixture. Mix well after each addition. Beat egg whites (at room temperature) until frothy; add cream of tartar, and beat until stiff peaks form. Fold into batter.

Grease three 9-inch round cakepans; line with greased waxed paper, and dust with flour. Pour batter into prepared pans, and bake at 350° for 25 to 30 minutes or until a wooden pick inserted in center comes out clean.

Spread mocha frosting between layers and on top and sides of cake. Store in refrigerator, or the cake may be frozen. Garnish with chocolate curls, if desired. Yield: one 3-layer cake.

Mocha Frosting:

1 cup butter, softened
2 to 2¼ cups powdered sugar, divided
1 tablespoon instant coffee granules
¾ teaspoon cocoa
¾ teaspoon hot water
2 egg yolks
1 to 1½ tablespoons almond extract
2 tablespoons rum

Cream butter and 1½ cups powdered sugar until light and fluffy. Combine coffee powder, cocoa, and water; stir into creamed mixture. Add egg yolks,

and beat 5 minutes. Stir in almond extract and rum. Add enough of remaining sugar to make spreading consistency (frosting gets quite firm when refrigerated). Yield: enough for one 9-inch layer cake.
*Anita Cochran,
Nashville, Tennessee.*

BLACK WALNUT CAKE

½ cup butter, softened
½ cup shortening
2 cups sugar
5 eggs, separated
1 cup buttermilk
1 teaspoon baking soda
2 cups all-purpose flour
1 teaspoon vanilla extract
1½ cups chopped black walnuts
1 (3-ounce) can flaked coconut
½ teaspoon cream of tartar
Cream Cheese Frosting
Chopped black walnuts
Red and green candied cherries, diced

Cream butter and shortening; gradually add sugar, beating until light and fluffy and sugar dissolves. Add egg yolks, beating well.

Combine buttermilk and soda; stir until soda dissolves.

Add flour to creamed mixture alternately with buttermilk mixture, beginning and ending with flour. Stir in vanilla. Add 1½ cups walnuts and coconut, stirring well.

Beat egg whites (at room temperature) with cream of tartar until stiff peaks form. Fold egg whites into batter.

Pour batter into 3 greased and floured 9-inch round cakepans. Bake at 350° for 30 minutes or until a wooden pick inserted in center comes out clean. Cool in pans 10 minutes; remove layers from pans, and let cool completely.

Spread Cream Cheese Frosting between layers and on top and sides of

cake; decorate cake with additional walnuts and candied cherries. Yield: one 3-layer cake.

Cream Cheese Frosting:

¾ cup butter, softened
1 (8-ounce) package cream cheese,
    softened
1 (3-ounce) package cream cheese,
    softened
6¾ cups sifted powdered sugar
1½ teaspoons vanilla extract

Cream butter and cream cheese; gradually add sugar, beating until light and fluffy. Stir in vanilla. Yield: enough for one 9-inch layer cake.
*Mrs. Leslie L. Jones,
Richmond, Kentucky.*

FIG PRESERVE CAKE

1½ cups sugar
2 cups all-purpose flour
1 teaspoon baking soda
1 teaspoon salt
1 teaspoon ground nutmeg
1 teaspoon ground cinnamon
½ teaspoon ground allspice
½ teaspoon ground cloves
1 cup vegetable oil
3 eggs
1 cup buttermilk
1 tablespoon vanilla extract
1 cup fig preserves, chopped
½ cup chopped pecans or walnuts
Buttermilk Glaze

Combine dry ingredients in a large mixing bowl; add oil, beating well. Add eggs, and beat well; then add buttermilk and vanilla, mixing thoroughly. Stir in preserves and pecans.

Pour batter into a greased and floured 10-inch tube pan; bake at 350° for 1 hour and 15 minutes. Cool in pan 10 minutes; remove from pan. Pour warm Buttermilk Glaze over warm cake. Yield: one 10-inch cake.

Buttermilk Glaze:

¼ cup buttermilk
½ cup sugar
¼ teaspoon baking soda
1½ teaspoons cornstarch
¼ cup margarine
1½ teaspoons vanilla extract

Combine first 5 ingredients in a saucepan; bring to a boil, and remove from heat. Cool slightly, and stir in vanilla. Yield: enough frosting for one 10-inch cake.
*Linda Barnett,
Birmingham, Alabama.*

Showy Sweet Soufflés

Turn dessert into a grand event by surprising guests with a pretty, airy soufflé. All of these lofty desserts are prepared in straight-sided soufflé dishes. If the extra support of a collar is needed, follow our detailed instructions given in the recipe.

CHOCOLATE SOUFFLE

1 teaspoon sugar
2 tablespoons butter or margarine
2 tablespoons all-purpose flour
¾ cup milk, scalded
Pinch of salt
2 (1-ounce) squares unsweetened chocolate
½ cup sugar
2 tablespoons brewed coffee
3 egg yolks, beaten
½ teaspoon vanilla extract
4 egg whites
Sweetened whipped cream
Grated chocolate (optional)

Lightly butter bottom of a 1½-quart soufflé dish; sprinkle with 1 teaspoon sugar, and set aside.

Melt 2 tablespoons butter in a heavy saucepan over low heat; add flour, stirring until smooth. Cook 1 minute, stirring constantly. Gradually add milk; cook over medium heat, stirring constantly, until thickened and bubbly. Stir in salt. Remove from heat; set aside.

Combine 2 squares chocolate, ½ cup sugar, and coffee in top of a double boiler; bring water to a boil. Reduce heat to low; cook until chocolate melts. Stir chocolate mixture into sauce.

Gradually stir about one-fourth of hot mixture into yolks; add to remaining hot mixture, stirring constantly. Stir in vanilla.

Beat egg whites (at room temperature) until stiff, but not dry peaks form. Gently fold into chocolate mixture. Carefully spoon into prepared soufflé dish. Bake at 350° for 50 minutes or until puffed and set. Serve immediately with whipped cream and grated chocolate, if desired. Yield: 6 servings.
*Lynne Teal Weeks,
Columbus, Georgia.*

BANANA DAIQUIRI SOUFFLE

½ cup sugar
2 envelopes unflavored gelatin
⅛ teaspoon salt
6 eggs, separated
1¼ cups water
1 teaspoon grated lime rind
¼ cup lime juice
¼ cup rum
2 tablespoons banana-flavored liqueur
½ cup sugar
4 bananas, diced
¼ cup lime juice, divided
1½ cups whipping cream, whipped
1 banana, sliced

Combine ½ cup sugar, gelatin, and salt in a saucepan; set aside. Combine egg yolks and water, mixing well; stir into gelatin mixture. Place over low heat, stirring constantly, until gelatin dissolves. Remove from heat; add lime rind, ¼ cup lime juice, rum, and banana liqueur. Chill, stirring occasionally, until slightly thickened.

Beat egg whites (at room temperature) until foamy. Gradually add ½ cup sugar, 1 tablespoon at a time, beating until stiff peaks form. Toss diced bananas with 3 tablespoons lime juice. Gently fold beaten egg whites, diced banana, and whipped cream into gelatin mixture. Spoon mixture into a 1½-quart soufflé dish. Chill until firm.

Toss sliced banana with remaining tablespoon of lime juice; arrange over top of soufflé. Yield: 10 to 12 servings.
*Sara A. McCullough,
Broaddus, Texas.*

CHILLED ORANGE SOUFFLE

2 envelopes unflavored gelatin
2 cups water, divided
4 eggs, separated
¾ cup sugar
1 (8-ounce) package cream cheese, softened
¼ cup orange juice
2 tablespoons Cointreau or other orange-flavored liqueur
¼ cup sugar
1 cup whipping cream, whipped
Orange slices (optional)

Cut a piece of aluminum foil or waxed paper long enough to fit around a 5-cup soufflé dish, allowing a 1-inch overlap; fold lengthwise into thirds. Lightly oil one side of foil; wrap around outside of dish, oiled side against dish, allowing it to extend 3 inches above rim to form a collar. Secure the foil with freezer tape.

Soften gelatin in 1 cup water in top of a double boiler; let stand 1 minute. Bring water to a boil. Reduce heat to low; stir until gelatin dissolves. Stir in remaining cup of water.

Beat egg yolks until thick and lemon colored; gradually add ¾ cup sugar, beating well. Stir into gelatin mixture. Cook over low heat 10 to 12 minutes or until smooth and thickened, stirring constantly. Beat cream cheese until smooth; gradually add yolk mixture, beating well. Stir in orange juice and Cointreau; chill until consistency of unbeaten egg white.

Beat egg whites (at room temperature) until foamy; gradually add ¼ cup sugar, beating until soft peaks form. Gently fold egg whites and whipped cream into cream cheese mixture.

Spoon into prepared soufflé dish, and chill until firm. Remove collar before serving. Garnish with orange slices, if desired. Yield: 8 to 10 servings.

Tip: Raw eggs separate more easily while still cold from the refrigerator, but let whites reach room temperature to get maximum volume when beating.

December 317

Recipes With Centuries Of Tradition

If you're visiting the holiday-spruced historical homes in and around Norfolk, Virginia, you'll find that food was as important in seasonal festivities centuries ago as it is today. We have collected recipes typical of the holiday season during the time periods represented by historic houses in the Tidewater area. Similar recipes were known to have been served in the homes by the former owners.

■ Wassail is still served at the Myers and Willoughby-Baylor Houses during the holiday season. At one time, the type of fruit floating in the serving bowl signified the financial status of the host. Wealthy sea merchant Moses Myers brought in oranges, lemons, and other tropical fruit from his vast travels to warmer climates. So clove-studded oranges for the wassail were not uncommon at his home. Less affluent Captain Willoughby would probably have offered his guests a cup of wassail from a bowl garnished with whole apples, which were widely available in Virginia.

WASSAIL

1 gallon apple cider
1 quart unsweetened tea
¼ cup sugar
3 small oranges
1½ teaspoons whole cloves

Combine first 3 ingredients in a large Dutch oven. Stud oranges with cloves, and add to cider mixture. Bring mixture to a boil; reduce heat and simmer, uncovered, 1 hour. Serve hot. Yield: about 4½ quarts.

HOT SPICED APPLE CIDER

1 gallon apple cider
2 (3-inch) sticks cinnamon
4 medium apples
2 teaspoons whole cloves

Place apple cider and cinnamon sticks in a large Dutch oven. Stud apples with cloves, and add to cider. Bring mixture to a boil; reduce heat and simmer, uncovered, 30 minutes. Serve hot. Yield: about 1 gallon.

■ In the days of Adam Thoroughgood of Virginia Beach, holiday visitors were likely to be offered Benne (sesame) Seed Cookies. The recipe was supposedly brought over by slaves, and believed to bring good luck.

BENNE SEED COOKIES

½ cup butter, melted
1 cup firmly packed brown sugar
1 egg, beaten
¾ cup all-purpose flour
½ teaspoon salt
¼ teaspoon baking powder
1 teaspoon vanilla extract
1 cup sesame seeds, toasted

Combine all ingredients in a large bowl; beat until smooth and creamy. Drop dough by ½ teaspoonfuls onto lightly greased cookie sheets. Bake at 350° for 8 to 10 minutes or until edges are browned. Cool slightly on cookie sheets; remove to wire racks. Yield: about 8 dozen.

■ The Willoughby-Baylor House displays Mrs. Willoughby's special pound cake each Christmas. Serving it upside-down shows off the rose-geranium leaf design baked into the bottom.

MRS. WILLOUGHBY'S ROSE-GERANIUM POUND CAKE

4 to 6 medium to large rose geranium
    leaves, oiled
1 cup butter or margarine, softened
3 cups sugar
6 eggs
3 cups all-purpose flour
½ teaspoon salt
¼ teaspoon baking soda
1 (8-ounce) carton commercial sour cream
2 teaspoons vanilla extract

Arrange geranium leaves, dull side up, in bottom of a greased and floured 10-inch tube pan; set aside.
Cream butter; gradually add sugar, beating well. Add eggs, one at a time, beating well after each addition.
Combine flour, salt, and soda; add to creamed mixture alternately with sour cream, beginning and ending with flour mixture. Stir in vanilla. Pour batter into prepared pan.
Bake at 350° for 1½ hours or until a wooden pick inserted in center comes out clean. Cool 10 minutes; remove from pan, and cool completely. Yield: one 10-inch cake.

■ Each year a local rabbi signals the start of the Hanukkah season at the Moses Myers House by lighting the menorah. Tourists present at this ceremony are served Latkes topped with applesauce or apple butter.

LATKES

6 medium potatoes, peeled and shredded
1 onion, peeled and grated
2 eggs, beaten
½ cup all-purpose flour
1 teaspoon salt
Vegetable oil

Squeeze shredded potatoes between paper towels to remove excess moisture. Combine potatoes and next 4 ingredients, mixing well. Drop heaping tablespoonfuls of potato mixture into 1 inch hot oil (350°). Fry until golden brown, turning once. Drain well. Yield: 12 to 15 servings.

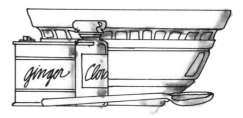

MINIATURE GINGERBREAD MEN

¾ cup butter or margarine, softened
1 cup sugar
1 egg
¼ cup molasses
2¼ cups all-purpose flour
1½ teaspoons ground cloves
1 teaspoon ground cinnamon
1 teaspoon ground ginger
Chopped raisins (optional)

Cream butter and sugar, beating until light and fluffy. Add egg and molasses; beat well. Combine next 4 ingredients; add to creamed mixture, stirring well. Cover and refrigerate several hours or overnight.
Work with one-fourth of dough at a time; store remainder in refrigerator. Place dough on a lightly greased cookie sheet; roll out to ¼-inch thickness. Cut dough with a floured 2¼-inch gingerbread man cookie cutter, leaving 1 inch between each cookie. Remove excess dough; combine with remaining dough in refrigerator. Decorate with raisins, if desired. Bake at 350° for 7 to 10 minutes or until lightly browned. Cool on cookie sheets 3 to 5 minutes; remove to wire racks, and cool completely. Repeat procedure with remaining dough. Yield: about 5 dozen.

From Our Kitchen To Yours

Pound cakes are a popular baked item for the holiday season, so brush up on techniques for making the perfect pound cake—one with excellent flavor and a smooth, velvety texture.

Begin with the best equipment—Choose a shiny, metal cakepan to reflect heat away from the sides and bottom of the cake. Dark pans will cause the cake to bake faster around the edges and brown more.

A pound cake is usually baked in a tube or Bundt pan. A tube pan has straight, high sides, whereas a Bundt pan is shallower with a fluted surface. Since pan sizes vary, we don't recommend substituting one pan for the other. Use the type recommended in the recipe. Most of our pound cake recipes are tested using a tube pan.

Once you have selected the correct pan, you'll need to grease and flour it. To keep the sides and bottom of the cake from browning too much, grease the pan with shortening instead of butter or margarine.

Use the right ingredients—Most of our pound cake recipes call for all-purpose flour, which is a blend of hard- and soft-wheat flour. Cake flour is a soft-wheat flour and weighs less than all-purpose, so these flours cannot be substituted.

Mixing procedures are important—To get the best volume, have butter or margarine, eggs, and milk at room temperature. This usually takes about 2 hours out of the refrigerator.

Creaming butter and adding eggs—For a light-textured cake, it's important to incorporate air by beating the butter until it's soft and creamy. Add sugar gradually, beating until mixture is light and fluffy—about the consistency of whipped cream. This takes about 5 minutes with a standard electric mixer and a little longer with a portable mixer. If you don't cream the mixture enough, the pound cake may have a coarse texture and be very compact. When adding the eggs, add one at a time, and mix just until the eggs are blended into the creamed mixture. Overmixing can cause the cake to flow over the pan's sides.

Adding flour and liquid ingredients—Before adding the flour mixture to the creamed mixture, stir dry ingredients together. Most all-purpose flour is presifted, so it is unnecessary to re-sift. It's very important to add the dry ingredients alternately with the liquid; be sure to begin and end with the dry ingredients, so batter will have a smooth finish instead of a curdled look. After the addition of each ingredient, stir just enough to blend. If you overmix at this point, too much air will be incorporated, possibly causing the cake to overflow and then fall. You may also have a heavy, compact texture or wet streaks throughout if you overbeat.

If eggs are separated and the egg whites added at the end, just fold in until whites are no longer seen. If you stir rather than fold them in, you may overbeat, causing the whites to have less leavening power.

Cooling—After the pound cake tests done and is removed from the oven, leave the cake right side up in the pan on a cooling rack for 10 to 15 minutes. Then remove the cake from the pan, and let it cool completely on a wire rack. Allowing the cake to cool first in the pan lets the cake become firmer and keeps it from breaking when it comes out of the pan. Be sure to keep the cake away from drafts while cooling, as that may cause it to fall.

POUND CAKE: Problems To Avoid

Problem	Possible Cause
Overflow of batter	Too much batter in pan Overmixing
Sticky top crust	Underbaking Too much sugar
Damp cake	Cooled too long in pan Underbaking
Tough crust	Overmixing Not enough sugar, fat, or leavening
Sinking in center	Underbaking Not cooled enough before removed from pan Exposed to draft during baking or cooling Too much liquid, leavening, or sugar
Heavy texture	Not enough leavening Old baking powder or baking soda Overmixing Wrong baking temperature Too much fat, sugar, or liquid

Beverages For The Season

What better way is there to relax during the hustle and bustle of the season than with a warm, soothing beverage. Hot Cranberry Punch does just that. For a quick and easy drink, make it with canned cranberry sauce.

HOT CRANBERRY PUNCH

½ cup firmly packed brown sugar
1 cup water
½ teaspoon ground cinnamon
½ teaspoon ground allspice
½ teaspoon ground cloves
¼ teaspoon ground nutmeg
2 (16-ounce) cans jellied cranberry sauce
3 cups water
4 cups unsweetened pineapple juice

Combine first 6 ingredients in a large saucepan. Bring to a boil; remove from heat, and add cranberry sauce, beating well. Stir in 3 cups water and pineapple juice. Heat to serving temperature. Serve hot punch immediately. Yield: about 2 quarts. *Mary Rudolph, Fort Worth, Texas.*

SYLLABUB

4 cups whipping cream
1 cup milk
1 cup sugar
¼ cup sherry or whiskey
1 teaspoon vanilla extract

Combine all ingredients in a large bowl; beat at medium speed of an electric mixer until frothy. Serve immediately. Yield: 7¾ cups.
Mrs. Elgin P. Straughn, Repton, Alabama.

Stop By For A Luncheon

It's 11 a.m. on a beautiful December day in Baton Rouge. The Christmas tree sparkles with tiny lights, poinsettias adorn each room, and the dining room table is laden with appetizers, salads, and desserts. The children, however, are still in school; the men are at work. What's the occasion? It's the annual shopping-stop luncheon at Mary McCowan's home.

Mary and Carol Anne Blitzer host the affair jointly. "It's our last chance to get together with friends before the children get out of school for the holidays," says Mary. Friends are invited to drop in for lunch while they are out shopping, and they come and go as they please.

Smoked Oyster Mousse
Spicy Homemade Sausage
Assorted Crackers
Holiday Turkey Salad
Tomato-Artichoke Aspic
Pineapple-Lime Salad
Sensational Salad
Toasted Pecans
Commercial Rolls
Cream Cheese Cake Squares
Teatime Tassies
Creamy Pecan Fudge
White Wine

SMOKED OYSTER MOUSSE

4 envelopes unflavored gelatin
1 cup water
2 (8-ounce) packages cream cheese
2 cups mayonnaise
4 (3.6-ounce) cans smoked oysters, drained and minced
¼ cup chopped fresh parsley
2 tablespoons Worcestershire sauce
1 teaspoon garlic powder
Dash of hot sauce
Cranberries (optional)
Fresh parsley sprigs (optional)
Spiced crabapples (optional)

Soften gelatin in water; set aside.
Combine cream cheese and mayonnaise in a heavy saucepan. Cook over low heat, stirring until cream cheese melts and mixture is smooth. Add gelatin mixture and next 5 ingredients to saucepan; stir until smooth.
Pour mixture into a well-oiled 6-cup mold. Cover and refrigerate several hours or until set. Garnish with cranberries, parsley, and crabapples, if desired. Serve with crackers. Yield: 6 cups.

SPICY HOMEMADE SAUSAGE

5 pounds ground beef
¼ cup meat cure mix
2½ tablespoons coarsely ground pepper
1 tablespoon crushed red pepper
2½ teaspoons mustard seeds
1½ teaspoons garlic powder
2½ tablespoons liquid smoke
Lettuce leaves (optional)
Apple (optional)

Combine first 7 ingredients; mix well, and chill 8 hours or overnight.
Shape meat mixture into five 5- x 3-inch logs. (Wear rubber gloves to prevent hand irritation.) Wrap logs individually in cheese cloth; tie ends with string. Place on a rack in a shallow baking pan; bake at 200° for 6 hours. Chill 8 hours or overnight; store in the refrigerator. Garnish with lettuce leaves and an apple, if desired. Serve with crackers. Yield: five 5- x 3-inch logs.

HOLIDAY TURKEY SALAD

11 to 12 cups diced cooked turkey
12 hard-cooked eggs, chopped
1 bunch fresh parsley, finely chopped
4 cups finely chopped celery
2½ cups mayonnaise
3 tablespoons lemon juice
1½ teaspoons pepper
1 teaspoon salt
1 teaspoon paprika
Fresh parsley sprigs
Paprika

Combine turkey, eggs, chopped parsley, and celery in a large bowl.
Combine next 5 ingredients; mix well. Spoon over turkey mixture; toss gently. Cover and chill thoroughly. Garnish with parsley sprigs and paprika. Yield: 20 to 25 servings.

TOMATO-ARTICHOKE ASPIC

4 envelopes unflavored gelatin
¾ cup cold water
5 cups vegetable cocktail juice
1 tablespoon lemon juice
1 teaspoon Worcestershire sauce
¼ teaspoon hot sauce
¼ teaspoon white pepper
5 carrots, finely chopped
1 (14-ounce) can artichoke hearts, drained and coarsely chopped
¾ cup finely chopped celery
½ cup minced fresh parsley
½ cup finely chopped green pepper
Lettuce leaves
Lemon halves (optional)
Paprika (optional)

Sprinkle gelatin over cold water, and let stand 5 minutes.
Bring vegetable cocktail juice to a boil; add gelatin, and cook over medium heat until gelatin dissolves, stirring constantly and scraping sides occasionally. Stir in lemon juice, Worcestershire sauce, hot sauce, and pepper; chill until the consistency of unbeaten egg white. Fold in next 5 ingredients; spoon into a lightly oiled 9-cup mold. Cover and chill until firm. Unmold on a lettuce-lined plate. Garnish with lemon halves sprinkled with paprika, if desired. Yield: 16 to 18 servings.

PINEAPPLE-LIME SALAD

1 (6-ounce) package lime-flavored gelatin
1 cup boiling water
1 cup cold water
1 (3-ounce) package cream cheese, softened
1 cup whipping cream, whipped
1 cup miniature marshmallows
1 (8-ounce) can crushed pineapple, drained
1 cup chopped pecans
Fresh parsley sprigs (optional)
Crabapples (optional)
Orange cups (optional)
Cranberries (optional)

Dissolve gelatin in boiling water; stir in cold water. Beat cream cheese until smooth. Gradually add gelatin; beat well. Chill until the consistency of unbeaten egg white. Fold in next 4 ingredients. Pour mixture into a shallow 6-cup mold; cover and chill. Unmold and garnish with parsley, crabapples, and orange cups filled with cranberries, if desired. Yield: 12 servings.

SENSATIONAL SALAD

2 cups vegetable oil
¾ cup cider vinegar
⅓ cup lemon juice
½ cup chopped fresh parsley
2 to 3 cloves garlic, minced
½ teaspoon salt
½ teaspoon pepper
2 cups (8 ounces) freshly grated Romano cheese
3 heads iceberg lettuce, torn

Combine first 7 ingredients in a large jar. Cover tightly, and shake vigorously until blended; stir in cheese. Toss dressing as needed with lettuce; store remaining dressing in refrigerator. Yield: 18 servings.

TOASTED PECANS

½ cup butter or margarine, melted
3 cups pecan halves
Salt to taste

Pour butter over pecans, stirring to coat well. Arrange pecans in a single layer on a baking sheet; sprinkle with salt. Bake at 275° about 1 hour; stir occasionally. Yield: 3 cups.

CREAM CHEESE CAKE SQUARES

1 (18.5-ounce) package yellow cake mix
    without pudding
½ cup butter, softened
1 egg, beaten
1 (8-ounce) package cream cheese,
    softened
2 eggs
2½ cups powdered sugar
1 teaspoon vanilla extract

Combine first 3 ingredients in a large mixing bowl; mix well. Press mixture into a lightly greased 13- x 9- x 2-inch baking pan. Bake at 350° for 10 minutes. Beat cream cheese at medium speed of an electric mixer until fluffy; add eggs, one at a time, beating after each addition. Gradually add powdered sugar, beating well. Stir in vanilla. Pour mixture over baked layer, spreading evenly. Bake at 350° for 35 minutes. Cool and cut into 1½-inch squares. Yield: about 4 dozen.

TEATIME TASSIES

¾ cup firmly packed light brown sugar
¾ cup chopped pecans
1 egg
1 tablespoon butter or margarine, softened
1 teaspoon vanilla extract
Dash of salt
Tart shells (recipe follows)
Sifted powdered sugar (optional)

Combine first 6 ingredients. Spoon mixture into tart shells, filling three-fourths full. Bake at 350° for 20 minutes or until browned. Dust with sifted powdered sugar before serving, if desired. Yield: 2 dozen.

Tart Shells:

1 cup all-purpose flour
1 (3-ounce) package cream cheese,
    softened
¼ cup plus 3 tablespoons butter, softened

Combine all ingredients; stir until well blended. Shape dough into 24 balls; chill. Place in greased 1¾-inch tart pans, shaping each into a shell. Yield: 2 dozen tart shells.

CREAMY PECAN FUDGE

3 (12-ounce) packages semisweet
    chocolate morsels
1 (7-ounce) jar marshmallow
    creme
1 cup butter or margarine
4½ cups sugar
1 (13-ounce) can evaporated milk
3 to 4 cups chopped pecans

Combine chocolate morsels, marshmallow creme, and butter in a large bowl. Set aside.

Combine sugar and evaporated milk in a heavy saucepan; bring to a boil, reduce heat, and cook over low heat 9 minutes, stirring constantly. Pour over chocolate morsel mixture; stir until chocolate melts and mixture is smooth. Add pecans; stir until well blended.

Spread mixture in a lightly buttered 15- x 10- x 1-inch jellyroll pan. Chill until firm; cut into squares. Cover and store in refrigerator. Yield: 10 dozen.

Southerners Share Their Family Traditions

More than any other holiday, Christmas is a time for families. The tree with heirloom ornaments, special gifts wrapped with love, and who could forget the wonderful aromas of dishes that capture memories of Decembers past.

GLAZED STUFFED HAM

1 (12-pound) fully cooked ham
½ cup chopped onion
½ cup chopped celery
2 tablespoons chopped fresh
    parsley
½ cup butter or margarine
6 cups soft breadcrumbs
¾ cup milk
1 egg, beaten
1 teaspoon rubbed sage
½ teaspoon dried whole thyme
¼ teaspoon salt
1 cup firmly packed brown sugar
½ cup dark corn syrup
½ cup orange juice
Watercress or fresh parsley sprigs
    (optional)

Remove skin from ham; place fat side up on rack in a shallow roasting pan. Bake at 325° for 2½ hours.

Sauté onion, celery, and parsley in butter until tender. Combine sautéed vegetables and next 6 ingredients; stir gently until well mixed.

Score ham in a diamond design, cutting 1½ inches deep and 1½ inches apart. Press stuffing into cuts.

Combine brown sugar, corn syrup, and orange juice in a medium saucepan. Cook over medium heat, stirring constantly, until sugar dissolves. Brush ham with glaze; reserve remaining glaze.

Insert meat thermometer, making certain it does not touch fat or bone. Bake at 325° for 40 minutes or until meat thermometer registers 140°, brushing ham frequently with glaze. Garnish ham with watercress or parsley, if desired. Yield: 24 servings. *Elizabeth Moore, Huntsville, Alabama.*

OLD-FASHIONED CORNBREAD DRESSING

2 cups cornmeal
2 teaspoons baking powder
1 teaspoon baking soda
1 teaspoon salt
2 eggs, beaten
2 cups buttermilk
2 tablespoons bacon drippings, melted
3 stalks celery, chopped
1 medium onion, chopped
2 tablespoons butter or margarine
12 slices day old bread, crumbled
2 to 2½ cups turkey or chicken broth
1 cup milk
2 eggs, beaten
1 teaspoon salt
1 teaspoon poultry seasoning
¼ teaspoon pepper

Combine first 4 ingredients in a large mixing bowl; add 2 eggs, buttermilk, and bacon drippings, mixing well.

Place a well-greased 10-inch cast-iron skillet in a 450° oven for 4 minutes or until hot. Remove from oven; spoon batter into pan. Bake at 450° for 35 minutes or until lightly browned. Cool; crumble cornbread into a large bowl.

Sauté celery and onion in butter until tender. Combine cornbread, sautéed vegetables, and remaining ingredients, mixing well. Spoon into a lightly greased 13- x 9- x 2-inch baking pan. Bake at 450° for 25 to 30 minutes. Yield: 8 servings. *Irene Payne, Columbus, Georgia.*

Tip: Whenever a recipe calls for a reheating process, the dish can be made in advance up to that point.

LAYERED CRANBERRY SALAD

2 envelopes unflavored gelatin
¾ cup sugar
1½ cups boiling water
1 cup ginger ale
1½ cups fresh cranberries, ground
2 envelopes unflavored gelatin
3 tablespoons sugar
½ cup plus 2 tablespoons boiling water
1½ cups commercial sour cream
1¼ cups lemon or pineapple sherbet,
   softened
¾ cup chopped walnuts or pecans

Combine 2 envelopes gelatin and ¾ cup sugar in a medium bowl; add 1½ cups water, and stir until gelatin is dissolved. Stir in ginger ale and cranberries. Pour into a lightly greased 8-cup mold, and chill until almost set.

Combine 2 envelopes unflavored gelatin and 3 tablespoons sugar in a medium bowl; add ½ cup plus 2 tablespoons boiling water, and stir until gelatin is dissolved. Add sour cream and sherbet. Beat at low speed of electric mixer until well blended; cool. Fold in walnuts; pour sour cream mixture over cranberry layer in mold. Chill until firm. Yield: 10 to 12 servings.   *Mrs. Guy Sillay,*
Norcross, Georgia.

COCONUT-PECAN CARROT CAKE

2¾ cups sifted cake flour
2½ teaspoons ground cinnamon
1½ teaspoons baking soda
½ teaspoon salt
1¼ cups vegetable oil
2 cups sugar
4 eggs, separated
¼ cup warm water
3 cups grated carrots
Coconut-Pecan Frosting

Combine flour, cinnamon, soda, and salt; set aside.

Combine oil and sugar; beat until smooth. Combine egg yolks and water; add to oil mixture, beating well. Stir in carrots and flour mixture, mixing until well blended. Beat egg whites (at room temperature) until stiff peaks form; fold into creamed mixture.

Pour batter into 3 greased and floured 9-inch cakepans. Bake at 350° for 25 to 30 minutes or until a wooden pick inserted in center comes out clean. Cool cake in pans 10 minutes. Remove layers from pans; place on wire racks, and let cool completely.

Spread Coconut-Pecan Frosting between layers and on top and sides of cake. Yield: one 3-layer cake.

Coconut-Pecan Frosting:

1 (13-ounce) can evaporated milk
1 cup sugar
½ cup butter or margarine
2 egg yolks
1 cup chopped pecans
1 cup flaked coconut
1 teaspoon vanilla extract

Combine milk, sugar, butter, and egg yolks in a heavy saucepan; bring to a boil, and cook over medium heat 12 minutes or until thickened, stirring constantly. Remove from heat, and add pecans, coconut, and vanilla; stir until frosting is cool and of spreading consistency. Yield: enough frosting for one 3-layer cake.   *Wilton H. Hogan, Sr.,*
Birmingham, Alabama.

CINNAMON TWIST COFFEE CAKE

2 packages dry yeast
⅛ teaspoon sugar
½ cup warm water (105° to 115°)
1 cup boiling water
¾ cup instant potato flakes
1 teaspoon salt
½ cup sugar
½ cup instant nonfat dry milk powder
½ cup butter or margarine, softened
3 eggs
About 5 cups all-purpose flour, divided
½ cup butter or margarine, softened and
   divided
⅔ cup sugar
1½ teaspoons ground cinnamon
½ cup chopped pecans, divided
2 cups powdered sugar
3 tablespoons milk
Candied cherries (optional)
Toasted slivered almonds (optional)

Dissolve yeast and ⅛ teaspoon sugar in warm water; set aside.

Combine boiling water, potato flakes, and salt in a large mixing bowl; beat well. Add ½ cup sugar, nonfat dry milk powder, and ½ cup butter; mix well. Add eggs and yeast mixture, beating well. Gradually beat in 3 cups flour; add remaining flour, ½ cup at a time, beating well after each addition.

Turn dough onto a heavily floured surface; knead about 10 minutes until smooth and elastic. Place in a greased mixing bowl, turning to grease top. Cover and let rise in a warm place (85°), free from drafts, 1 hour or until doubled in bulk.

Punch dough down; divide dough into 6 equal portions. Roll each portion into a 12-inch circle.

Place one circle on a lightly greased 12-inch pizza pan. Spread 2 tablespoons

butter over top of dough, leaving a ½-inch margin. Combine ⅔ cup sugar and cinnamon; sprinkle about 2½ tablespoons cinnamon-sugar mixture and 2 tablespoons pecans over dough. Place a second circle of dough on top of first. Repeat process with butter, cinnamon-sugar mixture, and pecans. Top with a third circle of dough. Moisten outer edge of circle and seal. Repeat process with remaining 3 portions of dough.

Place a 2½-inch cookie cutter in the center of 1 loaf (do not cut through dough). Cut dough into 8 wedges, moving from cookie cutter to outside edge of dough. Gently lift each wedge, and twist several times to form a spiral pattern. Remove cookie cutter. Repeat process with second coffee cake. Cover cakes, and let rise about 45 minutes or until doubled in bulk.

Bake at 350° for 20 to 25 minutes or until golden brown. Cool 10 minutes.

Combine powdered sugar and milk; drizzle over cakes. Decorate with candied cherries and almonds, if desired. Yield: 2 coffee cakes.   *Kathy Hunt,*
Dallas, Texas.

SPICY PUMPKIN PIES

2 (16-ounce) cans pumpkin
1 cup firmly packed brown sugar
1 cup sugar
4 eggs
2 tablespoons molasses
1 tablespoon pumpkin pie spice
½ teaspoon salt
2 cups milk, scalded
2 unbaked 9-inch pastry shells
Sweetened whipped cream (optional)
Pecan halves (optional)

Combine first 7 ingredients; beat at medium speed of electric mixer 1 minute or until smooth. Gradually stir hot milk into pumpkin mixture, beating until well blended.

Pour filling into pastry shells; bake at 400° for 10 minutes. Reduce heat to 350°, and bake 1 hour or until a knife inserted halfway between center and edge of pie comes out clean. Cool before serving. Garnish with sweetened whipped cream and pecan halves, if desired. Yield: two 9-inch pies.
Peggy H. Amos,
Martinsville, Virginia.

HOT MULLED CIDER

6 cups apple cider
3 tablespoons honey or light brown
  sugar
16 whole cloves
8 lemon slices
8 (4-inch) sticks cinnamon
¾ to 1 cup light rum

Combine cider and honey in a medium saucepan. Place 2 cloves in rind of each lemon slice. Add prepared lemon slices, cinnamon sticks, and rum to cider. Bring to a boil; cover, reduce heat, and simmer 5 minutes. Remove cinnamon sticks and lemon slices; set aside for garnish, if desired. Serve immediately. Yield: 7 cups.

Mrs. H. G. Drawdy,
Spindale, North Carolina.

Cooked Fruit In Minutes

Overcooking is the easiest way to ruin fruit, whether it's canned or fresh. That's why the microwave oven is ideal for cooked fruit side dishes like the recipes you'll find here. All you do is mix the ingredients together, and microwave about 10 minutes or less.

SCALLOPED PINEAPPLE

1 (20-ounce) can crushed pineapple,
  undrained
6 slices white bread
¼ cup plus 1 tablespoon butter or
  margarine
3 eggs, beaten
¾ cup sugar
½ teaspoon ground cinnamon

Drain pineapple, reserving ⅓ cup juice; set aside. Trim crusts from bread, and cut bread into 1-inch cubes; reserve crusts for other uses. Cut butter into ½-inch pieces. Combine reserved juice, pineapple, bread cubes, butter, and remaining ingredients in a mixing bowl, stirring well. Pour mixture into a lightly greased 2-quart casserole; cover and microwave on HIGH 8 to 10 minutes or until set, stirring at 3-minute intervals. Yield: 6 to 8 servings.

GINGER PEACHES WITH RUM

1 (16-ounce) can peach halves,
  drained
1 tablespoon butter or margarine
2½ tablespoons brown sugar
½ teaspoon ground ginger
2 tablespoons light rum

Place peaches in a 1-quart casserole; set aside. Place butter in a 2-cup glass measure. Microwave at HIGH 35 seconds or until melted. Add remaining ingredients to butter, stirring well; pour over peaches. Cover with heavy-duty plastic wrap, and microwave at HIGH 3 to 5 minutes or until peaches are hot. Let stand 2 minutes, basting peaches occasionally with juice mixture. Serve hot. Yield: about 6 servings.

WINE-POACHED ORANGES

7 large oranges, peeled and sectioned
1 tablespoon sugar
¼ cup dry white wine
3 tablespoons orange juice
½ teaspoon grated lemon rind
1 tablespoon lemon juice
Orange slice halves (optional)
Fresh mint sprig (optional)

Place orange sections in a 1½-quart casserole; set aside. Combine next 5 ingredients; stir until sugar dissolves. Pour wine mixture over orange sections; cover and microwave at HIGH 3 to 5 minutes or until thoroughly heated. Serve warm or chilled. Garnish with orange slice halves and mint, if desired. Yield: 6 to 8 servings.

SPICY APPLE RELISH

6 cups chopped, unpeeled cooking
  apples
⅓ cup chopped onion
¼ cup raisins
¼ cup firmly packed brown sugar
¼ cup water
1 tablespoon lemon juice
½ teaspoon ground ginger
½ teaspoon ground cinnamon
¼ teaspoon ground cloves
Dash of salt

Combine all ingredients in a 2-quart casserole, mixing well. Cover and microwave at HIGH 10 to 12 minutes, or until apples are tender, stirring at 4-minute intervals. Serve warm or cold with pork or poultry. Store in refrigerator. Yield: 6 servings.

Please Dieters At Your Next Open House

Put up the wreath, and hang the garlands—Christmas is the time for an open house. As you decide on the menu, remember that some of your guests will probably be dieting. One of the best gifts you can plan for them is a menu that's light in calories. You may be wondering how diet food can taste good enough for an open house—read on and see how "Cooking Light" readers have trimmed the calories in several delicious party treats that will delight dieters and nondieters alike.

MARINATED STEAK-AND-CHESTNUT APPETIZERS

2 (1-pound) flank steaks
½ cup dry red wine
¼ cup sesame seeds
¼ cup soy sauce
1½ tablespoons oyster sauce
2 (8-ounce) cans sliced water chestnuts,
  drained
Vegetable cooking spray

Trim excess fat from steaks. Partially freeze steaks, and slice across grain into thin slices; cut slices into 4-inch pieces. Combine next 4 ingredients in a shallow dish; add steak, stirring to coat. Cover and marinate overnight in refrigerator, stirring occasionally.

Remove steak from marinade; thread each steak strip lengthwise onto a wooden pick, weaving steak around 2 water chestnut slices. Coat rack of a broiler pan with cooking spray; place kabobs on rack, and broil 6 inches from heat 5 to 6 minutes, turning once. Yield: about 32 appetizers (about 50 calories each).

SHRIMP DIPPERS

3 cups water
1 pound large fresh shrimp, unpeeled
¼ pound fresh snow peas

Bring water to a boil; add shrimp, and cook 3 to 5 minutes. Drain well; rinse with cold water. Chill. Peel and devein shrimp; set aside.

Arrange snow peas in a steaming rack, and place over boiling water; cover and steam about 1 minute. Remove snow peas, and chill.

Separate snow peas lengthwise into 2 pieces. Wrap a snow pea half around each shrimp, and secure with wooden pick. Yield: about 26 dippers (about 12 calories each).

SMOKED SALMON SPREAD

1 (15½-ounce) can salmon, drained and flaked
1 (8-ounce) package Neufchâtel cheese, softened
1 tablespoon lemon juice
2 teaspoons grated onion
2 teaspoons prepared horseradish
¼ teaspoon liquid smoke
3 drops of hot sauce
2 tablespoons chopped fresh parsley

Combine first 7 ingredients; stir well. Spoon into serving bowl; cover and chill several hours or overnight. Sprinkle with parsley just before serving. Serve with melba rounds. Yield: 2 cups (about 38 calories per tablespoon).
Alice Van Nada,
Lowell, Indiana.

DILLED GARDEN DIP

2 cups low-fat cottage cheese
2 tablespoons tarragon vinegar
1 to 2 tablespoons skim milk
1 tablespoon finely chopped green onion
1 tablespoon chopped fresh parsley
½ teaspoon dried whole dillweed
Dash of freshly ground pepper
Pimiento strip (optional)
Fresh parsley sprig (optional)
Shrimp Dippers

Combine cottage cheese and vinegar in container of an electric blender; process until smooth. Combine cottage cheese mixture and next 5 ingredients. Cover and chill 2 hours. Spoon dip into a serving bowl; garnish with pimiento strip and parsley sprig, if desired. Serve with Shrimp Dippers or raw vegetables. Yield: 2¼ cups (about 9 calories per tablespoon).
Dolly D. Green,
Birmingham, Alabama.

CINNAMON WAFERS

¾ cup margarine, softened
½ cup sugar
2 egg yolks
1 teaspoon vanilla extract
2 cups all-purpose flour
1 teaspoon baking powder
1¼ teaspoons ground cinnamon
⅛ teaspoon salt

Cream margarine; gradually add sugar, beating until light and fluffy. Add egg yolks, and beat well. Stir in vanilla.

Combine dry ingredients; add to creamed mixture, beating well. Shape dough into 1-inch balls. Place 2 inches apart on ungreased cookie sheets; flatten with a fork. Bake at 300° for 20 minutes or until edges begin to brown. Remove wafers to wire racks, and cool completely. Yield: 4 dozen (about 52 calories each).

SHERRIED AMBROSIA

12 medium oranges
2 medium grapefruit, peeled, sectioned, and seeded
2 ripe pears, unpeeled and cubed
2 Red Delicious apples, unpeeled and cubed
2 cups seedless red grapes, halved
1½ cups unsweetened orange juice
½ cup dry sherry
2 tablespoons lemon juice
½ cup flaked coconut

Cut oranges in half crosswise. Carefully remove sections (do not puncture bottom); remove seeds, and set aside. Carefully remove membranes inside orange shells; set shells aside.

Combine orange sections and next 4 ingredients in a large bowl. Combine orange juice, sherry, and lemon juice; pour over fruit, and toss. Chill. Spoon fruit into reserved orange shells using a slotted spoon; sprinkle each with 1 teaspoon coconut. Yield: 24 servings (about 82 calories per serving).

HOT APPLE PUNCH

2 (12-ounce) cans frozen unsweetened apple juice concentrate, thawed and undiluted
1 quart water
2 cups fresh cranberries
2 (3-inch) sticks cinnamon
6 whole cloves

Prepare apple juice according to directions on can; pour into a large Dutch oven, and add next 4 ingredients. Bring to a boil; cover, reduce heat, and simmer 30 minutes. Strain mixture, discarding cranberries and spices. Yield: 1 gallon (about 72 calories per ¾-cup serving).
Diane Stokes Sockwell,
Baltimore, Maryland.

Christmas Aromas Set A Festive Mood

Would you like to make a batch of Christmas spirit? Try our "recipe" for Christmas Scent or Decorative Ribbon-Spice Balls. These spicy concoctions are for smelling rather than tasting, but their rich, sweet aromas will add Christmas flavor to your home.

Put on a pot of Christmas Scent and let it simmer while you're entertaining holiday guests. Or enjoy the delicious fragrance while you're wrapping presents or doing your Christmas baking.

Make Decorative Ribbon-Spice Balls to use throughout the house—hang some in the kitchen, mix some in a bowl with fresh red apples or clove-studded pomanders, tie them on packages, or even hang them on the tree. They're easy to make, and with the orris root in the mixture, they'll keep for several years.

For two delightful Christmas smells that you can mix up in the kitchen, make Christmas Scent and Decorative Ribbon-Spice Balls.

DECORATIVE RIBBON-SPICE BALLS

½ cup ground cinnamon
3 tablespoons ground allspice
3 tablespoons ground cloves
2 tablespoons ground nutmeg
2 tablespoons orris root powder (optional)
1 cup applesauce
4 yards ¼-inch red satin ribbon, cut into 12-inch lengths
12 whole cloves
3⅓ yards ¼-inch red satin ribbon, cut into 10-inch lengths

Combine first 5 ingredients, blending well. Stir in applesauce; mix well. (Mixture will be stiff.) Roll into 12 smooth balls about the size of walnuts.

Fold a 12-inch length of ribbon in half (shiny side to the outside), and use a thin crochet hook or hooked wire to pull loop through one of the spice balls. Place a whole clove in the loop, and pull the ribbon taut to anchor clove. Smooth out dough around clove after pulling ribbon taut. Tie a double knot on the other side of the spice ball, being careful not to pull too tightly. Arrange knot so that the ribbon hangs straight. Smooth out the dough.

Repeat procedure for remaining spice balls. Let dry completely, 5 to 10 days, on a metal tray, turning occasionally.

Using 10-inch lengths of ribbon, tie a small bow around knot of each spice ball, arranging ribbon so that bow ends hang in same direction as first length of ribbon. To hang spice balls, knot together ends of first length of ribbon.

After Christmas, carefully wrap spice balls in tissue paper, pack in an airtight container, and store in a cool, dry place. Yield: 12 spice balls.

Note: Orris root powder is available at some pharmacies. Spice balls can be made without it, but the fragrance will not last as long.

CHRISTMAS SCENT

3 (4-inch) sticks cinnamon
3 bay leaves
¼ cup whole cloves
½ lemon, halved
½ orange, halved
1 quart water

Combine all ingredients in a teakettle or saucepan, and bring to a boil; reduce heat and simmer as long as desired. Check often, and add additional water, if needed. Mixture may be stored in refrigerator several days and reused. Yield: 4 cups.
Marilyn Salinas,
Fort Worth, Texas.

Citrus Salads Brighten Meals

Cool and refreshing citrus salads add a little bit of sunshine to winter meals. These salads complement the flavor of a hot meal, even on a cold day.

Winter is the peak season for fresh citrus, so don't be fooled by the color of the fruit in the grocery store. A green-tinged peel does not mean the fruit is underripe. Cool weather makes citrus color up, and if warm weather predominates, an orange or grapefruit can be as sweet and ripe and still have a green blush. Citrus does not ripen further once picked, so state regulations require it to be ripe when sold. This is monitored by measuring the amount of sugar and acid in the fruit before harvesting.

ORANGE-CARROT SALAD

2 cups shredded cabbage
1½ cups shredded carrots
1½ cups coarsely chopped orange sections
½ cup raisins
½ cup chopped pecans
½ cup mayonnaise or salad dressing

Combine all ingredients in a large mixing bowl; toss gently to coat. Chill several hours. Yield: 6 servings.
Mrs. G. E. Hull,
Arlington, Texas.

ORANGE-ROMAINE SALAD

¼ cup vegetable oil
2 tablespoons sugar
2 tablespoons vinegar
½ teaspoon salt
Dash of hot sauce
6 cups torn romaine lettuce
5 cups torn iceberg lettuce
1½ cups orange sections
¼ cup slivered almonds, toasted
2 green onions, sliced
¼ cup cooked, crumbled bacon

Combine first 5 ingredients in a jar. Cover tightly, and shake vigorously until well blended; set aside.

Combine next 5 ingredients in a large bowl. Pour dressing over lettuce mixture immediately before serving; toss gently. Sprinkle salad with crumbled bacon. Yield: 4 to 6 servings.
Charlene Keebler,
Savannah, Georgia.

CONGEALED GRAPEFRUIT SALAD

2 envelopes unflavored gelatin
½ cup cold water
2 (16-ounce) cans unsweetened grapefruit sections, undrained
1½ cups sugar
1 (8-ounce) package cream cheese, softened
¼ cup half-and-half
½ cup chopped pecans

Soften gelatin in cold water; let stand 5 minutes.

Drain grapefuit, reserving juice; add enough water to juice to measure 2 cups. Combine liquid and sugar in a saucepan; bring to a boil. Remove from heat; add gelatin, stirring until dissolved. Stir in grapefruit sections.

Combine cream cheese and half-and-half; beat at medium speed of an electric mixer until smooth. Stir in chopped pecans. Pour half of gelatin mixture into a lightly oiled 8-inch square dish, and chill until partially set. Spread cream cheese mixture evenly over top; spoon on remaining gelatin mixture. Chill until salad is firm. Yield: 9 servings.
Gigi Vincent,
Bunkie, Louisiana.

GRAPEFRUIT SALAD

3 grapefruit
2 (3-ounce) packages lemon-flavored gelatin
1 cup boiling water
2 tablespoons plus 2 teaspoons sugar
2 teaspoons all-purpose flour
⅓ cup pineapple juice
1 tablespoon lemon juice
1 egg yolk
4 large marshmallows
⅓ cup whipping cream, whipped
Lettuce leaves

Cut grapefruit in half; scoop out pulp, discarding membranes and seeds. Reserve shells, pulp, and juice.

Dissolve gelatin in boiling water. Stir in grapefruit pulp and juice; add enough water to gelatin mixture to measure 4 cups. Pour mixture into grapefruit shell halves; chill until firm.

Combine sugar and next 4 ingredients in a heavy saucepan. Cook, stirring constantly, until thickened. Add marshmallows, and stir until melted. Cool completely. Fold in whipped cream.

To serve, cut each shell into quarters; place on lettuce leaves, and top each serving with a dollop of sauce. Yield: 6 servings.
Ann Harris,
Lenoir City, Tennessee.

MOLDED WALDORF SALAD

1 (11-ounce) can mandarin orange
  sections, undrained
1 (8-ounce) can pineapple chunks,
  undrained
1 (3-ounce) package lemon-flavored
  gelatin
1 cup boiling water
1 medium apple, unpeeled and diced
1 medium banana, sliced
¼ cup coarsely chopped pecans
Lettuce leaves

Drain fruit, reserving liquid; set
aside. Dissolve gelatin in boiling water;
stir in reserved liquid, and chill until the
consistency of unbeaten egg white. Fold
in fruit and pecans; pour into a lightly
oiled 5-cup mold. Chill until firm. Unmold on lettuce leaves. Yield: 8
servings.   *Bettye Cortner,*
Cerulean, Kentucky.

Ham-and-Vegetable Quiche is a great way to use leftover ham. Fresh vegetables and cheese are mixed with the meat for this flavorful entrée.

Ham And Turkey The Second Time Around

If the holiday leaves the refrigerator
with leftover ham or turkey, these recipes can help you stretch what's left.

When storing leftover turkey, remember to remove any dressing from the
bird and store both separately in the
refrigerator. Cooked turkey and dressing should be used within 1 or 2 days.
Keep cooked ham well wrapped in the
coldest part of the refrigerator for no
longer than 4 to 5 days. If you have a
large amount of ham or turkey left, you
may want to freeze some of it.

CHEESY HAM-AND-POTATO CASSEROLE

2 tablespoons chopped onion
¼ cup butter or margarine
¼ cup all-purpose flour
1 teaspoon salt
½ teaspoon dry mustard
Dash of pepper
1½ cups milk
2 cups (8 ounces) shredded Cheddar
  cheese, divided
2 cups cubed cooked ham
6 cups cubed cooked potatoes

Sauté onion in butter in a large saucepan until tender. Add flour and seasonings, stirring until smooth. Cook 1
minute, stirring constantly. Gradually
add milk; cook over medium heat, stirring constantly, until thickened and
bubbly. Add 1½ cups cheese, stirring
until cheese melts. Add ham and potatoes, tossing gently. Spoon into a
greased 2-quart shallow baking dish;
bake, uncovered, at 350° for 25 minutes. Sprinkle with remaining ½ cup
cheese; bake an additional 5 minutes.
Yield: 6 servings.   *Debbie Dermid,*
Horse Shoe, North Carolina.

HAM-AND-VEGETABLE QUICHE

Pastry for 10-inch pie
½ cup chopped cauliflower
¼ cup chopped carrots
¼ cup chopped onion
¼ cup chopped green pepper
⅔ cup chopped cooked ham
1 cup (4 ounces) shredded Cheddar cheese
3 eggs, beaten
1 cup milk
½ teaspoon salt
Fresh cauliflower flowerets
Fresh parsley sprigs

Line a 10-inch quiche dish with
pastry; trim excess pastry around edges.
Prick bottom and sides of pastry with a
fork; bake at 425° for 5 minutes. Cool.

Cook next 4 ingredients in boiling
salted water to cover 5 minutes or until
crisp-tender; drain well. Layer ham and
vegetables in pastry shell; sprinkle with
cheese. Combine eggs, milk, and salt;
beat well. Pour into pastry shell. Bake
at 375° for 40 to 45 minutes or until set.
Let stand 10 minutes before serving.
Garnish with cauliflower flowerets and
parsley. Yield: one 10-inch quiche.
          Gloria Pedersen,
Brandon, Mississippi.

TURKEY-AND-DRESSING PIE

2½ cups prepared cornbread dressing
3 tablespoons butter or margarine,
  melted
1½ cups finely chopped cooked turkey
1 cup (4 ounces) shredded Swiss cheese
4 eggs
⅔ cup half-and-half

Combine dressing and butter; mix
well. Press on bottom and sides of a
9-inch quiche dish; bake at 400° for 5 to
7 minutes. Cool.

Combine turkey and cheese; spread in pastry shell. Combine eggs and half-and-half; beat well. Pour over turkey mixture; bake at 325° for 35 to 40 minutes or until the pie is set. Yield: one 9-inch pie. *Mrs. James S. Stanton, Richmond, Virginia.*

TURKEY CASSEROLE

4 ounces uncooked elbow macaroni
¼ cup butter or margarine
¼ cup all-purpose flour
3 tablespoons instant nonfat dry milk powder
1 cup water
1 teaspoon salt
⅛ teaspoon pepper
1 (10¾-ounce) can cream of mushroom soup, undiluted
¾ cup frozen English peas, cooked
1 cup chopped cooked turkey
½ cup (2 ounces) shredded Cheddar cheese
½ cup soft breadcrumbs
1 tablespoon butter or margarine, melted
Paprika

Cook macaroni according to package directions; drain and set aside.

Melt butter in a large saucepan over low heat; add flour and milk powder, stirring until smooth. Cook 1 minute, stirring constantly. Gradually add water, cook over medium heat, stirring constantly, until mixture is thickened and bubbly. Stir in salt, pepper, and soup; cook until bubbly, stirring often.

Add cooked macaroni, peas, and turkey to sauce; stir gently. Pour into a lightly greased 1½-quart casserole; top with cheese. Combine breadcrumbs and butter; mix well. Spread over cheese; sprinkle with paprika. Bake at 350° for 20 to 25 minutes. Yield: 4 servings.
Eleanor Glading, Snow Hill, Maryland.

Discover Dried Beans

If you think dried beans are too basic and bland to be good, think again. You may want to try Vegetarian Chili. Spiced with chopped green chiles and chili powder, this hearty dish is sure to help take the chill off winter evenings. And for a Caribbean flair, try Spanish Black Beans; meaty ham hock and vinegar combine to give this recipe interest.

The vinegar is added after the beans are cooked; a delay in the softening of dried beans can occur when acidic ingredients are added too early in the cooking process.

SPANISH BLACK BEANS

1 (16-ounce) package dried black beans
3 medium-size green peppers, chopped
2 large onions, chopped
2 cloves garlic, minced
½ cup olive oil
5 cups water
1 pound meaty ham hock
3 bay leaves
1 to 1½ teaspoons salt
¼ cup white wine vinegar
Cooked rice (optional)

Sort and wash beans; place in a large Dutch oven. Cover with water 2 inches above beans; let soak overnight.

Sauté green pepper, onion, and garlic in olive oil in a skillet until tender. Drain beans; stir in vegetables and next 4 ingredients. Bring to a boil over medium heat; reduce heat to low and cook, uncovered, 1 to 1½ hours or until beans are tender, stirring occasionally.

Remove ham hock and bay leaves from beans; scrape meat from bone. Add meat and vinegar to beans; stir well. Serve over rice, if desired. Yield: 8 to 10 servings.

VEGETARIAN CHILI

1 cup dried pinto beans
4 cups water
1 (17-ounce) can whole kernel corn, undrained
1 (15-ounce) can tomato sauce
1 large onion, chopped
1 (4-ounce) can chopped green chiles, drained
1 clove garlic, minced
1 teaspoon salt
2 teaspoons chili powder
1 teaspoon dried whole oregano
1 bay leaf
1 cup (4 ounces) shredded Monterey Jack cheese (optional)

Sort and wash beans; place in a Dutch oven. Cover with water 2 inches above beans; let soak overnight.

Drain beans; add 4 cups water, and next 9 ingredients. Bring to a boil; cover, reduce heat, and simmer 2½ hours or until beans are tender. Remove bay leaf. Ladle into serving bowls; sprinkle with cheese, if desired. Yield: 6 to 8 servings.
M. B. Quesenbury, Dugspur, Virginia.

MEXICAN BLACK-EYED PEAS

1 (16-ounce) package dried black-eyed peas
2 pounds bulk pork sausage
1 medium onion, finely chopped
1 (28-ounce) can whole tomatoes, undrained
½ cup water
2½ tablespoons finely chopped celery
2 tablespoons sugar
2½ tablespoons chili powder
2 teaspoons garlic salt
¼ teaspoon pepper

Sort and wash peas; place in a large Dutch oven. Cover with water 2 inches above peas; let soak overnight.

Brown sausage in a heavy skillet, stirring to crumble. Add onion, and cook until tender; drain.

Drain peas well; stir in sausage and remaining ingredients. Bring to a boil; cover, reduce heat, and simmer 1½ hours. Add additional water, if necessary. Yield: 10 servings.
Mrs. Robert L. Lamb, San Angelo, Texas.

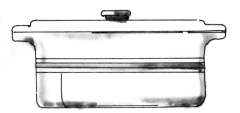

MOLASSES BAKED BEANS

1 (16-ounce) package dried navy beans
2 teaspoons salt
⅓ cup firmly packed brown sugar
⅓ cup molasses
½ teaspoon dry mustard
¼ teaspoon ground cloves
½ pound bacon, diced
1 medium onion, sliced

Sort and wash beans; place in a large Dutch oven. Cover with water 2 inches above beans; let soak overnight.

Add salt to beans, and bring to a boil. Cover, reduce heat, and simmer 45 minutes. Drain, reserving liquid.

Add next 4 ingredients, mixing well. Layer half each of bean mixture, bacon, and onion in a greased 2½-quart casserole. Repeat layers. Add reserved liquid to barely cover beans. Cover and bake at 300° for 2 hours and 15 minutes. Uncover and bake an additional 15 minutes, or until liquid is absorbed. Yield: 10 to 12 servings. *Virginia B. Stalder, Nokesville, Virginia.*

RAZORBACK BEANS

1 (16-ounce) package dried pinto beans
1 pound ground beef
1 medium onion, chopped
1 (16-ounce) can whole tomatoes,
  undrained
1 (4-ounce) can chopped green chiles,
  drained
1 (4-ounce) can taco sauce
1 teaspoon salt
1 teaspoon chili powder
½ teaspoon cumin seeds
½ teaspoon dried whole oregano
½ teaspoon garlic salt
½ teaspoon pepper

Sort and wash beans; place in a large Dutch oven. Cover with water 2 inches above beans, and bring to a boil; cook 2 minutes. Remove beans from heat; cover and let soak 1 hour.

Drain beans; cover with water. Bring to a boil; cover, reduce heat, and simmer 1 hour or until beans are tender. Drain 2 cups liquid from beans; discard remaining liquid.

Combine ground beef and onion in a skillet; cook until beef is browned, stirring to crumble. Add beef mixture and remaining ingredients to beans. Bring to a boil; cover, reduce heat, and simmer 1 hour and 15 minutes. Add additional water, if necessary. Yield: 8 to 10 servings.   *Donna Gershner,*
North Little Rock, Arkansas.

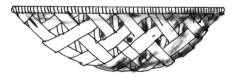

Snacks To Serve Anytime

When you're looking for the right snack for a casual gathering, these recipes will fit the occasion. Mix some tiny crackers or a party mix for your guests or your family.

SNACK-ATTACK PARTY MIX

1 (1½-ounce) can potato sticks
1¼ cups bite-size Cheddar cheese crackers
1¼ cups goldfish-shaped crackers
1¼ cups thin pretzel sticks
1¼ cups mixed nuts
3 tablespoons butter or margarine, melted
2 teaspoons Worcestershire sauce
½ teaspoon seasoning salt

Combine first 5 ingredients in a 15- x 10- x 1-inch jellyroll pan; set aside. Combine butter, Worcestershire sauce, and salt; drizzle over snack mixture, tossing gently. Bake at 250° for 45 minutes, stirring every 15 minutes. Yield: 6½ cups.   *Mary Kay Menees,*
White Pine, Tennessee.

CHEESE CRACKER NIBBLES

1 cup all-purpose flour
Dash of red pepper
⅔ cup grated Parmesan cheese
½ cup butter or margarine, softened

Combine flour and red pepper in a mixing bowl; add cheese; mixing well. Cut in butter until mixture resembles coarse meal. Mix with hands until dough is smooth; shape into a ball.

Roll dough out onto a lightly floured surface to ⅓-inch thickness. Cut into desired shapes with 1-inch cookie or canapé cutters. Place on an ungreased baking sheet; bake at 350° for 12 minutes or until lightly browned. Yield: about 5½ dozen.   *Jane Syers Hancock,*
Madison, Alabama.

Add Flair To Carrot Dishes

As favorite foods go, carrots are usually far down the list. Although they have a well-deserved reputation for goodness and nutrition, we tend to associate them with unimaginative dishes. But it doesn't have to be that way. We've rounded up some zesty carrot recipes that are packed with taste and variety and look good, too.

SCRUMPTIOUS CARROT CASSEROLE

3 pounds carrots, scraped and cut into
  ¼-inch slices
2 tablespoons butter or margarine
2 tablespoons all-purpose flour
1 cup half-and-half
½ teaspoon salt
⅛ teaspoon pepper
¼ teaspoon dry mustard
½ cup commercial sour cream
1 tablespoon prepared horseradish
4 slices bread, torn into small pieces
3 tablespoons butter or margarine

Cook carrots, covered, in a small amount of boiling salted water 10 to 12 minutes or until crisp-tender; drain. Spoon carrots into a lightly greased 2½-quart casserole; set aside.

Melt 2 tablespoons butter in a heavy saucepan over low heat; add flour, stirring until smooth. Cook 1 minute, stirring constantly. Gradually add half-and-half; cook over medium heat, stirring constantly, until mixture is thickened and bubbly. Stir in salt, pepper, dry mustard, sour cream, and horseradish; pour over carrots.

Sauté bread in 3 tablespoons butter until golden. Sprinkle over casserole; bake at 350° for 25 minutes. Yield: 10 to 12 servings.   *Susan W. Pajcic,*
Jacksonville, Florida.

CARROT PUFF

3 cups scraped and sliced carrots
½ cup butter or margarine, melted
3 tablespoons milk
2 eggs
2 tablespoons light brown sugar
Dash of ground nutmeg
Dash of pepper

Cook carrots in a small amount of boiling water 12 to 14 minutes or until tender; drain and mash. Spoon into container of electric blender; add butter. Process on high speed until smooth, stopping to scrape down sides with a rubber spatula as necessary. Add milk and eggs; process 1 minute. Add remaining ingredients; process until mixed well. Pour into a lightly greased 1-quart casserole; bake at 350° for 35 to 40 minutes or until set. Serve immediately. Yield: 4 to 6 servings.
Mary Frances Donnelly,
Roanoke, Virginia.

TASTY CARROT BREAD

1½ cups all-purpose flour
1 teaspoon baking soda
¼ teaspoon salt
1 teaspoon ground cinnamon
1 cup sugar
½ cup vegetable oil
½ cup buttermilk
2 eggs
1 cup shredded carrots
½ cup chopped pecans
1 teaspoon vanilla extract

Combine first 4 ingredients in a small mixing bowl; set aside.

Combine sugar, oil, buttermilk, and eggs in a large mixing bowl; beat at medium speed of an electric mixer for 1 minute. Add dry ingredients; mix at low speed just until blended. Fold in carrots, pecans, and vanilla.

Spoon batter into a greased and floured 8½- x 4½- x 3-inch loafpan; bake at 350° for 55 to 60 minutes or until a wooden pick inserted in center comes out clean. Cool 10 minutes in pan; remove to wire rack, and cool completely. Yield: 1 loaf. *Elaine Gray, Lebanon, Tennessee.*

TARRAGON CARROTS JULIENNE

7 to 8 large (about 1½ pounds) carrots, scraped and cut into 2-inch pieces
¼ cup butter or margarine
½ teaspoon dried whole tarragon
¼ teaspoon salt
Dash of coarsely ground black pepper

Position slicing blade in processor bowl. Arrange carrots horizontally in the food chute; slice, applying firm pressure with food pusher. Stack carrot slices, keeping ends even. Position slicing blade in processor; place carrot slices in bottom of food chute with cut sides parallel to chute sides. Replace processor lid, and slice again to make julienne strips.

Sauté carrots in butter 10 to 12 minutes or until crisp-tender. Sprinkle with tarragon, salt, and pepper; toss lightly. Yield: 6 servings.

Note: Carrots may also be cut by hand into matchstick-size pieces.
Sallie Chasteen, Atlanta, Georgia.

The delicate flavor of Lemon Vermicelli makes it a particularly good side dish. Garnishing with lemon slices and parlsey adds to its overall appeal.

Combine milk and butter in a saucepan; cook over low heat until butter melts. Set aside, and keep warm.

Cook vermicelli according to package directions; drain. Rinse with warm water, and drain again. Place in a bowl, and toss with lemon juice; let stand 1 minute. Add Parmesan cheese and warm milk mixture, tossing well. Garnish with parsley and lemon twists. Yield: 6 servings. *Jean Pashby, Memphis, Tennessee.*

add milk; cook over medium heat, stirring constantly, until thickened. Add 3 cups Cheddar cheese, process cheese, and pepper; stir until smooth. Stir in macaroni. Pour mixture into a lightly greased 3-quart casserole. Bake, uncovered, at 350° for 20 minutes. Sprinkle with remaining 1 cup Cheddar cheese, pimiento, and paprika; bake 5 minutes. Yield: 8 to 10 servings.
Libby Johnston, Marshall, Texas.

Spotlight Pasta Side Dishes

If you're tired of serving rice or potatoes at every meal, consider adding a pasta side dish to the menu. Vermicelli, fettuccine, noodles, and macaroni get along equally well with a variety of main-dish companions.

LEMON VERMICELLI

⅓ cup milk
3 tablespoons butter or margarine
1 (7-ounce) package vermicelli
¼ cup lemon juice
⅓ cup grated Parmesan cheese
Chopped fresh parsley
Lemon twists

THICK-AND-RICH MACARONI AND CHEESE

1 (12-ounce) package elbow macaroni
¾ cup finely chopped onion
1 large green pepper, finely chopped
½ cup butter or margarine
2 tablespoons all-purpose flour
1 (13-ounce) can evaporated milk
¼ cup milk
4 cups (16 ounces) shredded sharp Cheddar cheese, divided
1 (8-ounce) package process cheese, cubed
⅛ teaspoon pepper
2 tablespoons chopped pimiento, drained
Paprika

Cook macaroni according to package directions; drain. Rinse with warm water, and drain again; set aside.

Sauté onion and green pepper in butter in a large saucepan until tender. Add flour, stirring until smooth. Cook 1 minute, stirring constantly. Gradually

FETTUCCINE WITH SPINACH SAUCE

1 (16-ounce) package fettuccine
1 (10-ounce) package frozen chopped spinach
¼ cup butter or margarine
1 cup ricotta cheese
¼ cup grated Parmesan cheese
¼ cup whipping cream
½ teaspoon salt
⅛ teaspoon ground nutmeg

Cook fettuccine according to package directions; drain well. Rinse with warm water, and drain again; set aside.

Cook spinach according to package directions; drain and set aside. Melt butter in a large skillet over medium heat. Add spinach, cheese, whipping cream, salt, and nutmeg; stir well. Combine spinach mixture and warm noodles, tossing gently. Yield: 8 to 10 servings.
Linda Keith, Dallas, Texas.

Appendices

EQUIVALENT WEIGHTS AND MEASURES

Food	Weight or Count	Measure or Yield
Apples	1 pound (3 medium)	3 cups sliced
Bacon	8 slices cooked	½ cup crumbled
Bananas	1 pound (3 medium)	2½ cups sliced, or about 2 cups mashed
Bread	1 pound	12 to 16 slices
	About 1½ slices	1 cup soft crumbs
Butter or margarine	1 pound	2 cups
	¼-pound stick	½ cup
Cabbage	1 pound head	4½ cups shredded
Candied fruit or peels	½ pound	1¼ cups cut
Carrots	1 pound	3 cups shredded
Cheese, American or Cheddar	1 pound	About 4 cups shredded
cottage	1 pound	2 cups
cream	3-ounce package	6 tablespoons
Chocolate morsels	6-ounce package	1 cup
Cocoa	1 pound	4 cups
Coconut, flaked or shredded	1 pound	5 cups
Coffee	1 pound	80 tablespoons (40 cups perked)
Corn	2 medium ears	1 cup kernels
Cornmeal	1 pound	3 cups
Crab, in shell	1 pound	¾ to 1 cup flaked
Crackers, chocolate wafers	19 wafers	1 cup crumbs
graham crackers	14 squares	1 cup fine crumbs
saltine crackers	28 crackers	1 cup finely crushed
vanilla wafers	22 wafers	1 cup finely crushed
Cream, whipping	1 cup (½ pint)	2 cups whipped
Dates, pitted	1 pound	3 cups chopped
	8-ounce package	1½ cups chopped
Eggs	5 large	1 cup
whites	8 to 11	1 cup
yolks	12 to 14	1 cup
Flour, all-purpose	1 pound	3½ cups
cake	1 pound	4¾ to 5 cups sifted
whole wheat	1 pound	3½ cups unsifted
Green pepper	1 large	1 cup diced
Lemon	1 medium	2 to 3 tablespoons juice; 2 teaspoons grated rind
Lettuce	1 pound head	6¼ cups torn
Lime	1 medium	1½ to 2 tablespoons juice
Macaroni	4 ounces (1 cup)	2¼ cups cooked
Marshmallows	11 large	1 cup
	10 miniature	1 large marshmallow
Marshmallows, miniature	½ pound	4½ cups
Milk		
evaporated	5.33-ounce can	⅔ cup
evaporated	13-ounce can	1⅝ cups
sweetened condensed	14-ounce can	1¼ cups
Mushrooms	3 cups raw (8 ounces)	1 cup sliced cooked
Nuts		
almonds	1 pound	1 to 1¾ cups nutmeats
	1 pound shelled	3½ cups nutmeats
peanuts	1 pound	2¼ cups nutmeats
	1 pound shelled	3 cups
pecans	1 pound	2¼ cups nutmeats
	1 pound shelled	4 cups
walnuts	1 pound	1⅔ cups nutmeats
	1 pound shelled	4 cups

330

EQUIVALENT WEIGHTS AND MEASURES (*continued*)

Food	Weight or Count	Measure or Yield
Oats, quick-cooking	1 cup	1¾ cups cooked
Onion	1 medium	½ cup chopped
Orange	1 medium	⅓ cup juice and 2 tablespoons grated rind
Peaches	4 medium	2 cups sliced
Pears	4 medium	2 cups sliced
Potatoes, white	3 medium	2 cups cubed cooked or 1¾ cups mashed
sweet	3 medium	3 cups sliced
Raisins, seedless	1 pound	3 cups
Rice, long-grain	1 cup	3 to 4 cups cooked
pre-cooked	1 cup	2 cups cooked
Shrimp, raw in shell	1½ pounds	2 cups (¾ pound) cleaned, cooked
Spaghetti	7 ounces	About 4 cups cooked
Strawberries	1 quart	4 cups sliced
Sugar, brown	1 pound	2⅓ cups firmly packed
powdered	1 pound	3½ cups unsifted
granulated	1 pound	2 cups

EQUIVALENT MEASUREMENTS

3 teaspoons	1 tablespoon		2 cups	1 pint (16 fluid ounces)
4 tablespoons.............	¼ cup		4 cups	1 quart
5⅓ tablespoons.............	⅓ cup		4 quarts	1 gallon
8 tablespoons.............	½ cup		⅛ cup......................	2 tablespoons
16 tablespoons............	1 cup		⅓ cup......................	5 tablespoons plus 1 teaspoon
2 tablespoons (liquid)...	1 ounce		⅔ cup......................	10 tablespoons plus 2 teaspoons
1 cup.......................	8 fluid ounces		¾ cup......................	12 tablespoons

HANDY SUBSTITUTIONS

Ingredient Called For	Substitution
1 cup self-rising flour	1 cup all-purpose flour plus 1 teaspoon baking powder and ½ teaspoon salt
1 cup cake flour	1 cup sifted all-purpose flour minus 2 tablespoons
1 cup all-purpose flour	1 cup cake flour plus 2 tablespoons
1 teaspoon baking powder	½ teaspoon cream of tartar plus ¼ teaspoon soda
1 tablespoon cornstarch or arrowroot	2 tablespoons all-purpose flour
1 tablespoon tapioca	1½ tablespoons all-purpose flour
2 large eggs	3 small eggs
1 egg	2 egg yolks (for custard)
1 egg	2 egg yolks plus 1 tablespoon water (for cookies)
1 (8-ounce) carton commercial sour cream	1 tablespoon lemon juice plus evaporated milk to equal 1 cup; or 3 tablespoons butter plus ⅞ cup sour milk
1 cup yogurt	1 cup buttermilk or sour milk
1 cup sour milk or buttermilk	1 tablespoon vinegar or lemon juice plus sweet milk to equal 1 cup
1 cup fresh milk	½ cup evaporated milk plus ½ cup water
1 cup fresh milk	3 to 5 tablespoons nonfat dry milk solids in 1 cup water
1 cup honey	1¼ cups sugar plus ¼ cup water
1 (1-ounce) square unsweetened chocolate	3 tablespoons cocoa plus 1 tablespoon butter or margarine
1 tablespoon fresh herbs	1 teaspoon dried herbs or ¼ teaspoon powdered herbs
¼ cup chopped fresh parsley	1 tablespoon dried parsley flakes
1 teaspoon dry mustard	1 tablespoon prepared mustard
1 pound fresh mushrooms	6 ounces canned mushrooms

METRIC MEASURE/CONVERSION CHART

Approximate Conversion to Metric Measures

When You Know . . .	Multiply by . . .	To Find . . .	Symbol
	Mass (weight)		
ounces	28	grams	g
pounds	0.45	kilograms	kg
	Volume		
teaspoons	5	milliliters	ml
tablespoons	15	milliliters	ml
fluid ounces	30	milliliters	ml
cups	0.24	liters	l
pints	0.47	liters	l
quarts	0.95	liters	l
gallons	3.8	liters	l

APPROXIMATE TEMPERATURE CONVERSIONS—FAHRENHEIT TO CELSIUS

	Fahrenheit (°F)	Celsius (°C)
Freezer		
coldest area	-10°	-23°
overall	0°	-17°
Water		
freezes	32°	0°
simmers	115°	46°
scalds	180°	55°
boils (sea level)	212°	100°
Soft Ball	234° to 240°	112° to 115°
Firm Ball	242° to 248°	116° to 120°
Hard Ball	250° to 268°	121° to 131°
Slow Oven	275° to 300°	135° to 148°

Fahrenheit to Celsius: Subtract 32 • Multiply by 5 • Divide by 9
Celsius to Fahrenheit: Multiply by 9 • Divide by 5 • Add 32

COOKING MEASURE EQUIVALENTS

Metric Cup	Volume (Liquid)	Liquid Solids (Butter)	Fine Powder (Flour)	Granular (Sugar)	Grain (Rice)
1	250 ml	200 g	140 g	190 g	150 g
¾	188 ml	150 g	105 g	143 g	113 g
⅔	167 ml	133 g	93 g	127 g	100 g
½	125 ml	100 g	70 g	95 g	75 g
⅓	83 ml	67 g	47 g	63 g	50 g
¼	63 ml	50 g	35 g	48 g	38 g
⅛	31 ml	25 g	18 g	24 g	19 g

TIMETABLE FOR ROASTING BEEF AND LAMB

Kind and Cut	Approximate Weight	Internal Temperature	Approximate Total Cooking Times at 325°F.
	pounds		hours
Beef			
Standing ribs* (10-inch ribs)...................	4	140°F. (rare)	1¾
		160°F. (medium)	2
		170°F. (well done)	2½
	6	140°F. (rare)	2
		160°F. (medium)	2½
		170°F. (well done)	3½
	8	140°F. (rare)	2½
		160°F. (medium)	3
		170°F. (well done)	4½
Rolled ribs.................................	4	140°F. (rare)	2
		160°F. (medium)	2½
		170°F. (well done)	3
	6	140°F. (rare)	3
		160°F. (medium)	3¼
		170°F. (well done)	4
Rolled rump.................................	5	140°F. (rare	2¼
		160°F. (medium)	3
		170°F. (well done)	3¼
Sirloin tip.................................	3	140°F. (rare)	1½
		160°F. (medium)	2
		170°F. (well done)	2¼
Lamb			
Leg.................................	6 to 7	180°F. (well done)	3¾
Leg (half).................................	3 to 4	180°F. (well done)	2½ to 3
Cushion shoulder.................................	5	180°F. (well done)	3
Rolled shoulder.................................	3	180°F. (well done)	2½
	5	180°F. (well done)	3

*Standing ribs (8-inch ribs) allow 30 minutes longer.

TIMETABLE FOR ROASTING SMOKED PORK

Cut	Approximate Weight	Internal Temperature	Approximate Cooking Times at 325°F.
	pounds		minutes per pound
Ham (cook-before-eating)			
Whole.................................	10 to 14	160°F.	18 to 20
Half.................................	5 to 7	160°F.	22 to 25
Shank portion.................................	3 to 4	160°F.	35 to 40
Butt portion.................................	3 to 4	160°F.	35 to 40
Ham (fully cooked)			
Whole.................................	10 to 12	140°F.	15 to 18
Half.................................	5 to 7	140°F.	18 to 24
Loin.................................	3 to 5	160°F.	25 to 30
Picnic shoulder (cook-before-eating)...............	5 to 8	170°F.	30 to 35
Picnic shoulder (fully cooked)......................	5 to 8	140°F.	25 to 30
Shoulder roll (butt).................................	2 to 4	170°F.	35 to 40
Canadian-style bacon.................................	2 to 4	160°F.	35 to 40

TIMETABLE FOR ROASTING FRESH PORK

Cut	Approximate Weight	Internal Temperature	Approximate Cooking Times at 325°F.
	pounds		minutes per pound
Loin			
Center...	3 to 5	170°F.	30 to 35
Half..	5 to 7	170°F.	35 to 40
End..	3 to 4	170°F.	40 to 45
Roll..	3 to 5	170°F.	35 to 40
Boneless top..	2 to 4	170°F.	30 to 35
Crown..	4 to 6	170°F.	35 to 40
Picnic shoulder			
Bone-in...	5 to 8	170°F.	30 to 35
Rolled..	3 to 5	170°F.	35 to 40
Boston shoulder......................................	4 to 6	170°F.	40 to 45
Leg (fresh ham)			
Whole (bone-in)....................................	12 to 16	170°F.	22 to 26
Whole (boneless)...................................	10 to 14	170°F.	24 to 28
Half (bone-in).....................................	5 to 8	170°F.	35 to 40
Tenderloin...	½ to 1	170°F.	45 to 60
Back ribs..		cooked well done	1½ to 2½ hours
Country-style ribs...................................		cooked well done	1½ to 2½ hours
Spareribs..		cooked well done	1½ to 2½ hours
Pork Loaf..		cooked well done	1¾ hours

TIMETABLE FOR ROASTING POULTRY

Kind of Poultry	Ready-to-Cook Weight	Oven Temperature	Internal Temperature	Approximate Total Roasting Time
	pounds			hours
Chicken (unstuffed)*	1½ to 2	400°	185°F.	1
	2 to 2½	375°	185°F.	1 to 1¼
	2½ to 3	375°	185°F.	1¼ to 1½
	3 to 4	375°	185°F.	1½ to 2
	4 to 5	375°	185°F.	2 to 2½
Capon (unstuffed)	4 to 7	325°	185°F.	2½ to 3
Cornish Hen (stuffed)	1 to 1½	375°	185°F.	1 to 1¼
Duckling (unstuffed)	3½ to 5½	325°	190°F.	2 to 3
Goose (unstuffed)	7 to 9	350°	190°F.	2½ to 3
	9 to 11	350°	190°F.	3 to 3½
	11 to 13	350°	190°F.	3½ to 4
Turkey (stuffed)†	4 to 8	325°	185°F.	3 to 3¾
	8 to 12	325°	185°F.	3¾ to 4½
	12 to 16	325°	185°F.	4½ to 5½
	16 to 20	325°	185°F.	5½ to 6½
	20 to 24	325°	185°F.	6½ to 7½

*Stuffed chickens require about 5 additional minutes per pound.
†Unstuffed turkeys require about 5 minutes less per pound.

TIMETABLE FOR COOKING FISH AND SHELLFISH

Method of Cooking	Product	Market Form	Approximate Weight or Thickness	Cooking Temperature	Approximate Total Cooking Times
Baking	Fish	Dressed	3 to 4 lbs.	350°F.	40 to 60 min.
		Pan-dressed	½ to 1 lb.	350°F.	25 to 30 min.
		Steaks	½ to 1 in.	350°F.	25 to 35 min.
		Fillets		350°F.	25 to 35 min.
	Clams	Live		450°F.	15 min.
	Lobster	Live	¾ to 1 lb.	400°F.	15 to 20 min.
			1 to ½ lb.	400°F.	20 to 25 min.
	Oysters	Live		450°F.	15 min.
		Shucked		400°F.	10 min.
	Scallops	Shucked		350°F.	25 to 30 min.
	Shrimp	Headless		350°F.	20 to 25 min.
	Spiny lobster	Headless	4 oz.	450°F.	20 to 25 min.
	tails		8 oz.	450°F.	25 to 30 min.
Broiling	Fish	Pan-dressed	½ to 1 lb.		10 to 15 min.
		Steaks	½ to 1 in.		10 to 15 min.
		Fillets			10 to 15 min.
	Clams	Live			5 to 8 min.
	Lobster	Live	¾ to 1 lb.		10 to 12 min.
			1 to 1½ lbs.		12 to 15 min.
	Oysters	Live			5 min.
		Shucked			5 min.
	Scallops	Shucked			8 to 10 min.
	Shrimp	Headless			8 to 10 min.
	Spiny lobster	Headless	4 oz.		8 to 10 min.
	tails		8 oz.		10 to 12 min.
Cooking in water	Fish	Pan-dressed	½ to 1 lb.	Simmer	10 min.
		Steaks	½ to 1 in.	Simmer	10 min.
		Fillets		Simmer	10 min.
	Crabs	Live		Simmer	15 min.
	Lobster	Live	¾ to 1 lb.	Simmer	10 to 15 min.
			1 to 1½ lbs.	Simmer	15 to 20 min.
	Scallops	Shucked		Simmer	4 to 5 min.
	Shrimp	Headless		Simmer	5 min.
	Spiny lobster	Headless	4 oz.	Simmer	10 min.
	tails		8 oz.	Simmer	15 min.
Deep-fat frying	Fish	Pan-dressed	½ to 1 lb.	375°F.	2 to 4 min.
		Steaks	½ to 1 in.	375°F.	2 to 4 min.
		Fillets		375°F.	1 to 4 min.
	Clams	Shucked		375°F.	2 to 3 min.
	Crabs	Soft-shell	¼ lb.	375°F.	3 to 4 min.
	Lobster	Live	¾ to 1 lb.	350°F.	3 to 4 min.
			1 to 1½ lbs.	350°F.	4 to 5 min.
	Oysters	Shucked		375°F.	2 min.
	Scallops	Shucked		350°F.	3 to 4 min.
	Shrimp	Headless		350°F.	2 to 3 min.
	Spiny lobster	Headless	4 oz.	350°F.	3 to 4 min.
	tails		8 oz.	350°F.	4 to 5 min.

Glossary

à la King—Food prepared in a creamy white sauce containing mushrooms and red and/or green peppers

à la Mode—Food served with ice cream

al Dente—The point in the cooking of pasta at which it is still fairly firm to the tooth; that is, very slightly undercooked

Aspic—A jellied meat juice or a liquid held together with gelatin

au Gratin—Food served crusted with breadcrumbs or shredded cheese

au Jus—Meat served in its own juice

Bake—To cook food in an oven by dry heat

Barbecue—To roast meat slowly over coals on a spit or framework, or in an oven, basting intermittently with a special sauce

Baste—To spoon pan liquid over meats while they are roasting to prevent surface from drying

Beat—To mix vigorously with a brisk motion with spoon, fork, egg beater, or electric mixer

Béchamel—A white sauce of butter, flour, cream (not milk), and seasonings

Bisque—A thick, creamy soup usually of shellfish, but sometimes made of pureed vegetables

Blanch—To dip briefly into boiling water

Blend—To stir 2 or more ingredients together until well mixed

Blintz—A cooked crêpe stuffed with cheese or other filling

Boil—To cook food in boiling water or liquid that is mostly water (at 212°) in which bubbles constantly rise to the surface and burst

Boiling-water-bath canning method—Used for processing acid foods, such as fruits, tomatoes, pickled vegetables, and sauerkraut. These acid foods are canned safely at boiling temperatures in a water-bath canner

Borscht—Soup containing beets and other vegetables, usually with a meat stock base

Bouillabaisse—A highly seasoned fish soup or chowder containing two or more kinds of fish

Bouillon—Clear soup made by boiling meat in water

Bouquet Garni—Herbs tied in cheese-cloth which are cooked in a mixture and removed before serving

Bourguignon—Name applied to dishes containing Burgundy and often braised onions and mushrooms

Braise—To cook slowly with liquid or steam in a covered utensil. Less-tender cuts of meat may be browned slowly on all sides in a small amount of shortening, seasoned, and water added

Bread, to—To coat with crumbs, usually in combination with egg or other binder

Broil—To cook by direct heat, either under the heat of a broiler, over hot coals, or between two hot surfaces

Broth—A thin soup, or a liquid in which meat, fish, or vegetables have been boiled

Capers—Buds from a Mediterranean plant, usually packed in brine and used as a condiment in dressing or sauces

Caramelize—To cook white sugar in a skillet over medium heat, stirring constantly, until sugar forms a golden-brown syrup

Casserole—An ovenproof baking dish, usually with a cover; also the food cooked inside it

Charlotte—A molded dessert containing gelatin, usually formed in a glass dish or a pan that is lined with ladyfingers or pieces of cake

Chop—A cut of meat usually attached to a rib

Chop, to—To cut into pieces, with a sharp knife or kitchen shears

Clarified butter—Butter that has been melted and chilled. The solid is then lifted away from the liquid and discarded. Clarification heightens the smoke point of butter. Clarified butter will stay fresh in the refrigerator for at least 2 months

Coat—To cover completely, as in "coat with flour"

Cocktail—An appetizer; either a beverage or a light, highly seasoned food, served before a meal

Compote—Mixed fruit, raw or cooked, usually served in "compote" dishes

Condiments—Seasonings that enhance the flavor of foods with which they are served

Consommé—Clear broth made from meat

Cool—To let food stand at room temperature until not warm to the touch

Court Bouillon—A highly seasoned broth made with water and meat, fish or vegetables, and seasonings

Cream, to—To blend together, as sugar and butter, until mixture takes on a smooth, cream-like texture

Cream, whipped—Cream that has been whipped until it is stiff

Crème de Cacao—A chocolate-flavored liqueur

Crème de Café—A coffee-flavored liqueur

Crêpes—Very thin pancakes

Croquette—Minced food, shaped like a ball, patty, cone, or log, bound with a heavy sauce, breaded and fried

Croutons—Cubes of bread, toasted or fried, served with soups or salads

Cruller—A doughnut of twisted shape, very light in texture

Cube, to—To cut into cube-shaped pieces

Curaçao—Orange-flavored liqueur

Cut in, to—To incorporate by cutting or chopping motions, as in cutting shortening into flour for pastry

Demitasse—A small cup of coffee served after dinner

Devil, to—To prepare with hot seasoning or sauce

Dice—To cut into small cubes

Dissolve—To mix a dry substance with liquid until the dry substance becomes a part of the solution

Dot—To scatter small bits of butter over top of a food

Dredge—To coat with something, usually flour or sugar

Filé—Powder made of sassafras leaves used to season and thicken foods

Fillet—Boneless piece of meat or fish

Flambé—To flame, as in Crêpes Suzette or in some meat cookery, using alcohol as the burning agent; flame causes caramelization, enhancing flavor

Flan—In France, a filled pastry; in Spain, a custard

Florentine—A food containing or placed upon, spinach

Flour, to—To coat with flour

Fold—To add a whipped ingredient, such as cream or egg white to another ingredient by gentle over and under movement

Frappé—A drink whipped with ice to make a thick, frosty consistency

Fricassee—A stew, usually of poultry or veal

Fritter—Vegetable or fruit dipped into, or combined with, batter and fried

Fry—To cook in hot shortening

Garnish—A decoration for a food or drink

Glaze (To make a shiny surface)—In meat preparation, a jelled broth applied to meat surface; in breads and pastries, a wash of egg or syrup; for doughnuts and cakes, a sugar preparation for coating

Grate—To obtain small particles of food by rubbing on a grater or shredder

Grill—To broil under or over a source of direct heat

Grits—Coarsely ground dried corn, served boiled, or boiled and then fried

Gumbo—Soup or stew made with okra

Herb—Aromatic plant used for seasoning and garnishing foods

Hollandaise—A sauce made of butter, egg, and lemon juice or vinegar

Hominy—Whole corn grains from which hull and germ are removed

Jardiniere—Vegetables in a savory sauce or soup

Julienne—Vegetables cut into strips or a soup containing such vegetables

Kahlúa—A coffee-flavored liqueur

Kirsch—A cherry-flavored liqueur

Knead—To work a food (usually dough) by hand, using a folding-back and pressing-forward motion

Marinade—A seasoned liquid in which food is soaked

Marinate, to—To soak food in a seasoned liquid

Meringue—A whole family of egg white-sugar preparations including pie topping, poached meringue used to top custard, crisp meringue dessert shells, and divinity candy

Mince—To chop into very fine pieces

Mornay—White sauce with egg, cream, and cheese added

Mousse—A molded dish based on meat or sweet whipped cream stiffened with egg white and/or gelatin (if mousse contains ice cream, it is called bombe)

Panbroil—To cook over direct heat in an uncovered skillet containing little or no shortening

Panfry—To cook in an uncovered skillet in small amount of shortening

Parboil—To partially cook in boiling water before final cooking

Pasta—A large family of flour paste products, such as spaghetti, macaroni, and noodles

Pâté (French for paste)—A paste made of liver or meat

Petit Four—A small cake, which has been frosted and decorated

Pilau or pilaf—A dish of the Middle East consisting of rice and meat or vegetables in a seasoned stock

Poach—To cook in liquid held below the boiling point

Pot liquor—The liquid in which vegetables have been boiled

Preheat—To turn on oven so that desired temperature will be reached before food is inserted for baking

Puree—A thick sauce or paste made by forcing cooked food through a sieve

Reduce—To boil down, evaporating liquid from a cooked dish

Remoulade—A rich mayonnaise-based sauce containing anchovy paste, capers, herbs, and mustard

Render—To melt fat away from surrounding meat

Rind—Outer shell or peel of melon or fruit

Roast, to—To cook in oven by dry heat (usually applied to meats)

Roux—A mixture of butter and flour used to thicken gravies and sauces; it may be white or brown, if mixture is browned before liquid is added

Sauté—To fry food lightly over fairly high heat in a small amount of fat in a shallow, open pan

Scald—(1) To heat milk just below the boiling point (2) To dip certain foods into boiling water before freezing them (also called blanching)

Scallop—A bivalve mollusk of which only the muscle hinge is eaten; also to bake food in a sauce topped with crumbs

Score—To cut shallow gashes on surface of food, as in scoring fat on ham before glazing

Sear—To brown surface of meat over high heat to seal in juices

Set—Term used to describe the consistency of gelatin when it has jelled enough to unmold

Shred—Break into thread-like or stringy pieces, usually by rubbing over the surface of a vegetable shredder

Simmer—To cook gently at a temperature below boiling point

Skewer—To fasten with wooden or metal pins or skewers

Soak—To immerse in water for a period of time

Soufflé—A spongy hot dish, made from a sweet or savory mixture (often milk or cheese), lightened by stiffly beaten egg whites

Steam—To cook food with steam either in a pressure cooker, on a platform in a covered pan, or in a special steamer

Steam-pressure canning method—Used for processing low-acid foods, such as meats, fish, poultry, and most vegetables. A temperature higher than boiling is required to can these foods safely. The food is processed in a steam-pressure canner at 10 pounds' pressure (240°) to ensure that all of the spoilage micro-organisms are destroyed

Steep—To let food stand in not quite boiling water until the flavor is extracted

Stew—A mixture of meat or fish and vegetables cooked by simmering in its own juices and liquid, such as water and/or wine

Stir-fry—To cook quickly in oil over high heat, using light tossing and stirring motions to preserve shape of food

Stock—The broth in which meat, poultry, fish, or vegetables has been cooked

Syrupy—Thickened to about the consistency of egg white

Toast, to—To brown by direct heat, as in a toaster or under broiler

Torte—A round cake, sometimes made with breadcrumbs instead of flour

Tortilla—A Mexican flat bread made of corn or wheat flour

Toss—To mix together with light tossing motions, in order not to bruise delicate food, such as salad greens

Triple Sec—An orange-flavored liqueur

Veal—Flesh of milk-fed calf up to 14 weeks of age

Velouté—White sauce made of flour, butter, and a chicken or veal stock, instead of milk

Vinaigrette—A cold sauce of oil and vinegar flavored with parsley, finely chopped onions and other seasonings; served with cold meats or vegetables

Whip—To beat rapidly to increase air and increase volume

Wok—A round bowl-shaped metal cooking utensil of Chinese origin used for stir-frying and steaming (with rack inserted) of foods

Recipe Title Index

An alphabetical listing of every recipe by exact title
All microwave recipe page numbers are preceded by an "M"

Cream Cheese Frosting, 201, 255, 315, 316
Cream Cheese Fudge, 111
Cream Cheese Glaze, 150
Cream Cheese Loaf Cake, 151
Cream Cheese Puffs, 151
Cream Cheese Tarts, 74
Creamed Spinach with Noodles, 29
Cream Filling, 37
Cream Horns, 137
Cream of Asparagus Soup, 111
Cream of Green Bean Soup, 111
Cream of Mushroom Soup, 5
Cream of Peanut Butter Soup, 29
Creamy Baked Fillets, 91
Creamy Coconut Cake, 43
Creamy Cucumber Mold, 164
Creamy Curry Dip, 206
Creamy Fruit Dip, 51
Creamy Fruit Salad, 265
Creamy Garlic-Herb Salad Dressing, 66
Creamy Ham Medley, 90
Creamy Lime Sherbet, 165
Creamy Mocha Frosting, 311
Creamy Orange Dip, 117
Creamy Orange Salad, 124
Creamy Peas with Mushrooms, 196
Creamy Pecan Fudge, 321
Creamy Potato Casserole, M113
Creamy Potato Soup, 112
Creamy Roquefort Dressing, 12
Creamy Strawberry Dressing, 161
Creamy Stuffed Eggs, 143
Creamy Turnip Soup, 279
Crème Pâtissière, 207
Creole Oyster Pie, 214
Creole-Style Tomatoes-and-Corn, 142
Crêpes, 186
Crescent Rolls, 267
Crisp Fried Onion Rings, 65
Crisp Sugar Cookies, 243
Crispy Chicken, 152
Crispy Chicken Rolls, 288
Crispy Fried Fish, 92
Crispy Fried Flounder, 93
Crispy Italian Croutons, 126
Crispy Marinated Vegetable Salad, 193
Crispy Rice Crust, 43
Croissants, 188
Crown Room's Shrimp-Stuffed Catfish, 182
Crudité Platter with Dip, 139
Crunchy Granola, 144
Crunchy Marinated Bean Salad, 197
Crunchy Pear Salad, 244
Crunchy Squash Casserole, 293
Crunchy Vegetable Medley, 254
Crustless Ham Quiche, 235
Crustless Spinach Quiche, 235
Crystal Candy, 299
Cucumber Delights, 117
Cucumber-Pineapple Salad, 124
Cucumber Sauce, M286
Currant Scones, 117
Curried Chicken Salad, 66
Curried Dressing, 115
Curried Mushrooms, 214
Curried Mushroom Soup, M89
Curried Shrimp, 110
Curry Sauce, M71
Custard Sauce Ambrosia, 256

Daffodil Cake, 161
Daffodil Sponge Cake, 315
Dark Mocha-Chocolate Cake, 311

Date Bars, 313
Date Cupcakes, 7
Date-Nut Muffins, 75
Decorative Ribbon-Spice Balls, 325
Deep-Fried Strawberries, 109
Deluxe Apple Tart, 227
Deluxe English Peas, 68
Deluxe Light Banana Cake, 314
Dessert Crêpes, 84
Devil Doggies, 37
Deviled Beets, 217
Deviled Brussels Sprouts, 248
Deviled Eggs with Smoked Oysters, 161
Dijon Lamb Chops, 277
Dill-and-Chive Vinegar, 300
Dilled Baby Carrots, 80
Dilled Cucumber on Tomatoes, 142
Dilled Garden Dip, 324
Dill Sauce, M70, 107
Double Apple Salad, 227
Double Mocha Cake, 311
Down-Home Buttermilk Dressing, 114
Dressed-Up Barbecue Sauce, 173
Dried Peach Cream Pie, 146

Easter Egg Bread, 94
Easy Beer Bread, 160
Easy Bloody Mary, 115
Easy Cooked Escarole, 85
Easy Fried Rice, 76
Easy Holiday Mints, 299
Easy Homemade Mayonnaise, 12
Easy Hot Fudge Sauce, 69
Easy Ice Cream Balls, 106
Easy Nachos, 30
Easy Pecan Tarts, 313
Easy Processor Biscuits, 218
Easy Scampi, 291
Easy Spaghetti, 72
Easy Tomato Soup, 14
Easy Vegetable Salad, 16
Edam-Sherry Spread, 257
Edenton Eggnog, 251
Egg-and-Cheese Casserole, 293
Egg-and-Sausage Tortillas, 42
Eggplant Casserole, 217
Eggplant Parmesan, 215
Eggplant-Sausage Casserole, 215
Egg-Rice Salad, 18
Eight-Vegetable Relish, 179
Elephant Ears, 18
Enchiladas Terrificas, 32
Endive Boats, 80
Escarole-and-Bacon Salad, 85

Fajitas, 233
Fancy Fruit Medley, 82
Fast Goodies, 206
Festive Cauliflower, 34
Festive Cherry Salad, 265
Festive Cranberry Freezer Pie, 306
Fettuccine with Spinach Sauce, 329
Fiesta Rice, 76
Fig Preserve Cake, 316
Fish Aspic, 190
Fish Chowder, M38
Fish in a Crust, 294
Fish Monterey, 293
Fish 'n Aspic, 190
Fish Surprise, 231
Flaky Biscuits, 228
Flamed Plum Pudding, 276
Flaming Cheese, 187

Flaming Pears, 313
Flavorful Meatballs, 206
Fluffy Buttermilk Biscuits, 102
Fluffy Omelet, 56
Fluffy Potatoes, 296
Four-Bean Salad, 82
Frank-Filled Potatoes, M11
Frankfurter Sandwiches, M11
Freezer Blackberry Jam, M181
Freezer Peach Jam, M182
French Lettuce Salad, 187
Fresh Apple Cookies, 36
Fresh Apple Muffins, 264
Fresh Apple Pie, 178
Fresh Cantaloupe Soup, 190
Fresh Cauliflower Soup, 279
Fresh Cherry Cobbler, 178
Fresh Cranberry Sauce, 275
Fresh Fruit Compote, 82
Fresh Fruit Tart, 178
Fresh Mango Salad, 126
Fresh Mint Dressing, 126
Fresh Peach Crêpes, 186
Fresh Radish Spread, 166
Fresh Spinach Salad, 15, 77
Fresh Tomato Barbecue Sauce, 172
Fresh Vegetable Omelet, 211
Fried Cauliflower, 248
Fried Dill Pickles, 206
Fried Grits, 78
Fried Ham-and-Cheese Balls, 221
Fried Rice, 197
Frosted Margaritas, 115
Frosted Mint Tea, 161
Frozen Cheesecake with Raspberry
  Sauce, 73
Frozen Mocha Dessert, 311
Frozen Rainbow Delight, 105
Frozen Raspberry Dessert, 192
Frozen Tomato Salad, 52
Fruit-and-Pecan Dressing, 252
Fruit-and-Vegetable Rice Pilaf, 196
Fruit Balls, 299
Fruitcake Fondue, 258
Fruit Dessert Orange, 314
Fruited Chicken Salad, 25, 290
Fruited Yogurt Dip, 171
Fruitful Turkey Salad, 197
Fruit-Topped Vanilla Cream Pie, 49
Fruity Granola, 148
Fry Bread, 140

Garden Macaroni Salad, 290
Garden Patch Potato Salad, 82
Garden-Stuffed Yellow Squash, 106
Garlic Butter, 108
Garlic-Cheese Sauce, M70
Garlic Pesto, 108
Garlic Potatoes, 296
Garlic Steak, 8
Gazpacho, 112
German Potato Salad, 18
German-Style Red Cabbage, 2
Giant Chocolate Chip Cookies, 119
Ginger Beer, 159
Gingerbread Men, 299
Gingerbread Pancakes, 242
Gingerbread Squares, 16
Ginger Cream Topping, 312
Gingered Tea Sandwiches, 116
Ginger Peaches with Rum, M323
Glazed Fruit Salad, 290
Glazed Onions, 104

Month-by-Month Index

An alphabetical listing within the month of every food article and accompanying recipes
All microwave recipe page numbers are preceded by an "M"

Month-by-Month Index   **349**

General Recipe Index

A listing of every recipe by food category and/or major ingredient
All microwave recipe page numbers are preceded by an "M"

Oranges, Desserts *(continued)*

    Cream, Orange Chantilly, 156
    Cream, Orange-Coconut, 24
    Crispies, Orange, 205
    Dip, Creamy Orange, 117
    Flan, Orange, 95
    Fruit Dessert Orange, 314
    Glaze, Orange, 161
    Poached Oranges, Wine-, M323
    Sauce, Pineapple-Orange, 14
    Soufflé, Chilled Orange, 317
Dressing, Marmalade-Fruit, 171
Granola, Sunny Orange, 212
Mandarin Catfish Amandine, 183
Noodles, Orange, 177
Pecans, Orange, 299
Pork Chops, Orange, 81
Salads
    Carrot Salad, Orange-, 325
    Carrot-Tangerine Salad, 16
    Creamy Orange Salad, 124
    Mandarin Orange Salad, 161
    Pear Salad, Orange-, 164
    Romaine Salad, Orange-, 325
    Shrimp Salad, Orange-, 197
    Spinach Salad, Orange-, 16
Sauce, Mandarin, 60
Sauce, Orange, M286
Shake, Orange Milk, 166
Spareribs, Orange-Glazed, 296
Sweet Potatoes, Coconut-Orange, 252

Oysters
Baked Oysters over Toast Points, 214
Bake, Oyster-and-Corn, 44
Casserole, Oyster-and-Spinach, 44
Casserole, Oyster-and-Wild Rice, 44
Deviled Eggs with Smoked Oysters, 161
Landmark, Oyster, 88
Loaves, Spinach-Oyster, 213
Mousse, Smoked Oyster, 320
Omelets, Smoked Oyster, 96
Pie, Creole Oyster, 214
Scalloped Oysters, 213
Soup, Oyster-Cheese, 213

Pancakes
Buttermilk Pancakes, 101
Gingerbread Pancakes, 242
Sausage Rollups, Pancake-, 42
Shredded Wheat Pancakes, 59
Strawberry Pancakes, 219
Pastas. *See also* specific types.
Broccoli Pasta, 176
Clam Sauce, Pasta with, 291
Fettuccine with Spinach Sauce, 329
Garlic Pesto, 108
Orange Noodles, 177
Oregano Pasta, 176
Pimiento Pasta, 176
Salad, Pasta, 139
Sausage and Mixed Vegetables, Pasta
    with, 249
Shrimp Marinara, 233
Verde, Pasta, 201
Vermicelli, Lemon, 329
Peaches
Chutney, Peach, 179
Cobbler, Peach, 178
Crêpes, Fresh Peach, 186
Frost, Peach, 164
Ginger Peaches with Rum, M323
Ice, Peach-Yogurt, 83

Jam, Freezer Peach, M182
Muffins, Special Peach, 74
Preserves, Cream Cheese and Peach, 264
Salad, Peach Party, 290
Sauce, Peach, 144
Peanut Butter
Bars, Peanut Butter, 243
Brownies, Chocolate Chip-Peanut
    Butter, 73
Cake, Chocolate-Peanut Butter, 240
Cookies, Monster, 36
Cookies, Peanut Butter-Cinnamon, 30
Cookies, Peanut Butter-Oatmeal, 72
Cooler, Peanut Butter, 115
Frosting, Chocolate-Peanut Butter, 240
Frosting, Peanut Butter, 153
Frosts, Peanut Butter, 153
Logs, No-Bake Peanut Butter, 211
Pie, Peanut Butter Meringue, 30
Sauce, Peanut Butter Ice Cream, 30
Soup, Cream of Peanut Butter, 29
Squares, Chocolate Chip-Peanut
    Butter, 118
Temptations, Peanut Butter, 29
Peanuts
Brittle, Peanut, 298
Puff Nibbles, 191
Pears
Cookies, Pear Mincemeat, 264
Flaming Pears, 313
Jam, Paradise Pear, 300
Mincemeat, Pear, 264
Pie, Pear Mincemeat, 264
Pie, Pear Streusel, 244
Poached Pears with Raspberry
    Sauce, 212
Salad, Crunchy Pear, 244
Salad, Orange-Pear, 164
Salad, Pear-Lime, 152
Salad, Royal Pear, 265
Peas
Black-Eyed
    Delight, Tomato-Pea, 196
    Hot-and-Spicy Black-Eyed Peas, 9
    Mexican Black-Eyed Peas, 327
English
    Casserole, Quick Fresh English
        Pea, 145
    Continental, Peas, 254
    Creamy Peas with Mushrooms, 196
    Creole Peas, Quick, 123
    Deluxe English Peas, 68
    Onions Stuffed with Peas, 68
    Potato Nest, Peas in a, M239
    Salad, Cheddar-Pea, 82
    Soup, Chilled Pea, 181
Salad, Three Pea, 290
Snow Peas
    Sesame Snow Peas and Red
        Pepper, 175
    Skillet Snow Peas with Celery, 123
    Stuffed Snow Peas, 80
Pecans
Butter, Orange-Pecan, 75
Cake, Apple-Pecan Coffee, 242
Cake, Bourbon-Pecan, 25
Cake, Kentucky Pecan, 263
Cake, Pineapple-Pecan Upside-Down, 25
Carrots and Celery with Pecans, 254
Chicken, Oven-Fried Pecan, 288
Cobbler, Apple-Pecan, M198
Cookies, Butterscotch-Pecan, 36
Dressing, Fruit-and-Pecan, 252

Frosting, Coconut-Pecan, 43, 322
Fudge, Creamy Pecan, 321
Honeycomb Pecans, 300
Muffins, Cinnamon-Pecan, 219
Muffins, Cranberry-Pecan, 269
Mushrooms, Pecan-Stuffed, 261
Orange Pecans, 299
Pie, Spicy Pecan, 240
Praline Delights, Spicy, 299
Sauce, Praline, 143
Tarts, Easy Pecan, 313
Tassies, Teatime, 321
Toasted Pecans, 321
Peppers
Chile
    Casserole, Chile Rellenos, 31, 234
    Casserole, Green Chile-and-Fish, 32
    Enchiladas, Green Chile-Sour
        Cream, 234
    Pie, Green Chile-Cheese, 234
    Squash, Chile, 77
Green
    Muffins, Cheese-and-Pepper, 139
    Relish, Pepper-Onion, 180
    Salad Dressing, Green
        Pepper-Onion, 12
    Sauce, Pepper-Onion, 125
    Sausage and Peppers, Italian, 9
    Sauté, Tomato-Pepper, 142
    Stuffed Peppers, 202
    Stuffed Peppers, Beef-, 154
    Stuffed Peppers, Corn-, 104
    Stuffed with Beef, Peppers, 72
Jalapeño
    Loaf, Jalapeño-Cheese, 76
    Potatoes, Jalapeño, 39
    Quiche, Cheesy Jalapeño, 31
    Salsa Picante, 108
    Sauce, San Antonio Hot, 291
Red Pepper, Sesame Snow
    Peas and, 175
Pheasants
Wine Sauce, Pheasants with Port, 252
Pickles and Relishes
Apple Relish, Spicy, M323
Beet Relish, 179
Chutney
    Cranberry Chutney, 265
    Peach Chutney, 179
    Plum Chutney, 179
    Tomato-Apple Chutney, 180
Corn Relish, 107
Cran-Apple Relish, 300
Eggs, Beet Pickled, 287
Eggs, Spiced Pickled, 288
Fried Dill Pickles, 206
India Relish, 179
Mincemeat, Pear, 264
Onion Relish, Green, 65
Onion Rings, Pickled Refrigerator, 265
Pepper-Onion Relish, 180
Salad, Relish, 121
Vegetable Relish, Eight-, 179
Watermelon Rind Pickles, 106
Pies and Pastries
Almond Combs, 136
Apple Cider Pie, 227
Apple Dumplings, Old-Fashioned, 226
Apple Foldovers, 136
Apple Pie, Fresh, 178
Banana Cream Pie, 48
Blackberry Pie, 141
Blueberry Cream Pie, 142

Puddings *(continued)*
Cranberry Pudding, 306
Plum Pudding, Flamed, 276
Raisin-Pumpkin Pudding, 315
Steamed Holiday Pudding, 275

Pumpkin
Bread with Cream Cheese and Preserves, Pumpkin, 264
Pie, Pumpkin Chiffon, 312
Pie, Sour Cream-Pumpkin, 263
Pies, Spicy Pumpkin, 322
Pudding, Raisin-Pumpkin, 315

Quiches
Blue Cheese Quiche, 52
Broccoli-Cheese Pie, 235
Crab Quiche, Quick, 96
Green Onion Quiche, Cheesy, 42
Ham-and-Vegetable Quiche, 326
Ham Quiche, Crustless, 235
Jalapeño Quiche, Cheesy, 31
Spinach Quiche, Crustless, 235
Squares, Quiche, 222
Tarragon Cocktail Quiches, 127

Raisins
Candy, Mixed Raisin, 111
Muffins, Breakfast Raisin, 59
Pie, Spiced Raisin, 148
Pudding, Raisin-Pumpkin, 315
Salad, Carrot-Raisin, 174
Sauce, Raisin, 91, 275
Sauce, Rum-Raisin, 7
Scones, Currant, 117

Raspberries
Bars, Raspberry, 212
Crêpes Suzette, Raspberry, 84
Dessert, Frozen Raspberry, 192
Jam, Raspberry Freezer, M181
Mold, Raspberry Holiday, 253
Punch, Raspberry Sparkle, 57
Sauce Flambé, Raspberry, 142
Sauce, Raspberry, 73, 213

Relishes. *See* Pickles and Relishes.

Rice
Beef and Rice, Spiced, 285
Brown Rice Parmesan, 196
Brown Rice, Spanish, 196
Casserole, Ham-and-Rice, 75
Chicken-Flavored Rice, M144
Chicken Livers with Rice, 292
Fiesta Rice, 76
Fried Rice, 197
Fried Rice, Easy, 76
Lentil-and-Rice Supper, 202
Lime-Flavored Rice, 175
Parsley Rice, 197
Pie, Tuna-Rice, 123
Pilaf, Fruit-and-Vegetable Rice, 196
Red Beans and Rice, 37
Salad, Brown Rice-and-Vegetable, 202
Salad, Egg-Rice, 18
Salad, Salmon-Rice, 289
Salad, Tangy Shrimp-Rice, 66
Sausage, Beans, and Rice, Texas, 296
Waldorf Rice, 281
Wild Rice-and-Shrimp Creole, 292
Wild Rice Casserole, Chicken-, 241
Wild Rice Casserole, Oyster-and-, 44
Wild Rice Casserole, Sausage-, 250
Wild Rice, Pork Loin Stuffed with, 35

Rolls
Butterhorns, 267
Cherry-Almond Rolls, M198
Crescent Rolls, 267
Low-Sodium Yeast Rolls, 228
Quick Yeast Rolls, 267

Salad Dressings
Artichoke Dressing, 126
Bacon Dressing, Hot, 12
Buttermilk Dressing, Down-Home, 114
Coconut-Fruit Dressing, Tangy, 171
Curried Dressing, 115
Dill-and-Chive Vinegar, 300
French Dressing, Tangy, 12
Fruit Dressing, Marmalade-, 171
Garlic-Herb Salad Dressing, Creamy, 66
Grapefruit Salad Dressing, 262
Herb Vinegar, Mixed, 107
Italian Salad Dressing, 12
Mayonnaise, Easy Homemade, 12
Mint Dressing, Fresh, 126
Olive Oil Dressing, 266
Onion-French Dressing, 283
Pepper-Onion Salad Dressing, Green, 12
Pimiento Dressing, Lettuce Wedges with, 212
Poppy Seed Dressing, 16
Roquefort Dressing, Creamy, 12
Strawberry Dressing, Creamy, 161
Sweet-and-Sour Dressing, 70, 161
Sweet-and-Sour Fruit Dressing, 125
Tangy Salad Dressing, 115
Tarragon Vinegar, 107
Tossed Salad Dressing, 115

Salads
Antipasto Salad, 66
Apple Crunch Salad, 232
Apple Salad, Double, 227
Apple Salad, Swiss-, 81
Asparagus, Congealed Salad with Crabmeat-and-, 86
Artichoke Aspic, Tomato-, 320
Avocado Salad, Congealed, 266
Avocado Salad, Grapefruit-, 16
Bacon Salad, Escarole-and-, 85
Bean Salad, Cold Green, 106
Bean Salad, Crunchy Marinated, 197
Bean Salad, Four-, 82
Bean Salad, Saucy, 18
Bean Salad, Speedy Green, 283
Broccoli Salad, Congealed, 266
Carrot-Raisin Salad, 174
Carrot Salad, Orange-, 325
Carrot Salad, Simple, 152
Carrot-Tangerine Salad, 16
Cauliflower Salad, 291
Cauliflower Salad, Marinated, 232
Cheddar-Pea Salad, 82
Cherry Salad, Festive, 265
Chicken
  Chicken Salad with a Twist, 221
  Coleslaw, Chicken, 2
  Curried Chicken Salad, 66
  Fruited Chicken Salad, 25, 290
  Mold, Chicken Salad, 163
  Tahitian Chicken Salad, 120
  Tarts, Chicken Salad, 257
Citrus Salad, Southern-Style, 262
Coconut Salad, Chunky Fruit-and-, 24
Congealed
  Apple Crunch Salad, 232
  Avocado Salad, Congealed, 266

Broccoli Salad, Congealed, 124
Cherry Salad, Festive, 265
Chicken Salad Mold, 163
Crabmeat-and-Asparagus, Congealed Salad with, 86
Cranberry Salad, Layered, 322
Cucumber Mold, Creamy, 164
Cucumber-Pineapple Salad, 124
Grapefruit Salad, 325
Grapefruit Salad, Congealed, 325
Melon Ball Salad, Congealed, 125
Orange-Pear Salad, 164
Orange Salad, Creamy, 124
Peach Frost, 164
Peach Party Salad, 290
Pear-Lime Salad, 152
Pear Salad, Royal, 265
Pimiento Salad, Sunshine, 124
Pineapple Daiquiri Salad, 232
Pineapple-Lime Salad, 320
Raspberry Holiday Mold, 253
Shrimp Salad, 221
Tomato-Artichoke Aspic, 320
Tomato Ring, Tangy, 164
Tomato Salad, Frozen, 52
Tuna Salad, Congealed, 163
Waldorf Salad, Molded, 326
Corn Salad, Tasty, 289
Crabmeat-and-Asparagus, Congealed Salad with, 86
Cranberry Salad, Layered, 322
Croutons, Crispy Italian, 126
Croutons, Vegetable-Flavored, 148
Cucumber Mold, Creamy, 164
Cucumber-Pineapple Salad, 124
Cucumbers, Cool, 152
Egg-Rice Salad, 18
Escarole-and-Bacon Salad, 85
Fruit
  Chicken Salad, Fruited, 25, 290
  Coconut Salad, Chunky Fruit-and-, 24
  Creamy Fruit Salad, 265
  Glazed Fruit Salad, 290
  Honeydew Fruit Bowl, 186
  Honeydew Salad with Apricot Cream Dressing, 191
  Layered Fruit Salad, 290
  Lemonade Fruit Salad, 24
  Medley, Chilled Fruit, 60
  Melon Ball Salad, Congealed, 125
  Melon Mélange, 139
  Sweet-and-Sour Fruit Salad, 125
  Tropical Fruit Salad with Fresh Mint Dressing, 126
  Turkey Fruit Salad, 244
  Turkey Salad, Fruitful, 197
  Watermelon Fruit Basket, 161
  Watermelon Sparkle, 191
Grapefruit-Avocado Salad, 16
Grapefruit Salad, 325
Grapefruit Salad, Congealed, 325
Grapefruit Winter Salad, 24
Green
  Blue Cheese Tossed Salad, 195
  Boston Tossed Salad, 85
  Cheesy Italian Salad, 33
  Chef's Salad Bowl, 66
  Citrus Salad, Southern-Style, 262
  Grecian Green Salad, 266
  Lettuce Salad, French, 187
  Lettuce Salad, Layered Spinach-, 266

Favorite Recipes

Record your favorite recipes below for quick and handy reference

Appetizers and Beverages	Source/Page	Remarks

Breads	Source/Page	Remarks

Desserts   Source/Page   Remarks

Eggs and Cheese   Source/Page   Remarks

Main Dishes   Source/Page   Remarks

Salads Source/Page Remarks

Side Dishes and Vegetables Source/Page Remarks

Soups and Stews Source/Page Remarks